K

At home on the world markets

At home on the world markets

Dutch international trading companies from the 16th century until the present

Joost Jonker and Keetie Sluyterman

Sdu Uitgevers, The Hague 2000

Photo research: Godelieve van der Heyden, Bussum

Graphic design: Marise Knegtmans, Amsterdam

Printing: Sdu Grafisch Bedrijf, Den Haag

ISBN 90 12 08805 4

Contents

6

Filled with pride and contentment, this chief merchant of the Dutch East India Company (VOC) points his stick at the VOC-ships lying in the roads of Batavia, ready for the return trip to the Republic. This painting by Albert Cuyp probably represents Jacob Mathieusen and his wife.

The Dutch term *handelshuis* or merchant house inspires associations with enterprising traders, warehouses along the Amsterdam canals, and the sturdy sailing ships of the Dutch East India Company or voc. During the 17th century, these firms laid the foundations for the economic prosperity and flourishing culture of the Republic of the Seven United Provinces. Traders and their international operations were a driving force in the economy of this Golden Age, innovative forces contributing to a positive self-image of the Netherlands in its formative stage. As they built Amsterdam into the hub of this prospering trade, they were literally 'at home on the world markets'. Portraits of these merchants, painted by world famous painters such as Rembrandt or Frans Hals, still testify to their pride, and to the riches which they amassed. To this day, the warehouses, the elegant residences along the canals, and the prominent city hall on the Dam Square in Amsterdam are visible proof of their wealth and power. What happened to these international traders and their firms in the centuries that followed, however? We know surprisingly little about that. After the 17th century, the merchant houses disappear from sight, as it were, but did they also disappear from business life? The answer is, of course, that the opposite is true. This book tells the story of the lasting role of the Dutch merchant houses. The initiative was taken by the Dutch firm of Hagemeyer, acting on the felicitous inspiration to celebrate its centenary in the year 2000 by commissioning a history of Dutch trading houses during the past 400 years.

9

TRADING HOUSES AS A SPECIES – A characteristic feature of the genus traders is a recurrent pessimistic prediction about their imminent disappearance. The death knell has been sounded for them many times, with the anxiety already sounding in the late 17th century, and still echoing today. The fact that such predictions surface again and again really means that traders have falsified them each time. Yet it also means that they faced constant threats to their position.[1] This book focuses on a species of the genus traders, the *handelshuizen*, firms running international operations across a wide product range and in various markets, with the goods traded not necessarily passing through the Netherlands.[2] The Dutch term does not have an exact English equivalent. Its literal translation, merchant houses or trading houses, sits somewhat awkwardly on

The Rotterdam firm of R.S. Stokvis & Zn. is a good example of an exceedingly flexible trading company. Starting as a local wholesaler in 1844, the firm rapidly developed into a company working on a national scale , with its own production plants and export operations. However, after the Second World War Stokvis gradually lost ground. This late 19th century photograph shows employees on a Stokvis waggon.

20th century firms, whereas *handelshuizen* can be used, and is used, to describe internationally operating traders today. On the other hand, the English term international traders fails to capture one essence of *handelshuizen*, i.e. their identity as firms with a degree of continuity and a certain business culture associated with Dutch commercial traditions through the ages. Rather than coining a new term, or create confusion by switching terms at a really undefined and thus more or less arbitrary moment in time, we have opted to use the terms merchant houses, trading houses, and international traders as synonyms for *handelshuizen*.

This book, then, analyses the positions of merchant houses in business and the changes to their functioning over time. Such firms are intermediary service providers in the supply chain between producers and consumers, as a rule without either producing goods themselves, or selling directly to the final consumers. Directing the flow of goods also gives them involvement with flows of money and of information. In its intermediary function, trading houses may be regarded as a species of wholesaling. The firms stand out from specialised wholesalers, selling farming products, for instance, or building materials, raw materials, capital goods, or consumer products, as operating in various product sectors simultaneously. Before turning to the collective history of individual firms, first a word about the economic function of wholesaling.[3] Since this book aims to explore the varying functions performed by traders over time, we have deliberately opted for a fairly wide definition of wholesaling.

The manifold economic functions of international wholesaling may be reduced to a few main categories, i.e. matching differences in location, in time, in quantity, and in quality. A trader ensures that goods move from one end of the world to another, or from a port to its hinterland. He has to possess the right information about, for example, products made in Venice that might find ready buyers in Africa. As often as not, he will also arrange the transport required, with or without using his own means of conveyance. A trader may come to own the goods he handles, but this is not necessarily the case. Traders

Trading companies often commissioned handsome photo albums as showcases of their subsidiaries all over the world. During the 1950s, Lindeteves had this album made of its overseas offices.

10

will also cover the time between the production of certain goods and delivery to retailers or consumers. Ice skates, for one, are produced throughout the year, but consumer demand for them has marked peaks and troughs. Wholesalers provide a match between supply and demand by keeping such goods in stock. The same may be said for differences in quantity. Wholesalers group small lots into bulk orders, or conversely, break bulk deliveries into small lots. Finally, wholesalers may enhance the quality of goods by adding services such as advice, technical support, or finance. Another opportunity to add value lies in assorting products to form a range targeting particular customer groups. All these functions help to make goods available more efficiently and more cheaply. Wholesalers translate the conditions at which producers are able and willing to supply into the conditions at which consumers are able and willing to buy.

Traders have often had a bad press, being described variously as parasites who do not produce anything themselves, or as speculators abusing the circumstances in times of scarcity. Such stereotypes do not fit at all. On the contrary, traders are really the lubricants of business, key links in the economy. Thus, in theory, wholesaling may perform a wide range of useful functions. Will individual traders assume them, however? Will they get the opportunity to do so? Economic theory lends plausibility to the argument that in the long run manufacturers will render the intermediation by traders redundant. However, using the same theoretical concepts one may defend the notion of traders as having qualities by which they remain indispensable.[4] This leads us to the question about the circumstances determining whether or not trading firms perform particular functions. What were the dynamics of commercial intermediation and the functional shifts in trading over time?[5] This book aims to provide answers to such questions. It explores the markets on which Dutch international traders operated, the products they handled, and the services they

SELECTION AND PACKING OF CINNAMON BARK AT PADANG.

performed. Particular attention has been paid to the impact of general economic and political circumstances, of the rise of manufacturing industry, and of the revolution in communications. Thus we have attempted to bring partially unexplored lands into production.

APPROACH – Two authors have collaborated closely in producing this book. Its concepts have been defined by common consent, and the results were extensively discussed. The rest of the work was split into two distinct parts, with Joost Jonker writing Chapters I to IV, and Keetie Sluyterman taking on Chapters V to VIII. The introduction and the conclusion were again a joint responsibility.

For their research, the authors have drawn on a variety of sources. First of all, they enjoyed free access to the archival collections held by Hagemeyer. These collections gave information about the company itself, and also about several companies acquired over the years, such as Borsumij, Geo. Wehry, and the Twentsche Overzee Handel-Maatschappij. Hagemeyer is presently considering to transfer this material to a public records office at some future date. Internatio-Müller kindly allowed access to its archives, which include a detailed inventory for the years up to 1970. In addition, the authors have consulted many archives in public collections. Information from published annual reports and various magazines supplemented the data from original records. Of course, we have also made extensive use of books and articles, available in particular abundance for the centuries leading up to 1900.

ACKNOWLEDGEMENTS – First of all, we want to record here our gratitude to the executive board of Hagemeyer for showing trust in us as authors when commissioning this book from the Onderzoekinstituut voor Geschiedenis en Cultuur (OGC or Research Institute for History and Culture) of Utrecht University. It was a particular pleasure for us to know that the board expressly wanted a book about Dutch merchant houses in general. Consequently, we have cast our net wide. Hagemeyer figures in the story as one example side by side with others. As history progresses, however, Hagemeyer appears to become ever more prominent.

We want to express a special word of appreciation for the members of the editorial committee for this project, who have shared with us their valuable comments on the manuscript as the work progressed. The Hagemeyer representatives on this committee were Ivo Manders, the company secretary, and Noor Verheul, secretary to the board. The academic world was represented on the committee by Dr. Thomas Lindblad, Senior Lecturer at Leiden University, Professor Leo Noordegraaf of Amsterdam University, Professor Jan Luiten van Zanden of Utrecht University, and Dr. Joost Dankers, coordinator of commissioned research at the Onderzoekinstituut voor Geschiedenis en Cultuur of

Utrecht University. We have found the discussions in the editorial committee very stimulating. In translating the book into English, Drs. Diederik van Werven supported Joost Jonker with words and deeds, for which this author is very grateful. We are also indebted to Stratagem Strategic Research BV/RAND *Europe*, and in particular to Drs. Bouke Veldman, for providing us with the secondment facilities required to work on this project.

Moreover, we want to thank Ivo Manders also for his zest and enthusiasm concerning the project which he liberally showered on us throughout. Noor Verheul was a great help in solving no end of practical matters for us. Without the greatly appreciated services of numerous staff members of libraries and record offices, this book could not have been written. Discussions with and comments from colleagues provided key ingredients for the final result. We want to mention in particular Professor Geoffrey Jones of Reading University, and our Dutch colleagues Drs. Oscar Gelderblom, Drs. Nico van Horn, Professor H.W. de Jong, Dr. Clé Lesger, and Drs. Co Seegers. Interviews with traders, both active and retired ones, have handed us clues about the daily business during the most recent past. A list of the persons interviewed can be found in the appendix. We have greatly enjoyed those conversations and drawn considerable profit from them.

Joost Jonker and Keetie Sluyterman
Utrecht, January 2000

During the 16th century, the Low Countries conducted a flourishing foreign trade, but it took another 100 years before trading firms with a distinct identity and continuity in business developed. The two illustrations depict the trade in two key consumer articles, woollen cloth and wine. On the left the Den Bosch cloth market, painted about 1500. The inset shows barrels of wine hoisted from a ship in Bruges harbour, an illustration portraying the wine month of October, in a manuscript illuminated by Simon Bening in 1530.

CHAPTER 1

Dutch trade has its roots in ages long gone by. Merchant houses only appeared towards 5, as the Dutch Republic entered a Golden Age of economic world dominance. They played a key role in developing the country's commercial power.

A LONG DAWN – Merchant houses with large-scale international operations first appeared in Renaissance Italy. As early as the thirteenth century, large and enduring trading firms arose, run by several partners and branching out into subsidiaries in Italian cities and across Europe. During the Quattrocento, merchant houses such as Bardi, Peruzzi and Datini became notable specialists in trade and finance. They drew a large volume of transactions from a wide network, and carried on their business from one generation to the next under the same name and in the same cities. The expansion of these large Italian concerns gathered momentum with the aid of new management techniques.

The firms deployed their activities from a head office linking subsidiaries and clients abroad by correspondence. They devised ever more accurate accounting methods to keep track of their capital position and the balances of partners and correspondents. This development culminated in the invention of double-entry bookkeeping, which Italian merchants pioneered during the second half of the fourteenth century. To facilitate settlements and advances, these firms already used bills of exchange, instructions for payments to be made in the firms' name.[1]

Local correspondents and subsidiaries of the Italian merchant houses disseminated the new commercial techniques in Europe. Only the great Flemish-Brabantine cities copied them eagerly, however, because elsewhere trade had not yet attained the required level of sophistication. Barter still figured prominently in transactions. Otherwise, merchants relied on coins for their payments, and only very rarely did they resort to rudimentary bills. Bottomry contracts provided credit secured on ships and their cargo. In this period firms did not have head quarters, permanent offices at fixed addresses, nor client networks maintained by regular correspondence. Merchants escorted their consignments abroad, often as acting as masters on their own ships. They conducted their business in person, assisted by local brotherhoods of fellow merchants from the same region or city, or by innkeepers who often doubled as brokers. For handling large volumes or spreading risks, merchants resorted to varying partnerships and business alliances. As a rule, such contracts served a limited purpose: a

particular trip, a trading partnership for one sailing season or for a specific transaction, though no doubt the agreements were extended when the joint venture proved fruitful. A business could also acquire a form of informal continuity when merchants would hand over their affairs to successors trained on the job. The trading partnership formed by the Amsterdam merchant Symon Reyersz and his nephew Reyer Dircsz. during the 1480s demonstrates this pattern. At first, the elder partner would sail to the Baltic for the trading season, while his nephew looked after the Amsterdam side. As a rule, Reyersz stayed in Gdansk (formerly known as Danzig) from March until October, employing an agent in Lübeck for the partnership's transactions there. Subsequently, Dircsz accompanied Reyersz to get first-hand knowledge of the Baltic trade. Finally, uncle remained in Amsterdam and let his nephew do the travelling. Unfortunately we do not know how Dircsz fared in business from then on.[2]

Partnerships like the Reyersz-Dircsz team form the prehistory of Dutch merchant houses, which stretched out as a long transitory phase between the Middle Ages and the Modern era. This phase saw the disintegration of the medieval combined captain-merchant businesses and the rise of the first specialised trading firms. Merchants continued to reside abroad during the sailing season. They increased their scope by authorising partners, servants, captains or innkeepers for their transactions. Sometimes they already employed agents elsewhere.[3] As often as not, such agents were relatives, who had emigrated and lived scattered across the Continent.[4] This transformation took at least a century. The Reyersz-Dircsz partnership emerged in mid-century. The business of Claes van Adrichem, a merchant active in the city of Delft during the last quarter of the sixteenth century, looked very similar. Van Adrichem undertook many joint ventures of limited duration, for particular trips or consignments. He acted as merchant-freighter, merchant-shipper or shipper-bookkeeper in turn, to suit the opportunity. His concerns focused on the Baltic trade, and Van Adrichem employed an agent in Gdansk.[5] At the same time however, the captain-merchant continued to be fairly common in some regions.[6]

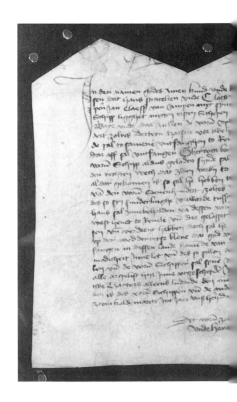

New commercial skills and accounting techniques spread across Europe from Italy, where trading houses flourished as early as the 14th century. This book for the instruction of double-entry bookkeeping, written in Dutch by Jan Ympijn Christoffelsz, was posthumously published in Antwerp in 1543. The title page shows a scholar at his desk surrounded by instruments and books, an illustration designed to emphasise the book's scientific pretensions.

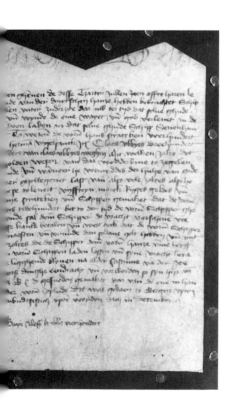

Trading thus gradually acquired a recognisable form as a business, connections with other cities, and a regular operating base. Even so, around the middle of the sixteenth century there were as yet no firms with an established continuity and tradition under the same name in the regions now known as the Netherlands. Nor were businesses very large. According to the ledgers for a tax on merchants' capital, most merchants had invested no more than 6,000-8,000 guilders in 1543. The largest was an Amsterdam partnership of three merchants, with an estimated capital of about 36,000 guilders.[7] The following year Arent Hudde headed the list of largest local exporters. He sent out more than thirty shiploads for a total amount of nearly 42,000 guilders. At that time, Amsterdam's trading network included no more than the surrounding countries, Scandinavia and the Baltic. The stock of goods traded was simple, mainly grain, fish and salt, beer, wine, raw wool and woollen cloth, wood, iron and copper.[8]

As a rule such tax assessments considerably understate the real amounts. Yet even when we take this fact into consideration, most Dutch trading concerns were small to medium sized compared to Antwerp merchants.[9] By 1500 this city had become the undisputed commercial metropolis of western Europe, with a voluminous and varied commodity market. Situated in the area now known as Belgium, Antwerp had road links with all corners of Continental

Europe, and shipping routes led to France, the British Isles, and the Baltic.

During the first half of the sixteenth century, the overseas expansion of Portugal and Spain added a new dimension to the Antwerp market. Western and northern Europe used to obtain limited supplies of gold, silver, spices and silk from Asia through the Levant by way of northern Italy and the overland routes across the continent. The discovery of sea passages to the Americas and Asia opened alternative and more direct sources of these luxuries. The Iberian peninsula started to supply steadily growing quantities to the European market, eclipsing the Italian cities. For most western and northern European markets, supply routes changed accordingly. The overland transport from Italy was superseded by ships carrying the prized commodities from Lisbon and Seville to Antwerp, which thus gained a key distributing function.[10] Between about 1530 and 1560, the city had its heyday as the most important commercial centre in Europe. Subsidiaries of Italian merchant houses introduced the latest management techniques, which were subsequently taken up and perfected by locals. In 1543, fifty years after the groundbreaking work of the Italian mathematician Luca Pacioli, an Antwerp printer published one of the first instructions about double-entry bookkeeping, written in Dutch by the merchant Jan Ympijn Christoffelsz.[11] At more or less the same time the negotiability of bills was put on a secure footing by the introduction of endorsement, the transfer of bills by a signature on the back.[12] During the sailing season the Antwerp citizens on the quays of the river Scheldt jostled with Germans, Britons, Bretons, Basques, Spaniards, Portuguese and Italians.

These crowds, the wide variety of goods traded, the power of the Antwerp bourse, and the wealth of local firms all camouflaged some striking weaknesses in the economic structure. Sea borne trade was being ousted by overland trade, which did not have deep roots along the Scheldt. The city remained a passive supplier of facilities to foreign merchants, who generated seasonal activities without strong linkages with local business. Merchandise mostly came to Antwerp in foreign ships, to be traded and shipped out again for further distribution or processing elsewhere. The river Scheldt was getting congested with the growing traffic. Some merchants started to divert their business to nearby ports such as Middelburg. Big local firms such as Della Faille operated in the Italian style with subsidiaries abroad. During the sixteenth century commission trading superseded this kind of organisation, being more flexible and most of all, cheaper. The new technique opened up opportunities for foreign ventures to medium sized merchant firms, provided they found a trusty correspondent abroad. This appears to have become ever easier, judging by the rapid spread of commission trading.[13] The dissemination of elementary bookkeeping reduced the scope for disagreement over settling accounts, so the dissemination of the new Italian-style principles helped to foster the change in business organisation. Ympijn's instruction of 1543 was published in French during the same year, and an English translation appeared four years later.[14] Even so, Antwerp had as yet little reason to fear a threat to its position. None of

By the mid-16th century, Antwerp had unmistakably become the biggest commercial centre in Europe. This anonymous panorama from about 1530 shows busy traffic and several different types of ships on the Scheldt river and in the harbour.

the nearby ports came close to it in economic power. Bruges had to resign itself to a secondary position once the city's harbour had silted up. The French and English ports served their respective hinterland and little more, as did Emden and Hamburg for north Germany. Middelburg profited from a licensed entrepot for wine, and from business spilling over from Antwerp, thus drawing a sizeable trade and an international merchant crowd. The city also had a voluminous shipping capacity at its disposal to support its trade, and yet remained anchored on the Scheldt as a satellite.[15] Dordrecht had lost its position as supra-regional trading hub after the curtailment of its centuries-old entrepot license, though the city retained a large distributive trade of iron, wood and wine coming down the Meuse and Rhine rivers. Rotterdam was as yet little more than a fishing port.[16] The annual fairs of Bergen op Zoom lapsed as the overland trade switched to alternative routes, and Antwerp attracted the remainder.[17]

THE RISE OF AMSTERDAM – Only Amsterdam, already the second commercial centre of the Burgundian Netherlands, could keep up with Antwerp's booming development. During the first half of the sixteenth century, and more strongly after 1540, the city experienced vigorous economic growth generated by a steadily expanding Baltic trade. This so-called 'mother of all trade' exported herring, salt, woollen cloth and wine, in return for grain, timber, rope and cables, tar and hides. Amsterdam and other ports on the west coast of the Zuiderzee reinforced their favourable location for this trade by organising dedicated transport. Ships from Holland sailed for the Baltic as early as weather allowed, enabling them to make two, or even three round trips each year. This was not really feasible from ports elsewhere. Since 1508 at least, the cities concerned jointly set the date of first departure in spring, so ships' masters could ensure collective security by sailing in convoy.[18] The sailing season edged ever closer towards winter. At the end of the sixteenth century, ships' masters already hazarded sailing well into December. On Christmas Eve 1593, a fleet of 100-150 freighters lay anchored off the island of Texel, when a sudden heavy storm created havoc.[19] The type of ships for the Baltic run, their particular design, equipment, rigging and crew number were all tailored to the needs of transporting the bulky commodities common on the route. During the 16th and 17th centuries freight rates accounted for 10-20% of grain bought at Gdansk. Cutting that cost by only a few percent thus had a considerable impact on the resale price.[20] Ownership of the freighters was spread over a large number of participants, often split down to a 1/32 or a 1/64 part, sometimes even smaller. The owners shared profits and losses with the ship's captain. This system spread the financial burden and risks of owning ships, thereby cutting running costs and lowering the entry barriers for shipping in general.[21] From Amsterdam and the surrounding countryside small shipping companies for the Baltic trade fanned out over the ports on the Zuiderzee, from nearby Hoorn and Enkhuizen, to Hindeloopen and Stavoren further away in Friesland. As a rule, merchants also held some shares in the freighters carrying their merchandise. Though some concentration of ownership occurred, they did not dominate the shipping trade as such. In these propitious conditions the Dutch fleet doubled in size from 300-400 ships in 1530, to 800 thirty years later.[22]

Amsterdam began its rise as a commercial centre mainly on the strength of its trade with the Baltic. In 1611, the engraver Claes Jansz Visscher visualised this relationship by depicting Amsterdam harbour with foreigners, including a Pole, a Swede, and a Dane, offering their wares to a maid symbolising the city of Amsterdam.

This dedication to bulk transport gave Dutch shipping a compound cost advantage from the late Middle Ages onwards.[23] After more than a century of hard struggle the north German Hansa towns had to submit to Dutch dominance in the Baltic, possibly because their strictly regulated trade could not compete with the freely operating Dutchmen. During the 1540s, the Hanseatic League tried one last time to fight off the feared rivals, but to no avail. At the Peace of Spiers (1544), Dutch shipping secured unrestricted access to the Baltic Sea. This did not free traffic from obstruction caused by wars in the area, a constantly recurring phenomenon until well into 18th century. However, once established, the right of free access remained unchallenged. The ports on the eastern coast of the Zuiderzee, such as Kampen, Zwolle, and Deventer, also submitted to the power of their rivals across the water. From the late 15th century these cities saw their trade with the Baltic and with France gravitating westward, and consequently their membership ties with the Hansa League weakened.[24] In return, the Zuiderzee ports became part of a hierarchical trade and transport system centring on Amsterdam. Ships would not head straight for their final destination, but would stop off at one port after another on the way, unloading some cargo and taking on board new consignments, before finally docking at Amsterdam. Regular shipping services between all ports welded the system into a network. Once connected, the participants could reap economies of scale for themselves and for their partners by specialising in what suited them best. The first connections were already in place by the 1540s, but it took another century to reach its greatest extension. From the late 16th century the system already included Hamburg. Dordrecht became the hub of a similar system, rationalising inland shipping.[25]

The Peace of Spiers firmly established Amsterdam's position as the main terminal for the Baltic trade and the most important grain entrepot in Europe. Four-fifths of the city's warehouses served to store grain. Consequently in 1564 merchants petitioned the Burgundian government in Brussels and complained about the shortage of warehousing to store other Baltic goods such as pitch, tar, potash, flax, and timber.[26] Mainly local merchants conducted an active trade, working on their own account, or handling commissions and consignations for principals elsewhere. Moreover, trade had strong links with other local sectors beside shipping, like industries processing imported raw materials into finished export products such as barrelled herring, soap, beer, oil etc.[27] Because of these linkages, business activities in Amsterdam lacked the marked seasonal pattern of trade in Antwerp, and they were spread more evenly over the year, though some fluctuations did of course occur from one month to another.[28]

With the Baltic trade firmly in their grip, Dutch merchants embarked on an expansion into southern Europe during the second quarter of the sixteenth century. They first seized the trade routes to southwest France and Spain, until then dominated by Breton and Basque shipping. This enabled the Dutch to buy salt and wine for the Baltic trade at source, though a large majority of the ships continued to sail through the Sound in ballast, as before. Portugal came next, mainly to buy spices. In 1560 the cities of Amsterdam, Enkhuizen and Hoorn jointly appointed a consul in Lisbon to assist their respective citizens in case of trouble, a sure sign of growing traffic. Around the same time Portuguese merchants appear to have ceded the northern trade routes to their new rivals.[29]

THE MERCHANTS' BUSINESS – The specialisation on the Baltic trade gave the Amsterdam market a certain lopsidedness. Nearly all other goods arrived via Antwerp or Middelburg, and compared to the cosmopolitan Scheldt ports the city looked somewhat provincial. A large number of immigrants and factors of foreign merchants lived in the town, but invariably they came from northern Germany or the Baltic towns. The local representative of Fugger, the great Augsburg merchants and bankers, Pompeius Occo, was originally from East Friesland.[30] The Amsterdam citizens realised the close connection between their prosperity and this immigration. In the 1564 petition mentioned above, merchants also complained that recent legislation had raised unreasonable obstacles to litigation by foreigners.[31]

In the Netherlands, the local and regional authorities usually showed their understanding of commercial interests, if only because economic necessity forced them to act against competitive threats. When the Burgundian government introduced a new tax on grain, the county of Holland bought an outright redemption rather than risk damage to Amsterdam's commercial artery and the related trade and industries throughout the province. The province of Zeeland decided against a redemption. Its grain trade would have profited greatly, but the province's various economic interests balanced each other. Thus Amsterdam kept its competitive advantage.[32] Moreover, the economy hinged on merchants, and that translated into political clout, though not necessarily into successful interventions.

The Netherlands could not exist without trade. Its economy had already become fully dependent on the surrounding countries, for the selling and buying of foodstuffs such as grain, beer, fish and meat, but also for trading raw materials and semi-finished goods like wool, fabrics, iron, copper, timber, rope, and cables. The constant tension between changes in demand and an unforeseeable supply increased this dependency. Bad weather, wars, epidemics and political circumstances all conspired to disrupt production or transport and destabilise supplies. Moreover, agriculture and industry were too small to organise their own sales, and thus depended on merchants. Trade, then, was essential to economic growth. For instance, when the Haarlem city fathers wanted to engineer an expansion of the local cloth industry, they had to develop far-reaching and innovative initiatives to generate trade. They started by offering export subsidies, but the amount of cloth produced remained too small to attract foreign wholesalers. The council then set up an office for the collective purchasing of raw wool in Calais, and selling the finished products of the Haarlem manufacturers to Spanish and Portuguese wholesalers in Antwerp. This office also enforced quality standards for Haarlem cloth. The city fathers' initiatives

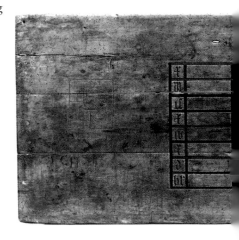

Calculating boards helped merchants to make rapid currency conversions. This is a German copy from the 15th century.

22

A portrait of Pompeius Occo, banker, merchant, and humanist. He was the Amsterdam agent of the leading Augsburg trading firm of Fugger, and as such a very important man in town. Painting by Dirck Jacobszoon.

succeeded in raising production and sales to unprecedented levels during the second quarter of the sixteenth century.[33]

Merchants not only pulled the commercial ropes, but also controlled money, credit and capital, essential factors in a society with ever feeble currencies and only rudimentary credit facilities. A vast variety of coins circulated, of uncertain intrinsic value and subject to constant exchange rate fluctuations. Money could disappear from circulation almost overnight, when a war drained reserves of gold and silver, or through hoarding after a currency debasement, or when an adverse trade balance caused an outflow. Under such circumstances trade reverted to barter, often with credit facilities to cover shortfalls. Both types of transaction depended on the kind of trust which is fostered only by prolonged relations among merchants with mutual interests. The production and transport of commodities, slow and irregular to modern notions, relied on merchants using their know-how of products and markets to offset the inherent long-term financial risks. A round trip Rotterdam-Gdansk-Amsterdam took about ten weeks in the last quarter of the sixteenth century, but in autumn this could easily stretch to twelve weeks or even fourteen. The typical salt run from

Amsterdam to the French salt ports, then to Gdansk and back to Amsterdam took at least fourteen weeks.[34] Upon delivery of the goods, the merchant's capital remained tied up until he could sell, which didn't always go smoothly. Consequently, the merchant's vital position in the supply of money and credit gave him a far wider economic function than trade alone.[35]

Big merchants usually maintained close links with the authorities, to obtain privileges such as licensed entrepots, patents and charters, to speed up court cases or avert litigation, or to get their bills paid, secure contracts, acquire offices and tender for public services such as tolls and tax farming. Conversely, the authorities constantly interfered with business. Sometimes they did so with the explicit aim of promoting development, as in the case of the Haarlem cloth industry mentioned earlier. As often as not financial considerations provided the impetus, a need for revenues or loans. Alternating motives resulted in one ad hoc decision after another. While balancing between competing business interests, the authorities had to be mindful of the precarious social stability, easily upset because of the low standard of living. Unemployment and sharp fluctuations in food prices could soon lead to famine and the threat of violent riots. Averting such disasters provided a strong incentive for maintaining the status quo. This consideration was not necessarily decisive, however, and it could only be carried with the support of businessmen vying for favours.[36]

The authorities thus found themselves caught between a variety of interests, susceptible to pressure, but themselves not really able to push. Merchants brought their influence to bear through city fathers, through connections in provincial representations, or by lobbying directly with the central Government in Brussels, in order to get something done or something scuttled, above all to keep as much freedom of action as possible. The Emperor Charles v, for instance, consequently did not succeed in enforcing a ban on trade with the French enemy. His edict was simply ignored. The authorities could only get some grip on this trade by setting up a permit system with expensive licenses.[37] Around the same time the English King Henry VIII failed in his efforts to ban the foreign bill traffic.[38] Even so, trade interests did not dictate public policy. Craft guilds provided a considerable counterweight. Moreover, trade interests were seldom homogeneous. From time to time, wholesalers and retailers held diverging opinions, provinces could also take different positions, as Holland and Zeeland did over the grain tax mentioned before.

We know very little about 16th century Dutch merchants and merchant firms. Probably, small partnerships like Reyersz and Dirksz remained dominant as before and led the expansion into Spain and Portugal. In 1577, for instance, two Dutch merchants living in Lisbon, Gaspar Cunertorf and Hans Snel, entered into a partnership with a man called Jan Janssen with the aim of trading between Portugal, the Netherlands and the Baltic.[39] Cunertorf and Snel provided capital, presumably of 27,500 guilders, Janssen added another 2,200 guilders and agreed to represent the partnership as profit sharing factor in Gdansk and

A mint master, portrayed by Maarten van Heemskerk in 1529. This man used to be identified as Pieter Gerritszoon Bicker, master of the mint and alderman of Amsterdam. When in 1578 Amsterdam switched sides and joined the revolt against Spain, the Bicker family became one of the strongest clans in the city.

During the second half of the 16th century, Dutch merchants began to expand their commercial operations southward, establishing themselves in cities like Lisbon. From there, they shipped salt, tobacco, and dyestuffs to the north. Anonymous 17th century panorama of Lisbon harbour.

Amsterdam. The contract allowed him to draw on his partners or on their Antwerp factor until he would have established his own credit locally. The few data available show the partners operating as wholesalers with a wide range of goods. Janssen shipped grain, wooden ship's parts, pig iron, hides, rope and textile to his partners, sometimes straight from Gdansk, sometimes via Antwerp, Amsterdam or other Dutch ports. In Lisbon, Cunertorf and Snel operated both as wholesalers and as retailers in these articles, presumably a fairly common combination at that time.[40] Their northbound consignments mainly consisted of salt from Setubal, spices, sugar, rice and dye wood. The partnership's internal organisation looked both modern and old-fashioned. Cunertorf and Snel drafted no regular mutual settlements and therefore probably had not yet adopted the practice of regularly closing their accounts. They treated their transactions as separate deals, not as part of a single and independent business. The partners were modern in wanting a quick turnover from their factors, if necessary by bartering for return consignments. Sales often proved very slow, however. In July 1577 Cunertorf and Snel sent 22 bags of pepper to Janssen, which arrived four months later. The last bag was sold in May 1580, so after nearly two years. The partnership also looked modern in its fairly intensive correspondence. Letters from Lisbon to Amsterdam took about 44 days, from Amsterdam to Gdansk at least another sixteen.[41]

26

A quayside in Riga harbour, with a
port crane and fluyt ships,
anonymous painting from the second
half of the 17th century. Fluyt ships
were specially designed for cheap
bulk transport, and as such provided
the mainstay of the Baltic trade or
'mother of all trade'.

The Delft merchant Van Adrichem, mentioned before, also wrote regularly with his Danzig factor, continuously exchanging information on actual or expected price changes, the arrival of goods or ships, sometimes several times a week. They also discussed other matters, for instance where to buy a new ship for their regular captain.[42] During the sixteenth century, Dutch shipbuilders developed special freighters for bulk transport on the Baltic run. These ships had a longer than usual keel, with a bulging hull tapering to a narrow deck at the top. This latter feature reduced the ship's toll dues on the Sound, levied by measuring the deck surface as a proxy for carrying capacity. By 1590 a specific type of ship had emerged, the *Fluyt*. These freighters combined a large carrying capacity with excellent sailing characteristics and required only a small crew. Further development of these characteristics extended the competitive cost advantage well into the 17th century.[43] A comparison of crew sizes underlines the importance of this advantage. On estimate, a 1620 Dutch fluyt of 200 tons could sail with nine to ten hands, whereas an English freighter of the same carrying capacity required a crew of nearly thirty.[44] By adding dedicated supply and marketing of bulk products to this cost advantage, merchants built a revolutionary logistic concept.[45]

Unlike Cunertorf and Snel, Van Adrichem and his factor Aper Jansz Delft kept annual accounts, presumably according to the principles of double entry bookkeeping. The principal took the interests of his factor to heart, warning him at one point against neglecting to charge his principals for postage dues on their account.[46] Aper Jansz apparently spent 50 guilders a year on postage and must have conducted a very voluminous correspondence indeed. Though this amount represented only 0.5% of estimated turnover on the Van Adrichem account in 1590, it equalled the price of three oxheads of French wine, sold for him in the Sound a few years earlier. In present day terms that would mean annual postage costs of 9,300 guilders, sufficient for 138 letters a week between the Netherlands and Poland of the kind exchanged by these two merchants.[47] Van Adrichem and Aper Jansz probably spent quite a lot of time and effort on collecting and exchanging information on products, prices, ships' movements, freight rates and insurance conditions. In addition they had their routine office duties: winding up transactions, taking delivery of merchandise or shipping consignments, converting commodity prices into other currencies and different weight units, keeping their ledgers up to date, visiting the bourse, etc. Descriptions of commercial business in the early modern era often depict an idyll of short office hours and a slack tempo supposedly contrasting with the hectic life of business people today.[48] Such contentions really mistake the speed of communications for the pulse of business. The point of view that, because transport in the past had a slower pace, men in trade did not have to work very hard, over-looks the fact that commercial business required a very large number of actions. Moreover, it fails to appreciate that merchants like Van Adrichem and Aper Jansz, or Cunertorf, Snel and Janssen, went about their business with the same restless energy as people do today, constantly looking for new opportunities, different products, better suppliers, cheaper transport, lower costs.

Another striking aspect of Van Adrichem's letters is that they do not sug-gest uncertain and deficient postal services, but rather the opposite, a regularity and frequency which indicate a firm organisation. Antwerp had already set up a city post office running messenger services to the main European cities. Ships' captains, wagon drivers and travellers would also carry letters for a small fee. The Dutch cities quickly copied Antwerp's example and appointed their own messengers, creating a firm communications network. Of course, some letters never arrived, others took longer than usual, because delivery was held up by adverse winds or other circumstances. Merchants had no choice but to rely on the post, because 'envoyer sans information, ce seroit une pure folie [shipping merchandise without information would be pure folly]', as the merchant Daniël van der Meulen wrote in 1592 to one of his many correspondents.[49] They num-bered letters so they could spot any missing links. Important documents such as invoices or bills of exchange were copied and sent by different routes. Fast yachts usually accompanied merchant fleets, sailing ahead on the last stretch to speed up the post. Trade margins must have covered the remaining risk of mail mishaps. As a result postal services were firm enough to allow complicated commercial traffic. As early as the last quarter of the 16th century for instance,

Merchants usually mailed several copies of their letters and other documents, as a precaution against loss. This chest full of undelivered letters of postmaster Simon de Brienne demonstrated the wisdom of such precautions.

freight contracts would bind captains to load French salt in the Bay of Bourgneuf and sail to the Sound. While waiting for the often lengthy completion of toll formalities, they would receive instructions as to their destinations.[50] These were decided on the basis of the quality of the salt, and price movements in the Baltic ports, always fluctuating with the arrival of ships and changes in demand. During the 17th century salt ships sometimes docked at Texel to deliver a cargo sample. The ships' charterers would then examine the quality and instruct their representatives in the Sound accordingly.[51] By that time, then, a regular postal service must have been in place, overtaking the freighters, allowing merchants better sales targeting. Sailors' taverns served as staging posts for correspondence between captains and their principals. The supercargo on an exploratory mission to Italy in 1589 had orders to pass Dover on his way back, where Mr. Spirituel, landlord of the White Greyhound, would hand him instructions about his destination.[52]

Van Adrichem was fairly familiar with bills of exchange and used them regularly for payments between the Netherlands and Danzig, also to some extent for speculative uses such as anticipating exchange rate fluctuations and differences between exchange rates and commodity prices. In 1590 he and Aper Jansz had a bill turnover of 10,000 guilders between them.[53] Presumably Jansz had the initiative in this. Because of the uncertainties and dangers still attached to using bills, Van Adrichem repeatedly urged his factor to be cautious, warning him to take an extra signature as precaution.[54] By this time, bills had become quite current in Dutch trade, but had not yet attained full independence as a

29

The office of postmaster was a position fit for wealthy citizens. M. de la Court painted this portrait of the Delft postmaster Lambert Twent with his sons in 1697.

commercial instrument. The Amsterdam mathematician and schoolmaster, Claes Pietersz, discussed the bill accordingly in his manual on double-entry bookkeeping published in 1576, the first such instruction printed in the northern Netherlands. He discussed the bill and its uses, but did not include a separate bill account in his system. This book represented an improvement on Ympijn's work in other respects as well. Pietersz made the accounts more transparent by grouping the individual commodity transactions, rather than keeping them separate as before. He also gave examples of consignment transactions, goods shipped or received with a simultaneous advance payment on the invoice by the addressee. Therefore, Amsterdam merchants must have used this technique at the time of Claesz' writing, which indicates both an advance in commercial technique, and increasing capital available for such advances.[55] Unfortunately, we do not know the size of this consignment trade, nor whether it concerned imports or exports.

Van Adrichem, then, ran a business similar in scale to that of Reyersz and Dircsz or Cunertorf and Snel, but much more advanced in commercial technique and organisation.[56] His range of commodities traded was also wider and always changing. As far as we know, many firms from the last quarter of the 16th century specialised in a certain product or in trade with a particular region. However, some firms dealt in anything judged profitable with any country, provided they could find the right correspondents. The small scale and flexibility of such commercial firms gave the Dutch economy great power of expansion. The one man bands or two-man partnerships may have looked puny, but together they developed a formidable might by combining full competition with coordinated operations where necessary. By contrast, the Hanseatic merchants always operated abroad as a regulated unit, which blunted their business acumen. English merchants excluded competition on the long distance runs, by uniting into companies with exclusive Royal charters. Dutch merchants had no such constraints and could freely switch between markets.[57]

Compared to the great Italian merchant houses, Dutch firms only lacked volume of operations and a continuity of business under the same name, the last defining element that sets apart the businesses tied to changing individual merchants, from that of merchant houses. Cunertorf and Snel might have achieved some form of continuity, but the partnership fell apart when Janssen proved unreliable and the two senior partners started to quarrel. Van Adrichem ran a typical one man effort, with varying joint ventures, as did Daniël van der Meulen until his death in 1600.[58] No names of enduring firms from that period in time have come down to us. Law courts accepted the principle of corporate bodies with severally liable partners during the last quarter of the sixteenth century. However, until well into the 17th century, legal theorists struggled to distinguish between merchants and their business proper.[59] A formal continuity of firms only became feasible when that distinction had emerged. Until then merchants passed on no more than their trade knowledge and relations to their successors, or nothing at all.

Dutch trade expansion boosted the development of cartography. This art achieved a peak with the publication of the famous Joan Blaeu Atlas in 1664-1665. The picture shows a map of the Baltic from this atlas.

Even so, a family business built up over several generations could definitely achieve a considerable informal continuity. Captain Willem Jansz Hooft for instance sailed on the Baltic route, probably as early as the first quarter of the 16th century, and he died on board ship in 1562 when he was 77 years of age. Some of his children stayed in the Netherlands, others emigrated far and wide to Danzig in Poland, Bergen in Norway, La Rochelle in France, and Aveiro in Portugal. Around 1630, descendants living around the Baltic still did business for their Amsterdam relatives, whose sons, however, had meanwhile opted to go to university. The Hooft clan may not have traded under a particular formal name, but we have to assume that when successive generations took over the existing business, the family name sufficed for Baltic merchants to continue relations with the sons as they had done with the fathers.[60]

The activities of all the firms mentioned took place against the background of a momentous breakthrough. The routes to France, Spain and Portugal seized by merchants from the northern Netherlands during the last quarter of the 16th century opened a direct supply of products which they had obtained from secondary sources before. In combination with Dutch dominance in the Baltic, and the strong local shipping sector, this posed a serious threat to Antwerp's position, from Amsterdam in particular. Perhaps the Scheldt metropolis would in time have had to concede defeat for the reasons mentioned above: the shallow roots of the international trade sector, the sea borne trade eclipsing the overland routes, and the congested harbour facilities. On the other hand, a bipolar system could well have come into existence, since Antwerp and Amsterdam complemented each other. Anyway, political developments intervened and prevented a direct confrontation between the rivals.

A TRANSFER OF POWER IN THE LOW COUNTRIES – On 25 October 1555, the emperor Charles v stood before the Estates General of the Burgundian Nether-lands and abdicated. His son and successor King Philip II of Spain continued his father's policies, but by his measures he soon estranged himself from his subjects to the point of open resistance. Unlike Charles v, Philip strove to achieve his aims without taking notice of the delicate political balance in the country. Admittedly, the circumstances allowed him very little time for patience. War with France had depleted the treasury, and long drawn out negotiations with the provincial representatives over tax increases provided insufficient relief. In 1557, Philip had to declare a formal state bankruptcy by suspending payments, a shockingly new experience which threw his provinces into turmoil. The nobili-ty turned against the King because he entrusted an increasing number of tasks to administrative councils installed by him, bypassing the traditional representa-tive bodies. Ruthless campaigns against heretics stirred unrest all over the country, because protestants formed a sizeable minority.

During the 1560s the situation escalated into a crisis. Philip proved inflexible when confronted with pleas for leniency. A series of bad harvests pushed up food prices and created a famine, fanning the prevailing unrest.[61] During the late summer and autumn of 1566, iconoclast mobs stormed church buildings, smashing windows, altars and statues. These riots were partly spontaneous outbursts of despair, generated by economic misery, and partly

The revolt against King Philip II of Spain led to the creation of the Republic of the Seven United Provinces, with Amsterdam as its main economic centre. Copy of a portrait painted by Anthonis Mor van Dashorst.

Forces from the breakaway provinces fighting Spanish troops at the battle of Oosterweel, near Antwerp, in 1567. Engraving by F. Hogenberg.

organised actions planned by Calvinist zealots. In response, Philip charged the Duke of Alba to restore order in the Netherlands with the aid of the Spanish army.

The Iron Duke's clampdown turned the crisis into an open revolt. In 1572, the provinces of Holland and Zeeland repudiated the King's authority and appointed the leader of the resistance, Prince William of Orange, in his place. Only the two provincial capitals, Amsterdam and Middelburg respectively, remained loyal to Philip. The ensuing civil war devastated Holland and Zeeland. Successive Spanish governors did not succeed in subduing the rebels, however, and the insurgents gradually gained support elsewhere in the country. In 1579 the northern Netherlands allied with the main cities in the south against the King, but the alliance came under severe strain after military setbacks and the death of Prince William in 1584. The defeat of the rebels seemed a matter of time.

However, from the late 1580s the situation improved. Philip II turned his attention away from the Low Countries, and Prince William's successor, Prince Maurice, managed to recapture large areas. The allied rebels now became known as the Republic of the Seven United Provinces. In 1596 both England and France formally recognised the Republic as an independent country. The war against Spain ebbed and flowed still, but mostly beyond the borders and at sea. After peace negotiations had come to nothing, the two countries signed a truce that was to last twelve years.

The Revolt and the war against Spain split the Low Countries politically and produced far-reaching economic consequences. The two main commercial centres, Antwerp and Amsterdam, both suffered from the war, but their

Once it joined the Revolt against Spain in 1578, Amsterdam rapidly grew into the leading commercial centre of Europe. The population rose, prosperity increased, forcing the city to expand its bounds. This was done in four steps. In the third quarter of the 17th century Claesz Pietersz Berchem depicted this process in an allegorical painting. On the right is the Maid of Amsterdam dressed in white, with a 1662 map showing the new city plan.

34

eventual fate was in complete contrast. Antwerp had Calvinism and the rebel cause close to its heart, but the city remained under Spanish occupation. At the same time it became isolated, because Zeeland blocked the Scheldt to thwart the enemy. The 1579 treaty appeared to bring relief. Antwerp joined the rebels and trade picked up again, until the Spanish army recaptured the city in 1585 after a long siege. Antwerp did not really recover from this blow. The Republic choked traffic on the Scheldt to a trickle, merchants and craftsmen emigrated in large numbers, foreign firms relocated to other cities. Europe's metropolis declined to a provincial city with a rich past. The future lay in the north.

Amsterdam had at first sympathised with the Revolt, but had nevertheless remained loyal to the King. Thus the city became politically isolated within Holland, just like Antwerp, and also suffered an economic blockade. Alba's campaign started a Protestant exodus from the city, with many prominent merchants amongst the refugees, and trade slowed to a halt. The Baltic trade largely went to Rotterdam.[62] As late as 1578 the city fathers switched their allegiance. Though the exiles returned, and trade connections were restored, recovery took a long time. The war continuously threatened the trade routes, and, well into the 1580s, the independence of the rebellious cities and provinces looked precarious. King Philip jeopardised trade with the Iberian peninsula by proclaiming an embargo against merchants from Zeeland and Holland. Consequently some Amsterdam merchants opted to prolong their exile, while refugees from the southern provinces often preferred to settle in German cities or Baltic ports rather than Amsterdam. Thus Hamburg, for instance, became a centre for the trade in sugar and spices until the mid-1590s.[63]

HALCYON DAYS – Ten years after the fall of Antwerp, it had already become plain that Amsterdam had taken over as the main European trade centre, and that further expansion was in full swing. The city grew at an enormous rate, from about 30,000 inhabitants in 1585 to 50,000 in 1600 and no fewer than 100,000 in 1620. At the start of the Twelve Years' Truce in 1609 the Dutch sea borne trade dominated the main routes within Europe and from there to Africa, South America, and Asia to an unprecedented extent, though perhaps the commercial organisation had not yet attained the flexibility and tensile strength of Antwerp.[64] The merchant fleet showed further vigorous growth, from about 800 ships in 1560, to an estimated 1,750 freighters for Europe alone in 1630.[65] The sea lay wide open for whoever dared to sail it. The great legal scholar, Hugo de Groot, argued in his epoch-making treatise *Mare Liberum* (1609), that the open sea belongs to the world's nations and is therefore free for all to roam. Twenty years later, Amsterdam merchants observed somewhat smugly in a memorandum that, since the Truce, their business sense and cunning had served them to outsail all rivals. They had redirected all trade to the Republic, and had served all countries with their ships.[66]

This singular expansion found its basis in the strong shipping sector, the firm grip on the Baltic trade, and the zest for business shown by the ships' masters and merchants who pioneered the routes to Spain and Portugal. These factors explain why the Republic could experience a sudden spurt of economic growth when Antwerp fell to the Spaniards. However, they do not account for the astounding spirit of innovation and tireless initiative which inspired the country between about 1590 and 1610. A new era seemed to have dawned, in which everything was possible and nearly everything permitted, an era of spectacular ventures and corresponding profits, an era in which the world belonged to fearless pioneers, with consequences to match: unbridled growth, basic institutional innovation, intoxicating and exceptional opportunities, which blurred the boundaries between honest business and plain piracy, meteoric careers sometimes covering dubiously acquired riches, but also merchants losing their bearings after a glorious start and ending as beached whales.

This spectacular show was partly carried by an influx of refugees from the southern Netherlands, of labourers, craftsmen, manufacturers, scientists, and merchants.[67] The flow gained full momentum once the Republic had attained a firm existence. One of the scientists was the preacher and cartographer Petrus Plancius. He brought to the Republic his state of the art knowledge about navigation and map making as practised in the southern Netherlands, and also practical information about sea routes and foreign ports. He found keen students of his worldly teaching in Amsterdam. The merchants came from all strata of the Antwerp community. Some of them brought their experience of Antwerp's extensive mercantile-financial business, something which had not yet attained a high level of development in the north. Others went to the Republic while still at the start of their careers. These specific immigrants from the large group coming to Amsterdam contributed something indefinable to the booming economy in the Republic around 1600. They often stood in the front rank when new schemes took shape, for the launch of trading companies, for sending missions to unknown cities or continents, or for stock exchange manipulations. On the other hand, the thrust of innovation never came from the southern immigrants alone. They always found adventurous local merchants with sufficient experience and capital, and ready for action, or even about to take off. Lambert van Tweenhuysen, Van Adrichem, and members of the Hooft family mentioned above, or else Elias Trip, Jan Jansz Kaerel and Jan Poppen, about whom more will be said shortly, are all good examples. Records do not admit of a precise assessment of contributions made by the different groups. We must be content to conclude that the particular mix of merchants provided the thrust.

The expansion required certain basic commercial facilities. More or less simultaneously, the main ports of Amsterdam, Rotterdam, and Middelburg all set up marine insurance chambers, offices for registering policies and settling disputes.[68] The Amsterdam chamber does not appear to have had a lot of work to begin with, for in 1629 prominent merchants explained to the city council that only full owners had their ships insured. The widespread practice of risk management by splitting ownership and spreading consignments over several ships apparently reduced the need for insurance. Presumably, the chambers were meant to bolster trust in Dutch marine insurance. Foreign consignments were probably covered in the Republic. These must have supplied an important, and possibly fast growing share in total trade. For that matter, the Rotterdam chamber was busier than the Amsterdam one.[69]

The same three cities commissioned the building of an exchange, following the Antwerp model, so merchants could meet each other for business regularly. Rotterdam and Middelburg had no such facilities to offer at all, and decided to start building in 1595 and 1598 respectively.[70] The Amsterdam council could afford to wait. As early as the mid 16th century, merchants congregated at one end of the main harbour bridge. In bad weather they moved to the nearby St Olof's Chapel at the end of the Zeedijk. When this became too crowded, merchants moved to the much larger Old Church, a little further into town. The bell in a guard's shelter on the quay side rang the beginning and end of trade. This shelter also received all incoming letters. In 1592 the city council drew up new regulations for the exchange, including stringent penalties for armed threats and violence. The huge expansion of trade during the 1590s must have made the need for dedicated amenities urgent. The city architect, Hendrick de Keyser, designed the building, with the council urging him to splash out on ornamentation. In 1608 Hendrik Hooft, the youngest son of the mayor, laid the foundation stone. Three years later the bourse opened for trading.[71]

The Fall of Antwerp (1585) caused an influx of refugees from the Southern Netherlands to the Republic. The Antwerp mayor and ship owner Gillis Hoffmann and his wife Margaretha van Nispen left the city in 1566. Portrait by Maerten de Vos, 16th century.

In the 16th century, Amsterdam did not yet have an exchange building. Merchants met on the bridge separating the IJ sea arm from the Damrak canal, with the bell from a watch house sounding the business hours. Incoming mail had to be delivered to the same watch house. Abraham Storck made this drawing of it in 1679.

De Keyser's exchange building consisted of a rectangular open courtyard surrounded by a double colonnade rising to three stories. Merchants gathered at numbered columns assigned to each particular line of business. The city commissioners charged with liquidating bankrupt firms guarded both entrances. Amsterdam business centred on the bourse until the 1920s. During exchange hours everyone went there for business and gossip: merchants, brokers, insurers, ships' masters, and bankers. There were no entry restrictions, so from time to time the entertainment provided would attract a large crowd of spectators. Moreover, the bourse became the outstanding symbol of the Republic's entrepot market and commercial power, a Capitol of Commerce, as the poet Joost van den Vondel put it. The nations of the earth mill about, the world's commodities are on sale, one might pick up any language, it serves as a church where Jews, Muslims, and Christians meet each other in peace, eulogised another poet, Jeremias de Decker.[72] Foreign visitors frequently showed themselves equally impressed with this temple for all creeds united in commerce. Around the time of commissioning De Keyser, the city council also established a commission of brokers charged with compiling a regular official price-current. This journal started at least as early as 1585, presumably earlier still. Around 1600 it listed quotations for more than 200 commodities, bullion, and exchange rates. Copies of the Amsterdam price-current circulated all over Europe.[73]

The city fathers broadened the foundations of the entrepot trade system by setting up the famous Wisselbank or Exchange Bank in 1609. Inspired by the Venetian Banco di Rialto, this bank was intended to eliminate the plague of a defective currency by providing merchants with a smooth payments system. The variety of coins in circulation was enormous. In the Republic alone, no fewer than 24 cities produced their own coin, as often as not of different weight and quality. Sound pieces were hoarded, reducing the circulation to worn-out and underweight coins. Large settlements required sackfulls of specie, and nobody could tell their true value. The Wisselbank provided a solution by accepting deposits in all current coins, calculating their value and crediting the depositor in banco money against fixed exchange rates. By council order, merchants had to settle bills of more than 100 Flemish pounds or 600 guilders via the *Wisselbank*. The city council guaranteed deposits. Even creditors in bankruptcy cases could not seize them. Merchants disposed over their deposits by giro transfers to each other. Deposits bore no interest, the account holders paid a commission over their transactions. The bank's statute prescribed 100% liquidity, so deposits could not be used for providing credit or loans. In spite of this, the city treasury and the VOC (Dutch East India Company) did in fact receive clandestine, short-term advances.

The Wisselbank was purposefully conservative in design, and not progressive, a regulator and not a pump fuelling expansion with credit facilities or innovations such as paper money. Presumably, at that moment there was no need for such an instrument. The bank fulfilled its intended task of reorganising

The interior of the exchange built by Hendrick de Keyser, painted by Emanuel de Witte in 1653. This building functioned as the commercial hub of the entrepot market, and it also served as a prime tourist attraction.

the payments system with extraordinary success. The creation of a fiduciary currency unit with a guaranteed value and a stable exchange rate signified an enormous advance for the settlement of commercial transactions. Nowhere in Europe did such means exist, though merchants all over Europe longed for it. Soon banco money commanded a premium or *agio* over specie and bullion transactions. Within a decade of its foundation the Wisselbank had more than 1,000 depositors, and over 2 million guilders of deposits, mainly from Amsterdam, but merchants from all over Europe opened accounts so they could use the facilities. Middelburg copied the Amsterdam example in 1616, Delft in 1621, and Rotterdam in 1635.

The Amsterdam council deployed even more initiatives. It set up a grain exchange and a city lombard bank, it published the Antwerp bill regulations and made them binding within the city, and appointed supervisors for the postal system.[74] The importance of such steps can hardly be overestimated, for several reasons. First, they made the Republic more transparent and thus more attractive as a market for foreign merchants. Second, the initiatives turned the commodity market into a hub of allied services, reinforcing the wide range of goods available and the cheap shipping, with price information, insurance, finance, and a secure settlement system, each individual component raised to the height of perfection. This extraordinary compound competitive advantage provided the basis for an unparalleled commercial expansion which set in during the 1590s.

THE WORLD LIES OPEN – Once the disastrous initial years of the Revolt had passed, a vigorously growing Baltic trade, and a fast expanding trade network heralded economic recovery in Amsterdam. Colonies of Dutch merchants settled at the spoke ends of the network, sometimes remaining there as late as the early 18th century.[75] The demand for grain rose sharply following the opening of new markets on the Iberian peninsula and in Italy. During the first half of the 17th century, Dutch ships transported an annual average of 50,000 lasts, or 100,000 tons, westbound through the Sound.[76] The eastbound trade also underwent a transformation. Dutch ships had always carried several high-value products to the Baltic: textiles, sugar, spices, wine, and Mediterranean fruit. Once established on the southern trade routes, Dutch merchants could offer these commodities from source, thus cheaper, resulting in rising volumes.[77] The northern section of the trade network expanded when the routes to Norway and Archangelsk were seized from competing English merchants. Partnerships of southern immigrants ran the Archangelsk trade at first, continuing businesses started in Antwerp.[78] After Archangelsk the Russia merchants established themselves in Moscow. The Russian trade consisted of a large proportion of luxuries, outbound ships carrying various commodities from central and southern Europe, Asia and the Americas, to return with caviar, hides, leather, and furs. These goods often went directly to Italy.

The Spanish embargoes hampered trade with the Iberian peninsula, but failed to do lasting damage. Both Spain and Portugal had meanwhile become too dependent on the Amsterdam-centred supply of grain, timber, rope, pitch etc. from the Baltic to allow complete disruption. Business continued as usual, camouflaged by false names and flags of convenience, with the Government of Philip II turning a blind eye.[79] Merchants went very far indeed to circumvent embargoes. In 1605, for instance, Lambert van Tweenhuysen received a warning from his correspondent in Seville not to sail for Spain with a Dutch ship or crew under any circumstances, following an edict putting new and harsh penalties on trade with the Republic. Consequently he instructed his captain to sail from Amsterdam to Archangelsk, deliver the cargo and take a new load on board. He then had to dismiss the Dutch crew and engage English, French or Scandinavian sailors for the return trip to Spain. If the captain could not get enough crew members in Russia, he had to pass Falmouth or Plymouth on the way down and try there.[80] Continuous warfare probably made such camouflage a routine precaution. After all, ships on a long voyage were likely to run into at least one of the enemies at that particular moment. Some merchants did not even need tricks to duck the Spanish embargo. The Hooft family's relatives in Norway and Portugal enabled the Amsterdam-based merchants to continue their trade in salt, stock fish and grain between the Baltic and Aveiro on Norwegian ships without any hindrance.[81]

Like the Spanish King, the Estates General of the Republic equally failed in their efforts to control trade with the enemy. Representatives from the main ports supported merchants in their constituency who ignored the ban, the admiralties badly needed the revenues from licences, and a lack of funds made strict enforcement of any bans impossible. When his captain was caught dodging convoy duties on the Italian route, the Amsterdam council supremo and grain merchant, Cornelis Pietersz Hooft, received only a light sentence, protected as he was by his connections with Johan van Oldenbarnevelt, at that time the dominant politician in Holland and in the Republic as a whole.[82] Such fiddling was in fact not the prerogative of a commercial and political elite, but a widespread habit of merchants and ships' masters, which seriously undermines the reliability of contemporary data.[83]

Meanwhile captains and merchants had ventured still further. Around 1590 the first Dutch ships with Baltic grain passed Gibraltar on their way to Italy. Again, immigrants from the south made a large contribution. Among them were Daniel van der Meulen and Jacques della Faille. The latter had heard rumours about English merchants doing good business there, and he wanted another try after a not very successful earlier trip in 1584. The merchants started by gathering extensive information on prices, currencies, markets, and Italian customs and traditions. A cousin of Della Faille in Venice supplied details. Once the merchants had decided to go ahead, they sent a factor over land to Genoa. In 1589 the ship The Black Horseman sailed to Italy with a supercargo carrying written and very detailed instructions to gather information about ports, prod-

The Republic's political and commercial elites were closely entwined. During his life the prominent merchant Andries Bicker, Lord of Engelenburg, occupied many positions, such as that of Amsterdam mayor and member of the Estates General. Portrait by Anthoni de Vries after Barholomeus van der Helst, 17th century.

ucts of potential interest, people to get in touch with, commercial customs, and so on. The supercargo also had to check a very wide range of products on their sales potential: from metal ware to monks' habits, weapons, sugar, potash, rowing oars, rope, trinkets, dried and salted fish. To reduce the risk of confiscation by enemies, and to mislead the competition, the captain received two sets of papers for his ship, one English and one German, from the port of Emden, with different names and home ports for use as and when the situation required. The supercargo obtained an English passport. In spite of all preparations, the trip yielded disappointing profits, one reason being the wrong choice and poor quality of goods sent out, mainly fish.[84] Grain proved a better proposition. Two years after the trip of The Black Horseman, Amsterdam merchants alone employed between 50 and 100 ships in the Italian trade, attracted by profits rumoured to be between 300 and 400%.[85] Cornelis Pietersz Hooft established connections with Italian merchants through a colleague from Flanders. Among other things, this resulted in his exporting grain to Italy and settling a few bills, enough business to provide his son Pieter Cornelisz with a place to stay on his grand tour.[86] During the first decades of the 17th century, Dutch trade also established itself in the Levant and in north Africa. From 1612 the Republic had an ambassador at the Turkish court, and six years later a consul was appointed in Izmir (formerly known as Smyrna), the main commercial city. Subsequently the Estates General established consular posts on the main islands in the Aegean Sea and along the north African coast.[87] The Tunis and Algiers consulates date from 1616. The latter post functioned less as a support for Dutch trade, which was not very voluminous, than as a means for smoothing relations with the local rulers, who could help to negotiate with Barbary pirates about freeing captured ships and crew. Algiers did offer unusual opportunities for merchants. The local market was too small for the pirates' booty, it had to be sold in Europe. The first consul, Wijnant de Keyser, ran a very profitable business doing just this, with his merchant brother in Leghorn (Livorno) acting as intermediary.[88]

Following the trail of the Portuguese, Dutch ships sailed to the Canary Islands and the Cape Verde Islands, around 1590, to buy salt and sugar, and from there further west to South America and the Caribbean, and southeast to west Africa and the Gold Coast. These voyages also offered exceptional profits, at least initially. Between 1589 and 1595, Van Adrichem chartered fifteen ships, one for a journey to Guinea, the rest for sailing between the Baltic, the Netherlands, France, and Portugal. Profits on the European trips averaged 328 guilders, with a peak of 1,500 guilders, and four trips ending in a loss. Profits on the journey to Guinea amounted to nearly 20,000 guilders.[89] Such new ventures thus carried very handsome rewards, though not everyone will have equalled the success of Van Adrichem and his partners on this trip. After a few years, merchants on west Africa started to complain about increased competition eating into profits and tried to form a cartel to protect their market. Around 1610 some twenty ships a year sailed to the Gold Coast, carrying goods worth an estimated 500,000 guilders in all.[90]

Dutch merchants and ships' masters ventured ever further. In 1590, they ventured from Portugal to the Canary and Cape Verde Islands. Experiens Sillemans drew this sketch of a Dutch ship loading salt near the Cape Verde Islands in about 1625.

Finally in 1595 four ships embarked on the first direct voyage from the Low Countries around the Cape of Good Hope, to Asia. After more than two years, three ships returned, their crews decimated, and carrying insufficient cargo to cover costs, but also with conclusive evidence that the sea route to Asia was open for those able and willing to go.

THE TRADING ACTIVITIES OF A MILITARY-INDUSTRIAL COMPLEX – As will be remembered, Dutch trading partnerships around 1590 were still very small compared to firms in Antwerp or Italy. The tradition of changing partnerships between one-man undertakings employing factors overseas, proved sufficiently flexible for Baltic traders to extend their operations into France and the Iberian peninsula, to trade a growing range of products, and to incorporate technical innovations like the bill of exchange into their business. After about 1590, however, turbulent growth created new strains. Longer voyages demanded more capital power. A trip to Italy could last four or five months, the journey to Guinea sponsored by Van Adrichem returned after a year and three months, perhaps because the ship wandered about for a while.[91] On the new routes, ships also encountered more danger. The Baltic run was a well-beaten track and, after the Peace of Spiers, largely free from threats from piracy and legal confiscations by malevolent officials. Consequently, freighters usually sailed unarmed through the Sound. This was less advisable on the route to France, because of the Dunkirk-based pirates who prowled the Channel and the North Sea. However, sailing in convoy with or without marine escorts offered a solution to that particular problem. On longer journeys, ships as a rule sailed on their own, carrying appropriate armament. Once the Truce had expired in 1621, trade with Spain and Portugal again suffered heavily from embargoes and the direct effects of war. On the Mediterranean, Barbary pirates and the Turkish navy posed a constant threat to shipping.

As a rule, the Northern European seas were safe enough for Dutch ships to sail unarmed. However, for trips further afield, to the Mediterranean, to Asia, or to South America, they had to be armed. In 1647, Wenzel Hollar published a series of etchings of Dutch ships, using this harbour scene as a title page. Cannon lie on the left, anchors right. The wooden crates in the right foreground carry marks such as those used by merchants to identify their goods.

Crossing the oceans to Guinea, the Caribbean, South America, or Asia raised incalculable dangers of an altogether different order. Such ventures also required huge investment. At first sight, De Houtman's pioneering voyage to Asia was still a fairly small-scale affair (Table 1.1). The final sum came to just over 70,000 guilders for each ship.

Considering the length of the voyage, this compares well to the 25,000 guilders invested by the partnership sending The Black Horseman on its much shorter journey to Italy in 1585.[92] However, De Houtman's sponsors did not have to pay for armament, which was donated by the Estates of Holland from the county arsenal.[93] Subsequent entrants in the game did not get this windfall and consequently had to pay an extra 100,000 guilders per ship. This money remained tied up for an unusually long time. A round trip to Asia took about two years. It was also a high-risk business. Between 1595 and 1601, 65 ships sailed for Asia, but only 50 returned, a loss rate of more than 20%.[94]

	Fleet size	Commander	Capacity	Fitting costs	Cargo value	Total
1595	4 ships	De Houtman	500 last	170,000 gld	120,000 gld	290,000 gld
1598	8 ships	Van Neck		372,312 gld	396,738 gld	768,466 gld
1598	2 ships	De Houtman	650 last			500,000 gld
1599-1600	10 ships	Van Neck/Wilckens		638,121 gld	294,500 gld	914,205 gld
1601	13 ships	Van Heemskerck/Harmensz	665 last	609,741 gld	704,900 gld	1.3 mln gld
1602	14 ships	Van Warwijck				1.7 mln gld

Table 1.1

The costs of the first voyages to Asia

(guilders)

Source: Gaastra, Geschiedenis VOC 25;

Van Goor, Nederlandse koloniën 29-30.

Merchants responded as of old by forming partnerships to share the risk and cost of journeys to Asia. The first one, the Compagnie van Verre or Company for Faraway Ventures, was founded in 1594. This consortium of nine Amsterdam merchants sponsored De Houtman's voyage. Disappointing profits failed to dampen interest in the long-distance trade, the more so because a Spanish embargo banned Dutch merchants from Lisbon in 1598, cutting their supply of spices. Pioneering travellers started publishing their tales of discovery, fuelling public enthusiasm to unprecedented heights. Every port sprouted partnerships for the Asia trade, Rotterdam even two, Amsterdam a second one. These were trade partnerships in the old mould, but with a difference. They split ownership and management like modern companies do. Partners appointed a board from their midst to run the company from day to day, and to report back to them.

In July 1599 the second expedition commanded by Van Neck returned, the four ships carrying a fabulously rich load of pepper. Twelve months later, Van Heemskerck arrived with two ships and a load of nutmeg. The following year Van Warwijck came back with two shiploads of cloves. In 1602 no fewer than fifteen fleets totalling 65 ships had made a round trip. By now, the journeys from the Republic to Asia far outnumbered those of the Portuguese pioneers.[95] A dangerous rush loomed. Everywhere feverish preparations started for new companies, each fitting out its own expedition, while returning fleets carried the first news of competition pushing up prices in Asia. Swelling supplies also put European spice prices under pressure. Finally, ruinous competition threatened to help the Spanish and Portuguese rivals by weakening the Dutch position. After intense lobbying by Johan van Oldenbarnevelt among others, the existing companies finally merged into the voc, or Dutch East India Company in 1602.

The new company had a capital of nearly 6.5 million guilders in transferable shares. Amsterdam merchants bought more than half the shares. A quarter of these shareholders originally came from the southern Netherlands. They owned nearly 40% of shares, and dominated the list of largest investors.[96] The voc obtained a 21-year monopoly on the Asiatic trade from the Estates General, together with instructions to help speed up the European war against Spain and Portugal by inflicting maximum damage to their possessions in Asia. The charter also bestowed sovereign rights to the voc for Asia, so the company acted in the name of the Estates General when building fortresses, appointing governors, stationing soldiers, and concluding treaties. In the Republic, the company consisted of six regional departments or chambers, one each in Amsterdam, Rotterdam, Middelburg, Delft, Hoorn, and Enkhuizen. The chambers were administered by managing partners from the merged companies. These directors appointed representatives to the executive council of the voc, called Heren XVII or XVII Gentlemen after the number of delegates, which met twice or three times a year to determine the company's policy.

The VOC marked a new phase in the long-distance trade between Europe and Asia, because of its novel form as a limited company with transferable shares, because of the scale of its operations, and because of its dual purpose combining trade with war. Normal freighters carried defensive armament, if any, company ships were armed deliberately for offensive aims.[97] Strictly speaking, the VOC has no place in a book focusing on international traders. True, trade formed its original design, and until its demise the company continued to run a large commercial business. However, the original purpose became subservient to the increasing burdens of administering an enormous Asian territory and the consequent need to maintain a large military presence. For that reason the term military-industrial complex fits the company better than international trader. On the other hand, without the VOC the story of Dutch trade would be incomplete, so it does merit attention here.

As a limited company with a large share capital, the VOC had a unique durability. Until then, participants could resign partnerships after each voyage, and this principle also applied to the first companies in the long distance trade. The Dutch East India Company ran no such risk. The contract bound shareholders to leave their capital in the company for ten years. After that period they would receive a full account of the company's performance, and could then reclaim their capital if they wanted to. However, the Heren XVII managed to evade both statutory obligations. They completely ignored the shareholders, and the idea that shares might be reclaimed was soon wiped off the table. This high-handed attitude raised storms of protests from shareholders, but to no avail. The company's business was so closely intertwined with affairs of state, that the Estates General backed the Heren XVII against all complaints.[98] As a result, the directors could nurse the business to maturity without much interference.

The relief from the mundane worries of corporate governance enabled the VOC to develop a long distance trade, which married a very large scale to a long-term perspective. The company set out to gain control over the production and supply of spices, and developed a sales policy aimed at keeping prices stable. The Heren XVII and the company managers in Asia, the Governor General with his Council of India, ran a taut organisation designed to maintain an optimal flow of information and, to deliver products in accordance with standards. Every year the Heren XVII sent a list to Asia stipulating the products to be bought and the maximum purchase prices. The council also set the minimum sales margins. In their turn, the authorities in Asia reported extensively to the Republic on the course of business. Textile had to conform to specified models and samples, agricultural products such as spices were subject to purity standards. The company used its power wherever possible to force the local population into a regimented production of spices, increasing yields and eliminating competition. Rivals such as the Portuguese could not match this tight organisation, and the English had a hard time to draw level.[99]

45

In 1595, Cornelis de Houtman led the first expedition sailing from the Republic to Asia. Seven years later the existing companies for the intercontinental trade merged to form the VOC or Dutch East India Company. Frederik de Houtman, a brother of Cornelis, served the VOC as first governor of Ambon during 1605-1611. Detail from an anonymous painting of the Dutch school, 1617.

This was an expensive and time-consuming policy. During the first charter, the Heren XVII received a barrage of criticism on the way they managed the business and on the poor results. The first dividend was declared as late as April 1610. Even then, liquidity constraints forced the company to pay only a trifle in cash and the rest in kind, i.e., pepper, bay leaves, and nutmeg. Over the years 1602-1622, returns averaged no more than 10% a year, which was rather disappointing considering the high expectations and equally inflated share price. Merchants such as Isaac le Maire complained bitterly that profits were too low to justify a monopoly. Getting established in Asia required particularly great sacrifices of money and manpower. The VOC started with a series of campaigns to drive the Portuguese from the Moluccan spice islands Ambon, Tidore, and Ternate, a goal finally achieved around 1605. This was of course only a start, the company continued operating on the alert for, or actually at war, with the European competition, with Asian rulers, or with the population of territories where it sought to settle. Local circumstances determined the form of settlement. In Thailand for instance the company could carry on its trade undisturbed after securing exclusive contracts, so a simple trade office sufficed. The same applied to the branches in Canton, Mocha and Persia.

However, circumstances in the Indonesian archipelago pulled the VOC deeper and deeper into the mire of local politics, sooner or later leading to military confrontations.[100] Moreover, its efforts to monopolise the spice trade at source trapped the company in a tough struggle with inhabitants. Successive Governor Generals took ruthless actions to break the resistance. In 1621 for instance, the VOC captured the Banda islands to get control over the production of nutmeg and bay leaves. Very few original inhabitants remained on the islands. They had fled, had starved to death during the siege, or had died in battle. A handful of survivors were deported to Java.[101] Similarly, the company obtained a near monopoly in cloves by capturing the island of Ambon. Thousands of Ambonese died, the survivors were reduced to virtual company slaves working a tightly regulated production system. 'They fought a war against Nature itself, and consequently a true war of extermination against the inhabitants, anything to maintain the monopoly'.[102] These were Pyrrhic victories for the Dutch East India Company. Maintaining control over cloves, nutmeg, and bay leaves cost so much money, that the profitability of this business remains disputed. 'They have many castles with much trouble and little profit', an English observer commented on the VOC's business in the Indonesian archipelago.[103]

Building a balanced trade business entailed a prolonged territorial expansion. European merchants had no products to sell in Asia, local manufacturers made textiles or metal ware of equal or superior quality. Consequently, the VOC had to redress the inherently negative trade balance by shipping silver, amounting to about 1 million guilders a year. The company also attempted to raise revenues by introducing the Republic's multilateral trade network in Asia, by developing commercial activities between the various regions. For quite some time this strategy proved successful, yielding commodities and revenues sup-

The foundation of the VOC in 1602 established the limited company as a suitable form of business organisation for the long-distance trade. The company combined commercial with military purposes. On the left a bird's eye view on the spice island of Ambon, with the portrait of governor Frederik Houtman as inset (Dutch School, 1617). On the right the VOC settlement at Hougli in Bengal, a painting by Hendrik van Schuylenburg, 1665.

porting the overall business. If only this particular diversification had not also required new branches, in Coromandel and Bengal to get the cotton needed for the spice islands, on Taiwan to obtain Chinese silk for the Japanese trade.[104] As a result the VOC needed a constant supply of staff, soldiers, military supplies, and warships to establish and to maintain fortresses which often provoked resistance, which incited further expansion in response, etc. The company's continuous expansion thus had a momentum and rationale entirely of its own. At its widest span, the network stretched from the Persian Gulf via India, Sri Lanka, Burma, Tonkin, Indonesia, Malaysia, Taiwan to the isle of Deshima in Nagasaki Bay. With this last branch the Republic possessed a unique trade monopoly with Japan, which lasted from 1636 until 1854.[105]

Around 1620 the company's affairs started to show some stability. In that year the central fortified settlement taking shape near Jakarta on Java was officially named Batavia. At that moment the VOC had as many as seven branches in Asia and 4,500 employees, half of which were sailors. Total staff in the Far East, including persons en route, numbered around 7,700. Sixty years later the total had risen to at least 16,000 Europeans scattered over more than 20 branches in Asia, as well as 3,600 local employees and 2,400 slaves.[106] War expenditure dragged down the business. Between 1613 and 1660 the VOC spent 36.7 million guilders on soldiers' pay and fortifications, 35% of total cost.[107] Around 1700 it possessed a navy in Asia bigger than the entire navies of middle ranking European countries like Denmark or Sweden.[108] These ships, by the way, did not appear on the balance sheets, nor did the warehouses, fortresses, and territorial possessions. Evidently, the management used states rather than trading companies as mental references when valuing its possessions.[109]

In the Republic the VOC also employed large numbers of people, but unfortunately we do not know how many. The company built ships in its own yards complete with forges, rope walks, and paint works. The Amsterdam chamber housed these activities in a factory complex on an artificial island in the harbour.[110] Coordinating this huge business concern engendered a voluminous correspondence between the governors-general and the Heren XVII. Answers to specific questions would take at least 18 months to arrive, so the managers in Indonesia usually had to act as they thought best.[111] When in 1649 disagreement arose, the then governor-general Cornelis van der Lijn wrote to the Heren XVII in a huff that they had had no time to consult them and had acted in the best interests of the company. He argued that they really had to entrust matters to the Asian managers, and not treat them like small children.[112]

Around 1620 the company at last also started to produce the long-awaited results. The business in Asia yielded growing profits, the annual number of ships between Europe and Asia continued to grow, and consequently the volume of tropical products shipped and sold. Between 1610 and 1620, 50 ships returned from Asia, 75 during the 1630s, and 127 during the 1660s. The value of products shipped rose in proportion, from more than 8 million guilders during the 1610s to 26.8 million in the 1660s. Return cargoes consisted for nearly 60% of spices, mainly pepper, for 25% of silk and cotton, with saltpetre, copper, sugar and indigo making up most of the rest (Figure 1.1).[113] Profit margins were phenomenal, for in as far as the VOC did not have a monopoly on the products, it occupied the position of biggest supplier with a profound influence

The VOC kept up a keen demand for soldiers to defend its colonial empire. Abraham Storck painted company soldiers embarking near the Montelbaans tower in Amsterdam during the second half of the 17th century. A Swedish soldier, Olof Eriksson Willman, left a description of such a scene. He had enlisted as a naval cadet on 23 November 1647, to serve for five years at a salary of 10 guilders a month in the Dutch East Indies. On the 29th of November he went with a group of soldiers to hear a reading of the company regulations and to swear an oath of allegiance. Next day he was mustered and, having received an advance of two months' salary, he embarked near the Montelbaans tower. That night the ship set sail for Texel on its way to Asia.

on prices. For that purpose the company kept the volume of supplies secret, and arranged sales in Europe with a fixed group of substantial merchants.[114] We have no detailed data on profits during the years up to 1640, but gross trading profits subsequently ranged between 250-300%. Dividends finally started to flow liberally, of at least 20-25% during the 1640s, in later years sometimes 40-45%, occasionally peaking at 65%. As a result, the company's share price soared to over 400%.[115]

Efforts to also bring trade on Africa and America under a monopoly company like the VOC were much less successful.[116] The first plans circulated as early as 1600, but private trade had already become sufficiently rooted to scupper them. When in 1621 the Twelve Years' Truce ended, the need for a company became more pressing, because Spain and Portugal renewed their fight against Dutch trade with South America, which supplied, among other goods, salt, sugar, and dye wood to the Republic.

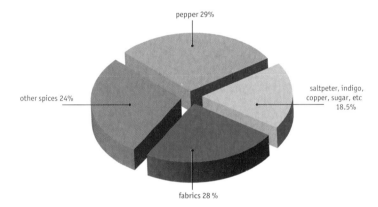

Figure 1.1

Composition of the VOC return cargoes,
1668-1670

That same year the West-Indische Compagnie (West India Company or WIC) was founded. Its organisation looked very much like that of the VOC, with chambers of shareholders managed by directors sending representatives to a central board. The WIC, however, had two directors more than the VOC, so a total of 19. Just like its sister, the new company obtained a trade monopoly and sovereign rights for its intended field of operations, Africa south of the Tropic of Cancer and west of the Cape of Good Hope, and the Americas. The WIC received express instructions to do maximum damage to the enemy, by privateering and by capturing Spanish and Portuguese colonies for settlement by Dutch immigrants.

The WIC faced a much harder task than the VOC. In Asia, Spain and Portugal possessed scattered settlements, but especially in South America they had struck deep roots. Since driving out the Spaniards and the Portuguese was going to be a very expensive business, the company aimed to raise a large capital. Investors dithered, however, after the experiences with the high-handed attitude of the Heren XVII towards the VOC shareholders. Presumably they also had their doubts about the profit potential of the tasks assigned. It took two years before the WIC directors had scraped together the 7.1 million guilders needed to make a start. And it was not enough. Within a few years the company had to call on the capital market four more times, until it possessed more than 17 million guilders in 1629, equal to the amount of shares and bonds issued by the VOC.[117] Even then the WIC muddled on from one financial crisis to another for the rest of its existence. This was caused by the effective failure to achieve its main goal, driving the Spaniards and Portuguese from South America. The company succeeded in doing great harm to enemy shipping; of all its activities, privateering was definitely the most profitable. Yet despite huge efforts, and not withstanding great financial sacrifices and temporary successes, like the capture of the Spanish silver fleet off Cuba by Admiral Piet Heyn in 1628, the WIC did not achieve its crucial aim. The company did manage find a footing in Brazil for a considerable time, but this strained the available resources to such an extent, that the Heren XIX had to water down their commercial monopoly on South America by giving merchants trade licenses. The lucrative privateering had also to be conceded to private enterprise. The WIC failed to exploit the available opportunities, whereas especially ship's masters from Zeeland knew how to make the most of them. Since the company's commercial failings were clear for all to see, the authorities in the main ports did little to stop merchants and pirate skippers from evading the monopolies, which did further damage to its business activities. Colonisation made little headway. Within the Republic few people were willing to go, if only because of the continuous wars. Once the Peace of Westphalia had brought the war with Spain to an end, the WIC started to withdraw from the captured territories, only holding on to settlements in Surinam and Curaçao. Thus a crucial reason for the company's existence disappeared.

The WIC faced an entirely different problem in North America. There was no need for territorial conquest, for the company possessed a number of suitable settlements on the east Coast, notably along the Hudson river, called the New Netherlands. Expansion required no more than a simple purchase of land from the Indian population. The colonists bought Manhattan island with merchandise worth 60 guilders. Moreover, the fur trade provided a good source of revenue. However, the WIC could not pursue an active colonisation policy because of a lack of funds. Inhabitants of the Republic showed little enthusiasm for emigration. The WIC had to recruit immigrants from other countries, and once in America the company left them more or less to their own devices. From time to time the New Netherlands ran a negative immigration balance: people

The attempt to repeat the successful setup of the VOC for trading on Africa and the Americas by setting up the WIC or West Indian Company, failed. For one, because the WIC faced an exceedingly difficult task. One of the directors of the WIC was the Amsterdam merchant Abraham de Visscher. A 17th century portrait attributed to Abraham Lambertsz van den Tempel.

returning home outnumbered immigrants arriving. Finding competent governors also proved a problem. Matters took a turn for the better only during the 1640s. With the appointment of Peter Stuyvesant as governor, the New Netherlands at last obtained a vigorous administrator. The WIC had to open up its north American trade to outsiders as well, inaugurating a period of economic growth and rising population. The looming of the second Anglo-Dutch War brought this to an end. In August 1664 a large English fleet sailed to New Amsterdam and forced Stuyvesant to surrender. When peace returned three years later, the Republic ceded its colony to Britain, New Amsterdam finally becoming New York.[118]

The WIC only made considerable headway in west Africa. The company captured a dozen Portuguese fortresses along the coast. These settlements provided the gateways for the trade in gold, slaves, ivory, wax, dye wood, and gum, which African tribes supplied from the hinterland. By value, gold was by far the most important merchandise. However, the slave trade came to occupy a central position in the company's business.[119] First of all because it required most of the available manpower, ships and money. In addition, the slave trade also formed the basis of a triangular trade. Ships from the Republic sailed for west Africa bringing guns and gunpowder, textiles, liquor, trinkets and cowrie shells. There they loaded slaves for sale in South America or on the Caribbean islands. With merchandise from that area, the ships returned to the Republic.

51

The West African trade supplied gold and ivory, but it gained its notoriety mainly because of the slave trade. The Republic exported Dutch gin and trinkets such as beads to Africa. Olfert Dapper made an engraving of gold divers and the gin trade in 1668.

Initially Brazil was the main market for slaves. Between 1636 and 1645 the WIC sold more than 23,000 slaves from Africa there.[120] When the company withdrew from the area, it also lost its dominant position in the slave trade. At the same time however, the plantation system spread to the north coast of South America and to the Caribbean islands. A much bigger market opened up, but also a more competitive one, with merchants from Britain and from the Republic and specifically the province of Zeeland joining the fray. The WIC's market share suffered a sharp decline. Dutch merchants transported an estimated 550,000 slaves from Africa to the Americas, 5% of the total. The WIC accounted for half of the Dutch number.[121] Spain remained the main customer. The right to trade with the South American colonies belonged to the King, who granted a charter or *asiento* to the highest bidding merchant. These so-called *asientistas* had to supply a set number of slaves. Since Spain did not have its own direct supply from Africa, the slaves had to be bought from English or Dutch traders, or the WIC. During the last quarter of the 17th century the brothers Balthasar and Joan Coymans managed to secure Royal charter for a number of years. They were Calvinists, who had first emigrated from the southern Netherlands to the Republic, and subsequently had settled in Cadiz. From there they continued trading with their brother Isaac, who remained in Amsterdam. Isaac Coymans did everything to harm the WIC, for instance founding a Danish company for trading with west Africa and South America.[122]

The WIC's trade was about half the size of the VOC's, at least initially. Around 1630 the West Indian Company's gross revenues from trade averaged 2.6 million guilders a year, against 5.9 million for that of its sister company.[123] As a business, the company was really a failure. In the long run, the debacle in North and South America easily outweighed the success of the African trade. And in Africa as well, the company had great trouble in fighting off the challenge of merchants evading the monopoly. The Heren XIX kept going with subsidies from the Estates General and the provincial authorities, and expensive bottomry advances. When the first charter lapsed in 1647, the WIC was, in fact, bankrupt. Even so the Heren XIX managed to obtain a new charter from the Estates General. They deftly manoeuvred towards a merger with the VOC. The Heren XVII showed no enthusiasm whatsoever, but succeeded in escaping only by paying a substantial ransom for the sister company's unwanted advances. In the end this did not really help the WIC. The company lacked a proper basis for existence, because the cost of the settlements in west Africa, on Curaçao and in Surinam simply outweighed the commercial revenues. At one point the problems became so acute, that the directors seriously considered licensing the gold trade to the VOC for an annual fee of 150,000 guilders, while at the time gold imports amounted to over 5 million guilders a year.[124] Long before the second charter was due to expire, the Heren XIX started lobbying the Estates General to express their interest for a renewal. This tactical move failed to ward off the company's bankruptcy. After prolonged wrangling with shareholders and bondholders, the WIC underwent a radical reorganisation in 1674. The company's shares and bonds were depreciated from a total of 23.5 million to 4.5 million guilders, the central board being reduced to ten members.125 Why did anyone bother at all to extend the life of the WIC and its monopoly? The company incurred losses most of the time, and it was out-competed by private enterprise on all fronts. Presumably, all parties concerned realised that, despite the losses, the WIC did remain the most practical way of maintaining the necessary harbours and forts in west Africa, Surinam and Curaçao. The trade with those regions could not do without. Rival nations could not wait to take over, and if that happened, the Republic would lose all its trade there. Merchants would not have been either willing or able to shoulder the burden. They preferred to ride piggy back on the WIC, pocketing the profits while leaving the company to pick up the bill. The Estates General had neither the financial means, nor the administrative resources to take over. Given the Republic's fragmented political organisation, offloading the WIC's losses onto the interested shareholders, cities and provinces included, was the most effective way of paying for a colonial presence, if not perhaps the most equitable one.

MOGULS AND MACHINATIONS – During the commercial expansion, merchants with varying partnerships could still compete successfully. At least, some merchants succeeded in doing so, like, for instance Daniel van der Meulen, an erudite man, member of the Estates General. He was born in Antwerp and married to Hester della Faille. After emigrating from the southern Netherlands, Van der Meulen continued his overland trade with southern Germany and Italy, apparently successfully, first from Bremen and subsequently from Leiden. As noted above, he and his brother-in-law pioneered the Republic's overseas trade with Italy, and with his brother he set up one of the first ventures to west Africa. Van der Meulen enjoyed great esteem as a merchant, and as a diplomat in the service of the Estates General, but his business does not appear to have been very large. A partnership set up in 1585 with his brother and two brothers-in-law for trading with the Baltic and the Mediterranean had a capital of 12,000 Flemish pounds or 72,000 guilders. That company was no doubt only one of Van der Meulen's business interests.126 In 1600, the year of his death, the city of Leiden imposed a capital levy of 1%. The tax assessors estimated Van der Meulen's capital at 120,000 guilders. With that sum he undoubtedly belonged to the top layer of society. However, his wealth does not appear very large when compared to the wealth of other merchants around that time, even when we take into account that the Leiden assessors probably used low estimates.127

The heyday of expansion gave free rein to merchants with a zest for new ventures, and some of them were rewarded accordingly, resulting in a fast growth of mercantile capitals of unprecedented sizes within the Republic's boundaries. The total tax assessment of wealthy Amsterdam citizens amounted to 9 million guilders in 1585, to 63 million in 1631, and to 158 million guilders in 1674.128 Jan Poppen may serve as a good example of the opportunities in

A panorama of the IJ sea arm with Amsterdam in the background, painted by Abraham Storck around 1700. Storck's depiction of busy traffic served to emphasise Amsterdam's commercial power, which was beginning to show some strain just then.

those heady days. He came to Amsterdam presumably in 1560, as an 18 or 20 year-old fortune seeking Danish immigrant, like so many others. In 1579 he was a Baltic merchant, subsequently also trading with Spain and Portugal. With others, he pioneered Archangelsk trade and organised the first expedition to Asia in 1595. Seven years later, the Amsterdam chamber elected this prominent merchant as their representative to the board of the newly founded VOC. When he died in 1616, he was one of the richest men in town. We have no precise records of his wealth, but presumably it amounted to half a million guilders, possibly more. That was not bad going, for someone who had started out barrelling herrings.[129]

Moreover, Poppen was hardly an exception. Hans van der Veeken emigrated from Mechelen to Rotterdam, soon becoming one of the most esteemed merchants there. Around 1590, he was among the first to send ships with grain to Italy. With Pieter van der Haghe he sent four ships to Asia, via Strait of Magellan in 1599. The expedition failed. Van der Haghe went bankrupt, but Van der Veeken managed to keep afloat on the strength of his reputation and his wealth. When he died, he had rebuilt his fortune to 600,000 guilders.[130] Jan Jansz Kaerel became a citizen of Amsterdam in 1578, the year the city switched sides to join the Revolt. He started in the milk business and quickly worked his way up. Kaerel became supplier to the Stadholder's Amsterdam residence, and branched out into wholesaling products from Asia and from Turkey. He supported efforts to reach China via a northern sea route in 1594, joining the outfitters of the first Asian expedition the following year. Around 1600 he bought an existing Italian glass factory in Amsterdam and pushed the business into expansion. Kaerel died in 1616, leaving an estate worth nearly 400,000 guilders.[131] Ten years later, Cornelis Pietersz Hooft's estate amounted to a similar capital size of 320,000 guilders.[132] According to the ledgers of a 1631 capital levy, 24 Amsterdam citizens possessed a capital of more than 200,000 guilders. At least two of them, Jacob Poppen and Elias Trip, were millionaires.[133] Another wealthy merchant and industrialist, Louis de Geer, received no assessment because he happened to live elsewhere at that particular moment. He also amassed a huge fortune. When he died in 1652, his estate came to 1.7 million guilders.[134] For comparison: in 1585 the richest Amsterdammer, the iron trader Dirck Jansz Graaf, probably owned no more than 140,000 guilders.[135]

These success stories contrast with some striking, indeed spectacular failures. Willem Usselincx, for instance, was an Antwerp refugee who worked in Middelburg and campaigned for unrelenting war against Spain. He was an initiator of the West Indian Company and an early opponent of both the conquests in South America and the slave trade. He made his fortune in the Atlantic trade, only to lose it again by bankrupting in 1617, having committed a great slice of his wealth to a land reclamation project, the expected profits of which came too late.[136]

The merchant Willem Usselinx was an assiduous pamphleteer, one of his concerns being the foundation of a company for the West Indian trade. He invested a very large sum of money into the reclaiming of the Beemster polder, and was bankrupted by the protracted delay of the returns. A painting of the Dutch School, 1637.

55

A fellow citizen of Usselincx, Balthasar de Moucheron, wrote fewer pamphlets than his compatriot, but he probably traded on a bigger scale, wherever possible, in the traditional mould of a one man undertaking encircled by temporary partnerships. He pioneered the Russian trade, and had a brother in Archangelsk. In addition, De Moucheron traded with the Canary Islands and the Cape Verdian Islands, west Africa, Britain, France, Italy, and the Levant, focusing on arms and gunpowder. He took part in the fruitless efforts to find a northeastern sea route to Asia, sponsored an exploration to the Caribbean, and founded the Veerse Company, which in 1598-1601 sent two expeditions totalling five ships to Asia. These last two ventures lost money, probably finishing De Moucheron as a merchant. His business foundered, and to escape his creditors, De Moucheron fled to France, where he tried to interest King Henry IV in a projected Asian trade company, but in vain.[137]

Finally, there was Isaac le Maire, still an Antwerp spice trader in 1584. Once established in Amsterdam, he did business with all important countries in the expanding trade network, also taking up unusual activities such as the trade in fish between Plymouth, Dartmouth, and Alicante. Like De Moucheron, Le Maire was an early victim of the temptations of the Asian trade. He took part in the New Brabant Company which sent four ships to Asia in 1599, reputedly making a 400% profit. This enterprise first joined forces with one of the Amsterdam companies, subsequently merging into the VOC. With an invested capital of more than 88,000 guilders, Le Maire became one of the biggest shareholders in the Amsterdam chamber and consequently one of the representatives to the VOC board. He gave up his seat after a row over an apparent fraud, but also because, like De Moucheron, he disagreed on principle with the company's monopoly which put an end to free trade in Asia. Le Maire now turned into a resourceful challenger to the VOC. Following De Moucheron's example, he approached Henry IV and proposed setting up a rival company. When that initiative failed, Le Maire organised the first documented bear syndicate on the Amsterdam exchange in 1609, aiming to force a change of policy by pushing down the VOC shares. His scheme collapsed, landing Le Maire into trouble. He had to leave Amsterdam, presumably because the VOC board moved to prevent him from meeting his obligations, and settled in a country village. From there, he continued to pursue his aim of free trade with Asia, now in a different way. Sponsored by a number of merchants from Hoorn, Le Maire sent two ships to Asia via the southern tip of America in 1614. The expedition discovered a new sea passage and called it Strait Le Maire, rounding cliffs which came to be known as Cape Horn, honouring the home town of both the expedition's commander and the sponsors. The VOC charter did not cover this route, but in spite of this, the company board ordered the ships to be seized on arrival in Java. Despite endless litigation against the company, Le Maire did not succeed in getting full compensation for his claims, justified though these certainly were, at least in part. He died in 1624. According to his epitaph he had lost 1.5 million guilders during a mercantile career spanning thirty years, but it does not men-

Barrowmen, carters, porters, and merchants crowding around the public weigh house on the Dam in Amsterdam, built in 1556. The building had seven gates with large scales, but it could not cope with swelling trade, so during 1617-1618 the large building on the Nieuwmarkt which had served as city gates was converted into an additional weigh house. Detail from a painting by Johannes Lingelbach, 1656.

tion how much Le Maire had left over, for instance as revenues from the real estate speculations which he practised in his countryside exile.[138]

Usselincx, De Moucheron, and Le Maire shared a common background as immigrants from the southern Netherlands in the Republic. Once there, they applied a truly boundless energy and great intelligence to the discovery of new markets and new routes to known regions. They ascended to the top of the commercial world, but failed to hold on to their position. Why? Did they make an awkward fit in the business environment? Or did they simply overplay their

The large family of Pierre de Moucheron, merchant of Antwerp and subsequently Middelburg. At least two of his sons followed a commercial career as well. Balthasar de Moucheron, the most prominent of them, also established himself in Middelburg, and set up large scale operations in every direction. One of his brothers was a pioneer of the Russian trade. Painting attributed to Cornelis de Zeeuw, 1563.

hand, only to raise the mercantile community's suspicions with their dashing speculations? All three shared a great commercial ability, a passion for daring ventures, and a brilliant individualism, though these factors will have acted differently in each case. We do not know whether such characteristics did or did not fit in with the other merchants of that time. Together the three careers adorn the period 1585-1620 with that unmistakable aura of a great economic boom, with its unprecedented opportunities and spectacular projects ending in drama.

That these three merchants were immigrants, will not really have mattered in the end. The Republic's economic success attracted a continuous flow of immigrants, to sail the fleet, to man the colonial army, or to work in trade and industry. The mercantile community always had sizeable groups of foreigners in all echelons. During the 17th century, immigrants made up about half of all Amsterdam merchants.[139] Rotterdam numbered so many English merchants, that the city became known as 'Little London'.[140] As a rule the immigrants assimilated quickly, without necessarily disappearing into the crowd without trace. The Sephardic Jews formed a distinct group of immigrant merchants.

The Republic attracted large numbers of immigrants. Some of them rose to great wealth and prominence. Jeronimo Nunes da Costa, who came from Portugal, had a palatial town house built for himself on the Amsterdam Herengracht, with a luxurious garden at the back. Engraving by Romeyn de Hooghe, about 1700.

The first of them, traders and processors of Brazilian sugar, came to the Republic soon after the fall of Antwerp. The Truce generated a new influx of Jewish immigrants from the Iberian peninsula. Among them was Bento Osorio, who conducted a large salt trade among other activities. He chartered more than 200 ships for the classic salt run Setubal-Republic-Baltic in the years 1615 to 1618 alone. Osorio was reputedly the richest Jewish inhabitant of the Republic. Around the middle of the 17th century Jacob Delmonte, Jeronimo Nunes da Costa, and Antonio Lopes Suasso held their own amongst the big Amsterdam merchants. They dealt mainly in Spanish wool and Portuguese diamonds. They also provided financial services to the Royal houses of both countries, and acted as their chargé d'affaires for diplomatic missions. Nunes da Costa commissioned an imposing city mansion for himself on the newly constructed Herengracht, with an exceptionally beautiful garden at the back. When at home, he received foreign nobility and diplomats with great hospitality.[141]

During the first half of the 17th century, indisputably the two biggest trade moguls were Louis de Geer and Elias Trip, brothers in law and business partners in numerous projects. Their main activities concerned the metal trade and by extension arms manufacturing and trading. They maintained close links with the iron industry around Liège in Belgium, managed to redirect the supply of Swedish copper to Amsterdam, and built up a commanding position by combining the trade in raw materials with selling arms made in their own workshops, or by subcontractors. In 1624 De Geer joined Elias Trip and his second cousin Peter in a partnership for trading arms with a capital of 70,000 guilders, increased to 400,000 guilders two years later. This business was rather capital intensive, because of the workshops required, but also because the Swedish King used its copper monopoly to impose large advance payments on merchants for supplies.[142]

The De Geer-Trip partnership combined their common interests, leaving the partners to their own separate ways, which crossed again repeatedly, as it happened. De Geer relocated most of his activities to Sweden. He took Swedish citizenship in 1627, and started building a large industrial mining and processing concern for iron and copper, complete with blast furnaces, foundries, and forges. The conglomerate also comprised textile factories, paper mills and flour mills. De Geer supplied most of his arms to King Gustavus Adolphus, who

The families of Trip and De Geer combined the trade in raw materials with the production of arms in their own plants. The respective family members, while each going their own way, from time to time embarked on joint operations with each other. Hendrick Trip owned a gun foundry in Sweden at Julitabruk, Södermanland. Painting by Allart van Everdingen, about 1644.

pursued Swedish territorial ambitions in the Baltic and in north Germany during the Thirty Years' War. De Geer's diversified concern could supply everything needed for a whole army, including the soldiers if required. The product range also included warships complete with crew. The retail trade also received De Geer's attention, leading to shops and travelling salesmen selling copper pans and kettles.[143] He was not the only Amsterdam merchant to integrate backwards from the metal trade into manufacturing. The brothers Abraham, Jacob and Willem Momma also invested in Swedish mines and foundries. Gabriel and Celio Marcelis did the same in Denmark and Norway, while their brother Peter joined a partnership of three Dutch entrepreneurs who set up a large iron foundry and arms factory south of Moscow.[144]

The Trip family on the other hand remained merchants first and foremost. Besides the partnership with De Geer, Elias Trip maintained a number of other trade interests. He joined a consortium of four big merchants which bought all the VOC's pepper supplies in 1620.[145] Together with his cousin Pieter, he headed a family firm engaged in the arms trade. This firm acted as De Geer's agents in the Republic, supplying large advances on consignments of artillery. In addition, the partners moved carefully to corner the Swedish copper supplies. In 1629 they came close to success when they secured a contract granting them an effective monopoly in return for annual advances on supplies of up to nearly one million guilders. However, the contract was never fully implemented. Five years later the firm formed a consortium with De Geer and several other merchants, raising 2.4 million guilders to buy all available stocks of Swedish copper, to redeem the outstanding loans of the Swedish Government, and to provide a new loan on the copper.[146] Members of the Trip family also traded on their own account, sending, among other things, grain to Italy and the Levant by their own ships.

In 1631 the De Geer-Trip partnership fell apart, and a few years later the Trip family firm also came to an end. Elias and Peter Trip continued to trade on their own, but in 1634 three nephews, the brothers Jacob, Louis, and Hendrick Trip, started a new partnership for the arms trade. As far as we know, this firm is the first one with a demonstrable, formal continuity as a business. Presumably the firm had already become generally known under the combined names of the three brothers. When Jacob resigned from the partnership in 1651, its name was changed to Louis & Hendrick Trip. However, when a new partner joined seven years later, the firm's name remained unchanged, underlining the separation between the business firm and the partnership running it. The trade in arms, iron, and tar remained the core business, with sidelines in grain and tobacco. The firm started with a capital of 200,000 guilders, rising to 800,000 guilders during the 1650s, but rapidly declined again to its former level in 1670, when the partners decided to refocus on trading iron. Profits on iron averaged 11% of turnover. The firm continued trading until well into the 18th century.[147]

The merchant careers of Louis de Geer and the various members of the Trip family are both exceptional and characteristic of circumstances on the Dutch entrepot market during its first fifty years of existence. They were exceptional because of their particular trade and its strong industrial linkages. The arms trade was a very lucrative one, because of the wars raging all over Europe at the start of the 17th century, and, of course, also because of the constant demand for armaments generated by the Republic's economic expansion and the inherent need for a proactive defence policy. The Estates General and the VOC belonged to the regular customers of these moguls. De Geer's profit on arms reportedly amounted to 40% of the purchase price.[148] The profitability, the large conglomerates, and the fortunes amassed do impress, but these factors cannot conceal the fact that the trade in arms and raw materials for arms production remained unrepresentative for Dutch trade overall, or at least just one

Factory buildings of Hendrick Trip's
gun foundry at Julitabruk in Sweden,
about 1644.

of the numerous trades on the Amsterdam exchange. The large fortunes are
also misleading, to some extent. After all, the merchant community was not
composed solely of exceedingly rich businessmen, but it formed a
very mixed bag. Small and medium-sized merchants made an equally vital
contribution to the economic success of the entrepot system.

On the other hand, these careers do reflect characteristics typical for their
time, at least in some respects. De Geer and the Trips were prototypes of the
modern business moguls, empire builders consciously striving for a position of
power from which they could control the market for their products and could
exploit any passing opportunities. The Dutch entrepot market offered unique
opportunities for them, combining as it did, a maximum of information supply
with the biggest available stock of most products. The sharp rise in the scale of
business also provided the top of the merchant community with the necessary
means to indulge. Consequently the entrepot market was marked by the constant appearance of cartels, combinations, and operations cornering the trade in
particular products. Usually such monopolies collapsed again after some time.
Firstly, because the market's continued expansion would break any cartels.
Secondly, competition put such agreements under pressure as well. Merchants
would take part in a consortium to buy the voc's spices on a regular basis, but
not necessarily with the same partners. Apparently the bidders did not form a
closed group.[149] Thirdly, a cartel could fall apart because of disagreement
between the participants, because high prices opened up new supplies, or
because of a charter expiring. As often as not, monopolies did not originate in
sinister manipulations, but in public and exclusive licenses granted by the
authorities of the producing country. Merchants could obtain such licenses by
granting loans to these authorities, as the Trips did to get their hands on the
Swedish copper supplies. In 1659, the Amsterdam merchant Jean Deutz secured
a monopoly for mercury in a similar transaction with the Austrian Emperor.
Such monopolies governed the trade in Bentheim stone, in Tuscan marble, Norwegian ships' masts, German oak timber, Russian caviar, and what not. Sometimes such licenses were given away as a Royal favour. In 1661, the great Dutch
Admiral Michiel Adriaansz de Ruyter received a special license for the export of
cod roe and cod liver from the Danish King, in recognition of services rendered.[150]

THE CHARACTER OF THE ENTREPOT MARKET – Of course, economic expansion fundamentally changed the geographical pattern and the composition of the Republic's foreign trade. On the eve of the Revolt, the main trading partners were the Baltic, Britain, France, and to a lesser extent, Spain and Portugal.[151] Some seventy years later the pattern looked very different (Table 1.2).[152]

Table 1.2

Estimated imports by sea to the Republic, 1636

*Revenue of commodities sold.

Baltic	12.5 mln gld	25.8%
VOC*	8 mln gld	16.5%
France	4.7 mln gld	9.7%
Britain	4,4mln gld	9.1%
Norway/Russia	3 mln gld	6.2%
Spain, Portugal, Italy	3 mln gld	6.2%
North-Germany	2 mln gld	4.1%
Other	0.8 mln gld	1.7%
West-Indies, Africa	10? mln gld	20.6%?
Total	48.4 mln gld	100

The Baltic remained the single most important trading partner, even more so if north Germany were added to it. Second came the triangle Africa-the Americas-west Indies, though not for very much longer. We have no figures for the trade with these regions. The north American trade did not amount to much, a few hundred thousand guilders a year at most. South America supplied much more to the Republic. Around 1640 merchants and the WIC shipped for about 3 million guilders a year in sugar alone to Amsterdam. In addition, the WIC imported a lot of dye wood.[153] Imports from west Africa may well have amounted to about 5-6 million guilders. For at the start of the 1670s the WIC's gold trade alone came to more than 5 million guilders, beside substantial ivory sales.[154] All in all, the Republic's imports from these regions may well have amounted to about 10 million guilders. Asia thus probably held third place, the other trading partners were of more or less equal importance with 3-5 million guilders a year.

By 1640 the Republic had become the main European trade centre, the entrepot market which could supply from stock all imaginable products all year round. Until the 1580s the product range remained simple: grain and ships' supplies such as timber, rope and cables, pitch, tar, and, in Middelburg, wine. Each new destination added a new product segment to the market: bulk commodities like sugar; vital raw materials such as iron, mercury, copper, gold, and silver; special materials like dye wood from the Caribbean and Brazil; luxury products such as Russian caviar, silk, or Asian spices. All these products had been available before, trickling to Europe in small quantities from various directions and via several intermediaries. Consequently supplies varied sharply, depending on the time of year and the market situation in the last port of despatch. Now these

Tropical dyewoods had to be rasped to obtain the dye, which was done by prisoners condemned to hard labour at the so-called Rasping House on the Amsterdam Heiligeweg. Anonymous pen drawing, about 1611.

commodities became available in wholesale quantities and usually from source, shipped by exceedingly cheap transport, with supplies arriving as regularly as sailing would allow, and stored in quantities to ensure regular deliveries. The entrepot trade was primarily a seaborne trade. We know very little about the Republic's overland trade, but it appears to have remained of secondary importance.

What made the Dutch entrepot market so revolutionary? First of all, its product range. During the Middle Ages, trade had been largely restricted to merchandise combining high value with low volume, in other words, luxuries which justified the high cost of transport. Relying on its sophisticated logistical concept, the entrepot market widened trade to bulk products. Low cost transport provided a key ingredient, but ultimately the logistic organisation was the decisive success factor.[155] Secondly, the market assembled such a large variety of merchandise, that it could serve each individual buyer best with the desired products. Medieval trade had really consisted of bilateral exchanges between producers, with a hierarchy of local and regional markets collecting commodities for sale. International trade centres at the top of the mercantile pyramid, such as Antwerp, had facilitated bilateral exchanges between groups of merchants from all corners of Europe.

The entrepot market however offered multilateral exchange. It acted, in effect, as an international wholesalers', bypassing intermediate markets to buy and to stock products from around the world for sale to European consumers. This essentially modern market function created added value by its product range, and by its balancing of supply and demand. Moreover, the bypassing of intermediate markets concentrated the best information on production and prices on the entrepot market, eliminating the disinformation created by data passing down a long chain. This factor was bolstered by the huge numbers of ships converging on the Republic, which offered a high frequency of connections in all directions and consequently raised the speed of communications. The entrepot market thus served as the main, year-round junction for both products and information from all over the world.

Having said that, we need to stress four points. First of all, during the period 1500-1750, all of European trade expanded powerfully. The Republic emerged as a main driving force and exponent of this growth, but was itself driven by much wider economic developments.[156] Secondly, the term entrepot market would appear to suggest that all goods traded were in fact shipped via the Republic. However, a large volume of trade bypassed the country, as it was transported directly from one country to another, Amsterdam serving as a virtual market, facilitating transactions and setting prices. This phenomenon of the *voorbijlandvaart*, or by-passing shipments, emerged as early as the 16th century. An analysis of Amsterdam charter contracts from the first quarter of the 17th century suggests, that by far the majority of shipments in the Baltic trade and in the Norwegian trade bypassed the Republic.[157] As mentioned above, direct shipments occurred in the Russian trade as well. There were sound commercial reasons behind this development. For reasons of cost alone, merchants in the Republic will have tried to avoid whenever possible the detour and storage inherent in the *stapelmarkt* concept. News about price, quality, and quantity of harvests, for instance, reached the Republic no earlier, as a rule, than the goods themselves, so merchants could charter ships at leisure and meanwhile start

Amsterdam may have been the commercial centre of the entrepot market, but the Republic had numerous port cities serving as secondary centres, such as Flushing, depicted here on a painting by P. Segaar, 1669.

searching for buyers. The *voorbijlandvaart* thus was a rational consequence of the creation of a multilateral market with well-organised channels of information. Consequently, the entrepot system carried the seeds of its own destruction. After all, buyers and sellers abroad had equal access to the information on markets and products gathered in the Republic, and they could use this to cut out the middlemen. This did not yet occur during the first half of the 17th century, but clearly the writing was on the wall, more or less from the start.

Thirdly, the entrepot market had its hub of greatest activity in Amsterdam but, in accordance with the specialisation between ports, other cities functioned as important secondary centres. Hoorn and Enkhuizen on the Zuiderzee for instance, focused on the Caribbean trade. Thus in 1602 no fewer than 70 ships from Hoorn sailed to the West Indies to buy salt.[158] Rotterdam, around the middle of the 16th century still primarily a town of shipping and fishing, became a centre of trade with France and Britain, eclipsing nearby Dordrecht as a sea port. The city also had a considerable share in the trade with Asia and the Caribbean.[159] Dordrecht did keep a key position in inland river trade, mainly in timber from the Rhineland. Middelburg lost its hinterland because of the Scheldt blockade, but it succeeded in seizing an important slice of the trade with the Caribbean, Brazil, and west-Africa.

This spread of economic activities explains why some prominent refugees from the southern Netherlands did not settle in Amsterdam, but for instance in Leiden, like Daniel van der Meulen, Dordrecht, in the case of Carlo della Faille, Haarlem, for his brother Jacques, or Middelburg, like Balthasar de Moucheron and Willem Usselincx. These provincial cities offered the merchants equal opportunities for profiting from the combined commercial power of the Republic's ports, if only because the lines of communication were sufficiently short to follow developments closely. Grain for the Amsterdam market was regularly stored elsewhere while awaiting sale, mainly in Hoorn or Enkhuizen, sometimes still further away. In 1630, the grain merchant Jan Gerritsz Hooft had 120 metric tons of buckwheat lying in Amsterdam warehouses, against 140 tons in Dordrecht.[160] Simultaneously with the intercontinental expansion, the Republic's western provinces took steps to improve their inland transport system. Between 1630 and 1665 a true revolution took shape with the building of canals of a total length of about 600 kilometres. City councils commissioned these works and financed them, usually by issuing bond loans. Regular barge services subsequently linked the points of the canal network. Postal services also underwent a fundamental improvement by the switch from foot messengers to transport by barges, wagons, and horses.[161]

Fourthly, the entrepot market derived its economic importance not just from the commodity trade, but also from the value added by industry and other services. The Republic built up a strong processing industry with close links to trade: mills for making paper, sawing timber, or pressing oil from seeds, sugar refineries, salt and soap boiling works, all engaged in turning imported raw materials or semi-finished products into finished export commodities. The Zaan

region, just north of Amsterdam, grew into an industrial heartland, but the other big ports all had similar factory concentrations. The range of goods traded enabled the Republic to offer unique products, for instance English cloth dyed with dye from southern Europe and Latin America for export to Russia.[162] Trade stimulated industry, and not only in the coastal provinces. The Brabant potteries, for instance, also profited, and concentrated on mass production of standardised earthenware for export.[163]

 As regards services, cheap shipping provided a vital link in the chain, for the obvious reason of cost advantage. Specialised freighters enabled Dutch shipping to undercut all competition. The entrepot market helped to increase this advantage. With a large variety of products available from every direction, ships' captains sailing to the Republic stood a good chance of picking up return cargo, and could thus spread expenses over two trips. At that moment in time, the British trade pattern for instance was still markedly bilateral. Outward bound ships often had to sail in ballast, so all expenses weighed on the return cargo.[164] The Baltic trade demonstrates this particular aspect of the entrepot market to good effect. Around 1560, 78% of Dutch ships sailed through the Sound in ballast, but this had declined to 40-50% sixty years later.[165] Captains often loaded ballast with some commercial value, such as bricks, tiles, and rooftiles. Castle Kronborg near Helsingør, Hamlet's Elsinore, was constructed with building supplies from the Republic, by a Dutch architect who brought his own builders. The elegant Dutch Renaissance design overlooked the Sound and Helsingør harbour, where ships had to pay the toll.[166]

The entrepot market derived some of its power from industries processing the imported raw materials and semi-finished goods into ready export products. The Zaan area north of Amsterdam was a key location for many of these industries. Windmills served to provide power for a range of activities, such as sawing timber, pressing oil, paper making, rolling copper, etc. Anonymous view on the Zaan area, 18th century.

Shipping also provided a welcome source of revenue. Freight payments provided 37% of total revenue on the fourteen European ships sent out by Van Adrichem around 1590.[167] Other accounts from shipping ventures from that time show similar percentages.[168] The supercargo sent to Italy by the Van der Meulen-Della Faille consortium in 1589 received extensive instructions to look for outward cargo, should he decide on a trip to Crete. He was to enquire in Genoa, Leghorn, and other nearby ports. If he received no offers, he was to sail for Naples and try there, and if he could not pick up any cargo, his principals instructed him to buy hoops and hazelnuts in Castel Amaro, five miles south of Naples, to sell in Crete.[169] In short, anything would be better than sailing in ballast. Perhaps cargo shipping offered insufficient returns as a straight investment proposal. The sustained interest of investors to buy shares in ships suggests the opposite, but the fragmentary data on freight revenues do not enable us to draw firm conclusions. From the perspective of the entrepot market, the question of returns is of no importance anyway, because transport was an integral part of the system.[170]

As mentioned above, the entrepot market attracted foreign custom with a vital cluster of services besides shipping, such as insurance, information supply, finance, and smooth settlements. These services also generated separate revenues, which supported trade in their turn. For trade between the various regions that were served seldom balanced. Trade with the Baltic and with Asia in particular suffered from a chronic imbalance, which had to be redressed by shipments of gold or silver, mainly the latter. Spain supplied most of this bullion, extracted from South America by the shipload. The Republic earned the surplus of bullion required on one hand through its usually positive trade balance with the Iberian peninsula, on the other with trade-related services.

The Sound with Dutch and Danish ships, painting by Hendrick Cornelisz Vroom, 1620. In the background Kronborg castle, built with Dutch building materials, partly transported as ballast in ships heading for the Baltic.

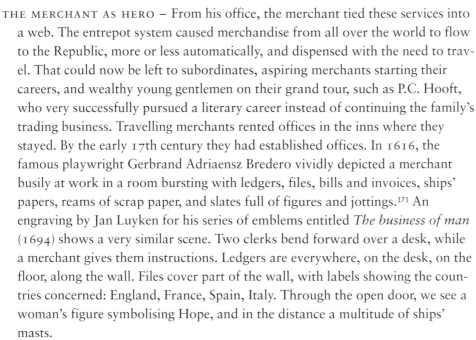

A director at his desk: Daniël Bernard, administrator and director of the VOC for forty years.
Portrait painted by Bartholomeus van der Helst in 1669.

THE MERCHANT AS HERO – From his office, the merchant tied these services into a web. The entrepot system caused merchandise from all over the world to flow to the Republic, more or less automatically, and dispensed with the need to travel. That could now be left to subordinates, aspiring merchants starting their careers, and wealthy young gentlemen on their grand tour, such as P.C. Hooft, who very successfully pursued a literary career instead of continuing the family's trading business. Travelling merchants rented offices in the inns where they stayed. By the early 17th century they had established offices. In 1616, the famous playwright Gerbrand Adriaensz Bredero vividly depicted a merchant busily at work in a room bursting with ledgers, files, bills and invoices, ships' papers, reams of scrap paper, and slates full of figures and jottings.[171] An engraving by Jan Luyken for his series of emblems entitled *The business of man* (1694) shows a very similar scene. Two clerks bend forward over a desk, while a merchant gives them instructions. Ledgers are everywhere, on the desk, on the floor, along the wall. Files cover part of the wall, with labels showing the countries concerned: England, France, Spain, Italy. Through the open door, we see a woman's figure symbolising Hope, and in the distance a multitude of ships' masts.

In his play, Bredero successfully captured the dynamics of his merchant's business: now on the exchange amongst his fellow merchants, now having meetings with shareholders in his shipping ventures, making complicated calculations in his head, daring to trade in securities, and being both big and bold enough to insure a ship and cargo on his own. And he had not even gone bankrupt yet, Bredero added sardonically. Well, if he had, it would not have been much of a problem, for shedding your creditors was easy, and no one held it against you. If only the Emperor's edict still applied, ordering bankrupts to be hanged in their own doorways, then it would not happen so often.[172] Presumably Bredero reflected popular opinions on the weak morals of merchants. The Amsterdam city fathers do not appear to have shared that pressing concern. Only in 1627 did they vote to establish an office for liquidating bankruptcies. Presumably the office went to work straight away, but the drafting of bankruptcy regulations took another sixteen years.[173]

Despite Bredero's misgivings, merchants meanwhile ascended to a very respectable status, as standard bearers of a new order built on trade and shipping. The spectacular economic success so soon after the revolt against Spain created a Republican self-imagery of a country of merchants, who had broken free from bondage to rule the world's oceans with daring and entrepreneurship. In 1658 the poet and playwright Joost van den Vondel waxed lyrical about the peace that reigned over the oceans now that Dutchmen had taken control. The world was for sale, opportunities abounded, insurance had become unnecessary now that all dangers had been eliminated. The straits were open, by rights the Republic owned the keys to the Sound, to the Channel, to Gibraltar, according to this patriotic poet.[174] The decorations on the facade of the new Amsterdam town hall, a majestic Dutch baroque palace designed by Jacob van Campen, reflected the same proud triad of trade, peace, and world dominance.[175] Building started in 1648, coinciding with the Peace of Westphalia which ended the Eighty Years' War. For the official opening in 1655, Vondel wrote a long poem eulogising the city's economic power and returning to the theme of trade, freedom and peace.[176]

A merchant in his office, engraving by Jan Luyken, late 17th century. This is one of Luyken's famous series of emblems called *The business of man*, depicting a range of economic activities with verses drawing moral lessons from them. Here, the merchant is admonished not to forget eternal salvation when striving for daily gain.

This new order of course required well-trained merchants. In 1632, Professor Caspar van Baerle gave his inaugural lecture at the Amsterdam Athenaeum Illustre and spoke at length about the *mercator sapiens*. According to him, this wise merchant was an *uomo universale*, a true Renaissance man, who needed a very wide and versatile knowledge in order to do his work properly. His actions had to be guided by ethics. Van Baerle pleaded for giving merchants a dedicated commercial education, combining scientific observations with practical insights.[177] It would take nearly another three centuries before the Amsterdam Athenaeum realised his recommendations.

Meanwhile a new genre of manuals appeared, fulfilling the demand for practical commercial information. These merchants' handbooks were hybrids between, on one hand the accounting manuals like those of Pacioli and Christoffelsz, and on the other the guidelines for foreign trade which circulated in some firms.[178] The 17th century commercial manuals offered a systematic compendium of details, mostly about European cities and countries, such as

Merchants crowd on Dam Square. The weigh house stands on the right, on the left construction is underway for the new city hall. The foundation stone for this building, designed as a monument of commercial power and wealth, was laid on October 26, 1648. Detail from a painting by Johannes Lingelbach, 1656.

measures, weights, currency, commercial law, current products, tariffs, insurance conditions, shipping, and customs. The first such books appeared around 1635, but the genre acquired recognisable form only with the publication of Jacques Savary's *Le parfait négociant*, in 1675.[179]

Within a century, the Republic had transformed itself into the main trade centre of the western World, with a large colonial empire. Around 1550, trade was still in the hands of one man firms with varying partnerships, small in size but extra-ordinarily dynamic and flexible. A hundred years later, the entrepot market had spawned a large number of substantial merchants, who dominated trade in all directions. Some of them already ran firms with unchanging identities from one generation to the next, proper merchant houses.

The commercial expansion generated a demand for practical information about the mercantile business. Special books appeared to fill that need, such as this one from the late 17th century.

The Republic's economic success led to conflicts with surrounding countries. In 1672, Britain, France, and the German princes of Münster and Cologne jointly declared war, after which this year passed into Dutch history as the notorious Year of Disaster. The large illustration shows the army of the French King Louis XIV besieging the town of Naarden on 20 July 1672, an unfinished painting by Adam van der Meulen, 17th century. The smaller illustration presents a tile tableau of the Battle of the Downs between the Dutch and the Spanish fleets in 1639.

ZEE SLAG IN DUYNS DOOR MARTEN HARPERS-TROMP

CHAPTER II

During the second quarter of the 17th century the Republic's trade position came under heavy fire. Neighbouring countries took political and military action against the entrepot market's supremacy. The Republic became embroiled in a long series of wars, and finally had to accept that its powers were insufficient to sustain the economic expansion. Other countries drew level with the seven provinces, some even overtook them. However, this did not mean an end to growth. The merchant houses managed to adapt their services admirably to the new situation, and succeeded in keeping the volume of the Republic's foreign trade at very high levels.

RUNNING INTO THE SAND – Of course the Republic's economic success did not pass unnoticed abroad. Competition arose. Sea routes had become common knowledge. Merchants' handbooks had disseminated information about conditions and products in various countries, printed price currents enabled merchants to follow markets and to obtain the information normally confined to insiders. Foreign merchants made increasingly successful attempts at beating the Dutchmen at their own game by building fluyt ships, for instance, to get products from source at the lowest possible costs, and by setting up companies for the long distance trade. Initially these efforts made little inroads as the Republic had an enormous lead. Around 1660 the Dutch merchant fleet was twice the size of its nearest rival, the British.[1] According to an English observer in 1685, London freight costs were still at least 10% higher than those in Amsterdam or Rotterdam.[2]

When open competition failed to achieve the desired economic ends, foreign governments adopted political and military means to break the Republic's hegemony. As early as 1610, Sir Walter Raleigh advised the British King James I to counter the influence of Dutch fishing, shipping and trade on the British isles by abolishing all obstacles to competition in business. Eight years later the King commissioned John Selden to write a reply to De Groot's proposition that the seas were essentially free for all. Entitled *Mare Clausum*, Selden's treatise claimed sovereignty over the waters around Britain from north to south and from east to west, and denied other nations an automatic right of free passage. Practical consequences followed only in 1651, when Parliament passed the first Navigation Act granting British shipping radical favours to the detriment of foreign competition. France felt humiliated by the Dutch commercial supremacy as well. The inhabitants of Nantes complained repeatedly about exploitation by merchants from Holland and Zeeland, who completely dominated the port's economy.[3] The Tuscan marble for the building of the Royal palace at Versailles came from Amsterdam, and not directly from Italy.[4] King Louis XIV and his minister Colbert drafted specific policies to fight this supremacy. Denmark and Sweden also harboured a growing resistance against the Dutch grip on the Baltic trade, and took steps against it.

In short, hardly had peace been signed with the arch enemy Spain, when new challengers appeared on the scene. During the second half of the 17th century, the Republic had to wage war for its very existence almost without a break, over and over, against Britain, against France, against one of the Scandinavian countries. These wars tested the Republic's strength to the limits. After all, for all its economic might, it remained a small country. There was no lack of fighting spirit, however, for the Estates General did not shy away from con-

An allegorical engraving about the Year of Disaster, 1672. A maid representing the Republic tries with all her might to uphold a stake crowned with the hat of liberty, which four enemies attempt to pull down. The Stadtholder lion is chained and cannot come to the maid's rescue. The Republic defended itself vigorously in the incessant wars of the late 17th century, but at the cost of spiralling financial burdens.

frontations. Usually, though, they carefully considered beforehand the chances of success and the likely damage to the country's own trade and industry. In 1655 they retaliated against the first round of shipping acts with a ban on finished cloth from England.[5] The struggle with France also meant first of all hitting French exports with import bans on wine, brandy, paper, sail cloth, and silk.[6] Denmark finally abandoned its protectionist policies after Dutch reprisals against Danish and Norwegian products.[7]

However, the Republic simply lacked the means to mobilise sufficient soldiers and armaments for repeated conflicts with the big European powers. The ever mounting cost of armaments was partly to blame for this. In time of war, the Republic used to expand its relatively small navy with armed merchant ships. Dedicated freighters, such as the fluyt, had become largely unsuitable for naval battles, however. They were no match for a new generation of warships, three-deckers armed with a hundred or more cannons. This first became apparent during the First Anlgo-Dutch War (1652-1654). Forty years later, it had become an acute problem.[8]

Raising defence expenditure was the only remedy, but this had already reached very high levels, pushing up taxation in the process. In 1600, the normal taxes of the province of Holland amounted to 7.27 guilders per head annually, with local taxes coming on top of that. One hundred years later, provincial taxes had risen to 16.59 guilders per head. Wage rises lagged far behind. At the beginning of the 17th century, a day labourer had to work ten days to pay the provincial taxes, by century's end this had risen to no less than eighteen days, and to around twenty in 1720.[9] Rising taxation also affected trade, for instance markedly impairing the Republic's competitiveness with Hamburg, which had very low customs tariffs.[10] And it still was not enough. Public debt spun out of control despite sharply rising tax revenues. At the end of the War of the Spanish Succession (1702-1713), the province of Holland had 310 million guilders of loans outstanding, against 128 million guilders at the start of the war. The Estates General also became burdened with large debts, though not nearly as heavily as Holland. In 1715 the united province's paymaster had to suspend payments for nine months because he had no money to meet the interest instalments due, causing in effect a state bankruptcy.[11] Such a disgrace had not occurred before.

THE FOREIGN TRADE DILEMMAS OF A SMALL COUNTRY – Could the Republic have safeguarded its commercial interests by other means than war? The Estates General tried trade treaties as an alternative. Between 1676 and 1684 the united provinces concluded such treaties with Portugal, Spain, Sweden, Denmark, and France. When matters came to a head, these devices proved too frail, being easily brushed aside or undermined, no more than a prologue for fighting.

Would the Republic have fared better by adopting protectionist policies itself? As early as the third quarter of the 17th century, calls began to be heard

The rising commercial competition from Britain became ever stronger. In 1688, the Dutch Stadholder William III and his English wife Mary ascended the English throne, but the Republic's international political position continued to decline, despite this personal union between the two countries. Ludolf Bakhuysen painted William III returning from Britain and landing at the Oranjepolder.

in favour of protection, in response to the first French measures against Dutch trade. Despite support from the influential Amsterdam mayor Coenraad van Beuningen, they went unheeded.[12] The Leiden cloth manufacturer Pieter de la Court argued the opposite case, in favour of liberalisation of trade and industry. According to him, all legislation and privileges restricting competition had to be abolished, including the guilds and the monopoly charters of the VOC and WIC.[13] The united provinces did not live by free trade principles, nor did any other country at that time. Imports and exports were subject to customs duties and other levies. These amounted to roughly 3-5% of the cargo value, low in comparison to neighbouring countries, but apparently higher than those imposed by rival German ports such as Hamburg and Bremen.[14] Very generally speaking, the customs duties checked transit trade and favoured the import of raw materials and the export of finished products, i.e. the entrepot market and the surrounding processing industries. Thus the wholesale trade and the processing industries suffered less than the traders only serving local consumers or those selling directly to the German hinterland.

However, the tariff system was not used deliberately as an economic instrument, for instance to protect manufacturing against cheap imports, or to create opportunities for import substitution. True, the Estates General voted to support specific new industrial sectors, for instance those producing brandy, silk, sail cloth, and paper. These measures were exceptional, and did not represent dedicated efforts to promote certain industries, but constituted actions against French exports.[15] The customs duties were a patchwork of fiscal expediency and ad hoc decisions favouring particular pressure groups. Competing economic interests prevented a unified stance. During the first debate on retaliation against France around 1670, Amsterdam, Leiden, and Haarlem sided against Rotterdam and Middelburg, that is to say general trading interests teamed up with the cloth producers against the wine importers. During the second round of debate, Leiden took the initiative, while Amsterdam prevaricated for a considerable time. During the Nine Years' War (1688-1697) Amsterdam, Rotterdam, and Middelburg united against Leiden over a complete embargo on the consumption of French products and on trade with France. The cloth city wanted the ban, the trading cities opposed it, with the thin excuse that a trading ban would render the wine captured by privateers worthless.[16]

The varying and shifting interests largely explain why calls for a radical change of tariff policy went unheeded. It even proved impossible to get an agreement over abolishing duties that encumbered trade. In 1681 the Amsterdam city council launched a scheme for a new tariff system which would have reduced the import duties considerably. Resistance from the West Frisian ports and from the province of Zeeland scuppered it.[17] A tariff revision completed in 1725 changed a few items and introduced some protective measures for manu-

The Republic failed to devise a proper defence against the economic warfare practised by the surrounding countries. Efforts towards a coherent tariff policy foundered on the fragmentation of trade interests, with cities dependent on cloth production taking a different view from those with, say, substantial wine imports such as Dordrecht. This anonymous 18th century painting shows wine traders in Dordrecht involved with customs declarations.

facturing and for fishing, but it did not amount to a fundamental policy change either way.[18] In effect, the United Provinces lacked the strong central administration necessary to push through and enforce any changes.[19] The free trade initiatives failed, not just because of the fragmented interests, but because of the woefully inadequate customs enforcement. Five regional admiralty boards collected the duties. City councils had nothing to gain from strict enforcement, quite the contrary. Captains and merchants knew exactly how to circumvent payment of duties by cheating or threatening violence, and they sent their ships to the cheapest port. For those not in the know, some ports had special customs clearers to help them with the authorities for a share of the savings. Customs evasion varied from 30-40% of duties in Amsterdam and Rotterdam, to no less than

80% in Zeeland. Growing trade rewarded cities which condoned such practices. Consequently, the Republic had free trade in all but name. Under such circumstances no one wanted a change of policy, which could conceivably lead to stricter enforcement.[20]

A protectionist customs policy would no doubt have been counterproductive for the entrepot market. After all, this system already suffered from an erosion of its competitive advantages. Protectionism would have raised cost, making matters worse. Nor could the Republic, with its small home market and dependency on foreign supplies of food and raw materials, really have afforded tariff barriers. However, in all probability industry did suffer from the absence of protective tariffs. Manufacturers had to fight on two fronts. Their export markets became less and less accessible, while free imports easily saturated their home market.

The Republic simply punched above its weight, and could not really compete with the big European powers. The lack of physical strength prevented further commercial expansion, indeed, holding on to established positions proved exceedingly demanding. The united provinces could still hold their own against Sweden or Denmark, but no longer against France and Britain. The navy made its presence felt in the Baltic repeatedly and with success, while operations in the Mediterranean went wrong more than once. During the War of the Spanish Succession the navy could no longer escort ships past Gibraltar. Consequently, the insurance premiums for the Mediterranean trade soared to 50% of the cargo value.[21]

To counter the dwindling military power, merchants set up trade associations by region. These organisations helped them to protect trade from war damage and to lobby the authorities on their behalf. As early as 1625, the Mediterranean trade, which suffered more than other trades from privateering and chicaneries, took the lead. At the suggestion of Cornelis Haga, the ambassador to Constantinople, merchants established the Board of the Levant Trade and Shipping on the Mediterranean. Seven Amsterdam merchants ran the board, assisted by representatives from the other main ports. The association functioned rather like a modern quango, i.e. a quasi-public body charged with certain prescriptive powers over its assigned field. Directors monitored trade, arranged convoys of freight ships, represented merchants and shipowners in consultations with the city council and with the Estates General, maintained good relations with the admiralties, paid ambassadors and consuls, and coordinated the sector's activities in wartime. The board also supervised the special embassy and consular funds for presents and bribes to local officials. Merchants from the Republic had to pay 2% of the value of their imports and exports into these funds.[22]

The Board of the Levant Trade, then, exercised public functions benefiting foreign trade. For a long time it remained the sole example of its kind. In 1663 the Amsterdam city fathers established a chamber of commerce with 26 members, to give its opinion on the state of trade and competition at the coun-

't Jaar 1 6 7 7.
Tegens Donderdag den 18 Maart,
Word UE. ter begravenis gebeden met het Lijk van

MICHIEL DE RUYTER,
HERTOG, RIDDER &c.
L. ADMIRAAL GENERAAL
van Holland en Weftvriesland.

Op 't Nieuwe Waals Eyland, als Vriend in huys te komen,
om ten een uur precijs uyt te gaan na de
NIEUWE KERK.
UE. Naem zal gelezen worden.

For a long period still, the Republic could make its power felt in the Baltic, but naval operations in the Mediterranean repeatedly ended in disaster. In 1674, the famous admiral Michiel de Ruyter was killed in a battle off Sicily. The picture shows an invitation for the official enterment of his remains, three years later.

78

cil's request or of its own accord.[23] The city council soon regretted its own initiative, for the chamber energetically set to work, and produced a succession
of reports on various subjects of keen interest to trade and industry. These calls
for action annoyed the city fathers so much that they moved to side-track the
chamber. As a result the members lost interest, and after two years the embryonic chamber of commerce disappeared. A similar institution functioned in
Rotterdam from 1677 until 1683.[24]

The Nine Years' War provided a new impetus towards the formation of
trade associations. Although they copied the example given by Board of the
Levant Trade, these particular organisations concentrated on their private functions, and did not engage directly in public tasks such as diplomatic and consular duties abroad. As usual during a war, the Amsterdam Baltic merchants
elected a committee for consultations with the admiralty on shipping convoys.
This Committee for the Baltic Trade was also charged with maintaining a fast
sailing galliot, to warn freighters against approaching enemy squadrons or privateers. The admiralty wanted to shed this commitment, presumably for reasons
of cost. The committee also acquired some powers of authority within the sector, such as official representations, the supervision over the grain exchange,
and consultations with authorities abroad over toll tariffs etc. For this latter
task the directors appointed agents in the Sound and in a couple of Baltic ports.
The expenses were paid by a levy on all ships sailing between the Republic and
the Baltic, the so-called galliot money.[25] The White Sea merchants set up a similar organisation called the Board for the Muscovy Trade, and the traders on
Norway and the whale fishers among others, did likewise. These associations
were not an Amsterdam phenomenon. Other ports also appointed directors for
certain sectors.[26]

After about 75 years of supremacy the Republic had to master the art of
compromise, to try and make the most of a weak political position. After the
trade wars with Sweden and Denmark the grip on the Baltic trade remained
firm, but the days of unchallenged hegemony were clearly over.[27] At the end of
the Nine Years' War the diplomats representing the Estates General participated
as equals in the negotiations leading up to the Treaty of Ryswick (1697). Fifteen
years later they were relegated more or less to the sidelines while Britain,
France, and Spain discussed the terms of the Treaty of Utrecht (1713). The
Republic fought no fewer than three wars with Britain, yet failed to achieve any
change in the British government's protectionist policies. The Treaty of Utrecht
granted Britain the *asiento*, the prized monopoly on importing slaves to South
America which gave its possessor an unbeatable lead in the commodity trade
with the Spanish colonies.

The repeated confrontations with France did succeed in containing Louis
XIV's territorial ambitions, but at the same time they failed to bring about a
change in his mercantilist policies. The Republic signed a fairly favourable trade
treaty with France as part of the Treaty of Utrecht, so the bilateral trade
remained of great importance. In 1716 about 30% of all French exports went to

The Peace of Utrecht (1713) marks a turning point in the Republic's international position. During the peace negotiations held in the Utrecht city hall, pictured here, the representatives of the Estates General were relegated to the sidelines while Britain, France, and Spain discussed terms. Engraving by I. Smit, 1713.

80

the seven provinces, which in their turn supplied 17% of French imports.[28] Still, France had unmistakably gained considerable ground. Marseille for instance, raised to a privileged position in the Levant trade by Colbert, had taken over from Amsterdam as the main distributor of Turkish mohair yarn to the cloth industry. The French cloth industry could now compete successfully with Dutch producers in Leiden and Haarlem in areas like yarn supply and the sale of finished cloth.[29]

The Treaty of Utrecht serves as a useful marker for the change from expansion to consolidation. For during the last quarter of the 17th century, the entrepot market tended to recover from war damage fairly quickly, and the customs revenues continued to rise. The War of the Spanish Succession broke this trend, however: customs revenue dropped, and went on dropping well into the 1720s, until after the end of the Great Nordic War (1700-1721). The number of ships reaching Amsterdam also fell. In 1721 only just under 1,400 freighters entered the harbour, fewer than in 1672, the famous Year of Disaster, when hostile French and British warships had blockaded the North Sea. There was a lapse of at least eight years after the cessation of hostilities, before a sluggish recovery finally got underway.[30]

IN SEARCH OF BETTER MARGINS – The expansion might have reached its highest point during the last quarter of the 17th century, but it was not followed by an absolute contraction. Judging by the customs revenues, the Republic's foreign trade remained at more or less the same level until the last quarter of the 18th century. Probably both value and volume increased slowly (Table 2.1).[31] In 1720 foreign trade totalled an estimated 200 million guilders, fifty years later it amounted to more than 240 million.[32]

	1720	1770
European maritime trade	151 mln gld	167 mln gld
Land trade on Belgium / Germany	16 mln gld	30 mln gld
Intercontinental	31 mln gld	46 mln gld
Total	198 mln gld	243 mln gld

Table 2.1

Rough estimate of the Republic's foreign trade

However, European trade meanwhile experienced very strong growth. The United Provinces failed to keep up, and consequently dropped ranks. Trade moved elsewhere, with both producers and consumers establishing direct links. As mentioned in Chapter 1, sooner or later the entrepot market was bound to start losing out to direct trade. After all, competing merchants could easily adopt the knowledge and skills involved, set out on their own, and save the cost of a detour to the Republic. The mercantilist protectionism of neighbouring countries and the ensuing wars were not in any way the cause of this process, as is sometimes claimed, they did no more than accelerate it. Therefore it does not come as a surprise that Dutch merchants faced increasing competition, and that they gradually lost ground. What amazes, however, is that they managed to keep the Republic's foreign trade at very high levels for more than a century, that the contraction which set in only around 1790 did not occur much earlier. The explanation for this phenomenon lies in a changing organisation of trade and shipping, deriving from efforts to hold on to trade flows by cutting the cost of the entrepot market through increased productivity and specialised services.

Shipbuilding again played a key role in the search for lower costs. The fluyt was developed into several subtypes, dedicated to the transport on a specific route. These ships had a slightly larger cargo capacity, but a smaller crew, and thus a higher productivity. On the other hand new, smaller, types appeared such as koffs and smacks, which compensated their smaller carrying capacity with an even better ratio of crew to cargo.[33] Increasing productivity kept Dutch shipping competitive despite the Republic's rising wage levels. According to the prominent Amsterdam merchant Thomas Hope in 1751, for cheap shipping ser-

vices nobody could beat Frisian ships' masters sailing with their sons or a few hired hands.[34] By the second quarter of the 18th century, the koffs and smacks had a large share in the Baltic trade.[35]

The new vessels offered several additional advantages over the fluyt. Shallow hulls enabled them to avoid enemy warships and privateers by hugging the shore.[36] This design feature also helped shipping to cope with the silting up which affected many sea entrances and harbour approaches. The big freighters coming into use towards the end of the 17th century had little trouble in entering the ports of Middelburg and Flushing in Zeeland, but entering Rotterdam or the ports on the Zuiderzee became more and more difficult. As early as the 16th century, the sea passage to Amsterdam harbour was a maze of shoals and sandbanks. In 1544 the Emperor Charles V prohibited the dumping of ballast by ships approaching the city. From 1575 the city council owned and operated a floating treadmill to dredge the harbour entrances. This invention by Joost Jansz Bilhamer was powered initially by men, later by horses. The British ambassador Sir William Temple complained that the sea crossing from the island of Texel to the IJ near Amsterdam posed more of a threat than a journey from Texel to Spain.[37] Tall ships such as the East Indiamen had to drop anchor near Texel and reduce their draught by transferring cargo into lighters. Even then the sandbanks near the island of Pampus a few miles off Amsterdam harbour posed an insurmountable obstacle for tall freighters until the invention of heavy lifting gear, the so-called ships' camels, in the 1680s.[38]

The approach to Rotterdam harbour was little better. The Meuse estuary had insufficient depth, forcing ocean going vessels to make a wide detour. Captains would first sail westward to the tip of the island of IJsselmonde, then around the island along the Oude Maas in an easterly direction, past the city of Dordrecht, veering south-west towards Moerdijk, and then via the Hollandsch Diep to the village of Willemstad. At that point they had the choice between a northern route passing through the Haringvliet, or a southern one through the Grevelingen. The trip from Rotterdam to the open sea normally took a few days, but with a bit of bad luck it could run to a fortnight or even more. Wags

The 18th century witnessed a notable trend towards the use of smaller ships, such as smacks and koffs. This wall painting by Aede Lutsens from the late 18th century shows a koff under construction at a Frisian yard.

The silting up of the harbour entrances became a permanent problem. The city of Amsterdam combated it with its own dredge mills, shown on the left in this painting by Abraham Storck, about 1675.

had it that Brouwershaven, the last village visible for outward bound ships, lay midway between Rotterdam and Java.[39]

Poor accessibility made Dutch harbours more expensive, but it did not in itself stop the use of taller ships. From a technical viewpoint, freighter size reached a design optimum around 1700. During the 18th century, rivals such as the British merchant navy also specialised by using ships of varying capacity rather than striving for ever larger ships.[40]

COMMERCIAL ORGANISATION AND ADDED VALUE – The most profound commercial change was the switch from trading for own account to trading in commission. For all we know, Dutch merchants mostly traded for own account during the age of expansion. Diagram A in Figure 2.1 depicts the directions of the resulting trade flows. Merchants or their supercargoes went abroad in person to buy, they operated in a partnership with emigrated fellow countrymen or relatives, or they appointed a local factor. Products were shipped back to the Republic for trading on the entrepot market. Or the other way around, merchants bought goods on the entrepot market and exported them for sale abroad by their supercargoes, partners, or factors. This was really an expensive business. Merchants took responsibility for the finance and the risk of a long chain, from purchase in one country until sale in another. They had little choice in the matter. During the pioneer phase merchants ventured into the unknown, they had to explore new markets, establish the connections and the mutual trust for regular business. Their foreign counterparts often had little or no experience with the sort of large-scale export trading so typical of the Dutch entrepot market.

Commission trading shifts the burden. A commission trader receives goods for sale from producers, usually abroad, or purchases goods on behalf of foreign buyers. In both cases the principal pays the merchant a commission for his services, a percentage of the invoice total, plus the cost of any supplementary services such as finance, transport, and insurance. From the Italian cities and Antwerp this technique had spread over Europe. Amsterdam merchants knew how to use it, but, as mentioned before, they did not use it for commercial expansion. As a matter of course, trade itself nursed suppliers and buyers towards the skills and capital power needed to start acting as their own exporters and/or importers and distributors. The Republic's intermediary function changed accordingly to diagram B in Figure 2.1.

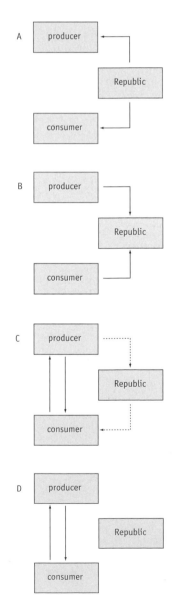

Figure 2.1

Producers would send their wares to a Dutch commission trader, or this trader would place an order with them on behalf of some foreign buyer. The initiative, the financial burden, and the risk of the transaction all moved to the principals, the commission trader arranged the transaction and took care of any supplementary services required. Commercial developments at either the producers' or at the consumers' end could give rise to configurations varying from one product to another and from period to period. For instance, an Amsterdam merchant would import goods for his own account and sell them to a commission trader executing an order from abroad. Or the other way around, a commission trader would sell commodities on behalf of a foreign supplier, to a trader exporting them for his own account, or for joint account with a foreign merchant.[41] Further development of the commission trade gave rise to an important variation, the consignment trade. This involved the commission trader paying to his principal a percentage of the invoice value of goods sent, as an advance to be paid back with the proceeds from sale of the goods. Such advances became so common, that the terms commission trade and consignment trade are often used synonymously, unjustly so.

The switch from trading for own account to commission trading was a very gradual one, impossible to pin down in exact periods in time. It amounted to a process of commercial emancipation, with four distinct phases. Developments in the tobacco trade between Britain and its North American colonies between about 1660 and 1740 illustrate these to good effect. At first, London merchants sent ships with a supercargo to Maryland and Virginia to buy tobacco, often bartering European products. In the second phase, the merchants appointed local factors to sell consignments and to buy tobacco. Around 1690, the roles reversed at the onset of the third phase. American tobacco planters and commission merchants started to consign shipments to British houses, who in their turn sent goods in commission to the Chesapeake. The fourth phase began during the second quarter of the 18th century. The planters and merchants on the East Coast set up warehouses in Britain managed by their own agents for the sale of tobacco and the buying of return shipments.[42]

Merchants on Dam Square near the weigh house, looking down towards the Damrak. Detail of a painting by Johannes Lingelbach, 1656.

Unfortunately we do not possess similarly detailed information about the Republic's various trade sectors. They must have followed the same pattern of development, though presumably developments generally occurred somewhat earlier. In all likelihood, the phases and the transitions between them differed, in timing and in duration, from one trade branch to another, depending on the speed of commercial development at either the producers' or at the consumers' end, and on the nature of the product. As for the latter factor, trading for own account could hold out longer in sectors where the key wholesaling functions of keeping stock, sustaining a product range, or grading products remained of particular importance, or where home demand accounted for a large share in total turnover. These factors enabled grain traders for instance to continue dealing for their own account on a considerable scale until well into the 18th century.[43] Merchants dealing in commodities with a final processing stage in the Republic, such as sugar or linen, were probably also late in making the transition to commission trading. And finally, trading for own account never disappeared completely. For, of course, commission merchants did not invariably operate in one and the same way. The daily variety of deals would not have permitted standard recipes. Merchants sold lots in partnership with the shipper, or half in commission, half for their own account. They bought odd batches or remainders, established market positions in anticipation of price rises, or sent out shipments to test particular markets. Such transactions were usually for own account, with or without a partner. For dealing with markets suffering under a dubious business mentality or an unsound currency, commission trading remained unsuitable anyhow. For these reasons, merchants' accounts as a rule show a variety of transaction types. In the final analysis, for each particular business the balance between commission trading and trading for own account can only be read from the items on the profit and loss account.

Trading madder on the Rotterdam exchange, anonymous painting from 1737. The merchant is negotiating with some suppliers, while on the right his servant draws a sample from one of the barrels. The barrels bear various marks. Rotterdam had a substantial trade in this red dyestuff, deriving from the large scale cultivation of madder in the nearby province of Zeeland.

Presumably, commission trading became dominant in the entire Republic during the third quarter of the 17th century. This is evident from the gradual decline of the Dutch merchant colonies which the commercial expansion had spawned along the main trade routes, from Archangelsk in the north, to Izmir and Aleppo in Asia Minor.[44] Commission trading undermined their continued existence. By now merchants could usually find a suitable local commission trader to deal with.[45] Consequently the need to let relatives or staff emigrate disappeared, and the colonies withered for lack of new arrivals. During the 18th century, most foreign ports would still have one or two resident Dutch merchants or firms, but the concentrations typical of the earlier part of the 17th century had dwindled. Around 1650 Bordeaux counted around 70 merchants from the Republic, Cadiz 30, Malaga 20, Leghorn about a dozen. The Dutch colony in Izmir reached its zenith by 1690, with 25 firms. Other Mediterranean ports usually had two or three. By 1700 only a handful of merchants remained: 17 in Bordeaux, a sole individual in Cadiz, Seville, and Malaga, 8 in Leghorn.[46]

Local circumstances largely determined the tempo of the decline. For example, foreign firms left Cadiz once Spain barred them from trade with its Latin American colonies, reserving it for Spanish houses. As a result foreign merchants established partnerships with Spanish traders, like Balthasar Coymans did, or they reverted to using supercargoes for their transactions, with Spanish firms supplying the papers and signatures required.[47] On the other hand, the Dutch merchant colonies in Izmir and Archangelsk remained strong when the others had already declined. In both cities particular commercial customs prevailed which required a local presence. By 1720 the decline started to affect these colonies, too, in Izmir following the diverting of the Levant trade to Marseille, in Archangelsk because of competition from newly founded St Petersburg.[48]

Of course, observers did notice this phenomenon at the time. Towards the end of the 1680s pamphlets appeared sounding the alarm over the dwindling merchant colonies abroad, as a sure sign for the entrepot market's alleged decay.[49] Some modern historians take the same position.[50] Even so this direct connection does not seem plausible. The merchant colonies disappeared, but the Republic's foreign trade retained a fairly stable volume with peak years not far below previous ones. As will be argued shortly, the trade pattern remained largely the same as well. Consequently the disappearance of the colonies must have been caused by the switch to commission trading.

This switch had another important effect. The capital power needed for the overseas trade declined markedly, because the cost and risk of transactions moved to the principals. A commission merchant could cover his remaining risks and his credit cost easily and cheaply by having them underwritten in ways detailed below. This opened up new opportunities for aspiring merchants to make a career in foreign trade. Quite often they would start trading with a particular region or in a specific product, and expand towards other regions and into other products as turnover rose. Sooner or later such merchants would also embark on shipping. The partnership established between Mrs Susanna van Eeghen-Blok and her son Christiaan in January 1725, was basically a wholesale business in fabrics with its own shop attached. The new firm started with 40,000 guilders worth of goods underway to foreign buyers, out of a total stock valued at more than 100,000 guilders. The Van Eeghens kept fabrics as their core business and concentrated on trade with the West Indian islands, though from time to time they sent shipments to other destinations. From its West Indian clients, the firm received consignments of tobacco, cocoa, hides, and indigo

There was no sharp boundary line between wholesale and retail trade until well into the 18th century. Van Eeghen, for one, continued to operate in both sectors for a considerable time. Its retail outlet may well have looked like this shop in silk and woollen fabrics. Detail from a painting by Johannes Schoenmakers, late 18th century.

for sale. As a matter of course, the commodity trade led to shipping activities and bottomry transactions.[51]

Such commission trading firms usually built up a capital of 100,000-200,000 guilders within a generation. J.I. de Neufville & Co., a linen trader, started in 1730 with just over 30,000 guilders. The first balance sheet of Poupart & Crommelin, dated 1737, shows a capital of 20,000 guilders. After twenty years, both firms traded with capitals of over 200,000 guilders.[52] That amount would appear to be a standard size for merchant businesses. Francis Pym's journals, covering the years 1737 and 1738, show an Amsterdam merchant with fairly extensive imports of various commodities. His capital presumably amounted to 160,000 guilders. Pym's commercial network had a pretty wide radius. He drew supplies from all the main ports of Europe, Curaçao, and North America, to sell all over the Republic.[53] Zeger van Son & Zn. ranged with the firms just mentioned, having a capital of 100,000 guilders in 1746. From its original Baltic trade, Van Son branched out during the 1750s, also dealing in tea, dye wood, and raisins.[54]

Commission trading, then, opened new opportunities for those with commercial ambitions. The very openness of trade and the all-round activities of commission traders prevents us from drawing set distinctions between their respective market functions. According to a classic but disputed conception, the market had three different groups of merchants. Firstly, the importers or *zeehandelaren*, literally sea traders, who imported commodities, each from his own

88

Jacob van Campen's city hall towering over its surroundings, a proud symbol of world power. The building was completed in 1655. When Gerrit Berkheyde made this painting, in 1672, that power had just come under simultaneous attack from four sides.

area of specialization. They sold to what became known as the 'second hand' or *tweede hand*, large firms specialising in particular commodities. These firms supposedly operated as the balance between supply and demand. They arranged and financed storage, sorting and grading, and, where necessary, processing of the commodities. A third group of merchants took care of the final distribution, ordering from the *zeehandelaren* for onward sales to the hinterland.[55] The market functions did exist, but there were no functionally separated trading firms. No doubt some merchants will have concentrated on one function only. However, the firms for which we have details operated a range of commercial activities and supplementary services, for their own account or in commission, for customers at home or abroad, to suit opportunities and possibilities.

Finally, commission trading provides the main reason why the Republic's foreign trade retained its very high volume until the end of the 18th century. Firstly, merchants could increase their activities considerably. For commission traders did not have to await shipments to arrive or to be sold before entering into new transactions. After all, they invested their capital into the supplementary services of finance, storage, and insurance, not in the commodities at hand. Consequently, compared to trading for own account, trading in commission lowered the amount of capital needed for a given product volume, so commission merchants could sustain a higher volume and speed of turnover. This effect probably gave the Republic a new lead over its commercial rivals. Secondly, commission merchants could use supplementary services as a lever to reinforce their grip on trade or to attract new business. As suppliers and customers emancipated towards independent merchants and set up direct connections, the United Provinces lost its attractiveness as a market. Merchants developed a range of sophisticated supplementary services to compensate for this loss, and to shore up their positions and retain as much business as possible.

Commission trading led to the rise of large merchant houses with a wide span of activities. These firms differed from the moguls dominating the commercial expansion first of all by their longevity. Several firms remained in business for over a century or even longer. Two of them still exist today under their own names, Insinger & Co. and Van Eeghen & Co. Moreover, the latter is still turning the same ground as three hundred years ago, the international commodity trade.[56] This apparent longevity of 18th century firms is partly coincidental, a matter of observation and the chance survival of records. Two key 17th century firms have disappeared from view, for instance. Louis de Geer's successors opted to stay in Sweden and to continue his business interests from there. No coherent records survive for the various merchants from the Hooft family. If they had, we might well have been able to construe from them business activities with a span and a longevity similar to those of 18th century firms.

Yet one crucial difference remains. During the era of economic expansion, merchants often traded in loose and varying associations, and did not seem to bother to hand over their business as a formal unit from one generation to the next. Guillelmo Bartolotti successfully continued trading in this way well into the 1650s. He died a millionaire in 1657.[57] Merchants followed in the foot-

steps of their fathers, fathers-in-law, uncles or former masters, and continued the business under their own name. They kept in touch with suppliers and customers mostly through correspondence. Such ties usually rooted in personal acquaintance, established during the aspiring merchant's years of travelling, and subsequently sustained by the factors or supercargoes who came to complete the transactions. Commission trading changed this. Business partnerships gradually consolidated into firm associations, some faster than others. A summons for a meeting of Baltic traders dated 1706, addresses 137 merchants, 18 of which traded in formal partnerships.[58] Perhaps the need for consolidation had not as yet reached the grain trade, at that moment probably still mainly carried on for own account.

In other trade sectors, firmer associations probably followed hard on the switch to commission trading. Suppliers and customers now came to rely on some commission trader abroad to handle their commodities, to use their name for chartering ships, for taking out insurance policies, for financial transactions. Personal relationships were not completely absent. Merchants' sons often received part of their education abroad from their fathers' business relations, and subsequently travelled around before establishing themselves in business. Direct personal relations between firms could then easily cease for decades on end. The business relations proper would come to reside in letters and other documents, conveyed by always varying intermediaries such as ships' masters or couriers.

Commission merchants, then, lived by their name and reputation, more so than traders for their own account. Consequently, such partnerships propagated a particular name for their business. Their successors had a fixed interest in continuing that identity, which they did by emphasising continuity above change in the inevitable partnership changes. For evident reasons, this happened first in firms which expanded into long-term financial transactions. The development of Jean Deutz' activities demonstrate this to good effect. Deutz father came to Amsterdam as an immigrant from Cologne. He must have done very well, for the son married Geertruid Bicker, and so into a powerful family of

By depicting merchants of different nationalities, such as Arabs and Baltic grain traders, Berkheyde underlined the city's extensive trade network in his 1672 painting.

patricians and businessmen. This made Jean Deutz the brother-in-law of Johan de Witt, the dominating politician of his day in the Republic. In 1659 Deutz acquired the exclusive rights to sell Austrian mercury in Europe. As usual, this trade went hand in hand with large advances on supplies to the monarch granting the right, in this case the Austrian emperor. De Witt then helped Deutz to get a large contract for mercury supplies to the Spanish crown, for use in the Mexican silver mines. After Jean Deutz's death, his widow continued the business under the name of Wed. Jean Deutz, Wed. standing for widow. When their son Jean Deutz, a lawyer by training, became a partner, the suffix '& Soon' was added. In 1695, the firm Wed. Jean Deutz & Soon floated the first regular securitised foreign loan on the Amsterdam stock exchange for its Austrian customer, a 1.5 million guilder issue for twelve years bearing 5% interest.[59] The Estates General guaranteed the loan to keep its political ally sweet during a war with France. The next alteration in the firm came when Willem Gideon Deutz, grandson of the founder, entered the partnership, his grandmother retiring at the same time. The partners now dropped the prefix 'Wed.' and named the firm Jean Deutz & Soon. On his father's death in 1719, Willem Deutz announced that he would continue trading under the name Jean Deutz & Soon as he and his father had done before.[60] The crystallisation of a particular business identity such as this one did not mean that merchants put all their interests together in a single firm. Next to the mercury and banking business, Jean Deutz owned a firm trading in silk. Willem Deutz also entertained other commercial interests outside the core business.

NEW SERVICE PATTERNS – More or less simultaneously with the switch to commission trading, the range of commercial services was profoundly improved. First of all, self-sufficient, independent occupations appeared out of subsidiary mercantile services delegated by the merchants themselves to separate agents. As mentioned above, merchants and ships' masters had grown apart during the 16th century. Now a new occupational split occurred, as ship owners emerged as a separate group, people owning and managing ships with no commodity trade worth mentioning. This presumably happened during the second half of the 17th century. Amsterdam's short-lived chamber of commerce had no ship owners amongst its members, but forty years later the Board of the Baltic Trade recognised their importance. The Board regulations laid down that delegations to the Estates General in the Hague or other political missions had to be made up from merchants and ship owners alike, suggesting potentially diverging interests between the two groups.[61] The rise of independent ship owners did not spell the end for merchants or ships' masters continuing to act as such, though. Until well into the 19th century such combinations appeared side by side with specialist ship owners.[62]

Next, ships' agents or *cargadoors* appeared, making a living from chartering ships and handling cargo. The term existed as early as the late sixteenth century, but the profession did not, at least not within the Republic. In 1598 the Rotterdam city council saw no need for a space for 'carrigadors' in the planned exchange building, apparently because there were none. Whereas notarial deeds from the first half of the 17th century occasionally mention ships' agents, the first partnership was presumably established in Amsterdam, as late as 1662. Specialised services must have developed rapidly since then. According to Le Moine de l'Espine, ships' agents were widely available around 1700, and forty years later Amsterdam had more than thirty of them. The profession also flourished in Rotterdam.[63] In effect, the *cargadoors* streamlined the land side of sea transport, intermediating between supply and demand for cargo capacity, super-

Travellers in front of the Nieuwe Stadsherberg (new city inn), a drawing by Ludolf Bakhuysen from 1698. This inn was built on a wooden platform moored in the IJ, and served travellers arriving after the city entrances had been closed for the night.

92

vising the loading and unloading of ships, arranging storage, and performing all necessary formalities and paperwork. As traffic managers for their particular regions, they provided a better balance between ships' movements and the demand for capacity, cutting costly idle time for both ship owners and shippers. This was an important step forward, because the speed of transport depended not so much on technical improvements as on better organisation.[64]

The emergence of independent ship owners and ships' agents marks an important moment in the development of the entrepot market. Clearly, trade and subsidiary services in combination had attained such volume, that delegation and specialisation made sense. The port of London reached this point considerably later. The first ships' agents appeared there only towards the end of the 18th century.[65] Such divisions of labour were logical consequences of the switch to commission trading. The merchant now became a manager coordinating a transactions chain to sell commodities. Managing and owning ships ceased to be core business, commission merchants could contract them in, as and when required, and charge them to their principal. It was not a matter of a stringent separation between tasks and occupations, but of increased choice, whether or not to keep services in-house. Merchant firms would now provide all services themselves, now contract out some of them, or even all. Whatever their choice, the competitive advantage created by the division of labour probably amounted to more than streamlined services alone. Spinning tasks into separate professions generated volume and competition for those services, initiating a virtuous circle of lower cost and higher volumes. Principals abroad quickly spotted the resulting cost savings. As early as the beginning of the 18th century, Amsterdam became the key centre intermediating between foreign merchants, shippers, and

A view of the Rotterdam exchange in 1720. The city's Wisselbank was housed in the so-called Blue Tower on the left. In the background ships moored along the Blaak.

93

ship owners, irrespective of the ship's flag, cargo, or itinerary. Subsequently these services grew into a shipping exchange used by shippers all over Europe.[66] By 1770 half of the charter contracts for the Baltic trade concerned foreign ships or ships bypassing the Republic.[67] Maritime insurance also acquired a firmer base and a European reach. During the last quarter of the 17th century insurers started to join in fairly large and durable syndicates, heralding the first limited companies which were established in 1720.[68]

Financial innovations complemented the commission trade and the new service pattern as a matter of course. Credit had been part and parcel of trade on the entrepot market during the era of commercial expansion, as mentioned in the previous chapter. Merchants used capital power to bind their suppliers, for instance by advancing money on products before the harvest, or in anticipation of supplies of say copper or mercury. They also offered unbeatable terms for payment.[69] Such arrangements continued, besides new ones dedicated to the commission trade, especially the consignment advances treated above.

The use of bills was expanded and perfected by the adoption of acceptances, in short a bill which a debtor or his banker has signed to guarantee payment on expiry. This signature, especially when given by firms of wide reputation, lent bills an extra security, which made them easier and cheaper to sell.[70] Suppliers abroad gladly received acceptances, because they could use them to pay outstanding debts in the Republic or elsewhere. English wool exporters, for instance, sold their acceptances received as payment from Amsterdam to London importers, who used them to pay ships' supplies bought in Gdansk. From there the acceptances would wander back to Amsterdam, as settlement for salt and wine received, or to be credited to the account of a Baltic firm. The possibilty offered by such triangular transactions greatly simplified international payments.

Two giro forms for transferring money in the Rotterdam Wisselbank, issued by the firm of Cordelois, De Vrijer & Mees, 1728 and 1732. Account holders used such forms to manage their accounts.

At the same time, acceptances created a new form of credit. A commission trader for example would grant his customers the right of acceptance. This meant that for a small commission he would accept payment of their bills, in effect extending credit until the bills fell due and customers redeemed their debt. A new and sophisticated occupation emerged mirroring the dedicated shipping services, that of merchants dealing in acceptances or the first merchant bankers proper. Of course the connection between volume of services, specialisation, and cost savings held here as well. Around 1760 Hope & Co. for instance charged 0.25% for supplying a bill. Another Amsterdam merchant, taken to task by a correspondent for his charging 0.33%, wrote back to defend himself by saying that Hope & Co.'s low commission reflected that firm's large business volume, whereas for him it would not be worth the trouble.[71]

The Antwerp bill regulations already described the acceptance technique. Merchants in the Republic presumably knew how to use it, but the first signs of widespread adoption appeared only around the middle of the 17th century. A legal textbook published in 1656 cited some rules concerning accepting bills.[72] The Amsterdam city council enacted a decree about the outward appearance of acceptances in 1660, and added another one laying down the terms of expiry three years later.[73] In 1664 the chamber of commerce pleaded for a change in the rules governing acceptances.[74] Apparently this particular financial technique went through a formative period during those years. There must have existed firms of sufficient reputation to allow the use of acceptances to strike roots, but we do not know them, nor the reach of their activities. Acceptances must have crossed the borders of the Republic very quickly as a matter of course. By 1711, the Amsterdam firm of A. Pels & Soonen did substantial acceptance transactions with Britain, and presumably also with France.[75] The War of the Spanish Succession generated the British acceptances in question, but from the size of Pels's business we may surmise that the firm had been similarly active before the war. More or less at the same time as Pels, the firm of Clifford & Zoonen

The perfection of financial techniques helped to raise the stature of merchants in the public imagination, as is demonstrated here by the frontispiece of Samuel Ricard's *Traité général du commerce* (1705). Enthroned at his desk, this merchant musters an acceptance, offered to him by two customers.

appeared on the scene as dealers in acceptances. Both firms grew very fast to become the main merchant bankers during the first half of the 18th century, surrounded by an ambience of wealth, fame, and mysterious powers.

Acceptances contributed to this aura. Exchange transactions anyway spread a suggestive atmosphere of deep and elusive mysteries, comprehensible to initiates only. In 1624, Gerard de Malynes published a merchants' handbook which named 'the three essential parts of trafficke (...) bodie, soule, and spirit of commerce, namely commodities, money, and exchange for money by bills of exchanges'.[76] According to this perception, bankers were really running a business of the spirit, unencumbered by the laborious fuss of lasts of grain or sacks of coin. Acceptances deepened that mystery still further. With this technique the spirit acquired command over a much larger soul and body, stretching over all of Europe, with limbs reaching out beyond view. And all that radiated around a desk. The frontispiece of Samuel Ricard's book *Traité général du commerce* (1705) gives a fine illustration of the merchants' business status as enhanced in public opinion by acceptances. We see a commodious room, presumably very light and airy, with a view onto a square with a public weigh house and the harbour beyond. The high walls are covered with filing cabinets from the floor to the ceiling, the doors labelled with names of cities and countries. Four clerks occupy themselves with ledgers and papers. In the foreground a merchant enthroned behind his desk, with a ledger open in front of him and a bank transfer ready in his hand. Turning to look over his shoulder, he musters an acceptance, offered by two submissive customers.

The financial service sector received another powerful stimulus from a currency reform and a very important new function created for the Wisselbank. Specie still performed a key role in international payments. However, merchants always had difficulty in finding large amounts of sufficient quality for payments abroad, because the coins in circulation were an endless variety similar only in their equally dubious weight and content. The Republic's provinces cheerfully increased this confusion. As many as fourteen mints produced coins of different type and weight. In 1659 the Estates General decided to introduce new and full-weight guilder coins as a first step towards a currency reform. The value of the guilder subsequently remained virtually unchanged until devaluation in 1936. Opposing interests between the provinces then blocked further progress, until in 1694 the reform was finally completed by bringing the mints under uniform control. This did not at all end the chaotic circulation. The reform had aimed to create above all a solid currency as a prop to foreign trade, the confusion within the country continued to reign as before. From now on, everyone could have bullion minted into so-called *negotiepenningen* or trade coins, with a fixed value against the guilder. Three such coins came into circulation: the ducat, *rijksdaalder* or rixdollar for the Baltic, the *leeuwendaalder* or lions dollar for the Levant, and finally the ducaton for Asia. These coins enjoyed a very wide circulation, built on the Republic's commercial power and their own fixed value.[77] A strong guilder did not mean a blessing for everyone, though. Linen manufacturers in the province of Overijssel petitioned the Estates General in 1704 and again in 1752, complaining about the adverse exchange rates making German linens up to 20% cheaper than their products. They demanded protective tariffs in compensation. The estates of Holland countered by claiming that the free trade in linens generated a strong demand at home and abroad, which benefited the Overijssel producers as well. Nothing changed.[78] Subsequent repeated controversies about currency policy and tariff protection between industrial and commercial interests usually had the same pattern, and also left matters as they were.

In 1683 the Wisselbank's board extended its brief to complement the currency reform underway. From then on, merchants could lombard bullion with the bank for a small charge. In return, they received a *recepis* or tradable receipt. This new facility turned the Wisselbank into the central depository for gold and silver in Europe. For it became very attractive indeed to send precious metals to Amsterdam, deposit them safely with the bank, and switch to trading with transferable paper in stable banco money. As specie substitutes, the receipts cut the cost of specie settlements which used to underpin trade. Amsterdam's central position in the international currency flows gained an entirely new dimension. The Wisselbank attracted large flows of gold and silver, which the board directed to the masters of the mint for coining into trade coins. The number of depositors and total deposits jumped. Until 1680, the bank's deposits rarely exceeded 10 million guilders, after the reform the amount usually ranged between 15 and 20 million. The *recepissen* found eager acceptance, so much so that cash withdrawals fell into disuse.[79]

During the 18th century, the entrepot trade proper lost ground to commission trading and financial services. Paulus Determeijer Weslingh began as a merchant in stock fish, but gradually developed a growing banking business. J. Quinkhard painted him and his servant in 1765.

The bullion receipts reduced the cost of specie settlements in some cases, and eliminated the need for them entirely in others. Settling debts and meeting standing obligations could now be done by transferring paper in stead of gold or silver. Moreover, the range of other available facilities enabled merchants to switch effortlessly between assets, from credit to coin, to paper, to bills, to commodities, to securities, and back again, depending on their opportunities, demands, or obligations at any moment in time. This lent their business increased flexibility and scope. Merchants within reach of the Amsterdam exchange had enjoyed such benefits for a long time, now acceptances and the *recepis* gave access to potential users living anywhere. Cashiers and bankers handled the transactions, there was no need to appear in person. It comes as no surprise that foreigners held a large share of the Wisselbank's mounting bullion deposits. At the end of the 17th century, they deposited about half of the silver on estimate.[80] Consequently, by that time foreign merchants must have begun using the local financial services for bills and acceptances very intensively indeed.

A NEW LEASE OF LIFE FOR THE ENTREPOT MARKET – Now, did this new service pattern amount to a new recipe for commercial success? In the past, this question has often received a negative reply. Commission trading and acceptance transactions have had to endure particularly severe criticism, some of it as early as the end of the 18th century, at a time when the Republic's economy deteriorated rapidly. Critics first of all blamed commission trading, which they deemed passive by nature. According to them, the economic debacle could have been avoided, if only merchants had shown more courage and continued trading for their own accounts. Acceptance banking and the emergence of independent shipping services made matters still worse in the eyes of these observers. For with these facilities merchants and bankers enabled the foreign competition to bypass the entrepot market. The increasing importance of banking services emerges from such accounts as a specific factor accelerating the disintegration, a sign of commercial passivity and laziness, a business fit for retired merchants.[81]

At the time itself, other commentators countered these suggestions by emphasising the true nature of commission trading, arguing the advantages of acceptance banking, and the inevitability of the economic decline.[82] Even so, a rumble of criticism sounds through the ages, muted but unmistakable. The switch to commission trading sometimes still counts as a deliberate choice for passivity, for a settled existence avoiding risks and travelling, an act with which the Republic consciously passed the initiative to foreign merchants.[83] Because commission traders did not handle their own goods, their business was supposedly without risk. They sat on fat margins, propped up by monopolistic practices and their own inflated self assurance. The separation of supplementary services from the core commercial business allegedly contributed to the entrepot market's disintegration, for this enabled the competition to turn their back on the Republic.[84]

Now there is certainly reason for some qualifying comments on the apparent success of commission trading, mainly because commission trading and the underlying services failed to halt commercial decline. The Republic's market position appears to have worsened overall between 1650 and 1750. The trend sketched in Figure 2.1 proved inexorable. Presumably around 1720, most sectors were still in the situation depicted under B, an active trade intermediation between demand and supply. However, by and by circumstances changed towards C. Suppliers and consumers moved to establish direct connections, with the Republic relegated to providing supplementary services. Possibly phase D, trade and services bypassing the entrepot market, already appeared on the horizon in some trade sectors. Under these circumstances, the division of labour into specialisms possibly created an overly rigid service structure which prevented radical economic change. Necessary adjustments may in that case have met with fierce resistance from a crowd of professionals, each fighting for his own special interests. After all, merchants and ship owners on the Board for the Baltic Trade did not necessarily agree with each other. Other indications for rigidity and resistance to change surfaced during the first half of the 19th century, as the next chapter will show. And yet this objection cuts no ice. It makes no sense at all to blame the generation of merchants active around 1680 that they should have prevented some problems emerging more than a century later, by not choosing what was for them the best economic option. From the viewpoint of commercial technique, Dutch merchants really had no choice. They had to switch to commission trading if they wanted to stay in the race. And finally, trading for own account did not disappear completely, as mentioned above: if it had really offered better opportunities than commission trading, merchants would definitely have not been slow to use it on a wider scale.

Also, the specialist services undoubtedly made it cheaper and easier for foreign merchants to establish direct connections, thus bypassing the Republic. Since the 1750s, critics have pointed to the *voorbijlandvaart* as a sure sign that the sophisticated services of commission traders, acceptance bankers, and ship owners, undermined the entrepot market and thus hastened the economic decline.[85] Though old and venerable, this reproach is unjustified. As mentioned above, the *voorbijlandvaart* was as old as the entrepot market, and by 1600 a considerable volume of shipping bypassed the Republic as a matter of course. Perhaps the direct routing of shipments increased during the 18th century. One would expect so. After all, to Amsterdam linen merchants executing orders for Silesian linen from English houses it made no sense at all to have the goods in the Republic. They instructed their suppliers to ship the fabrics from Hamburg directly to Britain, unless the customer wanted them bleached in Haarlem.[86] And how many ships were involved anyway? The old route from France to the Baltic and back suited the *voorbijlandvaart* best. Around 1750, an estimated 400 ships each year sailed directly either way without landing in the Republic.[87] At that time the number of ships entering Amsterdam harbour averaged roughly 3,000 a year, and had done so for decades.[88] It appears unlikely then that direct routing can have done a great deal of damage.

DE
OOPMAN,
OF
YDRAGEN
TEN OPBOUW
LANDS KOOPHANDEL EN ZEEVAARD.

ERSTE DEEL.

MSTELDAM,
RRIT BOM. 1768.

The magazine De Koopman attributed the decline of Dutch trade to merchants resting on their laurels and neglecting their duties. The magazine's title page shows a scholar at work, with the commercial handbooks by Le Long, Ricard, and Gregory King at hand. Engraving by Reinier Vinkeles, Amsterdam 1768.

Moreover, blaming the specialised services for the erosion of the entrepot market is tantamount to confusing cause and effect. The market's progression from phase A to phase D in Figure 2.1 was an entirely natural and unavoidable one. Suppliers and consumers will always try to cut out the wholesaler and do business directly. They will succeed in this, unless the wholesaler continues to offer sufficient added value, with logistics, product range, or other dedicated services. The commission traders and acceptance bankers did exactly that. They aimed to make a profit from offering services which helped to make the entrepot market as cost effective as possible. If they failed to compensate the market's disadvantages, then clearly foreign customers found the service facilities an attractive commercial proposition, but that no longer went for the market. That was not the fault of the commission merchants and acceptance bankers, of course, but a collective failure due to the Republic's size and the mercantilist policies of surrounding markets. Contemporaries must have been flabbergasted. The Republic had very powerful merchants, who ruled the world from behind their desks, who amassed huge wealth for all to see. And such businessmen would be unable to give their home market a share in their success? Then they simply did not exert themselves sufficiently. Clearly they put private wealth and idleness above the common weal. In stead of the sound trade of their forebears, they gambled with securities. Instead of travelling all over the world, they collected public sinecures, and bought feudal titles to play the squire on their manors along the river Vecht, or in the dunes bordering the North Sea. This essentially moral condemnation of the commercial elite, as failing in their proper duties, appeared in periodicals such as *De Koopman* (the Merchant), but also in novels and plays.[89]

Of course, commission trading was hardly a passive and risk-free business with cast-iron margins. Firstly, though the commodities themselves no longer tied up a commission merchant's capital, the underlying financial services did so to a large degree: the consignment advances, the acceptances, and other credit lines to customers. Terms of payments still stretched out over a long time, at least 9-12 months in the linen trade, for instance.[90] Secondly, a commission merchant had to prove the value of his margin by selling the goods at hand as best he could. Failure to do so would lose him a customer to someone else. Past opinion suggested that commission traders effortlessly made large profits. Manipulations and market imperfections would often have enabled them to dictate prices.[91] This interpretation does not ring true. Neighbouring countries competed keenly with the Republic. The home market was open and, to all appearances, hotly contested as well. Monopolies and cartels rarely succeeded in maintaining themselves in the face of ineradicable smuggling, unless the merchants concerned had a contract with a bonafide supplier. For instance, some merchants in the Archangelsk trade had a firm grip on the supply of Russian leather, and still unofficial imports undermined their efforts to push up prices.[92] Even Hope & Co., without doubt the most powerful and the most skilful European merchant firm of its day, could not bend the market to its will. Between 1787 and 1794 the firm lost millions of guilders in a deliberate effort to manip-

ulate the price of cochineal, a dyestuff.[93] At the beginning of the 18th century, the Amsterdam city monopoly on price currents disappeared. By that time commission merchants and brokers distributed so many private price lists to win customers, that upholding the official monopoly no longer made sense.[94] The officially appointed brokers could not handle the growing business volume, forcing the city authorities into tolerating a large crowd of unofficial brokers.[95] In 1735 the prominent Rotterdam merchant firm J. Senserff & Co. wrote to an English client 'We seldom encourage our friends to engage in any commodity because we daily finde by experience how little there is to be depended upon, trade being overdone on all sides'.[96]

The continuing immigration alone would have thwarted merchants' efforts towards a closed shop with inflated margins. A sample of bill protests suggests that, at the beginning of the 18th century, Amsterdam's inhabitants were a very colourful variety of nationalities. When a bill expired but remained unpaid, notaries drew up a so-called deed of protest. The sample showed that of the merchants protesting a bill between 1701 and 1710, 38% were French Huguenots, 30% Dutch, 18% English, and the remainder German, Russian, or Jewish.[97] These nationalities of course had an important position in the trade with their countries of origin. During the 18th century, for instance, the Dutch Levant trade moved more or less entirely over to immigrated Greeks, Armenians, and Levantine Jews.[98] The various regional trades could reflect a similar variety of nationals, though. In the early 18th century, 30% of the merchants trading with Britain was English, against 28% Huguenot, 21% Jewish, 13% Dutch, and about 8% Germans and Italians.[99]

During the late 17th and 18th centuries, immigrants kept coming to the Republic. Commission trading, after all, offered good perspectives to build a fortune from scratch. Newcomers did not appear to have any lasting difficulties in settling down and climbing the commercial ladder. In 1723, a French merchants' manual praised Dutch merchants for their openness and trust towards correspondents of all nations.[100] An anonymous editor, who published a new and revised edition of Ricard's by now famous manual in 1781, had a similar opinion. 'Nowhere is it easier for foreign merchants to establish themselves', he wrote, 'although it does take a long time before newcomers get credit. The Amsterdam commission trade would wither without firms of foreign origin, for these houses continuously create new connections and new business.'[101] Certainly, immigrants did face some obstacles. An anonymous commentator in the periodical *De Koopman* denounced them, advocating to give dissenters, Jews, and Catholics the same rights as Dutch Protestants.[102] Only adherents of the official Dutch Protestant religion could hold official positions. That principle did not prevent immigrants from achieving prominence in their chosen trade within a generation, even if they happened to be, for instance, Mennonites, Jews, or Catholics. To all appearances the careers and the assimilation of immigrants could progress very quickly, in the 18th century just as before. There always were firms established and managed by foreign merchants among the first rank houses: Clifford, Hasselgreen, Hogguer, Deutz, Thomas & Adrian Hope, Braunsberg, Senserff, Osy, to name but a few. Thus the market's openness and the keen competition renders it unlikely indeed that commission traders could overcharge systematically.

On the other hand, the complaints about passiveness, high commissions, and commanding positions may still have some truth in them. These phenomena may have occurred in trade sectors which the Republic could hold firmly in its grip because of its geographical location or by historical happenstance. The trade in Asiatic products was one such sector, for instance, although competition on this particular market increased considerably after about 1720. Other sectors succeeded in developing a new service, as lateral reservoir, once direct connections had robbed them of their original wholesale functions of product range and central reservoir. In this capacity merchants absorbed surplus products which the regular channels could not accommodate, to release their stock when prices had recovered. This niche strategy presumably originated in trades with a marked cyclical production pattern, such as grain or wine.

Credit facilities were a crucial ingredient for this particular marketing mix. According to Ricard, Amsterdam's large business volume ultimately rested on finance: merchants could always sell for cash, or else lombard their goods.[103] The linen trade provides a good example of lateral reservoirs developing. Silesian linen used to be distributed over Europe via the Republic. As we have noted above, Hamburg gradually became the main port for shipping linen from the German hinterland, for Dutch merchants as well. When manufacturers found sales slow or prices too low in Hamburg, they would ship their goods to the Republic. Dutch merchants would give them consignment advances of 75%, allowing the producers to await better prices with cash in hand.[104] Consequently, linen merchants such as the Amsterdam firm of J.I. de Neufville & Co. had no need to find customers in a hurry. Buyers would appear automatically when prices recovered. Their charges must have mirrored this particular market strategy. In 1757 the London linen merchant Thomas Nash, a customer of De Neufville, complained about his commission charges: 'We are exceedingly sorry to see that your charges are not modern, but according to the old fashion, where little business was attended with great profit'. Time and again he urged his Amsterdam colleague to change tack and aim for a high turnover with low margins, instead of the other way around as now, 'quick sales being infinitely most agreeable, though with small profits', and a few years later 'a quick sale (…) is the very life of trade'. Nash wrote that he preferred to lose a commission rather than run the risk of having goods on his hands for too long.[105] For De Neufville however, the opposite was true.

Here we have the origins of the commercial conservatism ridiculed by a famous 1830s novel, Hildebrand's *Camera Obscura*, in which Uncle Stastok prefers to let his goods rot in the warehouse, rather than spoiling the market by cutting his prices.[106] The competition with other commercial centres inspired the likes of De Neufville to use the available facilities for creating a niche market with higher margins, rather than turning their trade into a brisker and more competitive one. Under the circumstances this was probably a very rational choice. Nash may have experienced a direct relationship between lower commissions and higher turnover, but this would not have worked for De Neufville. The London merchant lived in a fast growing city with almost 700,000 inhabitants around 1750. This metropolis served a hinterland with roughly 7 million inhabitants, protected against foreign competition, but open and without serious commercial obstacles to Nash. Moreover, he could profit from a privileged position in the burgeoning Atlantic trade. Between 1720 and 1770 the value of British foreign trade doubled, from an estimated 145 million to 290 million guilders.[107] More than two thirds of that trade went to London.[108] By contrast, De Neufville's home market counted only 2 million inhabitants in a stagnating population. Foreign competition had free access, whereas the surrounding hinterland remained heavily protected. By 1750, the Republic's trade lagged behind the British. Between 1720 and 1770 the estimated value of foreign trade rose from 180 million to 240 million guilders.[109] Consequently, London had become a much bigger market than Amsterdam. In 1753, London's foreign trade amounted to roughly 150 million guilders, against only 85 million guilders for Amsterdam.[110]

Fiddling with commission charges or with customs duties would not have sufficed in this situation, only very radical and all-round cost cuts might perhaps have succeeded in restoring the entrepot market to vigorous growth. Perhaps. For its range of products, once unique, was by now commonplace. Trade and shipping had progressed to eliminate the need for central stocks. And finally, on most foreign markets, tariff protection remained, whatever the Republic did

The editor of the magazine De Koopman was not alone in his essentially moralist criticism on 18th century business life. The engraver of this print about the 1763 commercial crisis clearly shared his opinion. Wealth distracts the Amsterdam Mercury, while Pride stands ready to lash him. A monkey acts as a bookkeeper, rats sniff the empty coffers. In the background the Amsterdam exchange building. The two round cartouches depict two classical stories of pride and fall: Phaeton and Icarus.

G. V. Nijmegen delin.

J. C. Philips fecit.

to change its conditions. Under such circumstances a defensive niche strategy was rational, not simply blind conservatism. Whether or not De Neufville and the linen trade were exceptions, we do not know. As argued above, the market was open and very competitive, reducing the chances of survival for any niches. De Neufville found this out to his cost. From the mid 1740s, the firm struggled against a steadily falling turnover of its main product, linen. After an attempt at diversification had misfired, the partners liquidated in 1764.[111]

Summing up, the new service pattern was a recipe for commercial success in as far as it helped to slow down the decline of the entrepot market. For more than a century after 1650, the Republic retained a voluminous foreign trade and a vigorous service sector. The criticism directed at the 18th century merchants really departs from a tacit, unrealistic premiss, i.e. that they could have and should have maintained the commercial lead more or less infinitely. That was simply impossible given the Republic's position, which made holding on to the status quo for so long a remarkable achievement indeed.

THE WANING OF A COMMERCIAL EMPIRE – This achievement becomes even more impressive when put in perspective by other factors. The changing trade pattern depicted in Figure 2.1 coincided with an erosion of the Republic's competitive position in other sectors. During the commercial expansion, trade had had close links with fishing and processing industries. Towards the end of the 17th century these sectors began to suffer from increasing competition. Surrounding countries started to cultivate their own industries with or without protective tariff walls. The French cloth industry has been mentioned, but this phenomenon occurred in all sectors, fishing not excepted. At the start of the 18th century industry fishing began to decline irreversibly, not in relative terms as with trade, but in absolute terms, measured in production and employment. Some sectors succeeded in maintaining their position for a considerable time, among them typical processing industries such as sugar refining and cotton printing. Others even showed growth, such as paint works and gin distilleries. However, most sectors went from bad to worse, for instance the vitally important textile industry, and fishing.[112]

This industrial erosion was an autonomous process. Merchants could do little to stop it, despite facing essentially the same threat: the Republic's vulnerable competitive position, as a small country, possessing little in the way of raw materials and having a small home market surrounded by much larger producers sheltering behind mercantilist protection. Possibly the Dutch wage levels, higher than elsewhere, were also a factor in the fall in exports.[113] Trade suddenly acquired two fresh problems. With the processing industries sinking into the economic mire, imports of raw materials and semi-finished products decreased, as did exports of finished goods, trade flows which had given the entrepot market its original power. Moreover, the supply of ready export products fell, creating a commercial handicap which would not be remedied until well into the 19th century.

Meanwhile the Republic reached structural economic limits as well. The Baltic trade shows these to best effect. This particular trade sector remained of uncommon importance, keeping on estimate about half of the merchant fleet occupied.[114] Imports amounted to roughly 10 million guilders a year around 1720, the export value will have been somewhat less.[115]

After the Great Nordic War, the Republic lost ground in the Baltic trade. The number of Dutch passages through the Sound rose, but the number of British and Scandinavian passages rose faster, so the Republic's share declined. Until 1660 Dutch passages averaged 60% of the total, sinking to less than 45% over the years 1660-1700, and to not quite 30% in 1700-1710. During the 18th century, the Dutch share averaged about 30%, with peaks of 50% in exceptional years (Figure 2.2).[116]

Thus, the famous 'mother of all trades' went through difficult times. Why? First of all, because the economic structure of the Baltic and the Scandinavian countries changed, and the required range of imports and exports with

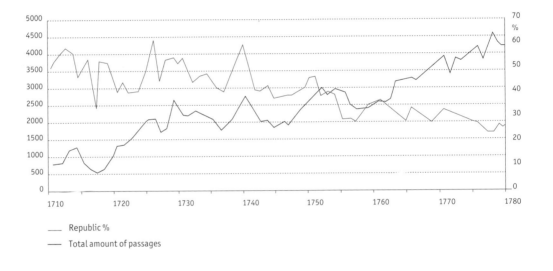

_____ Republic %

—— Total amount of passages

Figure 2.2

Total number of westbound passages through the Sound (left scale) and the percentage headed for the Republic (right scale), 1710-1780

it. Bulk products such as grain, salt, herring and wine, declined in importance compared to, for instance, fabrics, colonial products, iron, pitch, hemp, leather, and hides. The Republic's rivals gained a growing market share for these products. Whereas Dutch ships' masters and merchants had initially provided services locally in short supply, most Baltic ports now had sufficient ships, crew, and traders of their own. Secondly, key trading partners began to close their market to foreigners. Sweden enacted shipping laws towards that end in 1722, and stepped up its trade protection from 1738. Consequently, trade with the

Republic fell, though from time to time returning to something like its former prosperity.[117] Prussia embarked on mercantilist policies, too.[118] Meanwhile the Russian trade moved from Archangelsk to St Petersburg, founded in 1707 by Tsar Peter the Great, with the explicit purpose of serving as a window facing the west. From the start, St Petersburg had a merchant community with a mix of nationalities, among them many English traders, whereas the Archangelsk trade had been dominated by Amsterdam firms.

A Frisian ship's master employed in the Russian trade, painting by Frans van der Mijn, 18th century.

Thirdly, The Republic also lost its dominance of the bulk trade, partly as a direct consequence of the trade wars. Until about 1660, for instance, Dutch ships carried two-thirds of all French wine through the Sound, and half of it came from stocks held in the Republic. Twenty years later, about 70% of the wine came directly from France, and Dutch ships carried no more than 40% of the total. The wine trade in the Republic suffered further setbacks during the War of the Spanish Succession. The Dutch share in the wine transport recovered slightly after the war, but the market share remained far below prewar levels. Less than 20% now came via the entrepot market, more than 80% straight from France.[119] This change translated directly into a sharp rise in the number of Dutch eastbound ships sailing in ballast through the Sound. Since the 1620s ballasted ships averaged 40-50% of the total, i.e. normally ships' masters picked up eastbound cargo, but years of food scarcity pushed up demand for grain, increased traffic, and as a result many more ships sailed in ballast. During the Nine Years' War however, the number of Dutch eastbound ships fell, while the percentage sailing in ballast rose to an average of 66%, peaking at nearly 80%. From about 1720 the earlier correlation between grain transport and ballasted ships returned, but with ballasted ships now averaging around 60%.[120]

Other factors than war eroded the Dutch market share in grain, herring, and salt: changing demand and the rise of new production regions for grain, shifting fishing grounds and Scottish competition for herring, the forward integration of production and refining at source for salt. The timing of the decline differed for each product. Grain demand started to fall during the second quarter of the 17th century, followed around 1660 by the demand for herring. Only salt remained stable until the Great Nordic War. The results were the same for all products, though. The total volume transported through the Sound rose, but the Republic's share stagnated or dropped, resulting in overall reductions from 60-80% of the total to 20-30% or even less. During the second quarter of the 18th century the same happened to high-value goods such as fabrics and colonial products.[121] Only the timber trade managed to retain its large market share until 1780, when decline set in there as well.[122]

The Republic, then, could not keep up with developments in the Baltic trade. Clearly, Dutch merchants failed to make the most of the available opportunities. What were the reasons behind this? Had they become satisfied with their achievements, did the assembled riches cause them to lose their knack and appetite for trade? This reproach sounded as early as the 18th century, and echoes can be heard even today.[123] Factors such as a loss of business acumen may of course have had some influence. On the other hand, we have countless

indications of Dutch ships' masters and merchants fighting against their declining market share. We have seen how they managed to compensate the loss of French wine as bulk ware in the eastbound trade, the percentage of ships in ballast dropping back during the 1720s. They tried out new products to replace those affected by falling demand. When the Hamburg market for herring became saturated, Amsterdam traders switched to sending oysters.[124]

Merchants constantly tried to improve their position, as we have seen above. Why then did they not succeed in keeping up with the competition? Presumably because the Republic had reached a crucial economic threshold, best demonstrated by reversing the question: could the Republic have kept up with the competition? A calculation of the shipping capacity needed to retain market share in the Baltic trade suggests it could never have succeeded in doing so. By 1780 about 9,000 ships in all passed through the Sound every year.[125] Dutch ships numbered 2,400 or 27%. At the beginning of the 18th century the Dutch share in the total was 45%. Consequently, in order to maintain position the number of passages around 1780 would have had to be 4,050. This would have required a considerable expansion of the merchant fleet. Assuming that ships passed through the Sound three times a year, this means a total of 1,350 freighters would have been needed.

Now around 1750 the Republic had a merchant fleet of an estimated 2,000 freighters, of which 870 plied the routes to Norway and the Baltic.[126] Probably, this fleet employed about 30,000 sailors.[127] Keeping up with the competition thus would roughly have meant an extra 500 ships, manned by 5,000-6,000 crew. However, the Republic had a very serious shortage of sailors. This manifested itself as early as the second half of the 17th century, and led to more and more foreigners being signed on. Around 1700, 25% of crews on Dutch ships were foreign, mostly Germans and Scandinavians. During the 18th century the number of immigrants on board ships continued to rise, reaching as much as 60% in 1774-1775.[128] The VOC had similar percentages of foreign employees in the years mentioned.[129] The Republic itself, then, could not supply enough sailors to maintain the strength of the existing merchant fleet. Expanding the

The Republic became dependent on attracting labour from abroad as early as the 17th century. In 1673, Ludolf Bakhuysen painted this press-ganged sailor sitting down in despondence. During the 18th century, labour shortages helped to curb the Republic's further economic expansion.

108

fleet would have meant attracting yet more labour from regions abroad with a surplus. Now, Dutch shipping, like the other economic sectors, already paid higher wages than shipping in other countries did.[130] In order to attract more immigrants, ship owners would have had to offer still more in comparison to what rivals like Scandinavia, Germany, or Britain paid their sailors. They had precious little margin to do so. After all, the entrepot market already competed at a disadvantage, involving as it did a detour for most products. Wage increases would have made the underlying cost problem worse, and would have dealt a further blow to this trade concept.

In conclusion, the Republic would not have been able to keep up with the growth rate of the Baltic trade because of the merchant fleet's labour shortages alone. Of course this is not the only reason why Dutch trade stagnated while the competition surged ahead. Yet the result of this calculation does indicate strongly, that trade had lost shipping as its driving force, a factor of key importance during the era of economic expansion. The loss of dynamism also becomes evident from the stagnation of the merchant fleet. After 1650 the number of vessels remained the same, the 2,000 freighters just quoted, and total capacity never exceeded 450,000 tons. By contrast, the British and French merchant navy showed strong growth. Presumably around 1730 both rivals drew level in this respect with the Republic, and fifty years later they had a firm lead.[131] So there did exist a strong demand for shipping, but apparently the ships' masters from Zeeland, Holland, and Friesland could not meet it despite switching to less labour intensive ships such as the smacks and the koffs.

The Republic, once the freight carrier for the whole of Europe, now had to rely more and more on the services of foreign shipping to fulfil its transport needs. Until about 1750, on average 70-80% of the ships leaving the Sound and heading for Amsterdam had their home port in the Republic. As the Baltic trade grew during the third quarter of the 18th century, this percentage declined to barely 60% in 1780. At the same time, the number of foreign captains sailing west through the Sound and heading for the Republic rose to 30% of the total.[132] Foreign shipping even made inroads on the Dutch home market, transporting products despite the local ship owners' advantage of geographical location. For instance, most Rhenish wine shipped through the Sound used to come from the Republic in Dutch ships. After the Great Nordic War the demand for this product fell. The Dutch trade share remained at 90%, but the transport share fell to less than 40%.[133]

THE CREEPING DECLINE OF THE TRADING COMPANIES – Structural problems also started to affect the two standard bearers of the Republic's overseas expansion, the VOC and the WIC. The radical reorganisation of the latter in 1674 raised hopes that the management of the West Indian colonies plus the West African trade in gold, ivory, and slaves, would give the new company a sound business foundation. To save cost, the directors began to outsource as many tasks as possible. Henceforth ships were chartered, and not built and main-

tained by the company's own yards. The WIC continued to run a considerable trade, the curtailment of its operations notwithstanding. During the years 1674-1735, the company chartered an average of sixteen ships a year. The much larger VOC sent around 30 ships a year to Asia at that time, while on average about 25 made the return voyage to Europe.[134] The last quarter of the 17th century was fairly successful for the WIC, but soon after the old bugbears appeared again: the competition from other merchants, the constant need to defend the settlements in Africa against other European countries, the drain of colonial management expenses on revenues. Whenever the charter came up for renewal, directors, shareholders, and merchants clashed with each other about the terms of the contract before the Estates General, and each time the company had to cede some ground. At the end of the 1730s it had been reduced to an administrative body which granted trade licences, and ran colonial establishments with the fees it raised.[135]

The VOC's problems centred on its business in Asia. During the last quarter of the 17th century, the company succeeded in adding virtual monopolies in the fine spices cinnamon, nutmeg, bay leaves, and cloves to its dominant position in pepper. However, the military expenses required to maintain that position proved to be very high. As a consequence, only some of the local branches, established to buy agricultural products, returned a profit. As a rule, the Factorij in Batavia also lost money. Finally, the tightly centralised business structure

Batavia was at the heart of the VOC's Asian business operations. The company built its own shipyards and warehouses on the island of Onrust (Unrest). On the left a ship on its side, to facilitate hull repairs. The ship on the right has just fired a gun salute. Painting by Abraham Storck, 1699.

translated into high and rigid costs. The VOC ran its Asian trade as an entrepot system. Instead of shipping products from source to the Republic, all goods were first went to Batavia and transferred to the regular return fleets. In the long run the company's intra-Asian trade could not really compete. The Taiwan branch had to be given up for good in 1662, making the VOC dependent on others for its China trade. The trade monopoly in Japan via the Deshima office lost much of its value by restrictive regulations imposed by the Japanese government. On the other hand, the big trading establishments in Bengal, Coromandel, Suratte, and Persia thrived on handling a variety of products: cotton and silk especially, but besides that also copper, silver, and saltpetre. Until about 1690 the company's Asian business made an overall profit of about 800,000 guilders, not much, considering the size of operations. Things went disastrously wrong after that. From 1692 the Factorij incurred losses of 1.5-2 million guilders a year.

To square the accounts, the company had to send increasing amounts of bullion from Europe to Batavia: twenty million guilders during the 1680s, forty million in the 1700s, more than sixty million in the 1720s. While the company's Asian business went into decline, its European market underwent momentous changes. The VOC had just asserted its dominance in the spice trade, when margins started to crumble. Until about 1670, European prices were about three times the purchase price in Asia. That margin fell to slightly over 2.6 during the years 1680-1720, and to less than 2.5 from then on.[136] No one outside the VOC knew about these problems. The Heren XVII gave no information whatever, and individual directors schemed to boost public confidence by pushing the company's share price.[137]

The Heren XVII did not complacently sit by and let circumstances deteriorate, far from it. As early as 1662 the secretary to the board, Pieter van Dam, raised two fundamental questions. He espoused a policy of halting territorial expansion in order to concentrate on improving the company's commercial efficiency, for instance by outsourcing some of the activities. Van Dam thought transport in Asia too expensive, and argued that private ship owners and merchants could operate more cheaply.[138] The directors did not adopt his recommendations, but did take a few other sweeping decisions. First of all, they freed capital by running down stocks, and attracted fresh capital by issuing bond loans. This enabled the Heren XVII to expand the staff and the fleet. Around 1670 the return fleet from Batavia averaged ten ships a year, sixty years later this had risen to thirty. The value of goods received trebled from about 3 million to nearly 9 million guilders in 1730. Sales rose from 9 million to 16 million guilders.[139] Diminishing returns reduced the effect of this expansion. During the 1680s, returning ships carried on average just over 300,000 guilders worth of products, but this amount sank to about 220,000 guilders in the 1730s.[140]

Directors also introduced radical changes to the product range, by vigorously raising the trading volume of cotton, silk, tea, coffee, and other products, such as china. These goods had been known in Europe for some time, but still remained luxuries. The VOC used to sell only fabrics in substantial quantities

(see Figure 1.*). Coffee and tea had a medicinal status.[141] Within a fairly short span of time, increasing supplies by the VOC helped to turn them into popular beverages, enjoyed by a wide public. To safeguard its own supplies, the company introduced the growing of coffee on Java. Figure 2.3 shows the consequences of the changes to the product range.[142] Around 1670 spices accounted for almost 60% of product value, seventy years later for only 30%. By 1740, the value of fabrics, coffee, and tea, all outweighed that of pepper, once so keenly sought after. However, with these products the VOC entered a very competitive market. The old rival, the British East India Company, sold them too. French merchants imported coffee from the West Indies to Europe, and succeeded in wresting for instance the Hamburg coffee market from Dutch merchants. [143] During the second quarter of the 18th century, merchants in Sweden, in Denmark, and in the Austrian Netherlands established companies for the Asian trade, as often as not with Dutch capital. These new companies did not have any territorial ambitions, and they favoured direct connections, buying tea in China and sailing straight back to Europe. By contrast, the VOC depended on tea supplied by Chinese merchants to Batavia. Consequently, the company were at

The VOC began trading in other luxury goods, such as coffee, tea, silk, and chinaware to compensate the shrinking margins on spices. This ivory plaque, made in China during the first half of the 18th century, shows European traders loading chinaware in a lighter.

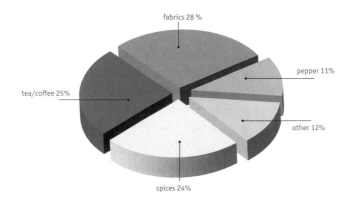

fabrics 28 %

pepper 11%

other 12%

spices 24%

tea/coffee 25%

Figure 2.3

Composition of the VOC return cargoes, around 1749. Source: Gaastra, Geschiedenis VOC, 134

Initially, the VOC shipped products from China to the Republic with a detour via Batavia. However, competition from Danish and Swedish merchants forced the company to adopt direct sailings between China and the Republic.

This anonymous early 19th century painting shows the Canton seafront with several European establishments.

an inherent cost disadvantage compared to the competition, without being able to control product quality. Meanwhile Swedish and Danish merchants flooded the market, in the Republic too. In 1737 and again three years later, a Rotterdam firm complained to a British correspondent about the Scandinavians controlling the supply of tea. The VOC only switched to direct sailings between China and the Republic after lengthy deliberations.[144] Finally, the Heren XVII instructed Batavia to meet the deficits by raising taxation. Thus, by 1720, the territorial possessions generated 30% of the VOC's revenues in Asia. However, the net effect of this policy remains in doubt, for the gains were partly offset by increased expenses of tax collection and administration.[145]

Despite all efforts the company failed to extract itself from the quicksand. The core business expanded, but profits stagnated. After 1730, sales revenues dropped again. The VOC worsened its predicament by continuing to pay high dividends, defying the deteriorating results.[146] Presumably the Heren XVII did not dare touch the dividend ratio. Financially, the company had become highly dependent on advances over expected product supplies and on bond loans at low interest rates of 3.5 - 4%. These debts rose from 2.3 million guilders in 1730 to 21.4 million guilders by 1760.[147] Admitting to the problems and changing tack would have pushed up the company's interest expenses, and might even have cut its life line by making investors shy of the bonds. The exchange had already become suspicious, for from 1732 the company's share price had started to slide. However, the board's dividend policy depleted the available working capital, thus reducing its options for change. From 1736 until 1739 the VOC had a negative cash flow: expenses exceeded the revenues from sales. At long last the directors gave in, and reduced pay outs, though leaving them still much higher than the situation warranted.

During the 1740s the situation appeared to take a turn for the better. A forceful Governor-General in Batavia, G.W. van Imhoff, succeeded in raising Asian revenues, by establishing a limited company for the opium trade, for instance. Bolstered by an official monopoly charter, this so-called Amfioensociëteit outcompeted the thriving opium smugglers between Bengal and Indonesia. High VOC officials privately held the 1.5 million guilders share capital, the VOC itself supplied the opium.[148] Imhoff also wrote a memorandum for the Heren XVII in which he analysed the company's failings. As causes for its decline, he mentioned first the high expenses stemming from the geographical overstretching, and subsequently the increased competition, the VOC's lack of flexibility in adapting to changed circumstances, and finally the lack of competent staff. Van Imhoff mainly sought the remedies in reorganisations.[149] He does not appear to have considered giving up occupied territories, as indeed the people most concerned with the tottering WIC did not either. The directors never acted on Van Imhoff's recommendations, by the way.

His successor Jacob Mossel continued his policy of increasing revenues. He also strove for a reorganisation of the company, but went beyond drafting plans and started a campaign to canvass support. Mossel's aim was not a very ambitious one, to present day standards. He calculated the company's capital to be 35.4 million guilders, and wanted to achieve a one percent rise in returns, from 5% to 6%.[150] The detailed proposals towards that goal found a better reception in the Republic than Van Imhoff's memorandum, among others with Thomas Hope, partner in the eponymous firm and at that time director of the

In some cities, Dutch merchant colonies continued to thrive for a considerable time. Local circumstances were responsible for this in one such case, Smyrna. Around 1770 Antoine de Favray painted this family scene of David George van Lennep, chief merchant of the Dutch establishment, with his wife, children, and servants.

VOC. They also had the desired effect. The VOC's revenues rose again, for one because the average cargo value on ships returning from Asia increased. For the first time since the late the 17th century, the amount passed the 300,000 guilder mark, to peak at more than 380,000 guilders during the 1760s.[151]

Increasing competition, then, ended the Republic's commercial expansion. After 1675 consolidation set in. Trade remained at very high levels, thanks to new patterns of commercial services. Merchants succeeded in holding on to trade flows by developing a sophisticated intermediation. Still, surrounding countries came ever closer, and finally managed overtake the Dutch. By 1750 the Republic had clearly lost its position in the front ranks. Britain and France now called the economic tune, the once mighty merchant fleet fell behind, industrial decay was rampant, the VOC failed to carry out necessary reorganisations. A dark horizon loomed.

Cargo list showing the goods transported by two VOC ships returning to the Republic from Asia.

115

Rotterdam, a view on the Blaak with the exchange on the right, anonymous painting from 1752. By the early 18th century, the city's original exchange building had become too small. After a long wrangle about plans for a new one, the city council finally took a decision in the early 1730s, and the building pictured here opened for business in 1736.

CHAPTER III

During the second half of the 18th century the Dutch trading houses could still muster sufficient capital power to keep up with the competition. Meanwhile, the country finally lost its commercial primacy to Britain. Wars and other coincidences then shook the foundations of the commercial services sector, once so successful. During the turbulent transition between the 18th and 19th centuries, the merchant houses managed to keep a considerable trade volume going, considering the circumstances. Soon after the establishment of the new Kingdom of the Netherlands in 1813, however, it became clear that the tables had turned, once and for all. How did a small country manage, without many locational advantages and surrounded by neighbours protecting their home markets and their fledgling industries?

WRITINGS ON THE WALL – The third quarter of the 18th century was a fairly prosperous one for the Republic's foreign trade. The transatlantic trade in particular experienced growth. Surinam and the Caribbean islands supplied rising volumes of coffee and sugar. In addition, these islands served as home bases for smuggling to North America, a thriving business created by the British Navigation Acts which excluded foreign merchants from trading with their colonies.[1] According to a well-known contemporary estimate, Dutch foreign trade amounted to more than 260 million guilders in 1780 (Table 3.1).[2] Whether or not these particular data tally with more modern calculations given above, such as the value of trade in 1770 or the value of the Baltic trade (Table 2.1 and p. 105), is of no concern here.

Such data will always diverge, because of the different hypotheses and approaches underlying them. The exact volume need not concern us for the moment anyway. What matters first of all, is the apparent growth in value during the 18th century, about which this estimate and modern ones agree.[3] Secondly, this contemporary estimate gives an impression of the geographical pattern of Dutch foreign trade. European trade accounted for the main component by far, with the Baltic, Britain, and France supplying more than 51% of the

Asia	35 mln gld	13.3
West-Indies / South America	28 mln gld	10.6
Baltic	55 mln gld	20.9
Britain	43 mln gld	16.3
France	37 mln gld	14.1
North America	2.3 mln gld	0.9
Other	62.7 mln gld	23.8
Total	**263 mln gld**	**100%**

Table 3.1

The estimated value of the
Republic's overseas trade in 1780

total. Each of these sectors on their own outweighed the VOC's activities. The preponderance of European trade must have been higher still, for the estimate does not specify the overseas trade with the Iberian peninsula, Norway, and the Mediterranean, and it does not take into account the overland or inland shipping trade with Belgium and Germany. The trans-Atlantic trade and the Asian trade appear to have been more or less equal in weight. That is not the whole story, however. In all probability, most of the Asian imports were re-exported, and much of the Republic's European trade depended on these key products.[4] Consequently, the VOC's economic importance extended beyond what the figures suggest about the volume or value of its trade. The company also provided employment for thousands of people. Around 1780 the Asian side of the business presumably employed 27,000 people. The chambers in the Republic had a few hundred staff, the company's shipyards may have had a thousand hands.[5]

However, the trade growth suggested by the various estimates camouflages a creeping economic contraction. The Republic was gradually thrown back on sectors in which the country could offer comparative advantages, because of geographical location, sophisticated services, or historical happenstance. Timber, wine, and iron from the Rhineland, or iron and glass from the Liège region sailed down the rivers to find natural markets in the delta region. Similarly, the Dutch grain trade had an advantage from its age-old focus on the Baltic. Finally, the trade in colonial products derived its continuing importance from the VOC's established grip on production in Asia. Other trade sectors gradually contracted to the size needed for supplying the direct hinterland, because producers and consumers established direct relations and cut out the Republic's intermediation. As a consequence, the focus of the Republic's foreign trade shifted to its immediate neighbours, to the detriment of more distant countries such as those around the Mediterranean, on the Iberian peninsula, and Russia.

A process of internal contraction mirrored this external contraction. Business tended to concentrate in Amsterdam, and to a lesser extent in Rotterdam. Regional centres such as Hoorn, Zwolle, Den Bosch, and Dordrecht lost out. During the era of economic expansion, these cities had served as key supports for the entrepot market, each with its own niche speciality: the West Indian trade in the case of Hoorn, or the wine trade for Dordrecht. The external contraction undermined these activities. They relocated to Amsterdam, or disappeared altogether.[6]

This dual process of contraction and concentration took shape only very, very gradually, over the course of about sixty to seventy years. The turning

VOC employees marching in support of the stadholder William V following the near civil war of 1787. The company must have had a large staff in the Republic, the Amsterdam chamber alone employed 1100 people on its shipyard by 1790. There are no exact figures about employment, however, only impressions such as this one.

points and the speed of developments differed for each trade sector and for each city. As mentioned in the previous chapter, sectors such as fishing and the wine trade encountered structural difficulties as early as the last quarter of the 17th century, while cloth manufacturing showed the first signs of decline only around 1740. Similarly, Hoorn and Enkhuizen suffered from a progressive economic decay from the early 18th century, whereas Zwolle managed to maintain its position after 1720, and Dordrecht and Nijmegen followed fluctuating trends.

KINGS OF COMMERCE – The merchant houses do not appear to have suffered much from contraction or concentration. Indeed, they did remarkably well, partly because of their financial services. First of all, the acceptance trade experienced a vigorous growth, stimulated by payments and credits generated by the War of the Austrian Succession (1740-1748) and the Seven Years' War (1756-1763). During these years, several new houses specialising in such transactions rose to prominence in addition to George Clifford & Zn. and A. Pels & Sn.: Hogguer, Muilman & Sn., R. & Th. de Smeth, and Thomas & Adrian Hope. Deutz was no doubt also active in this particular field. Of this group, only Pels and Muilman originally came from the Republic, the other firms were founded by immigrants.

Hope became the undisputed leader of the Amsterdam merchant houses, and consequently of the Republic. The firm operated as agents to the British government during the Seven Years' War, running its bill transactions and its payments to its allies and army commanders. In addition, Hope placed war loans on behalf of the government. Between 1757 and 1763, the British public debt doubled, to 132 million pounds sterling. A considerable part of that amount was arranged by Hope, with Clifford also taking a slice.[7] At the same time the firm had a varied commodity trade, presumably on a very substantial scale. We have it on Thomas Hope's authority that the firm chartered at least 50 ships a year for timber alone.[8] The partners employed private couriers to get price data early. This enabled the firm, for instance, to monitor closely the effect of the French Revolution on grain prices during 1789, a year of scarcity. That was presumably also the reason why the Amsterdam city fathers approached Hope to purchase grain for them.[9] The firm probably operated as a commission

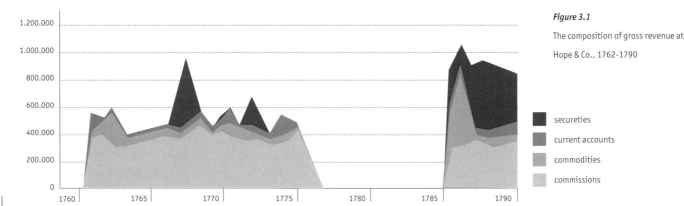

Figure 3.1

The composition of gross revenue at Hope & Co., 1762-1790

■ secureties
■ current accounts
■ commodities
■ commissions

trader in these transactions, for its own trade no longer amounted to very much, at any rate by the 1760s (Figure 3.1).[10] Commissions generated most of the revenue by far, and financial transactions such as the selling of bills and the issuing of loans would be included under this heading by Hope. Other merchant bankers with extensive financial services, such as Clifford or Pels, also continued to entertain sizeable commodity interests. Until well into the 19th century, trade and financial services remained intertwined. They fed each other reciprocally, but trade came first. Trade generated the connections, the services, and the information on which the merchant bankers depended for their existence. To be able to manage their risks, they had to have a close knowledge of commodity prices, ships's movements, and harvest prospects. This precept held true even if their financial services became an important, or even the key component of their business. Maintaining close links with the commodity trade lent such firms greater scope for financial engineering, for instance for offsetting the effects of exchange rate fluctuations on interest payments or loan instalments. The literature often takes any merchant house providing substantial financial services for a banker, but this term does not do justice to the business as essentially composite.[11] The merchant bankers were bankers because they specialised in financial services in addition to their commodity trade, and could thus charge lower rates for them. This dual business differed from that of, for instance, R. Mees & Zn. in Rotterdam, which concentrated on arranging payments, trading in bills, and by extension, providing credit.

Amsterdam ce 1er. Janvier 1762.

Madame)

...s avons l'honneur de vous informer que nous avons pris en Societé M.
...OPE, fils de notre Sieur THOMAS HOPE, & M. HENRI HOPE notre
...raison fera deformais, a commencer de ce jour, HOPE & Compagnie.
...ec ci-bas nos Signatures (excepté celle de M. JEAN HOPE que nous ne
...vous donner qu'au retour de fes voyages) auxquelles feules nous vous
...jouter foi.
...ous flattons Madame) que ce changement n'en mettra point
...entimens pour notre maifon & que vous agréerez les efforts que nous
...en meriter la continuation.
...ons l'honneur d'etre.

Madame)

Vos trés humbles & trés
obeiffans Serviteurs

T. H. S. THOMAS HOPE,

.H. S. ADRIEN HOPE,

.H. S. HENRI HOPE.

121

The Keizersgracht between Molenpad and Runstraat. Hope & Co.'s business complex is on the left, Henry Hope's town residence stands somewhat further along the canal. Painting by H. Keun, third quarter of the 18th century. When established at this spot, Hope & Co. reached its absolute zenith as the most powerful merchant house of its day.

Around 1760 the firm of Thomas & Adrian Hope reached a size not seen before in Amsterdam with a capital of four million guilders on assets of eight million guilders. Ten years later the capital had grown to more than seven million guilders, exceeding the VOC's 1602 founding capital.[12] The firm dwarfed its rivals. Pels, for instance, not far behind Hope in standing and reputation, had as little as 500,000 guilders in capital in 1755.[13] Travellers admired the firm's imposing headquarters between the Keizersgracht and the Herengracht near the Molenpad, complete with warehouses, offices, and flats for the partners and their families.[14] At that moment in time Hope appears to have employed a staff of 26 people.[15] The business derived its unprecedented power and elasticity from two very competent partners, who had nursed it to greatness with energetic prudence since 1734. As economic advisers to the Stadholder, Thomas Hope caught the public eye more than his brother. For William IV he wrote the famous 1751 proposal to turn the Republic into a free trade area.[16] He represented two successive Stadholders on the board of the VOC, and was instrumental in the efforts to reorganise the ailing company.[17] In 1762 two new partners joined the firm, one of whom was Henry Hope, a Boston born nephew of the founders. On this occasion the firm's name was changed into Hope & Co.[18] Very soon Henry Hope occupied a position hardly less distinguished and powerful than that of his uncle Thomas. Popular lore had it that no prices were quoted on the Amsterdam exchange until he appeared.[19] Under Henry Hope the firm entered a new era.

For in addition to the acceptance business, another type of financial services came to flourish in abundance during the second half of the 18th century, i.e. large securitised foreign loans. This started with a series of loans to plantations on the Caribbean islands and in Surinam. Deutz again took the lead, issuing the first such loan in 1753. For the firm it was really a diversification of its scheme of advances on mercury supplies developed for the Austrian emperor. Merchant houses with trading interests in the region supplied long-term mortgages to plantation owners in return for exclusive product consignments, split the loans into bonds, and sold these to investors. Interest payments and loan instalments were paid from the proceeds of the product consignments. The securities market in the Republic, flush with capital, eagerly snapped up these issues. The receiving countries could not really cope with the sudden flood of capital. A slump in agricultural production and financial malpractice took the steam out of this particular loan business during the 1770s.[20] Meanwhile the merchant bankers had shifted their main activities to lending to the governments of, among other countries, Sweden, Denmark, Spain, and Austria. Like the plantation loans, these loans were often issued by merchant houses with close commercial links with the countries in question. Thus J. & C. Hasselgreen acted for the Swedish government, and J. Dull & Co. for Denmark. Goll & Co. became the agent for the Austrian emperor when Deutz liquidated in 1754, after the death of its senior partner. During the 1760s and 1770s the Republic exported annually an average of 11-14 million guilders' in capital.[21]

This was only the beginning. The American War of Independence brought a vigorous increase of the customary smuggling between the Republic, the Caribbean islands, and North America. The Fourth Anglo-Dutch War (1780-1784) interrupted this business, but not before very long trade resumed and continued to grow strongly for a considerable time. Merchant houses with American connections showed exceedingly powerful growth. The two biggest firms, D. Crommelin & Sn., and P. & C. van Eeghen, achieved total assets of 2-2.5 million guilders during the 1790s.[22] As usual, loans followed trade. In 1782 the first loan to the fledgling republic was issued, and Amsterdam merchant bankers supplied a total of 30 million guilders until 1794. At the same time Hope & Co. issued loans totalling 53 million guilders on behalf of the Russian emperor. The firm's capital grew accordingly to more than 15 million guilders, on total assets of 25 million guilders. This last amount equalled total assets of the famed Wisselbank. By now Hope & Co. had become clearly too big for the Amsterdam market (Figure 3.2), for the return on capital dropped parallel to the increase in assets. Compared to other businesses, the firm's profits were fairly high. The partners received interest over their share in the capital, which was deducted from gross revenue. If these payments are added to the net profit payouts, returns on capital averaged about 12%, double the rate which Mossel aspired to for the VOC. Even so this percentage does not appear to be very high considering the nature of the business, the risks, and the stories about exorbitant profits surrounding these affairs. During the 19th century, Hope & Co.

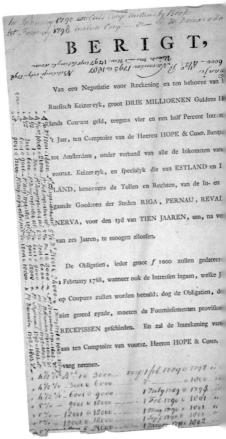

Announcement of Hope & Co.'s first Russian loan, 1788, with scribbled notes about converted bonds. The firm extended the first large loans to the Russian empire, and remained its court banker until well into the 19th century.

122

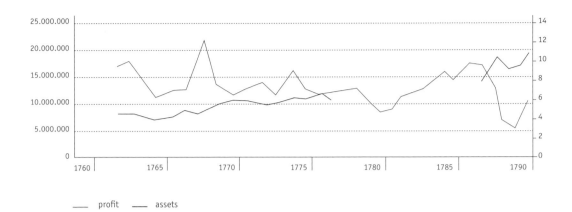

Figure 3.2

Total assets (left scale) and net profits as percentage of capital (right scale) of Hope & Co., 1762-1790

Source: as Figure 3.1

____ profit ____ assets

Henry Hope had a palatial country house built for himself, in addition to his imposing city residence on the Amsterdam Keizersgracht. This house, called Welgelegen for its beautiful location, now serves as the residence of the provincial government of North Holland. Engraving by B. Comte after a drawing made by H.P. Schouten.

would become far more profitable.[23] The focus of these activities, by the way, was Amsterdam, but the Rotterdam firm of Joan Osy & Sn., for one, developed similar banking activities. [24]

Within about forty years, the merchant houses thus created the first proper modern and versatile capital market of international stature. The firms also achieved a new level of public appreciation, by the span of their trading activities and financial interests, and by the close ties between the two. Top merchants assumed a royal style of life in magnificent country mansions, commissioned portraits of themselves and their families from fashionable society painters such as Hodges or Liotard, and collected paintings. In these respects as

in the others Henry Hope was the uncrowned king. In Amsterdam he lived on the Keizersgracht, a few houses away from the firm's business complex, in a huge house which mainly served as a background for his very impressive collection of old masters. Near Haarlem Hope built a splendid mansion hugging the dunes, named Welgelegen and fit for a king indeed.

Presumably, Amsterdam still had a small lead on its nearest rival London as regards financial services, based on experience, flexibility, sheer capital power, and the close links between the commodity trade and the money market. The former city also had merchant firms of a size unknown in Britain. Firms with assets of about a million guilders were exceptional in London during the last quarter of the 18th century, in Amsterdam hardly so.[25] What these firms achieved by way of transactions between 1770 and 1794 had never been shown before. It did not last very long, either.

FROM CRISIS TO CRISIS – The previous chapter already mentioned that around 1750 Britain must have had a considerable commercial lead over the Republic. Its foreign trade turnover and the tonnage of its merchant fleet were by now far bigger, and they showed fast growth. London must have been a much bigger market and harbour than Amsterdam at that time.

Consequently, London had probably also become the biggest provider of commercial services. Amsterdam will still have supplied some of them, notably banking transactions such as loans, bill transactions, bullion trade and securities arbitrage. For example, by the early 1790s the London market did not as yet possess the required technical know-how and experience to issue foreign loans, to the extent that merchant bankers in the Republic did. The interest coupon on securities was unknown, and the investing public willing to buy foreign securities remained quite small.[26] On the other hand, London must have attracted an increasing share of the commercial intermediation, transport, warehousing, and insurance for third parties, if only because its volume was so much bigger, and conditions consequently more competitive. The city's financial services also became increasingly important. At least two Amsterdam Jewish securities traders established a London office during the third quarter of the 18th century, among them the father of the renowned economist David Ricardo.[27] Amsterdam would necessarily have lost its preeminence in this field, too, because it had reached the limits of its capacity. Hope & Co. might dominate international commerce with its huge capital, but that went hand in hand with sharply decreasing returns, as we have seen. London had boundless opportunity for growth. More or less coincidental circumstances determined the moment when Amsterdam lost the last vestiges of its commercial leadership, just as had happened two centuries previously in the case of Antwerp.

For the Republic entered into a very turbulent period indeed, which lasted for about fifty years. A series of political and economic shocks destroyed the basis under its commercial services. It all began with a financial crisis in 1763, followed by a second and more severe one ten years later. This last crisis had a

Het uittrekken der *PATRIOTTEN* uit *UTRECHT*.

G. Balth. Probt. excud. A. V.

The ignominious defeat in the Fourth Anglo-Dutch War generated political strife between the Patriot and Orangist or Stadholder factions. The Republic stood on the brink of civil war, when in 1787 the Prussian King invaded the country to restore order. J.B. Probst made this engraving of Patriot militia fleeing the city of Utrecht before the Prussian advance.

serious aftermath in the form of a prolonged recession, which really ended only around the time of the American Declaration of Independence (1776). The war with its former colonial overlords forced the United States to seek alternative trade routes, finding them on the opposite side of the North Sea. However, this brought the Republic into conflict with Britain in the Fourth Anglo-Dutch War (1780-1784). The united provinces suffered humiliating defeats on all fronts, and with far-reaching consequences. A sharp political clash broke out between Orangists and Patriots about the causes of the disaster. The country slid towards civil war, avoided only by an invasion of the Prussian army which restored order.

Meanwhile two pacemakers of the economy, the VOC and the Wisselbank, ran aground. The VOC had suffered very severe damages during the Fourth Anglo-Dutch War. Britain had captured a great number of ships returning to Europe with products, and also conquered key bases in Asia. The directors did take some initiatives to try and salvage the business, for one by a radical reorganisation of communications by establishing intermediary post offices and services with fast packet ships.[28] The scope for such actions had become too limited by now, because the company suffered from a liquidity crisis which led to a formal suspension of payments.[29] The VOC kept floating only by virtue of large advances supplied by the Wisselbank on the orders of the Amsterdam city fathers. These advances were illicit. After all, the bank's charter forbade the giving of credit, the directors had to leave the deposits untouched. Of course the news leaked that the rules were being disregarded. Confidence in the bank guilders started to slide, and consequently the celebrated agio, the premium paid for banco money over cash, declined. Foreign depositors moved their assets and bullion flowed away, to Hamburg and especially to London.[30] The WIC had already disappeared from the stage more or less unnoticed. The American War of Independence brought the company a sudden windfall in the shape of increased revenue from trading licences, but the war with Britain dealt a blow from which it did not recover. The Heren x kept going with subsidies from the Estates General, and when the charter expired in 1791 the assets were nationalised.[31]

In this utterly unstable situation the Republic again had to face a war, this time siding with Britain and Austria against the revolutionary regime in France (1793). This coalition achieved very little. French troops made rapid advances into Belgium, heading for the Republic. In the autumn of 1794, Hope & Co. moved its business to London, leaving caretakers in the Amsterdam office to look after current affairs such as interest payments. A few months later the French had occupied the entire country. The Batavian Republic was proclaimed. The new government nationalised the bankrupt VOC, and tried to keep trade with Asia going through other channels, but with little success. The Wisselbank's agio sank below par when the city council finally came clear, which sent worried depositors scuttling to get their money back. Repeated efforts failed to breathe new life into the moribund bank.

The Batavian Revolution marks the beginning of the so-called French Era (1795-1813). The Republic was independent in name only, France called the tune. As a consequence, the Netherlands automatically changed sides, and now found itself at war with Britain again. The colonies were all lost save for some West African fortresses and Deshima. Trade had to find ever more ingenious routes to circumvent British embargos. At the same time, Napoleon in his turn attempted to weld the European continent into an economic bloc with his Continental System, hoping to bring Britain to its knees by isolating her. These

126

Because of the weather, the famed Dutch Waterline proved worthless as a defence when France invaded the Republic. Severe frost had frozen all defensive canals, rivers, and lakes, so the French army could advance more or less without hindrance. On 21 January 1795, the enemy crossed the ice on the Meuse river at IJsselmonde towards Kralingse Veer, on the way to Rotterdam. Drawing by Dirk Lagendijk.

When in 1806 Napoleon made his brother Louis Napoleon King of the Netherlands, J. Andriessen drew this sketch of a conversation between two gentlemen summing up the public reaction to the news: 'Have you heard today's news? Well there were rumours on the exchange that Prince Louis has been appointed governor-general here Share prices have dropped sharply'.

wider political aspirations left little room for the little independence still left to the Batavian Republic. The country was first brought to heel as a puppet kingdom with a brother of Napoleon as King (1806-1810). When that proved insufficiently effective, the Netherlands were simply annexed as part of the French empire (1810-1813). At last trade and shipping could be put under strict controls. In 1806 about 1,500 ships entered Amsterdam harbour, four years later only just over 200, and a year later again not a single one.[32] Rotterdam harbour had a peak of 1,720 arriving ships in 1802, but around 1810 the shipping ground more or less to a halt there as well.[33] Decimated by British and French privateers, the Dutch North Sea fishing fleets no longer dared to leave port. The faltering foreign trade dragged industry into an acute crisis as well. The lack of raw materials and export opportunities forced key sectors such as shipbuilding, fabrics, sugar refineries, soap boiling, cotton printing, and tobacco cutting to curtail their production, resulting in a sharp rise in unemployment. The big cities saw their population decline, as inhabitants sought better opportunities for survival elsewhere and immigration halted. Fishing towns, manufacturing centres and commercial cities saw the number of poor living on charity swelling rapidly, to as much as 30-40% of the population.[34]

THE END OF AN ERA – The experience of this enforced idleness led contemporaries to conclude that foreign oppression had broken the back of the Republic's trade empire. According to I.J.A. Gogel, minister of Finance under three successive regimes during this period, the Netherlands continued to function as the market and trade entrepot for the whole world until Napoleon's annexation.[35] Presumably Gogel meant to say, that until then the country still had had active trade links with all continents supplying a wide range of products. Now, until well into the French Era the foreign trade volume did remain considerable. War circumstances of course caused sharp fluctuations from time to time, but presumably, when taken overall, neither the volume nor the composition of imports and exports differed very much from the situation around 1750. On estimate, total foreign trade amounted to about 180 million guilders as late as 1809, just before Napoleon imposed his controls.[36] Nor does the economy appear to have been completely disrupted. At any rate, the number of bankruptcies, though significantly higher during the last quarter of the 18th century than before, showed a clear downward trend after 1795.[37]

The trading houses flourished as a whole, though with some exceptions. P. & C. van Eeghen went through fairly hard times, one reason being coincidental business disruptions such as the death of one of the partners. A number of prominent firms liquidated during the French occupation. As often as not they were old firms: Muilman & Sn., for instance, established in 1727, W. van Brienen & Zn., dating from about 1719, or Hogguer, active under various names since 1722. Perhaps these firms suffered adversity, but in each of the cases named the partners retired in the full enjoyment of their accumulated wealth, suggesting that they left business because they had seen enough of it.

Cartoon lampooning the efforts of the Batavian government to boost the economy. The Committee for Trade and Shipping, consisting of a merchant with a basket of match sticks, a smith with a bent anchor on his anvil, and a sailmaker mending a torn sail. A dilapidated sloop with a useless sail rides the waves. Sixth print from the series Hollandia Regenerata by D. Hess, 1797.

HET COMMITTÉ VAN KOOPHANDEL EN ZEEVAART.

128

Some well-known firms went under. As far as we know, this mainly happened to firms predominantly active in foreign loans, such as J. & C. Hasselgreen, R. & Th. de Smeth, or Wed. E. Croese & Co.[38]

These cases are outweighed by numerous examples which prove that the commodity trade continued to offer excellent business opportunities. For example, between 1797 and 1810 the Amsterdam ship owners and merchants Retemeyer & Boissevain saw total assets triple to nearly 450,000 guilders. Between 1804 and 1810, the partners of Couderc, D., & M.P. Brants shared profits of 200,000 guilders each year. They ploughed most of it back into their business, pushing up the firm's capital from 400,000 guilders to 1.4 million guilders. Goll & Co. also prospered.[39] New firms jumped into the market and went all the way to the top in a very short time. Willem Borski began his career in 1789 as a broker on the Amsterdam exchange. Six years later, at the time of the Batavian Revolution, he called himself a merchant, trading, among other things, in grain, rice, and indigo. At the same time Borski developed substantial financial services. By 1800 he presumably had become the biggest commission trader in foreign securities, Hope & Co.'s indispensable linchpin for issuing their loans. The commodity business must have declined in importance relative to finance, though Borski continued to follow it closely. In 1812 he had become a millionaire several times over, and one of Amsterdam's richest inhabitants.[40]

Anthony van Hoboken also entered the commercial fray during the

Republic's final years, though a little earlier than Borski. He established himself as a trader in milk, butter, and cheese in 1774. By the end of the year 1780 he started trading with the Cape of Good Hope and the Dutch East Indies. An old custom of the VOC gave a ship's crew the right to stow a quantity of commodities for sale en route. On the eastbound voyage especially the crew's cargo could be quite voluminous. Ships going to Asia had plenty of room to spare, giving sailors ample opportunity to take merchandise with them. The company took little notice of the eastbound trade, more or less limiting itself to shipping bullion to balance the deficits. Still, the growing European community in Asia of course had a demand for all kinds of products. As the VOC went downhill, the private trade of sailors transformed from an insignificant phenomenon to a fully fledged and independent business. When Van Hoboken tried it for the first time, he shipped consumer goods to Asia for as much as nearly 40,000 guilders, including cloth, iron ware, and smoked salmon. Just to compare, the company's return cargoes usually averaged about 300,000 guilders per ship during those years, so the VOC let considerable opportunities pass by unused.[41] With other freighters Van Hoboken shipped barrels of beer, wine, cheese, glass ware, Gouda chalk pipes, and writing paper. Agents on the Cape and in Batavia sold his consignments, and bought return cargoes, mostly coffee, sugar, and spices. In addition, Van Hoboken nursed a strong interest in exotic animals, which fetched good prices in Europe: monkeys, canaries, ostriches, everything including young elephants and rhinoceroses. Meanwhile his core business remained the trade in butter and cheese, probably involving sizeable exports to Britain. In 1790 Van Hoboken bought his first ship. After the French occupation, he expanded his shipping activities vigorously by buying one ship after another. High freight rates enabled him repeatedly to recoup his investment within a year. By 1800 he possessed at least eleven ships, mostly without any other shareholders. Most of his ships plied the European routes. Van Hoboken's classic trade network stretched from the Baltic via France, Spain, Portugal, and Malta to the Levant. He also chartered freighters to sail from Hamburg to Asia, at a time when the British authorities prevented Dutch ships from doing so. In the end he bought his own East Indiaman. In 1802 this ship sailed to Asia, carrying for example wine, beer, Dutch gin, iron bars, and a number of paintings, advertised as being in accordance with the latest taste and extra beautiful. On the occasion of his marriage, Van Hoboken declared in the presence of a notary that his capital amounted to half a million guilders. This included a country mansion on the river Schie, provided with greenhouses growing peaches and grapes.[42] Finally, the career of H.G.Th. Crone, less spectacular than those of Borski and Van Hoboken, equally demonstrates that the apparently unfavourable circumstances left sufficient room for new initiatives. Crone came to Amsterdam in 1790 as a German immigrant. He took a job as an office clerk, and began a trading business on the side, drawing on contacts established during his trainee years with German firms in Soest (Westphalia), Bremen, and Zwolle. Within a decade he was running a varied overland trade with a turnover of nearly 200,000 guilders.[43]

129

During the exceptionally tumultuous period 1790-1813, Willem Borski managed to build a large fortune from trade and banking within a short time. After his death, his widow Mrs. J.J. Borski-Van de Velde continued the firm's business, confirming the position of Wed. Borski amongst the first rank of Amsterdam finance. This portrait of Mrs. Borski is a copy, for she took the original with her into the grave.

So there appeared to be little to worry about for people restricting their view to the situation at home, like Gogel. And yet the Netherlands had already lost its position as market and trade entrepot for the world to London. In 1805, the British foreign trade turnover was six times the Dutch one.[44] London had also taken over as pivot for international services. The unusual economic and political instability affecting the Republic in its last years had broken the confidence required for this particular function. A substantial number of the ships which had transferred to flags of convenience during the Fourth Anglo-Dutch War did not return to the Republic. Apparently, ship owners and captains had come to prefer having their domiciles abroad.[45] Most of the crew were foreign anyway.

A document signed by the US Secretary of State James Madison concerning the purchase of the Louisiana territory in 1803. The US government bought this territory from Napoleon for 15 million dollars, and paid with the proceeds from a loan jointly arranged by Baring Bros. and Hope & Co.

Holders of maritime insurance policies encountered increasing difficulties in getting claims recognised and paid. The political disturbances of the 1780s in particular decimated the private insurers which dominated the market. Moreover, Dutch insurers still relied on often ambiguous, partly handwritten contracts drawn up for each individual case, whereas London had adopted standard policies in 1779.[46] The collapse of the Wisselbank proved the final straw, for with it the bullion stock disappeared that had served as the hinge for the bill trade and the settlements system. In the meantime, London had also built up superior financial resources. In 1794, for instance, Austria issued a loan in London totalling 55 million guilders. A transaction of such magnitude would have been beyond the power of Amsterdam, for all its financial muscle. During the 1780s, peak years for the foreign loan business, the market never took more than 20 million guilders a year. The biggest borrower, Russia, never issued more than 12 million guilders a year, and Hope & Co. took care to split such loans into four tranches to avoid saturating the market.[47] During the Napoleonic Wars Britain could fall back on its own channels to place government loans and effect payments to armies and allies on the Continent. As late as the Seven Year's War, such transactions used to be carried out by merchant bankers in the Republic. In 1807 the Amsterdam price current stopped quoting the price for bills on London, so traffic on this artery must have declined to a trickle. Consequently, Amsterdam lost its position in the international payments system, the trade in bills and bullion which was closely linked to it, and the voluminous arbitrage trade, which all worked together to balance claims and debts between trading regions.[48] True, the city did partake in some spectacular transactions, such as the 11 million dollar loan with which the United States bought the French territory of Louisiana from Napoleon. However, the leading role had clearly passed to London. Just as with the commodity trade, this switch came about simply because Britain generated a bigger volume of transactions and adopted the necessary skills, though coincidences determined the moment in which it happened. So only those people who restricted their view to the situation at home, could safely blame French tyranny for the decline of trade and shipping. The true battle had been fought, and lost, much earlier and through different causes.

The main sectors of the Dutch economy, aquatint after W. Kok, 1794. Trade dominates the scene, industry has all but disappeared. On the bottom row in the middle clerks working in a merchant's office, flanked by the Rotterdam exchange (left) and the Amsterdam exchange. The next row shows from left to right: mining, the wine trade, farming and grain trading, tobacco cutting and coffee trading, and trading in tea, spices, and fabrics. The second row from the top depicts peat digging, shipbuilding, a view of Amsterdam with Dam Square, the timber trade with saw mills and paper mills, and the island of Texel. On the top row from left to right weaving, butter and cheese making, herring fisheries, and whaling.

TACKING TO AVOID ENEMIES AND OCCUPYING FORCES – The merchant houses could fall back on wide experience to keep trade going during wars. The Republic had always taken a pragmatic stance about war and trade or, depending on one's point of view, not a very scrupulous one. In war time two principles applied: the prohibition of trading with the enemy was practically impossible and worked to the benefit of commercial rivals only; and 'free ship, free goods', or 'the flag covers the cargo', i.e. the term contraband goods, products under a trade embargo because of their potential contribution to warfare, should be interpreted narrowly to safeguard the commercial interests of neutrals. Common opinion held armaments to be contraband, and that was it, preferably for all time. Given the Republic's geographical location, the Estates General had no alternative options, probably, if they wanted to avoid damaging the country's economy unduly. After all, in the wide hinterland there were always neutral nations ready to spot commercial opportunities. Ships' masters and merchants from the Republic itself, moreover, had become used over the centuries to let their freighters or transactions switch colours according to circumstances. Sweden enacted protective navigation laws in 1724, for instance, reserving the country's shipping to Swedish nationals only. At a stroke the share of Swedish ships' masters in the trade with the Republic trebled. However, nearly half of these captains paid galliot money in Amsterdam to the Board for the Baltic Trade, and consequently they must have remained Amsterdammers.[49]

This kind of camouflage had achieved a high level of perfection by the end of the 18th century. And necessarily so, for by now the Republic could no longer command the military power required to uphold its narrow interpretation of contraband against for instance Britain, which had always upheld a much wider definition and accordingly categorized ever more products as such. During the American War of Independence this difference of opinion became an open conflict. The voluminous smuggling conducted by Dutch trading houses between the Caribbean islands and North America angered Britain, the more so because of the arms supplies involved. To end this trade, the Royal Navy patrolled the seas and boarded neutral shipping, the slightest whiff of contraband sufficing for a ship to be seized and taken to port as a prize. The righteous indignation in Amsterdam and Rotterdam formed a direct cause for the Fourth Anglo-Dutch War. To keep business going, merchants bought flags of convenience for their ships on a massive scale. These could be had more or less around the corner. In north western Germany, ports such as Emden had special offices which, for a small charge, arranged Prussian identities for ships and commercial transactions, including all papers needed to make the fictitious home port of ship, crew, and cargo look convincing. The Belgian port of Ostend offered equally hospitable facilities under the Austrian flag. Merchants who thought the options nearby too transparent, had plenty alternatives in Hamburg, Altona, Copenhagen, or the Baltic ports. Dutch notaries developed smooth standard transactions for the sham purchase of ships by foreigners.

As a result, the maritime traffic to and from the Republic remained more or less at peacetime levels, despite the emergency circumstances. Only the

During the Fourth Anglo-Dutch War, Britain occupied the Republic's possessions in the Caribbean to end the smuggling from there to the US. On 20 December 1780, British troops plundered the island of St-Eustatius. Engraving by C. Brouwer after P. Wagenaar, 1782.

nationality differed. According to observations by officers of the Dutch navy, about half the freighters passing the isle of Texel and heading for Amsterdam in 1782 carried the Danish or Prussian flag. The traffic in the sea passages around the south western islands had become at least 80% Austrian. This charade became ever more elaborate, because British prize courts of course knew what went on, and quickly picked out the most obvious tricks. Sometimes the courts were powerless. In August 1781, 70 freighters set sail from the Republic to the Baltic, escorted by a navy squadron commanded by Rear Admiral Zoutman. Near Doggersbank Zoutman was drawn into a battle with the British navy. The confrontation ended without a clear victory for either side, but the freighters had not managed to get through and returned to port. A few weeks later the same ships left port again, now under the Swedish flag and escorted by a Swedish warship.[50]

After the French occupation, merchants immediately reached for their trusted box of tricks. Circumstances demanded an ingenuity and an adroitness yet greater than before. Britain urged its allies against France to a radical curtailment of the neutrals' rights. The principle of 'flag covers cargo' went overboard, the alliance declaring everything belonging to French subjects to be contraband. Moreover, the allies proclaimed a comprehensive trade embargo, including food. Warships and privateers were ordered to stop and search neutral ships for contraband thus defined, and to tow offenders to a British port. In reaction France, of course, adopted similar policies against her opponents. Neutral shipping was thus trapped between the two sides, each trying to outdo the

During the Napoleonic Wars, British and French privateers scouring the North Sea inflicted heavy damage on the Dutch fishing fleet. On Scheveningen beach, near the Hague, fishing vessels have been put under military protection. Engraving by Teerlinck, 1803.

other in devising new measures to harm the opponent's economic interests.[51] As a result, Dutch ship owners, however effective their camouflage, had to guard against ships from both the British enemy and from the French ally. French privateers stalked the North Sea from bases on the Scheldt river. Captured ships were taken to prize courts in occupied Antwerp. The authorities in the Batavian Republic had to look on gnashing their teeth, their French ally turning a blind eye to what was going on. To add insult to injury, ships confiscated by the courts were sometimes auctioned back in the Batavian Republic, in Rotterdam. Van Hoboken bought them for his fleet.[52] Of course, these practices were not only directed at Dutch shipping under a neutral flag. Genuine neutrals also suffered from them. Danish and American ships took over a substantial part of the traffic between Europe and the rest of the world, as often as not chartered by Dutch merchants. Both Denmark and the US encountered so much obstruction from the British surveillance and piracy, that in the end they went to war with Britain.

The authorities also assumed a radically new position and attitude, with profound consequences for the freedom of action in business. Under the Republic, officials at the local and regional level had always left trade and industry very much to their own devices. Opposing interests between the provinces prevented the Estates General from passing restrictive legislation. The Batavian Republic, however, evolved into a centralist state within a few years. The revered provincial autonomy was replaced by a central government run by ministers and departments from their administrative seat at The Hague. This new administration quickly showed a keen interest in economic matters. Ministers and civil servants began charting the Netherlands by systematically gathering information on a range of subjects, directing requests for detailed information to local authorities. Actions followed quickly: policies, statutes, licence systems, and checks covering more or less every aspect of society.[53] Whereas before local and regional authorities had lived side-by-side with the trade and industry under their jurisdiction, the civil servants from The Hague now holding the reins were not bothered by such direct concerns, and were consequently less inclined to allow organized evasion. In the case of foreign trade, the French also exerted considerable pressure to get their way, by allowing privateers to roam and by stationing inquisitive customs officers in the main ports.

To modern eyes this may not have amounted to very much, perhaps. Moreover, smuggling remained very voluminous: over land, via canals and rivers, or along routes opened by coincidence. When, for instance, the British invaded Walcheren for a time in 1809, this opened an immediate and copious flow of colonial commodities to this island.[54] Still, compared to what went on before, this administrative revolution amounted to a clear break. The systematic dodging of regulations, as practised by mayor Hooft and his contemporaries, became a thing of the past. From now, crisis situations would force merchants to spend a lot of time in getting the right papers such as licences, exemptions and permits, sometimes more time than they needed to find suppliers or customers. Of course, this did not put an end to illegal activities, how could it have done so, but from being the rule it became the exception.

In 1809, British troops occupied the Dutch island of Walcheren and laid siege to Flushing. Aquatint by A. Lutz after J. Jelgerhuis.

Government interference during the French occupation was not just detrimental, though, business certainly reaped some benefits too. First of all the new regime started to demolish the existing barriers to internal trade, such as the lack of firm long-distance roads, the widespread differences in weights, measures, taxes, and excises between provinces and between individual cities. The finishing touch to these initiatives had to be postponed for a lack of funds. Parliament began to overhaul the patchwork of local customs and regulations. An official commission of legal experts was entrusted with the task of drafting a new code of commercial law. The professors had not yet finished their work when the annexation to the French Empire made it redundant by the introduction of Napoleon's Code du Commerce. Secondly, the government gave trade and industry formal representative organs in the shape of chambers of commerce. The Rotterdam city council established one on its own initiative in 1803, the rest of the country were given Chambres du Commerce in the Napoleonic mould at the annexation eight years later. Because of the association with the French occupation regime, the new institutions failed to raise widespread enthu-

A view on the Gapersbrug in Rotterdam, with on the left the exchange. In 1803, the Rotterdam city council took the initiative to set up a chamber of commerce, with offices in the exchange building. Anonymous sepia drawing, around 1800.

siasm. Van Hoboken accepted a nomination for membership of the Rotterdam chamber, but several Amsterdam merchants declined it, perhaps because they feared to be made jointly responsible for the very unpopular French trade policies.[55]

Detailed information about Van Hoboken's activities allows us to get a fairly detailed impression of the barriers to trade during the French occupation, and about the way in which merchants circumvented them. At the time of the Batavian Revolution, his core business was still the export of butter and cheese to Britain, and he was the biggest such trader in Rotterdam. His turnover with one cheese wholesaler in Edam amounted to 100,000 guilders.[56] The new regime put a trade embargo on these exports. Immediately Van Hoboken rerouted his trade to neutral territory. His suppliers in Edam and Friesland received instructions henceforth to send deliveries to an agent in Amsterdam, who transferred the goods to scheduled freighters sailing under the Danish or the Prussian flag to Emden, Hamburg, or Altona, at that time a Danish city. Local firms in those ports then forwarded the consignments to London. From time to time, Van Hoboken asked his London correspondents to order goods from Spain. These consignments followed the same route, in the opposite direction.[57] If the North Sea appeared to be safe, Van Hoboken risked sailing directly from Rotterdam to London. The correspondence with his London customers of course had to find surreptitious routes, too. Letters to Britain were usually sent in triplicate: the original for instance via Ghent in Belgium, one copy via Ostend, and another directly with Dutch fishermen from Katwijk on the coast.

Danish and east Frisian merchants acted as figureheads for Van Hoboken's ships. The east Frisian independent mini states of Kniphausen and Papenborg, just over the border between Prussia and the Republic, supplied a complete set of ships' papers for about 400 guilders a year. Captains and crew obtained identity papers to match after spending one night in the statelet concerned. Such papers were antedated on request. Count Bentinck tot Rhoon,

The near continuous warfare forced ships' masters and merchants to use every kind of camouflage imaginable if they wished to continue their business. This ship on the Meuse river near Rotterdam flies the flag of Kniphausen, a land-locked mini state just over the border with Germany. Watercolour by Gerrit Groenwegen, 1795.

Lord of Kniphausen, even appointed a consul in Amsterdam to smooth this paper trade. His landlocked manor of about two square kilometres had suddenly turned into a nice little money spinner.[58] With such artful manoeuvring Van Hoboken succeeded admirably in keeping his business going, and in profiting from the sharp rise in butter and cheese prices caused by wartime circumstances. This attracted jealousy and anger in Rotterdam. During the summer of 1795, a pamphlet circulated which accused Van Hoboken of dodging the export embargo. He jumped to defend himself. He put an advertisment in the *Rotterdamsche Courant* newspaper protesting his innocence, and lying straightfacedly that he only served the inland market and never exported.[59]

Van Hoboken's ships were more than carriers of his commodity trade. Judging by the substantial freight revenues, chartering them to other merchants in the Netherlands and abroad may have been much more important. He had a friendly and familiar relationship with his captains. If Van Hoboken did not have an established correspondent somewhere, he let them act for him in the old style of the 16th century. The captains were often entrusted with a small cargo of merchandise not listed in the bill of lading, say some chests of cheese or Dutch gin worth a few thousand guilders. They had to sell them for their owner at the ship's destination, in return for a commission or a share in the profits. Van Hoboken's trust was sometimes thrown back at him. One captain disappeared without trace, pocketing the revenue of forty barrels of salt meat, sold as instructed in British Guyana (Demerary).[60] This was an old problem. Guillelmo Bartolotti repeatedly experienced similar disappointments during the first half of the 17th century.[61]

Van Hoboken's shipping business did lose some ships, despite his precautions and camouflage: three during 1797 alone, a few more in the following years, now to the French, now to the British. Though he could claim the damage from his insurers, replacements were hard to find. Van Hoboken had people search for him all over Europe. The captains had standing orders to ask around for ships to buy. When he got wind of an impending large auction of confiscated freighters in Bordeaux, he sent someone down immediately. In the end the auc-

In August 1795, anonymous pamphlets accused the merchant Anthony van Hoboken of unpatriotic behaviour for ignoring the ban on the export of butter and cheese. He defended himself by placing this notice in the Rotterdamsche Courant newspaper of 1 September, firmly denying all allegations. Meanwhile he continued his export business using a variety of covers.

Den Ondergeteekende, bewust van zyne onfchuld, en zich daarop verlatende, heeft tot hiertoe met bedaardheid en ftilzwygen aangezien, de lasteringen, waar mede hy overladen word, in zekere periodique Gefchriften, genaamt *Kroegpraatje*, *Coolcingels Burger-* en *Boerepraatje*, en *Koffypraatje*, dan heeft gemeent niet langer te mogen zwygen, na dat hem in handen gekomen is No. 9, van het *Coolcingels Burger-* en *Boerepraatje*, waarin hy niet flegts befchuldigd word, op een bepaalde tyd, des nagts, met behulp van veertien Knegts, 800 Vaatjes Boter geladen te hebben, maar waarin men zich bovendien niet ontziet, zyne Medeburgers tegen hem voor in te nemen en optchitfen; en verklaart dienvolgens: voor eerst, dat de aantyging van het laden dezer 800, meerder of minder Vaatjes Boter op den bepaalden of eenige anderen tyd, des nagts, volftrekt onwaar en valsch is: Ten tweede, dat zyne Negotie in Boter zich *altoos*, en *nu nog* bepaald tot het verkoopen aan Ingezetenen van deze Stad en Provincie, en dat hy nooit, het zy voor eigen Rekening, het zy in Commisfie, eenige Boter naar buiten 's lands heeft afgefcheept of verzonden; terwyl hy eindlyk belooft een Premie van *Twee Honderd Dukaten* aan den Schryver van het bovengemelde No. 9; indien dezen zich wil bekend maken, en hem in rechten bewyst de Inlading van 800 Vaatjes, een meerder of minder getal, op den bepaalden of eenige anderen tyd, des nagts, geladen te hebben; nemende de Ondergeteekende aan, zoo haast de Schryver, in tegenwoordigheid van twee of drie Getuigen, of wel by Notariale Acte, zich als zoodanig zal bekend gemaakt hebben, de Twee Honderd Dukaten, of de waarde van dien in Zilver Geld, in de Wisfelbank dezer Stad te configneren, met overgifte, dat die fomme aan den Schryver zal worden uitgereikt, op het oogenblik, dat dezelve zyne befchuldiging zal bewezen hebben. De Ondergeteekende vleid zich, dat zyne onpartydige Medeburgers hier door zullen overtuigd zyn van zyne onfchuld. Hy kende geen beter middel ter zyner zuiveringe; verlangt men egter iets meer, en kan men hem een beter middel aan de hand geven, hy zal er zich met dankbaarheid van bedienen.

Rotterdam den 1 September 1795.

A. V. HOBOKEN.

B. WEDDELINK zal, op Woensdag den 9 September 1795, even buiten Rotterdam, in de Hartmanslaan, op den Binnenweg, en den 10 September 1795, in de Boslaan, ingaande op de Goudfche Cingel, by de Schouw, en in de Warmoefierslaan, ingaande op den

tion did not take place, but the captain concerned stayed there for two years and bought seven ships for his principal.[62] This expansion of the fleet really came too late, because circumstances had changed radically for the worse. First the neutral flags had gone, one by one. Denmark went to war with Britain, Napoleon occupied east Friesland and went on to conquer Prussia. By that time Papenborg and Kniphausen had already lost their credibility as bonafide bases for shipping. Moreover, the belligerent countries tightened their mutual economic blockade. Obligatory licences forced commodity exports into ever narrower channels, consignments from the Batavian Republic to neutral ports included. Ship's masters had to acquiesce in time-consuming inspections of their ships and their papers. Incoming ships sometimes had to await clearance, lying off Texel for four to six weeks, in the Vlie or in the Meuse estuary. The Continental System (1806) was a logical culmination of this evolution. The Republic's foreign trade was entirely subjected to approval in advance by the authorities, acting on instructions from Paris.[63]

And yet there remained loopholes. Finding them and obtaining the right permits and exemptions made merchants into temporary kings. After all, commodity prices rose as the supply dwindled.[64] Getting the papers sometimes required elaborate detours. In 1807 Van Hoboken sent one of his captains to Bordeaux as commander of one of his newly bought ships. He gave him extensive instructions to load salt and get the papers for Antwerp. However, the captain had to try to enter Ostend, Flushing, or Goeree near Rotterdam instead, asking permission from customs to disembark for receiving orders. If they refused to let him, he was to make for Dover or London, have his cargo marked for re-export, and get papers for a trip to Rotterdam from one of Van Hoboken's London correspondents. Van Hoboken urged his captain to have pretexts ready at all times, and to keep his true destination a secret from his crew.[65]

The annexation to France brought fresh complications. Ship owners had to apply for a special licence to send their ships on a given trip. Applications were dealt with in Paris, which could easily take six to nine months. Van Hoboken had to appoint a special agent to work on the officials concerned. He also sent a nephew to speed up his applications. After some time they knew the ropes and were able to obtain the necessary licences, though from time to time it happened that a licence came through and had to be accepted without anyone knowing the kind of cargo which it covered. Dispatching imports also involved supplying full and detailed accounts to Paris. Despite all his efforts, Van Hoboken's shipping gradually came to a halt, and presumably the overland trade in food gained prominence within the business.[66]

For the maintenance of his growing fleet, Anthony van Hoboken bought his own shipyard, named Rotterdams Welvaren (Rotterdam's Prosperity). This 19th century engraving by Gerrit Groenwegen shows a Government yard on the left, with on the right a koff and a frigate lying in Van Hoboken's yard.

138

A cartoon about the Continental System, the economic blockade against Britain enacted by Napoleon in 1806. On the right an Englishman sits on a bare rock, shouting in despair that he will starve miserably. On the left a soldier (Russia) attempts to climb a rock. The Queen of Prussia dangles from his hair saying that she has no support but him. The Prussian King hangs on to his wife's skirt. Coloured engraving, signed 'Forioso fecit'.

Other merchant houses must have gone about their business more or less in the same way as Van Hoboken did, but we have no details about them. As far as we know, Van Hoboken formed an exception only in his extensive shipping commitments. P. & C. van Eeghen, though suffering a slight setback, still kept a fairly voluminous trade with the US running. Imports were mainly coffee, sugar, rice, and tobacco, the first two products coming from Asia in American ships. Van Eeghen exported cheese, fabrics, and Dutch gin. The constraints on the overseas trade made the firm try and shift its focus to the direct hinterland. Even so business had come more or less to a halt by 1811, when only five letters a month were posted.[67] Trade turnover with the US remained considerable for D. Crommelin & Sn. as well. In addition, both firms were among the biggest lenders in the repo market, giving three months' credit on collateral of securities.[68]

Hope & Co. did not at first experience any adverse effects from its move to London. Until about 1808 the firm remained active with a massive commodity and financial business. As of old, the transactions stretched all over Europe, with important offshoots to the US and South America. Trade with the US reached a peak in 1807 with purchases of 10 million guilders. In Britain, Hope & Co. operated in close collaboration with Baring Bros. & Co. At the same time, the Amsterdam office provided a vital base for transactions in mainland

Europe. The firm was a pivot for elaborate triangular transactions. Hope & Co. financed in 1804, for instance, deliveries of Russian ships' supplies to the French navy. France paid for the supplies with the proceeds from the sale of Louisiana to the US, i.e. with American government bonds, issued by Hope and Baring. The money did not go to Russia, however, it remained in Amsterdam to pay for interest and instalments on Russian loans, issued by Hope & Co.

Loans to Portugal and to Spain had similar ingenious constructions. The Portuguese transaction rested on deliveries of dye wood and diamonds from Brazil. Spain issued bills in return for its loan, which gave the firm access to Mexican silver. The silver was partially shipped directly from Mexico to Britain on behalf of the East India Company, which had a great demand for it. The rest went to Hope's US agents, who used it to run commodity transactions between the US, Europe, and Mexico, Spain having granted licences to trade with the latter country as part of the loan conditions. The agents also bought bills sent in payment to US exporters by their European importers, and returned them to Hope & Co. for cashing on expiry. Such schemes worked, because each of the countries concerned gave priority to its own interests, and accepted into the bargain that opponents benefitted as well. For devising and negotiating schemes, Hope & Co. could rely on the exceptional talents of its partner Pierre César Labouchere. Born in the Hague, he had French origins and received part of his training with the firm of an uncle in Nantes. This uncle recommended him to Henry Hope. In 1790 Labouchere started in the Amsterdam office as a clerk. Three years later he was given the authority to sign for the firm. By his marriage to Dorothea Baring he personified the close collaboration between the two firms. According to a famous story, Labouchere asked Hope & Co.'s partners if he would be admitted to the firm should he come to marry her. When they said yes, he then presented himself to Francis Baring as a prospective partner of Hope & Co. and asked permission to marry his daughter, thus gaining both his love and the desired admission to the firm. The anecdote is presumably apocryphal, but does illustrate Labouchere's qualities for multilateral transactions.

However, even he could not halt the firm's gradual decline after about 1808. Tighter trade embargoes cut the links with the continental market. The Spanish-American transactions became stuck as war raged on the Iberian peninsula. Labouchere had to run the business more or less on his own. Henry Hope was now over seventy years old and lived in semi-retirement. The other partners were pessimistic about the firm's future prospects, and in 1813 the partnership broke up. Alexander Baring bought the dismal remnants of what had once been the world's greatest merchant house.[69]

140

Hope & Co. managed to maintain its position among the chief European merchant houses until about 1808. The firm derived its continuing strength partly from the energy of its partner Pierre César Labouchere, the main driving force behind the business during this tempestuous period.

With the end of the French occupation Napoleon's hated customs officers, who had personified the severe trade restrictions, finally disappeared as well. In this cartoon, pedlars hawk customs officers at ten a penny. Anonymous coloured engraving, 1813.

'A long pull and a strong pull and a pull altogether', a cartoon depicting Napoleon's downfall and concerted efforts to get trade moving again. From the rock on the left, a Russian, a Spaniard, and an Englishman attempt to pull merchant ships into the sea, with Dutchmen ashore pushing them. Napoleon and his brother Joseph look on in despair. Coloured engraving by Thomas Rowlandson, 1813.

A FALSE START — More or less at the same time, the French empire also came to a rapid and inglorious end. Harried by Russian and Prussian armies, Napoleon retreated to France and abdicated. On the last day of November 1813, the Prince of Orange returned from exile to the Netherlands and accepted the title of Sovereign Prince. The hated French customs officers had already disappeared, the trade embargoes had been lifted, privateers and warships had returned to base. Napoleon's short-lived return as French emperor appeared to endanger the new Kingdom of the Netherlands for a short time, until the Battle of Waterloo definitely put an end to French supremacy.

Dutch politicians and merchants took for granted that trade would revive as soon as the seas had reopened. Such had always been the case, following the Year of Disaster 1672, and also following the Fourth Anlgo-Dutch War. The expectations appeared to come true. The ports soon filled up with ships bringing commodities from all corners of the world. In June 1814 the first ship bound for Asia left Amsterdam. Pent-up demand created a post-war boom, and subsequently poor harvests during the years 1817-1818 generated large grain shipments from the Baltic. The foreign trade turnover rose to an estimated peak of more than 260 million guilders, more than respectable in comparison to 18th century levels.[70] With Labouchere and three Amsterdam businessmen, Alexander Baring established a new partnership under the name Hope & Co., and the trusted partnership Baring-Hope straightaway reclaimed its prominence in international finance with a loan to France and the reorganization of the Austrian government debt. A few prominent Jewish banking firms from Germany established branches in Amsterdam. Merchant houses such as D. Crommelin & Sn. had record years with net profits of 15% and more.[71] To all intents and purposes it seemed as if old times had returned, as if the economic power of the Republic lived on in the new Kingdom.

Nevertheless, the business community must have grasped very soon that something had gone irretrievably wrong. For the boom did not spread throughout the economy, as used to be the case before. Agriculture flourished, but that was really an exception. The securities trade developed vigorously, but after some initial successes it became very clear that London firms had the reins of international finance firmly in their grip. Those firms now dwarfed the Amsterdam houses. Around 1815 the two largest firms, N.M. Rothschild & Sons and Baring Brothers & Co., had capitals of more than 10 million guilders each.[72]

141

The new Hope & Co. returned to Amsterdam with a capital of more than 1.5 million guilders, the partners of D. Crommelin & Sn. shared equity of just over 2 million guilders at that moment.[73] Only Russia remained a regular customer in Amsterdam, and that, by the way, not entirely of its own accord.

All other economic sectors remained stuck in a bad slump. Industry, which had become very vulnerable during the last quarter of the 18th century, now went into a free fall. Napoleon's trade barriers around the continental market had given some manufacturers a welcome shield against the competition, but now foreign products flooded the market. An official enquiry from 1816 showed a dreary decline over more or less the whole range of industry. Three years later the picture was hardly less depressing.[74] Fishing only kept going by government subsidies.[75] The merchant navy was less than a shadow of its former self during the latter years of the Republic. In 1824 the fleet had only 1,100 ships left with a total capacity of 140,000 tons. During the Fourth Anglo Dutch War the tonnage had still been about three times that amount.[76] Once the Republic's freighters had served the whole of Europe, now they could no longer meet domestic demand. About 60% of traffic in Dutch ports carried a foreign flag, and no longer for camouflage purposes.[77] The international settlements system had in the meantime become firmly established in London, reducing Amsterdam's once world-spanning trade in bills and bullion to a rudimentary level fit to serve regional needs. The city no longer even possessed a central position for this trade in its own country. The intensive local traffic with Britain enabled Rotterdam bankers for instance to pull the trade in bills on London to their own city. Amsterdam merchants and bankers tried frantically to resuscitate the Wisselbank, a pitiful shadow by now, to act as a flywheel for the trade in bills and bullion. This failed completely, because there was simply no need anymore for an institution like this. In 1819 the bank was finally dissolved.[78]

In short, the mutual link between Dutch foreign trade and the inland production of goods, transport, and other services no longer existed. This particular connection had been the basis for the Republic's original economic success: a powerful shipping sector, which on the one hand brought raw materials and semi-finished goods to the entrepot market and shipped the finished goods to their destination, and on the other hand supplied its services to third parties. Around 1700 the first cracks had started to appear in this successful commercial recipe. Manufacturing and fishing had begun to lose foreign marketshare, partly because of rising protectionism. The merchant navy stagnated because of a manpower shortage. The trade sector could not, of course, remedy these shortcomings, but the merchant houses did succeed in holding on to a large slice of European trade by starting to offer specialised services: commission trading, shipping, insurance, settlements, finance, and finally the large scale foreign lending. That lever gave the Republic a very considerable foreign trade turnover. Meanwhile, however, the service sector and manufacturing parted company to go their separate ways. The former managed to retain a leading position in Europe, the latter shrank to a level sufficient to meet local or regional demand, because the Republic offered no locational comparative advantages which could

In 1822, the old VOC warehouse on the Amsterdam harbour suddenly collapsed, probably because the structure had been overloaded with stored grain. As a consequence, the city skyline was robbed of this landmark building, a leftover from the now long-gone company. Watercolour by C. Overman.

compensate foreign protectionism. Robbed of its linkages with other economic sectors, the service sector became a giant with feet of clay. Once toppled by the late-18th century turmoils and Napoleon's Continental System, the giant failed to find its feet again. The lever had broken. From 1819 the Dutch foreign trade turnover, the sum of imports and exports, fell remorselessly, to a nadir of 125 million guilders in 1830.[79] An additional problem made matters worse. During the 1820s international trade began to display signs of gradually shifting functions. Scheduled shipping services brought more regularity into transport. This usually led to wholesale functions shifting to the producing countries. Formerly independent importers in the consuming countries lost their position, being replaced by agents. Both phenomena first appeared in the Atlantic trade. After about 1850 this trend spread rapidly to other sectors, aided by the telegraph and technical improvements to steam ships.[80]

The trading houses attempted in vain to counter the decline by applying the usual tested remedies. D. Crommelin & Sn. for instance, second only to Hope & Co. among the Amsterdam firms, bought ships' shares for a total of about 25,000 guilders in 1817. However, despite the shipping interests the firm's US trade, formerly its main activity, failed to revive. Presumably Crommelin could not compete with a few active rivals. The Dutch trade turnover with the US amounted to about 4 million guilders, which Crommelin should easily have been able to handle on its own, considering its capital of 2 million guilders. At least five other firms vied with Crommelin for a share, amongst them Van Baggen, Parker & Dixon, the firm of the US consul in Amsterdam. These firms served a niche market anyway. British ports distributed the main product flows from the US to Europe and nothing was going to change that, with the shifting wholesale function and the lack of suitable export products from the Netherlands. On the contrary, the Dutch market became less and less attractive for US exporters, the Dutch share in US exports halving between 1820 and 1840.[81] In addition to his US commodity interests, Crommelin ran a flourishing tea trade and banking activities, mainly securities lombards and securities trading. During the early 1820s Crommelin lost a considerable amount on the ships' shares, and the partners reduced their investment to a small sum. Around 1835 however, they reconsidered their approach. The firm restarted its commodity trade and in support again bought ships' shares for greater amounts than before, 40-50,000 guilders invested in six to eight ships. This investment was profitable in itself, returns averaging 14% a year. However, the hoped-for substantial rise in consignment again proved illusory, and after a few years the partners allowed their shipping interests to run down gradually.[82]

Other firms used their capital power to attract customers. This was only successful really in the grain and seeds trades, sectors with cyclical surpluses which found their way to Amsterdam as of old on the continuing strength of the Baltic trade.[83] Hope & Co. vigorously jumped into commodity speculations during the early 1820s: sugar, tea, coffee, timber, spices, and tobacco. Moreover, during 1826-1827 the firm also joined a consortium of mainly foreign firms led by the Dutch consul in Liverpool, Daniel Willink, which attempted to corner the British cotton market. Just as the attempt to corner cochineal supplies at the end of the 18th century, this commercial coup misfired completely. The other speculations also mostly brought losses, and Hope & Co. had to write off 1.7 million guilders in total.[84]

The once closely interlinked services now really went separate ways. The maritime insurance still served foreign clients, but no longer as a derivative of commodity transactions. The German merchant house Johann Bernhard Hasenclever ran a substantial trade covering most of Europe and South America. The firm directed its bill transactions through London. Nearly three quarters of its insurance policies were underwritten in Amsterdam, however, yet the firm did hardly any other busines there.[85] Foreign merchant houses and bankers used the Amsterdam money market on a wide scale for short-term loans, but this had no effect whatsoever on the volume of foreign trade. The stock market had a very large trade in foreign securities, with the exception of Russian loans all issued by London firms, which as a consequence profited most. And if some foreign banker did approach Amsterdam firms with a loan proposal, this invariably concerned leftovers or unattractive issues refused by London firms.

Trade now declined to the level required for the demands of the direct hinterland. This was not a very big market. The Netherlands had just over 2 million inhabitants. The unification with Belgium added another 4 million people, but this combination fell apart in 1830, before the two countries had achieved an economic unity of sorts. In terms of time, trouble, and cost per unit, the direct German hinterland was still remote from the Republic, much more so than many of the sea ports with which the country had had frequent services. Road transport was far inferior to shipping by sea in speed and capacity, if only because of the deplorable state of most roads.[86] Of course, there was some

trade. Dutch merchants toured Westphalia to buy fabrics as early as the 17th century. Linen was sometimes transported by road from Silesia via Leipzig to the Republic.[87] During the early 19th century, this traffic turned from pull to push. Merchants in fabrics from Westphalia started to expand their activities towards the Netherlands using an innovative retail concept, in essence the formula used by modern chain stores and department stores. One such pioneer was Anton Sinkel. He started with a shop retailing fabrics on the Nieuwendijk in Amsterdam, which had a fast expansion due to Sinkel's ground-breaking sales techniques such as the selling of remainders at deep discounts on special days. In 1822 Sinkel reopened after extensive rebuilding works had added adjoining properties to his shop. Fabrics and clothing remained the core business, but in addition Sinkel started selling a very large range of household utensils. Within a few years, he opened branches operating the same concept in other cities, Utrecht, Leeuwarden, and Leiden. Sinkel travelled to the German trade fairs to do his own purchasing, personally conducting the waggon caravan laden with new stock back to the Netherlands.[88]

In addition to the overland trade, there was a substantial trade along the Rhine: timber, iron ware, and wine downriver, coffee, spices, and sugar upriver. Rhine shipping suffered under a large number of tolls, and, like the road transport, faced some restrictive bottlenecks. Barges on their way from Amsterdam to the Rhine first sailed over the Zuiderzee past the island of Pampus, then cut inland to enter a stream near the town of Muiden leading them past Utrecht and

Wijk bij Duurstede and finally into the river. They had to pass no fewer than 22 bridges and 4 locks, losing much time and money on the way. Utrecht took a considerable slice of both, for the city owned an old privilege granting a monopoly of hauling barges through its canals to a group of women. Rotterdam had much better river connections with Germany than Amsterdam had, but even so a journey to Cologne could easily take a month. Transport between the Dutch and the German Rhine ports was in the hands of barge skippers running scheduled services. Their vested interests frustrated any attempts to improve transport, for instance by using steam powered barges.[89] Moreover, Dutch ships going upstream paid higher duties than German or French ones on the German stretch of the river, so the trade from Amsterdam or Rotterdam operated at an automatic cost disadvantage. In its turn, the Netherlands itself restricted transit traffic with various protectionist measures designed to protect trade and shipping in the river delta. The government of King William I tenaciously maintained its protectionist stance, to the point of antagonising its mighty Prussian neighbour. This policy has come in for some considerable criticism, for its alleged legalistic refusal to come to terms with changed circumstances. Yet the resistance did have a basis in reality. After all, it made no sense to lift restrictions on shipping through Dutch territory as long as the restrictions upriver beyond the borders remained in place, such as the higher duties on the German stretch of the river. The Mainz Rhine Treaty (1831) finally gave equal treatment along the whole river to all citizens of states bordering the Rhine. With this treaty, the Netherlands at last acquired a wide entrance to its German hinterland. Within a short time the Rhine trade became a growth sector.[90]

In 1831, the Netherlands and Prussia resolved their long-running dispute about the mutual restrictions on free shipping on the river Rhine. As a consequence, shipping on the river rose rapidly. This anonymous 19th century panorama of the city of Arnhem, taken from Hotel de Belle Vue, shows the Rhine with busy traffic in the background.

Allegory on the trade between Europe, Asia, Africa, and the Americas, about 1845. The oval inset on the left shows the new Amsterdam exchange built by the architect J.D. Zocher during the 1840s. On the right the Rotterdam exchange.

GROPING FOR A WAY OUT – The first half of the 19th century has long been regarded as an era in which economic stagnation and self-satisfied apathy held each other in an oppressive embrace, with time more or less standing still for manufacturers dabbling in verse writing and for merchants stuck in their paternal cities, watching the world more often from their regular coffee house tables than from behind their desks.[91] The commercial agent and writer E.J. Potgieter sneered about a 'Jan Saliegeest', a listlessness to be observed everywhere, a shortage of guts and entrepreneurial spirit. Posterity has paid him the compliment of raising his sharp rebuke into a proverbial expression. Circumstances appeared to prove him right. Widespread unemployment and grinding poverty prevailed. In Amsterdam, for instance, a quarter of the population depended on charity at normal times, but in times of scarcity this rose to more than a third.

At the same time, neighbouring countries such as Britain, a little later followed by Belgium, the Ruhr area in Germany, and northeastern France, showed a dynamic industrial growth. The Dutch economy failed to follow their lead, however. The introduction of innovations such as a widespread mechanisation of manufacturing, the railways, or steam powered ships, lagged behind the pioneers. The Dutch development of banking also deviated, with commercial joint-stock banking appearing as late as the 1860s. Everything seemed to lag fifty years behind the rest of western Europe, and the German poet Heine joked that in the Netherlands, even the Last Judgement would be delayed by half a century. Initiatives towards change, for instance the introduction of bonded warehousing in the big port cities, or changes in standard trade conditions, aroused the opposition of merchants who tried with armoured conservatism to resurrect the Golden Age rather than change their ways. Moreover, big enterprises such as the railways, steam shipping, commercial joint-stock banks, and canal companies usually saw the light of day only after lengthy tussles and loud bickering in the press and sometimes in parliament, too.

Meanwhile the securities trade continued to flourish. Consequently, the market absorbed foreign loans without much trouble. As a result, investors were blamed for the tardy economic development. They were regarded as faint-hearts, averse to risk and apathetic coupon cutters, who preferred foreign government bonds for their money, rather than making it work towards the progress of national enterprise. The conviction took root that the Netherlands no longer possessed sufficient enterprising spirit, no zest or daring to roll up the sleeves and catch up with the pace of world developments, resulting in a remorseless downward economic spiral. With regards to trade, this view found confirmation in a memorandum written by Claude Crommelin. In 1854 he analysed the development of his firm since 1836, and decided to liquidate. To him it made no sense to continue with the commodity trade, for the business had mostly operated at a loss. To defend his opinion against his partner R.D. Wolterbeek, he listed the merchant firms which he had seen disappear from the exchange since his first visit in 1812.[92]

Potgieter's denunciation looks so convincing. The Dutch economy withered. Other countries demonstrated how the problems should be tackled, but this did not happen in Holland. Money was no object, the country had capital aplenty. Consequently, a weak mentality must have prevented the passing of available opportunities. And yet this reproach of listlessness no longer cuts ice. First of all, because research has now shown that the Dutch economy performed better than used to be thought. Its pattern of development, however, differed from those countries with an early industrialization. There were simply no comparative advantages such as available raw materials or a big internal market which could have generated an industrialization spurt in the foreign mould. As a result there was no widespread switch to factory production. Economic development followed a more even course, spreading equally over the different

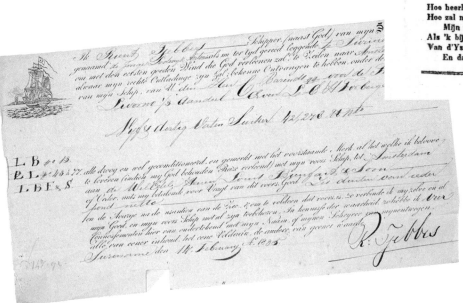

Bill of lading signed by ship's master Rient Tjebbes for transporting 35 barrels of sugar from the Surinam plantation of Livorno for delivery to the Amsterdam merchant house Louis Bienfait & Soon, 1835. In the left margin the marks with which the sender had marked the barrels for Bienfait, all of them variations on the firm's initials.

Nou spreekt de Trekschuit.

zal men kijken en met reden,
heelhuids met uw heeft gereden,
Tot Haarlem, en wil verder gaan;
schoon zijn zaken stoom vereisschen,
moet, al bulkt hij met afgrijzen,
Uit armoed in mij, Trekschuit! gaan.

Nu spreekt de Spoorwagen.

ht maar, er zullen tijden komen,
gij nog ãars van Joost zal droomen,
Want als mijn roem gevestigd is,
t ras een broertje mij daar groeten,
zult gij op uw blooten voeten,
Mij smeeken om erbarmenis.

Nou spreekt de Trekschuit.

g snorker! van uw groot vermogen,
aan kan op moerasgrond bogen,
Die misschien zakt in korten tijd,
aat uw vuile maag aan 't braken,
t dan, ondier! in Pluto's kaken,
aar uw nog heet're gloed verbeid.

Nu spreekt de Spoorwagen.

zal ik in mijn vaart naar boven,
menschelijk vernuft nog loven,
n vloeken uwen slakkengang;
zoolang als ik blijf in 't leven,
den Handel voordeel geven,
n uw steeds houden in bedwang.

ij de Prinsengracht, N°. 1.

After a protracted wrangle, the first Dutch railway line connecting Amsterdam with Haarlem opened in 1839. Until then, this used to be one of the busiest stretches of barge traffic, inspiring an anonymous writer to compose a fictitious discussion between barge and railway about the future of passenger transportation. Despite public misgivings he forecast a glowing future for the railway, with benefits for trade in particular.

sectors of agriculture, services, and industry. New technology, by the way, was immediately applied, when market circumstances allowed. As often as not, initiatives towards change foundered for sound economic reasons: the high cost of equipment and raw materials in relation to existing technology or the size of the market, a rigid excise structure which hampered the reaping of returns on investment in some sectors, low returns in comparison with alternative investment opportunities, or resistance against giving up existing margins in return for the uncertain gains of change.

In any case, the merchant houses did what they could. The striking aspect of their behaviour is not conservatism, but the tenacious will to keep on going, despite losses and setbacks. Crommelin's repeated efforts to attract new commodity business through shipping activities have already been mentioned. Van Hoboken succeeded where Crommelin failed. The French occupation had hardly ended, when the Rotterdam firm restarted its European trade, and at a profit. Van Hoboken sold a classical range of products over an equally classical network stretching from the Baltic to Izmir: butter, cheese, Dutch gin, pottery, stock fish, dried fruits, opium, tapestries, and wine. As soon as circumstances allowed, Van Hoboken also sent out ships to South America, the Caribbean, and the Dutch East Indies. The ventures to South America and to the Caribbean proved disappointing, but Asia became a success as before. The firm prospered. When in 1832 the founder took his sons into partnership, he furnished a capital of 1 million guilders. With this amount, Van Hoboken equalled the Amsterdam merchant houses.[93] L. Bienfait & Soon also had a combined shipping and trading business. French wine was one of its key products. After the French occupation, the firm diversified into trade with the Dutch East Indies, and returned to Surinam, where it had had interests in plantations for decades. These connections supplied Bienfait with the products denied to Van Hoboken.[94] Why did Van Hoboken and Bienfait succeed in rebuilding a profitable commodity business through shipping, and why did Crommelin fail? Perhaps Crommelin remained fixated on its original core trade, the US, for too long, without considering switching to, for instance, Europe or the Dutch East Indies. Initially profits from other activities, including the issuing of a US loan, may have rendered a serious reconsideration of the business strategy less pressing. When that changed, it had become too late to start up trade with the Indies, as we shall see in due course, because of the establishment of a semi-official company for just that sector.[95]

For reasons explained above, the merchant houses always tried to keep their commodity business going, whether or not their main interest had shifted to finance. Even Hope & Co., by far the most specialised merchant banker, retained its commodity interests.[96] The business mix differed from firm to firm. H.G.Th. Crone had a varied European trade, presumably on a modest scale, with an important offshoot to Surinam.[97] At Determeyer Weslingh & Zoon commodities and finance more or less balanced each other. In both activities the firm ran transactions for joint account with firms in Belgium, Germany, Paris, London, and Genoa. In addition the firm tried out virtually everything: consign-

On 30 November 1813, the eldest son of Stadholder William V returned from exile, and landed on the beach at Scheveningen, near the Hague. He assumed the title of Sovereign Prince, and reigned as King William I.

ments for own account of any commodity imaginable to all corners of the earth, in shipments of usually about 20,000 guilders at a time, at most 100,000 guilders. If a venture lost money, the partners spiritedly tried once more, with the same goods or with something else. Stadnitski & Van Heukelom had a more pronounced securities trade than Determeyer Weslingh & Zn., but this firm also continued to run a very varied and partly speculative commodity trade.[98] For Van Eeghen & Co. finance and maritime insurance evidently provided the dual core business during the second quarter of the 19th century. At that time, the firm really looked more like an investment trust for family capital than a merchant house. For commodity transactions were a subordinate activity, lombarding and trading securities generated most of the revenues. The firm kept its focus on the US and constantly tried to find new correspondents there. Van Eeghen had a good entry position as director of the Holland Land Company, an investment company set up by a number of Amsterdam merchant bankers to run a failed speculation in US property. This directorship generated an attractive income and some commodity consignments for Van Eeghen. Even so, like Crommelin, the firm could not keep up with the competition either. In 1832 four ships from the US entered Amsterdam harbour with exclusive consignments for Van Eeghen & Co., a record for the firm. During that same year, however, Van Baggen, Parker & Dixon handled no fewer than 27 ships consigned to it.[99]

Time and again, the merchant firms tried to resurrect one trade sector or another. The West African trade, for instance. The Netherlands still possessed a string of fourteen mostly dilapidated fortresses on the coast, inherited from the WIC. These had once served to protect the trade in gold, ivory, and slaves between the region and the Caribbean.[100] The abolition of the slave trade in 1814 had reduced traffic to less than a trickle. Still, the Dutch government did not want to give up any outposts of empire and spent just over 40,000 guilders a year maintaining enough staff to hoist the flag every day. The Amsterdam firm of Johannes Boelen & Co. sent a ship there once in a while starting in 1834, apparently not without success.[101] Van Hoboken also repeatedly sent ships to West Africa, chartered by the Colonial Ministry to pick up black soldiers and transport them to the Dutch East Indies.[102] However, a company launched in 1840 to begin regular trading with the region failed miserably, despite an ambitious capital of 1 million guilders.[103] In 1847, the Rotterdam merchant Huibert van Rijckevorsel tried again with fabrics. At that time palm oil was the area's most important export product. Van Rijckevorsel took the Dutch governor of the area, Anthony van der Eb, as a partner. To seal the association, he named a ship after the governor, and pulled some strings with the government in the Hague to get him a royal decoration. The same connections ensured that Van Rijckevorsel's interests carried weight against British overtures to the Dutch government to start levying customs duties on the West African coast. Twenty years after Van Rijckevorsel started trading to what is now known as Ghana, the Dutch gin brand Van der Eb had an excellent name there still.[104]

So the merchant houses did not form a uniform group which vainly continued to apply outdated recipes, far from it. Their business pattern had too many differences, and the vicissitudes of individual businessess did so, too. As far the available data are at all sufficiently detailed, they show contrasting developments. Only the assets of D. Crommelin & Sn. followed a declining trend from the early 1820s onwards, the other firms experienced the usual mixed fate of good years alternating with bad ones.[105] So apparently they did succeed in finding new business to replace the disappearance of old activities.

Moreover, the firms showed a keen eye for promising new companies. They invested with relish in, for instance, the Amsterdamsche Stoomboot-Maatschappij (ASM), founded in 1825 to start a regular steam shipping service to Hamburg and London, or in the Koninklijke Fabriek van Stoom- en andere Werktuigen, an engineering company set up in 1826. Braunsberg & Co. had a standing credit facility for an engineering company in Tilburg during 1824. Arie van der Hoop, a partner of Hope & Co., lost a small fortune in the bankruptcy of an Amsterdam engineering company in which he had invested. Van Eeghen & Co. supplied consignment credits to cotton manufacturers in the Twente region, which eventually led to the firm investing in a steam powered cotton mill. As a rule there was no shortage of support for new ventures, unless the prospective profits held out by the founders appeared too meagre. The merchant houses stood to gain in more ways than one. Their investment could generate commodity transactions, and if the company concerned took off, they would be able to sell their shares at a profit.[106]

The reproach that merchants preferred to stay at home, neglected their foreign correspondents, and consequently were out of touch with the overseas markets, does not ring true either. Crommelin listed several firms with family connections overseas in his 1854 memorandum.[107] There was a Dutch merchants' community in Izmir at least until about 1840.[108] As before, aspiring young merchants travelled to visit foreign connections during their trainee years. Hope & Co. exchanged such trainees with Baring Bros. on a regular basis, but less prestigious firms, such as Crone, also sent their intended successors abroad. Partners of Van Eeghen and of Crommelin visited the US during the 1820s to reconnect with old acquaintances. In 1845, Van Eeghen & Co. sent an agent to Java for a survey of prospects in the tobacco trade. Two years later, a partner went there as well to sustain the firm's now rapidly expanding business.[109]

Moreover, the energetic regime of King William I spared no efforts in stimulating the economy. The so-called merchant King harboured neo-mercantilist economic opinions.[110] In his view, the government had to steer developments, to take initiatives, and to step in where necessary with money or protective legislation. The centralised administration inherited from Napoleon presented the King with the means to realize his vision. He jumped into action. Within six months of his return, for example, William signed the decree to establish the Nederlandsche Bank, the intended circulation bank for his kingdom. To help the bank off to a good start, the King bought a substantial stake in it.[111] He took a keen and active interest in the building of and improvements to roads, canals, and port facilities. The government developed practical policies to stimulate industry, on one hand by protective tariffs, on the other by setting up a fund for industrial development and enacting regulations to promote the use of products made in the Netherlands. In addition, ship building received special attention with subsidies to eliminate the cost differential with foreign yards. On his own behalf, William I invested money into a variety of businesses which he deemed worthy of his personal support, ranging from steam shipping companies, engineering factories and a company for the China tea trade, to a company supporting a uniquely small category of tenanted farmers in the province of Groningen.[112]

Of course, these initiatives were definitely not all equally clever, effective, or successful. Some of the interventions even proved distinctly counterproductive, because support only postponed the necessary radical reorientation, and thus raised its inherent cost, so the taxpayer had to pay twice. Other interventions soon lost their impetus, as conflicts of interests between the Netherlands and Belgium, or a shortage of funds prevented further progress. Possibly the policies also lacked a well-thought out strategy, however, elaborate the considerations which had gone before. For example, in preparing a draft act laying down new customs tariffs in 1815-1816, a government commission made detailed comparisons about costs facing the transit trade on Germany in Dutch ports and the costs of alternative routes.[113] The whole set of measures demonstrates that the King and his ministers attempted with some purpose to improve the Dutch competitive position by strengthening comparative advantages, or by eliminating disadvantages.

As time went by, however, the desired effects failed to materialize. The foreign trade balance, still positive during French Occupation, turned negative, and the gap widened rapidly. Imports of mainly manufactured products kept rising, whereas exports dropped sharply.[114] The Dutch economy had little more to offer than agricultural products. The merchant houses faced a nearly insoluble problem. The home market supplied insufficient products for their international trade. They could rarely compete on the world markets with foreign products, because the detour via the Netherlands was inherently more expensive than direct trading. Consequently, the merchants became dependent on consignments from abroad. These were slow in coming, for the lack of ready exports mentioned made the Netherlands an expensive destination for shippers. The German port of Bremen, for instance, had a substantial traffic of emigrants to the US, which kept freight rates low and in turn served as a lead for US tobacco consignments.[115]

Once again, the periodical public debate about the dreary position of Dutch trade flared up, firing all customary passions. Pleas were heard to lift the restrictions on the transit trade, but they found no support either in Amsterdam or in Rotterdam.[116] The Hollandsche Maatschappij van Wetenschappen (Dutch Society for Science) again, fifty years after the previous one, held a competition for essays analysing the commercial decline and offering suggestions towards a solution. The prize, a gold medal and 150 guilders, went to a retired Amsterdam merchant and former ships' agent J. van Ouwerkerk de Vries. His winning essay gave a good overview of the decline, but failed to offer solutions beyond some ornate commonplaces and practical remarks of limited scope, such as improving the harbour approaches.[117] The Amsterdam Chamber of Commerce unleashed vociferous differences of opinion in the capital's commercial circles with its efforts to reform the standard conditions of sale. As it was, each product had its own peculiar customs concerning true weight, tare, and terms of payment, each with different corresponding discounts on quantity and price. Additional commercial services such as those of the public weigh house staff, dockers, porters, packers, and lighter crews were all separately added to the final bill. The city council did make regulations about the conditions of sale, but it failed to monitor them. Consequently, the circumstances were really somewhat murky. Those unfamiliar with the Amsterdam market remained more or less in the dark whether or not the quantity of goods supplied or the final amount on invoices received was reasonable. Press stories alleged that the inherent abuse scared foreign customers away. This inspired the Chamber to strive for lower transaction costs and a more transparent service structure.[118]

The Chamber's proposals ran into widespread opposition. Contemporary observers branded the resistance an expression of blind conservatism, and historians have eagerly copied their denunciation, and not without reason. Presumably, the supply chain did have too many links in relation to the much reduced market it served, so a rationalisation made sense. The Amsterdam mercantile crowd was not susceptible to such changes, irritated as it was by the inexorable erosion of both its economic position and its political power. The King's constant interventions had rubbed salt into these wounds: he had imposed De Nederlandsche Bank and abolished the Wisselbank; he imposed his will again and again when it came to major public works such as harbour improvements, the projected Groot Noord-Hollandsch Kanaal providing a new link to the open sea, and the building of bonded warehousing; and he refused to let his ambitions be tamed by the Amsterdam-controlled capital market. So the slightest

Changes in shipping required better port facilities. In 1831, P. Kiers painted the construction of new locks in Amsterdam's eastern docks.

hint had everyone up in arms, in angry defence of their margins, whether or not the initiatives merited serious consideration.

Yet the resistance against the reform of sales conditions did find its foundation in sound economic sense. The existing conditions enabled the Amsterdam merchant houses to keep staff numbers to a minimum, and to charge additional services directly to the customer. After the French Occupation, the famous firm of Hope & Co. did not return to its large business complex near the Molenpad, but set up office at the Keizersgracht 579, in a somewhat shabby room over the stables backing on to the house at Herengracht 478, the senior partner's residence. The firm probably employed no more than ten or at most fifteen staff. Other firms at least assigned proper rooms in residential accomodation to their offices. In 1830, Van Eeghen & Co. had a staff of two plus an unpaid trainee in a room on the lower ground floor of the senior partner's home. H.G.Th. Crone was little bigger. The founder himself bought an upright writing desk for four persons in 1805. New furniture became necessary only in 1883, when the firm expanded its staff with two new members.[119]

The sales conditions must have been abused, perhaps more, perhaps less than happened in other ports. The Chamber of Commerce failed to unearth systematic malpractice. Possibly the Amsterdam conditions raised local expenses above the level of the competition, but this must be set against the customs duties, which were substantially lower than those in, for instance, French or British ports.[120] That was not the point, however. Reforming the conditions really meant cutting the supply chain into pieces and a subsequent realignment of the established functions and margins. And all that for uncertain gain. Foreign merchants who avoided Amsterdam will gladly have mentioned the local commercial customs as the reason why. The true cause, of course, lay much deeper: the city was no longer a keen market on a European level as before, but a regional centre. Fiddling with the sales conditions could not change that position in any fundamental way. So the whole system would have to be overhauled without tangible advantages. It is not surprisding, then, that the proposals generated deep hostility. For similar reasons both Amsterdam and Rotterdam merchants resisted the lifting of restrictions on the transit trade and the building of public bonded warehouses. This would give foreign rivals a firm base in the Netherlands, but Dutch merchants would not gain a better footing abroad at the same time. In other words, margins would shrink, but only the competition stood to gain from the expected higher turnover. Under those conditions, keeping the door shut was really a sensible option.[121]

The journalist J.W. van den Biesen found out to his cost that pointing to margins angered Amsterdam merchants. He came to know the exchange thoroughly as a trainee with a tobacco broker. His patron sent a private market circular to his clients every fortnight, and this inspired Van den Biesen to launch a newspaper in 1828, the *Algemeen Handelsblad*. Commercial information was given a central place in the paper. Van den Biesen himself gathered commodity prices and securities quotes on the exchange, and added all sorts of information about market moods, rumours, and prices from the after hours trading in the stock brokers' club and the coffee houses along the Kalverstraat. This quickly won the paper popularity and a wide readership. However, the exchange crowd, and more specifically the stock broking fraternity, looked askance at Van den Biesen's success. Their margins were coming under pressure, because the *Algemeen Handelsblad* published narrower bid-offer spreads than the official price current did. When during the autumn of 1830 Van den Biesen gave vent to impopular opinions concerning the newly erupted Belgian Secession, things got out of hand. On the 28th of October he came to blows with the prominent securities trader A.J. Saportas in the Fransche Koffiehuis, a coffeehouse frequented by stock brokers since the 1720s at least. The next day, an angry mob chased Van den Biesen from the exchange. He fled into a nearby house, from which he had to be rescued by the police. The paper did not appear next day.[122]

Meanwhile William I had devised new and more powerful means to boost the economy. He directed his dynamic attention to a field in which the Netherlands had a large potential competitive advantage, the colonies in Asia.

BUILDING A NEW ENTREPOT MARKET – After the Napoleonic Wars, the Netherlands had been restored in most of its colonial possessions by Britain. The government then took the decision to leave trade with the colonies in Asia free on principle, and not to create a new monopoly like the VOC had possessed. After all, the economic shortcomings of such exclusive charters had become very obvious during the last decades of the 18th century. Immediately, merchant houses in Rotterdam, Amsterdam, Middelburg, Dordrecht, and Ghent resumed trade with the Dutch East Indies. In support, the colonial government intro-

Anthony van Hoboken was among the first to resume trade with Asia as soon as the new Kingdom of the Netherlands had been founded. He sent his ships to the Dutch East Indies and from there also to Japan, where the Dutch establishment at Deshima near Nagasaki had survived the Napoleonic Wars. This water-colour on silk, dating from 1820 and attributed to Kawahara Keiga, shows a view of Nagasaki Bay with two Van Hoboken frigates, Arinus Marinus and Ida Aleyda.

duced customs duties discriminating against foreign trade. Shippers from the Netherlands, for instance, paid nothing, exporters from other countries had to pay a 12% levy on the value of goods sent. The port duties were changed in a similar discriminatory way.[123]

Van Hoboken was the first to jump at the new opportunities. In the autumn of 1814, he sent the first ship to the Dutch East Indies. Five years later, his ships had already made six return trips. One ship had gone on to Japan. In 1821 Van Hoboken's fleet included six East Indiamen, partly modern ships which could sail to Asia and back in eight to ten months. Since the 1770s, shipping had made considerable strides, both technically and in the charting of optimal routes. As a result, the duration of the trips fell sharply. During the last quarter of the 18th century, a trip to Asia lasted about 212 days. By the early 19th century, this had fallen to only 176 days, and in 1830 no more than 121. Four years later, the fastest ships sailed to the Dutch East Indies in 85 days, and it became possible to do a round trip in seven months.[124] Initially Van Hoboken spread his risks by letting his ships sail in joint account with the shipping and trading firm of N.J. de Cock & Frère in Ghent. After a few years the agreement was terminated, because Van Hoboken refused to have his ships unload in Antwerp, he wanted to direct all business to Rotterdam.[125] He switched to an old scheme for his subsequent trips. He took shareholders for his ships, and acted as their bookkeeper and manager. The shareholders shared in profits and losses of a trip, and Van Hoboken always made good with the administrative charges.[126] Claude Crommelin looked down on such schemes, by the way.[127] Van Hoboken bought his own yard to maintain his fleet. After a few disappointing experiences with local agents, he sent a trusted clerk to Batavia to represent him. This clerk went into partnership with a local merchant as the firm of Ten Brink & Reijnst, and subsequently appointed correspondents in Semarang and Surabaya.[128] We have no detailed data on the results. The gradual expansion of

Van Hoboken's trade with the Dutch East Indies suggests that he made an overall profit, no doubt due to the particular way in which he had organized the shipping side. The shipping itself and the outward journeys were probably profitable, because of lucrative government contracts for the transport soldiers and officials. However, Van Hoboken alleged that he lost 3% over the return shipments of colonial products.[129]

Within a few years, trade with the east had returned to substantial proportions. As early as 1819 the volume of goods shipped surpassed previous levels by a wide margin, for in that year 37 Dutch ships coming from Asian ports passed customs with a total capacity of more than 30,000 tons. In addition, 44 foreign ships of unknown capacity entered Dutch harbours. If these latter had the same capacity as the Dutch ships, total incoming tonnage from Asia amounted to more than 65,000. During the 18th century, the average annual tonnage of returning VOC ships never rose above 25,000 tons.[130] The value of trade also overshadowed the company's achievements. In 1819, imports from the Dutch East Indies totalled nearly 31 million guilders on estimate, whereas the VOC rarely shipped for more than 10-11 million guilders a year from Batavia to the Republic.[131] According to contemporary reports, British and US firms handled 40% of Dutch imports from Asia.[132] Even then Dutch merchants together still imported at least as much, and probably more, than the VOC used to do, i.e. about 18.5 million guilders. The product range was, true enough, less varied than before. After all, the Asian trade network which had supplied silk, cotton, and tea to the VOC had disappeared, so imports consisted mostly of coffee, sugar, spices, and tin. Still, the trade did not drop in value. During the last quarter of the 18th century, VOC ships used to carry return loads with an average value of 400 guilders per ton, against an estimated value of 475 guilders per ton for return cargoes in 1819.[133] About 70% of exports from Java went to the Netherlands, the rest mainly to Singapore and other Asian destinations.[134] Only the Dutch eastbound trade carried very little overall weight. The lack of suitable export products prevented the merchant houses from raising their import share to more than a pitiful 15-20%.[135] In itself that low figure was no reason for anxiety. After all, the VOC had had a constant negative trade balance as well, and had compensated this by shipping out bullion. However, a European rival had now succeeded in turning the tables. British merchant houses saturated the Asian market with superior industrial goods, chiefly cotton fabrics.

So taken overall, the decision to leave trade with the Dutch East Indies open to competition proved a success. True, in some years during the French occupation imports had been much higher, but the merchant houses achieved far better results than the VOC at any time during the 18th century. Van Ouwerkerk de Vries said as much in his prize essay for the Hollandsche Maatschappij.[136] Yet support grew for the notion that competition could not be maintained in principle. Alarming news arrived from the Indies that the commercial hegemony by foreign merchants would sooner or later lead to political dominance by foreign powers.[137] Moreover, bad harvests reduced exports of agricultural products. Dutch merchant houses found it increasingly hard to compete with their rivals, who could spend more on purchased goods because they had ready import products. An increase of customs duties on foreign imports to 25% had failed to raise the market share of Dutch importers. Exports to the Netherlands fell to just over 50% of the total.[138] A survey of firms in Amsterdam, Rotterdam, and Ghent painted a bleak picture of heavy losses, pessimism, and merchants switching from trading for own account to commission business.[139]

These reports made a deep impression on the King. His realm stood to lose an important economic activity to the competition. Worse still, the colonial possessions in Asia were at stake. Though trade between the Dutch East Indies and the Netherlands had become substantial, this would not last if foreigners

During the early 19th century, the Caribbean colonial possessions supplied more tropical commodities to the Netherlands than the Dutch East Indies did. This anonymous watercolour from 1750 shows a panorama of the cocoa, coffee, and banana plantation Cornelis Vriendschap in Surinam.

dictated margins and Dutch firms withdrew. After all, a similar penetration had driven the VOC from the Indian subcontinent at the end of the 18th century. The situation on Java also contrasted sharply with circumstances on the Caribbean possessions. There, Dutch firms controlled the market, and at that moment in time imports from the West Indies outstripped those from the East Indies by far.[140] The imminent decline of trade with the Dutch East Indies appealed strongly to the King's thirst for action, which had earlier manifested itself repeatedly in grand projects. Monopolies and anti-competitive injunctions might have had their day, but William I thought that capital power could achieve the desired results.[141]

During the winter of 1823-1824 the King drafted plans for a huge trading company designed to solve three interrelated problems at one stroke. First of all, the company was to embark on world-spanning trade and to create markets for Dutch products. Secondly, it would set up a systematic and large-scale commercial business to recapture the colonial trade from the competition. Without

Official portrait of William I, painted by Joseph Paelinck in 1819. The King continuously devised projects to boost the Dutch economy. On receiving alarming reports from the Dutch East Indies about the imminent collapse of Dutch trade there, he took the initiative to found the Nederlandsche Handel-Maatschappij (NHM) to counter this threat.

export products, the Netherlands stood no chance of regaining its economic power. Consequently, carefully targeted orders would have to nurse Dutch industry towards producing the right goods. The King's blueprint envisaged a company with a capital ranging from 12-24 million guilders, so its scale of business would be substantial indeed, which would lower the cost and risks of the Asian trade. Finally, the projected company was to reinforce the financial position of the colonial government by exporting the agricultural products which it received as taxes in kind. These products would be shipped to the Netherlands and sold by auctioning, preferably twice a year, as of old, to be able to feed the market. In addition, the company could be entrusted with other varying tasks on behalf of the government, such as the transport of troops and the farming of the opium monopoly.

The conception of a big trading company to shore up trade with the Dutch East Indies of course owed its inspiration to the VOC. A government commission had floated similar proposals in 1803. At that moment, circumstances had prevented their being carried out. When the French occupation ended, the merchant houses had been very keen to prove themselves on an open market, though the colonial government had warned as early as 1817 that they would make little headway.[142] The King's project diverged from its illustrious predecessor in a few crucial respects. The company would not be entrusted with public powers or functions. That was to remain the preserve of the colonial government, though of course the government and its regular commercial agent did

work together as an opaque hybrid. Nor would the company get a formal trade monopoly, only some privileges designed to create a dominant position, together with the prospective scale of operations. And lastly, the company was to act as an intermediary, a commission trader, whenever possible, and commission private firms to do the work. On the 29th of March 1824 the official gazette published the Royal decree founding the Nederlandsche Handel-Maatschappij (NHM or Dutch Trading Company), as it had been named. One of Van Hoboken's ships carried the mail to Batavia with copies of the decree.[143]

On being asked, Van Hoboken had declared himself against the King's plans, by the way. In his opinion the colonial trade was better left to private enterprise, though he had no objections to creating particular advantages for Dutch firms.[144] The senior partner of D. Crommelin & Sn. also recognized the danger that the merchant houses now stood to lose their entry to Asia and more specifically to the Dutch East Indies. For his firm was active in the tea trade, a branch which had formerly belonged to the VOC.[145] The two businessmen stood more or less alone in their opinions, however. The Royal decree generated a wave of euphoria: a big trading company which would resurrect the entrepot market, which would show the Dutch flag on the world's oceans again, and above all, which would bring an end to the humiliations inflicted by foreign competition! And without much risk, too, for the King himself bought a large share in it and in addition personally guaranteed a dividend of 4.5%. On Monday 12 April 1824 the share subscription opened at the country's ten biggest chambers of commerce. An overwhelming rush occurred. Amsterdam investors alone had pledged a total of almost 32 million guilders before midday. At the end of the afternoon, the Antwerp chamber closed on a total of 14 million guilders, Rotterdam on 11 million, Brussels on 8 million. Within a day nearly 70 million guilders had been subscribed. After ample deliberations the government set the company's capital at 37 million guilders, and business could open. As a gesture towards the shareholders in Belgium, the head office was established in The Hague, which of course dampened the enthusiasm in Amsterdam. The company was to move to the capital only after the Belgian Secession.

The NHM was not, in all fairness, a merchant house as defined in this book. As often as not, such houses performed a variety of other tasks subordinate to trade. The NHM's priorities were the other way around, however. Its commercial business served a much wider purpose, the regeneration of the Dutch economy and anything that could bring this about. The company's board interpreted its mission in the widest possible sense, running the NHM as a body generating economic activities and spreading them with distributive justice over Dutch business down to its smallest segment. This conception certainly produced results. For example, the NHM only chartered ships built in the Netherlands, and paid very handsome freight rates into the bargain. In addition, the government paid subsidies over new ships built since 1824. These policies combined started a ship-building boom which pulled the yards from the crisis which had gripped them from the end of the French Occupation. Until 1868, shipyards and ship owners received subsidies estimated at a total of more than 84 million

The NHM's first register of shareholders, showing the ranking of subscribers. At the top is the King's subscription for 4000 shares. The governor of the province of North Holland, Tets van Goudriaan, ranked second, taking 25 shares. The third entry was for the chairman of the Amsterdam chamber of commerce, L. Bousquet, who bought 600 shares for himself and his merchant house together.

160

guilders.[146] Van Hoboken jumped at the opportunity, launching a company for the exploitation of four new East Indiamen with a capital of 300,000 guilders in 1825.[147] The maritime insurance sector also veered up when the NHM began to hand out generous premiums. Out of principle, the company behaved contrary to commercial sense. The board did not aim to cut out middlemen and to cut margins, quite the opposite, it strove to use as many intermediaries as possible, it maintained or reinstated margins, it organized its sales towards giving all merchants a chance to buy, and finally, it spread the unloading and storing of goods over Amsterdam, Rotterdam, Dordrecht, Middelburg, and a little later also Schiedam, to give work to the maximum number of people.

Keeping people in work was definitely a worthy purpose, given the country's crushing unemployment. This led to conserving the status quo, however, regardless of economic efficiency. Moreover, the company did not care for constant reassessments of means and ends, so markets became distorted. Fat premiums built a lazy and heavily fragmented maritime insurance market which, for instance, developed hardly any interest in statistical methods and risk analyses.[148] Generous freight rates created a structural overcapacity in shipping. Ship owners took to ordering new freighters more or less randomly, knowing that they could recoup their investment with two or three trips for the NHM.[149] Clever merchant houses used the subsidies for the Asian trade to diversify.

The high freight rates paid by the NHM generated a wave of speculative ship building. When Cornelis Smit commissioned a ship for himself, he received an NHM guarantee for two trips to Asia and back, which nearly repaid his building costs. Smit christened his ship 'Dankbaarheid aan de NHM' (Gratitude to the NHM) in recognition. Watercolour by Jacob Spin, 1840.

Van Rijckevorsel, for instance, used them to start his West African trade.[150] Claude Crommelin, senior partner in the eponymous Amsterdam firm, considered that the NHM had debased shipping and maritime insurance to charity work. The high rates enticed one and all to set up in business, peddling shares to keep going. He thought it beneath him.[151] A one-sided demand for ships meeting the NHM's requirements starved ship yards of stimuli towards technical change, instead leading them to build old-fashioned freighters along established lines. Spreading the activities over five ports did not produce the desired effects either.

The agencies established in Dordrecht, Middelburg, and Schiedam remained too small to generate any derivative commercial services. Sales were conducted through the company's auctions in Amsterdam and Rotterdam. The other ports really served only for storage and transshipment of their fixed share in the company's imports, a privilege jealously guarded by the city authorities concerned.[152] Fundamental changes in policy, or even minor amendments to the standard conditions, encountered serious difficulties. With its efforts towards economic regeneration, the NHM itself created various vested interests which effectively curtailed the company's room to move. Attempts towards change always unleashed a storm of criticism which soon rattled the windows of palace and parliament, putting the board under heavy pressure to review its objectives. Thus the NHM, notwithstanding its good intentions, reinforced tendencies towards sclerosis rather than helping to bring about reorientation and change.

Yet the company did have an open mind for innovations. The board stimulated, for instance, the warehousing of commodities using tradeable warrants, standard documents which smoothed the transfer of ownership or the lombarding of particular lots as required. Agencies were established all over the country, and instructed to search actively for manufacturers of export products. This network spread the NHM's conditions and practices as standards throughout the Netherlands, and sometimes even far beyond. The company's trade mark gradually became a grade for high quality fabrics within the textile trade in the Dutch East Indies. In 1839, the board commissioned two brokers to develop a standard for sugar samples, resulting in a wooden box with eighteen numbered flasks holding sugar grades from dark brown to white. This made the sugar trade more transparent, for merchants now could rely on numbers in stead of vague descriptions such as 'pale brown'. The so-called 'Dutch standard' was adopted rapidly by the international sugar trade, and also by customs authorities in Japan, New Zealand, and the US, which levied duties on sugar using its colour as a gauge.[153]

The company's commodity trading got off to a rather difficult start. In accordance with its instructions, the NHM embarked immediately on a wide ranging trade reaching out to all continents. A total of 1 million guilders was lost in ventures to America and the Caribbean, and 2 million guilders in expeditions to China. Within a few years, the board therefore limited its ambitions to the core business originally intended, trading with the Dutch East Indies. In 1826 the company established a branch in Batavia called the Factorij, really a fairly independent subsidiary which ran the Asian side of operations. During its financial year 1824-1825, the NHM shipped commodities worth 2.8 million guilders to the Netherlands, mostly coffee and spices. Four years later exports totalled as much as 12.5 million guilders, a considerable growth to a hardly impressive total, considering the huge capital involved.[154] Dutch imports of colonial products did not rise to the same degree. Clearly the NHM did not succeed in capturing a substantially bigger share of the exports than the merchant houses had had before, possibly partly because agricultural production on Java suffered major damage as a result of an insurrection against the Dutch colonial

Wanting to boost the sugar trade by establishing uniform product descriptions, the NHM board commissioned two brokers to develop a standard. This resulted in a wooden chest with 18 numbered flasks holding different sugar samples ranged by colour. From now, sugar traders could refer to numbers rather than vague descriptions of colour.

government led by Dipo Negoro. Meanwhile the Dutch market share in imports did rise as desired, helped by a further rise of the differential customs duties to 35% and a coincidental drop in British imports. In 1826 Dutch shippers supplied 33% of all imports, and the figure continued rising until it stabilized at about 40%. At that moment the Factorij imported for about 4 million guilders a year in the Dutch East Indies.[155] So here, as with the colonial exports, capital power did not succeed in forcing the hoped-for breakthrough, it could at most consolidate what had been achieved by other means before. During its first years the NHM made some profits on trading for its own account with the Dutch East Indies, but these were wiped out by heavy losses in 1828 and 1829. The six years in business closed with a positive balance only because of a loan to the colonial government, shipments on behalf of the Dutch government, and the farming of the opium monopoly, with which the NHM followed in the footsteps of the VOC's Amfioensociëteit. The profits were small, however, too small to pay the promised 4.5% dividends to shareholders. Until 1834 the King had to meet a shortfall with his own money every single year. Finally, at the end of the 1820s the company's capital was reduced to a more realistic 23 million guilders.[156]

A radical change in colonial policy finally helped the NHM to unlock its potential during the 1830s. The Dutch government, taking its cue from Governor-General Johannes van den Bosch, introduced the so-called Cultuurstelsel or Cultivation System on Java. Under this scheme, the local population had to cultivate specific products on 20% of its land, and supply these to the colonial government in lieu of taxes and colonial servitude. The colonial government consigned these products, mostly coffee, sugar, and the dyestuff indigo, to the NHM, which transported the goods to the Netherlands and auctioned them there. The system of forced cultivation succeeded in raising commodity production and exports at very fast rates. Exports rose from 12 million guilders in 1830 to more than 60 million by 1840. At last the Dutch share in exports climbed back to more than 70%. On average, the NHM sold 47 million guilders worth of colonial products every year between 1840 and 1850, more than twice as much as the VOC at its peak had managed to do. Revenues flowing to the Dutch exchequer rose and rose, totalling 500 million guilders during the years 1831-1869. These so-called Indian revenues provided the cork on which the Netherlands came to float.[157]

The government and the NHM worked in harmonious cooperation towards building a conglomerate of processing industries around the fast-growing colonial trade. Scaled import duties on rice created opportunities for mechanized rice mills, which peeled rice from the Dutch East Indies and then re-exported it. The sugar duties were targeted to give refiners export subsidies which rose as productivity increased, thus putting a very effective premium on a continuous rationalisation and mechanization of sugar production. During the early 1840s the first refiners switched to steam powered refining. In 1849 the biggest refinery was reorganised into an NV or limited liability company with a

The Dutch excise system put an effective premium on continuous productivity increases, leading to the building of large steam sugar refineries in the Amsterdam Jordaan area. This painting by J.D.C. Veltens shows the factory of Beuker & Hulshoff on the Lauriergracht.

164

capital of 2.8 million guilders. This made the company probably the biggest industrial venture in the Netherlands by far, and the first one to bypass the merchant houses in size. The NHM supported the sugar trade from beginning to end. The Factorij gave sugar planters in the Dutch East Indies consignment advances, which tended to degenerate into long-term loans on the collateral of plantations and sugar processing installation because of the sector's strongly cyclical nature. At the end of the 1830s the NHM had several millions of guilders outstanding in such loans, or better laid up in them, for as a rule there was no question of regular interest payments, nor any prospect of repayment. To please Dutch refiners, the company organized its sugar auctions at frequent intervals, so they had no need to keep large stocks of raw sugar. Flexible arrangements for paying raw sugar purchases added to the refiners' own floating capital. Between 1842 and

1849 two sugar refiners owed a total of 1 million guilders to the NHM in this way. These credit facilities were as immovable as the advances to planters, as both refiners had used the money to modernize and expand their premises and equipment.[158] In its turn, the core of colonial processing industries generated growth in supply industries. The engineering company Koninklijke Fabriek van Stoom- en andere Werktuigen, one of the key suppliers, used NHM credit as well, for exporting sugar equipment to the Dutch East Indies.[159] From time to time the NHM created additional special facilities as a stimulus for particular trade sectors. During the 1840s this happened successively for tin, coffee, and wool.[160]

Still another economic sector received targeted support. After the independence of Belgium, the company developed a commitment to the Dutch cotton industry. For the export products formerly supplied by manufacturers from Belgium now had to be found in the Netherlands proper. The NHM left no method untried to assist cotton producers: consignment advances, product lombards, shareholdings in mills, anything was put to use in the hope of raising production levels. The board established an agency at the village of Nijverdal, close to the main cotton producing area in the east of the country to serve as a bridgehead towards the industry. It was headed by an English cotton expert, Thomas Ainsworth. He founded schools to train the local population in cotton weaving, introduced the latest skills and equipment, and provided a key link between trade and production. Meanwhile the NHM had reached an agreement with the government over ways to raise sales in the Dutch East Indies. In a secret contract, the company promised to increase its shipments, insured for any losses by a government guarantee. This collective effort produced remarkably quick results. In 1832, the NHM sent calicoes worth 6,000 guilders to the Dutch East Indies; eight years later cotton exports had risen to more than 6 million guilders. At long last Dutch imports passed those of the British rival. Even so the competition certainly did not disappear, the market share of Dutch imports barely attaining 50%. It has to be said that the company's support for the cotton industry was part charity, but it did succeed in creating an export market for companies which proved viable in the long run.[161]

Taken overall, the NHM's activities had a strong banking element in them: the board used flexible credit arrangements to create markets and to favour its customers. It was an old and tested recipe, which, through the company's business volume and through the way in which the board interpreted its mission, had a very special impact, almost on a national scale. This translated to the revenue side, of course. Interest charges made up more than 20% of the company's gross revenues up to and including 1849. Trade for own account and for the government's account supplied another 25%, commissions over 35%.[162] During the 1830s finance dominated the company for a time, but for a special reason. Belgian independence brought the government's financial position into complete disarray, and ministers approached the NHM to get money without parliamentary permission. The board did not dare to refuse, on account of the close ties with the company's founder and holder of a substantial share, King William I.

An Indian merchant carrying rolls of cotton over his shoulder, coloured lithograph by A. van Pers in A.J. Duymaer van Twist, *Nederlandsch-Oostindische Typen*.

165

Initially the company just supplied advances over expected shipments of government products, a very common trade custom which, however, very soon degenerated into loans for indefinite terms and more or less without collateral. The NHM itself had to raise increasing sums at the exchange to keep afloat. In the end, the government owed nearly 40 million guilders to the company, which at that moment had total assets of 58 million. Then the game was up. The NHM experienced increasing difficulties in finding credit, because the exchange smelt a rat, sending the share price down. In November 1839 the board refused to comply any longer, forcing the government into giving parliament full disclosure of the facts, the prelude to political developments which led to the King's abdication a year later.[163]

Had the NHM by that time fulfilled its mission as defined by its founder? Dutch foreign trade had risen considerably at any rate, largely due to the stimulus from the tropical trade. Around 1850 colonial products made up about 50-60% of Dutch imports. Most of them came from the Dutch East Indies, Surinam's share having fallen away. The same products supplied 30-40% of Dutch

After his abdication, King William I became a target for public lampooning, partly inspired by his subsequent marriage to the Belgian countess Henriëtte d'Oultremont. This anonymous 1841 lithograph entitled 'The household of William the Cheesevendor', in the top row shows the King leaving the ship of state (left) and liquidating his business concerns. Middle, he warms himself near an open fire and falls in love with the countess (left) before departing for Germany. There he marries Henriëtte d'Oultremont (bottom left), and she becomes pregnant.

The huge scale on which the NHM operated was seen by many as a threat to private enterprise. This cartoon, published in 1840, depicts the company as a sea monster gobbling up trade and shipping.

exports. Total foreign trade turnover in colonial commodities amounted to an estimated 129 million guilders on a total of 300 million, or 40%.[164] Consequently, trade with the Dutch East Indies had become considerably more important for the Netherlands than before. The Asian share in the Republic's foreign trade turnover around 1780 has been estimated at 13% (see Table 3.1).[165]

In other respects the company's performance record does not look too impressive at first sight. After all, the flourishing tropical trade was a consequence of the Cultivation System, and not the NHM's merit. Private merchant houses, less restricted in their operations, would probably have managed the product flows with considerably more efficiency. After all, the NHM was not allowed to seek the best market, but had to sell in the Netherlands. Repeated efforts to obtain higher prices by directing commodities to various European ports met with immediate protests from interested merchants.[166] Low returns on capital reflected this lack of freedom. The company's profits were considerable, but not spectacular. During its first 25 years in existence, dividends averaged 7.5%.[167] The shareholders of another of William I's creations, the Nederlandsche Bank, received no more than 6% over the years 1814-1849.[168] However, the partners of most merchant houses usually wrote their returns on capital in double figures.[169]

In addition, the relief policies for Dutch industry had had little overall effect. Only the sugar refineries and the cotton industry struck deep roots, of all the sectors supported. However, both industries radically changed course after about 1850, confronted with increasing competition as the favours granted by the government and by the NHM gradually disappeared. Protection thus had hampered them, at least as much as helping them.[170] The remaining sectors did not survive the end of protectionism, or barely so. The carefully fostered margins and middlemen disappeared. Maritime insurance foundered. Rice mills closed. The engineering companies surrounding the colonial entrepot market did manage to keep afloat, but their heyday was clearly over. The market share of ship building and ship owning plummeted, both in the Netherlands and in the Dutch East Indies. The NHM's historian, Mansvelt, concluded therefore that the relief efforts had achieved very little at great cost, because the prosperity generated had been artificial and temporary, not did not last.[171]

And yet almost two generations of, for instance, sailors or ship yard labourers had had work which they probably would not have had without the NHM's relief policies. Private merchant firms would have operated more efficiently in the commodity trade, but they could never have achieved comparable effects on employment. Whether policies directed at a radical adjustment would have produced better results than neomercantlism, remains open to question. The international protectionist climate would not have changed any sooner, at any rate. Opening the home market and setting the transit trade free would have been a useless sacrifice of existing margins without corresponding policy changes abroad. Radical adjustment would, moreover, have increased unemployment and consequently lowered home demand, opening the threat of a vicious circle. From that perspective, the NHM's comparatively poor economic

167

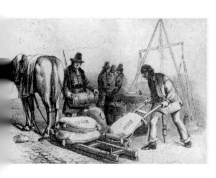

Unloading an NHM cargo, wood engraving by Henry Brown.

performance becomes less significant, measured against the excellent social returns, the creation of jobs to get through a period in which the Dutch economy proved unable to generate sufficient means of existence for its population by other means. This argument only works, however, by leaving the Dutch East Indies out of the equation. At that time, people regarded it as a territory for exploitation. Providence had allotted its treasures to the Netherlands to use, so by rights the mother country could extract a maximum of revenues. The colonial government did use a modest part of the revenues for investments in roads, irrigation projects, and other public works. However, such investment was invariably directed towards improving the efficiency of the Cultivation System, and increase its yields. All other tasks of colonial administration were equally systematically neglected. For a long time, the government paid no attention whatever to how Java's population coped with the forced cultivation. During the 1840s there were repeated famines and epidemics on the island which claimed hundreds of thousands of victims, consequences of the commercial exploitation having gone too far, to the detriment of food production. If the Cultivation System was subsequently readjusted to prevent such disasters, and even if the system did not damage Javanese society quite so badly as has previously been supposed, the misery thus caused has to be booked on the debit side of the economic regeneration policies for the Netherlands implemented by the government and the NHM.[172]

The horse changing station near Surabaya, anonymous photograph from the album 'Souvenirs de Voyage 1891-1892'.

RULERS OVER A CRUMBLING REALM – Meanwhile the old merchant houses went downhill. A 1773 estimate puts the capital of the Amsterdam merchant houses at 30 million guilders in all.[173] We know nothing about the underlying data for this figure, so we cannot determine the margin between guessing and accuracy. There is no doubt, however, that during the 19th century the amount was lower, and that it continued to fall. Estimated total capital of the thirteen merchant houses with an 18th century provenance for which we have quantitative data, or at least some indications, amounted to over 13 million guilders. Fifteen years later three firms had disappeared, and the remaining ten together barely possessed 10 million guilders. Around 1850 only seven firms were still in business, with nearly 7 million guilders in capital, so almost half of the 1820 figure. The true total must have been higher, of course, for each of the years mentioned, because in many cases we know little more than a merchant firm's name, and this is true even for some respected firms. Luden & Van Geuns, for instance, or Insinger & Co., both presumably second only to the big firms such as Hope & Co., D. Crommelin & Sn., or Van Eeghen & Co., and reported to have been keen in business. Insinger managed to keep going, and still exists as a bank today. Luden & Van Geuns was in business as late as the last quarter of the 19th century, and we have no date for its liquidation.[174] The awareness of so many missing details does little, however, to alter the clear downward trend. After all, we do have certainty about the biggest firms concerned, such as Hope & Co., Van Eeghen & Co., Crommelin, Determeyer Weslingh & Zoon en Stadnitski & Van Heukelom.[175]

According to the chronicler of this decline, Claude Crommelin, the merchant houses became stuck without fail between on one hand dwindling commissions, and on the other the NHM's dominance of the Asian trade. His 1854 memorandum appears to be convincing. Here is someone who had experienced this development at first hand, so he knew what he was writing about. And yet, was the decline so inexorable as Crommelin makes it appear? Did the NHM rob the merchant houses of the desired opportunities? They definitely had an impact on trade with the Dutch East Indies. Private merchants had an estimated share in

Announcement of an auction of Java coffee, plus a poster listing auction prices, 1827. To uphold the markets for its products, the NHM organised regular auctions rather than selling on arrival.

the Dutch tropical imports of about 30-40%, and they presumably supplied about 40% of calico exports to the Dutch East Indies, too. Some cotton manufacturers took the export of their products in their own hands, with or without consignment advances from merchant bankers.[176] However, in the colonial trade the merchant houses had really very little room for manoeuvre. On Java, they could hardly buy products cheaper than the NHM, which had exclusive supplies from the biggest seller by far. Van Hoboken had connections in official circles which from time to time helped him to prise commodity lots out of the colonial government, much to the company's chagrin, for the officials took such opportunities to spell out to company staff how much cheaper the Rotterdam firm operated.[177] Such connections were vital. Free product supplies were not very substantial, and as a rule strong competition for them kept prices down. At the other end, European sales took their cue from bidding at the NHM's auctions, which the board could manipulate, but the merchant houses could not. The company's inefficiency and its efforts to keep prices of tropical products high did create an wide trade margin. At the same time, however, the NHM's social mission helped to spread European distribution of colonial commodities over as many firms as possible. So in this respect Crommelin was presumably right, this sector offered too little scope for the merchant houses.

Crommelin's other complaint, dwindling commissions, appears puzzling at first sight. For not only the colonial trade grew, foreign trade rose in other sectors as well. In 1820 the estimated Dutch foreign trade turnover excluding tropical products amounted to 76 million guilders, rising to 174 million guilders thirty years later.[178] So there was scope for growth, only Crommelin, and other merchants leaving the stage, failed to make the most of it. They simply could not get a hold on the commodity flows which passed under their noses. Why not, then? Because of their original position in the supply chain. Crommelin's conception of his business centered on shipments in commission or in consignation of grain, timber, salt, wine, sugar, potash, hides, tobacco, coffee, tea, drugs, dyes, silk, and spices, in short, the products for which the Republic had once organized the European distribution. Now these commodities trickled in only to satisfy regional and local demand, coffee, grain, timber, and sugar excepted. More and more such supplies were shipped by producers on direct orders from merchants or wholesalers in the hinterland, which would entrust the contact with suppliers, the customs formalities, and the goods forwarding to agents like Potgieter. By virtue of modern office inventions such as the copy press and the steel pen, he could run such a business more or less on his own, and with a minimum of capital. And still he found time to travel around regularly visiting his customers, and to edit *De Gids*, a literary and political monthly magazine of liberal leanings with a wide readership, which Potgieter had helped to found in 1837.[179]

If the merchant houses could not compete with such agents, it was not for a lack of Potgieter's almost manic energy. The merchant houses' conception of trade was different, focusing as it did on essentially international wholesaling: handling commodities by the shipload, followed by sorting, grading, and stock keeping, to sell them on in smaller lots to inland wholesalers or importers abroad. That particular function, crumbling since the Republic had lost its central distributive functions, was now gradually becoming entirely redundant, as mentioned above, with the market changes following the higher regularity of shipping with the introduction of scheduled services and steam ships.

The merchant houses battled in vain against that trend. It was a world wide phenomenon, not a particular problem of the Dutch market. Producers no longer shipped consignments in commission to their correspondents, and sat back to await what happened, they began selling on specified orders only.[180] As a consequence, the Dutch trade system decentralised. Commercial agents and provincial wholesalers found their way in Britain or Germany, for instance to import American tobacco from Bremen, or to ship coffee and sugar to Hamburg, to Bremen, or down the Rhine, bypassing the large scale and capital intensive handling and distribution offered by the merchant houses.[181] This

decentralization levelled the traditional hierarchical trade pyramid. The number of merchants rose, most palpably at the distributive end of the chain. In 1850, the Amsterdam business tax assessed 3,202 persons as merchants, against only 2,419 in 1826. The category of big merchants or *zeehandelaren* at the pyramid's apex hardly grew in number, the next group of foreign merchants increased somewhat more, but the number of inland merchants at the bottom rose sharpest.[182] So trade offered plenty of opportunities, only not for the kind of wholesaling business which had previously directed the trade chain.

So Crommelin was right, too, in the second part of his diagnosis: the merchant houses lost ground because the foreign consignments dried up. Some historians have concluded from his account, that the whole of Amsterdam trade, or even Dutch foreign trade overall, declined during the first half of the 19th century.[183] The rising foreign trade turnover and the growing number of merchants in the Amsterdam licence tax suffice to refute that opinion. The specific business operated by the merchant houses went downhill, not Dutch foreign trade: other firms took over their functions. The decline of the merchant houses was not caused either by their blind adherence to obsolete recipes like commission trading, and their refusal to take risks and switch to trading for their own accounts.[184] These firms possessed far more energy, business acumen, risk acceptance, and tenacity than Crommelin's melancholy memorandum suggests. The available records demonstrate that they tried anything at least twice, trading for own account included. Dogged persistence appears a better term for these firms. For the energy with which they clung to their positions, the ingenuity and daring with which they tried again and again to justify their commercial view, does win respect. We have seen how D. Crommelin & Sn. repeatedly experimented with shipping ownership and trading for own account, how for instance Determeyer Weslingh & Zn., or Stadnitski & Van Heukelom, constantly tried out commodity consignments of varying volume and composition. They may have been running against the tide; they might have been better off cashing

To support its new strategy, Van Eeghen & Co. again set up its own shipping operations. This watercolour by G.L. Kiers shows the firm's frigate Amsterdam being launched, 1872.

their chips and leaving, as Crommelin did, or face the facts and downgrade their business to an agency. Presumably they never really came to a decision. After all, their business may no longer have been a goldmine, but there was always something going. Because finance provided most firms with steady revenues, they never really felt the need to rethink their business from the ground upwards, for instance as a wholesaler for the inland market.

Crommelin's memorandum does not give a representative survey of Dutch or even Amsterdam commerce, but really only the personal reasons why the senior partner of a respected merchant house wanted to liquidate. He wrote as a desillusioned merchant looking back on a mercantile career spanning forty years. With his partners, he had tried everything, but had made unlucky choices at crucial moments. He had passed through two deep commercial crises. After the second one, in 1848, his brother had resigned from the partnership, taking nearly half the firm's capital with him. In the year of his writing, 1854, a sudden squall had shaken the Amsterdam colonial trade, bankrupting as many as fourteen firms.[185] New technologies, such as the telegraph, had not made Crommelin's life any easier, and he did not expect it to change his business for the better. He was nearing sixty years of age, and could not muster the courage to change tack and begin anew with trading for own account, as his partner Wolterbeek had proposed to do. Crommelin wrote his memorandum to convince Wolterbeek that this would be inviting disaster. The vicissitudes of the Amsterdam merchant houses offered him arguments in abundance, resulting in an exagerrated account of irreversible decline. To understand the memorandum correctly, the reader has constantly to keep in mind that Crommelin *did not want* to see opportunities anymore: firms which in fact flourished at the time of his survey, such as Hope & Co. or Van Eeghen & Co., are mentioned only in passing. The partners failed to come to an agreement, and the firm was dissolved. Crommelin continued in business on his own until his death in 1859. Wolterbeek possessed too little capital to venture into trading on his own, and in the end he settled for the risk free existence of a director at the Nederlandsche Bank.[186]

Others noticed, as Wolterbeek had done, that a particular field began to offer opportunities for the large scale commodity business of the merchant houses. During the mid-1840s a new generation took the helm at Van Eeghen &

Co., which devised a new lease of life for the trusted formula. After close study of foreign trade and freight rates in the Dutch East Indies, the firm decided to embark on consignment trading in calicoes, anticipating an imminent collapse of the Cultivation System and a consequent liberalisation of trade. The cotton venture became a success, because local firms, such as Van Eeghen's correspondent Paine Stricker & Co., succeeded in getting substantially better prices than the NHM's Factorij managed to do.[187] Business expanded rapidly. In 1850 the firm commissioned an Amsterdam yard to build ship for its trade with Java. Growth soon outpaced capacity: in 1852 a second ship was launched, and a third the following year.[188] Meanwhile the first cracks had appeared in the Cultivation System.

After the French Occupation, the Dutch economic hegemony was clearly over, forcing the country to begin more or less from scratch. The merchant houses set to work with zest and ingenuity to resurrect their trade, but they were only partially successful. The entrenched competition and structural changes in international trade curtailed the demand for their particular kind of intermediation. After about 1830 Dutch foreign trade grew, but the product flows took different routes. Initially, trade with the Dutch East Indies offered good opportunities, until the Nederlandsche Handel-Maatschappij more or less seized this sector. As a consequente, the ranks of merchant houses had become seriously depleted by 1850. At that moment in time new opportunities appeared on the horizon.

173

In 1854, the Amsterdam merchant Claude Crommelin wrote a sombre memorandum about the decline of the merchant houses which he had personally known on the exchange. The picture shows his remarks about Van Eeghen & Co. Having embarked on new ventures with the Dutch East Indies, this firm was undergoing a remarkable renaissance that very moment. Crommelin was loath to follow this example.

A clerks' room in the NHM headoffice on the Amsterdam Herengracht, watercolour by C.A.J. Hamburger, 1880.

The steamer Queen Elisabeth sailing through the Suez canal, 1870. The opening of the canal drastically reduced the travelling times between Europe and Asia, while the more or less simultaneous introduction of the compound steam engine gave steam shipping a decisive lead over sailing vessels.

A train on its way from Haarlem, still visible in the background, to Amsterdam, a painting by Wouterus Verschuur, about 1855. The watchman waves a white signal to the driver to indicate that the track ahead is free. On the right hand side of the track an optical telegraph pole stands side by side with posts for an electromagnetic telegraph line. The electromagnetic lines introduced by the railways were the first ones to link the three big cities Amsterdam, the Hague, and Rotterdam with each other.

CHAPTER IV

Around 1850 international trade suddenly accelerated. The industrial

revolution spread from one country to another, and new, faster means

of transport and of communications became available. Protectionism,

until then a pervasive influence, proved to be no longer viable as an

economic policy, and free trade began to break down the barriers

erected around countries. These developments generated a powerful

expansion of trade, which went hand in hand with deep structural

changes. The commodity trade specialised, and new intermediaries

appeared who handled industrial products. Meanwhile, the surviving

merchant houses managed to stay in business by specialising in colonial

trade.

THE HEYDAY OF LIBERALISM – The systematic exploitation of the Dutch East
Indies through the Cultivation System and product consignments handled by
the NHM came under public attack before it had been in operation for a good
ten years. Initially, opponents concentrated on the company's economic inefficiency, the same objection which Isaac le Maire had raised against the VOC. In
1839 the liberal lawyer Dirk Donker Curtius published an anonymous pamphlet denouncing the NHM as a costly joke at the expense of the public interest.
An extended edition appeared nine years later at a piquant moment in time.
The 1848 changes to the Dutch constitution had unequivocally entrusted the
supervision over colonial policy to Parliament. Donker Curtius had just
become Minister of Justice, the NHM's shareholders faced a decision over continuing the association for another 25 years, and the terms for a new consignment contract between the company and the government had been agreed, but
the contract itself had not yet been signed. The Amsterdam merchant Joan
Muller publicly sided with Donker Curtius in a devastating brochure branding
the NHM as a failure. A press debate began. The economic activities generated
by the company were brushed away as artificial by the Rotterdam liberal
newspaper *Nieuwe Rotterdamsche Courant*.[1] Several members of Parliament

put the matter into a broader perspective, voicing moral objections. Was it really permissible that the Netherlands pocketed colonial revenues worth tens of millions of guilders, without doing much in return?[2] This criticism did not result in immediate changes. The shareholders voted to continue the association, and Parliament approved the new contract by a small majority.[3] However, colonial policy had now become a subject for open debate. A political campaign ensued which within twenty years brought about the dismantling of the whole system.

The attack on colonial policy was definitely not an isolated incident, but part and parcel of a powerful, all embracing push towards a liberalisation of trade, transport, and industry. Public opinion became persuaded that protection was counterproductive, by raising prices and thus restricting consumption and growth. Britain was the first country to adopt a new policy. After a prolonged tussle between interest groups, a liberal government headed by Robert Peel first abolished the import duties on grain and meat, and subsequently in 1849 repealed the Navigation Acts, which had favoured the country's own merchant navy for nearly two centuries. Foreign ships' masters and owners gratefully seized the resulting opportunities to pick up cargo. As early as 1850 more than 200 Dutch ships sailed from British ports to Asia.[4] This example was followed everywhere, countries replacing the chauvinistic favours to their own trade and transport by equal rights regardless of nationality, and fostering international cooperation.

A series of profound technical innovations accompanied the liberal tide. Industrialization spread from the core countries Britain, Belgium, Germany, and France to the countries surrounding them. A second phase started, with steel, chemicals, and electricity taking the place of steam and coal as leading sectors. Mechanization and factory production spread to more and more sectors of the economy, creating an ever widening range of industrial supplies, from food products such as milk, cheese, flour, soap, salt, margarine, and biscuits, to utensils like candles and steel pens, and to consumer durables as like ready-made clothes and shoes. Advances in transport and communications constantly opened up new markets for these products. As a consequence, world trade grew faster than industrial production in this era.[5] The telegraph connected the continents into a market which learned to count the hours and minutes, sometimes already the seconds, instead of the weeks and months. Essentially, this innovation vastly increased the speed differential between transport and communications, until then not a factor of huge importance in the long-distance trade. After several fruitless attempts, the first permanent line between Europe and Asia opened in 1865, followed by a transatlantic cable a year later. These lines had many teething problems. Speed was restricted to about ten to fifteen words per minute. Messages became garbled from being repeated frequently by intermediate stations without proper command of the language concerned. A despatch from Britain to India took five to six days.[6] New calculating techniques enabled merchants to process a flood of figures in no time. Around 1850, the American John E. Fuller started to produce what he called a *Telegraphic computer, by which business calculations of every possible variety are*

An 1876 quittance from the records of Van Eeghen & Co. for the sending of a telegram to Surabaya costing almost 200 guilders, a very substantial amount. The firm's messenger did not have to walk very far to the nearest telegraph office, which was located just around the corner.

176

instantly performed, a circular slide rule for the fast calculation of prices.[7] Long-distance transport underwent a transformation, too. The railways introduced cheap overland bulk transport. Compound steam engines sharply raised the efficiency of steam engines, sending maritime freight rates down. Sailing simply could no longer compete with faster, cheaper, and more reliable steam shipping.[8] The opening of the Suez Canal in 1869 substantially reduced the length of shipping routes between Europe and Asia.

THE PRAGMATIC LIBERALISM OF A FREE TRADING COUNTRY – The Netherlands scrapped its own navigation laws two years after Britain had done so. Soon after a trade and shipping treaty was signed with the German Zollverein, which cleared the last formal hurdles for trade with the hinterland. Its was not principled liberalism which inspired the Dutch government to take action, but fear of not being allowed to make the most of the opportunities created by Britain and Germany, unless it reciprocated them.[9] At that particular time, the vanguard of liberalism was still formed by a small group of people. The taking apart of the carefully assembled complex of import duties, legislation, premiums, and favours for Dutch products ran into opposition from well-entrenched interests. Liberal newspapers such as the *Algemeen Handelsblad* or the *Nieuwe Rotterdamsche Courant* served social circles which were as influential as they were small. The Rotterdam paper lost more than 13,000 guilders a year until 1855. It remained in business only by virtue of its dedicated shareholders, a group of merchants supporting free trade led by Huibert van Rijckevorsel, and nicknamed 'Amicitia liberals' after their elite city club.[10] In addition to these papers, a number of magazines, such as *De Gids*, *De Economist*, and the *Tijdschrift voor Nederlandsch-Indië*, worked hard to extol the blessings of liberalism over the perils of protection.

Gradually parliament and public opinion were won over, not so much for principled liberalism, as for the pragmatic view that the interests of a small country require the trade of goods and services to be free. By 1870 this argument had won the day. From time to time protectionist protests continued to be raised, invariably so when foreign suppliers looked set to win a substantial order, inspiring Dutch suppliers to stir nationalist sentiments in the hope of getting a second chance. In 1861, manfacturers founded the Nederlandsche Vereeniging van en voor Industriëlen, a lobby organization with the express purpose of keeping government commissions in the Netherlands whenever possible. Agitation in favour of protection could score only isolated successes, and failed to achieve fundamental adjustments to liberal policy.[11] The liberals' most important goals had been achieved by 1870. After two revisions, the customs tariff had been reduced to levies for purely fiscal purposes. Trade policy took free trade for its basic principle, working through most-favoured nations clauses.[12] Recasting colonial policy took considerably more effort, because of the complex of interests concerned, and because of the complicated legislation needed for a change of direction. The Culture System, moreover, had meanwhile been virtually dismantled, and private enterprise had gained free access to the Dutch East Indies.[13]

The famous term of 'laisser-faire' falls short as a hallmark for the liberal efforts, for the government did not restrict itself to clearing obstacles that hampered private enterprise. It also took initiatives to create facilities in the public interest. New legislation enshrined the Chambers of Commerce as independent representatives of local economic interests with the government.[14] The 1850 Post Act instigated a radical overhaul of postal services, including lower postage and the opening of post offices in every municipality. Immediately the number of letters sent rose sharply, inspiring further innovations: the introduction of post boxes and post cards, followed by further postage reductions culminating in the adoption of the uniform 5 cents tariff.[15] The 1852 Telegraph Act required the government to build a national telegraph network, two Railway Acts (1860/1863) did the same for building and running a national railway service.[16] In 1862 Parliament passed legislation providing the framework for the building of new and badly needed direct channels to the sea for both the Rotterdam and the Amsterdam ports.[17] The following year, the Bank Act 1863 was entered in the statute book, formally confirming the Nederlandsche Ban*k* as the national circulation bank with a bank note monopoly. Here, then, principled liberalism was defeated, though only after a heated debate on the merits of free competition for circulation banks.[18]

With these reforms, the current notions about publicity began to shift. During the first half of the 19th century, both government and private business as a rule kept economic information to themselves. Reports from the Chambers of Commerce, company statements and turnover data, even the interest rates at the Nederlandsche Bank were considered to be sensitive information, unsuitable for publication. Limited liability companies allowed their shareholders to consult handwritten balances and revenue statements at their headoffice prior to annual meetings, but outsiders were excluded, such information being none of their business. The Hollandsche IJzeren Spoorwegmaatschappij (HSM), the main railway company founded in 1837, pioneered a different attitude, submitting monthly traffic statements and an annual report to the press. It took more than ten years before other companies followed suit. In 1852, the Nederlandsche Bank's board, on the initiative of its energetic secretary W.C. Mees, decided to start publishing monthly balance statements. The Amsterdam Chamber of Commerce issued its first public report in the same year, as an appendix to the city's annual report. By and by the notion took root that, as a rule, such information should be public.[19]

In 1863, Parliament also passed an act to improve public secondary education, introducing new school types concentrating on modern European languages, commercial skills, and science.[20] The city councils of Amsterdam and Rotterdam used the powers assigned under the act to set up schools dedicated to train commercial skills. Despite continuous pleas for improved commercial education, this remained a matter of entirely practical training until the middle of the 19th century. After primary school, an aspiring merchant would join a

The 1850 Post Act brought a radical and urgently needed reorganisation of the Dutch postal services. One of the changes introduced shifted the paying of postage from receivers to senders, who paid for the conveyance of their letters in advance by the affixing of stamps. This 1851 manual explained how the new system worked.

firm as junior clerk, work his way up and nose around at some other firm at home or abroad, until he had learnt enough to become a manager, or to start his own firm. The *Nederlandsch Handels-Magazijn*, a commercial dictionary, published yet another extensive plea for better commercial education in 1843, including a design for such a school and a draft budget.[21] Three years later, the prominent Amsterdam medical doctor and social reformer Dr. Samuel Sarphati, started a private school for commercial education. Such institutes really extended the pupils' first training phase, from thirteen years to fifteen or sixteen, with selected economic subjects, after which the customary practical training with firms took its usual course. From the 1880s, office staff trade unions, such as Mercurius, started evening classes in foreign languages, book keeping, and, a little later, in shorthand and typing as well. The Amsterdam municipal school, by the way, was housed at Keizersgracht 123, known as Huis met de Hoofden because of the sculpted busts in its facade, and famous because it once had belonged to the arms magnate Louis de Geer.[22] In 1887 G.M. Boissevain, J.A. Hoogland Azn. and M. Mees set up a society, the Vereeniging Het Buitenland, with the purpose of stimulating young men to take up traineeships abroad. The society gave interest-free loans to candidates and helped them to find suitable firms, supporting about five young persons a year in this way.[23] Those who could afford to do so, arranged their sons' training themselves. The Rotterdam ship owner Willem Ruys sent his two sons to a Brussels boarding school. One of them went from there first to a German secondary school for commercial education in Lübeck, and then to traineeships with firms in London, Bordeaux, and Copenhagen. The other took practical training only, first with a London bank, moving from there to a Manchester firm to get to know the cotton trade.[24]

A view of Amsterdam's western port area, painted by C.C. Dommelshuizen in 1870. On the right the round Lutheran church on the Singelgracht. With the exception of the steam tug on the left, Dommelshuizen showed sailing vessels only, which were just then starting to lose out in the competition with steam shipping.

179

Higher education such as that provided by the German commercial colleges still remained a devout wish in the Netherlands, Barlaeus' pleas in the 1630s notwithstanding. The economist and banker N.G. Pierson, a self-taught teacher of economics at the Amsterdam commercial school, did not consider these colleges to be sufficiently useful, and he steered his nephew J.L. Pierson towards the customary practical training.[25] Plans for a national commercial college came and went, without anything happening. In 1905, the Amsterdam Vereeniging voor Voortgezet Handelsonderwijs, a society devoted to further commercial education, started dedicated classes to fill the gap. Eight years later Rotterdam finally opened a Handelshoogeschool or college for advanced commercial education, and in 1922 the Amsterdam university established a faculty for the commercial sciences. Prominent businessmen like Ernst Heldring supported this latter initiative, while retaining their conviction that trade had to be learnt in practice, and not by academic studies.[26]

MARKETS IN A MAELSTROM – The liberalization of international trade gave a powerful economic stimulus to the Netherlands. Having had to manoeuvre long and hard to shore up a crumbling market position, the country suddenly discovered its geographical position and hinterland as a prize asset. An era of prolonged economic growth began, the like of which had not been experienced for decades and more. Reversions like the crash of 1873, or the long depression during 1879-1895, did interrupt growth for a time, but each time the recovery started with growth rates achieving somewhat higher levels than before. Industrialization spread rapidly throughout manufacturing. The unlocking of markets made industrial production grow faster than trade or agriculture.[27] The eastern region of Twente experienced a rapid mechanization, the founding of large steam spinning and weaving mills, and the establishment of the Stork engineering company. Similar developments could be perceived in numerous economic sectors all over the country. In 1850 more than a quarter of the Dutch labour force worked in manufacturing, predominantly in small, almost craft-like firms. Sixty years later, this figure had gone up to more than a third. The number of people working in agriculture dropped correspondingly, from a third of the total to a quarter. Employment in trade, transport, and financial services remained more or less constant at nearly a fifth.[28]

From 1890 onwards, moreover, a strong growth manifested itself in medium-sized to large businesses, and a decline in small-scale production. Sometimes, the switch to large-scale mechanized production followed immediately on the lifting of restrictive legislation. It did so in the case of steam flour mills and steam breweries, where changes in the excise system finally opened up long dormant opportunities. Similarly, the production of electric light bulbs took off during the 1890s, following the abolition of patents.[29] A strong growth of demand both at home and abroad, however, provided the main driving force behind economic growth and industrialization, with demand itself driven by rising incomes, population growth, the disappearance of trade restrictions, better

Until about 1850, the textbooks used and the curriculum followed by adolescents set on a commercial career hardly differed from what used to be common during the 17th or 18th centuries. This 1802 textbook looked remarkably close in approach to the one shown on page 71. Fundamental changes only came with the 1863 Secondary Education Act.

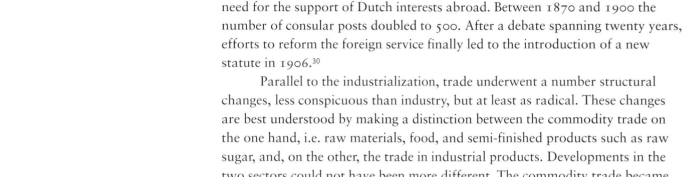

transport, and expanding markets. This expansion is well reflected by a growing need for the support of Dutch interests abroad. Between 1870 and 1900 the number of consular posts doubled to 500. After a debate spanning twenty years, efforts to reform the foreign service finally led to the introduction of a new statute in 1906.[30]

Parallel to the industrialization, trade underwent a number structural changes, less conspicuous than industry, but at least as radical. These changes are best understood by making a distinction between the commodity trade on the one hand, i.e. raw materials, food, and semi-finished products such as raw sugar, and, on the other, the trade in industrial products. Developments in the two sectors could not have been more different. The commodity trade became ever more polarized, as the improvement in transport and communications reinforced the trend, visible as early as the 1820s, towards a concentration of trade functions at the outer ends of the commercial chain. By contrast, the industrial products trade generated new links. Its volume and product range made it into an entirely new sector with marketing requirements entirely different from either the commodity trade or the trade in craft products before it.

Let us turn to the commodity trade first, where marked polarization became noticeable, making intermediate links redundant, or relegating them from independent operators to dependent agents. For more and more products, sorting and grading shifted from customers to shippers or producers, the telegraph connected sellers and buyers during transport, and favoured the emergence of futures markets to balance fluctuations in supply and demand. At the ports of destination, brokers or agents took delivery and handled the cargo, arranged transshipment, temporary storage, and forwarding. Breaking bulk and making markets was done at the final destination by inland wholesalers or provincial commission traders who would have purchased the goods from the importing merchant houses in the ports. This process of concentration presumably also led to further commercial specialization. Merchant houses used to keep a broad product range in addition to a particular speciality, say timber or linen. During the second half of the 19th century, firms in the commodity trade tended to concentrate more and more on one commodity, like grain or iron ore, timber or cotton.

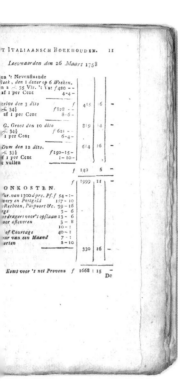

These tendencies did not manifest themselves in all sectors simultaneously. The margins of Liverpool cotton traders came under pressure around 1860, those of the London grain trade some twenty years later.[31] In 1879, the Rotterdam grain merchants, Gebr. Van Stolk & Co., ran a thriving consignment business, whereas eight years later the firm wrote to its agent on the Black Sea that this particular type of business had become outdated.[32] Chicago possessed a mature futures market for grain in 1865, Liverpool opened a clearing house for cotton transactions in 1876, and six years later the first European futures market for coffee started in Le Havre.[33] In some sectors, the intermediate links managed to hold on to their position, because they had the special skills required to determine the varieties and the quality of the products concerned, and to set prices accordingly. This applied to coffee and tobacco, which had a wide quality range depending on the plant variety, the producer, the weather, and harvest circumstances. Tobacco leaves from a single plantation sometimes received dozens of different trade grades.[34] The standardization of product descriptions sometimes did not take place until the 20th century.

In 1858, the Amsterdam merchant P.N. Muller predicted that, within a decade, agents would have replaced independent merchants in most trade sectors.[35] Three years later he wrote an article concentrating on the consequences of the telegraph and steam transport, noticing the shrinking margins, the disappearance of price differentials between distant markets, and the resulting relegation of formerly independent intermediaries to a dependent position. Shopkeepers had drawn level with merchants, he alleged, for the former could now order their goods from abroad as easily as the latter used to do. Capital had become a worthless privilege to merchants. Banks supplied any trader with what he needed, and the speed of transport reduced that need anyway. According to Muller, the commercial scope was now disappearing for true merchants, men running independent ventures for their own account as once on the entrepot market.[36]

Muller straddled the past and the present. He observed acutely how the increased speed of communications worked on the commercial chain, and also how the chain's management no longer depended on capital power, stock keeping, and stamina, but on product range, customer network, and speed of action. However, he extolled an idealized entrepot trade, run by wealthy merchants working for their own accounts, over and above commission trading as waged services. Like many of his contemporaries, Muller associated trading for own account with the daring and the business acumen which once had made the Republic a great commercial power. He consequently felt the switch to commission trading as a national decline. In 1875 he wondered why Dutch merchants appeared to cling anxiously to commission trading, except for speculations, which they did for own account, and often recklessly so.[37] Trading for own account stood for taking calculated risks with long-term speculations based on skill and experience, contrasting with commission trading as the timid shifting of someone else's goods without any risk involved, a simple shop. No matter that commission trading had established itself as the norm across the world for centuries or more, no matter that the Netherlands hardly offered any special advantages as a centre for the international wholesale trade for own account in bulk commodities, no matter that commission traders would have to take risks if they were not to lose their principals: Muller blamed the disappearance of the international wholesale trade on the commercial ineptitude of his time.[38]

With due respect for Muller's experience and knowledge, but he was off the mark on this point. It is hardly likely that the merchant houses clung to commission trading from submissive timidity, just as it had not been risk avoidance which had inspired the switch to commission trading during the last quarter of the 17th century. The supply of the commodities traded by the merchant houses in Europe was usually marked by a strong variation in quality and in quantity, so the value of shipments could be assessed only on arrival, months after their dispatch. Merchant houses trading for own account had to rely blindly on the shipper, whose skills and fidelity really determined their margins. For that very reason Van Hoboken had sent a trusted clerk to Batavia as early as 1821, to set up a firm with which he could embark on mutual trade and the exploitation of plantations. The concentration in the commodity trade, and more specifically the speeding up of communications from the 1850s and the standardization of product descriptions, did create the kind of close ties between suppliers and customers which allowed trading for own account, first of all in the Atlantic trade. However, during the third quarter of the 19th century, few Dutch merchant houses possessed sufficiently close ties abroad to take the risk, at least in the colonial trade. A joint-venture such as that between Van Hoboken and Ten Brink & Reijnst in Batavia was still an exception.[39] Probably the merchant houses took to commission trading in products which depended on specialist skills, as the polarization of the commodity trade progressed. And, in any case, the merchant houses did trade for their own accounts: no doubt sometimes for speculations, reckless or otherwise, in addition, however, for the undertaking of specific ventures in cooperation with trusted partners, and for shipments to try out particular markets or products. In the last two cases success meant finding correspondents for regular consignments in commission. Consequently, should trading for own account have been more successful than commission trading, the merchant houses would have noticed, and would definitely have used it more frequently. Circumstances changed only around the turn of the century, as will be explained in more detail below.[40]

Muller also overlooked the opportunities created by the revolution in communications and transport. Merchants did see them, and used them to create new intermediary positions. In the cotton trade, the telegraph and steam shipping made the detour via once almighty Liverpool redundant. At the end of the 1860s, Amsterdam merchants succeeded in establishing a cotton market of more than just regional significance. Despite vigorous support from the NHM, earlier efforts to do the same had foundered repeatedly because the circum-

The Chinese quarter in downtown Batavia, a photograph from 1872. Chinese traders were key links in commercial business in the Dutch East Indies, and already operated as such during the days of the VOC.

stances were not yet ripe.[41] Rotterdam coffee traders created a flourishing market in South American beans by underwriting a regular shipping link with Brazil, which a German shipping line began in 1893.[42] Around 1900, a similar attempt by Amsterdam merchant houses cooperating with Wm. H. Müller & Co. to set up a market in South African wool failed, however, because of strong competition from Antwerp and London.[43] By 1875 the Amsterdam cane sugar market had already disappeared, as the Java producers started to sell supply contracts in London for direct shipments to the buyers.[44] This made Van Eeghen & Co. switch to selling beet sugar from Germany and Belgium.[45] Futures markets offered another means to reinforce intermediary positions, since they enabled merchants to hedge price fluctuations for their customers. In the Netherlands, futures markets were created for coffee (1888), tin (1890), pepper (1892), cloves (1898), copra (1899) and sugar (1902).[46] Faster communications also allowed some merchants to increase their trade volume. In 1905, the Borneo-Sumatra Handelmaatschappij (Borsumij) reported a satisfying strong growth in its forest products trade, resulting from the recently opened option of selling by telegraph from the remote locations in the Dutch East Indies where the company operated. This had reduced the risk of price fluctuations, so Borsumij had been able to increase the sales volume.[47]

In other trade sectors, particular circumstances favoured the position of the wholesale trade. As soon as the river trade had been fully liberalized by the Treaty of Mannheim (1868), the Rotterdam transit trade profited from a strong growth in demand for bulk commodities such as grain and ore from the German hinterland, because the goods had to be transferred from ocean going vessels into Rhine barges. The grain trade to move back from Antwerp to Rotterdam, for river transport now became cheaper than the so-called 'Iron Rhine' rail

Borsumij used the attic of its the Hague headoffice for storing and showing some of its tropical imports, such as rattan, lying in bundles everywhere on the floor.

link through Belgium to Germany. German importers down the Rhine handled some of this business, with forwarding agents or cargo handlers to represent them in Rotterdam. However, local firms succeeded in attracting a substantial share by offering services which combined transshipment with grading and storing. The Amsterdam warehouse companies spotted this opportunity, and began to develop new facilities in the Rotterdam harbour, the Vriesseveem in 1871, the Blaauwhoedenveem a few years later.[48] Developments at Gebr. Van Stolk reflected the changes in the sector. In 1847 the firm started selling Dutch grain and imported flour. During the early 1860s Van Stolk abandoned the flour business to concentrate on grain supplies for German customers, building a network of correspondents in Southern Russia, the Danube basin, and the US. The firm established agencies and warehouses all along the river to support its business, keeping stocks as far away as Mannheim when supplies ran high.[49]

The fast growing trade in ores showed the same pattern, the establishment of wholesaling for own account based on transshipping and the transit trade. For a long time, by the way, this particular sector escaped the notice of contemporary observers, even those committed to trade. As late as 1877 the annual report issued by the Rotterdam Chamber of Commerce paid hardly any attention at all to the transit trade in ores, though it handled about 60,000 tons a year for the Krupp works in Essen alone.[50] Wm. H. Müller & Co., a leading company in this sector, covered the whole supply chain, from exploiting its own mines in South America to transporting and selling the products. The rise of South America as a supplier of ores, grain, guano, meat, and coffee, brought a revival of the trade relations with that continent, though Dutch exports remained too small to sustain an independent shipping line.[51] Both the ore trade and the grain trade used technical innovations in cargo transfer, such as electrical wharf cranes, grain elevators, and dedicated warehousing, to defend their position against competing German traders.[52] Coal shipments remained small until about 1890, but they took off with the setting up of the Steenkolen Handels-Vereeniging (SHV or Coal Trading Association, 1896), which obtained a monopoly on Dutch sales from a German producers' cartel, the Rheinisches-Westfälisches Kohlensyndikat.[53] An attempt at a similar monopoly for potash foundered, however, when agricultural purchase cooperations established an organization for the joint purchase of fertilizers, the Centraal Bureau (1900).[54] In yet another trade sector subject to strong German competition, timber, Dutch merchants equally succeeded in maintaining their position. In 1876 the Noordzeekanaal opened, giving Amsterdam easy access to the North Sea. The Houthandel v/h William Pont subsequently moved its premises from Edam to Zaandam, near the canal, now an ideal port for timber imports by virtue of its vastly improved access for bulk transport. Favoured by this infrastructure, the company began an impressive expansion. Pont bought timber production forests in Finland, Russia, and the Baltic, and set up an office in Duisburg to support German sales.[55]

THE EXPANDING MARKET FOR INDUSTRIAL PRODUCTS – The Rotterdam
hardware wholesaler, R.S. Stokvis & Zn., exemplifies the opportunities for new
intermediaries created by the trade in industrial products. The firm was founded
in 1841 as a shop retailing food and hardware. Three years later, the founder
Raphael Stokvis switched trades, to sell British hardware and stove ornaments.
By the mid-1860s the firm had an annual turnover of more than 500,000
guilders, rising to more than 1 million guilders in 1872, and to more than 2 million guilders eight years later. Initially, Stokvis imported its products from Germany, Belgium, France, and Britain. From that basis the company expanded to a
conglomerate, extending from the production of screws, bicycles, and various
kinds of equipment to distributive activities. As early as the 1860s, Stokvis
exported its products, selling them in far-away countries such as the Philippines
and Brazil.[56]

While Stokvis captured the market, a long-established rival, Joh. Frederik
Hoffmann & Zn., quit. The firm originated in the 18th century, a wholesaler in
ironware and glass with its own production up the Rhine and Meuse rivers.
During the early 1800s Hoffmann reached its zenith with assets of 750,000
guilders, with which the firm allegedly was the biggest of its kind in Europe.
During the first half of the 19th century, the partners started to encounter
adversity. They attempted several diversifications to keep going, but in vain: the
firm liquidated around 1880.[57] We do not know precisely why Stokvis succeeded where Hoffmann had to give up. Presumably the partners failed to find a
new business mix. Moreover, one of them, J.F. Hoffmann Jr., developed a taste
for public offices, which reduced the time he could spare for the business.

Stokvis traded a broad and varied product range which the company
itself imported, perhaps with a broker or agent for cargo handling, but certainly
without intermediation by merchant houses. This bypassing of independent
importers and wholesalers was adopted by others, too, also by intermediaries
further down the line. We have seen above how Sinkel did his own importing.

The Rotterdam firm of R.S. Stokvis &
Zn. developed from a retailer in stove
ornaments into a hardware
wholesaler with a huge product
range, partly produced by its own
plants. These photographs of the
company's showrooms, taken around
1900, demonstrate this range to
good effect.

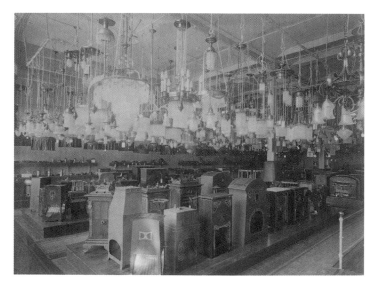

During the last quarter of the 19th century, department stores with a new marketing mix, such as the Bijenkorf, still in existence, arose to take over from pioneers like Anton Sinkel. This 1895 photograph depicts Arthur Isaac Goudsmit with his staff posing in front of his Bijenkorf shop on the Amsterdam Nieuwendijk shopping street.

His innovative retail empire brought him great wealth. His estate was worth 1.4 million guilders, shops included, in 1848. This put Sinkel on a par with the big Amsterdam merchants for wealth, but they would probably not have condescended to notice a shopkeeper like him.[58] Meanwhile B.J.J.F. Bahlmann, a former employee and compatriot of Sinkel, had copied his retail formula, building his own chain of ten shops starting out from the same Amsterdam street.[59] In 1866, A.J.G. Verster began a firm under the name of Perry & Co. on the Amsterdam Kalverstraat, really a franchise shop selling English articles ranging from steel pens to tea, chocolate, games, and overcoats. Verster bought these products from a British manufacturing and trading concern, which had already successfully introduced the formula in other European cities.[60] Sinkel, Bahlmann, and Verster heralded the dawn of retail chains and department stores, which began in the Netherlands during the last quarter of the 19th century. In 1876, the cooperative society 'Eigen Hulp' (Self Help) opened its first shop, expanding into a chain and adding its own wholesale business during the late 1880s. During this period, the grocers Simon de Wit and Albert Heijn started their first shops, and P. de Gruyter diversified from food production into retailing. Bazaars, department stores, and ready-made clothing chains appeared in the cities, replacing the pioneers Sinkel and Bahlmann.[61] After the agricultural crisis of the 1880s and 1890s, cooperative sale and purchase societies sprang into existence all over the countryside, which first cut out the retail trade and then moved into wholesaling by setting up the Centraal Bureau mentioned above.[62]

The example of Perry & Co. shows yet another aspect of the structural changes effected by the trade in industrial products, i.e. direct selling by manufacturers linked to the development of branded products marketed across countries, not just locally or in a particular region. Trade marks were common as early as the Middle Ages. Merchants used signs to identify goods as theirs in the hold of ships, or in warehouses. As often as not they used their stylized initials, or those of the firm. City authorities and guilds laid down the use of particular trade marks to certify the origin and quality of goods produced under their jurisdiction. This enabled them at the same time to eliminate unfair competition and to give the products a guaranteed identity on the market.[63] Fabrics were given a stamp or a lead seal, silver and gold objects carried a relief stamp indicating their fineness and their maker. In 1613, the Estates of the province of Holland passed a ban on the counterfeiting of such trade marks.[64]

Within the confines of small-scale craft production, trade marks mainly served as information for resellers, who often finished the goods. The producer's information never reached the consumer, it was replaced by the reseller's reputation. The roll of fabrics was cut off into lengths, or made into a coat, iron and glass parts assembled into a lamp, bags of coffee roasted and mixed to the desired blend, chests of tea weighed and repacked into small bags, cutlery sorted into elaborate sets.[65] Consequently, the value added to products by resellers, and the scope of their reputation, mattered most in consumer choice. Industrial production caused this moment to shift to producers or wholesalers, who took over

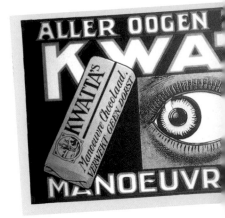

the finishing from the resellers, to supply ready packed and branded products for retail purposes. This shift turned trade marks into modern brands, designed to create an unchanging product identity along the whole trade chain from producer to consumer.

The first such modern brands originated in the 18th century, when manufacturers began to use their own labels. Between 1720 and 1732, two competing Amsterdam velvetmakers fought bitterly over the use of a particular label.[66] A yarn spinner from Den Bosch adopted a trade mark as well, probably in 1760, and had to put up with rival manufacturers grabbing a share in his success by imitating his brand.[67] The incorporation of the Netherlands into the French Empire introduced the protection of trade marks by law, for which they had to be filed with the local law court. Court clerks will hardly have noticed their new task. Until 1838, when a new commercial code became law, the Amsterdam court registered only two brands, one of them belonging to the inventor of powdered cocoa, C.J. van Houten.[68] The NHM registered various trade marks used by the company with the court in 1876.[69] The surviving records of merchant houses often contain many bound volumes with labels of the firms' brands, complete with the date of their registration. Dutch patent law may have been abolished by the liberalization, but the protection of trade marks had survived. A typically modern brand product was the Manoeuvrereep, the first pre-packed chocolate bar in the Netherlands sold under a brand name, produced by the Breda chocolate manufacturer Kwatta from about 1890.[70]

Theoretically, branded products posed a threat to the position of resellers, because their marketing scope allowed mass advertising, which made

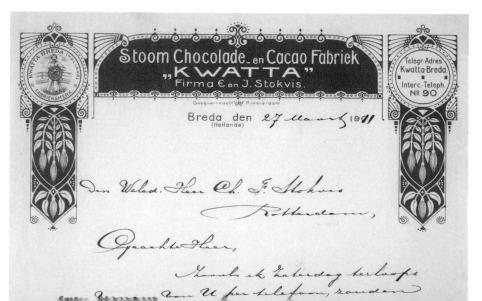

The Stokvis family became known for more than just wholesaling hardware. Two sons of one of the R.S. Stokvis partners bought the Breda chocolate factory Kwatta in 1893.

The Stokvis brothers pushed the
Kwatta factory into an impressive
expansion. For years and years,
Kwatta's Manoeuvre brand and its
slogan, depicted here, were
household words in the Netherlands.

the resellers' local or at most regional reputation largely redundant. However, resellers hardly suffered from this effect, at least until 1914. Both retailers and wholesalers maintained position, because the industrial revolution vastly increased the supply and the variety of products: various brands of tea, of soap, of margarine, different sorts of dyes, watches or glass products in varying qualities, sundry raw materials for new products such as margarine. Producers became dependent on the intermediate links in the chain for keeping this huge array well-organized for customers by sorting it into neat product ranges. In addition, manufacturers could establish a product identity by mass advertising, but for the time being they still had to rely on the resellers' ability to push products with individual retailers and customers. As industrial production developed and mass transport became ever cheaper, the geographical distance separating producers from consumers continued to increase. Without merchants knowing the ins and outs of local conditions, manufacturers simply could not sell their own products, least of all on distant and sprawling markets such as the Dutch East Indies. Finally, the market expanded more or less continuously until the First World War, so manufacturers gladly concentrated on producing and left the marketing to the existing intermediaries.

The marketing efforts of H.C. Heybroek Wzn. & Co. demonstrate to good effect how these factors combined to favour the continued existence of independent wholesalers. This firm, a forerunner of the Technische Unie which still exists today, was founded in 1880 as a wholesaler in lighting products: paraffin lamps, wicks, and Bohemian glass ornaments. Heybroek employed three travelling salesmen who toured the main cities in their respective districts every four months, accompanied by ten large boxes holding the new product range. They received their customers in hotels with special rooms to display their goods and, always on the road due to the not quite perfect means of transport, often built up close and jovial ties with their clientele there.[71] The manufacturers of products traded by Heybroek could never have afforded such exertions each for his own article. Heybroek's grouping of products into a range spread the marketing costs, thus bridging the distance between producers and their continuously extending market.

OUTPOSTS IN THE UNKNOWN – The structural changes in trade, then, did lead to shifting functions along the commercial chain and insurmountable difficulties for some firms, but did not result in the complete disappearance of independent resellers as predicted by Muller. On the contrary, the position of merchants appears to have become stronger. The merchant houses also succeeded in turning the new circumstances to their advantage, but only because of a more or less fortuitous factor, i.e. the Dutch colonial presence. They managed to get a hold on both the export of colonial commodities and on the export of consumer goods to the colonial possessions. It was really a niche function built on a geographical advantage founded in history, with an imaginative use of the opportunities created by the revolutionary technical advances during this era.

Rotterdam firms developed the African trade as a special feature. Curiously enough they showed little interest in Southern Africa, despite the old ethnic and language ties with the Boer population.[72] Van Rijckevorsel's trade with West Africa continued to expand, and this success inspired another Rotterdam firm, Kerdijk & Pincoffs, to start trading with the Congo. Having taken over

A European with a gun in his arms lying in a hammock carried by two Africans, with the one at the back clasping a liquor bottle, a late 19th century Congolese sculpture.

the interests of a British firm in the area, Kerdijk & Pincoffs set up two trading posts in 1857 and began selling a broad range of consumer products: fabrics, earthen ware, glass, hardware, arms, and liquor. A substantial part of the products was ordered from Britain. The firm exported palm oil and palm kernels, ground nuts, ivory, rubber, and some coffee. Apparently Kerdijk & Pincoffs succeeded in tapping a market which others had not been able to find. A French rival withdrew from the area in 1863, giving the firm further scope for expansion. In 1870 the turnover in African exports alone amounted to 1.5 million guilders. Nine years later the explorer Henry Morton Stanley confessed to having been impressed on a visit to the Congolese branches. He praised the comfortable housing, the abundant food, and the medical facilities for the local staff, concluding that 'The Dutch are, as usual, far ahead in the style, arrangement, and solidity of their structures'. Stanley's compliments were presumably not entirely disinterested, for Kerdijk & Pincoffs had sponsored his trip on the Congo river.[73] Another Rotterdam firm, Dunlop & Mees, attempted to set up trade with East Africa along similar lines as Kerdijk & Pincoffs, but it was much less successful.[74]

In their home town Rotterdam, Kerdijk & Pincoffs enjoyed great esteem. Supported by prominent businessmen such as the banker Marten Mees, Henry Kerdijk and Louis Pincoffs reorganized their firm first to a private limited partnership, and then in 1869 to a limited liability company, the Afrikaansche Handels-Vennootschap (AHV, African Trade Association) with a capital of 2.2 million guilders. Pincoffs possessed both great flair and energy. He maintained extensive political commitments: a seat in the Rotterdam city council and in the Provincial Estates, followed in 1872 by the membership of the First Chamber of Parliament, as the first Jewish Dutchman elected to the upper house. In addition, Pincoffs provided the main driving force behind a series of ground-breaking business initiatives: the Rotterdamsche Bank (1863), the Nederlandsch-Indische Gas Maatschappij (1863), the Holland-Amerikalijn (1871-1873) and finally the Rotterdamsche Handels-Vereeniging (RHV, 1873). The RHV was really a property developer designated to build and run harbour facilities and warehouses on the southern bank of the river Meuse, a project which Pincoffs had personally steered through the city council. Meanwhile the AHV had sunk into the mire. The company lost money, and to cover this up, Pincoffs trapped himself with financial manipulations and false accounting. In May 1879 he was caught out, but managed to escape to New York just in time. A financial panic ensued which brought several Rotterdam banks and companies into trouble. The press scoffed at the non-executive directors of the AHV, including Marten Mees, deeming them culpable for having neglected their supervisory duties. Alledgedly they had even helped Pincoffs to escape. Only the *Nieuwe Rotterdamsche Courant* kept a low profile on the case. The paper's readers, the elite 'Amicitia liberals', had not admitted Pincoffs to the club for his being a Jew, but they had otherwise supported him. Now these progressive businessmen and politicians looked pretty silly together. Moreover, the lawyer H.H. Tels, both the paper's editor and legal adviser to the AHV, had succeeded for half a day in delaying the public prosecutor from taking action against his client. As a consequence, he had to resign as dean of the Rotterdam law society. When the dust settled, the final damage turned out to be limited. After a reorganization, even the AHV was able to continue in business under a new name, the Nieuwe Afrikaansche Handels-Vennootschap (NAHV, New African Trade Association). Only the unfortunate Kerdijk, duped by Pincoffs as the non-executive directors had been, went to prison as a scapegoat.[75]

The reorganization of the AHV was led by H. Muller Szn., brother of the Amsterdam merchant and commentator P.N. Muller and, like him, an outspoken free trader. During the second half of the 19th century, Hendrik Muller became the most prominent businessman in Dutch trade with Africa. In 1850, he had gone into partnership with his Rotterdam brother in law Van Rijckevorsel, continuing the business under his own name from 1861. As before, his

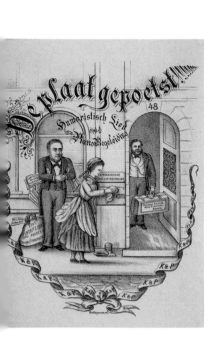

In 1879, the Pincoffs affair attracted huge public attention. One of the products was this song entitled 'Clearing out', about Pincoffs timely flight. On the left, Pincoffs in the office of the Afrikaansche Handels-Vereeniging, surrounded by papers concerning his business affairs and other social interests, and by a large bag of magic vanishing powder. On the right he steps out of the door, disguised and carrying a valise bearing an assumed name.

ships sailed to what is now known as Ghana, but they also regularly called at trading posts in Liberia. Muller's Liberian agent also acted as the Dutch consul-general there, while Muller became the Liberian consul-general in Rotterdam, such compound interests effectively pre-empting competition. And still the free trader Muller complained that his business went downhill because of insufficient support from the government.[76] When Dunlop & Mees was reorganized into the Handels-Compagnie Mozambique (HCM, 1875), Muller became chairman of the supervisory board. The HCM traded a range of products to East Africa, similar to what Hendrik Muller & Co. traded in Liberia and Ghana: arms, liquor, hardware, and fabrics, and as return cargo hides, ivory, oil seeds, and wax. Like its predecessor, the company never made much profit, and soon it had to be reorganized again into the Oost-Afrikaansche Compagnie (OAC, East African Company, 1883). A key consideration in keeping the business going was the expected demand for Mozambique oil nuts by the fast growing margarine industry. This demand never really materialized. Eventually the OAC transferred its interest to Liberia by taking over of Hendrik Muller & Co.[77]

Whenever the Rotterdam traders suffered setbacks in Africa, they were quick to stir the Dutch Foreign Office into dispatching a gunboat. Van Rijckevorsel had done so, the AHV and Muller followed his example. In 1879, the timely arrival of HMS Alkmaar commanded by lieutenant-colonel G. Doorman helped to limit the damage to the Congolese trading posts following Pincoffs' escape and the suspension of payments by the AHV.[78] Yet Muller failed in his attempts to goad the government into action over the partitioning of Africa by the European powers during the last quarter of the 19th century. The economic interests in Africa were considered too small, and moreover far outweighed by other foreign policy interests, such as Britain's attitude towards the Dutch East

The premises of Hendrik Muller & Co. in Elmina seen from the river, a photograph dating from about 1883. The African trade was the preserve of Rotterdam trading houses, led by Hendrik Muller.

Indies, or the aspirations of neighbouring Germany in Africa.[79] In 1872, the Dutch government at last handed the Ghanese fortresses over to Britain, despite Muller's vigorous campaign to prevent it from doing so. This sent Dutch trade with the region into decline, and Muller & Co. forcibly restricted itself to Liberia. By 1880 business there also went downhill, so Muller probably welcomed the appointment as general manager of the NAHV.[80]

Potential repercussions for the Dutch East Indies also inspired the Dutch government to remain passive on the 1884-1885 Berlin Conference, called to draft rules governing trade and shipping on the Congo and Niger rivers, and to provide a frame for the seizing of African territories. To all appearances, the Dutch delegation succeeded in achieving its aims, free trade for Dutch subjects, in other words the NAHV. A British-sponsored ban on importing arms and liquor, key articles for the company, was not accepted. However, in bilateral negotiations with Belgium, the Netherlands acknowledged the territorial claims of the Association Internationale du Congo. This organization pretended to have scientific and humanitarian aims, but it was in fact a cover for the neo-imperialist ambitions of the Belgian King Leopold III. Stanley acted as figurehead for the Association.[81]

The Berlin Conference gave Leopold a free hand. His Association began to carve out a colonial territory and to exploit its resources, mainly rubber and ivory. Joseph Conrad used the terrors inflicted by the exploiters on the African population for his novel *Heart of Darkness* (1899). He knew from first hand experience what he was writing about, for he had served on a Belgian ship in the Congo during the early 1890s. Perhaps it goes too far to accuse the NAHV of complicity to the atrocities, but the company did profit substantially from the

193

A few huts with a Dutch flag flying are all that indicate the Dutch trading post at Sinoë (now Greenville) in Liberia. A photograph dating from around 1870.

results. It was by far the biggest exporter in the region, with a trade turnover of about 12 million guilders in 1890, and 50 trading posts employing a staff of 200 Europeans plus 2,000 Congolese. From time to time, the punitive expeditions were undertaken to keep the indigenous population under the company's yoke.

The formal partitioning of Africa ended the NAHV's expansion. Diplomatic manoeuvring by the Belgian government pushed the company back step by step, while the Congolese colonial authorities began to interfere more and more with its day-to-day business. In 1890, the company probably helped to distribute a brochure which denounced the Congolese atrocities and called for a revision of the international conventions concerned, but that was to no avail for the time being. It was another fifteen years before an international protest movement succeeded in forcing the Belgian government to change its colonial management. Official support for the NAHV, by the way, had meanwhile virtually disappeared. The minister for Foreign Affairs W.H. de Beaufort considered defending the interests of a trader in arms and liquor not an attractive proposition. The company's board reacted to its worsening position in the Congo by transferring the trading activities to the surrounding Portuguese and French colonial territories. When France also began to raise obstacles, the NAHV changed tack and swapped its own settlements for participations in locally operating French companies. This worked, and the company resumed its business in Belgian Congo with similar participations. By 1910 the Rotterdam traders had rebuilt their presence to 30 trading posts and a small fleet of river boats. The company appears to have lost its momentum, however, for assets stagnated, and probably turnover as well.[82] Thus, in the long run, the trading houses found themselves slowly edged out of Africa because the Netherlands refused to build up a territorial presence there. Until about 1880, this factor was of no importance. Trade flourished, if and when necessary with the support of gunboats. The scramble for Africa by the European powers changed this. The merchant houses faced increasing restrictions on their business, and had to work hard to keep afloat.

THE TRAFFIC REVOLUTION AND THE COLONIAL TRADE – Circumstances in the Dutch East Indies were crucially different. Dutch rule expanded further and further over the archipelago, and did not really have to fear competition from other countries. The scrapping of the Cultivation System laid the production and exports of tropical commodities open to private enterprise. Simultaneously, the speeding up of transport and communications intensified the connections within the archipelago, and between the Dutch East Indies and the Netherlands. The carriage of passengers and mail was revolutionized by the opening of the so-called 'overland mail' by the British P&O Line in 1844: by steamer to Alexandria, then crossing the isthmus to Suez, from where a steamer would carry them on to India. It was a fast route, but expensive and uncomfortable. After completion of the railway between Alexandria and Suez, a trip from the Netherlands to Batavia took only fifty days.[83] Until 1869, freight had to sail around the Cape of Good Hope, the fastest sailing barks and clippers taking at least eighty days. A round trip could last eight to nine months, however, because of adverse weather or the sometimes long wait for return cargo. Sail ships were perfected by simplifying the rigging and by the introduction of new capstans around 1850. These innovations brought substantial labour savings. By 1875, ocean going vessels

STOOMVAART MAATSCHAPPIJ

ROTTERDAMSCHE LLOYD

KONINKLIJKE NEDERLANDSCHE POSTVAART

VEERTIENDAAGSCHE MAILDIENST
van ROTTERDAM naar JAVA via SOUTHAMPTON en MARSEILLE

HOOFDAGENTEN
RUYS & C°.

Rotterdam. Amsterdam. Antwerpen. Marseille.
JAVA AGENTEN: INTERNATIONALE CREDIET-EN HANDELSVEREENIGING. ROTTERDAM
BATAVIA. SAMARANG EN SOERABAJA

195

Within a decade of opening of the Suez canal, Amsterdam and Rotterdam steam shipping lines operated a fortnightly service to Batavia, a voyage now reduced to about 40 days. Eventually the two companies entered into an agreement establishing a weekly service. This publicity poster of the Rotterdam Lloyd dates from about 1890. In the Dutch East Indies, the merchant company Internatio acted as agents for the Lloyd.

had a crew of about 28 instead of the 50-60 hands which used to be the norm.[84]

A year after the opening of the Suez canal, the Stoomvaartmaatschappij 'Nederland' started a regular service with steam ships between Amsterdam and Batavia. In 1872, the Rotterdamsche Lloyd, managed by Wm. Ruys & Co., inaugurated services from Rotterdam. The canal cut travel times between the Netherlands and the Dutch East Indies to 40-45 days, from which cargo transport could now profit as well. New and direct connections from the two main harbours to the sea, the Nieuwe Waterweg for Rotterdam (1872) and the Noordzeekanaal for Amsterdam (1876), brought further reductions in travel time. Finally, the extension of the railway network offered passengers and mail the option of short cuts. For that purpose, the shipping lines made regular stops at ports with international railway connections. On 7 January 1880, the *Algemeen Handelsblad* reported as news the receipt of letters from Batavia dated 5 December 1879, so their conveyance had taken about a month.[85] Initially, the 'Nederland' line ran a monthly service to the Dutch East Indies, but the frequency was soon increased, during the late 1870s, to fortnightly. A few years later the company entered into an agreement with the Rotterdam Lloyd to run an alternating weekly service. This inspired the *Bataviaasch Handelsblad* to start a mail edition for the Netherlands, to keep the Dutch public informed about colonial business developments.[86]

The Suez canal, then, cut travel times, whereas steam shipping meant higher speed, more volume, and greater regularity of transport. Moreover, the introduction of the compound steam engine halved coal consumption and operational costs.[87] For the commodity trade, this transport revolution translated into lower freight rates, faster delivery, and shorter terms of payment. These factors intensified trade, for the range of goods suitable for long-distance trading increased sharply. By 1885 sail transport had finally become outdated.

Meanwhile, the telegraph had revolutionized communications. An expensive and slow cable had linked London to Singapore since 1865. Repeated attempts for an extension to Batavia failed, but despatches could be sent and received via a special Dutch telegraph service in Singapore. In 1870 a new and better cable between London and Singapore became available, and at the same time the long-awaited cable Batavia-Singapore. Reynst & Vinju in Batavia, successors to Ten Brink & Reijnst, immediately bought a code book for communications with Van Hoboken & Zn. in Rotterdam.[88] At that time, a 20-word telegram to the Netherlands cost over 70 guilders, more than three-and-a-half months' wages for an experienced hand in the cotton industry, and more than well-to-do Amsterdam citizens earned in a week.[89] It was, then, an expensive facility to begin with. The price of telegrams dropped steadily, however, and various coding skills were developed to ensure secrecy and to reduce the number of letters sent. Moreover, the merchant houses really had no choice in the matter. Telegrams offered an ideal way for the quick exchange of price fluctuations and other vital news with overseas branches, fast reactions on such information repaying the money spent on it. Competition simply forced them to use it. Consequently, the cable traffic between the Netherlands and the Dutch East Indies rose fast. In 1875, 13,000 telegrams were sent, or an average of over 35 per day. By 1900 the annual total had climbed to 100,000, more than 270 a day.[90]

In addition to intensifying traffic between the Netherlands and the Dutch East Indies, the transport revolution also helped to bind the islands in the Indonesian archipelago closer together. From the 1850s, steam shipping services started to spread, partly run by the Nederlandsch-Indische Stoomvaart Maatschappij (NISM), partly run by shipping lines established in Singapore and Penang. In 1891, the Koninklijke Paketvaart Maatschappij (KPM), a joint venture set up by the Dutch lines 'Nederland' and the Lloyd, took over the NISM's services. The KPM built a transport network which in the end covered the whole archipelago. The company's expansion was part and parcel of the twin extension of Dutch power and the economic penetration by Dutch business in the so-called Outer Provinces, the islands surrounding Java.[91] The colonial government asserted its power over the islands by treaties with local princes, but more specifically with a number of brutal military campaigns, among them the atrocious Atjeh War which lasted thirty years in all.[92] Private enterprise started the economic exploitation in tandem, aided by various arrangments and regulations

During the second half of the 19th century, the Netherlands gradually expanded its authority over the Indonesian archipelago. This sometimes resulted in long and bitter military campaigns, such as in Atjeh. In 1882 Jozef Israëls painted the departure of colonial troops from Amsterdam.

Around 1870 large-scale production of tobacco began on Sumatra. This picture, taken about 1890, shows Chinese coollies cutting tobacco on the Bekioen plantation in eastern Sumatra. The expertise needed for the tobacco trade enabled trading houses such as Van Eeghen & Co. to assume a wholesaling function distributing tobacco in Europe.

which created a luxurious climate for businessmen and employers. In 1856 a Rotterdam merchant house opened a branch in Padang on Sumatra, the next year another one followed.[93] The Nederlandsche Handel-Maatschappij and the Javasche Bank established their first agencies outside of Java.[94] Between 1870 and 1900, the Deli-Maatschappij and the Tabaksmaatschappij 'Arendsburg' developed large-scale tobacco plantations on the east coast of Sumatra, coal mines started production on Sumatra and on Borneo, the Billiton Maatschappij finally succeeded in overcoming the obstacles which had dogged the production of Billiton tin for years, three oil companies did the first surveys for oil on Java, Sumatra, and Borneo. The islands were tied closer together administratively and economically with each other, and especially with Java. Consequently, Batavia finally came to fulfill the functions of a capital which until then the city had only nominally possessed.[95]

By the early 20th century, the process of territorial consolidation had been completed. The Outer Provinces now supplied a third of the exports, against barely a quarter in 1880.[96] Exports from the Dutch East Indies rose from 170 million guilders in 1870 to 670 million guilders in 1914. The sharpest rise occurred after 1904, a consequence of the very strong economic growth which the country experienced during that period. Until 1880 the lion's share of exports went to the Netherlands, which in its turn supplied most of the imports. The two countries then started to drift apart. The value of mutual trade kept rising, but the respective market shares declined. In 1910, the Dutch East Indies drew only a third of its imports from the Netherlands, equal to 4% of Dutch exports. Conversely, about 4% of Dutch imports came from the Dutch East Indies, or about a quarter of colonial exports. This relative erosion of the mutual interests was a direct consequence of trade and transport opening up the Dutch East Indies, and the diversification of the two countries' economic relations with the growth of world trade. In addition, the Dutch East Indies broadened its range of export products. Oil, copra, and rubber provided a third of exports by value in 1914. Only a small amount of those products went to the Netherlands. Oil and rubber were sold on the world market by multinationals. The presence of an important margarine industry in the Netherlands meant that the country imported substantial quantities of copra, which together with tobacco, coffee, and tin, represented 75% of imports from the Dutch East Indies. Tea, quinine, and some kapok, made up the remainder, compared to which spices, once of such importance, hardly mattered. Dutch purchases of the traditional plantation commodities also declined. Around 1900 over 70% of the East Indian coffee went to the Netherlands, but this share had declined to less than 50% by 1910, and it continued to lose ground against the competition from South American coffee.

As mutual trade declined, the financial ties intensified. In 1900, Dutch investors had invested an estimated 1 billion guilders in the Dutch East Indies, more than 12% of the Netherlands' total financial assets. On the eve of the First World War, investments had doubled, and their share in the assets had risen to 14%. The portfolio consisted predominantly of shares in plantations (45%),

and mines (20%), with the rest spread over trade and industry, mainly the former. Dutch capital provided by far the biggest share of colonial foreign investment, with over 70% of the total.[97] Dutch investors financed the advance of private enterprise after the demise of the Cultivation System, and more in particular the powerful growth after 1900. In 1880 the Amsterdam stock exchange quoted no securities issued by colonial companies, except for the NHM and the Nederlandsch-Indische Handelsbank, a colonial bank with a Dutch headoffice. Twenty years later, the official list showed about 95 companies, among them trading firms such as the Handels-Vereeniging Amsterdam (HVA) and the Internationale Crediet- en Handelsvereeniging 'Rotterdam', plantations like the Delimaatschappij and the Tabak-Maatschappij Arendsburg, mining companies, and a string of railway and tramway companies.[98] Between 1904 and 1914, colonial companies floated shares and bonds for a total of 275 million guilders on the Amsterdam market, not counting the issues floated by *Royal Dutch Shell*. This amount represented a quarter of total company issues, and it outstripped the capital demand from Dutch industry, trade, or transport taken separately.[99]

THE FRUITS OF MODERN IMPERIALISM – Dismantling the Cultivation System really meant executing four economic reforms, i.e.:

› Abolishing the forced cultivation of tropical products by the indigenous population on behalf of the colonial government;
› Replacing the consignment of tropical products to the Netherlands by open sales on Java;

The Netherlands lost its voluminous trade in cane sugar when European farmers began to cultivate sugar beet, which coincided with Asian producers starting to use the telegraph for selling delivery contracts for sugar in transit. Meanwhile, sugar production concentrated in the cultivation areas. This 1872 picture shows a sugarfactory on Java.

› Abolishing the differentiated customs tariffs which favoured Dutch trade;
› Establishing a legal framework for the ownership and lease of property.

In 1857, the colonial government initiated the liberalization of trade and transport by starting to sell its sugar in Batavia. By 1875 the process had been more or less completed. Forced cultivation continued in the case of coffee, but the production and sales of other products had become free. The customs tariff no longer discriminated in favour of Dutch trade. Property ownership and lease holds had been given a legal basis. Europeans were excluded from owning land, but they could take up long leases with sufficient legal security for business purposes such as investment and mortgages. Finally the financial relationship between the Netherlands and the Dutch East Indies underwent a crucial change with the 1854 Currency Act, which introduced the guilder as the colony's currency. Until then, the Batavia exchange rates on Amsterdam fluctuated so strongly, that the exchange risk on remittances discouraged private firms from increasing their business volume.[100]

The chief consequence of these reforms was the splitting of a cumbersome government organization for producing, selling, shipping, and financing of tropical products into separate, market-oriented businesses, and in addition, the laying down of conditions for transferring them to the private sector. Indignation about the excessive misery which the Cultivation System had imposed on the indigenous population certainly did provide an important motive for its abolition, an indignation voiced in scathing terms by the liberal press, and immortalized by Multatuli's novel *Max Havelaar* (1860). However, the policy changes drew their inspiration in at least equal measure from the glaring inefficiency and unproductivity of government-run affairs, which left insufficient scope for key economic principles such as competition, cost control, product improvement, market functions, and profit maximization, terms which the liberal regime held closer to its bosom than any other, including nationalist feelings. In 1863 the colonial government granted the exclusive licence to run regular steam shipping services in the archipelago not to a Dutch company, but to a British one, whose bid was cheaper by 1 cent per nautical mile, for a difference of over 400 guilders a year.[101] At the very same time, the NHM organized two auctions a year for coffee selling parcels holding tens of thousands of bales each. These parcels contained beans of the same variety, but of vastly different quality. The auction samples usually represented the lowest quality in the parcel, but prospective buyers were in no position to gauge the parcels' overall quality, turning the bidding into a gamble.[102] No surprise that such inefficiency raised protests.

Deprived as it was of the general management of the colonial government's commodity business, including the incumbent privileges and obligations, the NHM embarked on a radical new course. The board introduced commercial conditions to handling calico shipments from the Netherlands. As a result the company lost all its manufacturing customers to private merchant houses, for these firms succeeded in selling the goods 10-13% higher than the NHM managed to do. From necessity, the board restricted its cotton trade to selling quality fabrics which could command a higher price under the NHM brand. This was not a very big market. By 1870, the company's turnover amounted to only

The Regent of Lebak, Z.H. Radèn adipati Karta Natta Negara, a colour lithograph by C.W.M. van der Velde from the book *Gezigten uit Nederlands Indië*. In 1856, the author Multatuli (Eduard Douwes Dekker) briefly functioned as a government official in Lebak, a poverty stricken area in the Bantam province of Java. The social circumstances there provided the inspiration for his epochal novel *Max Havelaar*.

199

about 1.5 million guilders a year, with a trend towards steady decline.[103] At the same time the Factorij in Batavia had to start competing to obtain the sugar, coffee, and spices which used to fall into its lap. This turnaround took considerable efforts. The company had not been used to looking for suppliers and customers, after all these had presented themselves, and they had accepted the conditions proposed. To obtain a regular supply of products, the Factorij expanded its credit facilities to planters again. Within a short span of time, it had once more frozen several millions of guilders in this way. Despite initial successes, the company did not succeed, either in achieving satisfactory returns, nor in sustaining open competition. Its commodity trade shrank continuously, though by 1900 sales were still as high as 50 million guilders a year, representing 20% of exports from the Dutch East Indies.[104] Finally, the NHM decided to switch to commercial banking. In 1874, the statutes were amended to allow trading in bills, and new amendments ten years later extended the company's business to full banking services. This arduous process of reforming the NHM into a market oriented company with a new mission was, by the way, masterminded by Hendrik Muller, a representative for the Rotterdam shareholders on the non-executive board since 1868.[105]

The liberalization of the colonial trade at last offered the merchant houses the commercial scope for which they had long been waiting. During the third quarter of the 19th century, one firm after another focused on the Dutch East Indies. Some authors lazily blame a shortage of keen and successful businessmen in Dutch trade for this late conversion.[106] We have noticed in some detail above, that this view is inconsistent with the facts. The merchant houses definitely proved themselves keen for trade, but until about 1850 the NHM had denied them sufficient breeding ground in the colonial trade. Van Eeghen & Co. developed into a merchant house in the 17th century mould as soon as trade opened up, i.e. a firm with a broad product range, extensive and varied services, and a commercial network spanning far and wide. The financial services which had kept Van Eeghen going during the first half of the 19th century did remain important. The firm traded in bills and in securities, and participated in syndicates to float securities when suitable opportunities arose. In addition, the partners embarked anew on a large scale commodity trade supported by their own shipping. The firm wanted to attract product consignments by offering low freight rates, so the shipping was hardly profitable in itself. Van Eeghen & Co. sold its last ship as late as 1887, when sail had finally lost the competition with steam.[107] The commodity trade involved exports of cotton fabrics to the Dutch East Indies, and imports of nearly all colonial commodities, with coffee and tobacco as core products. For the latter product, the firm organized large auctions in the Frascati building on the Amsterdam Nes street, the centre of the Dutch tobacco trade.[108] The partners used commercial techniques to suit circumstances: commission or consignation transactions, trading for own account or in joint account with trusted partners, sometimes simply passing orders from others on to business connections. Van Eeghen & Co. did not aim for exclusive relationships, trading all its products with a group of suppliers and customers.

During the 1880s, the Nederlandsche Handel-Maatschappij began transforming itself from a trading company into a commercial bank. Its President Balthasar Heldring masterminded this change of strategy.

In 1850, Jan van Eeghen moved house to Herengracht 462, taking the firm of Van Eeghen & Co. with him. This drawing by Christiaan Andriessen depicts the partners' office in 1806, when the house was occupied by the firm of Pizzagalli.

200

The firm also arranged finance and insurance for transactions. Consignation advances automatically led to supplying capital to cotton manufacturers in the Twente region, and to plantation owners in the Dutch East Indies. As Van Eeghen's commercial renaissance progressed, the number of staff rose. In 1850, the firm moved with its senior partner Jan van Eeghen to the Herengracht No. 462. This stately canal-side house had a separate entrance for the lower ground floor. Office staff and visitors descended a few steps to enter a passage ending in a staircase at the back of the house. The stairs led to a waiting room with a counter. The room behind the counter housed seven clerks, seated on high stools at sloped writing desks. A screen in the corner hid the privy. The firm's partners had a room overlooking the canal. A narrow passage linked it to both the clerks' office, and to a third room for meetings and for exhibiting samples.[109]

Van Eeghen & Co. was not the only merchant house which experienced a striking revival, though it did remain an exception with the dynamic approach commissioning its own ships. Rival Amsterdam firms such as Van Heekeren & Co. and H.G.Th. Crone also established a successful colonial trade which, however, never matched Van Eeghen's for size. Since the 1830s, Crone imported hides, tobacco, and spices from the Dutch East Indies, exporting a variety of goods. Like van Eeghen, the firm maintained commercial relations with a group of correspondents, without exclusivity either side. The liberalization of the colonial trade first of all pushed up its exports to the Dutch East Indies, and subsequently its imports of colonial commodities, too. Even so, until the late 1880s the two partners could handle all business with a staff of two or three, accomodated in a single room with a high writing desk made for four persons, which the firm's founder had bought in 1805.[110] Van Heekeren acquired prominence in the creation of the Amsterdam cinchona market.[111]

Curiously enough, Rotterdam houses were less successful in keeping pace with developments. Like his brother-in-law Van Rijckevorsel, Hendrik Muller had traded with the Dutch East Indies in addition to his West African trade. This business never became very substantial, despite the free reins given to private enterprise. From 1884 Muller's firm predominantly operated at a loss.[112] Van Hoboken & Zn. embarked on a course opposite to that of Van Eeghen & Co. After Van Hoboken's death in 1850, his sons switched from shipping and commodity trading to finance, apparently because they spotted better opportunities there. The firm abandoned its European trade and cut back its fleet, building up extensive commercial relations with colonial plantations instead. In 1850, Van Hoboken signed a contract with the concessionaires for the exploitation of tin on the island of Billiton, granting them a credit of 500,000 guilders in return for product consignments. Exploring the prospective mining sites and getting production started required large amounts of money and ever increasing patience. At the founding of the Billiton Maatschappij in 1860, the new company owed 600,000 guilders to Van Hoboken. Having expanded shipping again for a time, the partners decided to wind up these activities when steam shipping appeared to win the day. On the 1st January 1876 the firm changed its name to Van Hoboken & Co., with new articles of association listing its mission as

Dutch East Indian trading companies often employed Chinese cashiers. The picture shows the cashier of Internatio's Surabaya office, Ang van Liong, behind his desk. It was taken in 1894, ostensibly in celebration of Liong's silver jubilee with the firm. On the right foreground a chest of one of Internatio's key principals, the cotton producer Koninklijke Stoomblekerij Nijverdal. The publicity poster of another key principal, the Rotterdam Lloyd, hangs on the wall, left (see p. 195).

banking, providing advances on colonial commodities, importing commodities, and private capital management.[113]

The opening of the Dutch East Indies to private enterprise also stimulated initiatives for new ventures aiming at large volume colonial trade. In 1863, a group of Rotterdam businessmen supported by Twente calico producers founded the Internationale Crediet- en Handelsvereeniging 'Rotterdam', Internatio for short, a limited-liability company with a paid-up capital of 1.5 million guilders. Internatio was intended as a general commission trader with the Dutch East Indies, specializing in calicoes. To direct the overseas operations, a Semarang firm was taken over and reorganized as head office for the colony, after which subsidiary offices in Batavia and Surabaya followed. Building a basis for a new

Offices on the main street in Batavia's business district, the Kali Besar, about 1870. The consulate of the German city of Bremen, at that moment in time still a 'Free Hanseatic City', stands in the middle.

business by taking over existing firms was a common approach. In 1879, Amsterdam businessmen set up the Handels-Vereeniging Amsterdam (HVA), with a paid-up capital of 1.2 million guilders. The HVA also focused on the colonial trade, and the company really operated as an extension of three firms, to wit H. Reineke (Amsterdam), Van Beek, Reineke & Co. (Batavia), and Wille, Gans & Co. (Surabaya). Among the company's other main shareholders were the gin distillers Blankenheym & Nolet and the engineering company Stork.[114] The opening of the Dutch East Indies of course also gave a powerful push to firms already established there. Within a short period of time, they developed from more or less passive importers handling consignments from European firms to independent importers placing orders elsewhere. A description from 1862 gives a good impression of office circumstances at these firms. The merchant houses in Batavia all had their offices on the so-called Kali Bezaar. Office hours were from nine o'clock until four. The *mandoer* or headman over the indigenous staff would arrive first and open up the office, with the regular porters sitting in a row along one of the outer wall, waiting for instructions. Then usually the Chinese cashier climbed behind his desk next to the entrance, after which the European staff entered one after another. Towards 9.30 the manager and the chief clerk would turn up.[115]

Internatio traded between the Netherlands and the Dutch East Indies in both directions, and for its own account and in commission for others. From an early stage in its existence, the company also undertook business with India, China, and Japan, and in 1878 it began to act as an agent for the Rotterdam Lloyd in the Dutch East Indies. Such agencies for other companies were a regular feature for overseas merchant houses. Lindeteves in Semarang was the main agent for the Nationale Levensverzekering Bank, a life insurance company, and the Trading Company Late Hegt & Co., operating in Burma from 1898, acted as agent for several Dutch steam shipping lines. In Medan, Güntzel & Schumacher acted for two German shipping lines plus a string of other companies, such as oil companies and fertilizer manufacturers. Borsumij had an agency for the insurance company 'De Nederlanden'. These insurance agencies sold fire and life assurance policies of course, but also so-called 'fidelity bonds', policies serving to guarantee a cashier's fidelity.[116]

Quite soon after Internatio's inception, a problem typical for the Dutch East Indies threatened to ensnare its business, i.e. advances to plantations. Planters could not get the required long leases or the labour needed without paying the indigenous population in advance, sometimes for up to five years.[117] Moreover, considerable time elapsed from the first planting until commercial crops became available, eighteen months with sugar, for instance. These bottlenecks were passed down the commercial chain. Planters would demand long-term credit facilities from the exporters of their products. Crone operated with consignment contracts which gave the producers three years to repay the credit given.[118] Thus the advances were really fixed capital for the plantations concerned. Consequently, bad harvests or other mishaps inaugurated a vicious circle which tied the creditor closer and closer to his debtors. All merchant houses

The plantation Maryland in east Sumatra, about 1885.

active in the Dutch East Indies had this same problem: without credit, no product exports. Internatio's board failed to exert sufficient control over its general manager on Java on the point of plantation advances, and because the agent also proved to have private business interests in the plantations at stake, the board dismissed him in 1866. Following these entanglements, Internatio went through a few difficult years around 1870. The nominal value of the shares was halved to compensated the losses sustained. From time to time the board went against its convictions and used accommodation paper as stop-gap credit, up to as much as 500,000 guilders. After 1872 the worst had passed, enabling Internatio to attract fresh capital. At the same time its plantation advances rose again, however.[119]

There were hardly any alternatives, really, considering the rudimentary state of the colonial banking system. The Javasche Bank operated as the circulation bank and main supplier of credit since 1827. Public orphanage foundations invested their surplus funds in secure long-term loans, and the Oost-Indische Maatschappij van Administratie en Lijfrente, a life insurance company founded in 1842 and operating in effect as a bank to plantations, supplied some loans to planters, too. The Nederlandsch-Indische Escompto Maatschappij came to reinforce this thin cast in 1857, to little avail. Confronted with a lack of regular facilities, planters and merchant houses took to drawing on their Dutch connections for money by issuing so-called 'pig on pork' bills, the name referring to the bills' role in creating credit between two departments of the same institution without an underlying commodity transaction to show for it. The NHM Factorij and the Javasche Bank gave the example for this practice. Now the demise of the Cultivation System cut the colonial government's advances to producers, and at the same time attracted a rush of new entrepreneurs seeking credit. The

204

In 1863, the Nederlandsch-Indische Handelsbank was set up with the specific purpose of remedying the rudimentary state of banking in the Dutch East Indies. The bank had its head office in Amsterdam, but the main operations were in Asia. The picture shows the Semarang branch in 1925.

shortage of available capital became acute. In 1862, a severe crisis broke out which paralysed the economy, emphasizing the need for new banks.[120]

Initiatives to meet that need already materialized the following year. The Chartered Bank of India, Australia & China opened a branch in Batavia. In the Netherlands, two new banks were founded, in addition to Internatio, with the specific purpose of financing colonial business: the Nederlandsch-Indische Handelsbank (NIHB) and the Rotterdamsche Bank. Both were meant as colonial banks, with head offices in Amsterdam and Rotterdam respectively for the general business management and the required links to the money market, and actual operations run by branches in the Dutch East Indies. The NIHB made a success of this concept and built a flourishing colonial business, the Rotterdamsche Bank, however, retreated in 1872 after repeated losses, to concentrate on banking in its home city.

The new banks did not solve the credit problem, quite the contrary. They did not develop the sort of long-term credit facilities required by the planters, but restricted themselves to commercial credit and bill transactions, thus really helping to increase the use of problematic credit facilities like the 'pig on pork' bills. The Dutch business world, comforted by more regular circumstances, did not want to have anything to do with such practices. And true enough, sometimes they smelt of fraud. As was the case with Bauermann & Co., an exporter on Celebes and a pioneer in the copra trade. Bad harvests hit the firm in 1878, and it liquidated. The owners continued their business under a different name, creating a famous scandal in 1884, by attempting a swindle on the Javasche Bank.[121]

That same year, the so-called Sugar Crisis broke out with such violence, that the Dutch business world felt its shocks. For some time, structural difficulties had undermined the base of the colonial economy. The two key products,

Crop disease was a constant threat for the colonial plantations. During the 1880s the two main crops, coffee and sugar, both suffered from severe outbreaks of disease, which helped to spark a prolonged economic crisis. Subsequently such outbreaks returned from time to time. Two researchers muster diseased sugar cane on the Gladah department of the Soekowide sugar factory, photographed in 1925.

coffee and sugar, suffered from the erosion of European prices caused by rising sales of beet sugar and Brazilian coffee. Planters of both crops in the Dutch East Indies also struggled with serious disease outbreaks. Sugar prices dropped, causing a liquidity crisis at the Nederlandsch-Indische Handelsbank and at the Koloniale Bank, as outstanding crop advances and credit paper could not be repaid. When the worst appeared to have passed, the greatly respected Semarang firm of Dorrepaal & Co. suspended payments. Dorrepaal, a merchant house by name, was really a bank which accepted deposits and had used them to build up very extensive plantation interests: in no fewer than 22 sugar refineries, 38 coffee plantations, and 53 other plantations. The whole conglomerate had been kept going by juggling bills, which had ended when the Nederlandsch-Indische Handelsbank and the Koloniale Bank ran aground. The firm's enormous size comes out to best effect by looking at the first reorganization plan drafted by Amsterdam merchants and bankers. A new company, the NV Dorrepaalsche Bank der Vorstenlanden, would continue the business, reinforced by 6 million guilders of fresh capital plus a bond loan of 7 million guilders, for a total of 13 million guilders. At that moment in time De Nederlandsche Bank, the national bank and the country' biggest, had capital and reserves of just over 20 million guilders.[122]

The Sugar Crisis failed to end the crop advances and accommodation paper, but it did lead to colonial firms subsequently being reorganized into limited liability companies in an early stage of their development, usually through the services of Amsterdam merchants and bankers. Merchant houses such as Crone, Van Eeghen, and Van Heekeren took the lead in this new field. As often as not, they knew the firms concerned from their commodity trade, and they possessed the connections in the Dutch East Indies required to take a look on the spot and arrange details. The firms knew the colonial trade inside out, and thus could assess the merits of plantations. Finally, they had the capital power and the money market connections to ensure a smooth sale of shares or bonds. Their intermediation usually resulted in the colonial company's seat being established in the Netherlands, usually in Amsterdam or in The Hague. This latter city had among its population a large group of repatriated civil servants and businessmen, a rock solid group of investors in colonial enterprises by virtue of their background and disposable funds. As often as not, the partners of the issuing merchant houses managed the company, appointing an agent to run the business on the ground.

Presumably these organizational changes in the production of colonial commodities engendered a switch from commission business to trading for own account. For the receivers in Europe could now rely on the required close cooperation with an agent in the Dutch East Indies, while exchanging telegrams reduced the scope for surprises. The reorganization brought the merchant houses into a pivotal position, too, within the whole of colonial production, trade, and finance. As a consequence, their partners came to occupy other prominent functions in the business world. S.P. van Eeghen collected by far the most non-executive directorships of all. 'Mr. S.P.' had a seat or the chair on the non-execu-

206

J. Zilver Rupe and A.E.F. Muntz return to Internatio's Surabaya office in the company carriage with the driver Djipo and the headman Sartiman. Photograph dated 25 April 1902.

tive boards of all important banks, shipping companies, and plantation companies, the result of his business acumen, but definitely also of the far-flung business interests of his firm.[123] Still, Van Eeghen & Co. remained a merchant house first of all. That is to say, it did not turn itself into a holding company for colonial companies, industrial concerns, or transport companies. The partners kept the commodity trade as their core business, in contrast to comparable British colonial merchant houses such as Butterfield & Swire, or Matheson & Co.. These firms transformed themselves, sometimes as early as the last quarter of the 19th century, into investment companies managing very varied interests in mines, shipping, manufacturing, and colonial plantations.[124]

During the late 1880s, Internatio had 3 million guilders of frozen loans to planters on total assets of 15 million guilders on account of the Sugar Crisis. The board succeeded in gradually reducing these obligations to acceptable proportions, but even so it took about twenty years, until 1905, before the company had finally digested the full consequences of the blow. Internatio subsequently held only small shares in colonial ventures, not all of them safe in every respect: one investment concerned a sugar plantation regularly visited by tigers.[125] Meanwhile the company grew into the biggest Dutch colonial trading concern, with branches in Batavia, Semarang, Surabaya, Cheribon, Telok Betong, and Singapore, in addition to booking offices for the Rotterdam Lloyd in Weltevreden and in Tandjong Priok. Exports to Asia remained a core activity, with a turnover of 24 million guilders in 1914. Cotton fabrics were still the main product, traded in commission for Twente calico producers as before. Having its own branches in the Dutch East Indies enabled Internatio to run a fairly voluminous trade for its own account from the start. Shortly after 1900, the board began to expand this particular activity, taking over a Singapore firm to push sales there. Exports of colonial commodities lagged far behind the imports. Internatio shipped produce worth only 7.5 million guilders to Europe in 1914.[126]

A company like Internatio, with branches extended over a wide area, depended for its survival on a tightly organized coordination. The general manager in the Dutch East Indies held together the various offices there by regular visits. In addition, the company's agents held a general meeting once a year to discuss the business. Internatio also widely used telegrams to exchange business data and instructions. This failed to prevent headoffice and agents from getting entangled in lengthy disagreements, as happened during the years 1876-1890. At that stage the Rotterdam board did not visit the Dutch East Indies for personal inspections. Of course, from time to time agents travelled to Europe on holiday, but it was 1914 before the first Internatio manager went to the Asian offices.[127] Until then, written admonitions had to make do with Internatio. In 1910, on getting wind of the Batavia agent's undiplomatic reply to complaints from the Rotterdam Lloyd about services provided, the Rotterdam board rebuked him for his high-handed conduct, and reminded him somewhat pedantically of the need to conduct correspondence in measured tones, since replies took two months to arrive. Write calmly, be modest but firm at the same time, never show irritation, least of all sarcasm, the board instructed.[128]

At the Borneo-Sumatra Maatschappij or Borsumij, the board kept in closer touch with its branches. This company was set up in 1894 as the successor to the private limited company J.W. Schlimmer & Co., which had taken over the NHM's trading activities on the island of Borneo in 1883. The Schlimmer family continued to hold a large share and predominant influence in the new company. Van Heek & Co., a Twente calico producer, also had a parcel of shares. It was a general colonial import and export business, supported by a small fleet of river boats and coasters. Core products were forest products such as gum and rattan, but Borsumij also exported coffee directly to the US, and very successfully exploited a coal mining concession. Surplus profits from coal sales financed the development of a rubber plantation on land adjacent to the mine. Borsumij offices sold paraffin in commission for the Royal Dutch. From its two offices in Palembang on Sumatra and Bandjermasin on Borneo, the company built up a network of branches in the archipelago. The Dutch company seat, moved from Arnhem to Amsterdam in 1898, mainly served as the link to its shareholders and customers. In 1912 the Borsumij head office moved again, now to the Hague. At its foundation, the company had a paid-up capital of 500,000 guilders, which rapidly increased with the growth of business, reaching

Borsumij ran its own shipping services between its various branches, much to the annoyance of the KPM, which claimed a monopoly on shipping within the archipelago. The photograph pictures one of Borsumij's river boats around 1900.

3 million guilders on assets of 7 million guilders in 1914. A separate general manager ran the operations in the Dutch East Indies, but even so, from the beginning the Dutch board regularly travelled to Asia. As early as 1903, agents submitted quarterly business reports to headoffice, and the non-executive board discussed their results six weeks later. Such close monitoring could not, of course, prevent accidents from happening. During the summer of 1904 the Palembang agent, W. Hissink, started to behave curiously. Letters to him went without reply, and he did not react to a board admonition to take his duties

In the early 1900s, HVA withdrew from general trading to concentrate on the production of tropical commodities. One of the company's plants, the sugar factory Jatiroto in east Java, was reputedly the world's largest, with a huge railway engine depot.

more seriously. After six months the board suspended the agent and commanded him to explain himself fully within three months. In June 1905 the manager for the Dutch East Indies went to Palembang for an inspection. The day before his arrival, Hissink committed suicide, in despair over the imminent disclosure of his mismanagement.[129]

Internatio led the group of Dutch colonial merchant houses which became known as the Big Five, and also included Borsumij, Geo. Wehry, Lindeteves, and Jacobson & Van den Berg.[130] The term presupposed that the group remained the same throughout, and thus distorts reality. Around 1900 the HVA certainly belonged to the top merchant houses, but by backward integration the company gradually moved into production. The colonial financial constraints proved stronger than its statutory restriction to trade alone, so like all others the HVA acquired plantation interests. Even so, it apparently weathered the Sugar Crisis effortlessly, though the experience inspired the board to amend the company statutes to include the management of industrial companies in addition to trade as its mission. By 1900 the HVA began to expand its capital and to extend its plantation interests, taking over selected companies, and reclaiming fallow grounds for the cultivation of sugar, rubber, cassava, tobacco, and a string of other crops. On East Java the company built the sugar refinery Jatiroto, at that moment reportedly the biggest in the world. Nor were the trading activities neglected. In 1904 the HVA opened sale and purchase branches in Manchester and in Singapore. However, after making an extensive tour of inspection of the Asian offices, the manager Reineke concluded that the commodity trade was insufficiently profitable. Margins on the imports into the Dutch East Indies consistently remained too low, because of the necessary customer credit. According to Reineke, the HVA possessed insufficient trade skills to improve its performance in the colonial commodity trade. As a result the HVA sold its general trading activities in 1910, though this arm had by then reached the not inconsiderable turnover of 12 million guilders a year. The company now became a very large and diverse colonial production company selling its own products. In 1914, capital and reserves had mounted to 14 million guilders, making the HVA into one of the biggest of its kind in the Dutch East Indies. Internatio and Crone bought the company's trade activities, Crone's trading for own account in colonial commodities rising sharply as a result.[131]

Going by size, Güntzel & Schumacher would have had to belong to the top group of merchant houses, too. This firm, founded in 1889, operated from Medan on Sumatra, importing general consumer products and exporting mainly timber and other forest products. Once reorganized into a limited liability company in 1906, Güntzel & Schumacher began to expand by taking over trading firms in Tandjong Balei, Tandjong Poera, and Taroetoeng. In 1914 the company had total assets of 2.4 million guilders, and offices both in Hamburg and in Amsterdam, as well as nine branches on Sumatra.[132]

Less is known about Jacobson & Van den Berg, and about Geo. Wehry. The former was set up in 1860, in Semarang, under the name of Jacobson & Co., but this had been changed to Jacobson Van den Berg & Co. by 1872 at the latest. In addition to the original Semarang office, Jacobson & Van den Berg established branches in Batavia, Surabaya, and Cheribon, plus an office in Rotterdam. As far as we know, the firm operated as a general import and export business, with interests in coffee and cinchona plantations. Geo. Wehry dated from 1867. It was the successor to a firm called Wehry & Wille, about which we know only that it had an office in Batavia, and in Europe, presumably Paris, to buy its imports. After four years in business, Geo. Wehry opened a branch in Surabaya, and moved its European office to Amsterdam. During the 1890s the firm set up three more branches in the Dutch East Indies. Originally, Wehry exported tobacco, coffee, and vanilla to Europe in commission for planters, importing consumer goods. Like the other traders, the firm possessed sometimes considerable interests in plantations. The range of goods traded gradually expanded with various other commodities: paraffin, cattle, milk, batik wax, and candles. Wehry also added tea, hides, and cinchona to its exports. Besides its commodity trade the firm managed a number of agencies for foreign firms.[133]

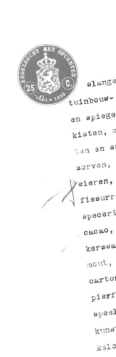

Trading houses often imported goods in bulk, for repackaging them into their own branded products. Such brands were registered with the local court, so counterfeiters could be prosecuted. The document below is the beginning of a long list of products which Geo. Wehry wanted to register.

n keukengereedschap, stal-,
en - gereedschappen, meubels
oratiematerialen, bedden, lijk-
derdeelen van muziekinstrumen-
chwaren, vleeschextracten,con-
it, vruchtensappen, geleien,
ijzenolie en -vet, koffie, kof-
siropen en stroop, honing, meel,
usen, azijn, mosterd, zout,
n, bakkers- en banketbak-
diëtetische voedingsmiddelen,
bordpapier, carton, papier- en
werkte grondstoffen voor de pa-
ier, photographie- en drukwerk,
den en plaatjes, letters, cliché's,
, aardewerk, glaswerk en mika-arti-
rd, opnaaisels, knoopen, kant, bor-
waren, riemen en tasschen, schrijf-,
tseerbehoeften, billard- en kleer-
aielen.

Lindeteves was set up in 1875, and operated from Semarang. The firm concentrated on the hardware trade, tools and equipment. In 1888 the Amsterdam banking firm of Vermeer & Co. arranged a reorganization into a limited liability company with a capital of 100,000 guilders. This inaugurated a period of fast growth. The company set up a branch in Surabaya which soon overshadowed the original main office. In 1901 Lindeteves floated a 1 million guilder share issue, two years later the company established an office in Amsterdam to coordinate the purchasing activities in the Netherlands, Britain, and the US. The capital was raised again in 1909, to 2.5 million guilders, to pay for the take-over of R.S. Stokvis' business in the Dutch East Indies. Renamed Lindeteves-Stokvis, the company developed into a dedicated wholesaler of technical supplies, with an important division for building complete installations such as production units.[134]

Now the Dutch East Indies had some trading companies much bigger than the Big Five, like the Handelmaatschappij Kian Gwan in Semarang. This extraordinarily successful business was founded in 1863 as the first limited liability company set up by Chinese inhabitants, the Oei Tjong Han family. Successive generations of this family built Kian Gwan into a dominating presence in the region, with a string of branches including eight outside of the Dutch East Indies. In 1892 the company had a capital of 3 million guilders, rising to no less than 15 million guilders twenty years later, double Internatio's capital.[135] Moreover, a substantial volume of trade bypassed the merchant houses. Many big companies, both in the traditional sectors of, for instance, tobacco and sugar, and in the new so-called 'automobile products' oil and rubber, combined production with trade.

As far as we can establish, the Dutch colonial merchant houses did not produce very impressive returns, that is to say, compared to other colonial companies they paid meagre dividends. Between 1889 and 1913, the average return for colonial trading companies was 6% at most, less than the average total for all limited companies.[136] Internatio never paid more than 10%, the HVA only after 1904, when the company had switched to production. The shareholders of Borsumij considered a 7% dividend outstanding, and on the eve of the First World War the company repeatedly paid as much as 9%.[137] Jacobson & Van den Berg, a private limited partnership, held the record, giving its partners 13.5% in 1913.[138] By contrast, a dividend of 20% meant a meagre year for shareholders in the Deli-Maatschappij, one of the biggest tobacco producers. Between 1890 and 1914 the company twice paid no dividends at all, yet the average for the period still touches on 41%.[139]

What, then, gave trading companies such as the Big Five their respected position and prominence within the colonial business world, even if in those surroundings they were not particularly big, and from an investor's viewpoint not very attractive? The traders derived their position from their function as versatile intermediaries, with strong connections in the retail trade, well-established in a huge and fragmented archipelago. The big growers of colonial commodities may have exported their products themselves, but numerous smaller companies remained, which depended on merchant houses to do it for them, not least because of the complicated relations with customers. Nearly all traders had very wide-ranging interests, agencies, and connections, from import and export to various plantations, to shipping, to insurance, to finance, to importers in other countries. Bringing all those strands together continued to be of great importance until the concentration in the production of colonial crops during the 1920s and 1930s. On the other hand, the merchant houses offered Western manufacturers and, not to forget, service providers such as insurance companies, ready access to a huge market with intricate local circumstances, something which these companies could never have achieved equally smoothly through their own agents. The merchant houses operated particularly successfully in giving European business, and more specifically Dutch business, this

Europeans were a distinct social group in the Dutch East Indies, living more or less separated from the indigenous population. The photograph pictures a party in the Batavia zoo, around 1900.

212

privileged access. Trade between the Netherlands and the Dutch East Indies gradually declined, but around 1900 the Dutch share in colonial imports was still five times higher than the Dutch share in world trade.[140]

The trading companies owed their prominence to this function, but presumably also to the peculiar Dutch East Indian situation, that enormous archipelago with a sprinkling of Europeans scattered far and wide, expats who depended for their contact with the wider world, and for the pleasures of Western consumer goods, on the Internatio offices, the Wehry agents, the Borsumij coasters, extending their services into the same far corners to make a living. Hendrikus Colijn, who as prime minister of the Netherlands would become the prophet of thrift during the great economic crisis of the 1930s, ran up large debts as an officer in the colonial army by ordering books, wine, and cigars

from home.[141] Back in the Netherlands, some people looked askance at the demand for consumer goods from the Dutch East Indies, even when they profited by it. In 1910, one of the Internatio directors, A.C. Mees, wrote a private comment on his memo pad on what he regarded to be the indulgence of some Dutch expats living in the Dutch East Indies, who wanted luxuries, Dutch tins and beer, a motorcycle or a car, regular visits to the cinema whatever the distance, tennis courts. Such people had to be reminded that colonial life was necessarily frugal and hard working.[142] In the opinion of people like Mees, luxury was a privilege reserved for the European countries, to be sustained by making money through thrift and enterprise in the colonies. This inspired a prolonged mutual misunderstanding, which repeatedly upset the relations between head office and the Asian branches, and not just at Internatio. Managing boards in Europe easily became convinced that staff in the Dutch East Indies took their tasks too lightly, the overseas branches had a thin skin for the constant pedantic admonitions from the Netherlands, and when it suited them they simply ignored the opinions of people without experience in colonial business.[143]

As part of its agency contract with the Rotterdam Lloyd, Internatio operated separate booking offices for the shipping line. This is the shipping department of the company's Batavia head office in the early 1900s.

213

AN IMPORTER OF CONSUMER PRODUCTS IN SURABAYA – With the demise of the Cultivation System, the Dutch merchant houses started to lose share in the market of importing consumer goods into the Dutch East Indies. As early as 1870, Reynst & Vinju noticed that products from the US, France, Britain, Switzerland, and Australia were supplanting their imports from the Netherlands.[144] Towards the end of the century, Crone, Van Heekeren, and Van Eeghen & Co. had to give up their exports to the colony. Presumably they could no longer compete because they had no local branches, and apparently, they did not want to establish any. Colonial companies such as Wehry, Borsumij, or Lindeteves had offices both in Asia and in Europe, while the Dutch company Stokvis set up its own operation in the Dutch East Indies, and so could do without further help from merchant houses.

However, by 1900 the traders operating in the Dutch East Indies also began to suffer from shrinking margins on their imports. This was really the consequence of the same structural changes which European wholesalers had been experiencing since about 1860. Erdmann & Sielcken (1875) initially traded in Dutch butter and cheese, plus British and Swiss fabrics, exporting coffee, sugar, and a whole range of other tropical products such as hides, rattan, and copra. The firm also dealt in bills and securities with the Amsterdamsche Bank and with Wertheim & Gompertz. Erdmann & Sielcken had branches in Semarang, Surabaya, and Batavia, an office in Amsterdam, and moreover, from the start, for its sugar transactions a permanent agent in London, in Mincing Lane, the street housing the merchants in tropical commodities. Around 1900, the firm abandoned its import business to concentrate on exporting and forwarding. The partners found it too difficult to find suitable staff for handling the mainly Chinese and Arabian retail trade, and they professed themselves to be fed up with the colonial custom of customer credit with its incalculable risks. Simultaneously, Maclaine Watson & Co., and Martin Dyce & Co., merchant houses of British origin, ceased to import as well.[145] In 1911, Internatio decided to run down its general consumer products trade and give priority to bulk products such as fabrics.[146]

To protect their margins, other importers adopted a new strategy, i.e. selling monopoly brands. Merchant houses obtained exclusive rights from manufacturers to sell their products in a given area. This relationship pivoted around industrial branded products. Instead of obtaining their merchandise from a group of correspondents, importing traders really entered into the service of one particular producer, to push a particular brand from a range of competing products. For that reason, advertising costs were often borne by the manufacturers. Reinforcing the specific wholesale function of dedicated pushing offered both parties potentially greater sales opportunities. The trader saw his competition eliminated, the manufacturer exchanged a fragmented representation by a motley group of merchants for dedicated market access. By the end of the 19th century, this new strategy began to take shape. In March 1899, Geo. Wehry approached a Manchester manufacturer to obtain exclusive product agencies formerly held by the bankrupted Semarang Trading Cy. At that moment, the firm already possessed a number of monopoly brands, including Pfaff sewing machines, and various brands of wines and spirits. And yet, in 1903 Wehry had an argument with the Twente cotton producer Jannink about not wanting to enter into an exclusive relationship, which Jannink was reluctant to do, too. Other cotton manufacturers had by then switched from open consignments to a range of merchant houses, to regular orders from a single agent. By 1920 this transition had been nearly completed for the consumer goods imports from Europe and the US, but presumably

214

The Willemskade in Surabaya, photographed during the early 1890s.

Johan and Anton Hagemeijer together with the latter's wife in Surabaya, 1900.

not yet for the bulk products such as fabrics.[147] Adopting the strategy demanded a novel commitment from wholesalers, a thorough understanding of brand products, plus the ability to cooperate closely with the retail trade. This latter factor was a key reason for established and respected firms such as Maclaine Watson & Co., or Erdmann & Sielcken to retreat.

As always, new entrants appeared who did spot the available opportunities. Around 1900, the brothers Johan and Anton Hagemeijer, sons of an Amsterdam wholesaler in watches and clocks, went to live in Surabaya, then a city with a population of just under 150,000 people. We do not know why they left the Netherlands during the late 1890s. Nor do we know for certain what the eldest, Johan, did for a living, as varying stories circulate. According to his private account book, Anton had a job as bookkeeper with the firm of E. Blavet & Co. in 1900, moving to a better paid position with Franz Wolff & Co. the following year. In addition, he did some work for a third firm.[148] In January 1900 Anton Hagemeijer, almost 26 years of age, borrowed 1,000 guilders for a trip to the Netherlands, where in the summer he married Catharina van den Bosch from the town of Alphen aan den Rijn. To all appearances he must already have nursed plans to start up in business, for he accepted 24 cheeses for selling in commission from the Alfensche Kaashandel, a cheese trader in his wife's native town. This consignment arrived in Surabaya by the steamer Sumatra, and were booked as sold in February 1901 under the heading 'net revenue No. 1'. The next shipment arrived the following month, no longer in commission but for joint account with the Alfensche Kaashandel. By September of that year, Anton's account book began to look like embryonic business accounts with debtors and invoice numbers. New products also appeared: kapok, cigars, somewhat later china, too. Johan, who took his meals with the newlyweds and may have lived with them, probably helped to run the business. When the accounts were closed on the 31st of December 1901, the brothers shared the business profit half and half. The initiative clearly rested with Anton.[149]

At that moment in time, the brothers had not yet established a formal partnership. Presumably they had only agreed to try out a business idea and see

Anton Hagemeijer behind his type-writer, around 1900.

how things would develop.[150] After nearly two years, Anton had built up suffi-cient confidence, and he left his job as a bookkeeper towards the end of 1902. The product range was considerably expanded, for the balance at year-end 1903 shows a large variety of goods under the heading 'products sailing': fabrics, ink wells, travelling bags, toothbrushes, clocks and watch chains, fruit wine, cigars, ladies' blouses, and cheese. This last item was still traded for joint account, the others belonged to the brothers. Turnover for 1903 amounted to over 60,000 guilders, on a capital of 16,000 guilders and assets of 38,000 guilders. In 1904, turnover doubled, and Anton and Johan decided to raise their cooperation to the status of a legal partnership. On 31 December 1904 they appeared before the notary B. ter Kuile in Surabaya to establish the firm of Hagemeijer & Co. The present company, then, has legally existed from that date. However, since business really began four years earlier, the year 1900 may justifiably be taken for its origin. Shortly after signing the contract, Anton left for Europe and established an office in Amsterdam. Until then, father Hagemeijer had probably done the purchasing for his sons. Anton developed the Amsterdam branch into the firm's head office and main administrative centre, setting up an index card system to keep track of the product range, and laying down the firm's rules and policies by despatching so-called 'Indian Instructions' to the other branches.

The Hagemeijer business was a classical consumer products wholesaler: importing a large and varied range of Western manufacturing products, not in bulk but in fairly small lots, selling to wholesalers and retailers in Surabaya and the surrounding country. Established firms in Batavia and Semarang abandoned similar activities at that very moment. The brothers must have been aware that there was still a market. Perhaps they had noticed the pace of economic growth quickening since the turn of the century, and the effects which this had on soci-

The first office of Hagemeijer & Co. on the Pnagoong in Surabaya, with the firm's two founders in the background. The photo must have been taken after the official incorporation of the firm in 1904, judging by the addition of the suffix '& Co.'

The stock room of Hagemeijer & Co., 1911.

The Hagemeijer brothers began trading by importing Dutch cheese. The firm still dealt in cheese in 1934, when it registered this label as its brand, a 'house brand' in the most literal sense of the word.

ety in the Dutch East Indies. Perhaps they had understood how the demand for consumer products was bound to rise as a consequence. And apparently the Hagemeijers were not intimidated by the irregular customs concerning payments and credit. They did not have any capital of their own for support, and availed themselves of facilities offered by the Nederlandsch-Indische Handelsbank instead. Interest charges rose in tandem with turnover, and turnover rose rapidly. In 1908 sales amounted to 500,000 guilders, reaching 1 million guilders two years later. The firm concentrated on branded products from the start, mostly for its own account. Some products were bought in bulk and given own brands, for other products the Hagemeijers obtained exclusive rights from European manufacturers.

On the eve of the First World War, the Hagemeijer brothers possessed a trading business with a capital of 800,000 guilders and a turnover of 2 million guilders, built up from scratch in fourteen years. The year 1913 had yielded a profit of more than 200,000 guilders for them to share, whereas Anton had earned roughly 3,000 guilders a year as a bookkeeper. Their firm was by no means a merchant house as yet, restricted as it was to importing and wholesaling. It was a small business, as Dutch East Indian commerce went. However, the brothers had clearly discovered a market neglected by others, which appeared to offer opportunities for unlimited growth.[151]

During this period of radical economic change, then, trade succeeded very well in maintaining its position. The commodity trade and the trade in manufacturing products faced plenty of new opportunities, as the distance between producers and consumers increased. With the demise of the Cultivation System, the traditional merchant houses discovered a huge new market in the Dutch East Indies. When this became dominated by branded products, some established firms withdrew, creating opportunities for new entrants such as the Hagemeijer brothers, who succeeded in building up a business within a very short time.

Unloading goods at Internatio's Semarang subsidiary on the Oude Boom, 1907.

Inset: During the First World War, trade between Asia and Europe became increasingly difficult. As a consequence, trading houses sought a way out by establishing themselves in other countries, such as Japan. 'Old friends finding each other again', the cartoonist Louis Raemaekers wrote as a caption under his drawing in the newspaper *De Telegraaf*, 19 April 1920.

CHAPTER V

During the years from 1914 to 1940, traders were forced into the defensive. The First World War imposed restrictions on trade, challenging merchants to find new ways. The same restrictions provided manufacturing industry with an incentive to assume functions until then belonging to trade, which threatened to eliminate wholesalers. Finally, traders had to find a solution to the economic crisis during the early 1920s, and to the long depression of the 1930s.

AN ERA OF CONFLICT AND PROTECTIONISM – In August 1914, after months of diplomatic tension, war broke out in Europe, abruptly cutting international economic ties, which had become ever closer during the last quarter of the 19th century. Borders were closed, trade routes blocked, and restrictions were imposed on the free transfer of capital. All the great industrial nations were drawn into the conflict, which disrupted the international economy so deeply, that some of its effects would last until the 1950s.

The war meant the end of the Gold Standard. Banknotes could no longer be exchanged for gold, and gold could no longer be exported freely. This made international payments much more difficult. During the late 1920s, after gigantic currency problems in Germany and in Austria, the Gold Standard was reintroduced in a modified form, but the system never returned to its pre-war efficiency. The curtain finally fell in the 1930s, with the devaluation of the pound sterling in 1931 carrying a substantial responsibility for the demise. Currency problems increased the commercial risks for the international traders. Governments began to intervene more and more, restricting the free development of trade. War circumstances in Europe stimulated the rise of industrial production in Asian and South American countries. When the war ended, these fledgling industries often received protection from European competition. In Europe itself, however, protection advanced, too, if only because of the birth of new national states with their own borders. Post-war difficulties with currencies and inflation reinforced tendencies towards raising barriers around national economies. The 1917 revolution in Russia installed a regime bent on creating a largely self-sufficient economy under centralized command. In Europe and the us, government interventions came as subsidies, inspections, and trade restrictions. Towards the end of the 1930s, nearly half of world trade was subjected to levies, and nearly thirty countries, of which nineteen in Europe, restricted imports by means of quota or licences.[1]

Consequently, the growth rate of world trade sharply declined, and trade patterns changed. The volume of world trade continued to rise, but average growth rates per head fell from 34% over the years 1881-1913 to only 3% over 1913-1937. In 1913, European trade represented two-thirds of world trade. This had gone down to half in 1937. Conversely, the US share rose, and the combined share of Asia, Africa, and Oceanea grew by a little. Africa, for instance, became an important supplier of tropical commodities such as cocoa, oil seeds, and edible fats. The dominant position of Europe in exports of industrial products diminished. In 1913, Europe supplied four-fifths of world exports of industrial products, but this share had gone down to two-thirds. This was due mainly to rising exports from the US and from Japan. Despite these changes, the trade flows largely remained unchanged in character, with exports of industrial products from the developed countries to the lesser developed countries, and conversely, mainly primary products from the lesser developed countries to the industrialized ones. Japan and India provided exceptions to this pattern.[2] The internationally operating traders would soon experience the consequences of all these long-term changes. First of all, they were confronted with the immediate problems following the outbreak of the First World War.

THE FIRST WORLD WAR – On the outbreak of war, the Netherlands declared itself neutral, and it was lucky enough not to get drawn into the violence by one of the belligerent sides. Even so, the war did make itself felt throughout the country in many ways. The conscript army was called up to protect the borders, and in the autumn of 1914 large numbers of Belgian refugees fled to the Netherlands. During August, the population reacted immediately with a run on the banks and the stockpiling of commodities. Though the government had little experience with economic interventions, it conferred with business leaders and proclaimed a series of measures to combat the chaos. The board of the Amster-

The war generated a wave of refugees to the Netherlands, which succeeded in remaining neutral. There was, however, anxiety about food supplies to feed the Dutch population, inspiring this 1917 cartoon in the magazine *De Amsterdammer*, captioned: 'Will there be enough for me?'.

The threat of war led to a run on banks during the summer of 1914, such as on the Haarlemsche Bankvereeniging pictured here, customers being anxious to get their deposits.

By hoisting the NOT-cone on its ships, the Dutch merchant navy hoped to keep trade going during the war.

dam stock exchange had closed the market for an indefinite period some days before the guns had actually started firing. The stock exchange reopened only on 9 February 1915. Gold exports were banned, so for practical purposes the Netherlands left the Gold Standard. As a result, traders were confronted with great uncertainties over exchange rates. The government tightly regulated exports with licence systems and prohibitions, to ensure that the population would continue to receive sufficient supplies of food and fuel. The war situation itself greatly restricted commodity imports.[3] Whereas the sailing under convenience flags had done a lot to alleviate the war impact on trade during the 17th century, the French Occupation had demonstrated the potential for devastation. A striking feature from the latter period was the administrative paperwork needed to keep at least some trade going. This returned during the First World War, though the Netherlands itself was not one of the warring parties.

The advantageous geographical position of the Netherlands, at the crossroads between the two expanding economies of Britain and Germany, now became a big disadvantage. Britain controlled the seas, and its embargo on supplying Germany with contraband, really on any goods needed in wartime, applied to neutral countries, too. The Dutch government did not want to assume responsibility for monitoring whether goods imported in the Netherlands would not in fact be forwarded to Germany. After all, this would endanger its neutrality. In order to safeguard the overseas imports, a group of prominent business leaders founded the Nederlandsche Overzee Trustmaatschappij (NOT, Dutch Overseas Trust Company) in November 1914. Managers from the big banks and from the main shipping companies filled the seats of the supervisory board of the NOT. Representatives from the merchant houses were conspicuous for their absence in this illustrious gathering. A.G. Kröller, partner in the combined shipping and trading firm Wm.H. Müller & Co., formed the sole exception. Kröller had apparently been the main inspiration for the NOT. He did not, however, have a seat on its Executive Committee.[4] The NOT acted as a guarantor towards Britain that contraband goods handled by the trust would not be forwarded to Germany. Its guarantee was implemented by contracts both with

221

transporters and with importers that the goods concerned served for use within the Netherlands only. Ships belonging to companies which had acceded to the NOT flew the NOT flag, a huge cone, and received a certificate from the trust. The NOT, by the way, did not possess any coercive powers over shippers and traders to back up its guarantee that goods would not be sent to Germany. Imported raw materials processed in the Netherlands and then exported to Germany posed a particularly delicate problem.

When the British government tightened its embargo in 1915, nearly all goods had to be accompanied by a 'certificate of origin'. However, typically Dutch products such as flower bulbs, cheese, butter, condensed milk, eggs, fish, candles, and gin were excepted. Re-exports of commodities coming from the Dutch East Indies also remained free, so trade in these goods grew strongly during the initial war years. Britain declared ever more goods to be contraband as the war continued, and as a result the NOT's administration turned into a bloated bureaucracy.[5] When writing his commemorative book on Internatio in 1938, the company's manager A.C. Mees celebrated the NOT as a stroke of genius, which had saved the Dutch trade in colonial commodities after they had been declared contraband.[6] Still, even the NOT could not prevent the circumstances for sending goods from the Dutch East Indies to Europe from worsening. Van Heekeren, a somewhat smaller merchant house, had a less positive opinion of the trust, complaining about the almost five years of being ruled by the NOT, its ever tighter regulations and sprawling ordinances replacing commercial experience and skills, and about the high administrative charges due on signing a contract with the trust.[7]

Trade did not suffer from regulations and agreements covering imports and exports alone. Mines and submarines proved at least as frustrating. Britain first laid a minefield closing off the southern part of the North Sea, restricting passage through the Channel to a narrow stretch of water close to the English coast. The Royal Navy scattered its mines very liberally, as was evident from both the number of ships hit by them, and by the about 5,000 mines drifting on to the Dutch coast during the war. In response, Germany declared the seas around Britain and Ireland including the Channel to be a war zone, in which neutral shipping would also be endangered. To impress the neutrality of Dutch ships upon the crews of German submarines, shipping companies emblazoned the visible parts of hull and superstructure with the Dutch flag.[8]

Towards the end of the war, Germany even began to attack all shipping, whether neutral or not. As a consequence, maritime transport declined dramatically. A total of 88 Dutch ships were sunk. The torpedoing on March 16, 1916 of the 'Tubantia', the flagship of the Koninklijke Hollandsche Lloyd, meant a particularly nasty shock to public opinion.[9] Traders and ship owners suffered another setback with the closure of the Suez canal in 1916, which forced them to switch to the old route via the Cape of Good Hope. From October 1917 until February 1918, Britain closed her submarine cables for telegrams, which severely handicapped trade between the Netherlands and the Dutch East Indies.[10]

The NOT's intermediation and regulations created a substantial bureaucracy.

Dutch public opinion was outraged when German submarines sank the steamer Tubantia. Joh. Braakensiek captured this mood in a cartoon for De Amsterdammer, with the sailor shouting: 'The rascals! And cowards: they won't even admit who did it!'.

Meanwhile, Albert Hahn lampooned the unchecked exports of food to Germany in the magazine De Notenkraker, 3 June 1916.

Finally, in 1918 Britain and the US requisitioned all Dutch ships lying in British or American ports. The consequent lack of transport meant that by the end of the war, stocks of primary products had piled up in the Dutch East Indies and other production regions.

Even so, the war did not prove to be one long sorry story of adversity and suffering for the merchant houses, for prices rocketed, and the opportunities for profit increased accordingly. During the first war years, Dutch trade and industry could in fact expand their business vigorously.[11] Germany exerted a strong demand on supplies from the Netherlands, so goods which could be traded freely under the regulations found a ready market. A substantial black market developed, which was inevitable under such circumstances. The strong pull from foreign demand even threatened to leave the Netherlands with insufficient supplies for its own needs. For that reason the Dutch government limited exports of a range of foodstuffs, and it also intervened extensively in the coal trade. After all, fuel was essential for both private households and for industry. Initially the Steenkolen Handels-Vereeniging (SHV) had attempted to organize an orderly distribution of coal by bringing private interests together in the Kolenbureau or Coal Bureau. The SHV occupied a strong position in the trade, having both agreements with a German coal syndicate, and secret connections with a company trading in British coal. However, its initiative generated so much resistance and distrust, partly on account of rising coal prices, that in 1917 the government took the distribution of coal into its own hands. The SHV anxiously wondered whether this would be a temporary measure, or the first step towards increasing government intervention in the economy.[12]

The colonial traders faced problems of an entirely different order. It became more and more difficult for them to transport goods from Asia to Europe and vice versa. As a result, they had to find new sources of supply and new outlets for sales. For sugar, Asia had already become the key market, but for the other products the Netherlands and the other European countries were the main trading partners. During the war, the US and Japan appeared on the horizon as suppliers and as customers.[13] The rise of the automobile industry made the US a keen customer for the new export commodities of oil and rubber. This country pioneered mass production and mass consumption. A huge variety of industrial mass products, from sewing machines, cameras, canned soup, and cigarettes to washing machines, cars, and farming machines found their way first on the American market, and then gradually also abroad. Japanese business gratefully used the disruption of trade between the Dutch East Indian archipelago and Europe to expand its shipping lines and trade network there. Trading firms from Japan discovered the way to indigenous consumers by nourishing their connections with the Chinese retail trade.[14]

The changes in trade routes did not lead to the complete elimination of the Dutch trading houses, though they had to adjust to having new rivals. In fact, as often as not, the established traders helped to open the new routes. This becomes evident from the fact that several trading houses established new

By the end of the war, transport had become a serious bottleneck, causing a stockpiling of commodities in the Dutch East Indian ports. The photograph shows the harbour of Tandjong Priok in quieter times, 1907.

branches in Japan and in the US. Anton Hagemeijer did so: he went to the US in 1915 to set up a purchasing branch, and somewhat later he established another one in Japan (Yokohama). With industrial products increasingly hard to obtain in Europe, he aimed to get them from these two countries. The same motive made Lindeteves-Stokvis establish branches in New York, Japan, South America, and China during those years. Internatio also became interested in having an office in Japan, which was an important buyer of sugar. In addition to getting new supplies, finding new sales outlets for colonial commodities provided another reason for setting up branches. This motivated the Amsterdam broker G. de Vries & Zn. to open a New York office in 1918. With it, the firm hoped to obtain a share in the commodity trade which had found direct routes from the Dutch East Indies to the US during the war.[15] By taking over the Van der Chys Handel Maatschappij in 1916, Borsumij opted for a diversification of sales which took it a long way from home indeed. The core activity of this trading company was selling tea in Russia. In his position as supervisory director of Van der Chys, J.G. Schlimmer, the director of Borsumij, knew that the company needed financial support. However, Borsumij was to get very little pleasure from its acquisition as a result of the Russian revolution in November 1917. Ceteco, active in Latin America, focused on the local trade and the transport between Latin American countries during the war. To meet the demand for transport, the company commissioned several sailing ships from the yards which had formed part of its original business as of old.[16]

Despite the many problems and restrictions, the First World War was a profitable time for the trading houses, as can also be derived from the dividends paid out.[17] However, increasing stocks and rising prices proved a cash drain, so trading houses began to attract more capital. New share issues found ready takers, no doubt partly because of an abundant capital supply and the high dividends. During the war investors had already shown a keen appetite for buying shares in trading companies, but their optimism reached a peak in the immediate post-war period. Europe yearned for commodities, and warehouses in the production areas such as the Dutch East Indies were full of them, ready to be taken on board of the first ship to arrive. Conversely, there existed a great

demand for all kinds of industrial products in the Dutch East Indies.

Between 1916 and 1919, Internatio expanded its share capital from 7.5 million guilders to 12.5 million guilders. Borsumij more than doubled its capital between 1918 and 1920, also in two steps, from 3 million guilders to 7.5 million. This last increase followed the take-over in 1919 of the Maatschappij voor Uitvoer en Commissiehandel (MUCH), which operated on Java. The Borsumij directors considered an expansion of the company's activities to Java important because of the opportunity to obtain exclusive agencies, also called 'monopoly relations'. Hagemeyer shared in the optimism during those days and reorganized the firm into a limited liability company with a capital of 4 million guilders, of which half were issued and paid up. Presumably this reorganization also had something to do with the death, on October 10, 1918, of Johan Hagemeijer, which necessitated a revision of the original partnership contract from 1904. When the firm became a limited company, Anton Hagemeijer and Johan's widow each received half of the shares issued. Anton and P.H.F. Heijnen, who had worked for the firm since 1908, were the company's two directors.[18] At that time, the company name was still variously spelled with the original Dutch 'ij' or with a 'y', as in Hagemeyer, depending on the keyboard of the available typewriters. We have not been able to establish when the directors formally adopted this spelling as the official one, and have chosen to use it from the point of the firm becoming a limited company.

With apposite pride, Johan
Hagemeijer (standing) and his
brother Anton pose to show their sales
ledger. The photograph was probably
intended to announce the formal
incorporation of their trading firm to
their family in the Netherlands.

In addition to the expansion of existing companies during these years, new combinations appeared. One such war creation was the Rotterdam trading company 'Transoceana', founded in 1918, an extension of the import of Argentinian grains and seeds run by Le Gué & Bolle's Handelmaatschappij. The oil producers U. Twijnstra's Oliefabrieken had a hand in this business as well. Another company which focused on Latin America was the Compania Mercantil Argentina (Argentinian Trading Company) which also dealt in grain. When founded in 1915, the shares issued amounted to a capital of 3 million guilders, which rose to no less than 20 million guilders by 1920. From 1916, the company concentrated mainly on inland trading, following the difficulties in the export trade. Its business drew support from illustrious names, such as S. van Deventer, A.G. Kröller, Dr. J.P. van Tienhoven, and W. Westerman. The last two people also had ties with the Internationale industrie- en handelsvereeniging in Rotterdam, established in 1917. Led by NV R.S. Stokvis & Zonen, this combination aimed to create new sales opportunities for Dutch industry during the war. The Internationale took over Stokvis's Russian trade, and was soon entirely taken over by the company. The shares issued reached an amount of 3.25 million guilders in 1920.[19]

Two of the combinations just mentioned demonstrated that industry was getting itself involved in trade. The war had made manufacturing companies painfully aware of their dependency on supplies of raw materials. Until 1914, unrestricted international operations and smoothly performing Dutch trading houses had always ensured that industry could meet its needs on the Dutch markets. The war had put an end to that, setting manufacturers thinking about the desirability of vertical integration. As early as 1917, the SHV directors noticed manufacturers beginning to threaten the position of trade: 'It will be plain to anyone who has kept his eyes open during this highly unusual period in our economic life, that producers will become steadily more influential as time passes, while the importance of the pure intermediate trade will steadily decline. We thus believe our goal should be to become as strong in this respect as our Limburg competitors by gaining influence over mines with an equally favourable geographical position, and which produce similar coal.'[20] The margarine producer Ant. Jurgens ascribed price rises for his raw materials more to traders than to scarcity. In 1916, he started trading in West African palm kernels, to bypass British traders in that product, but also with an eye on the expansive developments which he expected after the war. Jurgens entered into secret agreements for copra supplies in the Dutch East Indies, and also invested in production units for processing the copra into oil.[21] All in all, the First World War and its aftermath appeared to have brought the Dutch merchant houses mainly prosperity and new opportunities. However, the bill was soon to be presented.

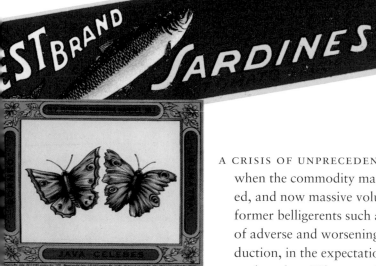

The sample room of Borsumij's The Hague headoffice in 1907, testifying to the large variety of consumer goods which found its way from Europe to the Dutch East Indies.

A CRISIS OF UNPRECEDENTED DEPTH – The year 1920 brought the great crash when the commodity markets collapsed. During the war, stocks had accumulated, and now massive volumes hit the market, flooding it. In addition, sales to former belligerents such as Germany or Austria-Hungary remained low because of adverse and worsening exchange rates. Industry had strongly increased production, in the expectation of a vigorous post-war demand, and stimulated by trade orders. When supplies turned out to exceed demand everywhere, prices collapsed, sometimes to levels under the cost of production. Banks and merchant houses faced a particularly difficult situation. The Dutch banks had relaxed their former reservations towards financial commitments to industry during the First World War, and had supplied finance for the expansion of production on a large scale during and immediately after the war. Collapsing prices revealed turnover and profit figures to be largely inflated. Losses sharply reduced the capital of manufacturing companies, but specifically also of trading companies.

The international traders found themselves in very severe weather. Firstly, they lost heavily on their stocks. In 1920, they still hoped for the best, but during the following year the full extent of the damage became clear. The Handelmaatschappij S.L. van Nierop wrote that the uncontrollable price falls had come down like an avalanche, sweeping everything in their path.[22] Moreover, the merchant houses often had orders outstanding with producers, which they could only cancel at a loss. Finally, they had often delivered orders to customers, which had run into trouble themselves and thus could no longer meet their obligations. Losses on debtors revealed themselves somewhat later than the losses on stocks, so many companies discovered the gravity of the situation only gradually. Trade turned out not to be a guarantee for profitability after all. As a result, the margarine producer Jurgens decided in 1921 to leave the commodity markets to traders. The cigar manufacturer Gebr. Philips of Maastricht also derived little pleasure from its adventure in the tobacco trade. The Tabak Unie, its joint-venture with the Internationale Tabakshandel, nearly bankrupted the company in 1922.[23]

The crisis years 1920-1922 wiped out old traders and new traders alike, but the crash hit new companies particularly severely. At the Handelmaatschappij 'Transoceanea' just mentioned, losses over 1920 amounted to 6 million guilders, equal to the entire share capital. The Compania Mercantil Argentina appeared to ride out the storm during 1920, only to run into losses of 18 million guilders in 1921, and that on a capital of 20 million guilders. Liquidation was unavoidable. One angry shareholder wanted an inquiry into the causes of the debacle, with special attention paid too the role played by the firm of Wm.H. Müller & Co. The Internationale industrie- en handelsvereeniging of Stokvis & Zonen went down in 1923. No doubt the Russian Revolution had speeded up its demise.

In 1924, Hobbe Smit painted dark clouds over Rotterdam harbour. By that time the clouds were just beginning to lift for the international trading companies, after a deep depression during 1921-1923.

Old firms foundered as well. The Handelmaatschappij v/h Huttenbach & Co. was declared bankrupt in December 1921, having operated in the Dutch East Indies since 1875. As an explanation for its failure, the company cited the fact that, like so many other colonial traders, it had bought a large volume of goods, the prices of which had sunk far below invoice value by the time of their delivery. In addition, the board blamed its banks for having withdrawn their credit facilities at the very moment when they were needed most. The Handelmaatschappij v/h Kerkhoff & Co. also complained that liquidation had become inevitable because its bank had refused further credit.[24] However, in other cases the banks did do their utmost to keep companies going, also from a thorough understanding of their own best interests. Van Nierop & Co.'s Handelmaatschappij was reorganized by splitting the company into its constituent parts, to save the viable activities from being dragged down by bankruptcy. Its liquidation in 1922 led to the formation of two new companies, the NV Handelsvereeniging Oost-Indië, a general trader, and the NV Huidenhandel and Leerlooierij Oost-Indië, a company dedicated to trading and processing hides. After 1923, the latter firm was renamed to Maintz' Productenhandel. This was no doubt due to the reorganization of Maintz & Co., which had also landed in trouble. In both cases banks played a leading role.

It comes as no surprise that Hagemeyer, after all a relative newcomer in this world, experienced severe setbacks as well during the early 1920s. In its report for 1921, the second year as a limited company, the board already referred to falling prices having pushed several trading companies, both big ones and small ones, to the wall. The board remained full of optimism over its own future, however. Most of the company's old stock had been cleared, and agreements had been reached with several suppliers about existing contracts. Moreover, the company had closed its branches in Manchester and in Medan, and had reduced staff numbers at the other offices. Losses of about 500,000 guilders were transferred to the following year. When that year brought another substantial loss, however, a financial reorganization became necessary.[25] The company's bank had sufficient confidence in both the board and the economic prospects to

continue its support, at the price of becoming sole proprietor of all shares for several years. This must have been a bitter blow to the Hagemeijer family. In 1924, the subscribed capital was reduced from 2 million guilders to 750,000 guilders.[26]

Internatio and Borsumij managed to weather the crisis with flying colours. Earlier crises had taught Internatio the importance of keeping substantial financial reserves, declared and undeclared. During the war, the board had already channeled some of the profits to a special price reserve account. This enabled the company to pay a 10% dividend even at the nadir of the crisis, 1921. With its interests spreading to production and shipping agencies, by the way, Internatio was a more complicated organization than most importing traders, but that did not necessarily make it less susceptible to economic fluctuations. Borsumij equally survived the crisis with ease. As a rule, its general manager J.G. Schlimmer favoured prudence. In June 1920, he resisted a dividend increase, asserting that top-heavy prices made the situation in Asia critical for importers. The large stocks and the deliveries under way created an enormous price risk, after all. If the company stuck to its cautious approach, it could afford to lose 1 million guilders without damaging dividends, Schlimmer argued. This policy of dividend consolidation enabled Borsumij to keep its pay outs at 9% during the early 1920s, and to achieve this the company had to dip into its reserves for one year, 1921, alone. In its own view, Borsumij escaped the full impact of the crisis because the company did not have such a large fabrics trade as the other importers had.[27]

In 1907, Borsumij moved its headoffice from Amsterdam to the Hague, which was probably the immediate reason for commissioning a series of photographs. The company's founder J.W. Schlimmer occupies a comfortable armchair in the boardroom, while his son J.G. Schlimmer is seated behind the desk. Though Borsumij had become a limited company as early as 1894, the succession by family members remained a matter of course.

RUNNING A BUSINESS BY REMOTE CONTROL, BUT NOT BLINDLY – Slow communications between the Netherlands and the overseas offices were among the reasons why the 1920 price collapse hit many traders so hard. Delays imposed by the scope of the existing means of communication were sometimes compounded by a defective business organization. It is probably no coincidence that Internatio and Borsumij, two traders older and bigger than the rest, withstood the price avalanche fairly successfully. Internatio in particular had developed an extensive administrative organization to monitor and steer its business. Thus the Rotterdam head office employed no fewer than 42 people in 1913, rising to 73 in 1924. The company's entire European staff numbered 606 in that year.[28] Moreover, the agents in the Dutch East Indies met each other regularly to discuss general business policy, staffing, and conditions of employment. Hagemeyer's fast growth within a short time probably meant that the company lacked a similarly efficient organization. At any rate, Anton Hagemeijer returned to the Dutch East Indies in 1921 to execute the required reorganization in person.

Of course, before the war Hagemeyer had already adopted an administrative system for processing requests from the Dutch East Indies, direct orders to various European manufacturers, and ship goods to Asia. The company built a card index for all products traded, from yarn, silk flowers, essences, chains, machinery, pipes, scissors, locks, and wine glasses, to china tea pots, both ordinary and heat resistant ones. The overseas offices were allowed to suggest changes to the system, but only the Amsterdam headoffice could implement them. The firm also drew up extensive instructions for insuring goods and for handling claims about shipments on delivery. Ever the practical merchants, the company advised that small claims had to be settled immediately, because as a rule in such cases, keeping the goods concerned meant that the final cost would be higher than the original claim, even without counting the loss in time and effort.[29] In 1921, the agents received a terse reminder that complaints about the

In anticipation of a post-war boom, the international traders collectively caused a flood of consumer goods in the overseas colonies. A sound administration with a rapid feedback to the headoffice proved to be a vital aspect of business organisation. On the left, Internatio's Batavia office around 1920. On the right: the unloading of goods directly onto the quay, without the use of lighters, helped to reduce damage.

Hagemeyer's first office in Surabaya had a tile wall panel showing an archer with the ambitious slogan 'We strike home'. This archer subsequently appeared in various guises as the firm's logo. Hagemeyer commissioned the artist Theo van Doesburg, later to become a key figure in the De Stijl movement, to design this 'Cubist Archer' trade mark. It was registered as such in 1920 for all articles, with the exception of fabrics and iron and steel products. Van Doesburg also designed stationery for the company.

quality of shipments should be well founded, and not just reflect on adverse market circumstances. Hagemeyer, by the way, had observed that during the boom of 1920, with huge deliveries leading to chaos, theft had risen considerably, as had the damages percentage. For window panes, breakage averaged 25%, for mirrors 18%, and for china, glassware, and earthenware the usual measure was 5%. For Batavia and Surabaya, where ships could unload directly onto the quays, these percentages were lower than for Semarang, where cargo had to be transferred into lighters, and choppy seas prevailed in the roads.[30]

One of the lessons which Hagemeyer distilled from the boom and the ensuing crisis, was the company's need for better and systematic data about the standing of its customers. As early as November 1920, the Surabaya agent commented that little had been done about collecting relevant information due to the booming market and the evident prosperity of most customers. Now that circumstances had changed, he expected nasty surprises from creditors' agreements, and bankruptcies.[31] Hagemeyer had mainly Chinese wholesalers for its customers, who supplied the numerous inland retail shops of daily utensils. The Amsterdam headoffice attempted to gauge potential turnover per area by scrutinizing population census figures. As this measure proved somewhat coarse, the staff also tried to assess a region's wealth by looking at the number of taxpayers and the number of cars. When turnover in an area lagged far behind what Amsterdam had defined as sales potential on the basis of such calculations, headoffice called its local manager to account.[32]

A.J.M.H.

232

To prevent renewed overstocking, the agents were under express instructions during the early 1920s not to buy for their own accounts. Amsterdam only wanted to execute direct orders from customers, with the exception, however, of products for which Hagemeyer had exclusive sales rights. In 1939, the Palembang agent wrote an interesting comment on the keeping of stocks. According to him the local market was too small for it. His small band of buyers would immediately notice the presence of stocks, cleverly sit and wait until he had exhausted his opportunities for selling, and then offer to relieve him at a discount.[33]

An instruction issued in 1921 forbade agents to place orders directly with manufacturers who had sales representatives stationed in the Dutch East Indies, for head office thought this threatening to the business. For one, because sooner or later these representatives would turn into commercial rivals, and also, because close relationships between sales representatives and the company's agencies depressed sales prices by too much.[34] Amsterdam issued further detailed administrative instructions for keeping track of orders, stocks sailing and on hand, and sales.[35]

Hagemeyer used the telegraph intensively. The company's operations, in fact, made the most of the available communications facilities. Exchanging information by telegrams had the disadvantages of high cost and insufficient security. Consequently, messages were often sent in a concise code known only within the company. This created an exclusive relationship between the purchase organization in the Netherlands and the sales operations overseas. In addition, the Amsterdam office grouped the overseas orders, and searched the European market for suitable products and manufacturers. Such connections could be maintained more efficiently and cheaply from Europe than from the Dutch East Indies. Each month the Hagemeyer agents had to cable their main accounting data to Amsterdam, and in its turn, Amsterdam at the start of each month cabled the volume of shipments and the volume of orders remaining with manufacturers during the preceding month. When KLM (Royal Dutch Airlines) established its regular air service between the Netherlands and the Dutch East Indies in 1930, the agents received instructions no longer to send their data by telegram but by air mail, since this was cheaper. The telephone did not initially assume a role of great importance in business. [36] Thus the magazine *Indische Mercuur* reported that in 1929, telephone conversations between the Netherlands and the Dutch East Indies had totalled 3,413, of which 915 for business purposes, and 2,498 for family chats.[37] Smooth communications between the overseas branches were important as well, by the way, for they had to assist each other with the monopoly agencies and with any potential losses.[38] The spread of wireless telegraphy during the 1920s specifically helped to improve communications within the huge archipelago.[39]

Another important crisis lesson for Hagemeyer found expression in the so-called Indian Instruction No. 34, Supplement No. 3, dated 22 December 1922. During the past years, this Instruction stated, the company had gained mostly bitter experiences with pay advances to the staff. Pay advances did not improve the performance of poor employees, and they spoiled good employees. After these disappointing experiences, the board had had to decide to end this practice for the European staff, much to its chagrin. An exception was made for the indigenous employees, who would remain eligible for advances of no more than a month's pay each on the occasion of Javanese New Year. This complaint should be seen from the perspective of a sharp drop in staff pay, of course. The system of bonuses and profit sharing had accustomed the managerial staff to benefits from rising profits during the years 1914-1919. Such rewards had equalled or even exceeded regular pay, so losing them required a great mental flexibility from the staff. Borsumij's general manager commented in 1922 that the company's employees continued to live in a 'fool's paradise', but that they would have to get accustomed to living within their means.[40]

From 1923, the colonial trading houses in general returned to profitability. The 1920-1922 crisis had been severe, yet short. The plantations entered a period of renewed growth, pulling the Dutch East Indian economy out of the mire. Foreign trade increased again, and the overall standard of living rose. The

The summer weather made tropical Christmases special. In 1928, Internatio organised a football tournament for the occasion. The picture shows employees arriving for the game between the Batavia and Semarang branches, ending in 3-1.

Dutch East Indies entered their 'Indian summer'. Most traders had cut costs, in particular by closing branches in Japan and in the US. Yet not all of the gains made during the war had been lost in the ensuing crisis. On balance, most firms ran a bigger volume of business in 1924 than they had done in 1914. Trade between the Netherlands and its colony did not return to its pre-war pattern. Dutch exports to the Dutch East Indies, made up of fabrics, capital goods, and a wide array of consumer goods, continued to decline as a percentage of the colony's total imports. Concerning exports from the Dutch East Indies, the Dutch share, which had sunk from 26% in 1913 to 16% in 1920, yielded another percentage point, falling to 15% in 1925. The Dutch market share remained especially high in a traditional crop like tobacco, whereas it was small in new products like oil and rubber. The Netherlands did have a reasonable share in copra exports, another new crop, but part of those exports probably served the transit trade.[41]

The violent fluctuations during the early 1920s manifested themselves in other world regions as well. Ceteco, active in Latin America, had operated profitably during the war with local trading. In 1919, imports from Europe recovered, but during 1920 it proved difficult to sell the imported goods. Declining prices for commodities such as coffee, cocoa, and hides seriously harmed the spending power of the local population, so Ceteco became stuck with its consumer products from Europe and from the US. Moreover, many debtors became unable to fullfil their obligations. In 1922, the worst had passed, and several years of rising sales and satisfactory results followed.[42]

The Twentsche Overzee Handelmaatschappij (TOHM) had been founded at the height of the post-war boom, in the summer of 1920, to export bleached cotton goods all over the world. The original intention had been to have the fabrics made by wage labour in Germany and Austria, and to sell them in India, East Africa, and North and South America. Two cotton producers from Enschede, the firms of Nico ter Kuile and B.W. & H. ter Kuile, had taken the initiative for the new company. When prices collapsed at the end of 1920, also hitting the market for cotton fabrics, these plans were scuppered. Within a few years the worldwide ambitions were reduced to exports to just two regions: India and East Africa. In the latter region, the TOHM developed from an importer to a general trader. Business diversified from cotton goods to other manufactured products. The TOHM also embarked on modest exports of raw

234

cotton, copra, and sisal from East Africa. In addition, the company acquired the agency of a shipping company, the Holland-Afrika Lijn. The board valued this representation very highly, because it added to the firm's prestige. This was especially important for a young business. After three difficult initial years, the TOHM's turnover rose until 1930.[43]

The label for cotton fabrics, or tjap, of the Twentsche Overzee Handelmaatschappij, which set out to conquer the world, but eventually found its niche in East Africa.

DOUBTS ABOUT THE VIABILITY OF WHOLESALING – The directional changes in trade flows and the difficulties which merchant houses experienced during the early 1920s, fired a debate in the Netherlands about the viability of wholesaling, focusing on the question whether or not intermediation by independent wholesalers still fitted into the existing economic structure. Admittedly, the rise of manufacturing industry and the appearance of branded products became manifest towards the end of the 19th century, but until 1914 the potential threats from these joint phenomena had been pushed into the background by the economic expansion. Markets had been sufficiently reliable and efficient for manufacturers to depend on them. The war and the ensuing crisis had rocked this trust, so manufacturers did have some reason to develop their own trading activities for securing raw material supplies and product sales.

The economist E.J. Tobi concluded that Dutch wholesaling was being threatened with elimination, since it had been too slow to adapt to the new circumstances. He did not have the quantitative data to back up his argument, but its logic was irresistible. Trade had to become aware of the fact that branded products had enabled industry to undermine the functions of wholesalers. Trade journals and mass advertising provided manufacturers with direct access to their customers, allowing them to assume two key functions of trade, selecting and pushing products. By employing their own travelling salesmen, manufacturers obtained a better grip on their sales, and a better feel for the market. As industry grew in size and developed financial muscle, it would naturally assume a third function, finance, too. Manufacturers producing a range of goods with related distribution channels could also take over the function of grouping orders. Direct relations between manufacturers and customers would also become the trend in the export business.[44]

Now did the rise of corporate manufacturing really lead to the gradual elimination of merchant houses?[45] Data from Dutch occupational censuses show that the number of people working in commerce, i.e. wholesale and retail taken together, continued to rise throughout the 20th century. Employment in trade also increased its share in the labour force, from 9.5% in 1899 to 12.5% in 1930.[46] Trade as a whole, then, offered more and more work, though retailing may have caused this rise more than wholesaling. Chapter IV has already mentioned the fact that chain stores assumed some functions of wholesalers. During the Interwar period, this evolution had lost its revolutionary edge. Having expanded at the time of the First World War, retail chains and department stores entered a phase of maturity characterized mainly by mutual competition. By expanding their product ranges and their services to consumers, such as free cups of coffee, stores like the Bijenkorf and Vroom & Dreesmann attempted to increase turnover.[47]

To what extent did industry assume wholesale functions? There are no data other than the occupational censuses, but sufficient reasons exist for supposing that this effect proved, on balance, not to be as bad as expected. Firstly, because industry generated an enormous expansion in the number of transactions, and partly integrated with functions which it had created itself to begin with. So that part of the integration was not detrimental to existing traders. Secondly, manufacturers often used a combination of strategies to buy supplies and sell products. For some markets or products, traders retained their importance, whereas manufacturers assumed trade functions for other markets and products. The above mentioned broker De Vries underlined this effect in the firm's jubilee book by referring to the Dutch Margarine Union's 1929 decision to concentrate its purchasing activities for copra, oil seeds, and many other raw materials in London. Since the company towered over the Dutch margarine industry, this decision appeared to threaten traders with disaster. In the end, however, things turned out to be not so bad, and traders succeeded in holding on to a fairly large share of the Union's supplies.[48] This example concerns the purchasing end of industry, but the same happened at the sales end. From the First World War, the light bulb producer Philips Gloeilampenfabriek in Eindhoven adopted a strategy of vertical integration. Towards that end, the company established numerous marketing companies abroad over the years. And still Philips continued to use traders and agents as well, first of all for the smaller markets. The Dutch East Indian market was always left to independent intermediaries. Secondly, traders were used to introduce new products. Having established a series of foreign companies selling light bulbs during the years 1919-1925, the Philips board did not consider it self-evident for these companies to market the subsequently developed radio sets as well. During 1925-1930, separate marketing companies were set up for radios, gradually taking over from the independent agents which had meanwhile pioneered the market. Philips definitely did take its agents' interests into account, because of their local knowledge, their experience, and their trading connections.[49]

Of course vertical integration was not the sole privilege of manufacturing. Traders could also adopt it. The Rotterdam wholesaler R.S. Stokvis & Zn. participated in several manufacturing companies, and it developed its own branded products, leading to well-known brands such as Erres, a name derived from the company's two intials, Fasto, and Inventa.[50] As representative for the Dutch market of a German coal mining cartel, the SHV succeeded in acquiring a prominent position in the coal trade. The company built its own river fleet, invested in port facilities, and took shares in mines. Its participations also stretched out into fishing and into several Dutch industrial companies. The SHV general manager, F.H. Fentener van Vlissingen, was even regarded as one of the key champions of Dutch industry. He took an active role in establishing ENKA, a

Department stores and retail chains assumed some functions of traditional wholesaling, but there was heavy competition between them. Publicity campaigns such as the household week advertised by this 1920s poster served to attract customers away from rival outlets.

nieuwe
ERRES
wasmachines

Some traders also moved into producing consumer durables. With this leaflet, R.S. Stokvis & Zn. advertised its own brand of washing machines, Erres.

rayon producer, in 1911, and also in setting up the Koninklijke Hoogovens, a steel works, in 1918. Van Vlissingen had many supervisory directorships, among them the sugar producer CSM, KLM Royal Dutch Airlines, and the engineering works of Stork and Werkspoor, and had seats in innumerable committees and representative boards.[51]

We may thus conclude that the links between industry and trade were subject to change. Exclusive sales agencies, no longer a new phenomenon during the 1920s, but certainly an increasingly prominent feature of trade, signalled an important aspect of this change. In 1925, Hagemeyer commented on the monopoly product trade expanding. The company had such agencies for products such as watches, soap, cigars, and whisky. At that moment in time, Hagemeyer was still a modestly sized merchant house, but this did not mean that it acted for small companies or for Dutch companies only. In a 1937 brochure, Hagemeyer listed as its patrons several big companies, among them the French perfume maker Coty in Paris, the US companies Procter & Gamble for soap, and Reynolds for Camel cigarettes, the British firm of Burroughs Wellcome & Co. for beauty products, and the German manufacturer Beiersdorf & Co.[52] Several Dutch companies also used Hagemeyer as their representative. The cigars of Willem II and the brown sweets called Haagse Hopjes by Frank Rademaker were exported to the Dutch East Indies by Hagemeyer, as were the milk and butter produced by the Lijempf.

According to the US business historian Alfred Chandler, the big US manufacturing concerns had a high degree of vertical integration, a typical feature which they developed towards the end of the 19th century. They gradually took charge of the whole production chain, from purchasing supplies to distributing the final products.[53] However, and this goes for American companies, too, the situation was never clear cut and uniform, for some markets agents remained important. After all, Hagemeyer represented Procter & Gamble and Reynolds on the Dutch East Indian market. The Ford Motor Company did set up a marketing subsidiary for the Netherlands in 1924, but granted Borsumij agencies for the more modest markets of Sumatra, Borneo, Biliton, and Banka.[54] And this, by the way, was only one of the many exclusive agencies handled by Borsumij.[55] Tels & Co., a somewhat smaller trading firm, prided itself in 1939 on its large number of exclusive agencies for well-known brands, particularly in fabrics, consumer products, and food.[56]

The publicity in the colonial magazines of those years allows us to catch a glimpse of the relationship between manufacturers and their agents. Thus Geo. Wehry advertised for Amstel Beer, Hagemeyer recommended Lilly Dental Paste as 'used the world over, sold everywhere', and Jacobson & Van den Berg drew the attention to Champagne Veuve Clicquot.[57] Lindeteves used advertisements to announce its agency for Lips locks and the Peugeot 301 car. However, Philips and Royal Dutch Shell advertised their own products, without mentioning an agent. The same was true for Senator cigars, in those days a household brand.[58]

Anton Hagemeijer considered billboards placed on busy roads an effective means of publicity. The company's Palembang office adhered to his opinion in 1938.

Trading in proprietary brands continued, in addition to agencies for branded products. Having proprietary brands enabled traders to switch suppliers without the customer having to know, something which of course they could ill afford to do with branded products. Proprietary brands meant that traders had to see to their own publicity. Anton Hagemeijer wanted his to be short, clear, and conspicuous. He considered frequent advertising in newspapers a waste of money, but he approved of doing so in the Saturday and Sunday papers, since these were usually read from A to Z on Sundays. As for other kinds of publicity, Hagemeijer thought bill boards, placards, and signs on busy roads to be the most effective means of attracting public attention.[59] Yet, as Hagemeijer assured his agents, giving a good service and personal attention remained the best publicity. The firm should offer its customers service as understood in the us, not just bare service, but service adding value for the customer without cutting the firm's profit margin to the bone. Customers who made money with and by the company's products returned automatically, Hagemeijer argued: the company must earn money, but enable its customers do so, too.[60]

238

Publicity did not stop at the threshold of Geo. Wehry's Cheribon branch. The bookkeeper's jubilee took pride of place, but did not obscure the fact that the company dealt in clocks, and acted as agents for Agfa photographic equipment and Duryea flour.

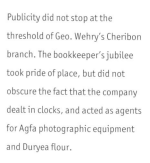

The lack of quantitative data renders it difficult to give a final verdict about the balance between the opposing tendencies towards the elimination of intermediaries on the one hand, and the increasing need for intermediaries on the other. A survey of developments in Britain formulated the following cautious conclusion: 'On balance it would appear that the wholesaler lost ground in the inter-war years but that the decline in his relative importance, taking the whole range of consumer goods trades into consideration, was not very great'.[61]

PROTECTION THROUGH CARTELS AND GOVERNMENT INTERVENTION – By the late 1920s most merchant houses were back to full strength. After 1923 the Netherlands enjoyed a period of vigorous economic growth, for which the expansion of the manufacturing industry provided an important driving force. Exports rose considerably. The service sector, including transport and transshipment, contributed to growth. These fortunate circumstances were not to last very long, however. The New York stock market crash of October 1929 heralded a period of economic depression which gripped the whole world until the mid-1930s. Commodity prices, by the way, had started a declining trend somewhat earlier. During 1930, the stock market collapse appeared to have only a limited impact on the Netherlands, but the Dutch East Indies' economy immediately became trapped in a downward spiral. When in 1931 Britain left the Gold Standard and Germany introduced exchange restrictions, the international depression began to exert a deep influence over the Netherlands, too. Export oriented companies faced severe difficulties in realizing profitable sales abroad, because the Dutch government clung to the Gold Standard until 1936.[62]

With the depression, the international traders entered a new time of worries. The merchant house Reiss & Co. provides a good illustration of what could happen. Since 1923 this firm strove to write off the losses suffered during

Suppliers began to issue warranty cards to convince customers of their excellent service levels. This 1916 warranty has been personally signed by a Stokvis director.

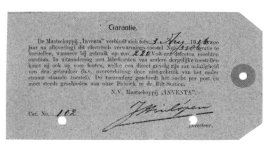

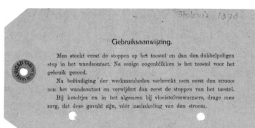

1920-1921. In 1929 Reiss appeared to be close to that aim, but before achieving it, losses mounted again following the difficulties encountered during the 1930s.[63] Commodity prices had already shown a tendency to decline during the late 1920s, but after 1930 they sank deeper and deeper. This had important repercussions for trade in general and for the trade of primary producers such as the Dutch East Indies in particular. First of all, trading volumes and profit margins declined. Commodity producers attempted to consolidate prices by cutting production, resulting in less land reclamation and less soil cultivation. Traders dedicated to supplying agricultural equipment saw their turnover drop sharply. Finally, the population's spending power declined, reducing the demand for everyday consumer goods. Around the world, prices dropped, companies had to cut back production, employees found themselves without work. The slump was all encompassing, whereas the crisis of the early 1920s had mainly hit banks and traders.

Warning of deep falls for those scraping the sky: cartoonist Tjerk Bottema commented somewhat moralistically on the New York stock exchange crash in De Notenkraker on 9 November 1929.

Various strategies were tried to combat the economic depression. Businessmen attempted to support prices by forming cartels, governments endeavoured to stimulate national recovery by trade restrictions, quota, licences, and customs duties, where necessary to the detriment of other countries. The 1930s became the heyday of mutual business arrangements to limit competition, by 'gentlemen's agreements' and conventions. Manufacturing industry made such mutual agreements, but they occurred as well between industry, wholesalers, and consumers.[64] Whenever industry had formed a cartel, traders were automatically forced to accept a corset of agreements. Doing this did not necessarily prevent

Following the New York crash with a slight delay, Dutch stock exchange tickers also began to register alarmingly low share prices.

them from flourishing. Developments in the Dutch coal trade were largely determined by the Dutch mines on one hand, and the SHV, as representative of a German coal syndicate, on the other. The SHV also possessed all shares in its main rival in the port of Rotterdam, the SSM, which sold British coal, though this fact remained a secret at the time. From 1930 the SHV began to take over local coal retailers to increase its grip on the distribution of coal. The inland coal trade had become a cartel in 1929, but this fell apart in 1932, causing such severe price competition that a new cartel agreement covering the Dutch market was signed within a year. The agreement laid down retail prices and quotas.[65] As Chapter IV has shown, the Centraal Bureau (Cebeco), which one may call the merchant house of the agricultural purchasing cooperatives, had been established to prevent the formation of a monopoly in the potassium trade. Having become the main importer of fertilizer and cattle feed, the organization in its turn entered into cartel agreements during the 1930s. This fitted into a policy supporting Dutch business. Cebeco expected only short-term gains from price competition.[66]

Some of the bigger wholesalers also drafted binding price agreements. In 1934, the big paper traders signed such an agreement with the paper manufacturers, with the wholesalers emphasized towards the producers the importance of not selling to traders who undercut the agreed prices. After all, the manufacturers equally benefitted from halting the murderous price competition.[67] These cartels branched out to the Dutch East Indies as well. Internatio, for one, sold 'caustic soda' for the worldwide cartel of ICI, IG Farben, and Alkasso.[68]

Importing wholesale traders in the Dutch East Indies drew together when negotiations loomed with the colonial government about import restrictions.[69] The colonial importers saw the increasing competition from Japan as a threat. As mentioned above, many traders had begun to buy products in Japan during

The coal trade was heavily cartellised. The port of Rotterdam, pictured here in 1936, continued to be an important transshipment station for coal.

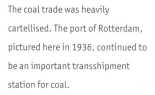

the Great War. Subsequently, Japanese importers and wholesalers had moved into trading Japanese products in the Dutch East Indies. The Japanese industry managed to imitate nearly all European and US products, but with a ratio of price to quality which the original producers could never match. In 1931 the yen was devalued by 60%, rendering Japanese products even cheaper. The Japanese share of total imports into the Dutch East Indies rose from 11% in 1930 to 30% in 1933. To a large extent the colonial traders were responsible for this rise, because they very eagerly added Japanese products to their ranges.[70] Many merchant houses again opened purchasing branches in Japan, among them Hagemeyer.[71] The Amsterdam head office did warn its agents, though, not to run a stock of Japanese products under any circumstances, since with successive ship loads goods always became cheaper again. All such stocks had to be depreciated immediately by 100% on the branches' balance sheets.[72] J.G. Schlimmer, general manager of Borsumij, could even wax lyrical about the Japanese people. In a meeting with the supervisory board, he commented on their energy, zest, and simplicity which made the country into such an inspirational one, contrasting with the West which offered no more than demands, apathy, and languishing businesses.[73] Jacobson & Van den Berg initially exercised restraint towards imports of Japanese products, on account of existing ties with European producers, and because any business with Japan had to be done for own account. In 1933, the firm switched positions after all, resulting in the board concluding in 1936 that the trade for own account far exceeded the commission business.[74]

However, the international traders were less happy with Japanese aspirations to take over the wholesale and distribution functions as well. Schlimmer thought that the Japanese went too far in this respect. Internatio's manager A. Hombrink agreed, commenting that if the Japanese succeeded in realizing their aims, the end would be nigh for the European importers. For that reason the

242

The Pasar Baroe shopping street in Batavia, with on one corner the Toko Bombay-Yokohama shop. During the 1930s, competition from Japan became a serious worry for the merchant houses in the Dutch East Indies.

Batavia importers had acted judiciously in warning the colonial government of this imminent threat, and in asking for support. After all, according to Hombrink, not just the import trade was under threat, but a much wider issue, for what would be the political value of a *Dutch* East Indies if trade and distribution had become 90% Japanese?[75] Internatio accordingly championed a trade organization of colonial importers, while the company also pressed the government for action. In East Africa, by the way, the TOHM also suffered from the competition of Japanese products.

The Dutch government, having hastily dropped its active stance in the wake of the First World War, could not but return to increasingly interventionist economic policies during the 1930s depression. To secure the exports of Dutch industry, trade treaties were concluded, often aiming to alleviate the consequences of protectionism introduced abroad. As a small country, the Netherlands did not have a very strong bargaining position, leading to necessarily limited results. Government support during the 1930s was mainly directed at agriculture, less so at manufacturing industry. Official intervention in trade mainly concerned retailing, with the introduction of legislation regulating the establishment of new shops, seasonal sales, and opening hours. The needs of wholesaling received far less attention. In 1938, the secretary of the Chamber of Commerce for Rijnland, P.G. Knibbe, in a blazing speech to the members of the Dutch association of grain and flour traders, pleaded for government regulation in wholesaling. According to him, the activities of the big companies on one hand, and the official crisis intervention in agriculture on the other, threatened to crush this sector between them. Knibbe appealed to the government to protect the position of wholesaling, for he deemed independent wholesalers essential to keeping the Netherlands and the Dutch people free from unwanted tyranny. It is unclear how many wholesalers shared these ideas. Most traders probably preferred to run their businesses without government intervention. Knibbe com-

243

Many international traders chose to meet the Japanese competition head-on, by opening their own offices in Japan and setting up in Japanese goods themselves. The picture shows Geo. Wehry's Osaka branch in 1933.

mented himself that the wholesale trade trod the road to the relevant ministries all too rarely.[76]

For a considerable time, businessmen in the Dutch East Indies failed to agree whether or not the colonial government had a regulating task to perform in the crisis gripping commodity production and trade. Initially the top plantation companies, which usually had a fairly strong influence on the market as well, held the opinion that the crisis should be allowed to run its natural course, weeding out the weaker businesses, and clearing the field for the most efficient producers. As prices continued their relentless decline, however, most businessmen lost their confidence in the efficiency of the market.[77] This also held true for the merchant houses with substantial plantation interests. As a consequence of the depression the HVA, which had really become a composite plantation company, had to cut back production sharply. Sugar production was completely halted.[78] Managing plantations had become the core business for H.G.Th. Crone. Its main interests were tobacco, rubber, and tea, sugar to a lesser extent, and as a consequence the firm did a little better than the HVA. Crone closed its commodity sales department, which had been taken over from the HVA in 1911, in 1928 after poor results. In 1931 the firm suffered a heavy loss, and during the remainder of the 1930s profits proved no more than meagre.[79] Van Eeghen & Co., which had also largely switched to the colonial commodity business, went into decline, partly because H.L. van Eeghen proved a less dynamic personality than his father S.P. van Eeghen had been. This firm, by the way, also occupied itself with capital management.[80]

In 1933, manager Hombrink of Internatio, which had substantial interests in sugar plantations, described the disastrous impact of the world crisis on sugar production. He returned to the Dutch East Indies after a four-year absence. Describing a landscape nearly empty of sugar cane, closed factories and empty loading bays already marked by a lack of maintenance, warehouses brimming with sugar turning into syrup, Hombrink confessed himself to be more moved by this industry's desperate situation than he had been after reading all relevant annual reports and statistics.[81] Gradually, and after lengthy negotiations international production restrictions were agreed for many commodities, helping to consolidate prices.

A range of measures introduced to regulate colonial imports also aimed to support Dutch industry. The colonial government designed a system of import licences to discriminate by country of origin and by quantities imported. The Twente cotton industry notably profited by these regulations. Internatio faced an interesting conflict of conscience as a result. In 1933 the Dutch East Indies' government imposed quota for imports of fabrics. Importers had to buy part of their assigned quota from producers in Twente, the rest being free. Hombrink wondered whether the free quota should be granted to Internatio's close customers in Twente, or better used to order in Japan. The solution was not so difficult. Profits on Japanese fabrics were three times higher than on the Twente products. Moreover, Hombrink, keeping an eye on the future, considered it prudent to nurse connections with Japanese producers.[82]

244

Tobacco supplies from the Dutch East Indies made Amsterdam into an important centre for the tobacco trade, which it remained until well into the 1950s. In the absence of uniform product standards for tobacco leaves, buyers had to muster the lots in person before the auction in the Frascati building, pictured here in 1926. Below, brokers scrambling to obtain the best deals for their principals at an auction in March 1929.

245

MANUFACTURING ACTIVITIES IN THE DUTCH EAST INDIES – In this way the colonial government attempted to combat the depression by restricting both exports of commodities and imports of manufactured products. Alternatively, the economy of the Dutch East Indies could be supported by stimulating an indigenous industry for import substitution. The colonial government had drafted schemes towards that end as early as during the First World War without really putting anything into effect, and during the prosperous 1920s the plans had been shelved. Several European and US manufactures, however, had established production units to get closer to the market. During the 1930s, the colonial government resumed its efforts. Several initiatives were developed in cooperation with the business community. A committee of prominent leaders from industry and banking was charged with analysing the opportunities for industrialization. The merger between two tin companies was considered, but it did not go through. Schemes were drafted for establishing an aluminium industry. The threat of war inspired a demand to set up an indigenous chemical industry. None of these ambitious government plans produced concrete results, however.[83]

Several merchant houses responded to the official aspirations to create local industries by devising more modest plans of their own, hoping to realize them with government support through guaranteed purchases or with market regulations. At that period, the colonial traders went through difficult times.

During the early 1930s, those trading companies quoted at the stock exchange all lost money, and were consequently forced to cut their business. Out of fifteen firms, only five paid any dividend at all in 1932, and the following year this number declined to three.[84] Setting up new activities thus became a matter of survival. The government's restrictions on Japanese imports did help the international traders to consolidate their position, but at the same time this made them conscious of how dependent they really were on free trade. Getting access to locally produced goods, in one way or another, appeared to be a sensible way to reduce this dependency. In 1938, both Internatio and Borsumij came to the conclusion that it made sense for them to safeguard turnover by increasing their interests in manufacturing industry.

Internatio was on familiar ground here, by the way, for together with the Papierfabriek Gelderland in Nijmegen, a paper manufacturer, and the trading firm Handelmaatschappij v/h Rupe & Colenbrander, the company had begun a joint venture for making paper from rice straw in 1921. The Papierfabriek Gelderland managed production, and Internatio marketed the paper. The colonial government supported the venture by agreeing to buy, every year for a period of twelve years, a set quantity of paper equal to almost half of the original production capacity. Prices were set for three years.[85] By the time that the guaranteed government purchases ended, the factory had become strong enough to do without support.

Difficulties with imports inspired Internatio to participate in a candy works set up by one of its principals, the British candy producer C. & E. Morton. Internatio and Morton jointly managed the production, and Internatio marketed the candy. The factory ran into fierce competition from Chinese and indigenous producers. In 1933, Internatio entered calico production by setting up the Preanger Bontweverij in Garut, a joint venture with several Twente manufacturers whose consignments the company had sold for many years. Internatio took the initiative for this venture, and purposefully approached the manufacturers to join. The Bontweverij became an important employer for the region, with a staff of 24 Europeans and over 3,000 indigenous employees in 1940.[86] Internatio also participated in a spinning mill, set up by a group of Dutch cotton producers. With the Chamotte-Unie from the Dutch town of Geldermalsen, a joint venture for the production of fire-proof building materials was set up in 1937. And Internatio finally added a small cigar factory to its tobacco trade. The company's industrial activities remained modest in size compared to its commitments to trade and colonial plantations.[87]

All Internatio's industrial activities were joint-ventures, the cigar factory excepted. The company preferred this as the best way to obtain the skills needed to run specific industrial production units. Internatio's board openly admitted that its commercial origins made the company a newcomer to industry. This meant that it should embark on manufacturing only with expert partners under the express condition that these had committed themselves to building up the venture concerned.[88] Internatio, then, entered into commitments with industry,

In the Dutch East Indies, merchant houses entered into joint-ventures with manufacturers. An early example was the Padalarang paper factory, set up by Internatio with the Papierfabriek Gelderland.

but did not want to assume the role of manufacturer. For production issues the company trusted the skills of its partners, while keeping the marketing for itself.

Lindeteves-Stokvis partly used the same strategy as Internatio, expanding its industrial interests through joint ventures. In 1934 the company founded a paint works in collaboration with the Dutch producers of Sigma paints, NV Pieter Schoen & Zoon in Zaandam. Lindeteves' engineering works, dating from 1920, merged with the colonial activities of the engineers De Vries Robbé & Co. in the Dutch town of Gorinchem. In addition, the company began the production of steel barrels.[89] Managing power stations and water companies became Maintz & Co.'s main activity, though maintaining its ties with several plantation companies. The company also managed a broadcasting station, the Nederlandsch-Indische Radio-Omroep Maatschappij.[90] Borsumij participated in various ventures, including a bicycle factory and a leather factory, considering these participations as experimental investments, designed to sustain turnover. For the board remained as yet unconvinced that the manufacturing activities would survive without the government's protection.[91] Hagemeyer limited its industrial commitments to a few short-lived investments.

Lindeteves-Stokvis and the Zaandam paint producer Pieter Schoen & Zn. (Sigma) jointly founded a paint works. Their Batavia paint shop, Toko Eltosin, opened in 1934.

RENEWED EXPANSION – During the late 1930s, the merchant houses entered into a new expansionary phase. This became manifest not just from the commitments to manufacturing, which ranged from extensive to limited, but also from a rising number of branches. In addition to the Japanese offices mentioned above, the traders developed an interest in branches in Singapore and Malaysia. These expansions increased the demands on staff management. In the early 1930s, most traders had had to cut staff numbers and to lower the remunerations sharply. When new scope for growth appeared by the end of the 1930s, a rising number of Europeans had to be hired and trained to run the branches, and they had to be found a proper place within the respective organizations. This was all the more complicated because of the arrangements concerning staff leave, which, depending on the firm, might last from six to nine months, and might be claimed by employees after a stay in Asia of five to eight years. Each company had its own customs concerning questions such as the amount of salary paid during leave, any compensation for the passage to Europe, and, if paid by the company, whether or not this covered family members travelling as well.[92] In 1939, Hagemeyer used an employment contract stipulating that the employee was obliged to work at any office in the Far East to which the board sent him. The contract began to apply on the day of the employee's arrival in Asia, and ended on the day when he left work for European leave. The timing and conditions of such leave would be granted at the board's discretion. The terms omitted to mention anything about salaries during leave. Hagemeyer paid annual bonuses, using a somewhat subjective assessment of each individual employee's contribution for setting the amounts. In 1922, the company had had an arrangment using gross profits as a gauge, but the resulting awkward disputes had inspired the board to adopt a simpler system.[93]

Staff management required a complex interaction between the respective Dutch headoffices and their overseas branches. On regular inspection trips, general managers from the Netherlands attempted to keep abreast with what happened in the offices overseas. Before the First World War managers would

248

undertake these expeditions a few times in their lifetime at most, but during the interwar years such business trips occurred very frequently. At this stage, head office managers often had experience of working in Asia during an earlier phase of their careers, so they knew the situation at first hand. During visits from head office, the overseas branch managers would strive to present themselves in the best possible light, in the hope of afterwards getting a good mark in the report. Such efforts shine through in reports like the one written in 1932 by T.P. Baart de la Faille, formerly Internatio chief agent and subsequently promoted to become one of the company's managers, about a visit to the Tandjong Karong branch, commenting on the spirited and skillful way in which the agent Den Hertog and his staff took the company's interests to heart. He had received an equally good impression from the Gawok branch, but had missed the necessary 'esprit de corps' at Surabaya, which would have befitted its new, spacious, and smart accommodation.[94] Such reports were sent in copious numbers to the Netherlands, to give headoffices an impression of business at the overseas branches, and of how various employees performed. By the 1930s most merchant houses had established some form of pension or a savings arrangement for their European staff.[95] There are few details about staff numbers, because annual reports failed to mention them. To give some indication, then: around 1939, Lindeteves-Stokvis had the following staff disposition: a total of 130 people worked in Amsterdam, London, and New York offices, the operations in the Dutch East Indies and in the Straits Settlements employed about 500 European staff, and in addition several thousand Chinese and indigenous employees.[96] In 1939, Internatio had 145 people working in the Dutch headoffice and 4,000 in Asia. This figure did not include staff at the plantation companies and the industrial joint-ventures.[97] Stokvis & Zonen, a wholesaler mainly active in the Netherlands, employed about 1,300 people in 1940.[98] Staff size at Hagemeyer is not exactly known. At the end of the 1930s, the Amsterdam headoffice employed an estimated 50 people. By that time the chief agency in Batavia, Hagemeyer's most important overseas office, had a staff of six Dutch people and more than thirty Chinese and Indonesians, while the other fourteen branches counted two Dutchmen at most. Thus total staff probably numbered between 100 and 200 people.[99]

In the final analysis, how did the merchant houses during the 1930s perform overall? The combined restrictions on both exports and imports of course proved a formidalble obstacle to free trade. Yet within those restrictions, the opportunities for profitable trade apparently expanded, for after 1935 most

249

The sarong weaving mill of the Preanger Bontweverij, a jointventure of Internatio with Twente cotton manufacturers.

Staff and customers celebrate the
opening of Geo. Wehry's new Medan
office in 1932.

traders succeeded in finding their way out of the thicket, benefitting from more
favourable economic circumstances. Figure 5.1 presents data on the dividends
of a number of merchant houses, and Figure 5.2 shows average dividends for
fifteen such firms. Both figures give the pay-outs as a percentage of a company's
nominal capital, the usual measure at that time.[100] Of course dividends reflect a
company's true profitability only to some extent. Even so the impact of economic fluctuations is clearly evident from these graphs. The years 1921 and 1933
show clear troughs, whereas the second half of the 1920s was favourable. The
First World War provided a peak in pay-outs, but the picture is a flattered one
because of the high inflation during that time. Figure 5.1 demonstrates the
extent to which the traders experienced the economic cycles in very similar
ways. In 1937 there was another peak, though a lower one. Optimism returned
to such an extent, that serveral merchant houses expanded their capital in 1937.
When Hagemeyer did so in 1937, its shares were simultaneously floated on the
Amsterdam stock exchange.[101] From then on, the company became subjected to
probing questions from investors, and to comments from stock analysts.
Prompted by the annual report for 1939, the weekly magazine *De Zakenwereld*
(*Business World*) wrote in April 1940: 'Not a bad investment for someone with
sufficient patience and with sufficient means to accept the inherent risk of colo-
nial securities.'[102] Patience was to be in sore demand, for in May 1940 the
Netherlands was drawn into the Second World War.

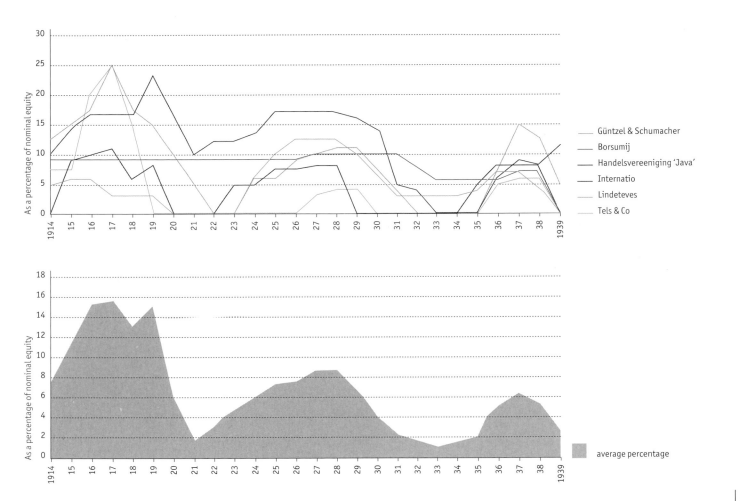

Figure 5.1

Dividends of 6 Dutch trading houses

Figure 5.2

Dividends of 15 Dutch trading houses

Legend (Figure 5.1):
- Güntzel & Schumacher
- Borsumij
- Handelsvereeniging 'Java'
- Internatio
- Lindeteves
- Tels & Co

average percentage (Figure 5.2)

During the years 1914-1940, the political and economic circumstances underwent profound changes. War and chauvinistic protectionism restricted the freedom of merchant houses, but offered them new opportunities, too. The international trading companies could survive only by deploying maximum flexibility, and by changing tack in time. Seeking new trade routes proved to be one of the solutions. Manufacturing industry assumed some trade functions, but with exclusive brand agencies the traders retained a worthwhile field of operations, which, moreover, could be extended to various markets. During the 1930s depression, traders sought protection from cartel agreements with manufacturing industry in the Netherlands, whereas they expanded their operations in the Dutch East Indies with manufacturing ventures.

On May 10, 1940, the Germans
invaded the Netherlands. A heavy
bombardment of Rotterdam
contributed to the Dutch capitulating
within a five days. Many Rotterdam
trading firms lost their offices.
Moreover, in 1944 the Germans
demolished the city's port facilities
and quays. As late as 1946 a lot of
clearing still needed to be done
before the harbour for Rhine shipping
could be rebuilt.

CHAPTER VI

Just as the First World War had temporarily suspended the growth of international economic linkages, the Second World War heralded a break with the past in starting the process of decolonisation. The overseas colonial empires disintegrated, forcing the colonial traders to grope their way through radically altered political circumstances. The merchant houses had experienced increasing political interference with their business as early as the 1930s. During the war government pressure intensified still further, and it remained a dominant fact of life for a long time after the war. Finding themselves in a world of military violence, political pressure, and uncertain economic circumstances, the international traders attempted to keep trade flows going and to secure their income.

TRADING UNDER ENEMY OCCUPATION – The Second World War broke out in September 1939, when German armies invaded Poland, causing Britain and France to declare war on Germany. Just as in the First World War, the Netherlands hoped to be able to maintain a neutral position, but in May 1940 the German invasion shattered this illusion. Queen Wilhelmina and the council of ministers fled to London, setting up an official Dutch government in exile there. As a consequence, Dutch companies with international operations suddenly faced two regimes, one in allied territory, and one under German occupation. Some of the international traders had used the temporary respite since September 1939 to anticipate the eventuality of the Netherlands being drawn into the fighting. As early as May 1939, the Ceteco board had issued a warrant entrusting the Curaçao managers with the overall control of the company's overseas business if and when the Netherlands should come to fall under enemy occupation. Internatio had managed to send a number of senior staff to the US in the nick of time. Other companies, such as Hagemeyer, effected a formal move of the company seat during the war. For this purpose, the exiled government set up a special commission to validate the legal formalities for such a move, and to appoint new executives and new supervisory directors. In cases like that of Hagemeyer the rupture of communications between the Netherlands and its overseas territories could have peculiar consequences, with two head offices drafting an annual report for 1939. Both the Dutch office and the one in the Dutch East Indies, by the way, concluded that the company was in good shape.

The Netherlands had carefully prepared for war by building stocks and by setting up official agencies, called Rijksbureaus, which controlled the distribution of industrial raw materials. Most overseas imports and exports fell away following the German occupation, but simultaneously the German market was opened for Dutch business, and this market had an almost insatiable demand for goods. As a consequence, the Netherlands was inundated with German orders. Selling products proved to be no problem at all, but over time the stagnating supply of raw materials imposed severe restrictions. Until the end of 1941, Dutch industry maintained satisfactory production levels. Farmers had the crucial task of supplying sufficient food. The retail trade had sufficient work to do, profiting from a faster goods turnover and opportunities for a gradual clearance of old stock. Amidst all this business activity, wholesalers also continued to find satisfactory employment.

As the war continued, its consequences became ever more pressing. During the winter of 1941-1942 a severe coal shortage left the population out in the cold, and forced some companies to close. The war had forced itself into the lives of the Jewish population much earlier and in a much more dramatic way. They had been isolated and stigmatised as a group more or less from the start. From 1941 Dutch Jews were deported to German concentration camps, from which only very few returned. In 1942 the Nazis began to round up Dutch workers to fill the need for labour in German factories. During 1943

Blowing up the river bridges failed to halt the German advance. The Dutch army vainly demolished the one crossing the Meuse here, in Maastricht. Capitulation followed on May 15, 1940.

they relented, considering it more sensible to let the Dutch produce goods for the German population in their own country, but in the spring of 1944 the German occupation regime intensified its efforts, forcing Dutch labour to work in the Reich. To increase economic efficiency, business had been grouped into sectoral organisations in the German mould, assigning the international traders to the wholesale group. However, the new organisation failed to solve the most pressing economic problem, the increasing scarcity of raw materials. Of needs, surrogates and alternative raw materials became the norm. In 1944, industrial production and productivity declined sharply, and after the liberation of the southern Netherlands in September 1944, hardly any serious work was done at all in the northern part of the country, which continued under occupation until May 1945. The population there had to spend most of its energy on its daily efforts to find food.[1]

War circumstances probably effected little change in the relationship between trade and manufacturing. A scarce supply of products made traditional wholesaler functions such as publicity and pushing new products largely redundant. Supplying credit also became less important, as most companies had more than ample liquidity. As a consequence, manufacturers could assume wholesaling functions without much additional effort. It remains to be seen whether they really did take the trouble of doing so, however, as the prevailing scarcity meant that goods sold anyway. At first, the balance of power between market parties favoured the manufacturers, but the rationing of products gave customers, and indirectly trade, more leverage, in a way shifting the struggle to obtaining the necessary rationing scrips.[2] From day to day government influence increased, more specifically the powers wielded by the officials running the *Rijksbureaus*, who distributed the scarce raw materials and assigned German orders. Working

Drawing on the lessons from the First World War, the Dutch government had prepared the rationing of food very thoroughly, including an experiment with the rationing of sugar. Goods for which scarcity was expected, such as coffee and tea, were rationed as early as June 1940, when this picture of an Amsterdam shop was taken.

closely with representatives of each sector, the Rijksbureaus tried to consolidate the pre-war circumstances as faithfully as possible in most cases. One sector in which this happened was the paper trade, where wholesalers successfully defended their position, even when direct selling from producer to consumer would have made economic sense under war circumstances. In their turn, whenever possible the paper wholesalers made a point of using pre-war sales figures as a basis for supplying their regular customers.[3] The principle of distributing scarce supplies according to pre-war ratios was assumed as right and proper more or less by everyone. Relations between wholesalers and retailers in the coal trade, for instance, completely rigidified along such lines.[4] Presumably this consolidation of pre-war circumstances tallied exactly with the intentions of most Dutch people. The Nazis attempted to reorganise Dutch business along entirely new lines, whereas the Dutch, particularly after 1942, mainly preferred to continue as best they could while awaiting the end of the war.

Of course some traders took the opportunity to profit from the scarcity, and to achieve a sharp increase of turnover and profits. Scarcity always creates black markets, and the appearance of war profiteers testified to that. It is hard to say whether this was a widespread phenomenon, and to what extent bona fide wholesalers engaged in it.[5] A comparison of the census of 1930 with that of 1947 appears to suggest that trade as a whole presumably remained a fairly stable occupation. During that period total employment in trade rose slightly, whereas people working in trade as a percentage of the labour force declined somewhat.

With the German occupation of the Netherlands, the head offices of the merchant houses operating in the Dutch East Indies had lost their main function, as the German invasion broke off nearly all contact with the world overseas. Consequently, these firms had to make a fresh start in domestic trade within the Netherlands, if only to meet the costs of their head offices. At first they could still trade available stocks which, ordered for overseas markets, could no longer be shipped there. Moreover, during the initial war years substantial imports of consumer goods continued, so we may assume that the traders succeeded in setting up new activities.[6] War circumstances or not, interesting transactions still remained possible, such as the export of flower bulbs to France in return for imports of French perfume for the Dutch market. Hagemeyer managed to keep its head office going, even realising a modest profit.[7] Immediately upon the end of the occupation P.H.F. Heijen, who managed the Dutch end of Hagemeyer during the war, described in a letter to staff in the Dutch East Indies, that the firm had begun the war with a large stock, some of it bought immediately after the occupation. Profits had been good, but nothing fancy, as pushing prices proved impossible under the circumstances. Revenues had just covered costs, and no more, whereas the war had offered opportunities for large profits. That would have required collaborating with the Nazis, however, and the company had been averse to that on grounds of principle. Moreover, Heijen had foreseen the eventual outcome all along, and considered the need for open seas all-important. Finally the heavy taxes had made huge inroads. Even so, the company could remain satisfied, for many of its rivals had had to run up large debts with their banks to keep their head office going.[8]

Lindeteves-Stokvis also managed to develop a business within the Netherlands to cover the costs of the Amsterdam-based operations.[9] Jacobson Van den Berg & Co. found an intriguing new field of operations in the Netherlands by getting involved with the official organisation running the rationing of fabrics. For a fixed fee per staff member per month, the Rijksbureau concerned, called Distex, hired Jacobson Van den Berg & Co. to run its operations by providing its staff, office, and all other requirements, including typewriters. To get the numbers required, the company even had to bring in additional personnel hired from Ruys & Co. By thus providing Distex with the experienced office services needed, Jacobson Van den Berg & Co. ensured work for its own staff under its regular management.[10]

In 1942, the Germans appointed *Verwalter* or special supervisors to all Dutch merchant houses with operations in the Dutch East Indies. Most boards tried to circumvent their *Verwalter* as best they could by suspending the regular meetings of shareholders or of supervisory directors. As a consequence, information about day-to-day business at these companies remains scanty. After the war, Lindeteves-Stokvis commented that its *Verwalter* had given the company very little trouble, for a cost of 26,865 guilders' salary.[11] To Germans such appointments probably offered an attractive opportunity for escaping front-line service, regardless of any question over exercising influence.

While Germany was still a winning side and full of optimism about

257

In 1942, the prominent Dutch national socialist M.M. Rost van Tonningen founded the Nederlandsche Oost-Compagnie or NOC, and he subsequently tried to enlist the support of merchant houses for colonising territories in Poland and the Ukraine under NOC colours. The company's logo, with its clear echoes of the VOC emblem, publicised these colonial ambitions.

From 1942, the German regime appointed *Verwalter* or supervisors to the boards of all colonial trading houses. The Austrian F. Jarl was assigned to Internatio. In February 1945, he became nervous about the Allied advance and fled back to his native country.

establishing its much-vaunted thousand year Reich, the Dutch Nazi collabora-
tor M.M. Rost van Tonningen developed plans for Dutch colonies in Eastern
Europe. He nursed hopes to interest companies such as the colonial trading
houses for his project, used as they were to operate in such circumstances. In
June 1942 the Nederlandsche Oost Compagnie was set up to coordinate business development in the prospective colonies. The plans failed, however, to raise
any enthusiasm in the Netherlands. Moreover, any plans soon got bogged down
in a bureaucracy, as the organisation at the German end was very opaque. In the
end the tide of war rendered all initiatives obsolete.[12] Consequently the Nederlandsche Oost Compagnie did not generate any employment for the trading
houses. To give their staff a semblance of work, the companies organised cours-
es throughout the war. The Internatio board, for instance, gave lectures on the
Dutch East Indies, confidently assuming a return to this field of operations in
due course. With the fuel scarcity getting ever more pressing, Dutch office hours
were cut anyway.[13] Meanwhile anxiety deepened about the overseas branches
and staff under Japanese occupation.

THE SITUATION IN THE DUTCH EAST INDIES – Until 1942 the trading houses in
the Dutch East Indies had succeeded admirably in continuing their business,
despite having been cut off so suddenly from their head offices in May 1940.
The Java Sumatra Handel Maatschappij saw itself faced with all kinds of questions and uncertainties, which had to be solved now without the usual recourse
to 'Amsterdam'. The Hagemeyer branches became confused about the matter
of sending their accounting data to the main Batavia branch, or to Anton
Hagemeyer who happened to be in Manchester when the Netherlands were
occupied. In the end the Batavia chief agent, J.H. Middeldorp, was entrusted
with the general management over the entire business. In 1941, the exiled
government's London commission sanctioning the formalities of company law
informed the Batavia managers that it had dismissed Anton Hagemeijer, who
had meanwhile moved to New York, as general manager. The board minutes
failed to mention any motivation for this decision. After the war it turned out
that the commission had dismissed Hagemeijer from his position for having
been a regular donor to the NSB, the Dutch Nazi party, before the war. His
prolonged travelling abroad had prevented him from discontinuing his donor-
ship after the German occupation. Meanwhile the Germans also considered
Hagemeijer as an enemy, confiscating his possessions in the Netherlands,
including his Blaricum home.[14]

Overall, the overseas branches proved exceedingly capable of continuing
in business under their own steam. At the request of the exiled London government, the traders began to build up large stocks in the Dutch East Indies, partly
with supplies bought in China and in Japan. However, their activities in the
Dutch East Indies came to an abrupt halt with Japan's lightning advance
through Asia and its subsequent occupation of the Dutch East Indies. In

Until the Japanese attack of March
1942, business in the Dutch East
Indies continued more or less as
usual. Bank transactions with Japan
also went ahead more or less
normally.

258

After the capitulation of the Dutch East Indian forces on 8 March 1942, Japanese soldiers triumphantly entered Batavia.

February 1942, Hagemeyer's general manager Middeldorp announced large losses following the Japanese capture of Malaysia. He still considered the company's position as sound, despite having been busy cancelling orders, and despite not knowing the results of his actions since the purchasing branches had failed to wire replies. Less than a month later, on the 8th of March 1942, the Dutch East Indian forces capitulated. Even so the Dutch succeeded in destroying some of the infrastructure, some productive units, and particularly the oil installations in the Dutch East Indies, whereas the German surprise attack in Europe had delivered the Dutch productive system more or less intact into the enemy hands. The Japanese had a clear interest in the continuation of economic activities, with sugar plantations and cinchona plantations receiving special attention, but even so they gradually began to remove all European staff, deporting them to concentration camps. The women and children of Europeans were subsequently also imprisoned. In a retrospect over these years, Lindeteves stressed the personal misery, the material damage, and the complete disruption of everything intentionally and systematically wrought by the Japanese occupation regime on the Dutch East Indies, in disregard of all laws of civilisation and humanity, and surpassing all that had happened in the Netherlands itself.[15] The post-war annual reports with their long lists of deceased staff provide a sad testimony to the large numbers of casualties suffered during the war in the Dutch East Indies. The long delay in drafting such reports underlines how difficult it was after the war to get any insight at all into what had happened to companies while the fighting lasted.

One of the few traders to experience positive effects from the war as well as negative ones, was Ceteco, which operated entirely within Allied territory. The branches on the Cape Verdian islands and Portuguese East Africa had to be closed, and a staff shortage also led to the closure of some South American branches. By contrast, the Santo Domingo branches with their mixed business of trade and industry did very well, and the industrial interests in Colombia yielded favourable results. The New York office succeeded in taking over some of the purchasing activities formerly done in Europe, just as in the First World War, so the relations with the company's overseas customers continued, and the marketing organisation remained intact.[16] In East Africa, the Twentsche Overzee Handel Maatschappij or TOHM also achieved a substantial increase of its turnover in both exports and imports during the war. Though the company did lose its customers in continental Europe, it established new relations with manufacturers in India, Britain, Southern Africa, and North America. As a producer of key raw materials, East Africa profited from the economic circumstances created by the war, which increased the population's spending power.[17] However, Ceteco and TOHM were favourable exceptions to the rule. For most merchant houses, the Second World War proved to be a nadir in their existence. From the summer of 1944, a heartfelt longing for an end to the fighting was felt by all.

The war years were fairly favourable for the Twentsche Overzee Handel-Maatschappij in East Africa. On the left the Tanga office, right the workshop and garage in Dar es Salaam.

IF THE DUTCH EAST INDIES ARE LOST... – The end of the Second World War did not bring a sudden and tempestuous revival of trade, such as had happened at the end of the First World War. The merchant houses faced a bleak situation to begin with. A glaring scarcity of goods and food reigned everywhere, but the opportunities for trading them remained limited in numerous ways. International trade was hemmed in on all sides. The German hinterland lay in ruins, and the Allied occupying forces clung to a policy of self-sufficiency. The transit trade offered few prospects for economic growth for the time being. The situation in the Dutch East Indies continued to be uncertain.

In the Netherlands, the advancing Allied armies had ended the German occupation in May 1945. When Germany capitulated, Allied and Dutch forces were present in the country to exercise authority. The situation in Indonesia was completely different. Japan, bowing to the unprecedented disasters caused by the detonation of two atomic bombs, capitulated sooner than the Allies had expected, on the 15th of August 1945. At that moment, no Allied armies had as yet landed in the archipelago. This power vacuum led to chaos. The Dutch government counted on its Allies to help restore its old colonial rule, though the Netherlands had been defeated both in Europe and in Asia. Dutch public opinion considered the potential loss of the Dutch East Indies as fatal to the country's economy, a feeling ably expressed in the then current saying 'If the Dutch East Indies are lost, all is lost'. With hindsight it is particularly striking that the Netherlands took the restoration of colonial rule for granted. Dutch business also expected that it could pick up the threads where they had broken in 1942. However, during the Second World War the political circumstances had drastically changed. Throughout the war, the Allies themselves had used terms such as political self-determination and democracy to inspire the soldiers fighting on their side, many of whom came from colonial territories. Nationalist Indonesians had been exhorted by Allied propaganda to start a guerrilla war against the Japanese, and after capitulating, the Japanese supported the nationalist movement. In August 1945, the Indonesian nationalists proclaimed the independent Republic of Indonesia, inaugurating a struggle for liberation lasting more than four years.

Australian soldiers land on the
Borneo coast near Balikpapan, 1945.
In the background dark clouds from
burning oil wells.

The chaotic circumstances that prevailed immediately following the capitulation are illustrated to good effect by the British supreme commander for the area, Admiral Lord Mountbatten, ordering the Japanese commanders to remain at their posts and await the arrival of the British forces. He also ordered the prisoners of war and the civil internees not to leave the Japanese concentration camps until Allied forces had arrived on the scene, since it appeared to be safer in the camps than outside them. During the entire autumn of 1945, fighting between Allied troops and Indonesian Republicans continued on Java. In late November 1945, the Hagemeyer board in Batavia wrote to its agents, describing the fairly heavy fighting which had raged in the city. Most offices remained closed, the Kali Besar and surrounding area being the scene of frequent disturbances. According to this circular, severe unrest had also affected Semarang, leading to the air service being suspended. The Batavia managers had lost contact with the branch in the city. Surabaya appeared to be calmer, but a formal state of war continued to apply there. From the Outer Provinces little or no information trickled through, but the situation was assumed to be fairly calm.[18]

For many Europeans in the Dutch East Indies, the end of the Second World War brought nothing but profound disillusion. In a letter to the Amsterdam head office, Hagemeyer's Batavia directors described this emotion of people having survived internment in concentration camps only to face renewed upheavals, filling them with fear. The managers no longer expected a full restoration of the old situation, considering that the support for that had come too late.[19] For some considerable time, the Indonesian population had little reason for optimism either, following the end of the war. Economic disruption had caused severe poverty and even famine in many areas. There was a pressing shortage of food, and moreover of clothing and of medical supplies.[20]

Many companies had lost their administration during the war, so they had great trouble in reconstructing their financial situation. Most of them published their first annual reports as late as 1948. According to these reports, the situation in the cities had meanwhile returned to some semblance of order, and the companies concerned had generally succeeded in regaining and repairing their former premises. As a consequence, financial losses turned out to be less than expected for the merchant houses, at least when compared to manufacturing companies, which had incurred more overall damage. The plantations had suffered most of all. Both buildings and crops were often heavily damaged, sometimes beyond repair. Dutch businessmen had as yet failed to regain access to all of their plantations. In some cases, nature had reclaimed them, leaving no trace of where they had once been.[21] In its annual report for 1948, Geo. Wehry announced that four of its plantations still remained inaccessible. One of its tea companies had to be liquidated immediately, the Japanese having uprooted all the shrubs. Despite the damage and the chaos, most businessmen showed themselves strikingly upbeat about the situation. Stokvis demonstrates how confident people were about the future profitability of business in Indonesia. When its joint-venture agreement with Lindeteves ended in 1948, the company bought a substantial stake in Javastaal-Stokvis NV, regardless of the strife continuing everywhere. Lindeteves proved itself as enthusiastic as Stokvis, boasting its organisation to be so sound and so dedicated that, as long as a modicum of calm, public order, and safety returned, the company would undoubtedly regain its former position in the future.[22]

During the war, the exiled government in London had already set up a number of organisations to speed up economic recovery in the colonies, and these attempted to combat the post-war chaos. The merchant houses were confronted with the NIGIEO, the Nederlandsch-Indische Gouvernements Import- en Export Organisatie, a quango charged with buying goods on behalf of the colonial government, and also with restarting trade and bringing some coherence into the flows of imports and exports. The former importers seconded some of their staff, in as far as they were fit for work again, to the NIGIEO for these tasks.[23] During the first post-war years it proved to be very difficult to find capable personnel. In 1950, one of H.G.Th. Crone's managers wrote somewhat cynically that good personnel deserved their holidays, and the rest had long been seconded to do other work, causing the firm to lose touch with them. One of its staff had been murdered by a gang, underlining the inherent risk of the working environment. By the end of 1946, the NIGIEO was reorganised into the Algemene Import Organisatie or AIO, which continued in existence throughout 1947. At first the Internatio board professed itself greatly alarmed by the government initiatives, fearing that they might lead to socialisation. When the extent of the confusion reigning in the Dutch East Indies, even months after the end of the war, gradually became clear in the Netherlands, the board came

The end of the Second World War spelled the beginning of the Indonesian war of independence. Many Dutch companies returned to find their buildings and plantations devastated. Borsumij's flour mill on Kotta Blata, photographed around 1949, had been completely destroyed.

round, however, commenting that in the chaotic circumstances it would be impossible for private enterprise to bear all the risks of trade. Consequently, the board expected the NIGIEO to continue for an indefinite period, despite all interested parties striving for an early dissolution.[24] Borsumij considered this particular organisation a visionary initiative from the colonial government, though perhaps private enterprise could have been allowed more opportunities earlier and to a greater extent. Hagemeyer also thought that, without government interference, the high risks involved would have greatly handicapped a recovery of the import trade.[25]

As the gradually patched up merchant fleet began to deliver the necessary goods to Indonesia, the country's balance of trade worsened. Raising exports thus became an urgent priority. However, with the forces fighting for an independent Republic of Indonesia controlling large areas of the country, many plantations and mines still remained inaccessible to Dutch entrepreneurs. During July and August 1947, the Netherlands attempted to regain control over the Indonesian archipelago by military force, officially camouflaged as extended police patrols, under the telling codename 'Operation Product'. These actions returned more than a thousand enterprises, most of them heavily damaged, to Dutch authority.[26] However, unrest, terrorism, and armed attacks continued unabated, forcing Dutch business in Indonesia to rethink its attitude. By and by, anti-republicanism made way for an acceptance of an independent Indonesia as the most realistic solution. As a consequence, the second military operation launched in December 1948 found little support among Indonesian business. Great relief greeted the agreement between the Republicans and the Dutch government in December 1949, formally acknowledging the existence of an independent Republic of the United States of Indonesia. The act transferring sovereignty was signed on December 27, 1949.[27] At last there appeared to be a basis for economic recovery and growth in Indonesia.

However, the agreement's Achilles heel was the matter of New Guinea. This island had been left out of the act transferring sovereignty, both parties agreeing to settle the matter at a later stage. Many businessmen in Indonesia were less than happy with this political compromise. An internal memorandum from Internatio voiced fears about the sudden enthusiasm for New Guinea becoming a bone of contention between Dutch companies and the Indonesian government, threatening to damage existing and greater interests.[28] Hagemeyer took an entirely different view, spotting an interesting opportunity to expand its business. In 1950, the company considered it an honour to be entrusted with a monopoly on the import and export trade in New Guinea for a year, granted by the Dutch Government.[29] The former Colonial Office, renamed Ministry for matters concerning the Union and the overseas parts of the Kingdom, had done so thinking that the market would be insufficiently attractive for trading houses to start operations in New Guinea, without the support of a guaranteed, temporary monopoly and government contracts. Officials had first approached the Moluksche Handelsvennootschap, which in the past had maintained some trad-

Hoping to bring their business back to prosperity under the new circumstances, Dutch companies adjusted to the likelihood of Indonesia's political independence earlier than Dutch politicians did. A group of Hagemeyer managers chose the expedient of paying a courtesy visit to Sukarno.

ing relations with New Guinea, but the company had declined for fear of exposing its dominating Indonesian interests.[30] Though Hagemeyer was also highly dependent on Indonesia, its board did not want to let the opportunity pass by. News of the monopoly granted to Hagemeyer surprised the other traders. Internatio reacted angrily in an internal document. The board saw few real commercial prospects in New Guinea, and doubted therefore whether rival Hagemeyer was to be congratulated on its monopoly. However, granting such a privilege without allowing others to consider its contents beforehand was disconcerting at the least.[31] Nor did the Dutch press receive the Hagemeyer monopoly more positively. The newspaper *De Tijd* commented that monopolies were always dangerous, usually undesirable, and definitely objectionable considering the Dutch-Indonesian atmosphere. On the other hand, the importance of the matter in scope and duration should not be exaggerated, the paper added, blunting the edge of its criticism somewhat. Perhaps there simply was no room for more trading companies.[32] The monopoly was granted for a year, and accordingly lapsed in the summer of 1951. The government acted in banking as it had in trade, allowing only one bank access to New Guinea, with the NHM stepping into this position.[33]

By 1950 people began to feel that the biggest problems had been solved, opening the way for a new period of economic growth in Indonesia, underpinned by Dutch experience and finance. This feeling was underlined by the fairly fast growth of the Indonesian national product between 1950 and 1957. This growth derived its momentum from the numerous repair works carried out everywhere, in which fairly modest investment achieved quick results.[34] And yet even after independence, armed attacks and political unrest continued to be part of daily life.

Though many Dutch businessmen had converted to the inevitability of political decolonisation during 1947, few had been aware of the desire for economic decolonisation which also manifested itself among the Indonesian population. The aspirations for economic independence would increasingly

During the 1950s, Indonesia experienced a period of rapid economic growth, as extensive repair works enabled a steep rise in production capacity within a short time. The photograph depicts bales of rubber being pressed on the premises of Borsumij's Bandjermasin branch.

266

come to influence developments in the young state. During the first years of independence, the Javasche Bank, which operated as the central bank, the railways and tramways, the airline, and several gas works and power stations had been brought under government control. The merchant houses were not nationalised, but in 1950 the government introduced a system of import licences and trade credit arrangements to promote the growth of Indonesian importers. This nationalist 'Benteng' policy proved successful in as far as that by the mid-1950s about 70% of imports was nominally traded by Indonesians. As often as not, though, they were not really responsible, acting as figureheads for Chinese importers running the business.[35] Dutch importers also found ways to continue their import trade, using their various exporting branches. Thus Borsumij had a substantial business in cooperation with Indonesian importers.[36] Hagemeyer did the same, sending goods to Indonesia from the Netherlands and from its other branches around the world, including New York and Japan. While they lasted, these exports to Indonesia provided a healthy revenue source.

Foreign investors siphoning off profits were often a delicate subject in the decolonisation process. Dutch businessmen in Indonesia invariably complained about controls on transferring profits. Immediately after the war, a shortage of foreign currency had made the Dutch colonial government restrictive in granting permission to transfer money from Indonesia to the Netherlands. This put the merchant houses in an awkward position. During the war most companies had run up large debts with their banks in the Netherlands, which they wanted to clear as soon as possible following the liberation. Funds towards that end gradually amassed in Indonesia, but the firms could use only small sums because of the restrictions on money transfers. Consequently many trading companies decided to avoid a drain on their liquidity by paying part of their dividends in shares. In the end, profits did arrive in the Netherlands until 1957, though with a considerable delay and cut in half by the deduction of taxes.

Rising wage demands in Indonesia posed more of a threat than the difficulties with transferring profits, for these undermined profitability itself. The labour intensive industries and the plantations proved particularly prone to strikes in support of wage claims. In its annual report for 1950, Borsumij commented that it might have to close some of its smaller and labour intensive industries, because with rising wages and declining productivity they were no longer profitable. These companies did begin to lose money the following year, but even so Borsumij refrained from closing them. The board reconsidered its position, concluding that having local companies made sense, as it had done in the 1930s, should imports be subjected to severe restrictions in the near future.[37] Wage rises hit the plantations, which were just beginning to recover from the damages inflicted on them, especially badly, because of falling commodity prices. In 1951, the Korean War had caused temporary price rises, and in 1955 rubber prices also peaked, but during the 1950s Indonesia's overall terms of trade worsened. Commodity prices generally lagged behind the prices of manufacturing products.

From the mid-1950s Dutch companies were increasingly confronted with an official policy then known as 'Indonesianisation'. The government, keen to promote the appointment of Indonesian staff to senior positions in business, began to restrict the influx of foreign staff. As a matter of fact Dutch companies were not averse to hiring more employees locally, for after all this would reduce the expense of sending people over from the Netherlands. Moreover, Hagemeyer had noticed that its European staff was less keen now to accept work in Indonesia. This made the board decide in 1956 to grant a premium of four months' basic pay, on top of the existing bonus arrangements, to employees willing to stay in Indonesia for the company at the end of their tour of duty. It may be doubted whether this decision had the desired effect, for the reluctance among staff for such appointments reached deeper than material considerations. Borsumij found that its European employees overseas were more apprehensive about the future than about their pay.[38]

Finding suitable local staff proved difficult, however, if only because the

Indonesian government exerted a strong demand for well-qualified personnel. Even so residence permits for foreign employees were refused, leading to shortages at some trading houses, notably Hagemeyer, Geo. Wehry, and Borsumij. This latter company complained that employees finished their in-house training only to leave and take jobs with Indonesian employers, who could offer better conditions deriving from special privileges. Nevertheless Borsumij reduced its foreign staff from about 320 to 160 between 1953 and 1957, simultaneously increasing the number of Indonesian employees to around 240. Hagemeyer chose to economise on its staff by reducing the number of branches.[39]

In 1954, Internatio decided to expand its interior distribution network, in particular aiming to bypass the Chinese intermediary traders, thus more or less falling in with the 'Indonesianisation'. Hoping to increase its public support and accommodate nationalist sentiment, the company set up seventy branches, mostly led by Indonesians, selling a product range largely supplied by local industries in which it held stakes. Internatio retained its commodity trade all along, and also continued to run the plantations under its management.[40]

Dutch merchant houses attempted to safeguard their position in Indonesia by seeking new opportunities and by adapting as much as possible to the demands of the new government. One may well ask why most companies showed such curious determination. Firstly, because alternatives proved hard to find, as we will show in due course. Secondly, in spite of all restrictions Indonesia continued to offer profitable business opportunities. Many traders emphasised the great importance of their activities outside Indonesia in their annual reports, but in 1955 Borsumij drafted an internal memorandum concluding that Indonesia

268

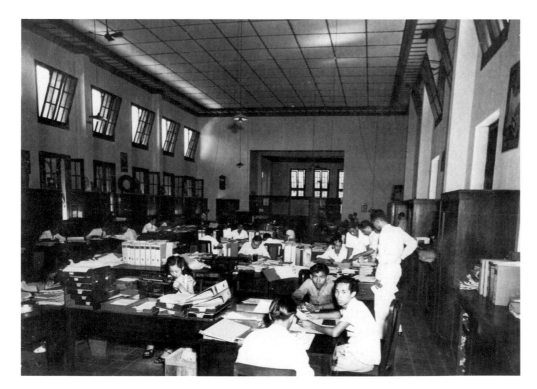

Under pressure from the Indonesian government, the international trading companies began to hire growing numbers of Indonesians, as demonstrated here by Geo. Wehry's import department in 1952.

continued to be the company's main revenue source, really the engine which kept the whole business going.[41] Wehry wrote in its 1954 annual report that it would still take time before the company's business activities outside Indonesia could compensate falling revenues from Indonesia.[42] And finally, Dutch businessmen stayed because they had a boundless confidence about being indispensable in Indonesia. A report from the Internatio board to the company's supervisory directors in the autumn of 1956 expressed this feeling tellingly. After stressing the deteriorating economic circumstances in Indonesia, and the increasing difficulties facing Dutch business there, the report concluded by pointing to the definitely useful, important, and hopefully lucrative functions performed by the company, as it were in compensation for the problems signalled earlier.[43]

Hagemeyer took a different view of the situation in Indonesia, and the company probably stood alone in this. Its business there decidedly was a welcome revenue source, but as early as 1954 the board considered the profits from the New Guinea and Singapore branches sufficient to sustain the existing dividend policy, even without revenues from Indonesia.[44] In 1956 the board seriously considered selling out to a big Indonesian group, but the deal fell through because the prospective buyers were short of capital and wanted to pay with future business profits.[45]

Nearly all companies woke up to a nasty surprise when in 1957 the curtain finally fell for Dutch interests in Indonesia. The New Guinea question dragged on and on, inspiring the Indonesian government to support employee sit-in strikes, which had started as spontaneous trade-union actions. In December 1957, all Dutch companies were put under government supervision, the management receiving orders forbidding all contact with the Dutch head offices. Most Dutch people took this as a signal for leaving the country, placing the management over the trading companies in the hands of Indonesian managers, hoping to return at some future time. Borsumij alone attempted to find a way for a continuation of active business in Indonesia, regardless of what had happened. At first the company planned to sell its trade organisation to Indonesians, and to hold on to it by retaining a minority stake. When it became clear that such a participation would still be unacceptable, and that only Indonesian staff could be used, Borsumij still tried to get some Dutch managers involved with the trading company by seconding them as advisors through a small firm, the Promoting & Trust Company. As late as 1959 the trading company continued to operate, under army supervision. The then general manager, E.E. de Haan, describes in his memoirs how he developed an efficient routine with a certain Captain Bagowi from the Indonesian army to impress visitors to the company, in particular those manufacturers' agents coming to announce a sudden termination of contracts in favour of Indonesian trading firms touting for Borsumij's business. The captain would follow the meeting at some distance, seated so as to be able to look the visitors straight in the eye, and wear down any opposition however hardened in business with a dark stare, if necessary

When granting independence to Indonesia in 1949, the Dutch government had retained its sovereignty over New Guinea or Irian Jaya. This created a continuous tension in the political relationship between the two countries. The worried-looking manager of Hagemeyer's Jakarta branch has rushed out to see slogans daubed on the wall, reading 'You must be swept from West Irian' (1958).

reinforced by fiddling with his army pistol. This hypnotic act and De Haan's arguments helped to save most agencies.[46] It was all to no avail. In December 1959 Borsumij saw itself forced to withdraw its last foreign employees from Indonesia.[47] Meanwhile the Indonesian parliament had passed an act nationalising all Dutch companies in December 1958.

The repatriated Dutch staff could lose their jobs as a result of the forced return to the Netherlands. When Borsumij considered repatriating all employees with their families in December 1957, the board decided to give the managers in Indonesia a free hand to do what they thought best. The directors did anticipate the need for substantial dismissals among the repatriated staff and employees on leave. In addition, an estimated third of the head office staff would become redundant. Indeed, the company immediately began to cut deeply into staff costs, although a core group of employees remained in Indonesia.[48] Geo. Wehry forcibly dismissed its entire staff working in Indonesia, and also gave notice to some employees at head office. Internatio had no positions to offer within the company to some of its repatriated staff either, understandably so because of Internatio's combination of trade with voluminous plantation interests. By contrast Hagemeyer, which had focused exclusively on trade, was able to offer all of its staff alternative employment in the company. The enforced retreat from Indonesia meant a heavy loss for all merchant houses, most of all for those which had had large investments in plantations and manufacturing industry. Their ability to recover from this blow depended mainly on whether or not they had meanwhile succeeded in setting up profitable businesses elsewhere.

270

– Had the trading houses spread their interests sufficiently during the preceding years to compensate the loss of their Indonesian operations? The uncertain circumstances in Indonesia immediately after the Second World War had made many merchant houses aware of the importance of spreading their risks by embarking on activities outside of the archipelago. Time was on the side of the traders in one key respect: after 1945, world trade reassumed its function of driving economic growth, rising faster than world production. From 1950 the world order showed a great stability, with regulated exchange rates and unprecedented productivity rises. World trade profited from all these factors. From the end of the Second World War until 1960, the growth of world exports in US dollars averaged 6% a year. This rise was even more impressive because the prices of goods traded were about as high in 1960 as they had been in 1948. The United Nations took the initiative for removing trade barriers by launching the General Agreement on Tariffs and Trade (GATT) in 1947, which aimed to reduce import duties and restrictions around the world. In prolonged rounds of negotiations, the participating countries succeeded in achieving slow but steady progress. Most trade took place between the highly industrialised countries of Europe, the US, and Japan. Moreover, these industrialised countries provided the key export markets for the rest of the world.[49] In 1950, primary products, i.e. agricultural products, fuel, and raw materials, accounted for 57% of world trade by value, against 47% for manufacturing products. A decade later, industrial products had just gained the upper hand with 55% of the total. This trend would continue during the 1960s.[50]

Politically, the times moved on, too. The Second World War had finally ended the existence of overseas colonial empires as a matter of course, inaugurating radical political shifts in both Asia and Africa. The Philippines had gained self-government just before the Second World War, in 1936. Decolonisation achieved a milestone in 1947, when India, the biggest of all colonial nations, became independent. The ensuing war between India and Pakistan immediately demonstrated the complexity of many liberation movements, independence often giving way to internal struggles by groups feeling oppressed in their turn. Moreover, the colonial boundaries were rarely the most logical or

271

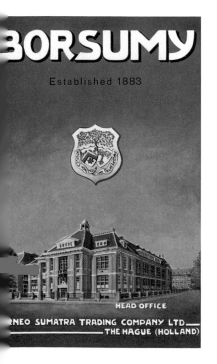

This publicity leaflet from Borsumij, designed for use abroad, shows an impressive headoffice on the outside and on the inside a large number of foreign branches scattered across Asia, Africa, America, and Europe. However, the company really remained strongly dependent on the revenues from its Indonesian operations.

desirable ones. Once India had become independent, other British colonial territories followed suit: Sri Lanka, Burma, Malaya, and Singapore, to name some of the countries in which the merchant houses operated. Decolonisation did not remain limited to Asia, subsequently spreading to Africa.[51] During the 1950s, Britain introduced limited forms of democratic government in its East African colonies, after which Uganda, Tanzania, and Kenya successively achieved independence between 1961 and 1963. This had been preceded during the early 1950s by the violent Mau Mau movement, which spread terror among the European community, in spite of the fact that many of its actions had been directed more at the African population. Nigeria became independent in 1960, though the British had as yet failed in their efforts for a democratic polity. The Belgian Congo was regarded as one of the most traditional colonies. As late as

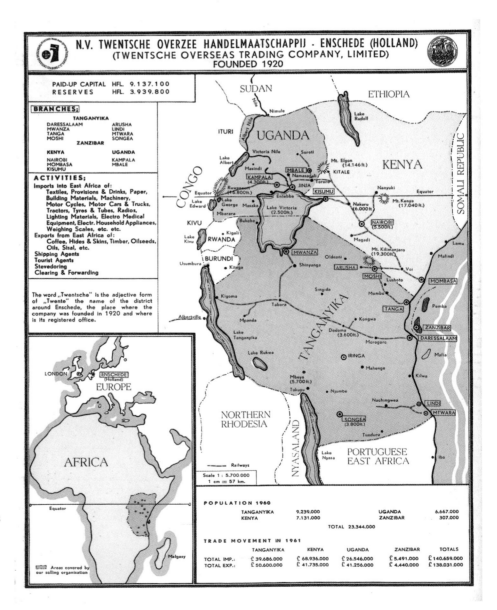

After the Second World War, the old colonial empires crumbled rapidly, and many new states arose in their wake. The Twentse Overzee Handel-Maatschappij initially operated simply in British East Africa, but the company's 1962 map shows branches in Uganda, Kenya, Tanganyika, and Zanzibar.

1955, the very idea of self-government within thirty years appeared far-fetched. During 1959, serious riots made the Belgian government change its mind, and a year later the independent republic of Congo was proclaimed. This abrupt declaration of independence was followed by years of fighting and chaos.[52] When during the early 1950s Dutch trading houses went into Africa, they did not know what lay in store for them.

The process of decolonisation meant that the traders were confronted time and again with changes in administrations and policies aiming to protect national economies from foreign pressures, such as restrictions on the transfer of profits, conditions for local participations, and difficulties with supplying work permits for foreign staff. As will become clear in the following section, finding profitable alternatives for the Indonesian operations proved to be no simple matter, despite the overall growth of world trade.

TO THE SURROUNDING ASIAN AREAS – Singapore, the city which occupied such a key position in the region as entrepot and transit port, was the first place in Asia where the merchant houses could restart their operations after the Second World War.[53] In December 1945, the Internatio board reported that work at the Singapore branch was again in full swing.[54] Hagemeyer also sent an employee to Singapore at the earliest opportunity, to set up a business selling products from Australia. These goods were purchased by G.L. Oostergo, a Hagemeyer agent who had gone to Australia immediately after the war, and who laid the basis for a Hagemeyer branch there by his activities. In March 1946, Hagemeyer's Penang agent, O. Bargman, described the situation there as boring and tiresome, as in Batavia, with everything still being run by the army and the local population showing a somewhat aggressive attitude. According to Bargman, the great freedom movement of the Orient had left its traces in Penang, and this would intensify once India had won its independence.[55] Meanwhile the Europeans living in the area enjoyed a standard of living higher than that in the Netherlands. When in August 1946 the Penang agent prepared to leave for the Netherlands, he was advised to take sufficient clothes with him, as these were practically unobtainable in the mother country, and to bring cigarettes and coffee, both scarce and keenly sought after on the black market.[56]

In addition to Singapore, many Dutch traders opened or reopened branches on the Malaysian peninsula, in Hong Kong, and in Thailand. One or two went to Burma, and in 1948 Internatio took over the Holland China Handelmaatschappij to gain entry to the Chinese market. With the communists seizing power soon after, the opportunities for trading with China probably remained limited, but this Hong Kong based trading company did give Internatio a foothold in a city with a future. Often new branches were set up as separate companies, the political unrest in the area of course increasing business risk. During the early 1950s, political risks in Asia were considered to be higher than in Africa. Business in Singapore and Hong Kong, moreover, depended

Seeking to expand their operations outside of Indonesia, the international trading companies first went to the surrounding Asian countries. Internatio established itself, for instance, in Penang (Malaysia) as the Rotterdam Trading Company (above), and also in Hongkong as the Holland-China Trading Company (left), which attempted to sell fertiliser in China.

274

heavily on developments in Indonesia and China, for the local population in these cities remained too small to generate sufficient demand. There was also a substantial barter trade between Singapore and Indonesia, much of it escaping registration in the official statistics.[57]

The trade links established immediately after the war did not all prove of lasting significance. Thus Australia, in the post-war era a supplier of scarce food and medical supplies, soon lost its importance as an exporter to Asia again. In 1948, once the Japanese government had lifted its ban on foreign traders entering the country, the Dutch firms returned, regardless of the experiences during the war. They attempted to get involved with both imports and exports, but the main importance of the Japanese branches turned out to be the purchasing of industrial products such as fabrics, batteries, radios, and building materials. Profits of the traders in Asia varied, being strongly sensitive to commodity prices on the world market, restrictions on imports and exports, import duty levels, and local bankruptcies. Thailand appeared to be particularly notorious for its debtor risks. Both Borsumij and Hagemeyer were generally satisfied with the result of their operations in Singapore, though no separate profit figures for the subsidiaries were published.

After a difficult start, Hagemeyer's New Guinea branch proved a financial success while it lasted. A separate subsidiary, the NIGIMIJ, ran the operations. Reports paint a vivid picture of the exceedingly primitive beginnings from which the company had to start. One Hagemeyer employee, V.P. van de Lande, fruitlessly attempted to reach the settlement of Kaimana by boat, having as sole indication of the landing place a description of a ruined warehouse on a silvery beach. A motor launch carried Van de Lande through the bay, swerving to evade the countless coral reefs, from one silvery beach to another, until he finally found the one indicated by noticing a deserted open tent with some empty oil drums. Having been carried to the shore through the breakers, Van de Lande found a mountain track leading to Kaimana, but it was so slippery that he gave up after half an hour.[58] Another employee, J.N. Elzinga, described how in March 1950 operations in Hollandia, the island's main town, started in a room belonging to the colonial administration from a camp bed which doubled as meeting table and filing cabinet. After some months the agent Van Bocken Maas had been given a small house by the administration, which served as living quarters, office, and workshop. This gesture had not really solved the accommodation problem. Rain entered freely into the house, sometimes leading the inhabitants to wonder whether they were inside or out. Even so Elzinga thought that it would still suffice as a business base for the time being.[59]

During the first years in operation, Hagemeyer had to make large investments into living accommodation and warehouses, and the company continued to expand in later years. Gauging the demands of the local population often proved to be difficult, more than once leading to stocks remaining unsold. Through the NIGIMIJ, Hagemeyer became involved with commodity exports for the first time in its existence, selling copra, gum resin, bay leaves, and crocodile

275

skins. As often as not the local population preferred barter to being paid with money. From 1953, the NIGIMIJ turned into a source of continuous profits for Hagemeyer, partly because of government contracts. When the company's Indonesian operations had to close, the staff could partly be transferred to New Guinea, though not all employees were keen on the move. After the closure of Hagemeyer's Indonesian business, the NIGIMIJ turned out to be the company's key revenue source, be it not the only one. This made Hagemeyer vulnerable, should the area be lost as a market. There was a very real chance of this happening, for the Republic of Indonesia claimed New Guinea as belonging to its territory. Consequently, Hagemeyer turned its attention to other continents.⁶⁰

In 1950, the Dutch government granted Hagemeyer a one-year monopoly as an import trader in New Guinea, an area with only modest economic development. After a difficult start, the company succeeded in building a profitable business there. When New Guinea was finally handed over to Indonesia, Hagemeyer left the country.

A TROPICAL ALTERNATIVE: AFRICA – During the 1950s, expectations about Africa were remarkably high. Immediately after Indonesian independence, many Dutch trading houses planned to settle on the continent, and in particular in its tropical regions. Judging that the operating conditions there were more or less similar to those in Indonesia, the firms thought they could put their knowledge and experience, built up over decades, to good use. They also expected a long delay before the process of decolonisation would reach the continent, though the British had already introduced a degree of self-government in Ghana in 1948. In 1959, the supervisory board at Lindeteves commented on 'the overbowling developments all over Africa, which nobody could have foreseen four or five years ago – on the contrary, everybody thought that Africa would remain calm at least for another 25 years'.⁶¹ The African economies grew during the early 1950s, stimulated by comparatively high prices for their exports, including coffee, cocoa, cotton, and minerals, and rising foreign aid and investments. As part of United Nations projects, the Netherlands also supplied some overseas development aid to Africa, particularly in the shape of knowledge and skills built up in the colonies.[62] Everywhere projects were launched designed to improve the standards of living, education, and infrastructure, and it appeared a matter of time until Africa would enter the era of mass consumption. The Twentse Overzee Handel Maatschappij or TOHM, which had operated in British East Africa since 1920, saw its turnover rise, and during the first half of the 1950s the company achieved very good profits. Concentrating on agencies, one for Philips radios and light bulbs among them, and commission trading, the TOHM developed an important business in cars, lorries, and farm tractors, building up an extensive service network in support. In 1958 the company reached its greatest size measured by the number of staff.[63]

From days long gone by, merchant houses of the 'general trader' type had worked in Africa. These firms traded in commodities with the aim of increasing the circulation of money among the population, and in addition they possessed general stores selling a variety of manufacturing products, such as fabrics and

During the 1950s, Dutch merchant houses established themselves in Africa, full of high expectations. They often dealt in a wide range of consumer products there, from radio sets and fabrics, to whisky and cigarette lighters. Offices often also served as sample rooms, as happened at Geo. Wehry (right). The agency business of Lindeteves, a wholesaler in technical equipment, included the selling of farming tractors. On the left, the company's Kenya garage in 1955.

tools. A typical example of the general trader was the United Africa Company or UAC, a Unilever subsidiary, which operated in West Africa. During the 1950s, the moment in time that many Dutch merchant firms went into Africa, the company was going through a process of strategic refocusing. The commodity trade was run down having lost most of its attraction, for in the areas under British rule marketing boards had appeared, increasing the competition from local merchants. The customary import and distribution of a large and undifferentiated range of goods also faced increasing competition, both from local traders and from overseas suppliers setting up their own sales and marketing operations. The only field of operations left was the import and distribution of specialised goods, like bicycles, radios, cars, medical supplies, and beer. Such products were no longer sold in general stores, but in department stores in the European mould. To protect its sales and to accommodate nationalist sentiment, the UAC also became increasingly involved with indigenous industries.[64]

How did the Dutch companies fare, entering Africa in the early 1950s as newcomers? The Dutch mainly settled in British East Africa, and in the Belgian Congo. At least five firms went to the former: Hagemeyer (1951), Lindeteves, Güntzel & Schumacher, Internatio (all three 1952), and Borsumij (1955), and four to the latter: Tels & Co. (as early as 1948), Borsumij (1951), Hagemeyer (1952), and Lindeteves (1954). Other areas which attracted Dutch merchant houses were Cameroon (Deli-Atjeh), Moçambique (Jacobson Van den Berg & Co., better known as Jacoberg after the war), and Ghana (Borsumij and Wehry). During the late 1950s, Nigeria began to attract attention. In 1951, the Handelsvereniging 'Amsterdam' (HVA), which had shifted its business focus entirely to plantations by this time, embarked on sugar production in Ethiopia.

Internatio operated in East Africa only for a short while. The company's chemicals trade, including pesticides, in Johannesburg proved a more lasting one, and from there Internatio sold all over the continent. Pictured here is Internatio's stand on the 1963 Rand Easter Show.

Dutch trading companies focused first of all on importing consumer goods. Sometimes they also became involved with exporting commodities, and in individual cases the firms participated in local industries. Thus when Borsumij went to Congo in 1951, the board decided to combine trading operations with a 50% stake in a company producing chocolate, bread, and biscuits, which had been founded by Ten Wolde, one of its key customers in Indonesia. Because ordinary bread was subject to price controls, by the way, the company had to concentrate on producing luxury bread. For the time being, profits lagged far behind costs. In 1953 Borsumij began operating in Ghana by entering into a joint-venture with a local company run by a team of brothers of Lebanese descent, but with British passports. British business connections considered this venture 'not in accordance with the company's standing', but the Borsumij board thought it could afford to remain aloof of such 'particularly British nationalist sentiment'. The joint-venture was not much of a success, and ended in 1956.[65] Güntzel & Schumacher expanded its operations to British East Africa, and Internatio also took recourse to this area. The company took over a small agency trader in 1953, followed some time later by a commodity firm. In 1960, Internatio withdrew again from the area, 'sadder and wiser'.[66]

Hagemeyer embarked on African operations in a grand way from the start, setting up three branches in British East Africa between 1951 and 1953, and almost simultaneously also entering Congo, beginning in Elisabethville and moving a few years later to Leopoldville, too. The company focused on importing bulk consumer goods, like watches, cigarette lighters, ballpoint pens, and fabrics, just as it had once done in the Dutch East Indies. Initially the Nairobi subsidiary returned modest profits, but when it expanded to open offices in Mombassa and Kampala, the revenues began to fall short of costs. In 1957, the Hagemeyer board came to the conclusion that too much had been set up in too short a time, and with insufficiently trained staff. The product range had been too varied, leading to excessive marketing costs. The situation in the Belgian Congo proved not much better, with the initial years constantly showing 'start-up losses'. By the mid-1950s these problems appeared to have been overcome, but then a recession began to cut into the population's spending power, which was never high to begin with. Additional difficulties were the long transport delays and the inevitable extensive credit terms. Finding suitable local staff proved difficult, too, necessitating the use of European employees, whose higher cost drained profits. Even so the Hagemeyer board thought that the area offered huge opportunities.[67]

After some years of toiling in this immense continent, many trading houses saw that they had overestimated the importance of their own experience, and that they would be wise to team up with locally rooted companies. The traders had not been discouraged, despite political unrest accompanied by outbreaks of violence having surfaced in the meantime. In 1954, the grave uncertainty of developments in Southeast Asia made Lindeteves decide to take over a company which had been based in Congo for a long time. A report issued by the Dutch

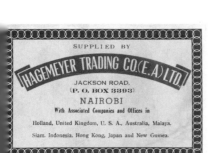

Because of the prevailing political instability in many countries, the international traders preferred to set up separate subsidiaries for their overseas operations. This also helped them to adapt to local company legislation. For its east African operations, Hagemeyer founded the Hagemeyer Trading Co. (East Africa) Ltd. in Nairobi.

federation of metal industries, issued after an exploratory visit to Congo, had inspired this move. Detailing the impressive economic strides of the area, the report argued that Congo represented a huge potential, unequalled by other overseas markets, for serious orders to the metal industry.[68] Lindeteves' take-over target was the Nieuwe Afrikaansche Handels-Vennootschap (NAHV), a typical general trader with branches in Congo and Liberia. Its product range included forest products, cotton, and the import of lorries and cars, for which the company also managed a chain of garages. The NAHV welcomed the bid, for its purchasing branch in the Netherlands urgently needed reinforcement, but the company lacked the capital for an expansion.[69] Its business experience was well-known. In 1956, Hagemeyer professed itself very satisfied with having poached some NAHV employees to set up its Leopoldville branch.[70] Lindeteves, once reinforced with the NAHV, probably became a force to reckon with. In 1958, Borsumij approached the company with an offer to amalgamate operations in Congo. At that moment Borsumij was possibly also pessimistic about its Congolese commitments, for the board had diagnosed the area as suffering from over-investment, oversupply of imports, scarcity of money, falling copper prices, and falling retail prices because of stock liquidations. Lindeteves rejected the Borsumij proposal to join forces in the Congo.[71] And, in addition, Borsumij had signed a joint venture with the TOHM, operating in British East Africa, three years before.

Hagemeyer did not achieve very encouraging results in Congo, losing about 1 million guilders in this country between 1952 and 1958. Even so, the board continued to keep an open mind about expanding the African operations. In 1958, one of the supervisory directors passed on information that the Handelmaatschappij v/h J.F. Sick & Co. was actively looking for a partner to merge operations and thus improve profitability. This Amsterdam merchant house operated in Ghana, Nigeria, and Cameroon, and thus had branches in areas where Hagemeyer had none as yet, and it also had an office in Venice for buying high-quality Muran glass beads, which still found a keen market in Africa. In addition, Sick & Co. possessed important agencies for photographic supplies. After negotiating for a year, Hagemeyer took over Sick & Co.[72] Take-overs such as this one suggest that the trading houses still thought that Africa offered sufficient business opportunities, but as yet operations there failed to amount to an alternative for Indonesia.

Newcomers found it difficult to obtain a foothold in Africa. Therefore, Lindeteves chose to take over the NAHV, which had been operating in Liberia and Congo for almost a century. On the left the company's stand at a trade fair in Leopoldville, right a garage and workshop in Bunia, both in Belgian Congo.

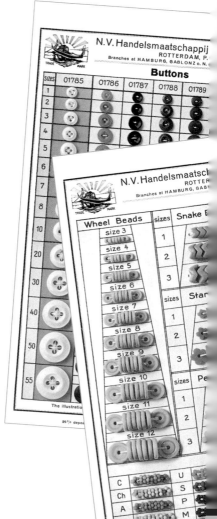

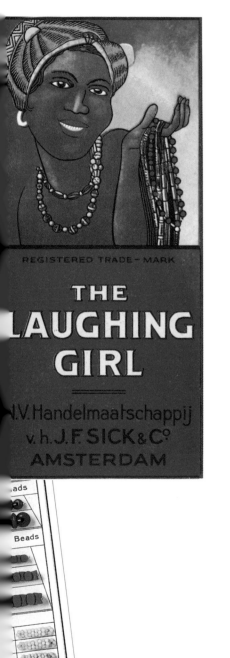

REGISTERED TRADE-MARK

THE
LAUGHING
GIRL

N.V. Handelmaatschappij
v. h. J. F. SICK & Cº
AMSTERDAM

TESTING THE WATER IN SOUTH AMERICA AND IN NORTH AMERICA – In addition to Asia and tropical Africa, the merchant houses turned their attention to South America. This continent had already shaken off its colonial masters at the beginning of the 19th century. The South American countries were characterised by strong economic fluctuations, and a regular return of galloping inflation. During the post-war era, many South American countries mapped out an economic course towards autonomy, which implied building up industries for import substitution.

As early as 1946, ten renowned companies drawn from the ranks of trade, banking, and shipping, took the initiative for a Nederlandse Maatschappij voor Zuid-Amerika, a joint-venture intended to operate in the Argentine, Uruguay, and Brazil. The group included Internatio, Lindeteves, and Jacoberg. The company failed, just as similar ventures to foster trade with South America, set up at the time of the First World War, had done, and it was liquidated in 1950. At that moment the Internatio board proffered the desperate financial circumstances in the countries concerned as an explanation for the failure. However, years later the Internatio director H. Stout wrote that at that moment in time, the company had lacked the right people to run operations, concentrating efforts on rebuilding its Indonesian business.[73]

Other efforts to gain a foothold in South America were much more modest. Internatio surveyed the opportunities from 1953 to 1956, and found them wanting.[74] Borsumij bought a small Peruvian trading company in 1954, and in 1957 Hagemeyer set up an equally modest branch in Paramaribo, the capital of Surinam. With many South American governments striving to build up indigenous industries by restricting imports, the climate was hardly encouraging for foreign trading companies. And yet Ceteco continued to demonstrate the trading opportunities available in the area, but then the company was familiar with the lie of the land from bygone days. During the Second World War the company had become involved with trading tropical commodities, only to refocus on consumer durables after the war, combining importing with the distributive trade. With the onset of protective policies to further South American industrialisation, Ceteco began to set up its own industrial ventures, and at the same time its range of imports changed from final products to semi-finished goods and raw materials.[75] By continuously adapting its operations to changed circumstances, Ceteco succeeded in keeping its South American business profitable.

After the liberation of Western Europe by the Allies, strong ties developed between Europe and the US, which emerged as economically and politically dominating in victory. The US strenuously attempted to rebuild Europe by granting Marshall Aid, and by encouraging European cooperation, aiming for a strong continent as a dam to contain the spread of communism. For Europe, the American economic progress served as a signal example. Wanting to master American production techniques and management skills, European businessmen embarked on study tours of the US.

For the colonial trading houses, the US had always been important as a market for tropical commodities, and as a supplier of consumer products and capital goods. During the 1950s, these firms began to look at the prospering Western countries with new eyes, as potential outlets for the distribution of industrial products. However, when attempting to establish themselves as importers there, the traders soon discovered that the inclination to protect home industries was not reserved for developing countries alone. After a tour of the US in 1952, the Internatio director H. Stout observed how the leverage of manufacturing interests made Congress increase trade tariffs when imports were considered to be threatening national production. He referred to a recent example affecting imports of milk, butter, and cheese, but argued that the same was true for bicycles, motorcycles, china, pipes, and for undifferentiated consumer goods in general.[76]

Though the merchant houses often bought existing businesses to establish themselves, it proved to be difficult to make headway as importers into the US and Canada. Borsumij attempted to build businesses importing building materials in New York, and fabrics in Canada, ending up with large unsaleable stocks in both cases.[77] During the 1950s, Dutch importers considered Europe much more attractive than the US as a market. Consequently, the Netherlands Chamber of Commerce in the US, despite being supported by the Dutch government with both money and dedicated policies, did not really succeed in increasing Dutch exports to the States.[78]

TAKING RECOURSE TO THE NETHERLANDS – In their searches for profitable potential markets, the colonial traders also surveyed opportunities in the Netherlands. As a rule the firms entered this particular market by taking over small and mostly specialised trading companies. During the 1950s, Dutch wholesaling remained more or less immovable, cemented as it was by the price covenants and other anti-competitive agreements concluded during the 1930s. Moreover, the Netherlands had a very flexible official cartel policy, far more flexible in fact than the one which would be introduced by the EEC. By taking over existing companies, the colonial traders were automatically admitted into existing agreements. In the mid-1950s Borsumij bought a wholesaler in fabrics and a pharmaceutical wholesaler. Hagemeyer concentrated on an old flame, clocks and electrical timepieces, the father of both founders having worked in

Hagemeyer dealt in clocks and watches for a long time, using this logo for persuading consumers to buy.

During the 1950s, the former colonial trading houses also attempted to expand their operations in the Netherlands. Lindeteves presented packaging equipment on a 1951 trade fair in the Amsterdam RAI exhibition complex.

that trade. In 1955, Internatio took over a number of specialised wholesalers in technical equipment. Maintz & Co. had begun sounding the Dutch market as early as 1948, when it bought Mijssen & Co., a company focused on engineering, a good fit with Maintz & Co.'s core activities in Indonesia, managing power stations and gasworks. It was of course not hard to foresee the imminent nationalisation of such public utilities in the wake of decolonisation, and this is exactly what happened. Lindeteves had developed operations in the Netherlands even earlier than Maintz & Co., i.e. during the Second World War.

Though immediately after the war Dutch economic prospects had not been particularly favourable, the country did enjoy a prosperous development. The Netherlands had entered the war as a colonial power of some stature, and consequently after 1949 it had to come to terms with being reduced to the status of a small, open economy. During the post-war years, the Dutch government exerted itself to achieve multilateral agreements by cobbling together bilaterals. This policy pivoted around the universally accepted importance of trade with Germany and overseas trade. In 1950, international settlements became much easier when the European Payments Union was founded. This created a multilateral clearing system between those European countries belonging to the Organisation for European Economic Cooperation since 1948, originally a framework for Marshall Aid. However, innumerable restrictions continued to weigh down trade with the most important trading partners. Even so the Dutch government remained somewhat ambivalent towards initiatives for a European Economic Community, fearing that a relatively small market would straightjacket a commercial country like the Netherlands.[79] Meanwhile the Netherlands profited greatly from the surge in world trade which began in 1950 and lasted until 1973. The Dutch market share rose, and export growth was particularly spectacular.

This need not surprise, for official policy had the promotion of exports as one of its key features, with manufacturing considered the prime supplier of export products. Consequently, the government supported industrial development in a variety of ways, in order to provide the population with sufficient means of existence. Between 1949 and 1963 a series of memorandums on industrialisation defined the policy outlines. The memorandums encouraged the Dutch population to begin seeing themselves as part of a modern industrial country, and no longer as constituting a colonial nation with a rich commercial tradition.[80] As a result, traders felt left out, misunderstood even. The Lindeteves annual reports expressed this sentiment very clearly. In 1949, the board emphasised the efforts, the time and the money required to gain access to foreign markets, the need to nurse a commercial business gradually, and the consequent lack of immediate and spectacular results. Unfortunately, the report continued, many manufacturers with whom the company would gladly join forces to promote exports showed insufficient understanding of these requirements, as did government officials, who all too often considered trade to be a superfluous and thus expensive link in the chain.

During these years, wholesalers began to feel uneasy, threatened by newcomers charging lower prices, be it for smaller product ranges. The rise of purchasing organisations, such as the Rijksinkoopbureau or Government purchasing office, generated suspicion, especially where the government supported such initiatives. Export promoters, such as the Stichting Nederlandse Export Combinatie or NEC, met with the same attitude.[81] The NEC was founded in 1952 by six manufacturers, who wanted to set up a joint foreign marketing organisation to ferry the sample chests and order books for all of their products around the world. This initiative tallied with the government's desire for export promotion, and as a result the opening of the NEC Utrecht head office in 1953, attended by about 50 manufacturers, was boosted by speeches from a member of parliament and from the head of the cabinet of the Utrecht mayor. In principle, the NEC admitted only one member for each product represented by the organisation. This turned out to be a successful recipe, fulfilling the needs of specific companies.[82] Some international traders regarded such initiatives by manufacturers as a threat. The Lindeteves board complained about it to its supervisory directors. Manufacturers might well embark on joint export marketing with official backing, the report said, but this by-passing of trade entailed greater risks than was often appreciated. It cited a recent example of a joint venture of small shipyards for marketing motor boats in the US, which had lost about 2 million guilders, to conclude that the direct costs of joint marketing were often much higher than manufacturers thought or hoped.[83]

The opening of the new Stokvis head-office in 1950. The company mainly sought to expand within the Netherlands.

Was wholesaling really a redundant link in the trade chain which raised the cost of goods, or was it a useful intermediary? During the 1950s, the 1920s debate about this point resurfaced. In 1955, an authoritative economic weekly, *Economisch-Statistische Berichten* or ESB, judged the disappearance of wholesaling in many sectors an historical fact: technical progress had made it redundant, or else the customers, whether or not united in cooperations, had assumed the wholesaling functions.[84] J.F. Haccoû, a professor in economics at Amsterdam University, was less pessimistic after a survey conducted by him in 1958, which confirmed that wholesaling continued to be of great importance to Dutch industry. Sales of the big industrial companies went mostly to smaller, craft-style companies, who took 28% of the total. Wholesalers came second with 26%, the retail trade bought 23%. For big and small manufacturers taken together, the retail trade proved slightly more important than wholesalers, taking 27% against 23% for wholesalers, with other companies again buying 28%. Haccoû explained the continuing importance of wholesaling as a marketing channel from its ability to lower distribution costs. Wholesalers enabled manufacturers to keep their marketing and transport departments simple, on the other hand offering customers a particular range of products supplied as and when required, enabling them to keep stocks low. Occupational censuses also showed a rise in the number of people working in trade, retailing and wholesaling as a percentage of the labour force increasing from 12.5% in 1930 to 13.5% in 1960.[85] In 1963, Haccoû forecast that wholesaling would become more prominent in the future, as a consequence of differentiating consumer preferences, increasing prosperity, and greater product variety. He thought that these developments would be reinforced by Dutch membership of the EEC.[86] Though the development of Dutch industry attracted all the attention, wholesaling proved to have a full lease of life.

STRIKING THE BALANCE: WINNERS AND LOSERS – What was the position of the colonial traders in 1959, once the official nationalisation of their operations in Indonesia had temporarily cut off their access to that country? Had they succeeded in spreading their activities sufficiently to compensate for the loss of their Indonesian operations since December 1957? As has already been mentioned in Chapter IV, around 1900 Internatio, Borsumij, Geo. Wehry, Jacobson Van den Berg & Co., and Lindeteves were regarded as the five main trading companies in the Dutch East Indies. Internatio had first concentrated on Africa and South America, before resolving to seek a way out in Europe. The company did not return any dividend at all in 1957, but it could resume such payments soon after, quite an achievement considering the fact that Internatio, with its extensive interests in plantations, had been hit comparatively severely by the nationalisations. Initially, Borsumij was less successful in finding profitable alternatives, because it stopped payouts in 1956. Four years later, the company decided to reinforce its position around the world by merging with Geo. Wehry, which had suspended dividends in the same year. The NHM had suggested this potential merger to Borsumij. Its attraction was less an expansion of operations, as the considerable cost savings deriving from a concentration in the Netherlands, Japan, Singapore, and America. Wehry's Amsterdam head office was closed.[87] It took another few years before the merged companies regained an upward trend.

Lindeteves, stretched out from Asia, to Africa, and to the Netherlands, only had to lower its dividend somewhat in 1957. After 1958, payouts did remain slightly below the levels achieved during the early 1950s, but meanwhile the company had merged with Jacobson & Van den Berg. For this latter company, still family-owned, no comparable dividend data could be traced. It was really a conglomerate of family firms, including the firm itself and the limited company Jacoberg Overseas. When the colonial business started to go downhill, the family shareholders considered that the time had come to dismantle the whole complicated array of firms and companies, thinking that the merger with Lindeteves would be the easiest way to achieve this. The Lindeteves board welcomed this proposal, reporting to the supervisory directors that both companies stood to gain. There was a partial overlap in operations, but the companies mostly complemented each other. Where they overlapped, cost savings could be made by merging branches. Elsewhere operations now run by one of the firms could be expanded cheaply by merging. Jacoberg appeared to have a very able board and a good staff.[88] After this report to its supervisory board, the Lindeteves board opened negotiations with Jacobson Van den Berg & Co., which led to a merger in 1958.

Meanwhile Güntzel & Schumacher, which sometimes used to be ranked with the 'Big Five' traders instead of Lindeteves, had now become one of the smaller merchant houses, possessing a share capital of 4 million guilders, against Hagemeyer, for instance, with 5 million guilders. After the loss of its Indonesian operations, the board presumably saw insufficient opportunities to

286

The trading company Tels & Co. found it difficult to keep going after the enforced departure from Indonesia, and it was taken over by Hagemeyer in 1963. The photograph shows Tels's Singapore branch.

L.E. TELS   tels   得力士洋行

continue the business. In 1960, the Rubber Cultuur Maatschappij Amsterdam bought the outstanding shares. Many smaller colonial traders simply disappeared. The Handelsvereeniging 'Holland-Bombay', which operated from Amsterdam, had liquidated as early as 1949. The Handelsvereeniging Java strayed far from its original field of operations by reorganising itself into a packaging company called A.E. Ruys Plasticverpakkingen in 1959. Reiss & Co. went into Africa, paid no dividends from 1957 until 1959, but managed to find its feet again subsequently. The Moluksche Handelsvennootschap relocated to Singapore and also bought a small pharmaceutical wholesaler in Paramaribo, but to no avail. The company paid its last dividend in 1954. Harmsen Verwey & Dunlop merged with Maintz' Productenhandel in 1957 to form Multitrade, which was taken over by Hagemeyer in 1960. Tels & Co. attempted to start afresh in Africa, but dividends dried up in 1956, and in 1963 it was bought by Hagemeyer. A remarkably large number of companies had to suspend dividends in 1957. This makes Hagemeyer's achievement all the more striking. The company paid a normal dividend that year, and even used a windfall from a favourable transaction with the tax authorities for an extra pay-out of 33.25% in 1958, with 25% paid in shares.[89] During the first fifteen post-war years, Hagemeyer had succeeded in overtaking a number of smaller colonial traders, and in getting closer to the leading companies. Undoubtedly, the board's decision to begin operations in New Guinea had contributed to this favourable result. On the other hand, Hagemeyer had always restricted itself to trading in Indonesia, thus escaping relatively lightly from the nationalisation policies, whereas companies such as Internatio, Borsumij, and Jacobson Van den Berg & Co. had suffered more because of their interests in plantations or local industries. Consequently, in the case of Indonesia, diversification turned out to be disadvantageous in the long run.

During the Second World War, trade operations assumed a provisional character. Companies in the Netherlands had to muster a lot of creativity to keep going, whereas business in the Dutch East Indies came to a complete standstill from 1942. After the war, the trading companies tried to pick up the threads again as soon as possible, but they had to grope for new ways in a world which was rapidly decolonising. The merchant houses remained active in Indonesia after its independence, optimistic about their indispensability, confident about the profitability of their operations, and really without sufficient profitable alternatives elsewhere. Commercial skills acquired in the Dutch East Indies were not necessarily successful in themselves, when transplanted to other regions. In 1959, the hour of truth sounded when the subsidiaries in Indonesia were nationalised. Some firms had to liquidate or to accept being taken over, others, such as Hagemeyer, went from strength to strength during this period. And yet, would the former colonial traders survive in the long run without their operations in Indonesia?

CHAPTER VII

During the 1960s the merchant houses began to concentrate their activities in politically stable regions. Here companies with a balanced business strategy and with sufficient energy could pick up on welcome opportunities, all the more so because these islands of political calm also enjoyed remarkable economic growth. This rising wealth offered scope for an expanding trade in consumer products. Some traders considered integration with manufacturing industry an attractive way of reducing their dependence on suppliers, and thus of bolstering revenues in the long term. However, this was to prove a hazardous course.

During the 1960s, Japanese consumer goods captured European markets. Borsumij and Hagemeyer both operated as agents for Japanese producers. Conversely, Internatio shipped fertiliser from Rotterdam to Asia, in this case to Thailand.

BELIEVING IN A CONTROLLABLE SOCIETY – As economic growth continued during the 1960s, it created an atmosphere of optimism about future prosperity for an increasing number of people. Between the end of the Second World War and 1960, world exports of the non-communist countries expressed in US dollars had risen by 6% every year. From 1960 to 1973, the annual growth of world exports averaged as much as 8%. By 1973, the turning point in this period, world exports by value in US dollars was seven times higher than in 1953, and four times by volume. During those years, the market share of industrialised countries had risen from 43% in 1953 to nearly 70% in 1973.[1] Japanese exports showed a particularly remarkable growth. During the mid-1970s the so-called newly industrialised countries in Asia and Southern America began to contribute to world trade. The GATT forum steadily worked towards reducing obstacles to trade, both in the form of levies and of quota restrictions. Even GATT could not, however, prevent the formation of regional trade blocks, such as the European Economic Community (EEC) which, incidentally, stimulated trade between the participating countries.

The dominant position of the industrialised countries also manifested itself in the kind of products traded. Around 1950, half of world trade consisted of primary products, i.e. agricultural produce and raw materials, the other half comprising industrial goods and semi-finished products. Until 1973, the share of industrial products rose to two-thirds of world trade by value. Within the category of industrial products, the importance of fabrics and clothing declined against machinery and vehicles, while during the 1960s chemical products boomed.[2]

By the mid-1960s, the decolonization process had been virtually completed, and the former colonies began to be grouped together under the term 'developing countries' or 'Third World countries'. Many of these countries found themselves in a vulnerable position. Their exports pivoted around a limited number of primary products, whose prices could fluctuate sharply, moreover. During the 1960s, however, high expectations prevailed about the potential to generate economic growth in these countries by giving them Western skills and financial aid, and by the selective boosting of trade. These aims found a typical embodiment in the United Nations Conference on Trade and Development (UNCTAD). During its first conference, in 1964, delegates pleaded for the

Meanwhile the international trading companies clearly lost their interest for investing in Africa. Only Nigeria continued to appear attractive for some time, boosted as it was by oil revenues. Hagemeyer operated a joint-venture there with Sigma Coatings, formerly known as Pieter Schoen & Zn., producing Sigma paints. Here a Hagemeyer retailer in Lagos.

adoption of measures to regulate the markets for raw materials, for granting exports from Third World countries preferential access to the markets of developed countries, and for development aid. Four years later the second conference accentuated these aims.[3] The international efforts to help the underdeveloped countries on the road towards economic growth inspired some merchant houses not to liquidate all of their investments in these countries, regardless of the losses sustained, and to monitor developments expectantly.

The optimism about the Third World's future mirrored a more general feeling in society of the world being essentially controllable. Thus economists and politicians believed that practical policy instruments derived from the Keynsian economic theories enabled governments to guide a country's economy in such a way as to prevent repetition of serious economic crises like the 1930s depression. This was referred to as 'dampening the economic cycles'. For businessmen, the dampening implied a lessening of their economic risk, raising confidence in making long-term plans. Business management theories blown over from the US reinforced this confidence. One such theory, propagated by the American Peter Drucker, reduced the managing of a business more or less to a matter of practical skills. According to Drucker, anyone could become an excellent manager by closely following his instructions.[4] The true leader of a company should not only know how to organise, but also how to map the future, i.e. develop a business strategy. Such a strategy would include an analysis of the company's strengths and weaknesses, plus a long-term analysis of its markets, both actual and potential. This would enable the board to take well-founded decisions about expansion, horizontal or vertical integration, or perhaps diversification towards building a business conglomerate.

Management consultants encouraged companies to develop long-term strategic plans, convinced as they were, that making sense of future developments was a viable concept. In his influential book *Corporate Strategy*, H. Igor Ansoff professed optimism about the idea of getting to grips with the future by analysing the present. In 1967, he wrote confidently: 'The shape of the firm in the 1980s, therefore, need not be dimly perceived through a crystal ball. It can be sketched by analysing and projecting from the present'.[5] That same year, H. Kahn en A.J. Wiener even dared to prognosticate on the future beyond the year 2000, on the basis of a belief that economic depressions were a phenomenon of the past: 'Today it is widely believed that, except possibly for China, almost all the communist and capitalist governments are coming to understand how to keep their economies reasonably stable and growing'.[6]

Such ideas about continuing economic growth and the need for systematic or even scientifically founded management became current in the Netherlands as well, penetrating the world of commerce. In 1969, G.H.J. Abeln wrote a typical report for the Federation of Dutch Wholesalers, entitled *The Dutch international trading house and economic growth*. Abeln argued first of all, that the volume of its investments in modern business necessitated a policy of continuity and stability. The factors of risk and coincidence had to be excluded wherever possible, and traders would have to relinquish their aversion to a scientific approach of commercial problems. It was dangerous to trust to intuition in business. Leadership over a company required analytical judgement most of all, and the ability to effect a synthesis of its constituent parts. Modern business simply no longer had use for traditional merchants, earning their living from taking chances, from risk and coincidence. The merchant houses had lost their positions in the developing countries largely because of the protectionism adopted by the newly independent governments. They had lost touch with industry in the wealthy western world through their failure to understand that the increasing demands placed upon products, marketing, and service, would lead to integration between production and sales. Abeln questioned whether traders had any future at all. He found that they might survive, if and when they developed from independent intermediaries into a conglomerate of trade and industry, acquiring manufacturing interests either by merging with industry, or by setting up their own production units from scratch. Traders would also have to reinforce the links with retailers by providing finance, after sales services, etc. The traditional trade functions of buying and selling no longer sufficed, these

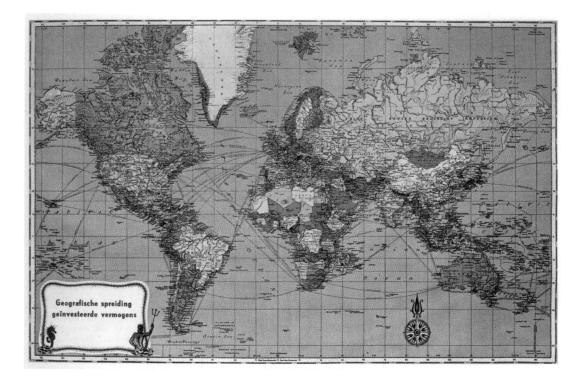

Africa and Asia became less attractive
for the international traders,
whereas they invested more and
more in Europe.

had to be expanded into marketing and sales promotion. Accordingly, Abeln envisaged the beginning of a phase of conglomerate mergers, underlining his argument by referring to the history of the United African Company, a Unilever subsidiary, and of Internatio. He expressly advised merchant houses to diversify their activities by embarking on industrial production.[7] Some of the Dutch merchant houses were already adopting his suggestions as a practical guideline that very moment, as will become clear below.

MIGRATING TO POLITICALLY STABLE COUNTRIES – During the 1960s, two overall trends dominated the trading houses, i.e. a desire to shift operations to politically stable countries, and aspirations towards diversifying their core business. The degree in which these trends left their mark differed from company to company, though. Table 7.1 shows the geographical spread of business of Borsumij Wehry, Hagemeyer, Internatio, and Lindeteves Jacoberg, as measured by their investment, since data on turnover were unavailable.[8]

		Europe	America	Australia	Asia	Africa
Borsumij	1962	35	13	8	24	20
	1972	69	10	-	12	9
Hagemeyer	1962	21	15	18	24	22
	1972	70	9	6	11	4
Internatio	1963	83	13	1	2	1
	1972	88	6	5	-	1
Lindeteves	1962	35	10	11	20	24
	1972	41	2	17	30	10

Table 7.1

Geografical spread of operations of four

international traders, in percentages of investment.

In fact, the growing preference for investment in politically stable countries mainly meant a shift from Asia and Africa to Europe, with a marked emphasis on the Netherlands. Despite a clear desire to establish a foothold in the USA, investments there relatively declined. Australia, though attractive from a political viewpoint, also proved a difficult field of operations for the Dutch international traders. Amongst these companies, Internatio acquired a particularly narrow focus on Europe, with 83% of its capital invested there in 1963, the first year for which the firm supplied data. Lindeteves Jacoberg occupied the opposite end of the scale, in 1972 still having only 41% of its investments in Europe and a continuing strong presence in Asia. Interestingly, Unilever's investments in Africa, through its United African Company subsidiary, amounted to 29% of its capital in 1955. This had declined to only 15% as early as 1965, inspiring Abeln, the economist mentioned before, to conclude four years later that only the biggest and strongest companies could afford to invest part of their resources in the newly independent countries.[9]

Before the Second World War, the trade flows managed by Dutch international traders were fairly straightforward. On one hand, they bought industrial products, mainly in Europe and to a lesser extent in the US, for the Asian and African markets. On the other, the firms bought crops and raw materials in Asia and Africa for sale in Europe and the US. This simple scheme underwent its first change following the rise of Japan as a producer of industrial products, and the trade pattern became ever more complex with the appearance of new industrialised countries. Some of the old trade flows continued to exist side by side with new ones. Hagemeyer, for instance, bought batteries from the Malaysian factory of a Japanese company, Matsushita, for selling in Africa, while at the same time marketing this company's consumer electronics National brand in Singapore, Malaysia, Australia, and subsequently in the Netherlands. The trade in primary products from Indonesia continued to be the main interest of the international traders' Singapore branches, and those established in Hong Kong shipped Chinese-made shoes to Europe. Borsumij Wehry sold tools produced in Poland on the US market. Both Hagemeyer and Borsumij Wehry built up a business importing Japanese products into Europe. During the colonial era, the trade in primary products had been closely linked with the possession or management of plantations for many merchant houses. The nationalization of Dutch possessions in Indonesia severed the organic links of this business, increasing the risks. In addition, the former colonial traders faced increasing competition from the direct buying of manufacturers, from the growing importance of specialised traders, and from governments in producing countries starting their own export operations.[10]

Transport changes during the 1960s stimulated the overseas trade in industrial products. In their turn, these changes were a response to the growth in world trade, and in particular, the fast growing trade in industrial products, which were usually transported not in bulk, but as general cargo. The transport revolution of these years centred around the rise of the container, large steel boxes for shipping cargo which enabled a cheaper and faster port handling of loosely packaged goods and small shipments. The container solution to the bot-

The container revolutionised maritime transport, particularly for general cargo, enabling more products to compete with each other worldwide. Internatio-Müller was closely involved with the foundation of Europe Container Terminus (ECT) in Rotterdam (1970). On the left the traditional way of cargo handling, right ECT operations during the 1970s.

tlenecks in port handling created scope for bigger and cheaper shipping. Moreover, containerization eliminated the need for repackaging during the transport from producer to consumer. This again meant faster goods turnover, lower costs of packaging, and less exposure to damage and theft, resulting in a wider range of goods competing with each other over longer distances.[11] Dutch sectors feeling the impact of rising imports from Asia included fabrics and electronics.

The rise of air travel and the declining cost of international telephone traffic also changed the operations of the international traders. It became ever easier for manufacturers to bypass traders and do their own overseas exports, seizing a growing slice of the merchants' territory. To keep their hand in that business, the traders had to increase their value added. In the developing countries the firms sometimes chose to do so by getting involved in retailing, in service organizations, or in production units, such as final assembly, leather tanning, paint making, or beer brewing. The old distinction between purchasing

The international trading companies were keen users of air travel, but their intermediary position suffered at the same time, for it became easier for manufacturers to keep in touch with their overseas customers.

branches and sales branches also began to blur following the progress in communications mentioned. Manufacturers now easily gained direct access to sales branches in various countries, without the intermediation of the purchasing offices. As a result, the former purchasing branches in Europe began to concentrate mainly on local wholesaling.

To a certain degree, the international traders went through similar experiences in the various regions. Political unrest was rife in many developing countries, and the Cold War fuelled it further. The merchant houses were continuously confronted, as they had been in Indonesia, with measures aiming for economic independence, not to mention wars and internal conflicts. The package of measures usually comprised restrictions on imports, limitations on the repatriation of profits, preferential treatment for local people, obligations for replacing European staff with indigenous people, and finally nationalisation of foreign companies, or at least substantial capital participations by local investors. Such interference could kill a business within a short time, as it did when Tanzania nationalised in 1966.[12] For the international traders, nationalist actions like this always came as an unpleasant surprise, and often as an incomprehensible one. One of Hagemeyer's supervisory directors vented a typical, somewhat despairing remark in 1964, following actions against Dutch companies in Singapore. He thought that such measures would not be greeted with enthusiasm by the population, considering the very high unemployment, although he had learnt from experience that it was impossible to foretell official actions in such politically less developed countries.[13] The economic uncertainty added to the political

Setting up an export subsidiary in Japan was easier than starting an import business there. Yet Borsumij Wehry succeeded in doing just this, on the strength of its agency for the Dutch milk factory DMV in the city of Veghel. This company sold milk products such as casein and lactose to Japan. Its sales of lactose became so important, that in 1991 DMV, now part of the Campina-Melkunie concern, dismissed Borsumij Wehry as its Japan agent.

suspense. For instance, the revaluation of the guilder in 1961 came as a shock after more than a decade of stable exchange rates. The board of Borsumij Wehry commented indignantly, considering the revaluation detrimental to international trade since it had seriously damaged the stability of the rates between the key currencies in world trade.[14]

However, the success or failure of a branch did not depend on general political or economical factors alone. The human factor also came into play, this agent or general manager running a branch better than that one. The transfer or untimely death of an agent could make a prospering business suddenly to collapse. Not everyone succeeded in getting to know the right people, and in securing the right agencies. Hagemeyer built up a magnificent business in Australia around the Matsushita agency, whereas Borsumij Wehry suffered disappointments on that continent and withdrew. As early as 1962, Internatio left Japan, though this did not, by the way, mean the end for the company's involvement in selling Japanese products. By contrast, Borsumij Wehry even succeeded in developing a thriving import business, quite an achievement considering Japan's focus on exports to the detriment of imports. Geo. Wehry had started this business in 1958.[15] Hagemeyer nursed a close relationship with the Japanese manufacturing concern Matsushita, which incidentally also had a joint-venture with the Dutch electrical concern Philips' Gloeilampenfabrieken. When the Amsterdam city council took the initiative for a trade mission to Japan, the Hagemeyer board considered whether or not to join the delegation, and decided against. It was the company's standard policy never to participate in trade missions to countries in which it already had a branch.[16] So, to all appearances, Hagemeyer did not care for maintaining relations with Dutch manufacturers and officials, the staple fare of such trade missions. Internatio withdrew completely from Asia in 1967, only to reconsider its decision ten years later. During the mid-1960s, Borsumij Wehry debated whether to run down its Asian investments outside of Japan, but in the end the board took no action.

The international traders' experiences in Africa were equally variable. From time to time the Congo branches operated profitably, but transferring profits to the Netherlands proved very difficult. The country suited businessmen with an adventurous streak. During the early 1960s, Hagemeyer had an employee there who effortlessly sailed through no end of difficulties and dangers, including those connected to smuggling profits out of the country.[17] A lack of import permits persuaded the company finally to terminate its operations there in 1967. Lindeteves Jacoberg persevered for somewhat longer. It took a considerable time before Hagemeyer operated profitably in East Africa, and when that phase had finally dawned, nationalist actions began to harm profits. During the 1960s, Nigeria experienced an economic boom powered by the oil industry, from which the international traders also profited for some years. For the merchant houses, however, the political uncertainty in the developing countries was decisive, even if the opportunities for profit were not inconsiderable, in making them prefer Europe as the target of new investments.

First of all, the familiarity of the political climate made Europe attractive. Admittedly, European politicians could also adopt measures unfavourable for the international traders, like, for instance, the introduction of import quota on a product the moment it became a success. Such measures, however, were usually less radical, and not as sudden. And as often as not, some room for negotiation remained. Secondly, from the 1950s onwards, Europe experienced a process of strong economic growth. Politicians strove hard to create a single European market. The growing wealth translated into rising consumer spending, and thus in booming sales of consumer goods. True, there were some clouds on the horizon, such as the scope of the EEC's impending cartel legislation, i.e. the question whether or not monopoly agencies and the many informal agreements between suppliers, wholesalers, and retailers, in the Netherlands would soon be outlawed. The intentions of the Brussels-based EEC officials were clear enough, but the practical consequences remained in the dark. For the time being, Dutch businessmen could continue with their collusive arrangements.[18]

Rising wage expenditure in the Netherlands became a pressing problem for the international traders. During the 1950s, employers' organizations and trade unions had cooperated with the government in adopting a policy of wage controls as a means to boost exports. This policy was torn apart in the 1960s, on one side by the unions demanding a bigger share of the economic growth, on the other by the competition among employers struggling to obtain ever scarcer labour. The first indication came in 1961 with the introduction of the five-day week, followed by an unmistakable sign in the form of the 1963 wage explosion. Labour costs rose substantially, forcing employers to find compensation for the cost increases one way or the other.

Borsumij Wehry and Lindeteves Jacoberg took rising wage costs as an incentive to focus closer on more specialised products requiring a better distributing organization and a higher service level than bulk products, in return for a generally better margin. However, specialisation required closer links with manufacturers to the point of the traders becoming dependent on them. This sensation of dependency was reinforced by manufacturing industry's remarkable expansion of scope during the 1960s.

THE STRAINS BETWEEN AGENT AND PRINCIPAL – For traders, their vulnerability in relation to manufacturers is a very real problem. The relationship between agent and principal is dominated by the classic dilemma that an agent's position is under constant threat, irrespective of his commercial performance. If an agent neglects his marketing duties, his principal will dismiss him for poor performance. However, an agent who succeeds in realising burgeoning sales also runs the risk of dismissal, because manufacturers will want to reinforce their grip on a market which has become important for them. Borsumij Wehry's agency for Olympia typewriters in Australia provides a good illustration of the first case. During the early 1960s, the company failed to achieve satisfactory sales for

During the 1960s, Dutch wages exploded, turning the Netherlands from a cheap labour country into an expensive one. The wage rises were inaugurated by the introduction of the five-day working week, an innovation feared by employers but greeted with enthusiasm by housewives. A cartoon by Behrendt, 22 April 1961.

As a rule, manufacturers continued to use the services of local agents longest for remote countries or for small markets. Borsumij, for instance, represented Philips in East Africa with window displays such as this one for radio sets, photographed in Nairobi in 1954.

these typewriters, so after a nine years' struggle the German manufacturer terminated the agency. Borsumij Wehry tried to persuade their principals to change their minds, but had to concede openly that the manufacturer did have a point in wanting to take the marketing into its own hands. Since the trader's Australian branch was highly dependent on the Olympia agency, the board reluctantly decided to close it.[19] Another Borsumij Wehry agency underlines the second case. In East Africa, the company marketed radio and television sets for Philips. For a considerable period of time, Borsumij Wehry cherished this agency, but it is not entirely clear whether their principal did so, too. Whatever the case, in 1972 Philips decided to tighten the screws on their agent, convinced that Borsumij Wehry made exorbitant profits on the sale of Philips products. Moreover, the electronics company had meanwhile become used to marketing through its own local offices. Borsumij Wehry refused to accept the proposed cut in its margins, arguing that the sales were not as profitable as Philips thought. Instead, the board proposed to set up a joint venture for the distribution, but this was turned down. As a counter move Borsumij Wehry began to add radio and television sets from a rival manufacturer to its product range. Consequently, Philips chose to take the East African distribution into its own hands.[20]

A principal did not have to terminate existing relationships to throttle revenue sources. In 1960, Borsumij Wehry somewhat reluctantly accepted an agency to market photographic equipment in the Netherlands and Germany from the Japanese manufacturer Canon. The board's reluctance concerned the obligation to start selling camera's in Germany, a country well-known for its production of high-quality camera's, so it did take some courage to begin selling Japanese-made equipment in the lion's den. However, within a couple of years winning German consumers for Japanese cameras proved a very viable concept. Once Europhoto, the subsidiary set up for this purpose, began to take off,

301

Canon became keen to participate in it. Initially the manufacturer bought a 40% stake in the marketing organization, but in 1975 Canon demanded a majority share, preferably 75%. Of course Borsumij Wehry was rather unhappy with its principal's demands, but the board acutely felt its own powerlessness, confronted with a manufacturer who could, if necessary, obtain the desired majority stake by force.[21]

Naturally Borsumij Wehry was not alone in its dependence on manufacturers. Matters could suddenly take an unwanted course, as Hagemeyer found out in Canada. The company ran a modest importing branch there selling Dutch food and tobacco products, and having among its agencies Douwe Egberts tobacco and the French cigarette brand Bastos. In 1966, Douwe Egberts wanted to begin production in Montreal. Hagemeyer put the company in touch with Bastos, since the cigarette manufacturer had spare production capacity there. As a consequence, Douwe Egberts and Bastos drew up joint marketing plans, which threatened to cut Hagemeyer out of the game. In the end the two manufacturers failed to reach an agreement, but even so Douwe Egberts did start its own distribution operations, taking over some of the Hagemeyer branch's staff for the purpose.[22]

Like Borsumij Wehry, Hagemeyer also experienced the pressure of a satisfied principal keen to protect sales. In 1975 Matsushita, producer of the consumer electronics brands National and Panasonic, signalled intentions to

302

The agencies for the Japanese consumer electronics manufacturer Matsushita in Singapore, Malaysia, the Netherlands, and Australia were Hagemeyer's key revenue source for years and years. On the right a Singapore shopping street, left a truck delivering consumer electronics of Matsushita's National brand to a Singapore retailer.

CHAPTER VII · Trade and industry, an awkward fit, 1960-1983

transfer the marketing activities for some areas to joint ventures with Hagemeyer. This would automatically involve the manufacturer directly with sales operations for its products, and the Hagemeyer board perceived Matsushita's intentions as a threat to the company's position. Director T.H. Bödeker immediately flew to Japan for top-level negotiations. By making some concessions concerning a joint-venture in Malaysia, Bödeker succeeded in securing the monopoly agencies in Singapore, Australia, and the Netherlands for a period of ten years, provided Hagemeyer continued to serve these markets properly. This agreement, by the way, was not formalised in a written contract, but remained a matter of mutual trust.[23]

Examples such as these only offer some illustrations of the tussles between agents and principals which litter the history of the international traders. Dependence always remains a threat in the background, even when the human relationships are good and the business links successful. This threat will be sensed more acutely under the pressure of intensifying competition. One way of ending the dependence once and for all, is by integrating production and trade into a single company. Another option to reduce the dependence on principals is diversification of the operations. Mergers and take-overs could serve to bring both aims within reach. During the mid-1960s the climate became particularly favourable for such concentration. Between 1960 and 1971, Europe experienced a wave of mergers, brought about by intensifying competition. This wave reached the Netherlands somewhat later and continued a little longer, the number of mergers and take-overs peaking in 1975.[24] The international traders entered this game with relish.

THE LURE OF INDUSTRY – When shifting their focus to Europe, the merchant houses had to solve the problem of what kind of operations they wanted to begin. Was it better to stick to international trade and distributive wholesaling, or should they choose to break new ground? In the end, the international traders expanded their operations in two directions. Some firms switched to manufacturing activities, with the purpose of achieving some degree of vertical integration. Others opted to build a conglomerate by a general diversification of operations, aiming to expand the business and to spread risk with activities not necessarily connected to existing ones or to each other. As time went by, however, most companies with a diversification strategy began to bring some integration of the old and the new activities, thus really retracting from becoming a conglomerate in the strict sense of the word. It has to be said, though, that the terms used to describe various business strategies suffer from a lack of firm definitions. This section looks into some forms of concentration, with particular attention for the coalescence of trade with manufacturing, for the optimistic expectations concerning such combinations, and to the generally disappointing results.

From the group of former Dutch East Indian international traders, Internatio was the first and the most determined in shifting its focus to Europe and in opting for a definite diversification strategy during the 1960s. The driving force behind the new strategy was H. Stout, member of the board from 1950 until 1974. His career track to the top had a trajectory common for trading companies. During the 1920s, Stout had been sent to Asia following a short training in the Rotterdam office. He returned from his long turn of duty abroad in the 1950s to receive a senior management position. Stout had become convinced that Internatio's future lay in Europe, and that the company's scope had to be widened. He also considered the scientific analysis of trade of paramount importance, so much so that in 1963, on the occasion of the company's centenary, he set up the Internatio Foundation with the purpose of stimulating research into trade. Stout wanted to end what he felt to be the relegation of trade in the league of economic sectors. All too often the representatives of industry, agriculture, shipping, and banking, carried the day on matters of commercial importance. Trade with remote countries overseas might be declining but, according to Stout, the primary distributive functions continued to exist. Indeed, the rising needs of modern society unmistakably added all kinds of secondary functions to the primary ones.[25] Stout saw no prospects in operations in the developing countries, and opted instead for investments in prosperous areas, such as Europe, Australia, and to a limited degree South Africa as well. The company's US branches remained important for the commodity trade, in which it continued to maintain an substantial stake. From Rotterdam, London, New York, and Boston, Internatio traded a wide range of crops, among them sugar,

To shift the focus of its operations from Asia to the Netherlands, Internatio acquired a string of Dutch companies, among them Roupe van der Voort's Industrie- en Metaal-Maatschappij in 1961. This firm's products included heating and bathroom equipment. During the 1960s, Internatio was to diversify its operations still further.

coffee, tea, cocoa, ground nuts, pepper, and rubber. In the Netherlands, the firm concentrated on wholesaling, taking over a large number of companies in this sector.

Wholesale businesses purchased by Internatio often included small production plants. As a consequence, Internatio assembled a group of industrial interests including a manufacturer of clamps and fittings for pressured air hoses, but also a producer of essential oils, scents, and aromatics, followed in 1961 by the acquisition of a manufacturer of lead and tin products, and a producer of lead oxide. This did not amount to a conscious diversification strategy. As late as 1965, Internatio still defined heating and air engineering and fitting as its second core business, taking over two important companies in this field, Van Rictschoten & Houwens and Gebr. van Swaay, three years later. These two acquisitions increased Internatio's total staff to 8,000 people. However, the variety of manufacturing activities continued to grow all along, leading to a redefinition of the company's mission into three parts: trade, fitting, and manufacturing. In the 1968 annual report the board wrote that the speed of growth justified Internatio's existence, for in modern society the future belonged to ever bigger business units. Economies of scale would dominate the pattern of competition. Accordingly, when the company merged with Wm. H. Müller & Co. in 1970, the board proudly announced that the new unit belonged to the top-fifteen of Dutch business. Through Müller, Internatio became involved with the trade in ore, river shipping, port handling, and general shipping. This merger again almost doubled staff numbers to a total of 15,000 employees.

Despite Internatio-Müller having widely diversified by 1970, the company had still not reached a high degree of industrialisation. This changed in 1972 with the last big transaction of the period, the take-over of Amalga, a company recently formed by the merger of three manufacturers of gas heaters and stoves, De Etna, Daalderop, and Diepenbrock & Reigers (DRU). The three producers had prospered following the introduction of natural gas, but when growth rates declined they felt threatened in their existence, and had therefore merged. At the very moment of Internatio's take-over, Amalga already suffered from very sluggish sales and consequent serious losses. It was hoped, however, that Internatio, with its capital power and proven marketing skills, would open up fresh prospects by investing in new products, and by opening new markets, foreign ones in particular. The take-over of Amalga raised Internatio-Müller's total number of employees to 17,800 people, 15,800 of which worked in the Netherlands, against only 2,000 abroad. Diversification had thus changed the company to an overwhelmingly Dutch business. It remained open to doubt, however, whether the strategy had really succeeded in spreading risk.

Hagemeyer's diversification strategy purposefully aimed at acquiring manufacturing companies, more so than Internatio did. During the 1950s, Hagemeyer had done very well in New Guinea, but business was terminated there in 1963. At the transfer of sovereignty in 1949, the question of whether or not New Guinea was to form part of the Indonesian Republic had remained unresolved. The Indonesian government continued to press its claims to the territory, and finally succeeded in getting them accepted by the United Nations. After a brief military campaign the Netherlands handed over New Guinea to the United Nations, which in its turn transferred it to Indonesia. For the remaining Dutch people in New Guinea, the transfer to Indonesia signalled that it was time to leave. This time Hagemeyer had sufficient time for an ordered liquidation of its business, so the company suffered no loss of capital. Quite the opposite, substantial hidden reserves suddenly became available. However, a crucial revenue source dried up. In 1961, 50% of profits still derived from New Guinea, creating a need to find suitable compensation.[26] Capital was no impediment, but it proved hard to identify the right opportunities. Hagemeyer continued its operations in Asia, Australia, and Africa, but the board really looked to the rich western world as the target for new investments. Propositions in prosperous countries such as Canada or the US were not necessarily successful, though. Irval Sales Co., a US importer taken over by Hagemeyer in 1962, returned losses from the moment it was bought until a disappointed board closed the business ten years later. In fact, until the 1970s Asia proved to be the area generating by far the highest profits in relation to investment.

Hagemeyer's conversion to manufacturing occurred during the mid-1960s. In 1962, the board still considered that taking over a manufacturing business was not in the company's interest, and so happily passed up the opportunity of buying a cigar manufacturer with the 'Uiltje' brand.[27] The board did fall for the leather industry, however, when in 1965 the opportunity arose to take over the Amsterdamse Leder Maatschappij NV. This company produced footwear in Oisterwijk, had just opened a unit recycling the waste of leather factories in Waalwijk, and also possessed a few small trading companies. Initially Hagemeyer's interest was mainly aroused by the company's seat, a stately property at a prime location on one of Amsterdam's canals, and less so by the manufacturing operations.[28] The board of supervisory directors raised the principle whether or not Hagemeyer should go into industry. Chief executive G.L. Oostergo affirmed that he would not have become interested in this particular industry, but for the considerable value offered by the various properties.[29] In subsequent take-over deliberations, the value of plants and warehouses was an equally decisive argument for the board. Once the take-over had been agreed, the Hagemeyer board began by inspecting its new acquisition. Visiting the Oisterwijk plant, the board members professed themselves to be overwhelmed by the sheer size of the complex and its equipment.[30] The price had been low, but then the returns were not very high either. Hagemeyer expected that reorganizations would soon improve matters, even though the board's practical management experience was almost totally oriented on trade, and had also been mostly built up abroad. On visiting offices Oostergo, for instance, used to limit his inspection to four essentials, i.e. the payroll, the debtor administration, the amount of stock, and the gross margins.[31] Manufacturing companies, however, required attention to entirely different aspects, too, such as production processes

306

During the mid-1960s, Hagemeyer became acutely conscious of its vulnerable position as a mere agent for strong principals, so the company began to diversify into industry. Its first acquisition, in 1965, was a leather works in Oisterwijk, followed in 1970 by a similar one in Waalwijk. The photograph shows their product range.

and product development. Yet Hagemeyer was confident that management skills applied to all businesses alike, so trade experience would suffice for running a manufacturing company. Initially this appeared to be true.

The Hagemeyer CEO Oostergo lacked a clear vision of how best to realise the company's diversification. He thought that on one hand acquisitions were preferable to starting new activities from scratch, but on the other hand he did not expect such acquisitions to generate similarly high returns as the trading activities for the time being. His expectations subsequently proved all too true. It was only towards the end of the 1960s that Oostergo began to emphasise the potential and the desirability for integration between trade and industry. Once the leather company had been acquired, the board dropped its reluctance over industrial commitments. During the following years, Hagemeyer bought the Nederlandse Uurwerkenfabrieken NUFA, a clock maker; two factories for

In 1968, Hagemeyer bought Berk-Beccon, a manufacturer of enamel pots and pans of some renown. One of its enamelling works was located in Doetinchem.

307

kitchen utensils, the Industriële Maatschappij Berk-Beccon and Emailleerfabriek 'De IJssel' (Edy), both producing the pots and pans with which Hagemeyer had once started operations in the Dutch East Indies; and a manufacturer of electrical household appliances, Electro-Kalorik, in Brussels. The size of these companies was still fairly manageable. However, in 1969 the company realised its first really substantial transaction by taking over Indola, which produced cosmetics, pharmaceuticals, plastics, and electrical appliances such as fans, power drills, and hair dryers. Indola was losing money at the moment of its acquisition. The company had undergone a whole string of reorganizations, all in themselves typical of the atmosphere during the late 1960s. The original Indola had merged in 1965 with Van der Heem to become Indoheem, a merger inspired by the need

for increasing business scope and efficiency in the face of mounting European competition. Van der Heem mainly operated as a subcontractor to the electrotechnical wholesaler R.S. Stokvis, supplying appliances under this latter company's Erres brand. Stokvis was also the main shareholder in Van der Heem. In 1966, before the Indoheem board had begun to realise the merger intentions, the core Van der Heem business, mainly the production of radio and television sets, was sold on to Philips. Indoheem kept part of the household appliances, and reverted to its original name of Indola.[32]

Hagemeyer now faced the task of creating new opportunities for this company. The supervisory board had not been very much in favour of the acquisition, but the executive board was full of optimism. Having come to the conclusion that Indola lacked sound commercial skills, the board thought that Hagemeyer could add real value, and it expected to return Indola to profitability within three years. Moreover, directors had become convinced of the need to embrace industry to counterbalance the threat of losing specific agencies.[33] The press statement about the take-over demonstrates that by 1969, the board had formulated a much clearer business strategy, referring as it did to the take-over as an integration between trade and industry which created new and better prospects for the sale of Indola products.[34] The composition of the Hagemeyer staff demonstrates the increasing importance of manufacturing within the company. Between 1965 and 1970 the number of employees rose from 1,300, all working in trade, to 6,600, of whom 2,600 in trade and no fewer than 4,000 in manufacturing.[35] As a consequence, the company changed its character. The need to foster integration inspired typical initiatives such as a Hagemeyer staff newsletter and an annual football competition between teams of the various subsidiaries. As a rule, teams from the manufacturing divisions won the latter.[36] The shareholders lavished praise on the board. In 1969, one of them approvingly quoted an article from the newspaper *De Tijd* arguing in favour of integrating trade with industry. According to the paper, trading companies which had refrained from getting involved with industry really had missed the boat.[37] Rival trading companies eyed the financial results with envious admiration. The business press called Hagemeyer a prime example of what could be achieved with judicious refocusing.[38] In the years following the big Indola acquisition, Hagemeyer bought a few more companies, one of them also in the leather sector, the Koninklijke Chroomlederfabriek 'De Amstel', and another, a plastics plant, the Ets. L.F. Laets. Inserting these companies into existing activities seemed an easy matter.

Borsumij Wehry showed considerably more restraints towards industrial involvement than either Internatio or Hagemeyer, but then the company possessed smaller resources. The enforced departure from Indonesia had seriously depleted Borsumij's power, and the merger with Geo. Wehry in 1960 had provided only limited reinforcement. At its formation, the new company's capital had been depreciated to 40%, partly because of the political instability prevailing in the less developed countries in which Borsumij Wehry operated, like Africa, Singapore, Malaysia, Borneo, and Burma.[39]

Hagemeyer's diversification strategy created the need for a company staff magazine, which was, of course, christened Boogschutter, or Sagittarius.

In 1968, Borsumij Wehry bought an aerosol factory, but this remained an exception. Declining sales and mounting losses persuaded the board to sell the factory again in 1975.

In 1971, Hagemeyer received the 'Mercurio d'oro' or golden Mercury award from a European trade and industry association.

Like Internatio and Hagemeyer, Borsumij Wehry refocused on Europe, and the company succeeded in obtaining some attractive agencies, including Sharp and Adidas beside the Canon representation already mentioned. In the Netherlands, Borsumij Wehry acquired a wholesaler in office equipment, but also a manufacturer of partition walls and warehouse storage racks. The company's fabrics operations included a production unit for ready-made suits. This did not really amount to a formal strategy of industrial activities, and the board clearly hesitated to adopt one. In 1968, the company took over a small producer of spray cans, the Aerosolfabriek 'Romance', a modest step potentially leading to another one, the acquisition of the Indoheem conglomerate mentioned above, at that moment not yet in the hands of Hagemeyer. Both trading houses glancing at the same manufacturing company demonstrates how the opinions on business strategy developed along similar lines in different boards during these years. As Borsumij Wehry analysed the situation, Indoheem possessed attractive premises, but had become stuck through poor marketing management. Providing this could be a good opportunity for Borsumij Wehry, but the board wondered whether a large manufacturing concern such as Indoheem would really make a good fit in its operations. Borsumij Wehry certainly made no haste in announcing itself as a potential bidder. Top executive J.H. Schlimmer appeared to be not very keen to incur industrial commitments in the Netherlands.[40] As has been explained, Hagemeyer took care of Indoheem, meanwhile renamed Indola, a little later. Nor did Borsumij Wehry convert to manufacturing during the years that followed. The Aerosolfabriek 'Romance', which soon experienced declining sales and mounting losses, by the way, was sold in 1975.

Not just the former Dutch East Indian traders watched industry. Ceteco had had industrial participations in Central and South America, a consequence of the local policies towards import substitution. The company's intention was to produce key consumer durables for its trading concerns, such as fridges, washing machines, radios, and televisions. In addition, Ceteco considered it advisable to expand its activities in Europe. This did not prevent the board in 1968, though, from buying the Amsterdam-based NV Zuid-Afrikaansch Handelshuis, a company operating as importer, exporter, and wholesaler in Angola and Mozambique. To fulfil its ambition of building a combination of trade and industry in the Netherlands similar to its business in Central and Southern America, Ceteco first acquired a wholesaler in electrical household appliances, a few years later followed by a string of companies, including an engineering company marketing industrial equipment, a heating radiator plant, and a sheet iron works. The company underlined its aspirations towards manufacturing in 1970 by adding the word *Industrie* or industry to its name, to form the NV Handel- en Industrie-Maatschappij 'Ceteco'.[41] It was not entirely clear how the board had envisaged integrating its Dutch operations. After all, the combined marketing of radiators and household appliances was not really a logical proposition. Ceteco had extensive experience with managing industrial companies in Southern America, and yet it did not have a very lucky hand with its Dutch acquisitions. Production at the radiator plant was made more efficient with new equipment, and initially this appeared to bear fruit. The sheet iron works and the industrial fitting company struggled against declining sales from 1971. The resulting radical scaling down of their operations necessitated dismissals and costly redundancy schemes. From 1974, a slump in the building industry also hit radiator sales, forcing the board to take drastic measures. Both the sheet works and the radiator plant could be kept going, be it on a much smaller scale than before, but the fitting company was sold in 1974. Having suffered severe losses in the Netherlands soon persuaded Ceteco to ditch its ambitions there.[42]

The annual reports of several other trading companies demonstrate just how much the desirability of integration between trade and industry was part of general business opinion. In 1968 Stokvis, for instance, which had some foreign subsidiaries but operated mainly in the Netherlands, wrote in its annual report that it considered trade a vital and irreplaceable link in the distributive process. However, trade would have to adapt ever faster to changing circumstances, if necessary by vertical integration. Merchant houses not wanting to take the initiative could always opt for linking up with an industrial company.

WHO TAKES OVER WHOM? – In the late 1960s, mergers and take-overs cast a spell on Dutch business, and the traders were no exception, as will have become clear from the acquisitions described. The former colonial traders, however, also regularly sounded out each other. How did they compare to each other around 1972, on the eve of the first oil crisis? Table 7.2 presents some indications in the form of staff numbers, turnover, and total assets.[43]

Internatio-Müller was still the biggest on all three counts. Hagemeyer had now overtaken both Borsumij and Lindeteves, despite their respective mergers

company	staff	turnover	assets
Borsumij Wehry	2074	396	171
Ceteco	4320	299	277
Hagemeyer	6471	864	435
Internatio-Müller	14500	2100	761
Lindeteves Jacoberg	2168	405	177
		million guilders	*million guilders*

Table 7.2

Comparison of five former colonial

traders in 1972

with Geo. Wehry and Jacoberg, to become second. Ceteco was the smallest by turnover, but in third position by staff size, a consequence of its labour-intensive retail operations in Central and South America.

In 1965, Borsumij Wehry explored a potential merger both with Ceteco and with Hagemeyer. Ceteco proved willing to take over Borsumij Wehry, but met with a firm refusal. Borsumij Wehry offered its Asian network for sale to Ceteco, but the latter company was mainly interested in the former's European operations. As regards the discussions between Borsumij Wehry and Hagemeyer, both parties came to the conclusion that the other still had too many commitments in developing countries, and neither wanted to get more of the same. The Borsumij Wehry executive J.H. Schlimmer felt that it would be a shame to sell the company now that the business appeared to be back on course. Hagemeyer was rather wary of the Borsumij Wehry executives Schlimmer and Van Schendel. The supervisory board considered them difficult and cunning, and advised caution in the discussions. The talks ended there.[44]

In 1968, Lindeteves Jacoberg and Hagemeyer entered into consultations with each other, but neither of them proved keen on seriously considering a

For over a century, the Schlimmer family played a leading role in Borsumij. J.W. Schlimmer founded the company in 1883, and in 1990 his grandson J.H. Schlimmer resigned as member of the company's advisory board. In 1969, he addressed an audience celebrating Borsumij's 75th anniversary as a limited company.

merger. The companies were really too different. Hagemeyer concentrated on consumer goods, whereas Lindeteves Jacoberg was heavily specialised in a variety of heavy technical equipment. During 1967, for instance, the company sold several British-made installations for the production of tufted floor carpets to manufacturers in the Benelux, shipped a push tug with twelve matching lighters to a Unilever subsidiary in West Africa, and finally delivered eighteen Dutch-made water towers to Iraq.[45] From time to time, the company helped to market Fokker aircraft. Lindeteves Jacoberg really sought to link up with technical wholesalers, and with its old partner R.S. Stokvis & Zn. in particular. From 1966 both companies were in regular discussions with each other about this subject. However, in 1970 Stokvis opted to merge with the Technische Unie Beheer, at that time the name under which the trading division of the OGEM-concern operated. OGEM, a company formerly operating in the Dutch East Indies, had made a successful business transition after its departure from Indonesia. During the 1960s, the company had rapidly acquired a string of wholesalers in electrotechnical products. OGEM had subsequently obtained a 60% interest in the Technische Unie by selling its businesses to this company.[46] Lindeteves Jacoberg, though warmly encouraged to join OGEM as well, fretted about the best course of action.[47] However, the board did consider the position of traders threatened by shrinking margins and the increasing scope of both suppliers and customers, so in order to retain some grip on the market participations in industry would become necessary.[48] These considerations became ever more pressing, because industrial companies had started to buy trading companies. During the early 1970s the steel manufacturer Hoogovens, for one, took over several wholesalers in building materials to boost its sales in the building industry.[49]

The merger between Internatio and Müller had drawn attention to the option of a merger between trading houses and transport companies. Continuing along these lines, the Nederlandse Scheepvaart Unie or NSU, a shipping company, invited Lindeteves Jacoberg for exploratory talks in 1972. The trading company nursed doubts about the synergy to be achieved, but did see the advantages of the NSU's ample financial resources, its international experience, and its business network. The board also considered that the NSU had come to grips with the consequences of a recent merger, more so than OGEM. Even so, nothing came of it.[50] A planned merger between Ceteco and another shipping line, the KNSM or Koninklijke Nederlandse Stoomboot Maatschappij, took a more concrete shape. In 1973 a press statement announced the companies' intentions to merge, seriously upsetting the Hagemeyer board which thought it had reached a mutual understanding with Ceteco about a merger in the foreseeable future. Hagemeyer had become interested in Ceteco, both because of its position in Central and Southern America, and because of its skills and experience in the field of light industry. Ceteco and KNSM invited Hagemeyer to join them in a merger, but failed to raise enthusiasm for their proposal. In the end, the announced merger between Ceteco and KNSM did not materialise either.[51]

In 1975, after five years of urging, OGEM finally succeeded in taking over Lindeteves Jacoberg. The OGEM board rejoiced over having secured this big coup, but Lindeteves Jacoberg had had some doubts about the wisdom of this step. A few years before the final take-over, one of the directors, an engineer named A.J. Klein, had written a somewhat desperate memorandum about the advantages to be expected from merging with OGEM/Technische Unie Beheer. Klein had had discussions with a director of Technische Unie Beheer R.F. van Heusden, and had found him unreceptive to the suggestion that the two organizations simply did not fit together. According to Klein, the respective product ranges required entirely different intentions and organizations, the Technische Unie Beheer selling lighting equipment, fridges, and switches, against Lindeteves Jacoberg's marketing of lathes, power generators for ships, and farm tractors. Consequently, the company's overseas branches would not be able to sell the Technische Unie Beheer products. Klein had argued in vain that he did not see any opportunities for Lindeteves Jacoberg in OGEM's operations in the field of industrial equipment and factory fittings, but he had failed to convince his counterpart. Klein considered better access to financial resources and to smoothly running management divisions as the sole advantages to be expected.[52] By 1975 the situation had not really changed from the one in 1970, and in spite of Klein's scepticism the take-over went ahead. In discussions with its staff, the Lindeteves Jacoberg board defended the merger with the additional arguments of better opportunities for job rotation, and increased involvement with property development.[53]

The OGEM-Lindeteves Jacoberg take-over became the business topic of the day, inspiring suggestions from Hagemeyer's supervisory directors that the company would do wise to follow a similar strategy. Was there not a lurking danger of Hagemeyer coming too late and being left standing alone? The executive directors responded by saying that they were fully aware of this danger, and consequently approached any proposed merger with an open mind, but strongly hesitated to give up the company's own independence. Again the sights were set on Ceteco. Both companies were well-disposed towards a merger, but Hagemeyer's industrial interests in the Netherlands were a formidable stumbling block. The Ceteco board had absolutely no wish to consider renewed deep commitments to Dutch industry, so shortly after having gradually surmounted its own difficulties in that respect.[54] Hagemeyer and Borsumij Wehry regularly conducted talks as well, but again Hagemeyer's manufacturing concerns proved to be a crucial obstacle. The Hagemeyer board, though, considered the chances for any cooperation between the two companies out of the question for as long as the Schlimmer family continued to exercise a strong influence on Borsumij Wehry. Even so the directors admitted to finding Borsumij Wehry an attractive candidate, as having more success in its import business than Hagemeyer itself.[55] As late as 1979, Hagemeyer contemplated a potential take-over by Van Ommeren, which would have created a combination of trade with transport. However, Van Ommeren discovered too many reasons for doubt, and thus ended the negotiations.[56] Hagemeyer continued under its own steam.

INDUSTRY UNDER PRESSURE – Now, did the move into industry bring the hoped-for expansion and stabilization of business performance? Managing an industrial company within a trading organization very soon turned out to be highly problematic. The trading houses had bought industries expecting to be able to increase turnover through their excellent commercial skills, thus generating economies of scale resulting in lower production costs, which would restore the companies' profitability. With an optimism typical for traders, the firms anticipated on their expectations by modernising and expanding the production capacity of their industrial acquisitions. However, the economic climate at the time hardly favoured a strategy of expansion through exports. During the 1970s

In 1973 the OPEC countries called for a boycott of supplies to the Netherlands, leading to price rises and fears of oil shortages. During the autumn of 1973 the government, led by prime minister Joop den Uyl, introduced a ban on car traffic on Sundays, so cyclists were suddenly free to roam the motorways. In the end oil remained plentiful, but the oil shock did inaugurate an economic recession lasting until 1983.

Shutting down loss-making operations became socially more or less unacceptable during the 1970s. The employees of the ENKA Breda works succeeded in preventing the plant's closure by staging a sit-in, but this proved to be no more than a postponement of the close-down.

circumstances changed completely, dashing the optimistic expectations about the future from the 1960s. First of all the system of stable exchange rates crashed when the US suspended the dollar's fixed gold parity in 1971. This step created deep anxiety on the currency markets and radical changes in the mutual rates of exchange. Then in 1973 the first oil crisis generated strong fluctuations on the commodity markets, conjuring up tentative indications of a return to the ghostly unemployment of the 1930s. Finally, the second oil crisis of 1979 heralded an economic slump. Many Third World countries struggled with a huge debt, in stead of being able to enjoy the fruits of economic growth. Suddenly the world turned out to be much more chaotic than many had thought or hoped.

The unfavourable economic developments hit Dutch industry particularly hard. High wages and a strong currency had undermined its international competitive position, resulting in stagnating exports. Rising oil prices also affected the performance of Dutch industry. From the mid-1960s, high wages and low energy prices had steered manufacturers towards buying labour-saving equipment with a disregard for fuel efficiency. These investments now became a liability rather than an asset, even more so following new energy saving requirements inspired by environmental concerns.[57] Moreover, the social climate of the 1970s robbed manufacturing of its flexibility, for redundancies were deemed unacceptable as long as the company concerned remained profitable overall. The sit-in at the Enka factory in Breda summarises the atmosphere of those days. By occupying the plant, the unions did succeed in preventing its announced closure for the moment, but ten years later the curtain still came down for Enka.[58]

Structurally weak sectors such as fabrics, ready-made garments, and footwear, suffered from declining sales because the competition from the newly industrialised countries or NIC's was particularly severe here. However, the pacemakers of the 1960s, the oil industry and the chemical industry linked to it, also faced rising raw material prices and a drop in turnover. Only food processing continued on an even keel. The electrotechnical sector and the engineering

315

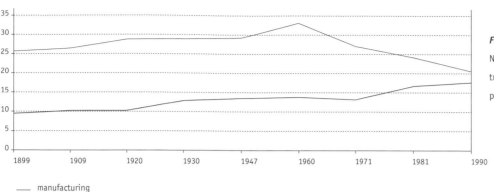

Figure 7.1

Number of people employed in
trade and in manufacturing, as a
percentage of total employment

— manufacturing

— trade

industry appeared to do comparatively well, with the exception of shipbuilding, but the building slump at the end of the 1970s also affected parts of the electrotechnical industry.[59] During the 1970s all efforts concentrated on maintaining the level of industrial employment, despite the fact that some sectors did appear doomed to fail in the end. Seizing the right moment to leave a business in decline is very hard, by the way, not just because of economic obstacles or social pressure, but also because of inherently flawed management perceptions. It is often impossible to obtain a timely assessment of disruptions in economic trends, if only for the time lag with which reliable data and relevant market information become available.[60] In this respect the 1960s optimism about the predictability of the future proved to be premature, to say the least.

Figure 7.1 depicts the number of people working in both trade and industry as a percentage of total employment.[61] This shows that during the 1960s, manufacturing declined as a source of employment, whereas trade rose at the same time. Remarkably, the trading houses became involved with industry at the very moment this sector began to lose ground in relation to other sectors. No surprise that this strategy failed to bring the successes expected by the traders.

DISAPPOINTING RESULTS – Developments at Hagemeyer demonstrate the potential problems of combining trade with industry to good effect. Time and again, the company's board started reorganizations with the best intentions and not a little confidence. At the Amsterdamse Lederfabriek, taken over in 1965, the new management had realised an improved performance within a few years, boosting this self confidence. At the acquisition of Indola in 1969, the board thought that three years would suffice to get the company back to profitability. Redundancies were not considered, the watchword was to expand European sales. This task was entrusted to the director M.P. Steijger, who had managed to return the subsidiaries in British East Africa to profit, and who had subsequently done such a good job at the Lederfabriek. However, he felt out of his depth at Indola, as became clear when Hagemeyer's supervisory directors asked him about the efficiency of the Indola management. Steijger voiced doubt, but admitted that his lack of technical training prevented him from getting the pic-

Indola failed to persuade enough
consumers into buying its products,
despite the colourful publicity
leaflets, and Hagemeyer equally
failed to realise rising sales for its
subsidiary. Indola's Utrecht plant
continued to operate at a loss,
notwithstanding endless
reorganisations.

ture straight. His comments about the company's efficiency had met with objections grounded in technical details which he failed to grasp, and Steijger thought that such details were only put forward because the management had no clear idea about the overall business.[62] This was no more than a technical problem, but two years later the executive board mentioned a most remarkable misunderstanding about the term 'order book' between the Indola plants at Utrecht and at Rijswijk. The latter adhered to the correct meaning, i.e. the tally of orders received from customers, but the former used the same term to describe planned production figures, leading the board members wrongly to assume the existence of substantial orders. By that time, both plants had been under the Hagemeyer umbrella for over two years.[63] The company's board was made up of managers who had been given a seat in recognition of their long and successful foreign service. However, the custom of rewarding toil under the tropical sun with a plush director's seat, as it were, had the inherent problem of creating a board whose members had really lost touch with the Netherlands during their long career abroad. None of the top managers had any experience with works councils, for instance. It is equally striking that they predominantly acquired companies in structurally weak economic sectors.

By 1970, the various manufacturing plants within the Hagemeyer company still had high order levels overall, but even so some of them made a loss. The combination of high wages and labour intensive production were largely responsible for this. Consequently, cost reductions through mechanization, automation, and improved production techniques became the norm. New and modern plants were built, sometimes with an increased capacity, as happened for instance with plastics production at Van Niftrik. From 1971, when turnover began to decline, one subsidiary after another entered upon a downward spiral. Losses would lead to the dismissal of the responsible managers, followed by a reorganization of production, which usually meant a cut in capacity enforced by reducing the working hours or by redundancies. However, as the fixed costs remained, the unit cost did not drop sufficiently to restore sales, so the losses continued or even worsened, turnover fell, and the newly appointed managers were dismissed. Now a new round of cutbacks began, which equally failed in sufficiently pushing down cost, in particular because turnover had meanwhile dropped further. All along, the reorganizations with their time reductions and redundancies demoralised the employees. Referring to Hagemeyer's logo, one of the shareholders indignantly commented in the annual general meeting that the famous archer was hitting its own side.[64] Total staff at Hagemeyer was the same in 1970 and in 1975, i.e. 6,600 people, but during the intervening five years a vast change had happened. Employment in trade had risen from 2,600 to 4,100, whereas the number of people working in manufacturing had dropped from 4,000 to 2,500. The industrial activities had undergone a contraction, not the envisaged expansion. The contraction would continue steadily after 1975.

There were various reasons for the disappointing turnover figures in manufacturing. The de facto devaluation of the dollar in 1971 had made the US market well-nigh inaccessible for the kitchenware Hagemeyer had hoped to sell. Competition from cheaper suppliers from Asia, from Hong Kong, for instance, added to that problem. The leather plants struggled to keep going as the west European footwear industry crumbled under the onslaught of imports from Italy and from the developing countries. Sales of Indola hair dryers stagnated because of a saturated market. A change in fashion towards more informal hair cuts, eliminating the need for a weekly wash-and-set, compounded the troubles. The power drills for the DIY market could not compete with Black & Decker. The production of plastics was dragged down into the mire because this plant mainly operated as a subcontractor to other Hagemeyer subsidiaries, so integration turned out to be a disadvantage in this case. The cosmetics and pharmaceuticals of Indola alone performed to satisfaction. Reorganizations had cost almost 29 million guilders between 1972 and 1975. However, the value of the company's property had meanwhile risen by nearly 20 million guilders, so the custom of closely watching this aspect when acquiring a business had at least produced a paper profit.[65]

By 1976 the time had arrived to hire a firm of management consultants. This firm calculated that at that moment, the majority of senior managers in the industrial subsidiaries had been in position for less than three years. Some subsidiaries had gone through a change of board two or even three times within a period of five years. All were sick of the constant reorganizations, and now badly needed stimuli towards commercial innovation after all that had happened. A most striking fact shone through this conclusion. To all appearances Hagemeyer had not succeeded in using its dedicated skills to best effect in its manufacturing companies. The synergy envisaged had not been realised. Building proprietary brands had remained of minor importance. The consultants had noticed the very low level of internal exchange within the concern, and commented on the trading subsidiaries being left free in their purchasing policy. They often chose outside suppliers, preferring straightforward commercial negotiations about prices to sticky talks about pricing and mutual margins with colleagues. The consultants also concluded that the profit rate of the manufacturing operations was too low, but not unfavourable in comparison to other Dutch industries suffering from the economic downturn, at least if Indola's disastrous Utrecht plant was left out of the consideration. Even so, in spite of this conclusion, the firm wrote a letter to the supervisory board recommending the dismissal of W. van Schaik, the executive responsible for running the manufacturing division. Van Schaik had been appointed in 1972 with the specific purpose of getting the division on to its feet again, but was considered to have made insufficient progress after three years.[66] The position of the executives who had bought the manufacturing operations in the first place did not come up for debate, however.

comfort voor u en haar

Changing fashions in hair dressing meant declining sales of hairdriers for Indola.

For some more years, Hagemeyer attempted to return the industries in its possession to profitability, but refrained from further acquisitions in this field. Meanwhile, general opinion about an integration between trade and industry had changed completely. In 1975, one of the shareholders suggested that the move into industry had been wrong as a matter of principle. Another one suggested three years later, that Hagemeyer's difficulties originated in their attempt to reconcile the contrasting mentalities of trading companies and manufacturing within a single organization. In 1979, a representative of the Vereniging voor Effectenbescherming, a society promoting the interests of private investors, once again emphasised this point by describing industrial activities within a trading business as fundamentally wrong. Hagemeyer countered such criticism by arguing that not every manufacturing company had lost money during the whole period, and by pointing to some successes, notably Indola Cosmetics and a few plants abroad. The company gradually withdrew from industry nevertheless.

Internatio-Müller's experiences with its manufacturing subsidiaries closely mirrored those of Hagemeyer, but there was a difference. Internatio-Müller had cast its net wider than just industry, and initially the resulting operational spread did facilitate the compensation of losses of one sector with the profits of another. On the other hand, the same spread ensured that the conglomerate was never without one problem or another. In the early 1970s the manufacturing companies appeared to be free from trouble, but the company's profits from manufacturing began to decline rapidly after the acquisition of Amalga Holding, and turned to losses from 1974. Internatio-Müller had expected, like Hagemeyer had, to raise the sales of its subsidiary in the light metal industry by using its international network. The company did not succeed in doing this, however, and the first oil crisis pushed the manufacturing subsidiaries into the familiar spiral of falling sales and rising costs. Each productivity rise was cancelled out by a new downturn of the economic cycle. And management consultants again concluded that the metal industry offered little scope for synergy. In 1978, Internatio-Müller resolved to refocus on the service sector, and in particular on transport, trade, and fitting operations. The manufacturing division gradually dwindled to a marginal position within the company. The production of pharmaceuticals terminated in 1980, the remnants of the interests in metal manufacturing were sold in 1991 and 1992.[67]

Did Stokvis and Lindeteves Jacoberg fare better, perhaps, having opted to join OGEM? During the 1970s, OGEM strove hard to acquire more companies and new operations, building a conglomerate of companies straddling the sectors of fitting, building, and trade. Each take-over resulted in reorganizations and rearrangements, giving the company a somewhat restless character. Businesses bought were often split into bits, and those parts then added to various existing divisions, a purposeful efficiency drive, but one which broke up familiar structures and networks. One part of Stokvis ended up with the main division Fitting, some manufacturing parts were put up for sale, and about half of the original company continued under the name of Stokvis BV. This rump did not succeed in realising expansion within OGEM, and it performed unsatisfactorily. Lindeteves Jacoberg became part of the Technische Handelsvereniging Internationaal or THVI, renamed OTRA in 1976. Lindeteves Jacoberg did not prosper within OGEM either. Conversely, OGEM directors later blamed Lindeteves Jacoberg as having contributed substantially to the conglomerate's downfall. In 1985 K. Fibbe, at that time the company's CEO, mentioned three factors which had soured the acquisition for OGEM. Firstly Lindeteves Jacoberg's large number of Asian branches, most of them small, independent, and involved in commodity trading, were opaque and hard to manage. Secondly a fraud which at one point had cost the company 18 million guilders within a week. Finally, management troubles with the Lindeteves Jacoberg board.[68] Of course the fraud case was an unexpected setback, but Fibbe should have grasped the import of Lindeteves Jacoberg's large number of small branches in Asia before launching a bid. The abstract concept of potential synergy had been insufficiently tested against business reality. An analysis of the mutual operations, as made by Klein in his 1970 memorandum, could have shown the lack of common ground. In 1978, Stokvis and Lindeteves Jacoberg merged into Stokvis Lindeteves, another reorganization which lasted less than a year.

That same year, OGEM's trade division discussed a crucial problem, the lack of communication within the conglomerate. As a result, the division's potential remained underused. The traders did acknowledge this, but argued in their turn for a freedom to choose suppliers as essential. If at all possible, customers and suppliers should not get the impression that OGEM subsidiaries would receive better conditions than they did. After all, the trading division realised only 1.5-2% of its turnover within OGEM.[69] Clearly, then, no synergy existed at all, and the desirability of closer links was even doubted.

The experiences of SHV, an international trader without old ties to Indonesia, shows just how much businessmen thought along the same lines, and thus landed into similar troubles. Specialised as it was in the coal trade, this company realised as early as the 1950s the desirability of widening its business scope. Initially the SHV opted to do so in the related field of oil, subsequently adding the exploitation of natural gas. During the mid-1960s the company began to operate in the sectors of building materials and heating equipment, which had at least some connection to the original core business. In its annual report for 1968, the SHV board stated as its aim to strive for growth both in line with existing operations, and through diversification. This took concrete shape in the setting up of Macro, a self-service wholesaler in the 'cash-and-carry' mould. In 1970, SHV took a logical next step by acquiring from the De Gruyter family and Unilever the company of P. de Gruyter & Zoon, a well-known grocer which combined a national network of supermarkets with its own production plants.[70] Two years later SHV went into property development by buying Melchior Verenigde Bedrijven. Meanwhile the company also expanded internationally. Macro proved to be a lasting success, and subsequent initiatives in this direction, such as Kijkshop and Xenos, also performed well. However, SHV failed to turn De Gruyter around, and the excursion into property development

During the mid-1960s SHV adopted a strategy of diversification. Its acquisition of the Xenos retail chain was targeted directly at consumers, while the purchase of Macro aimed at selling products in bulk to volume users.

was a failure. The board commented later that this had been one of the few absolute acquisition mistakes. Geveke Groenpol, bought in 1970, gave more trouble than profit. In 1980, the SHV management wrote a memo summarising the experiences of the 1970s:

> 'The history of the past few years has demonstrated that the benefits of synergy can often be overestimated and that it is wise not to be overly optimistic in this regard (..). The social problems associated with the acquisition of companies with large workforces, especially in the Netherlands, were underestimated in a number of cases. The same applies to the problem of integrating companies with entirely different cultures'.[71]

All these examples demonstrate that widening the business scope of trading companies was an arduous process. The core business overall performed better than the new operations which had been attracted with the very purpose of expansion and spreading risk. The traders' efforts to get involved with manufacturing were particularly unsuccessful, as managing an industrial company proved to be entirely different from managing a trading business. Manufacturers have to think in long periods of time, whereas traders are inclined first of all to react rapidly and flexibly, seizing opportunities when they spot them as true opportunists. Sometimes their assessment of those opportunities proves too optimistic, but overstocks can be cleared in a matter of months. Turning around a factory often takes years. Hagemeyer and Internatio both underestimated the cost and the patience required for industrial reorganizations. Moreover, it was exceedingly difficult to achieve the hoped-for synergy. The expectation that the dedicated marketing organizations would boost sales of the goods produced by the manufacturing subsidiaries turned out to be an illusion. Nor did the international marketing organizations appreciate the availability of industrial production within their company, a logical attitude since proprietary products never became more than a fraction of turnover. In addition, the marketing organizations greatly valued being free to buy goods where it suited them best, and to buy only what fitted best into their product range. Thus embarking on manufacturing had not lessened the dependence on principals.

Interestingly enough, the vicissitudes of the Dutch trading houses closely resembled those of British trading firms. During the 1960s, these also showed a growing interest in investing in Europe, with the political risks in the developing countries serving as a key argument. The trading houses' investments went both into distribution and into manufacturing, reaching a peak during the 1970s. The United Africa Company or UAC, a subsidiary of the Anglo-Dutch Unilever concern, presents a telling example of this strategy. To reduce its exposure to Africa, the UAC began to acquire a series of small companies in Europe, covering a wide field from the trade in building materials and the distribution of cars to the production of pharmaceuticals and office supplies. By the early 1980s it became clear that the diversification had failed. Of course the economic circumstances were unfavourable, but this factor was compounded by the small size and the lack of coherence of most acquisitions, which prevented efforts towards an integrated business and added value. Most manufacturing investments of other merchant companies also proved failures, inspiring one historian to conclude that 'The firms misjudged their core capabilities, imagining that running a brewery in Spain was the same as in Nigeria, or that they were "merchant adventurers" who could turn their hands to anything'.[72]

A PERVASIVE SLUMP – During the 1970s, the Dutch trading companies made sufficient overall profits to compensate the losses of their manufacturing operations. From time to time the commodity trade in particular generated substantial profits, but with a snag, for it was a highly speculative activity, and one dominated by specialised commodity traders and big customers. Internatio-Müller still performed well in the early 1970s. The company's board, however, put this into perspective by mentioning as a well-known fact that commodity trading generally performs better with rising prices than with falling prices. In 1980 Internatio-Müller suddenly had to accept a large loss at its New York subsidiary, underlining the truth of this statement.[73] Hagemeyer's coffee trade did very well at that particular moment, only to land into trouble some years later. In the early 1970s the company had also twice suffered severe setbacks through its Multitrade subsidiary, in 1973 even inspiring comments about a catastrophe.[74] Having lost its Indonesian plantations, the HVA attempted to continue operating in the commodity trade by buying and selling for own account, but the company was ultimately unsuccessful. As a result, the former HVA manager A. Goedhart concluded that, despite its name, the HVA had not been a trading firm in the true sense of the word.[75]

The wholesaling operations abroad performed variably. The rise of newly industrialised countries in Asia and South America might pose a threat to Dutch industry, but for Dutch traders this opened up new opportunities for intermediation. Borsumij Wehry built up a prospering trade in fabrics and in footwear based on purchasing in Asia for selling in Europe. For a considerable time, govern-

Initially the economic recession appeared to be modest, held up by combined government and consumer spending. The average family already possessed a television set, watching it preferably with open curtains all evening. During the 1970s, however, most consumers switched to colour sets, while the video recorder began its advance in the late 1970s.

323

ment expenditure and consumer spending softened the impact of the economic recession in the Netherlands, so consumer products continued to find a ready market. Television sets, video recorders, and single-lens reflexcameras still enjoyed substantial sales. As a result the seriousness of the economic situation remained obscured, until the recession struck with redoubled vigour after the second oil crisis of 1979. Interest rates rose to unprecedented levels, and as a result companies which had financed their expansion with loans faced severe difficulties. Bankruptcies became the order of the day, unemployment increased rapidly.

Because of their varying operations and markets, the peaks and troughs of the international traders were not exactly synchronised, but nearly all suffered from the recession. Figure 7.2 shows the ups and downs of four firms, using official figures on profits and losses. These have been expressed in

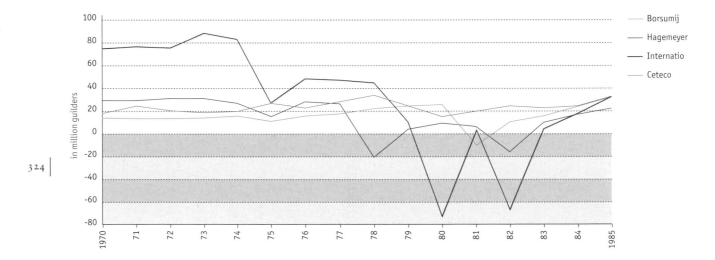

Figure 7.2

The sharply fluctuating results of
four international traders

constant 1990 prices to eliminate the effect of inflation as much as possible. Hagemeyer lost heavily in 1978 and in 1982, Borsumij Wehry had a trough in 1981, and Internatio-Müller faced large losses in 1980 and in 1982. Ceteco alone, with its business focus outside of Europe, did not show any difficulties deriving from the second oil crisis.

These years also demonstrated that building a conglomerate did not guarantee a more stable business performance, quite the contrary. The 1980s witnessed some spectacular bankruptcies of big companies, some of them conglomerates, such as the paper manufacturer Van Gelder Papier, the RSV (Rijn Schelde Verolme) shipyards, and OGEM. The demise of RSV in particular drew substantial media attention, for the government had formed this conglomerate and had supplied very large subsidies to keep it going, as an employment policy. The debate concentrated on the failing of these aspirations as much as on the correctness of the policy itself. The downfall of both OGEM and Van Gelder Papier

Huge government subsidies failed to save the RSV shipbuilding conglomerate. Two employees of the Rotterdamse Droogdok Maatschappij, part of RSV, stare gloomily into the company's empty repair docks.

led to the interesting discovery that a great number of subsidiaries, once rescued from bankruptcy, proved to be quite viable businesses in themselves, thus providing a fitting illustration to the limits of building conglomerates. A lesson which was not lost on the international traders.

During the favourable economic circumstances of the 1960s, the former colonial trading houses achieved a strong expansion of their operations. They nursed a high expectation concerning the potential added value for their business of an integration between trade and industry. However, the firms were bitterly disappointed in their expectations, partly a matter of making wrong choices, partly a matter of wrong timing. Most of all, however, from the perspective of trading vertical integration made less sense than it did from an industrial standpoint. The possession of a limited number of manufacturing companies did not make the traders' relations with manufacturers any less fragile. During the 1970s and 1980s, most manufacturing operations were either closed or sold. Stagnation and even contraction replaced expansion. Would trading houses still have a function after all?

In the 1990s, investing in shares began to attract an ever wider public outside the circles of professional investors. Share options, as an incentive for company employees became very popular, too. The picture shows the floor of the Amsterdam options exchange in 1999.

CHAPTER VIII

Developments in the 1970s demonstrated that integration with industry was not the best option for the international trading companies to shore up their position. This inspired a search for alternative solutions. The economic crisis of the early 1980s, and the spectacular failures of some conglomerates, reinforced existing doubts about the viability of diversification. A new business philosophy spread, summarised as 'back to the core business'. What, then, was the core business of the international trading companies? And what kind of operations should they embark on to realise the full potential of their core business? How much room did trading intermediaries really possess, and to what extent could merchant houses as a line of business continue to offer added value? The vicissitudes of a few key trading companies will serve as a guide in the search for the core of their business.

THE REHABILITATION OF FREE ENTERPRISE – The year 1982 was the turning point of the economic slump in which the two oil crises had precipitated the Netherlands. During this year, unemployment continued at alarming levels and the number of bankruptcies attained an ignominious record, but everything was to improve from that point onwards. Economic performance regained its upward trend from 1983, though growth slowed down temporarily around 1991-1992. The same year 1982 also marked a change in public opinion about the government's role in the economy. Government expenditure was cut to lower the tax burden, and a debate began about the government's role in guiding economic development. Subsidies had failed as a means of supporting industry, so it seemed preferable to give businessmen a free hand in devising ways to let their companies thrive and prosper. It was expected that this would also be the best way to combat unemployment. In 1982 the government, employers' organizations, and trade unions, together signed an agreement for limiting wage rises to boost employment, by improving the international competitive position of the Netherlands.

During the 1980s, opinions on entrepreneurship took on a more benevolent aspect once more, quite a change from the regular vilification as capitalist exploitation of the 1970s. Enterprising businessmen created employment and prosperity after all. Moreover, it had become evident that continuity in business was not a matter of course, even large and well-known companies could still go under. Thus, entrepreneurship was an achievement, and consequently the businessman as a person, and the individual style of leadership, merited closer attention. In the early 1980s companies focused on restoring profitability and hiving off loss-making operations. Companies had to concentrate on their core activities, on what they had traditionally been good at. From the mid-1980s new scope for expansion appeared, which was realised through mergers and take-overs dominated by a central concern for a company's internal coherence.

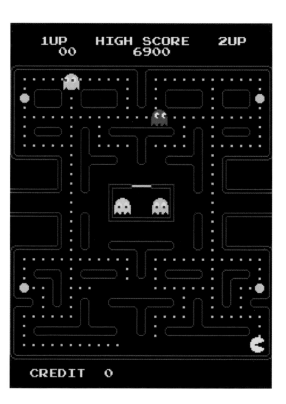

The market for childrens' toys entered a phase of fierce competition between traditional games and computer games, many of them made in Japan. Other markets, too, felt the Japanese competition breathing down their necks. Many companies responded to these competitive pressures by returning to what they designated as their core business. During the 1990s business managers faced a stark choice between gobbling up rivals or being gobbled up themselves, just as in the popular computer game Pacman.

Consequently, take-overs were accompanied by selective de-mergers. The more substantial mergers were often effected by the purchaser bidding for the equity of the company to be taken over, and paid for by the purchaser issuing new shares. Share price thus became a key factor for companies wishing to expand, raising the priority of keeping shareholders and business analysts sweet. Showing a regular increase in the profit per share was the best way to do this. As a consequence, Dutch companies clearly turned to the Anglo-Saxon tradition of creating shareholder value, publicising their tireless efforts to raise profits per share. By the late 1990s a shift in emphasis became noticeable. Falling more into line with Dutch traditions, companies professed a desire to create value for

328

all stakeholders, i.e. all parties connected to the business concerned, suppliers, customers, shareholders, and employees.

The poor performance of Dutch industry during the early 1980s inspired interest in other economic sectors, which appeared to weather the economic downturn better than manufacturing. This resulted in wholesaling being redis-covered, so to speak, and regularly being dubbed an unknown giant, to express the sector's vital economic importance in obscurity from the public at large.[1] Two developments appeared to hold out promises for the traders, provided they succeeded in devising the right ways of capturing them: industrialization in Asia and South America, and the disintegration of the business conglomerates. In 1983, the economist W.J. van de Woestijne argued that the newly industrialised countries elsewhere in the world should inspire the Netherlands to turn its

The rise of newly industrialised countries threatened European manufacturing industry, but it gave international trading companies new opportunities for selling their services. Loading and unloading at the juice and milk industry Imlaca in Valencia (Venezuela), 1998.

329

attention back to trade. He thought this option attractive both from a quantita-tive and from a qualitative viewpoint. For most products, consumer prices amounted to twice the production costs, so trade added a similar value to man-ufacturing. The qualitative aspects of trade were equally attractive, according to Van de Woestijne. Facilitating smooth connections between transport, finance, warehousing, and insurance required a sound infrastructure, plus much skill and experience. It was not to be expected that the newly industrialised countries could perform this difficult task immediately. He concluded, therefore, that this created a potential function for the Netherlands similar to the one performed during the 17th century.[2]

The disintegration of business conglomerates and a rising trend towards outsourcing, i.e. contracting out non-core business, combined to form the second development that opened up new opportunities for trade. As diversified companies fell apart, their trade divisions regained their independence, as happened to OGEM's OTRA division. However, hiving off services could also create new work. Multinational companies, for instance, attempting to reduce bureaucracy within the business, began to cast a critical glance at their central purchasing departments. Local production plants were given more scope to buy their own supplies from wholesalers if they wanted to do so.

During the early 1980s, the state of world trade still gave cause for anxiety to trading companies. Strong competition from the newly industrialised countries in Asia and Southern America led the European countries towards protectionism. Wishing to safeguard the achievements of the welfare state, the same countries were less and less willing to lower customs tariffs, and they increasingly resorted to other means for obstructing imports. The Poitiers customs office was one notorious example of such obstruction. To clamp down on the imports of video recorders into France, the French government in 1982 transferred the customs clearance of video recorders from Le Havre to an understaffed customs office at Poitiers. This reduced the number of video recorders imported from 64,000 a month to no more than 10,000.[3] The merchant house Borsumij Wehry keenly felt the effects. Its subsidiary Sharp France had a warehouse with 10,500 video recorders waiting for clearance in November 1982, and four months later not a single one had passed customs. Consequently, Sharp France ended the financial year 1983 with a loss.[4] As a result,

A shopping centre in Hongkong, for international traders the key city for locating operations in mainland China. First Pacific, which for a long time held a substantial stake in Hagemeyer, has its headquarters in Hongkong, too.

330

both Japan and other European countries lodged complaints against the French measures with the European Commission. The French government terminated the 'Poitiers import restrictions' once Japan had agreed to a 'voluntary' restriction on exports of video recorders. Though such measures raised no objections, agreed restraints were not conducive to the growth of world trade either.

To halt the rise of protectionism, the GATT opened new negotiations during the mid-1980s, drafting an agenda which included the liberalization of the trade in primary products and the supply of services. This so-called Uruguay round lasted longer than expected, but agreement was finally reached in 1994, after which the GATT was reorganised to become the World Trade Organization in 1995. The results achieved during the Uruguay round boosted world trade, though trade conflicts between the US and Europe, particularly those over agriculture, turned out to have some life in them yet.

The floating market in Bangkok.

While the GATT negotiations were still in full swing, the political situation in Europe changed profoundly. A turn in the political climate of the Sovjet Union, instigated by Gorbachev, signalled the end of the Cold War. In the autumn of 1989 the Berlin Wall dividing East Germany and West Germany fell, after which the communist regimes in Eastern Europe and in Russia fell like dominoes. An extensive potential trade area opened up. The political regime of these countries might have changed very rapidly, but their economies proved slow in adapting to the Western world. The high expectations concerning the speed of economic change had to be readjusted quite soon.

At the same time, the European Community had just embarked on building a single internal market, on one hand removing barriers to trade within the community, on the other drawing sharper boundaries with the world outside it. During the mid-1980s the member states had agreed to strive for a completely liberated internal market by 1992. In 1990, the European Commission commissioned research into the expected consequences of the internal market for wholesaling. The final report included the forecast that the growing scale of trade spelled the disappearance of small wholesalers in particular. Employment in wholesaling would fall, or at most remain stable, following scale increases and mounting competition.[5] Neither forecast has come true, at least not in the Netherlands. Both the number of firms in wholesaling and employment have kept rising after the liberalization was completed in 1992. The new opportunities created by the internal market probably explains this favourable development.

Dutch wholesaling overall had a prosperous time during the 1980s and 1990s. In contrast to manufacturing, employment in wholesaling remained fairly stable in the early 1980s, and rose sharply during the second half of the decade. Together with financial services, wholesaling belonged to the fastest growing sectors of the Dutch economy. Moreover, wholesaling performed a vital role in Dutch foreign trade, facilitating about 40% of all imports, and more than 25% of total exports. Wholesaling was thus a key link in the Dutch economy, for at that time the Netherlands imported nearly half of its GNP, and exported slightly more than that. In 1988, there were about 42,000 firms operating as wholesalers, employing a total of 350,000 staff, more than a third of the number of people working in industry. Subsequently, employment in wholesaling continued to rise, reaching 425,000 people in 1997.[6] Almost 40% of the wholesaling firms were classified as businesses run by a single person, but more than 300 had a staff of more than 100 people, and at the time belonged to the top of Dutch business by turnover.

During the early 1980s, however, the number of big Dutch international trading companies remained limited. For after all, the defining feature of such firms is that they operate in varying countries, and in varying products. Ranked by turnover, the 100 biggest Dutch companies active in manufacturing, transport, and trade, included a number of specialised wholesalers during the first half of the 1980s, among them Cebeco-Handelsraad, which concentrated on farming products, the dealer in tropical commodities Deli-Maatschappij, VRG and Bührmann-Tetterode in paper and printing equipment, the technical trader OTRA, and pharmaceuticals wholesaler OPG. Only a small number of firms could be categorised as international traders. With its two divisions of energy and retailing, SHV was also more a specialised wholesaler than a trading house. Particularly the former colonial traders Borsumij Wehry, Internatio-Müller, and Hagemeyer, continued to operate internationally in several areas.[7] The present chapter deals mainly with developments at these three companies.

During the 1980s and 1990s, the international traders faced three crucial developments: the continuing internationalization of business, suppliers and customers rising in scale, and rapid changes in information technology. None of these developments was essentially new, but each of them reached a new qualitative stage, forcing the trading houses in their turn to find a new and proper response. For all three factors affected the position of wholesaling as an intermediary. Internationalization threatened local markets and local brands. Scale increases undermined agencies and forced wholesalers into expansion if they wanted to keep their market presence. Information technology created new competition.

The fall of the Berlin Wall in 1989 was a source of widespread exhilaration. However, for a considerable time the political landslides in eastern Europe failed to generate substantial economic growth.

AGENCIES: WONDERFUL YET VULNERABLE — As we have seen above, trading companies and principals maintain a love-hate relationship. In their annual reports, the international traders proudly listed the famous brands which they served as marketing and distribution agents. Hagemeyer, for instance, mentioned the following agencies in its 1991 annual report: National / Panasonic / Technics, JVC, Maxell, AT&T, Moulinex, General Electric, Arnold Palmer, Wrangler, Christian Dior, Givenchy, Olympus, Cognac Otard, Nestlé, Wasa, Toblerone, Saab, Lancia, Philips, Siemens, and 3M. However, the merchant houses also keenly felt the vulnerability of these commercial relations, and struggled with the eternal question of how much longer they could hang on to their agencies.

333

The creation of a single market within the EU compounded this problem. It was generally expected that the disappearance of internal boundaries would lead to scale increases in both trade and industry. Because agencies always apply to strictly defined geographical areas only, the international traders were usually unable to expand their operations to cover Europe, since manufacturers had licensed rival firms to represent them in other countries. Indeed, manufacturers felt a need to integrate their business across boundaries on a European level. For them, the simplest way to raise production and marketing to a European scale was taking the distribution of their products into their own hands. Only the agents which showed an exceptionally good and efficient performance were allowed to remain in play, but even those risked being excluded by principals developing a European strategy.

During the 1960s, Borsumij Wehry had succeeded in acquiring an imposing range of very good agencies, and in this respect the company clearly had a lead over Hagemeyer.[8] However, in the 1980s Borsumij Wehry began to find its strength becoming a weakness at the same time. The company had sold cameras for the Japanese manufacturer Canon for years and years and with great success. By the early 1980s this agency had lost some of its shine, and as a consequence Borsumij Wehry lost money on its marketing of photographic equipment in Germany, the Netherlands, and Belgium. Parallel imports were a thorny problem. French dealers, for instance, exported cameras to the Netherlands, and

As a rule, agencies are transitory in nature. In 1984, Borsumij Wehry lost the Benelux agency for US manufacturer Mattel's famous Barbie doll. The company had succeeded in building very large turnover figures during the 1970s for Adidas, the manufacturer of sports goods, but even so this agency terminated in 1996.

undercut the official dealers, i.e. the customers of Borsumij Wehry, because they had no publicity or service costs. Such practices could not be prevented under EU regulations, and the Borsumij Wehry board thought it incumbent on its principal to take steps. When Canon's efforts proved insufficient, the board began to suspect that by allowing parallel imports, Canon really wanted to make life miserable for them so that they would be happy to relinquish the agency for a song.[9] True enough, in 1985 Canon started its own marketing in Germany, paying a handsome price to Borsumij Wehry for that company's 40% stake in Canon Europhoto. The following year Canon also terminated the agency contract for the Benelux. In its annual report, the Borsumij Wehry board showed resignation over the end of this relationship. The Benelux turnover in Canon products had declined to only a fraction of total turnover, and had become relatively insignificant as a revenue source. Still, it was a matter of regret to see the termination of a 25-year collaboration which used to be so profitable. Borsumij Wehry would remain proud of having achieved, in its agency areas, market shares for Canon products which were amongst the best in Europe.[10] Similar developments hit the company's agencies for Sharp in France and in the Benelux. The manufacturer began by cutting margins, and then offered to buy the agencies, arguing that it wanted to merge its European representation into a single organization. The French agency was terminated in 1990, two years later the Benelux agency went the same way. The successful Benelux agency for the German manufacturer of sports footwear and clothing Adidas, with which Borsumij Wehry had achieved a jump in turnover of 1,200% during the 1970s, was reorganised into a joint-venture in 1994, leading to its end two years later.

Of course the termination of agencies was not a new problem, but growing European union did provide manufacturers with an additional reason to approach the European market as a single unit, and thus end relations with any national representatives. Hagemeyer also experienced the vulnerability of its agencies, though possessing a less impressive range than Borsumij Wehry did. During the 1970s, the Matsushita agency for Singapore and for the Netherlands was Hagemeyer's most important profit source, on which the company largely depended for its existence. For that reason the Dutch marketing subsidiary, Haagtechno, switched to concentrate exclusively on selling the Matsushita

334

Hagemeyer's Matsushita agency for the Dutch market was the company's mainstay for many years, and it was still going strong in the year 2000. The Haagtechno subsidiary became totally dedicated to the interests of this principal and its consumer electronics brands, including Technics and Panasonic.

brands National, Panasonic, and Technics in 1977. Such a dedication to one principal fitted in with the Japanese tradition of opting for a partnership. Haagtechno's switch implied stretching the wholesaler's commitment to the retail trade. Whereas before the wholesaler used to deliver products to the retailer and leave him to find out how best to sell them to customers, now the emphasis shifted to providing the retailer with every possible support, ranging from extensive product information to advice about creating an attractive shopping environment, for moving Matsushita products out of his shop and into the hands of consumers. During the 1980s Servicom, a service subsidiary acquired by Hagemeyer with the 1969 Indola take-over and subsequently reorganised into the company's after-sales service provider, was completely dedicated to the interests of the main principal. Hagemeyer considered the providing of service as an integral part of this agency. The arrangement still exists to the satisfaction of both parties, side-by-side with Matsushita's developing pan-European approach. The Singapore agency for Matsushita was terminated in 1994, by the way, as part of the manufacturer's pan-Asiatic policy.[11]

H.J.J. Birner, A.H. Land, and J.J. Hollenkamp on a visit to Matsushita, around 1992. Two years later, the more than 20-year old Matsushita agency for Singapore terminated.

335

In 1994, Hagemeyer began a joint-venture with the Swiss Cosa Liebermann group. This company, termed Hagemeyer Cosa Liebermann or HCL for short, combined the operations of both international traders in the Asia-Pacific area, for the purpose of resuscitating the old Hagemeyer formula of marketing agencies there. Geographically, the two parent companies complemented each other perfectly. Hagemeyer operated mainly in Asia and Australia with brands such as Olympus, Moulinex, JVC, General Electric, Christian Dior, and Givenchy, whereas Cosa Liebermann worked predominantly in East Asia, China, and Micronesia, its agencies including Rolex, Puma, Bally, Chanel, and Shu Uemura. Consequently, HCL could offer consumers a range of brands for sports wear, life style products, household appliances, and photographic equipment. In 1996, Hagemeyer acquired Cosa Liebermann's 50% stake in the joint-venture.

Agencies still are an esteemed part of operations at the international trading companies but, as has been observed before, they do not really fit in a strategy of increasing the scale of business across national borders. Agencies do not provide a sufficiently firm base for a pan-European strategy of the traders themselves, either. Finally, agencies are full of uncertainty. Borsumij Wehry's CEO once put the problem succinctly by commenting on the constant change affecting company's operations, with the board worrying over managing an agency one day, only to lose it the next.[12]

MARKETING PROPRIETARY BRANDS – One way for trading companies to escape the dependence on agencies and to realise an increasing scale of business with their own means, was through creating their own brands. As Chapter VII has shown extensively, integrating with manufacturing was also an option, but this did not prove to be a very attractive one for the Dutch international traders: profits, if any, always turned out to be short-lived, while reorganising manufacturing subsidiaries was a difficult and expensive affair. Until well into the 1980s,

A consumer presentation of Christian Dior cosmetics and perfume in Singapore. Hagemeyer was exporting French perfume to Asia as early as the 1930s.

Borsumij Wehry succeeded in creating a substantial turnover in clothing, produced in China and marketed under its own brands in Europe. Goods returned by the company's large customers were dumped on local markets.

both Internatio-Müller and Hagemeyer struggled with the liquidation of their manufacturing interests. Thus, traders had meanwhile come to prefer creating their own brands, in combination with the outsourcing of production. The rising industrialised countries in the Far East appeared to hold out particularly appealing prospects as producers, the more so since the international traders already possessed a network in this area. However, promoting proprietary brands meant that the trading companies had to build an identity for the products concerned. This factor imposed restrictions on the strategy from its inception, for brands increasingly needed a world-wide image and presence to succeed. Local brands could not really compete with global ones.

As early as the 1970s, Borsumij Wehry set up a prospering textiles trade, selling its own designs produced in the Far East. A purchasing subsidiary and trial production plant were established in Hong Kong. The marketing initially targeted Germany, but subsequently widened to encompass other European countries. Applying the same recipe for a fabrics business in the US failed, however. The board mentioned staff having difficulty in coping with the wide differences in time zones as one of the reasons for the failure. There was a difference of seven hours between Hong Kong and Europe, and on top of that came the difference between the US and Europe. Employees had to answer the phone at all hours, which according to the board resulted in clear cases of premature exhaustion.[13] This was probably not the only problem, the modest size of its US textiles trade must have been a major obstacle for the company. Whatever the reason, the efforts to penetrate the US market with fabrics were terminated.

Borsumij Wehry supplied six groups of customers, i.e. wholesalers, mail order businesses, department stores, joint purchasing organizations, manufacturers, and market salesmen. This latter category was a vital channel for offloading the goods returned by the big customers. For the mail order firms, representing more than half of total turnover in textiles, as a rule returned an average of 10% of goods. In 1985, Borsumij found that its textiles turnover was very high and continued to rise, but that even so the high costs kept profit margins very modest indeed. Competition mounted, as many customers made regular visits, and thus came to know the tricks. The board hoped to create a new dimension for the fabrics business by relocating production to China, since this country continued to be unknown territory for most of its customers, so they would need an intermediary. The Borsumij Wehry board even decided to expand its textiles business substantially with production in China and subsequently Indonesia, and supported this expansion by heavy investment in automation. In 1987 the company shipped 40 million pieces of clothing from Asia to Europe. Unfortunately, the profits did not keep pace with turnover. The management lost their grip on the expanding business. Some deliveries arrived too late, others had the wrong specifications. There was no proper production control: the company placed orders, but did not follow them up with weekly monitoring of production and delivery times of the manufacturers. The cumbersome financial reporting system operated too slowly, and failed to warn of imminent problems. As a consequence, the textile division suffered heavy losses in 1989, which continued into 1990. The Borsumij Wehry board reacted with deep cutbacks in the business, but it could not prevent renewed huge losses from occurring in 1994. In the end it even proved impossible to sell Borsumij Textiles, so it shut in 1996.[14] Was this a matter of management failure or of a recipe which had had its day? Hindsight does not make it easier to decide, but it is a fact that companies such as the clothing chain C&A or Neckermann, a mail order giant, had begun purchasing in the Far East themselves. So it really boiled down to a classic case of a wholesaler ousted from a position by the retail trade. Moreover, small traders had developed a still cheaper way, buying containers full of unsorted mass textiles from China and selling the goods in Europe at rock-bottom prices. Of course this approach did not allow the development of a proprietary brand strategy.

With its Pollyflame subsidiary, Borsumij Wehry had a more lasting success. Initially, this company concentrated on marketing articles for smokers. By the early 1980s, Borsumij Wehry observed anti-smoking campaigns having reduced the popularity of cigarette lighters as birthday presents or business gifts. An agency for disposable lighters did provide Pollyflame with an attractive revenue source, but the Japanese principal had already given notice for it. Seeking to regenerate its business, Pollyflame found a new revenue source in gift articles, in particular business gifts and publicity related products, building a business in many European countries and even in the US with its own designs, produced in the Far East. Initially the company also introduced a proprietary brand, Enzo Varini, but as the board considered media advertising too expensive, the retail trade had to make do as a means to spread brand recognition. Eventually proprietary brands such as Marksman fountain pens or Spirit of St Louis for watches and hi-fi gained a certain recognition. Pollyflame responded perfectly to a curious phenomenon, the rising interest in gadgets in the rich western world, where many people already own all daily utensils. A merger with Edelman BV, which marketed plants and ceramics, added marketing opportunities in the sector life style and cosy home products. Renamed Pollyconcept after the Edelman merger, the company continued to nurse agencies, including the representation of Zippo lighters, since Zippo had succeeded in creating fashionable lighters suitable as business gifts. Thus a market which Borsumij Wehry had almost jettisoned in the early 1980s proved to have new life in it after all.[15]

During the late 1970s, Hagemeyer adopted a strategy of marketing proprietary brands, with the express intention of outsourcing the production. These brands would be targeted at consumers in the rich western world. With the brand Smith Family Toys, Hagemeyer entered the field of traditional toys, to face strong competition from the leading brands. Moreover, traditional toys struggled to compete with the new computer games. A second initiative was the Rolykit, a patented storing system, which looked splendid, but failed to find buyers.[16] Yet another attempt at establishing a proprietary brand led to the takeover of TEC in Germany, a second-rank or B-brand for consumer electronics.

The Borsumij Wehry subsidiary Pollyflame developed from an agency business for cigarette lighters into a purveyor of business gifts and publicity articles produced from its own designs.

The company focused mainly on portable radios, and introduced a walkman before the term even existed: the Bone Fone, a shawl with a built-in radio.[17] It was a big acquisition for Hagemeyer, and the company made large losses from the beginning. The board succeeded in getting the business almost back on track, but nevertheless this particular brand proved to be a downhill affair.[18] In the US, Hagemeyer operated a similar concept of low-priced hi-fi with the brands Yorx and GPX. For a number of years, GPX especially generated fabulous profits. The products invariably came from the Far East, China in particular. Initially the combination of a cheap production source with the market strategy of B-brands resulted in sufficient margins, but other businessmen also got wise to the trick. During economic recessions B-brands appeared to make some headway, consumer preferences shifting to price rather than brand name, but no sooner had the producers of prime brands cut prices, or B-brands proved to be in an exceedingly vulnerable position. Faced with narrow price differences, consumers preferred the leading brands, and the B-brands were pushed out of the market. With markets increasingly spanning the globe, brand products had to be sold and marketed all over the world. Small brands struggled to be noticed under the onslaught of the blanket advertising of world brands. The power of US department stores and retail chains compounded the problems there. In marketing its GPX hi-fi brand, Hagemeyer had to fall in with the retailers' standard clause of allowing customers to return goods more or less without restrictions. When Hagemeyer refused further deliveries on such conditions, GPX turnover fell dramatically. Occasionally the company did succeed in developing its own brand for niche markets, as happened with Case Logic, a producer of bags and storage systems for portable hi-fi.[19]

Having had varying success with promoting proprietary brands from the late 1970s, Hagemeyer in 1986 reaffirmed its ambitions to reduce the dependence on agencies by expanding the turnover of own brands to 50% of the company.[20] Nothing came of it, however. In 1993, the company's brands generated no more than 14% of turnover. The aspirations to reduce the dependence on a few principals did succeed, though, for turnover generated by agency sales had declined to less than half, i.e. 44%. Traditional wholesaling operations, rather than proprietary brands, had meanwhile developed into a key alternative to agencies, generating 42% of turnover.[21] Such operations typically formed a network that collected products from a large number of manufacturers, and they were thus dubbed 'multi-principal'. Perhaps, then, Hagemeyer had begun reconstituting itself from an international trader to a local wholesaler?

MULTI-PRINCIPAL – During the second half of the 1980s Hagemeyer, recognising the vulnerability of agents towards principals compounded by the difficulty of generating a substantial turnover with proprietary brands, began to search for a new field of operations. The board now redefined its strategy to be 'multi-principal', i.e. focusing on operations bringing together a large number of manufacturers or principals needing sophisticated distribution skills and logistical processes. Hagemeyer now really opted for a switch to specialised wholesaling, though the board expressly added the condition that the operations should be suitable for international expansion as a continuing distinction from wholesalers with only local business.[22] Two sectors appeared to be particularly attractive: pharmaceuticals and electrotechnical products.

Internatio-Müller had been operating in pharmaceuticals since 1964, when it acquired a combination of wholesalers gradually welded into a sound and coherent business named Interpharm. This company supplied drugstores, dispensing chemists, hospitals, and other health care institutions. By developing its own retail templates, Interpharm tried to get ever closer to its customers, and by the mid-1990s the company occupied the third position on the Dutch market, after OPG and Brocacef. It was a prosperous sector, as consumers spent increasing sums on health care. This drew the attention of the Hagemeyer strategists. Though pharmaceutical wholesaling primarily sold in the Netherlands, purchasing pharmaceuticals and drugstore products was an international business, drawing on a large number of suppliers. Hagemeyer considered Medicopharma an attractive opportunity to enter this market. The company itself nursed ambitions for international expansion, which fitted well with Hagemeyer's plans. A merger in the form of an equity swap was announced in 1989, but nevertheless foundered later. The Medicopharma shareholders considered the offer too low, and Hagemeyer did not want to risk a higher bid.[23]

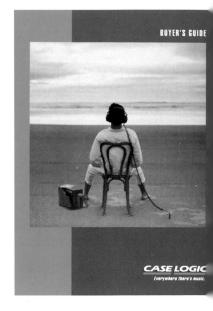

Launching proprietary brands in competition with established manufacturers' brands proved a thorny road for the international traders. However, Hagemeyer did manage to capture the niche market of bags and storage systems for personal hifi with its Case Logic brand.

340

Markets in which thousands of suppliers seek many thousands of customers are natural habitats for wholesaling, with a minimal risk of being cut out. Internatio-Müller succeeded in finding such an attractive market in pharmaceuticals with its Interpharm subsidiary, here with its company stand at the 1992 Farmavisie trade fair in the Amsterdam RAI exhibition centre.

Disappointed with the failed Medicopharma merger, Hagemeyer immediately set to work seeking entry to the other field of operations defined as attractive, the wholesaling in electrotechnical products. The company bought the wholesaler J.W. Bernard & Zn based in Capelle aan den IJssel, near Rotterdam, which had eleven subsidiaries all over the Netherlands. This company had been founded in Rotterdam in 1955 by J.W. Bernard, his son E. Bernard leading the subsequent expansion. Its product range comprised more than 25,000 items, supplied by about 200 principals in the Netherlands and abroad. As a consequence, the business was a truly multi-principal one.[24] While thus entering the field of traditional wholesaling, Hagemeyer nursed clear aspirations towards moving its boundaries, and the board hired a senior manager from the nearest rival in the field, OTRA, to explore the opportunities for international acquisitions in the sector. OTRA, by the way, a subsidiary of the French company Sonepar, had itself just embarked on a program of expansion in Northern Europe, too. Having meanwhile built up sufficient financial resources, Hagemeyer could straightaway target key companies, something which Bernard could never have done on its own. The acquisitions were thoroughly prepared. As a new entrant to this market, Hagemeyer only wanted to bid for solid companies, led by a sound management willing to continue in their positions after the acquisition. The board concentrated its search on national market leaders, preferably ranking first, second, or at most third, thus aiming for expensive but smoothly running companies.

Between 1989 and 1997, Hagemeyer bought electrotechnical wholesalers in Germany, the UK, Switzerland, Austria, Sweden, Norway, and Finland. As regards the Swedish market, the board had originally targeted Selga, which ranked second, the third ranking, Storel, having already been bought by OTRA. The acquisition of Selga fell through, however, so in 1997 Hagemeyer, for want of an alternative, successfully bid for the leading company, Asea Skandia.[25] The

341

Hagemeyer entered a new field of
operations in 1989 with the take-
over of J.W. Bernard & Zn., a
wholesaler in electrotechnical
supplies. The board considered this
an attractive sector, being what it
termed 'multi-principal'. During the
1990s, Hagemeyer acquired a string
of other electrotechnical
wholesalers.

Finnish wholesaler also possessed subsidiaries in Eastern Europe, enabling the group to take soundings in that direction as well. With these acquisitions, Hagemeyer created a strong Northern European group dedicated to supplying products such as cables, switches, bulb fittings and light bulbs to fitters in the building industry and installers of factory equipment. The subsidiaries all retained their autonomy, but Hagemeyer did stimulate them to exchange skills and experiences. The group's combined business made it into an attractive partner to big suppliers, such as Philips, Osram, ABB, Pirelli, Alcatel, and Siemens. Conversely, the group aimed to expand its services to manufacturers by exploring new markets, supporting marketing and distribution, and helping to defend their market positions.[26] Working as it did with many hundreds of manufacturers supplying tens of thousands of products and finally selling to thousands of customers, this group did not run the risk of being cut short by principals. Moreover, the international collaboration gave the group a head start over national wholesalers. Thus Hagemeyer had discovered a new and successful recipe to operate as an international trader. An additional attraction of electrotechnical wholesaling was its status as a business-to-business market, i.e. one without the joint purchasing organizations and retail chains dominating the market for consumer products. Quite the contrary, the desire among companies to outsource non-core business created new services opportunities here.

From 1988, Hagemeyer built up an import business for specialty foods in the US, guided by a similar concept of multi-principal operations. Andrew Land, senior manager and subsequently Hagemeyer's CEO from 1985 until 1999, nursed high expectations about this business. It went back to one of the company's long-standing subsidiaries in North America, a Canadian firm in foods, of modest size but profitable. Land confronted its management with a choice between growth or de-merger, and growth it was to be, of course. A substantial division of Specialty Foods was created by acquiring a large number of existing companies scattered across the US and Canada. The group concentrated on buying, marketing and distributing delicatessen, exotic products, and other fine foodstuffs. It had a sufficiently strong position towards its suppliers, but whether the division really had enough muscle to ward off its customers was another matter. For the big food retail chains were the main customers, and they became ever more powerful through mergers. During the 1990s this process of concentration rapidly accelerated, resulting in retailers which could dictate prices and conditions to their suppliers, and which proceeded to cut the margins of importers and wholesalers to the bone. As a result, the performance of Hagemeyer's Specialty Foods division suffered. Faced with a choice between further substantial acquisitions to bolster its position towards the retail chains, or selling the entire group, the board opted for the latter and sold it to Wessanen in 1999.[27]

Hagemeyer's latest acquisition also operated according to the multi-principal concept, although it served a somewhat smaller group of suppliers. In a period of fifteen years the Sydney-based Tech Pacific, bought in 1997, had developed into an important distributor of computer hardware and software, telecommunication equipment, and information technology in Asia and the Pacific area. The company occupied a leading position in Australia, New Zealand, Hong Kong, Singapore, and Malaysia, and also operated in Indonesia, the Philippines, Thailand, and India. Tech Pacific collaborated on a non-exclusive base with more than thirty principals, both manufacturers and software firms, including Hewlett Packard, Microsoft, Motorola, Intel, IBM, Compaq, and Toshiba, giving them access to its network of 20,000 retailers. As a dealer in information technology, the company of course used an on-line system which

Andrew Land, chairman of Hagemeyer's executive board from 1985 until 1999, sitting casually in a chair designed by the famous Dutch architect Gerrit Rietveld. Land steered Hagemeyer through a phase of vigorous expansion.

gives dealers any information required, from the availability of products to data about the balance of their account current with Tech Pacific.[28] With this acquisition, Hagemeyer also obtained information technology skills, a field offering attractive opportunities, but harbouring threats to wholesaling, too.

THREATS FROM LOGISTICAL SERVICE PROVIDERS AND FROM THE INTERNET

During the 1990s renewed warnings sounded about the looming downfall of Dutch wholesaling, even though the sector prospered in those years. Two developments fuelled this pessimism: the competition from logistical service providers, and the rise of the Internet. Information technology, moreover, closely linked the two phenomena together. In 1998, the transport sector trade rag *Logistiek Actueel* published an article under the challenging headline 'Will wholesaling survive until 2001?'. In it René Kreileman, general manager of Sentai Software Europe, voiced strong doubts about the continuing viability of wholesaling. According to him, manufacturing, transport companies, and retail chains had invested heavily in increasing their logistical efficiency, thus widening margins, but these developments appeared to have bypassed wholesaling.[29] The business magazine *Management Team* forecast in 1999, that the age-old Dutch commercial spirit was nearing its end, with wholesaling under threat.[30] Most remarkably, the magazine published its forecast side-by-side with an observation about the unavailability of data for 1999 preventing a quantitative substantiation for the slow extinction of wholesaling. Indeed, the data for 1998 pointed in the opposite direction. What then inspired this belief in the ultimate demise? It was based on the potential threat by new information technology, and particularly by the new phenomenon of the Internet.

At that moment information technology was hardly new for wholesalers. In the early 1970s the computer began to be adopted by traders, mainly for making the processing of voluminous administrative data, such as orders, deliveries, invoices, debtors, and creditors, faster and more efficient. As one advantage, managers could obtain information about available stocks much more often and quicker than before, enabling them to reduce the volume of products stocked. Better accuracy in delivering orders was another potential advantage. Reducing mistakes meant fewer products returned to the wholesaler. Large mainframe computers formed the backbone of this automation. Some trading companies began to set up their own computer departments. During the 1980s a new type of computer came on the market, the micro computer, also dubbed personal computer or PC. This was a much smaller machine, less conducive to administrative scale increases and centralization than the mainframes. The PC was ideally suited for the desks of individual employees, serving both as a high-grade typewriter and a calculator. The offices with typists busily battering away disappeared, as most employees began to draft their own letters and reports. As a consequence, administrations decentralised, and computer departments were closed.[31]

Hagemeyer attempted to build a substantial US business importing specialty foods and delicatessen, such as chocolate easter bunnies. However, the ongoing concentration among the company's customers made this market less and less attractive. In 1999, the division 'specialty foods' was sold to Wessanen.

Initially, the PC led to computer use becoming more isolated, but once it became possible to connect PCs, new and interesting perspectives opened up for creating computer networks. Information technology now turned into a strategic competitive weapon. From the preserve of technical departments, computerisation rose to be a vital part of the overall business strategy. Initially computer networks operated within companies only, but advances in telecommunication technology enabled the steady expansion of such networks, crossing the boundaries of organizations and countries alike, finally creating a world-spanning network. From an instrument for storing and ordering large amounts of data supporting management decisions, the computer and the information technology connected to it became an essential part of the entire business strategy. Networks assumed a crucial role, both for internal communication and for keeping in touch with the world surrounding a business. The system of running an organization through annual budgets in tandem with regular budget checks clearly demonstrates the surplus value of computer networks for the internal management of organizations. Such methods of communicating with each other would have been unthinkable without the computer technology. Networks also revolutionised customer relations. Armed with a portable computer or laptop connected to a telephone socket, salesmen visiting customers could obtain the most recent information on the spot, and when they reached an agreement, immediately pass this information back to the company.[32]

Letting systems communicate with each other, as in the Electronic Data Interchange or EDI, was the next step in external communication. This necessitated the creation of uniform protocols for data about products and transactions, such as for instance the bar code. It succeeded only where one party was sufficiently powerful to lay down a protocol for the others to follow. In the Netherlands, for instance, the food retail chain Albert Heijn, and the department store De Bijenkorf with its DIY subsidiaries Praxis and Hubo, proved strong enough to reach an agreement about a uniform standard. Moreover, such systems paid mainly in sectors handling a wide product range with a high order frequency, and without frequent and rapid changes in composition. Consequently, the sectors food and DIY were particularly suited to EDI. Creating these systems was exceptionally expensive, putting an effective brake on the general

Laptop computers and mobile telephones made employees ever more flexible.

adoption of EDI.[33] For wholesalers, EDI posed a threat in as far as enabling producers and customers to establish direct links with each other, bypassing the wholesale trade. Retail chains and joint purchasing organizations especially began to exploit that possibility, prompting the Verbond Nederlandse Groothandel or association of Dutch wholesalers in 1997 to launch a plan for developing a dedicated wholesalers' network. This facility aimed at permitting wholesalers to offer all the participants in the business column additional administrative services, like sales registration, financial management, analyses of turnover and sales, and profitability calculations. According to the association, the wholesale trade had to take an active role in developing EDI, thus securing its pivotal commercial position.[34]

The development of the Internet possibly posed an even greater threat than EDI had done. This revolutionary system allowed computers to communicate with each other regardless of brand, type, or operating software. The Internet created the possibility to send electronic mail across the world in a few seconds, including entire documents, and to use the world wide web for searching or offering information. By searching for information, customers also supplied data to those offering information, making the Internet doubly attractive from a commercial viewpoint. In contrast to EDI, the Internet is accessible to all, and at a much lower cost. There appear to be no limits to the spread of the Internet, whereas videotext, which raised high expectations during the 1980s, achieved only a modest penetration.[35] The practically unlimited possibilities to send and receive information through the world wide web makes data about the various markets around the world more widely available, increasing the transparency of markets. This poses a very real threat to wholesalers which, after all, earn their

Does the Internet pose a new threat to the international trading companies, or will it open new opportunities for providing services to them?

living as intermediaries mainly from a lead in knowledge. The best way for wholesalers to meet the threat of the Internet, just as with EDI, is to grab the initiative. The opportunities for expanding services are fascinating. *The Economist* magazine drew a sketch of a US retail chain which supplies builders with materials. Customers can order through the Internet and have the goods delivered on site, either immediately or exactly the moment when needed, as the customer wishes. If the builder happens to need a plumber or electrician as well, he may send data about the work and its location to the trader, who will then act as a labour exchange. The potential for extending the service are numerous, speed in realising the opportunities present is all that counts: 'It is no longer about the big beating the small, it's about the fast beating the slow'.[36]

Did Dutch wholesaling take an active stance towards information technology? A 1997 report took an exceedingly optimistic view, concluding that wholesaling was the most highly computerised sector of the Dutch economy. The penetration ratio was 90%, i.e. 90% of companies used computers and/or employed information technology specialists. Wholesaling was even dubbed leader in EDI, which meant that, in 1993, 10% of wholesalers used it. One fifth of the firms used e-mail at that moment. These figures have only limited value, considering the rapid developments in the field. The wholesalers surveyed mentioned as advantages of using information technology a greater efficiency and accuracy of invoice administration and bookkeeping, faster handling, more information, and a clearer picture of the overall business. However, some disadvantages had surfaced as well. The technology was expensive and required a more highly skilled staff, and implementing it often took longer than planned. Moreover, rapid changes in software created the need for constant modifications. Finally, the traders were concerned about losing touch with what actually happened in the market through the flood of misinformation.[37]

However appealing the visions about the future of the Internet may be, it does remain a virtual world. Eventually goods still have to be shifted and delivered. In addition to providing information, wholesaling has always performed a very practical function in facilitating the transport and stocking of goods. However, by the late 1980s new providers began to enter this particular market. Hauliers restyled themselves as logistical service providers, encouraged by the transport pressure group Nederland Distributieland. Other companies specialised in storing goods. The old private warehousing companies assumed a new profile as public warehouses. Wholesaling does indeed run the risk of being cut out by new logistical service providers from markets where the distance between manufacturers and retailers is a very short one, for instance because of powerful joint purchasing organizations. On the other hand, wholesalers themselves also use opportunities to outsource services. Research conducted in 1991 by the economic research institute for small and medium-sized businesses, EIM, showed that wholesalers outsourced transport and related services in particular, while keeping information management and stock control more or less completely in-house. Wholesalers expected to transfer storage to outside providers

at some point in the future. Cost was the main driver for outsourcing services, whereas service levels and flexibility provided the main arguments for keeping everything in-house. Wholesalers really considered logistical service providers more as subcontractors for dedicated services than as competitors.[38] In the final analysis, wholesalers continued to hold a trump card, i.e. after sales services. Once products had been ordered and delivered, there was always the chance of a problem, the need for repairs, or a need for advice. Backed by their product know-how and their service organizations, wholesalers could fulfil that need better than logistical service providers, unless the latter had meanwhile evolved into wholesalers themselves.

The international trading companies, as always keen to remain flexible, opted both for outsourcing services and for stretching the services provided. Hagemeyer's various subsidiaries developed their own recipes, guided by the parent company's preference for providing services adding value over merely shifting boxes. This left them sufficient room for manoeuvre. The Dutch distributor for Matsushita products, Haagtechno, decided to concentrate on marketing and after sales services, by outsourcing transport, storage, and handling with a logistical service provider. By contrast, electrotechnical wholesale subsidiaries considered their stock room as an essential part of their marketing concept. One of them, the German company Fröschl, succeeded in expanding its business services by developing an industry concept. Fröschl offered big manufacturers, for instance car producers, to take care of the entire supply of electrotechnical parts, from simple ignition locks to dedicated equipment. This approach freed the companies concerned from a bothersome administration and reduced their stocks, and it had the additional attraction of having an almost unlimited potential for expansion. Fröschl successfully operated the scheme for its customer Audi.[39] Far from being cut out by suppliers or customers, this particular wholesaler had become deeper involved with its customer than before, by falling in with the industrial trend towards outsourcing non-core activities as much as possible.

The determination and ingenuity of merchants to gain a position in the distributive chain for themselves outweighs any considerations about whether or not some wholesaling functions may be better performed by other links. The centuries-old Amsterdam merchant house Van Eeghen & Co. presents a good

Despite the boundless opportunities created by Internet, goods will have to be physically transported at some stage. Transport companies began to use the new ICT options to transform themselves into logistical service providers, seizing functions of the international trading companies.

example of merchants using their ingenuity to find new ways time and again. This firm dates from 1662. In 1999, it still operated as a trader, it was still a family business, and the firm was led by a Van Eeghen as before. During the early 1990s, the firm sold coffee, tea, spices, and dried vegetables, including onions. The commodity trade was subsequently terminated, being too speculative for its small margins. Turnover of the trade in spices and dried vegetables remained important, but profit margins became less attractive. The firm then switched to an entirely new field of operations by entering the trade in neutraceuticals, i.e. health-care ingredients for food. Specialised know-how about product development enabled Van Eeghen to provide links between suppliers and customers, by connecting ingredients produced by the former to products being developed by the latter. Simultaneously Van Eeghen arranged practical matters, such as transport, storage, and just-in-time delivery of the goods concerned. The firm developed its own brands as hallmarks for the quality and purity of the ingredients. Van Eeghen & Co. is now sounding out the possibilities of e-commerce and the Internet as ways of providing its customers with tailored services in the future.[40]

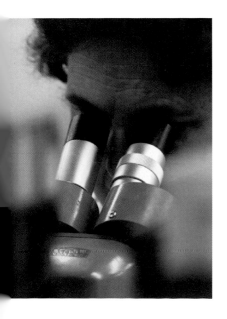

Laboratory research at Denofa, a Norway principal of Van Eeghen International. This company produces fish oil, which is rich in Omega-3 fatty acids. Such acids belong to the fast-growing category of neutraceuticals, ingredients with health-enhancing properties for food products.

INTERNATIONAL REALLY MEANS EUROPEAN – The search for the most suitable
and the most profitable sector also implied spreading operations across countries. How internationally oriented were the three key Dutch trading houses in
the early 1980s, and how did they subsequently develop in this respect? During
the 1960s and 1970s, the firms had focused more and more on Europe, and
within Europe, on the Netherlands. Internatio-Müller had added substantial
operations in transport and fitting technical equipment to its core, reducing the
importance of trading in overall turnover. In the 1980s, the company was predominantly active in the Netherlands, which generated 65-70% of revenues.
The rest of Europe generated 10-15%, making a European total of roughly
80%. Europe was hardly less important for Borsumij Wehry, but the parts were
more evenly matched, with about 45% of turnover coming from the Netherlands, against 30-35% from the rest of the continent. Out of these three firms,
Hagemeyer alone still had a balance of operations on several continents. In
1977, management consultants from McKinsey commented that Hagemeyer
had until then failed to gain a strong position as distributor in the two most
prosperous areas, Europe and the US. According to McKinsey, the company's
efforts had been unsuccessful, for lack of a clearly defined strategic concept,
compounded by a lack of experience and insufficient preparation. The report
concluded by recommending Hagemeyer 'to build a strong agency business in
Europe and North America'.[41] This recommendation was easy to write, but
hard to follow, as the markets mentioned were equally attractive for the
manufacturers themselves. They needed the services of an intermediary for small
markets or distant countries, less so for Europe or the US. In the early 1980s,
Hagemeyer realised 40-50% of its turnover in Europe, 20-25% in Asia, and the
rest from Oceania, Africa, North America, and the commodity trade.[42]

The interest shown by foreign companies in Dutch wholesalers presents
another angle on the sector's measure of internationalization. After the OGEM
debacle, the electrotechnical wholesaler OTRA was sold to the French company
Sonepar. This collaboration enabled OTRA to expand by acquiring companies
abroad as well.[43] Another important case in this respect is the interest in Dutch
trading houses demonstrated by the Indonesian Liem Group through its Hong
Kong investment company, First Pacific. In 1982, the Hagemeyer board raised
the company's equity to give First Pacific a majority share. One could call it
somewhat ironical that an Indonesian group thus came to own a Dutch trader
which had once risen to prosperity in the colonial economy. What made the
Liem Group take this step? During the 1970s, Hagemeyer had attempted to
supplement the traditional trade in consumer products by creating a new
source of profits with industrial ventures, but this had misfired. Indeed, on
balance large amounts of money and a lot of energy had been wasted. In 1980
Hagemeyer's supervisory board had appointed an energetic manager coming
from outside the company, Ruud Bom, to the executive board, hoping that he
would open up new perspectives. In order to build the financial muscle required
for expansion, Bom proposed to raise equity and give First Pacific a majority

In 1982, the Indonesian Liem Grou[
acquired a majority stake in
Hagemeyer through its investment
company First Pacific. It was sold
again in 1999.

350

stake. Reluctantly, the supervisory board accepted his plans. The agreement's full significance, Hagemeyer formally becoming a subsidiary of First Pacific, was not emphasised to the outside world, because the new owners considered the company's Dutch identity a commercial asset. The Liem Group's main interest for Hagemeyer derived from its expectation that, as an old trading house with a substantial coffee business, the company might become useful in marketing Asian commodities on the world markets. Coming from outside, they could not know that after internal debate Hagemeyer had just decided to terminate its coffee trade because of the large risks associated with commodity trading. However, the collaboration with the Liem Group made Hagemeyer postpone its plans to stop trading coffee for an indefinite period.[44]

The Indonesian Liem Group was not alone in showing interest in Dutch trading companies. During the early 1980s, the leading US retail company Sears, Roebuck & Co. had thrown itself into exporting US manufacturing products through its subsidiary Sears World Trade or SWT. The underlying vision was to create a world-spanning trade company modelled on the Japanese Sogo Shosha. SWT was launched with tall ambitions, but after three years, the company still operated at a loss, inspiring the magazine *Fortune* to comment: 'Sears Roebuck wanted to be the premier U.S. international trading company. It hired big names, talked big ideas, and spent big money. But the names did not bring action, the talk has turned quiet, and the money is flowing much less freely.'[45] In 1984, SWT approached the Borsumij Wehry board seeking to buy the company or at least a substantial majority stake in it, no doubt aiming to acquire a bridgehead for getting US goods flowing into Europe. However, Borsumij Wehry

Throughout the 1980s and 1990s, Borsumij Wehry and Hagemeyer concentrated on trade, whereas Internatio-Müller also focused on fitting technical installations and on transport. The company's logistical services to shipping lines and to shippers were expanded to other European ports, as far away as St.-Petersburg in Russia.

feared that swt wanted to use the company for buffering its own losses, and declined the honour.[46] swt then approached Hagemeyer's manager Bom. As it happened, the two companies already operated a joint-venture selling DIY products in the UK. Bom gave the Americans a much warmer welcome. He thought that swt could learn a lot from Hagemeyer's commercial know-how, and First Pacific was alive to the political interest involved in obtaining links with a key US company through its subsidiary. It remained an open question whether the products of swt and Hagemeyer were really compatible. However, meanwhile Hagemeyer had landed into serious trouble through its coffee trade, which made the extra cash injection generated by selling part of the company to swt more than welcome. So there was a striking contrast in perception between Borsumij Wehry and Hagemeyer: the former feared that the collaboration would lose money in the long run, the latter jumped at having secured short-term income. As of 1 January 1986, swt took a 20% stake in Hagemeyer. Bom departed to Sears' US head office, full of optimism about the advantages of the association. As part of the agreement, Hagemeyer shut down its coffee trade after sustaining heavy losses. However, the partnership with Sears was not to last long. For Hagemeyer, 1986 was not such a bad year, but swt lost so much money that before year's end, Sears Roebuck had decided to dissolve swt and to end the participation in Hagemeyer. Hagemeyer bought its own shares back with dollars which meanwhile had become considerably cheaper after a drop in the exchange rate. This windfall helped Hagemeyer to make a fresh start after 1986.[47] Sears Roebuck returned to its familiar US retail trade. In 1991 First Pacific attempted to acquire another Dutch merchant house, Internatio-Müller this time, with the aim of letting it merge with Hagemeyer, but the transaction fell through, as we will see below.

Reports studying the increasing internationalisation of the trade sector through cross-border mergers, take-overs, equity participations, and joint-ventures, also showed that Dutch trading companies acquired more foreign companies than the other way around. In 1989, 40% of all mergers and take-overs in wholesaling were cross-border, and this figure rose as high as 70% for equity participations and joint-ventures. This last form of collaboration proved particularly popular for associations with companies operating at some distance, geographically or culturally. These ratios remained more or less the same during the years that followed, with even a slight increase for the number of mergers and take-overs of companies abroad. These occurred mainly with companies located in the UK, Belgium, France, and the US. With regards to acquisitions, wholesaling was the most active sector of Dutch business after the financial sector. Conversely, foreign companies showed remarkably little attention for Dutch wholesalers, taking initiatives for only a handful of acquisitions.[48]

352

Big wholesalers in particular effected the mergers and take-overs. How did this strategy affect the geographical orientation of the three Dutch international traders Borsumij Wehry, Hagemeyer, and Internatio-Müller? To start with the last mentioned, during the 1990s Internatio-Müller continued to operate predominantly in the Netherlands, which generated 72-80% of turnover, because the pharmaceutical wholesaler and the fitting companies were mainly active in that country. About 90% of turnover came from Europe as a whole. Internatio-

First Pacific took a keen interest in a prospective collaboration of its Hagemeyer subsidiary with the US company of Sears Roebuck & Co.

Müller had really wanted to sell its ships' agencies, the logistical service providers to ships' owners and shippers, but when that failed, the board decided to build a North European network instead. This network now stretches from France to Latvia, Lithuania, and Russia. As regards the world outside Europe, during the mid-1980s Internatio-Müller recognised the desirability of increasing its presence in the Pacific and in North America. This desire proved hard to fulfil. In 1984, the company drew 15% of its turnover from Australia and New Zealand. The area showed no further growth, however, on the contrary, its contribution gradually declined during the following years, partly because the results lagged behind expectations. The US, South Africa, and Asia together supplied only a few percentages of turnover.[49]

Europe had an equally great importance for Borsumij Wehry, generating about 80% of turnover. During the 1980s the Netherlands was more important than the rest of Europe, but by 1994 the exact opposite had become true. For a considerable time, Borsumij Wehry had trade in consumer products as its core business, purchasing mainly in Asia and selling in Europe. Initially Asia was the

In 1993, Borsumij Wehry acquired the international trading company Ceteco, whose operations included the La Curaçao retail chain, with shops all over Central and Southern America.

company's main region after Europe with 16% of turnover, but this figure gradually declined. The US generated 10% of turnover in 1983, but it was a rare peak unmatched either before or since. By 1991 this share had sagged to 1%. Getting profitable operations off the ground in the US time and again turned out to be exceedingly difficult. In 1988, Borsumij Wehry's senior manager, M. van der Klooster, vented his disappointment by commenting that at least during the last 30 years, America had spelled nothing but trouble.[50] The company had had to struggle with powerful unions, but also with domineering customers. Africa no longer figured at all, once the trade in hides and skins had been terminated after heavy losses, and after the 1982 closure of the leather tanning plant in Kenya.[51] For the first time in its existence, Borsumij Wehry obtained a substantial presence in South America with the acquisition of Ceteco in 1993.

Hagemeyer's geographical spread showed strong fluctuations, alternating take-overs and disinvestments constantly shifting the emphasis between areas. During the early 1980s, the company still derived about 7% of its turnover from Africa, finally leaving the continent only as late as 1990. The Hagemeyer board aspired to spread risks by expanding the company in three important growth markets, i.e. Asia/Oceania, North America, and Europe, but as things stood it failed to realise the intended balanced spread. In the US, varying operations generated about 15-20% of turnover. Asia and Oceania contributed 25-30%. Finally, Europe realised about half of the company's turnover, but after the mid-1990s that share increased somewhat to 63% in 1998. Hagemeyer's annual reports did not make a breakdown of results achieved in Europe and the Netherlands. The bulk of the US operations, the entire food division, was sold early in 1999. During the autumn of 1999, part of the proceeds were spent on the acquisition of two US wholesalers, one dedicated to marketing safety equipment, the other operating as an electrotechnical wholesaler.[52]

Thus all three merchant houses retained a marked European focus. In addition to the Netherlands, Europe meant above all the neighbouring countries Germany, Belgium, the UK, and somewhat further away France and the Scandinavian countries. All three companies did show some interest in Eastern Europe, but none of them derived substantial business from the area for now. In 1984, Borsumij Wehry established a management staff division for Eastern Europe,

354

which began small-scale operations in the countries behind the Iron Curtain, imports and exports based on standing orders. For some years the division yielded fair results. Initially it appeared as if the end of the Cold War would boost trade with Eastern Europe, but at least by 1991 this had not really materialised. In its 1993 annual report, Internatio-Müller reported having set up a joint-venture in Prague, but the following year this company was no longer mentioned. Hagemeyer waited until 1991 before setting up an 'East European Trade Desk', which concentrated on trading with Russia. The results raised sufficient expectations to start a joint-venture with a Russian group in 1992. A number of transactions were effected, but it proved impossible to bring about a regular exchange of goods. Russian goods usually failed to meet Western quality standards. Conversely, whereas Russia exerted sufficient demand for Western goods it became progressively less feasible to obtain payment in dollars for them, so the joint-venture did not survive for very long. Trade with Russia is really only possible through a personal network using ingenious schemes, to which small merchant houses such as Van Eeghen are better suited than large companies. Meanwhile Hagemeyer has a foothold in several Eastern European countries by way of its electrotechnical wholesaling subsidiaries.[53]

Until now, none of the three Dutch international trading companies has managed to maintain profitable operations for a longer period of time in the US. This is all the more remarkable because other Dutch service groups, such as banks, insurers, and retailers, did succeed in doing so. Might the US be unsuitable as a country for wholesalers? As early as the 1970s, the American business historian Alfred Chandler argued that from the early 1900s, the room for wholesalers in the US has been squeezed out of existence by the market presence and the financial power of producers on one hand, and joint purchasing organizations and retailers on the other.[54] The Dutch trading companies indeed faced a running battle with domineering market parties. It hardly made sense to begin on a small scale in this market, but as yet the merchant houses lacked the muscle required to make a big start. Moreover, the US market was more transparent than the European one, which translated into narrower margins. Finally, accidental developments could also upset a successful business. Borsumij Wehry ran an agency in the US for the Polish Universal company, marketing nails and other steel products. In 1979, this trade was hit by new import duties introduced by the US administration. During 1982, US dock workers refused to unload Polish ships for months on end, out of solidarity with political struggles there. Consequently, Borsumij Wehry again suffered a serious loss of turnover for both its import business and its distribution organization, for half of the company's US turnover derived from the Polish goods. Repeated cuts failed to restore profitability to this particular business.[55]

Yet none of this made the trading houses resolve to leave the US for good. In 1991, a Borsumij Wehry strategy memorandum raised the almost rhetorical question of whether, as an international trader, the company could afford not to be present in North America, replying in the negative.[56] Hagemeyer always con-

After the fall of the Berlin Wall, European companies rushed to establish themselves in eastern Europe and in Russia. Western brands such as Heineken beer finally reached the luxury GUM department store in Moscow, pictured here in 1998.

355

sidered a presence in this country of great importance for its regional and currency risk spread. However, the board also appreciated the market's quality in foreshadowing the shape of things to come. For that reason, Hagemeyer rekindled its acquisition ambitions after selling the food division. Van Dorp Despec, a wholesaler in office products, shared this desire to have an ear to the ground in the form of a US interest, to survey market developments. Another wholesaler, Buhrmann, went one step further in 1999, and bought the company Corporate Express.[57]

The high expectations about business with eastern Europe led to early disappointments, but gradually trade began to pick up. Hagemeyer acquired a foothold in Prague through one of its electrotechnical subsidiaries.

MERGERS AND ACQUISITIONS – As will have become clear from the above, the international trading companies nearly always effected changes in their operations by mergers, acquisitions, and disinvestments. Dutch wholesaling demonstrated an increasing appetite for mergers, acquisitions, and collaborations, during the second half of the 1980s. Apart from the internationalisation already mentioned, this rising interest derived its impetus from the ample liquidity built up by companies during the 1980s, and from industry and retailing growing in scale. A few large companies laid down the rules in this concentration game. During the years 1987-1989, ten companies accounted for 40% of all transactions. The firms taken over were mostly smaller, independent, and regionally operating wholesalers. Businesses with less than 10 staff failed to generate much interest, however.[58] In 1991 and 1992, the number of mergers and take-overs declined considerably. Those years were difficult ones overall for wholesaling, though some companies weathered them better than others. From 1994, mergers and acquisitions rose again by leaps and bounds.[59]

Wholesaling unmistakably went through a process of scale growth in the sense that a few very large companies came into being, but still the average number of staff in Dutch wholesaling did not rise. Quite the contrary, during the 1980s this figure hovered around eight people, and it declined to seven in the 1990s. This apparent contrast stems partly from the limited reliability of statistical data about the number of companies counted.[60] Yet on the other hand, there is a sound explanation for this phenomenon at hand, and that is the constant flow of newcomers to the business. Wholesaling has always been characterised by low entry barriers. Setting up a business requires only modest capital, and no licences or official qualifications. Moreover, trading companies do not necessarily face cost penalties for being small, since trade offers fewer economies of scale than industry does. Buying in bulk of course gives better margins, but this is offset by large companies having higher administrative costs and more bureaucratic delays between decision and action than small companies do. However, keeping an established business going is not such an easy matter, so the influx of new businesses is balanced by an outflow almost as large. Even so, time and again there appears to be room for new dedicated wholesalers. They provide a key element in the dynamics of wholesaling and, once such businesses achieve a certain size, they form an attractive object for acquisition in the eyes of the big trading companies.

During the 1990s, companies looking for acquisitions clearly favoured winners. In the 1960s, Hagemeyer had bought some poorly performing businesses at keen prices, hoping to get them back on track again, but in the 1980s and 1990s the board only wanted to buy well-run companies. All acquisitions had to contribute to the profit per share from day one, and the incumbent management remained in place. Because Hagemeyer had opted for a decentralised approach with a small head office, the board could impossibly free managers to bring a poorly performing subsidiary back to par. So lame ducks with a promising potential were purposefully avoided, as Andrew Land put it in 1995.[61] Borsumij Wehry also preferred taking over companies with a sound management. As a minimum requirement, profits per share had to remain the same after the acquisition, and the new subsidiary had to contribute positively in the longer run.[62]

Borsumij Wehry did not always succeed in realising these aims, by the way. Acquisitions happened at various levels in the company, and the risks differed accordingly, though take-overs always harboured some risk. As J.H. Schlimmer, vice-chairman of Borsumij Wehry's supervisory board, commented in 1983, managers offering their company for sale always know more about the business than the potential buyer.[63] Sometimes take-overs concerned small companies bought as a welcome supplement for subsidiaries, a strategy sometimes termed stringing beads. In such cases, the bidder already had some knowledge about the sector concerned, and about the various companies in it, including the take-over target. As a consequence integration would usually be rapid and smooth.

At other times, companies of some consequence were acquired to start in a new direction, as was the case, already mentioned, with the Bernard take-over which set Hagemeyer on the road to electrotechnical wholesaling. Such cases were really a step in the dark entailing considerable risks, because the bidder still had to muster the relevant skills for the particular sector. Borsumij Wehry learnt this at great cost when acquiring a hire-purchase company, Favoriet Verhuur, in 1988. Not only were the kind of operations new to Borsumij Wehry, but it was also a company which had started from scratch with the idea of renting out hi-fi equipment and video recorders, giving customers the option to buy at the end of the rental period. One of the company's attractions appeared to be that Favoriet Verhuur did not compete with the retail trade, to which Borsumij Wehry sold a large volume of equipment through its subsidiary Fodor, Dutch agent for brands like Akai, Samsung, Fuji, and Olympus.[64] A little earlier, Hagemeyer had taken over the Allwave retail chain, but Borsumij Wehry preferred to avoid indirect competition with its customers.[65] Five years later, by the way, Hagemeyer sold Allwave again for a lack of success. To all appearances there is a great difference in approach between wholesaling and retailing. Favoriet Verhuur made a flying start and rapidly built up a large turnover, but payments lagged way behind. Moreover, it proved impossible to reclaim equipment when customers failed to meet their obligations. The business proved to have shaky foundations, so liquidation entailing large losses was the only way out.[66] On the other hand, with the Fodor acquisition Borsumij Wehry had hit a bull's eye, even though initially the board had shown some hesitation over the price.[67] This subsidiary became one of the pillars supporting Borsumij Wehry.

If the international trading houses were really only interested in smoothly operating companies, one might well ask what they had to offer in the way of added value by taking them over. What was the advantage of belonging to a large concern? Not only journalists, but also supervisory directors regularly raised the thorny question of whether the head office had more to offer than any investment trust. In Andrew Land's opinion, it was up to Hagameyer's head office to lay down an overall strategy, to draft standards for the administrative and financial management, and to monitor the subsidiary's performance closely and supportively.[68] He wanted a smallish staff to do this, a head office with 40 to 50 people should suffice to manage dozens of subsidiaries. After all, the specific skills of products and markets rested with the subsidiaries themselves, each of them responsible for their own personnel management. Land was rather sceptical about the concept of forcibly creating synergy. In 1993, Borsumij Wehry had a central staff of about 35 people, responsible for the general management, the financial management, and staff management. Cebeco-Handelsraad, the wholesaler for the agricultural purchasing and marketing cooperatives, developed a more or less similar approach to its head office, cutting staff numbers within a decade from about 1,200 to just over 30 people planning general strategy, financial management, and human resources.[69] From the mid-1980s, the Internatio-Müller head office went through a continuous trimming process. The company aspired to a flat and decentralised structure with efficient management systems and controls. It was tentatively suggested in 1997 that the company should aim to create synergy between the existing business and new acquisitions. The question arose whether the head office had not reached a critical limit to trimming, and whether it would be possible to effect greater interaction between the subsidiaries by alternative means. Thus acquiring companies and bringing them together in a holding company might become more beneficial.

Hoping to boost sales of Matsushita's Technics and Panasonic consumer electronics, Hagemeyer bought the Allwave retail chain in 1989. This excursion into retailing proved a disappointment, however, and the subsidiary was sold again in 1992.

TALKS BETWEEN THE THREE BIG INTERNATIONAL TRADING COMPANIES –
Finally, in addition to the take-overs surveyed until now, there have been mergers of whole concerns. These transactions carried most risk, because of their size, but also because of their impact on the entire corporate culture. The previous chapter has already mentioned the regular discussion between the three big former Dutch East Indian trading houses about potential mergers. As a rule, companies experiencing a momentary weakness took the initiative. Thus in 1984 Hagemeyer, urgently looking for new and profitable operations, sounded out Borsumij Wehry for its interest in merging. This proved not to be the case at all. Borsumij Wehry argued that the mutual agencies clashed, and that its interests in Indonesia could not be squared with those of the Liem Group, after all Hagemeyer's majority shareholder through First Pacific.[70] Figures 8.1 to 8.3 offer a comparison of developments at the three Dutch merchant houses with regards to turnover, staff, assets, and dividends.[71] To eliminate the effects of inflation as much as possible, turnover and profits have been recalculated into constant 1990 prices. The data on turnover clearly demonstrate the stagnation of the 1970s and the early 1980s, markedly so for Internatio and for Hagemeyer. Staff totals also reflects these developments. Hagemeyer embarked on a new and vigorous expansion in 1985, but Internatio followed this example as late as 1997. At Borsumij Wehry, both turnover and profits showed a fairly even upward trend, until its independent existence came to an end in 1995. Moreover, the profit figures demonstrate that Internatio suffered a severe loss still in 1991, whereas during those years Hagemeyer saw its rising turnover rewarded with equally rising profits.

Next, Hagemeyer and Internatio-Müller discussed merging. In this case the initiative had come from First Pacific, which had bought a substantial stake in Internatio-Müller in 1991, though without consulting Hagemeyer about this move beforehand. Hagemeyer nursed some doubts about the desirability of the proposal. On one hand, the board had a keen interest in the pharmaceutical wholesaler Interpharm, but on the other hand the recently acquired interests in electrotechnical wholesaling made a poor fit with Internatio-Müller fitting sub-

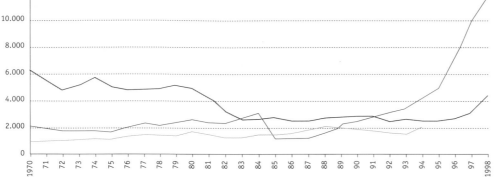

Figure 8.1

Turnover at three trading houses

(million guilders, constant 1990 prices)

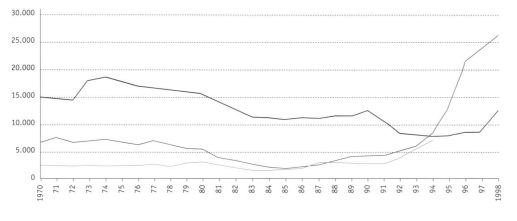

Figure 8.2

Staff numbers at three trading houses

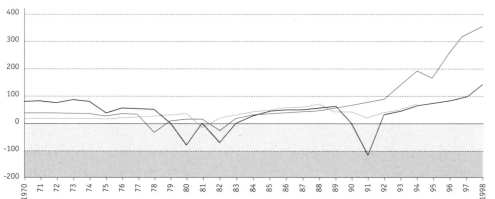

Figure 8.3

Profits at three trading houses

(million guilders, constant 1990 prices)

sidiaries. After all, some customers of the electrotechnical wholesalers competed head-to-head with Internatio-Müller subsidiaries, which could negatively affect wholesale turnover in case of a merger.[72] Internatio-Müller proved even less keen on a merger. Though the company was undergoing a reorganization process, the board preferred to get back on track without outside interference, and it had already drawn up a strategic plan towards achieving this.[73] In 1989, the motto had been growth through acquisitions, but two years later the management decided to shift the emphasis to reinforcing profitability. Internatio-Müller would subsequently focus on trade and fitting. The remaining manufacturing operations were sold. Transport was also no longer regarded as belonging to the core business, but when the planned sale of the ships' agency

HAGEMEYER

operations fell through, the board decided not just to hold on to them, but to begin an expansion. The new strategy brought closer integration to the fitting group, which was renamed to Imtech in 1993. Simultaneously the head office was trimmed back. In 1991 Internatio-Müller had to take a substantial loss in book valuations, the biggest in its history, partly because of the reorganization which had just begun, but profitability improved again subsequently. Led by P.J. Groenenboom, a former Philips manager, the company concentrated on providing integrated services, meaning, for instance, that projects commissioned could be supervised from the drawing room until final delivery, if the customer so desired. The technology division began to expand over the borders by acquiring companies in Belgium and in Germany. Internatio-Müller created an international network for its port handling operations. The pharmaceutical wholesaler also embarked on cross-border expansion. The trade in technical products, including the timber trade, were run down. By contrast, the chemical products trade was allowed to expand, and towards this end the company acquired British Petroleum's chemicals distribution business in 1998. As a consequence, Internatio-Müller returned to an expansionary phase from 1996, after performing poorly for many years.[74]

After 1991, talks between the three traders recurred regularly as before. There were even tripartite talks in 1994, codenamed Orange. McKinsey was to be commissioned to write a report about the prospects for this arrangement. Borsumij Wehry preferred a merger with Internatio-Müller, but developments were to take a different course.[75] During the 1990s, Borsumij Wehry worked hard to return to the right track. A very poor performance in 1991 had underlined the need to change tack. That year had seen a fierce price competition in consumer products, unleashed by bitterly disappointing sales in Eastern Europe. Borsumij Wehry's new CEO, Jan Noordam, had tried to keep a straight face, calling the losses accidental and inherent to trading companies, which in their essentially marginal existence always had had to reckon with regular ups and downs.[76] Even so, Borsumij Wehry decided to map a new course. In 1986 the company still had boasted with some pride that 85% of its turnover was in consumer products, and sold in Western Europe to boot. From now on, however, Borsumij Wehry began to strive for a greater geographical spread of operations, and a shift towards products other than consumer articles. Towards the latter end, Borsumij Wehry acquired Overtoom, a mail order company supplying office products and furnishings, canteen implements, storage necessities, and workshop fittings. This business achieved nation-wide brand recognition with a television commercial of a hooting delivery van and a customer exclaiming 'Hey, that's quick!'. Having been taken over by Borsumij Wehry, Overtoom gained permission to export its recipe to surrounding countries, but encountered more resistance than expected. Rather than continuing a solitary expansion, Overtoom sought and obtained a friendly take-over by the French company Manutan.[77] The acquisition of the technical wholesaler Stokvis also fitted in with Borsumij Wehry's attempts to reduce its dependence on consumer products, clearly keeping a watchful eye on the strategy followed by its rival Hagemeyer.[78] The expansion was shaped by acquisitions, the result being that about half of its operations had belonged to the company for less than five years by 1994.

Borsumij Wehry now began to raise capital for further acquisitions by floating subsidiaries on the stock exchange. Ceteco, a trader operating in Central and South America, was the first to go. The company had just been through a few turbulent years. In 1987, Ceteco had merged with Van Ommeren, assuming the ambitious name of voc. Perhaps the managers conducting the merger were not aware of the original voc's inglorious final downfall. Anyway, Ceteco did not prosper in the new combination. Turnover halved, and the results did not give much to cheer either. In 1992, Borsumij Wehry bought the now very

In 1983, Borsumij Wehry acquired Overtoom with the aim of expanding its business-to-business trade. The hoped-for international expansion of the Overtoom formula failed to materialise, however, so the company was sold in 1995. Borsumij Wehry's 1994 acquisition of Stokvis similarly aimed for an expansion of its business services.

much reduced company, attracted by its South American operations. Expectations were that the area would stabilise politically, and economic growth had meanwhile attained very decent levels. Even so, Borsumij Wehry's wish to spread risk made its board opt for a partial flotation of Ceteco.[79] This step also fitted in with a strategy giving subsidiaries greater independence. For other subsidiaries the board prepared partial flotations as well. In addition, Borsumij Wehry issued a subordinated debenture loan with warrants in December 1993.

This bond issue would have far reaching consequences for Borsumij Wehry, for the following year it brought the company's senior management into disrepute with accusations of insider share trading, since the issue had almost coincided with the acquisition of Stokvis. The stock exchange began to question transactions in warrants by a few Borsumij Wehry senior managers.[80] In the spring of 1995, the board decided to sound out Hagemeyer about a potential merger, even though the investigations were still pending.

At that moment Hagemeyer was experiencing a phase of vigorous expansion. In 1986 the company's CEO, Andrew Land, defined its strategy as expan-

362

sion by acquisitions. Autonomous growth was of course equally welcome, but according to Land this would not suffice to achieve critical mass at the right time. Land defined critical mass firstly as occupying a leading position in a particular market, with sufficient strength to counterbalance suppliers, customers, and competitors. Secondly, critical mass had organizational connotations, too. Each subsidiary had to have sufficient volume to be able to afford sound professional management, which could operate successfully with the tight budget controls introduced by Land into Hagemeyer. Subsidiaries which failed to make the grade were given the choice between accelerating growth or de-merger. Land also strove to achieve both stability and predictability in the company's performance. International trading companies, even those with Land's critical mass, could not influence some developments, such as macro-economic fluctuations, currency oscillations, or political vicissitudes. Companies could only try to spread their risks by geographical diversification. As mentioned above, Hagemeyer had targeted Europe, North America, and the Asia-Pacific area as the most attractive regions for its operations, because of their sound economic growth, political stability, and consumer spending power. However, the ups and downs of merchant houses are also strongly influenced by product life cycles, by the continuity or otherwise of the relations with their principals, and by seasonal factors. Such factors had to be anticipated by spreading operations over various product sectors and markets.[81] Translated into business terms, this meant that Hagemeyer reduced the overall importance of the agency-centred trade in consumer products in favour of the trade in professional products connecting numerous suppliers with numerous customers. Economic expansion and greater predictability were both key ingredients for the ultimate goal: realising an above average growth of profits per share for shareholders year-in year-out. With these principles, Hagemeyer had succeeded in realising an impressive growth in turnover and in profits between 1986 and 1994, achieving a size sufficient to approach other international traders for mergers. During the 1990s, the company held talks with the Danish East Asiatic Trading Company, and with the UK Inchcape group. None of these soundings led to anything, however.

Now, how did a merger with Borsumij Wehry fit into this strategy? Borsumij Wehry reinforced the emphasis on Europe, as it was somewhat heavy anyway. Through Ceteco, Borsumij Wehry offered an opening on the South American market, which until then Hagemeyer had branded as a not very attractive market. By 1994, Land had changed his mind somewhat, however, commenting that an international trader really needed a presence in South America. Finally, Borsumij Wehry contributed a package of agencies, whereas Hagemeyer had just begun a tentative withdrawal from this business. And Hagemeyer had no appetite at all for entering the fabrics trade which the merger would entail. Of course, Borsumij Wehry did possess some attractive subsidiaries which made a merger worthwhile considering, such as Stokvis, Fodor, and Pollyconcept. Yet the opportunity for making a forward leap in Hagemeyer's aspirations to achieve critical mass through a merger with

Borsumij Wehry outweighed any considerations about the individual sub-sidiaries. Moreover, the company's financial ratios would be strengthened by the merger. However, the risks also increased for, like Hagemeyer itself, Borsumij Wehry had strongly expanded through acquisitions during recent years. As a consequence, several subsidiaries had changed hands at least twice within a few years. This made it difficult for a new owner to obtain a proper understanding of what was going on, while such constant changes demotivated the incumbent management.

The Hagemeyer board must have felt a sense of triumph at being offered on a plate its nearest trade rival, which not only was much older, but which also had been much bigger and more successful than Hagemeyer for many years. In 1977, the Hagemeyer board had opined that Borsumij Wehry would not be ripe for acquisition for as long as the Schlimmer family had a say in the company.[82] In 1990 J.H. Schlimmer, grandson of the company's founder J.W. Schlimmer, retired as supervisory director, and five years later the board put Borsumij Wehry up for sale. An opportunity not to be missed, Land reacted.[83] Following the definitions of the economist Hans Schenk, professor at the Katholieke Universiteit Brabant, this merger was a typical battle for market position centring on independence and reputation, rather than on the creation of economic value.[84] In May 1995, Hagemeyer issued a provisional bid on the Borsumij Wehry equity, proposing to effect the transaction by a share swap using newly issued Hagemeyer shares. In September, after the definitive bid had been issued, 99% of the Borsumij Wehry shareholders accepted the conditions. The process of integration could now begin.

INTEGRATING TWO TRADING COMPANIES – Taking over a trading company is comparatively simple, Andrew Land told a journalist of the business magazine *FEM* in 1992. There is no laborious process of integrating different production processes, and Hagemeyer gives its subsidiaries a free rein to grow and prosper in their respective markets. The Hagemeyer name serves a purpose in the financial world alone.[85] Both Hagemeyer and Borsumij Wehry had small head offices and largely independent subsidiaries, so integrating the Borsumij Wehry companies into the Hagemeyer organization proved fairly simple in that respect. Still, the two companies did have a different approach, which could largely be reduced to differences in cohesion and in discipline.

The international traders had always allowed their managers operating abroad a large degree of freedom, a necessity grown from business practice. The Dutch head offices were seldom in a position to assess situations on the ground

properly, and thus had to rely on the judgement of their local managers. Head offices allowed managers who succeeded in building up a profitable business, which they often achieved through a personal network of acquaintances and friends, a free hand in expanding their operations. With admiration and appreciation, the head offices would each year collect the profits which these creative and dynamic managers generated. As a downside, the trading companies sprouted little kingdoms operating as if no head office existed. This was not a great problem as long as profits kept flowing, but once turnover or performance began to decline, the head offices found it exceedingly difficult to take appropriate actions. Usually, the energetic managers on the spot initially responded by denying the seriousness of the situation, playing down the matter as a temporary setback with things now back under control. If the situation worsened, boards tended to issue guidelines. However, managers which for years and years had become used to running their own business in complete independence, did not accept such interference. They were the experts on the spot, after all. Dutch boards then had no other option but to fire their intractable manager, yet as a rule this did little to solve the problems of the subsidiary. On the contrary, the manager concerned had personally moulded the business to such a degree, that successors had a hard time taking over.

From 1985, Land and his chief financial officer Phil Betsch had introduced a stringent budget system within Hagemeyer to give head office a better grip on its subsidiaries. Managers of the subsidiaries were made entirely accountable for their budgets. They were summoned to Naarden to defend their proposed budgets, and they had to account for any deviations at the end of term. Moreover, modern information technology enabled head office to follow turnover and performance and to discuss them with managers more or less on a daily basis. As a consequence, the board could take action much quicker when business flagged.[86] It did so, too, without hesitation, convinced of the commercial wisdom that taking losses early keeps them small. In addition, the board set up an International Policy Council in 1989, made up of the CEOs of the main subsidiaries. The Council met every quarter to discuss the common strategy and the situation at the various subsidiaries, thus boosting the company's internal cohesion. It took some years before the organization became used to the new budget discipline. The system fostered a different type of manager. Smooth salesmen no longer came top, but instead managers who could interpret financial data and act accordingly. Developing initiative and focusing on performance remained important: stand and deliver, became the message, and that meant achieving the often ambitious targets. Work hard, earn good money, and create value for shareholders was Hagemeyer's corporate culture in those days. In 1992, the Hagemeyer staff magazine published a fable summarising this attitude, entitled the competitor's creed:

'Every morning when the sun comes up, the gazelle wakes, and he knows that he will have to outrun the fastest lion, or he will be eaten. When the sun comes up, the lion also wakes. He knows that he must outrun the slowest gazelle or he will starve. In the end it does not really matter whether you are a lion or a gazelle. When the sun comes up, you'd better be running.'[87]

Though Borsumij Wehry had changed tack somewhat later than Hagemeyer, the company was really treading the same road. During the early 1990s, an atmosphere of small kingdoms and individual privileges still hung around. Some successful managers could be approached only with great circumspection. From 1992, Noordam attempted to end this situation, introducing a business plan towards this end. Some veteran managers had never worked in this way before, and they clearly had difficulty in getting used to it. Borsumij Wehry also set up a Policy Council to get a wider group of managers involved with the business strategy. For the managers of Borsumij Wehry subsidiaries, the merger with Hagemeyer reinforced a trend towards tighter budget disciplines which had already begun. Thus Borsumij Wehry had been accustomed to quarterly reports, whereas this became monthly when Hagemeyer took over. Internatio-Müller, by the way, operated with similar controls through budgets. In an interview, Groenenboom commented on the stringency of this system, the seriousness of budget

The atmosphere of the 1990s was one of scrambling for existence, with awards for outstanding customer service increasing the pressure to perform.

discussions sealed by drinking life-giving elixirs, the commitment to agreed targets, and his impatience with excuses if these were not met.[88]

In the end, none of Borsumij Wehry's executives or supervisory directors were given a seat on one of Hagemeyer's boards, though J. Noordam and A.J. van der Graaf both acted as advisers for some time. Perhaps the difference in corporate culture was also responsible for the small number of staff moving from the Borsumij Wehry head office to Hagemeyer. For them, it was a considerable change indeed from the stately head office on the Carnegielaan in the Hague to Hagemeyer's functional offices alongside a motorway near Naarden. The Borsumij Wehry staff must have been disappointed that it was Hagemeyer taking over Borsumij Wehry and not the other way around, which for many years had been far more likely to happen. Most Borsumij Wehry subsidiaries could continue their operations as before, the fabrics division excepted. One part of it managed to establish itself as an independent business, the rest was shut. In a few isolated cases subsidiaries of Borsumij Wehry merged with Hagemeyer companies, as happened between Borsumij Wehry's Stokvis and Hagemeyer's ARM.

The history of Stokvis demonstrates how some companies wander from one holding to the next, now being stripped, now being rebuilt in the process. Stokvis is a remarkable example indeed. At the beginning of the 20th century it was a proud technical wholesaler with international prestige, quoted on the stock exchange and possessing its own production plants. When taken over by OGEM in 1972, the company disintegrated into several parts, with its fitting division ending up as part of the Technische Unie. Its international trade operations merged with Lindeteves into OGEM Trade International or OTI. After OGEM had collapsed, OTI appeared doomed to go down with it as not viable to continue on its own, until the Gulf Group of the Pakistani Gokal brothers presented itself as a buyer. When this group also ran into trouble, the Stokvis companies plus some Lindeteves subsidiaries were acquired by an investment company of the NMB bank. In 1993, the assembly was bought by G. van den Brink, who in his turn sold it on to Borsumij Wehry.[89] Finally, Hagemeyer merged Stokvis with its ARM subsidiary. This latter company, founded under the name of Amsterdamsche Rijtuig Maatschappij, had a less exciting past, though in 1964 it had almost passed into the hands of Reindert Zwolsman, a controversial business tycoon of the time. ARM was founded in 1881 as a company for hiring carriages with horses and coachmen, and it continued in the transport sector since then, leasing cars, running garages, and running marketing agencies for well-known brands such as Saab and Renault. In 1988, Hagemeyer acquired the business.[90] During recent years, the ARM-Stokvis combination succeeded in realising a substantial growth of turnover and profits.

Financing the merger between Hagemeyer and Borsumij Wehry required much ingenuity. Hagemeyer had built up some considerable skills in this respect during the preceding years.[91] The Borsumij Wehry take-over raised a problem in as much as Hagemeyer's majority shareholder, First Pacific, wanted to retain its

stake so it could keep the Hagemeyer results in its consolidated accounts. Hagemeyer's strong expansion forced First Pacific to buy ever more shares each time
its subsidiary financed a new acquisition by issuing new shares. With the acquisition of Borsumij Wehry First Pacific reached its limit. A creative solution had
to be found, resulting in the issuing of cumulative preferential shares by a foundation designed for this purpose, the Stichting Administratiekantoor Preferente
Aandelen Hagemeyer. The shares were placed with institutional investors, but
the foundation retained the voting rights tied to them, and used these in accordance with First Pacific's instructions. Thus First Pacific could retain its formal
say, even though its stake had meanwhile declined to 39.7%.[92]

Two years later, the situation had already changed completely. With an
economic recession hitting Asia, First Pacific wanted to sell its Hagemeyer
shares. A merger with KNP-BT, a conglomerate of paper manufacturing and
trading with a wholesale business in office products which had just begun to
split itself into separate units, appeared to offer an elegant way out. The respective executive boards, which had used the same office building during the preceding years, had already drafted a blueprint of the new company, but the negotiations foundered in meetings between the supervisory boards. This made First
Pacific and Hagemeyer decide to put the former's very considerable share holding on the market. In March 1998, a publicity campaign accompanying the
resale focused on marketing and logistic services as Hagemeyer's dedicated
skills.[93] Securities analysts were very positive about Hagemeyer in general, and
about the company's presence in South America in particular. The merchant
bank MeesPierson, for instance, wrote in February 1998:

> 'One of Hagemeyer's major strengths is its balanced spread of activities
> across geographic regions and product cycles, which reduces the risk of heavy
> exposure in certain areas. As an illustration, whereas certain Asian countries
> are in difficulties, Latin American business is still buoyant, the US economy
> continues to grow strongly and the outlook for Europe is brightening'

With regards to South America, the bank's analysts concluded: 'no real threat
expected, but sentiment might be weak'.[94] First Pacific's shares were successfully
resold, but then some dark clouds began to gather above Hagemeyer's Ceteco
subsidiary. The Asian economic recession spread to South America, leading to a
serious drop in turnover. The situation worsened when during the autumn of
1998 two hurricanes, named George and Mitch, created havoc in the Domini-
can Republic and in Central America. Ceteco, also termed 'a bank which also
sells washing machines', was confronted with numerous debtors unable to meet
their obligations. Despite a 66% stake in the company, Hagemeyer considered
Ceteco as a financial participation, yet tried to keep it going by providing financial support. In 1999, once Ceteco had filed for bankruptcy, however, Hagemeyer wrote off its entire stake. Over the first six months of 1999, the company had
to announce its first loss in fifteen years.

A girl carrying a plank inscribed 'Capital' in the city of Tegucigalpa, Honduras, amidst the devastation caused by the hurricane Mitch in 1998. Natural disasters that hit Central America contributed to Ceteco having to apply for a suspension of payments in 1999.

The predictability of performance remained difficult to achieve, notwithstanding the spread of operations over various regions and products. With the Borsumij Wehry take-over, Hagemeyer had unmistakably bought into some problems. However, the company also had reason to establish with some satisfaction that after a century, it had become the most successful Dutch international trader. Hagemeyer now was really one of the few companies remaining from the rich colonial past. The journalists Van Hezewijk and Metze ranked the company fourth in their list of the 25 best performing businesses over the years 1982 1997, taking increases in market capitalisation and/or equity as measure. Only the insurer Achmea Groep, the fabrics producer Schuttersveld, and publishers Reed Elsevier had done better. Van Hezewijk and Metze failed to explain Hagemeyer's success, though they did indicate that the leaders of successful companies, such as Andrew Land, were able to lay down a clear strategy, and to hold on to it. They also knew how to overcome setbacks.[95] If we analyse the operations with which Hagemeyer earned its rising turnover and profits per share, it becomes clear that for most years, autonomous growth lagged behind growth bought by acquisitions. Consequently, Hagemeyer has succeeded during the past years in obtaining a large number of companies which contributed positively to the overall results within a short time. In addition, insufficiently profitable operations were systematically demerged. A necessarily provisional assessment suggests that the electrotechnical wholesale operations, and more in particular the purposeful expansion of this division to a group of European calibre, provides the key to Hagemeyer's recent successes.

In 1997, the list of leading Dutch companies showed wholesaling undergoing considerable change. The wholesalers in paper and printing equipment VRG and Bührmann-Tetterode had merged in 1992 with the paper producers Nederlandse Papierfabrieken into KNP-BT, but this combination had meanwhile started to disintegrate, from which Buhrmann emerged as a specialised wholesaler. SHV had sold nearly all of its retail operations, consequently shifting its focus back to the energy sector. Borsumij Wehry had been taken over, as mentioned, by Hagemeyer.[96] Except for Internatio-Müller all other wholesalers on the list, such as OTRA, OPG, and Van Dorp-Despec, came into the category of specialised wholesalers. Thus Hagemeyer formed an exception in that respect. From an international perspective, it is also one of the very few merchant houses to uphold the principle of bringing various products, marketing approaches, and countries together in a single company. Most of the comparable British international traders have disappeared during the last twenty years, having sold their operations in Latin America, Africa, and Asia to local companies or investors. Other firms disintegrated into their component parts under the pressure of the UK capital market with its demands for a clear focus and annual profit rises.[97] Hagemeyer continues to strive for a marked international spread of operations. However, in the strategy as defined in 1999 by the board under its new chairman Rob ter Haar, Hagemeyer will concentrate more than before on professional markets, and will place more emphasis than in the past on developing into a specialised service provider. Creating synergy between similarly focused subsidiaries has meanwhile been given high priority.[98]

The tiles which adorned Hagemeyer's first office in Surabaya were shipped to the Netherlands when the company had to leave Indonesia.

The archer with the motto 'We strike home' is the centrepiece, the words expressing the essential optimism which is natural to traders.

At the end of the 20th century, we may conclude that, by virtue of constantly renewing and adapting their business, independent trading companies continue to provide key links in the chain from producer to consumer. Trading companies returned to their function as intermediary as their core business. During the 1980s and 1990s, the merchant houses succeeded only partially in resuscitating their trusted agency recipe. A strategy of proprietary brands only yielded satisfactory results in niche markets. For the 1990s, the successful recipe was raising the traditional local wholesaling to a European level. Specialised wholesalers had already begun to adopt this approach, but an international trader such as Hagemeyer succeeded in realising it on a large scale within a short time. The logical next step is to raise specialised wholesaling from its European scale to a world level.

The rhythm of goods transport used to be determined by the force of the wind, or the power of horse and man. By the turn of the 20th century, loading and unloading ships had become a 24-hour business, computerised but still controlled by operators, such as here at the Rotterdam ECT terminal. Inset: a detail from Johannes Lingelbach's painting of the Dam with the fish market, 1656.

Conclusion

This book has traced the development of Dutch merchant houses over a span of more than four centuries, from the dawn of the Golden Age up to the threats and opportunities created by modern information technology. In the final analysis, how vulnerable were the traders, or how strong? As intermediaries, were they puppets on the strings of market parties, or did they control markets as spiders from their web? Were they parasites, redundant links in the chain, or did they really perform an essential economic function? We have analysed how the position of trading houses in the supply chain changed over time, with trading firms responding now by specialization, now by integration and diversification. This book focused particularly on traders handling different products between various countries. The conclusion will take a closer look at three forces bearing on the performance of merchant houses throughout the ages: political circumstances, the relationship between trade and industry, and developments in communication. Political circumstances greatly affected product flows. The rise of corporate industry relegated traders into second position as dynamic forces. The revolution in communication accelerated both product flows and information exchanges, creating new opportunities for interaction between them. In close mutual interaction, these three forces drew the boundary lines within which the trading houses had to find their way.

THE POLITICAL CIRCUMSTANCES – Political factors were a key force affecting the development of merchant houses. Wars, protectionism, and government privileges continuously created obstacles, but such restrictions could also work as incentives for finding new ways or developing new business schemes. Some traders proved better at this than others, resulting in a continuous coming and going of firms, reputable names disappearing while newcomers gained a place in the sun.

For example, the fall of Antwerp and the blockade of the river Scheldt in 1585 boosted the rise of Amsterdam as the hub of world trade, but a transfer of business from Antwerp to Amsterdam predated it. Initially, Dutch merchants operated on their own, or in small family partnerships. They succeeded in building up a strong position in the Baltic trade by developing a transport concept making effective use of the Dutch Republic's favourable geographic location. A strong shipping sector subsequently enabled the merchants to expand their commercial entrenchment by seizing hold of the trade routes between North and South Europe. The Amsterdam city fathers proved exceedingly active in promoting their city's business climate by developing initiatives in the field of insurance, exchange facilities, a price current, and money. Such official initiatives helped to make markets more transparent, in turn boosting economic growth. The support for business did not remain limited to general measures. Licences, charters, and official monopolies were designed to foster the commercial interests of insiders over those of outsiders. The most striking example of such a privilege is the voc, a public limited company uniting commercial aims with military purposes. Around 1650, the Republic reached the summit of its economic and political power. Mighty merchant houses directed a flow of products from around the world to the Republic, and redistributed them among customers all over Europe. The merchant represented the nation's self-image.

This leading position could not but inspire envy and competition in neighbouring countries. As a consequence, the Republic was embroiled in endless trade wars and specifically targeted protectionism, particularly from the side of Britain and France. The country could not keep up with the rate of economic growth in surrounding countries, either. Finding ship crews alone imposed clear limits, which even the drafting of large numbers of immigrants failed to alleviate. Office staff was no problem, by the way, for until well into the 19th century the work could be done with a few clerks. During the 18th century, Dutch trade shifted from expansion to consolidation. Merchants defended their position vigorously now, by switching to commission trading and by developing dedicated services. Thus ship owners and ships' agents became separate occupations. This specialization meant a decline of trading for own account, but it promoted an increase in the services provided to foreign traders. For a long time, the Republic maintained a leading position in financial services. Even so London, with its rising political power and its much bigger hinterland, gradually took over Amsterdam's hub function.

The recurrent wars during the 17th and 18th centuries were less ruinous to trade than one might have thought. Wars not only offered ready opportunities for an extensive arms trade, but they also pushed up prices in all sectors, so risks and profits rose more or less in tandem. Moreover, a large volume of transport could be kept going by using flags of convenience and false ships' papers. The Napoleonic wars wrought distinct changes here. During 1812, Dutch overseas trade was forced to an almost complete standstill by a British naval blockade and by French occupying forces who kept a tight grip on the sea ports from the land side. This period also introduced merchants to the need of having to spend more time in obtaining licences, concessions, and permits, than in finding suppliers and customers, a phenomenon which was to return in ever more pronounced forms in subsequent wars. During the First World War, the merchants' administrative chores would assume enormous proportions, even though the Netherlands itself was not a belligerent. In the Second World War, the Dutch merchant firms lost all contact with their overseas branches, and not even paper forms could offer any solace. Only the international traders located outside occupied territory could maintain a profitable business in the Second World War.

On 17th-century paintings of the Dam Square, merchants figured prominently, especially foreign ones. M. Monnickendam painted this colourful city scene of the square with on the right the exchange built by J.D. Zocher in 1903, the year in which the building was demolished.

Government policy now fostered, now hindered the development of merchant houses. After the French occupation, for instance, King William I attempted to revive Dutch trade and industry with targeted government support. For private merchants, this policy was counterproductive, though. They only returned to a new phase of prosperity when world trade began to be freed from the shackles of chauvinist protection and favours. Transit traffic along the Rhine boomed, and for the colonial trading houses it appeared as if the heydays of yore had returned. They profited unmistakably from the increasingly close ties developing between the Netherlands and its overseas colony in Asia. The merchant houses expanded their operations in the Dutch East Indies from trade to the management and ownership of plantation companies, or agencies for shipping companies and insurers. Sometimes these firms also developed banking functions. The international traders' success in expanding their operations derived from their know-how of local circumstances and from the strong demand for entrepreneurship in the fast growing economy of the Dutch East Indies.

The return of protection after the First World War was generally unfavourable for the international traders, if only because the Netherlands continued its free trade policies for a considerable time still. This changed during the 1930s, when the government began to protect both Dutch agriculture and the colonial economic interests. Trading houses profited from this protection as far as their representation of Dutch industry stretched, but their imports of Japanese products suffered. The trade barriers erected around the Dutch East Indian market inspired the traders to set up links with import substitution industries.

When the process of decolonization began after the Second World War, the international traders saw themselves confronted with a distinct reversal in their business. Having belonged to the world of the colonisers, they were now branded as hostile strangers, guests in a foreign country having to adapt to local rules and customs. The interests of the Indonesian population came first, and this did not necessarily mean the objective interests, but only the interests as interpreted by the new nationalist governments. When they eventually lost their possessions in Indonesia, the merchant houses were thrown back a long way, especially those with large plantation interests. The Dutch houses now faced increasing uncertainties, both politically and financially. In addition, they experienced difficulties with the transfer of profits, with employment permits for foreign staff, and with systematic advantages granted to local entrepreneurs. This required a great deal of flexibility and resilience from the international traders. In the long run, many firms proved insufficiently equipped or insufficiently inclined to continue operating in such conditions.

Considering the strong impact of political circumstances on the performance of trading houses, it would appear obvious to suppose that the firms tried to win political influence. Did they gain access to the networks of politicians and civil servants, though? During the 17th century, merchants generally maintained close links with officials to obtain privileges and defend their interests. As a rule, both merchants and officials belonged to the same social layer anyway. And yet traders did not always get their way, for their interests always varied, and thus could conflict. It would appear as if the international traders lost their interest in gaining political influence once the Netherlands had lost its position as a world power. As if they doubted whether the Dutch government could really do anything to support them. The directors of the big plantation companies, the banks, and the shipping companies with colonial interests jousted with government departments to defend their interests, but the directors of merchant houses were far less active, unless they had plantation interests. During the 1930s traders seldom visited the Dutch government offices, contrary to the representatives of farming and industry. After the Second World War, firms such as Hagemeyer on principle never joined trade missions to countries in which they had a subsidiary. The traders probably preferred to pickle their own onions.

THE LINKS BETWEEN TRADE AND INDUSTRY – During the 16th century, trade began to assume a key role in promoting export industries. Until the late Middle Ages, merchants had largely limited their operations to handling goods with a ratio of value to volume, trading them over a series of intermediate stations. Ships' masters and merchants from Holland and West Friesland developed a radically different concept for the Baltic trade, i.e. bulk transport as directly as possible to the Netherlands, linked to the processing of raw materials and semi-finished products to export products by Dutch industry. During the 16th and

From the 1870s, the international traders came into their own again, profiting from the ties between the Netherlands and the Dutch East Indies. Geo. Wehry was one of the firms spotting the new opportunities. The company celebrated its 50th anniversary in 1917, and on this occasion the staff donated the commemorative plaque pictured here.

17th centuries, the merchants adopted this scheme for one market after another, until the Republic controlled the supply of goods from all corners of the earth. This situation did not last for very long. Competitors copied the successful scheme, and protectionism eliminated the Republic's comparative cost advantage. The detour via the entrepot market gradually became too expensive compared to direct transport from producer to consumer. Even so, Dutch merchant houses managed to retain a strong grip on international product flows by further specialising their services. The levels of foreign trade and of the allied services remained very high for another century at least. However, meanwhile the once powerful processing industry crumbled, robbed of the supply and demand on which it had once fed.

After the French occupation, the merchant houses attempted to regain their position. They struggled in vain against the entrenched power of the British market, if only because the Netherlands produced little in the way of suitable export products by this time. The German hinterland remained under lock and key as a result of a political dispute about mutual market access. Important producers such as the US had meanwhile acquired sufficient commercial skills of their own to act as wholesalers. This left the Dutch international traders very little room indeed, only the Dutch East Indies continued to offer some opportunities. By 1850 a new phase dawned. Traders in an increasing number of producing countries began to do their own wholesaling, stimulated by technological revolutions such as the telegraph and more efficient steam shipping.

With the rise of corporate industry, manufacturers joined merchants as the dynamic driving forces of business. From the 16th century, the task of bringing new products to the attention of consumers had fallen to merchants. The rise of corporate industry seized part of that function from traders, and gave it to manufacturers. Industrial producers now became the sources of innovation, or at least the creators of products with features suggesting innovation, not just on a local scale, but on a large scale and for large groups of consumers. The introduction of branding underlined the particular properties of manufactured products. Manufacturers could establish a direct link with their customers using publicity, reducing traders to the more modest role of intermediary. Whether or not manufacturers would use these services came to depend on circumstances. Industry posed a potential threat to wholesaling, enhanced by the rise of retail chains which accompanied industrialization. Traders could easily get squeezed between these two links in the chain from producer to consumer. Predictions about the imminent elimination of wholesaling surfaced time and again.

However, during the years 1870-1914 this remained a latent problem because of sufficient economic expansion and free trade. Industry could rely on trade, both for supplying raw materials and for marketing its products, so manufacturers felt no great urge to perform these functions themselves. Indeed, industrialization created entirely new opportunities for the merchant houses: operating as marketing agents for industrial products. Both parties came to

Industrialisation and the rise of mass consumption posed a double threat to merchant houses, with both manufacturing and retail chains making inroads on classic wholesale functions. The manufacturer Perry & Co. bypassed wholesalers by setting up his own retail outlets to sell his products.

strive for an exclusive relationship applying to a certain geographical area. Operating as agents for manufacturers was an attractive option for the international traders, but also a delicate one. Firms which failed to achieve reasonable sales for their principals, the manufacturers, were bypassed without much ado. If they did succeed in creating a substantial turnover they also risked being dumped, having made their principals dependent on sales to such a degree that the latter preferred to take up marketing themselves.

The Great War rather changed the relations between traders and manufacturers. Trade restrictions caused by the war inspired industry to turn its attention to securing supplies and sales by integrating trade functions. Wholesalers felt themselves threatened, and with some reason. Some manufacturers really integrated some trade functions, though the urge to do so rapidly declined again during the prosperous latter half of the 1920s. Traders still had enough do to, however. Firstly, because industrialization continued to push up the number of transactions. Secondly, because trade remained an attractive marketing channel for reasons of the services offered, such as selecting products into ranges, keeping stock, and extending credit. Economic fluctuations also had an impact on the degree to which traders and manufacturers tended to collaborate or to begin integration of each others' functions. During the 1930s depression, the emphasis clearly shifted to collaboration, and not to integration. This derived from a desire for mutual solidarity on one hand, and on the other from companies in hard times shying away from additional responsibilities. Consequently, trade and industry supported each other by entering into cartel agreements, but deliberately stopped short of merging. In the Dutch East Indies, collaboration tended to lead to joint-ventures, and not to integration either.

After the Second World War, Dutch hopes of economic prosperity focused on industry as the main provider. There was hardly any interest in the

378

specific needs and desires of merchant houses. The decolonization process fundamentally changed their business, however. As a result the traders shifted their attention from the Third World to the wealthy western world. During the 1950s and 1960s, Europe and the us experienced tempestuous economic growth, which the trading houses were keen to join in. The range of products which average households desired to possess in order to feel happy multiplied. In principle, all these products and the transactions related to production and distribution could create new opportunities for trade, from the supply of raw materials and semi-finished products to marketing final products. During the second half of the 1960s, increasing competition coincided with economic prospects remaining favourable. In such situations it becomes attractive for companies to integrate or to diversify their operations. By the mid-1960s a process of integration and conglomerate building did indeed begin. Some trading houses enthusiastically joined it, partly motivated by a desire to spread risk, in which case the manufacturing operations and trade not necessarily had to form an extension to each other. However, the traders also partly strove for vertical integration, expecting to realise voluminous sales through their international marketing network, and conversely, to support their marketing network with consumer goods from their own plants. However, the combination of trade and industry proved a failure. Following acquisition, the manufacturing companies that were taken over often had to be radically reorganised immediately, which entailed arduous rounds of job cuts. In the atmosphere of the early 1970s redundancies were socially acceptable only when the survival of the entire company hung in the balance. The merchant houses failed to achieve much in the way of increased sales through their international marketing network. Running a manufacturing plant also proved to be entirely different from managing a trading company. Traders are by nature optimistic and opportunistic, accustomed to react rapidly and flexibly to signs coming from the market. By contrast, manufacturers adhere to long term developments, because of their substantial fixed investments, and they have to anticipate, because production processes cannot be changed at short notice. Possibly the traders, newcomers to industry after all, did not buy the right companies. The economic cycle turned against them, moreover, with the whole of Dutch industry entering a difficult phase after the first oil crisis in 1973.

From the perspective of manufacturing, integration and conglomerate building were not a decisive success either. Joining forces with trade proved no guarantee for continuity and profitability. Consequently, trade and manufacturing distanced themselves from each other again, both returning to concentrate on their respective core businesses. During the 1990s, the traders even began to extend their services to manufacturers, perhaps reflecting that industry increasingly relied on market forces following a new period of economic growth. Outsourcing operations, by the way, concerned the supply of raw materials and semi-finished products more than the marketing of final products. The rise of newly industrialised countries also offered the merchant houses attractive

International traders succeeded in creating new functions by acting as agents for manufacturing industry, in particular on remote markets such as those in African countries. The heart on the label of this Dutch gin bottle may indicate that the company acted for the well-known De Kuyper gin brand in Africa, or perhaps the NAHV had simply imitated its label.

379

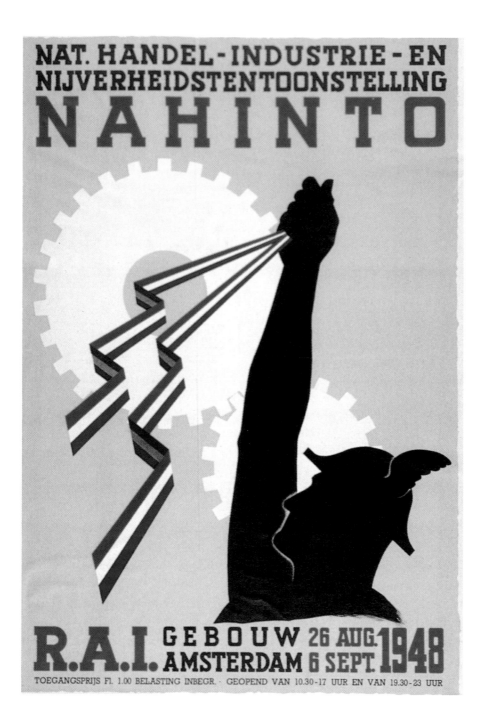

A publicity poster for the national trade fair for trade, industry, and crafts, held in 1948 in the Amsterdam RAI halls. The official designation NAHINTO may have put trade first, but during the post-war reconstruction of the Dutch economy, industry attracted most attention as the sector on which all hopes were pinned.

opportunities for expanding their operations, in addition to the outsourcing by manufacturers. Thus industrialization has not, on balance, eliminated trade.

Threats to trade did not come from industry alone, but also from retailing. The rise of retail chains and joint purchasing organizations has unmistakably seized part of the wholesale functions. Just like the trading houses, retail companies also became converts to owning their own manufacturing plants during the 1960s, and these operations were gradually terminated again, too. During the 1990s, retail chains increased their power considerably by the formation of international companies. As a consequence, international traders such as Hagemeyer increasingly focused on providing services to businesses.

CHANGES IN COMMUNICATION – The communications options open to the various links in the logistic chain, of course, have an impact on the functioning of the intermediaries effecting transactions between them. This holds true for both the flow of information and for the actual flow of products. Wars and protectionism could alter those flows, but technological developments were at least as important. Thus Amsterdam's rise as a hub of the entrepot trade was favoured by the overland trade declining in importance against maritime trade, for which this city was excellently located. The development of the fluyt ship enabled Dutch merchants to profit twice over from the rising importance of maritime trade, for the low operating costs of this vessel gave them a large competitive advantage over the foreign competition. The dense trade network to all corners of the earth translated into frequent and regular communications, a very positive influence on the business climate. After 1650 shipping no longer functioned as a driver for economic expansion, but the development of smaller ships brought a further rise in crew productivity, relieving pressure on a scarce production factor at that time. Moreover, smaller ships could also hug coast lines, offering greater protection in war time. The era of cheap bulk transport overland arrived with the railways in the 19th century, and more or less simultaneously steam shipping considerably increased the speed and regularity of maritime transport.

The invention of the magnetic telegraph meant an exceedingly important breakthrough in communications, reducing the speed of information flows from months, weeks, and days, to hours or even minutes. As early as the 16th century the papers embodying transactions not necessarily accompanied the goods which they covered, but the speed of conveying both messages and goods remained more or less equal. The telegraph brought a decisive change here. The information about prices and about sales opportunities could now be connected almost instantaneously, reducing the risk of transactions. This boosted turnover,

The Batavia telegraph office around 1900. The telegraph provided faster connections between production, prices, and sales, an evident advantage in trade between the Dutch East Indies and the Netherlands.

in turn lowering margins. Though the merchant houses continued to operate in the commodity trade for many more years, this sector increasingly became the domain of specialised companies, which often also had interests in the respective regions of production.

The telegraph favoured a type of trading house serving overseas markets with goods purchased in their original home country. Dutch traders usually had a head office in the Netherlands to purchase goods from manufacturers all over Europe, and to arrange finance and transport, acting on orders from their overseas subsidiaries. However, the telegraph was expensive to use, and its messages were open to scrutiny by outsiders. Consequently, firms developed codes open to initiates only, which meant that the telegraph fostered intra-company communications first of all.

The telephone and wireless communications supplemented the changes wrought by the telegraph, but they also reduced the exclusivity of rapid communications. This also held true for the rise of air transport, which not just accelerated the mail, but enabled people to travel faster between countries and continents, too. Trading houses felt the impact on their operations: it became ever easier and cheaper for importers to get in touch with overseas manufacturers. A rapid exchange of information by telegraph required knowledge of each others' codes, but the telephone did away with the need for that. Air travel, moreover, brought managers of manufacturing companies within ever closer reach of countries supplying raw materials, or key sales regions. After the Second World

The Sail Amsterdam manifestation offers every opportunity to marvel at the historical development of maritime sail transport. In 1995, a number of vintage sailing vessels arrived in Amsterdam harbour, led by a replica of a VOC ship and accompanied by thousands of smaller vessels.

War, these effects gradually manifested themselves. Manufacturers discarded traders as redundant intermediaries, but the business organization of the merchant houses themselves changed as well. In the 1930s it had still been efficient for them to concentrate European purchases in the Netherlands, because it was faster and cheaper to communicate within Europe from that single point than it was between Asia and Europe. During the 1950s and 1960s, however, the marketing subsidiaries increasingly began to bypass their head-office and place orders directly in Europe or elsewhere. This gave the overseas offices a greater independence, and reduced the advantages of having a network of branches, a change which actually occurred very gradually.

By that time the merchant houses no longer concentrated either on directing raw materials from Third World countries to the wealthy western world, and manufacturing products from Europe and the US to Third World countries. From the 1950s, Japan and other Asian countries began to supply increasing volumes of industrial products to Europe. Improvements to maritime transport boosted this process, because more goods could be shipped to Europe at lower cost. The spread of container shipping made a notable contribution to lowering cost, which really meant that manufacturing products could compete over longer distances. The merchant houses of Borsumij and Hagemeyer both took an active lead in marketing products from Japan and from other Asian countries in Europe. Such agencies, however, had an inherent vulnerability in the fundamental dependence of the agent on his principal.

Information technology drives the latest revolution in communications. The ability to monitor the supply chain from beginning to end with computers and networks offers unparalleled opportunities to integrate and to control the chain. Staying outside a network means running the risk of being excluded

The telephone and air travel posed new threats to the international traders by cutting distances between suppliers and customers.

altogether, for the Internet, after all, makes markets ever more transparent. However, rising information volumes create problems of selection, a key traditional function of wholesaling. Moreover, in the end goods will have to be transported, cleared for customs, stored, and delivered: all functions of traders. Of course, traders may expect competition from logistic service providers entering the same field. As things stand, however, the merchant houses have fully embraced information technology, determined to expand their services by creative mining of the opportunities offered by the world wide web.

THE TRADING HOUSES AFTER FOUR CENTURIES – By the end of the 20th century the firms on which this book focused, operating in various types of products in various countries, appear to have almost disappeared from the Netherlands. Its last representative was Hagemeyer, but that company has opted for a new strategy in the 21st century. This strategy features specialization on a limited number of sectors, though still in a multitude of countries. The Netherlands now looks likely to follow the road taken by the UK, where the old mer-

chant houses have already either disappeared completely, or have disintegrated into their constituent parts. Of course this does not mean that traders operating internationally have disappeared, only international traders with diverse operations have. The internationalization of trade appears to be increasing continuously. On one hand, internationally operating Hagemeyer turns out to be specialising, while on the other the specialised wholesalers have begun to internationalise, in a restless process of adaptation and change which fully characterises trade.

A trader's work really boils down to knowing consumer preferences, retail markets, purchasing markets, products, the logistic opportunities and obstacles, local customs, and local politics. It is all-important to know about people and openings, and to devise practical solutions for them. If all is well, traders will have a lead in such knowledge, while simultaneously realising that it cannot be protected or monopolised. Others can acquire the same information, enter the market concerned and reduce profit margins to such a degree that to retire becomes the only solution. At that moment traders will have to start searching for a new perspective, a new product, a new market, or a new marketing approach. These circumstances explain why merchant houses survive only by continuously shifting their focus. Knowing openings, knowing how to organise efficiently and how to react flexibly to new opportunities, that is the hallmark of trade, and the hallmark of traders feeling at home on the world markets. For each door that closes a new one opens somewhere, but traders will have to succeed in finding it, and then make up their own mind whether or not to pass through it.

385

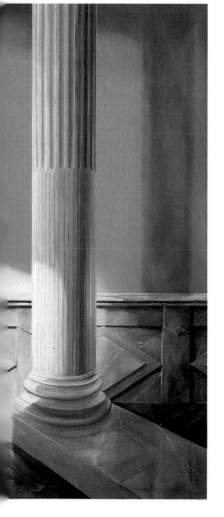

'The spirit of free trade', a painting by Max Kreijn in 1987, commissioned by Hagemeyer as a symbol for the company's international trading operations.

List of persons interviewed

O. Bargman,

 Hagemeyer employee from 1937 until 1977, 10 June 1998. His stationings
 included Singapore and East Africa, after which Bargman became managing
 director of the Haagtechno subsidiary.

W.M. van Eeghen,

 partner of Van Eeghen & Co., 13 April 1999.

G.M.A.M. Fagel,

 who worked for Hagemeyer from 1951 until 1985, latterly as member
 of the executive board, 6 April 1998.

Drs. ing. H.J. de Graaf,

 member of Hagemeyer's executive board from 1994 until 1999,
 16 June 1999.

Drs. P.J. Groenenboom,

 chairman of Internatio-Müller's executive board, 23 September 1999

Drs. R. ter Haar,

 chairman of Hagemeyer's executive board since April 1999, 21 October 1999.

P.A.J.M. Hagemeijer,

 youngest son of Anton Hagemeijer, 6 April 1998.

H.W.N.A. Jansen,

 since 1977 managing director of Hagemeyer's Haagtechno subsidiary,
 28 April 1999.

Drs. D. Jansen,

 since 1990 Hagemeyer's Director Staff and Organisation, 23 June1999.

M. van der Klooster,

 from 1983 until 1991 chairman of Borsumij Wehry's executive board,
 27 July 1998.

A.H. Land,

 from 1985 until April 1999 chairman of Hagemeyer's executive board,
 8 June 1999.

A.A.M. Lauxterman,

 who after a career with Lindeteves Jacoberg and OGEM became Hagemeyer's
 director for general affairs and staff from 1979 until 1990.

Drs. W. van Schaik,

 from 1972 tot 1977 member of Hagemeyer's executive board responsible for
 the manufacturing operations, 1 November 1999.

A.A.B. Teves,

 since 1991 member of Hagemeyer's executive board, 15 June 1998.

Notes

Introduction

1 N.J. Polak, W.J. van de Woestijne and S.C. Homan, *De functie van de groothandel* (Rotterdam 1966); E.J. Tobi, *Uitschakeling van den groothandel in industrieele producten* (Roermond 1928).

2 *Het Jaarboek Groothandel 1990*, a publication of the wholesalers' association Verbond Nederlandse Groothandelaren, defines merchant houses as organizations focusing on international trade, not necessarily via the Netherlands. Their services are usually markedly diverse. Large merchant houses have subsidiaries all over the world.

3 This survey is derived from: J. van Dalen, *Quantitative studies in wholesaling* (1992); J.F. Haccoû, *De groothandel, functies, dynamiek en perspectieven* (Leiden 1969); W.J. van de Woestijne, *Werken in de groothandel* (Leiden 1985).

4 M. Casson, 'The economic analysis of multinational trading companies' in: G. Jones, ed., *The multinational traders* (New York/London 1998). In his article, Casson uses the transaction costs theory which may serve both to explain integration of trade by industry, and to argue for the plausibility of a lasting position for traders.

5 Taking his departure point in industry, H.W. de Jong infers a relationship between forms of integration, conglomerate building, and collaboration on one hand, and product life cycles and economic fluctuations on the other: H.W. de Jong, *Dynamische markttheorie* (Leiden 1989).

Chapter I,
The unfolding of a commercial world empire

1 R. de Roover, 'The organization of trade', in: M.M. Postan, E.E. Rich, E. Miller, ed., *The Cambridge economic history of Europe*, III, *Economic organization and policies in the Middle Ages* (Cambridge 1963) 42-118, ibidem 70-78, 106-109.

2 N.W. Posthumus, *De oosterse handel te Amsterdam, het oudst bewaard gebleven koopmansboek van een Amsterdamse vennootschap betreffende de handel op de Oostzee 1485-1490* (Leiden 1953) 3-4, 11-36.

3 M. van Tielhof, *De Hollandse graanhandel 1470-1570, koren op de Amsterdamse molen* (The Hague 1996) 189-190; according to W. Brulez, *De firma Della Faille en de internationale handel van Vlaamse firma's in de 16e eeuw* (Brussel 1959) 365-375, circumstances were very different in the Southern Netherlands.

4 M. Bogucka, 'Dutch merchant's activities in Gdansk in the first half of the 17th century', in: J.P.S. Lemmink, J.S.A.M. van Koningsbrugge, ed., *Baltic affairs, relations between the Netherlands and Northeastern Europe 1500-1800* (Nijmegen 1990) 19-32, ibidem 20-21, specifically about agents 22-25.

5 A.E. Christensen, *Dutch trade to the Baltic about 1600, studies in the Sound toll register and Dutch shipping records* (The Hague 1941) 189-200; the correspondence between Van Adrichem and his agent was published by P.H. Winkelman, ed., *Bronnen voor de geschiedenis van de Nederlandse Oostzeehandel in de zeventiende eeuw* (The Hague 1971-1983, 6 vols.) III, 469-531. H.A. Enno van Gelder, 'Zestiende-eeuwse koopmansbrieven', in: *Economisch-historisch jaarboek* 5 (1919) 136-191 published a selection.

6 Van Tielhof, *Graanhandel* 170, 172.

7 P.A. Meilink, 'Gegevens aangaande bedrijfskapitalen in den Hollandschen en Zeeuwschen handel in 1543', in: *Economisch-Historisch Jaarboek* 8 (1922) 262-277. The ledgers for other big mercantile cities such as Middelburg are missing, but their total lies far below the Amsterdam amount.

8 N.W. Posthumus, *De uitvoer van Amsterdam 1543-1545* (Leiden 1971) 151.

9 P.G.A. de Waal, *Van Paciolo tot Stevin, bijdrage tot de leer van het boekhouden in Nederland* (Roermond 1927) 110-111.

10 H. van der Wee, 'Handel in de zuidelijke Nederlanden', in: D.P. Blok a.o., ed., *Algemene geschiedenis der Nederlanden*, VI, *Nieuwe tijd* (Bussum 1979) 75-97, ibidem 93-95; more in detail about the shift P. Jeannin, 'The seaborne and the overland trade routes of Northern Europe in the XVIth and XVIIth centuries', in: *Journal of European Economic history* 11 (1982) 5-60

11 De Waal, *Paciolo tot Stevin* 92-119. Pacioli's name is often spelt in different ways. I have stuck with the most common modern version.

12 J.A.F. Wallert, *Ontwikkelingslijnen in praktijk en theorie van de wisselbrief 1300-2000* (Amsterdam 1996) 87-88.

13 Brulez, *Della Faille* 367-370; Van der Wee, 'Handel' 94-95.

14 De Waal, *Paciolo tot Stevin* 95.

15 W.S. Unger, 'Middelburg als handelsstad, 13e-16e eeuw', in: *Archief Zeeuwsch Genootschap voor Wetenschappen* (1935) 1-173; see however V. Enthoven, *Zeeland en de opkomst van de Republiek, handel en strijd in de Scheldedelta* (Leiden 1996) 13-16.

16 A. van der Schoor, *Stad in aanwas, geschiedenis van Rotterdam tot 1813* (Zwolle 1999) 120-121.

17 J.A. van Houtte, 'Handel en verkeer', in: idem a.o., ed., *Algemene geschiedenis der Nederlanden* IV (Utrecht 1952) 154-201, ibidem 181-182.

18 T.S. Jansma, 'Hanze, Fugger, Amsterdam', in: *Bijdragen en mededelingen van het Historisch Genootschap* (1976) 1-26, ibidem 5.

19 M. Manders, 'Raadsels rond een gezonken Oostzeevaarder' in: R. Daalder, ed., *Goud uit graan, Nederland en het Oostzeegebied 1600-1850* (Zwolle 1998) 70-81, ibidem 80-81.

20 Van Tielhof, *Graanhandel* 114.

21 In other countries, most ships appear to have had a single owner at that time: Posthumus, *Uitvoer Amsterdam* 70.

22 Van Tielhof, *Graanhandel* 107.

23 Van Tielhof, *Graanhandel* 114.

24 F. Ketner, *Handel en scheepvaart van Amsterdam in de vijftiende eeuw* (Leiden 1946) 185-186; W.G. Heeres, 'De heffing van het paalgeld door Kampen en Amsterdam', in: *Economisch en sociaalhistorisch jaarboek* 46 (1983) 128-141, ibidem 128-133.

25 C.Lesger, 'Intraregional trade and the port system of Holland, 1400-1700', in: C.A. Davids, L. Noordegraaf, ed., *The Dutch economy in the Golden Age* (Amsterdam 1993) 186-217, ibidem 194-199; Postumus, *Uitvoer Amsterdam* 125-126; E. Baasch, 'Hamburg und Holland im 17. und 18. Jahrhundert', in: *Hanseatische Geschichtsblätter* 16 (1910) 45-102, ibidem 45-46.

26 J.G. van Dillen, *Van rijkdom en regenten, handboek tot de economische en sociale geschiedenis van Nederland tijdens de Republiek* (The Hague 1970) 38.

27 J.G. van Dillen, *Amsterdam in 1585, het kohier der capitale impositie 1585* (Amsterdam 1941) XIII.

28 J. de Vries, A. van der Woude, *Nederland 1500-1815, de eerste ronde van moderne economische groei* (Amsterdam 1995) 433; Posthumus, *Uitvoer Amsterdam* 228-230.

29 Van Tielhof, *Graanhandel* 117, 118; cf. K. Glamann, 'European trade 1500-1750' in: C.M. Cipolla, ed., *The Fontana economic history of Europe* 4, *The sixteenth and seventeenth centuries* (London 1974) 427-526, ibidem 446.

30 Posthumus, *Uitvoer Amsterdam* 120-121; Jansma, 'Hanze'.

31 Van Tielhof, *Graanhandel* 186-187.

32 Van Tielhof, *Graanhandel* 186-187.

33 H. Kaptein, *De Hollandse textielnijverheid 1350-1600, conjunctuur en continuïteit* (Hilversum 1998) 148-158.

34 Winkelman, *Bronnen Oostzeehandel* III, 536.

35 B.S. Supple, 'The nature of enterprise', in: E.E. Rich, C.H. Wilson, *The Cambridge economic history of Europe*, V, *The economic organization of early modern Europe* (Cambridge 1977) 394-461, ibidem 394-399.

36 Supple, 'Nature enterprise' 400-402.

37 Van Houtte, 'Handel en verkeer' 195.

38 A.M. de Jong, 'Zestiende- en zeventiende-eeuwse denkbeelden over de wisselkoersen', in: *Economisch-historische herdrukken* (The Hague 1964) 319-343, ibidem 321-322.

39 The following is based on J. Nanninga Uitterdijk, *Een Kamper handelshuis te Lissabon 1572-1594, handelscorrespondentie, rekeningen en bescheiden* (Zwolle 1904).

40 H.A. Enno van Gelder, 'Recente gegevens omtrent de 16e eeuwsche koopman', in: *Tijdschrift voor geschiedenis* 35 (1920) 199-223, ibidem 206-207.

41 Nanninga Uitterdijk, *Kamper handelshuis* LXXXVI-II. A closer analysis in Christensen, *Dutch trade* 202-208, 382-388.

42 Van Adrichem (Delft) to Aper Jansz Delft (Danzig), 13 January 1590, Winkelman, *Bronnen Oostzee-*

handel III, 495. A last is 2,000 kilos.

43 J. van Beylen, 'Scheepstypen', in: L.M. Akveld, S. Hart, W.J. van Hoboken, ed., *Maritieme geschiedenis der Nederlanden*, II (Bussum 1977) 11-71, ibidem 28-32; Van Tielhof, *Graanhandel* 108-110.

44 J.R. Bruijn, 'Productivity, profitability, and costs of private and corporate Dutch ships during the seventeenth and eighteenth centuries', in: J.D. Tracy, ed., *The rise of merchant empires, lond-distance trade in the early modern world, 1350-1750* (Cambridge 1990) 174-194, ibidem 176.

45 M. van Tielhof, *The mother of all trades, the Baltic grain trade in Amsterdam from the late 16th to the early 19th century* (forthcoming).

46 Van Adrichem (Delft) to Aper Jansz Delft (Danzig), 13 January 1590, Winkelman, *Bronnen Oostzeehandel* III, 495.

47 Enno van Gelder, 'Recente gegevens', 220. The three oxheads were sold for 46 guilders and 3 stivers. An oxhead of wine equals 232 liters, making a total of 700 liters, or 933 bottles. At 10 guilders a bottle this totals 9,330 guilders. The turnover of 10,000 guilders for 1590 calculated by Christensen, *Dutch trade* 233.

48 For instance J. Romein, A. Romein-Verschoor, *Erflaters van onze beschaving, Nederlandse gestalten uit zes eeuwen* (Amsterdam 197712) 285.

49 G. Jongbloet-Van Houtte, *Brieven en andere bescheiden betreffende Daniël van der Meulen 1584-1600*, I, *augustus 1584-september 1585* (The Hague 1986) LVI.

50 For instance Winkelman, *Bronnen Oostzeehandel* III, 256-257.

51 F. Breedvelt-Van Veen, *Louis de Geer (1587-1652)* (Amsterdam 1935) 42-43.

52 J.H. Kernkamp, A.J. Klaassen-Meijer, 'De rekeningen betreffende de exploratietocht van den Swerten Ruyter naar het Middellandse Zeegebied in 1589/1590', in: *Bijdragen en mededelingen van het Historisch Genootschap* 73 (1958) 3-53, ibidem 25.

53 Christensen, *Dutch trade* 233.

54 Christensen, *Dutch trade* 233.

55 De Waal, *Paciolo tot Stevin* 165, 167; Kool, *Die conste vanden getale, een studie over Nederlandstalige rekenboeken uit de vijftiende en zestiende eeuw, met een glossarium van rekenkundige termen* (Hilversum 1999).

56 A comparison in Christensen, *Dutch Trade* 394-399.

57 Cf. J.M. Price, P.G.E. Clemens, 'A revolution of scale in British overseas trade, British firms in the Chesapeake trade 1675-1775', in: *Journal of economic history* 47 (1987) 1-43, ibidem 2.

58 Jongbloet-Van Houtte, *Brieven Daniël van der Meulen* LVI.

59 W.F. Lichtenauer, *Geschiedenis van de wetenschap van het handelsrecht in Nederland tot 1809* (1956) 97-102.

60 S.A.C. Dudok van Heel, 'Hooft, een hecht koopmansgeslacht', in: R. Breugelmans a.o., *Hooft,*

essays over P.C. Hooft (Amsterdam 1981) 93-115, ibidem 94-108. Van Heel mentions a partnership contract between Cornelis and Willem Pietersz Hooft from 1584, but he does not make clear what kind of business this was. Anyway, Cornelis subsequently entered into various partnerships with other merchants. Unfortunately we have no further details. Father and son Guillelmo Bartolotti must have had a similar business continuity in the eyes of their fellow merchants: G. Leonhardt, *Het huis Bartolotti en zijn bewoners* (Amsterdam 1979) 40-82.

61 Besides the well-known petition of the League of the Nobility, a League of Merchants also petitioned for leniency: M. Dierickx, 'De eerste jaren van Filips II, 1555-1567', in: J.A. van Houtte, ed., *Algemene geschiedenis der Nederlanden* IV (Utrecht 1952) 305-349, ibidem 314.

62 Van der Schoor, *Stad* 166-168.

63 W. Brulez, 'De diaspora der Antwerpse kooplui op het einde van de 16de eeuw', in: *Bijdragen tot de geschiedenis der Nederlanden* 15 (1960) 279-306; J.I. Israel, *Dutch primacy in world trade 1585-1740* (Oxford 1989) 32-36.

64 That was Willem Usselincx' opinion in a 1608 pamphlet cited by A.E. Sayous, 'Die grössen Händler und Kapitalisten in Amsterdam gegen das Ende des sechzehnten und während das siebzehnten Jahrhunderts', in: *Weltwirthschaftliches Archiv* 47 (1938) 115-144, ibidem 693. However, Usselincx had an axe to grind after the scuppering of his efforts to found a trading company for the Americas: Israel, *Dutch primacy* 83-84.

65 J.R. Bruijn, 'De vaart in Europa', in: L.M. Akveld, S. Hart, W.J. van Hoboken, ed., *Maritieme geschiedenis van Nederland* II (Bussum 1977) 200-241, ibidem 200.

66 Quoted in Van Dillen, *Rijkdom en regenten* 20.

67 Cf. O. Gelderblom's forthcoming PhD dissertation 'Zuidnederlanders en de opkomst van de stapelmarkt 1578-1630'.

68 Bruijn, 'Vaart Europa', 202; until then, Amsterdam and Middelburg had had subsidiaries of the Antwerp insurance chamber: Van der Schoor, *Stad* 217.

69 Quoted by C.A. Davids, 'Zekerheidsregelingen in de scheepvaart en het landtransport, 1500-1800', in: J.L.J.M. van Gerwen, M.H.D. van Leeuwen, ed., *Studies over zekerheidsarrangementen, risico's, risicobestrijding en verzekeringen in Nederland vanaf de Middeleeuwen* (Amsterdam 1998) 183-203, ibidem 183; about Rotterdam idem, 199.

70 K. de Gast, '…ten dienste van de commercie', vierhonderd jaar Beurs in Rotterdam (Rotterdam 1998) 23-25; Sneller, 'Beurshandel' 138; Van der Schoor, *Stad* 180-181; Dordrecht converted a convent into an exchange in 1594-1596, idem 138-139.

71 M. van Rooy, *Amsterdam en het beurzenspektakel* (Aarlanderveen 1982) 11-14; J.C. Overvoorde, *Geschiedenis van het postwezen in Nederland vóór*

1795 met de voornaamste verbindingen met het buitenland (Leiden 1902) 316.

72 Quoted by R. van Gelder, R. Kistemaker, *Amsterdam 1275-1795, de ontwikkeling van een handelsmetropool* (Amsterdam 1983) 93.

73 Van Dillen, *Rijkdom en regenten* 9; J.J. McCusker, C. Gravesteijn, *The beginnings of commercial and financial journalism, the commodity price currents, exchange rate currents, and money currents of early modern Europe* (Amsterdam 1991) 43-52; N.W. Posthumus, *Inquiry into the history of prices in Holland*, I (Leiden 1946) XXVI-XXVIII.

74 A. Houwink, *Acceptcrediet, economische en bankpolitieke beschouwingen over den in het bankaccept belichaamden creditvorm* (Amsterdam 1929) 18; H.A.J. Maassen, *Tussen commercieel en sociaal krediet, de ontwikkeling van de bank van lening in Nederland van lombard tot gemeentelijke kredietbank 1260-1940* (Hilversum 1994) 115-122; Overvoorde, *Geschiedenis* 78.

75 J.W. Veluwenkamp, 'Merchant colonies in the Dutch trade system (1550-1750)', in: C.A. Davids, J.M.F. Fritschy, L.A. van der Valk, ed., *Kapitaal, ondernemerschap en beleid, studies over economie en politiek in Nederland, Europa en Azië, afscheidsbundel voor prof.dr. P.W. Klein* (Amsterdam 1996) 141-164; J.I. Israel, 'The Dutch merchant colonies in the Mediterranean during the seventeenth century', in: *Renaissance and modern studies* 30 (1986) 90-99 en idem, *Nederland* 363-364; M.C. Engels, *Merchants, interlopers, seamen and corsairs, the 'Flemish' community in Livorno and Genoa (1615-1635)* (Hilversum 1997).

76 P.W. Klein, 'De zeventiende eeuw', in: J.H. van Stuijvenberg, ed., *De economische geschiedenis van Nederland* (Groningen 1977) 79-118, ibidem 103; De Vries/Van der Woude, *Nederland* 483; J.A. Faber, 'The decline of the Baltic grain trade in the second half of the seventeenth century', in: W.G. Heeres a.o., ed., *From Dunkirk to Dantzig, shipping and trade in the North Sea and the Baltic 1350-1850* (Hilversum 1988) 31-52; J.Th. Lindblad, 'Nederland en de Oostzee, 1650-1800', in: R. Daalder, ed., *Goud uit graan, Nederland en het Oostzeegebied 1600-1850* (Zwolle 1998) 8-27, ibidem 15-17.

77 Cf. Israel, *Dutch primacy* 96-101, perhaps emphasising the trade in luxuries a little too much as a new phenomenon.

78 Israel, *Dutch primacy* 45-47.

79 J.H. Kernkamp, *De handel op den vijand 1572-1609* I (Utrecht 1931) 220.

80 S. Hart, 'De eerste Nederlandse tochten ter walvisvaart', in: *Jaarboek Amstelodamum* 49 (1957) 27-64, ibidem 58; about Van Tweenhuysen also H. den Heijer, *De geschiedenis van de WIC* (Zutphen 1994) 21.

81 Dudok van Heel, 'Hooft' 101.

82 J.H. Kernkamp, *De handel op den vijand 1572-1609*, II (Utrecht 1934) 93, 348-349.

83 Van Dillen, *Rijkdom en regenten* 53-54, 61; see

also C. Lesger, 'Over het nut van huwelijk, opportunisme en bedrog, ondernemen en ondernemerschap tijdens de vroeg-moderne tijd in theoretisch perspectief', in: C.A. Davids, J.M.F. Fritschy, L.A. van der Valk, ed., *Kapitaal, ondernemerschap en beleid, studies over economie en politiek in Nederland, Europa en Azië, afscheidsbundel voor prof.dr. P.W. Klein* (Amsterdam 1996) 55-76, ibidem 72-74.

84 J.H. Kernkamp, 'Scheepvaart en handelsbetrekkingen met Italië tijdens de opkomst der Republiek', in: *Economisch-historische herdrukken* (The Hague 1964) 199-234; Kernkamp/Klaassen-Meijer, 'Rekeningen exploratietocht' 7, 10-14, the instructions on 15-28.

85 S. Hart, 'De Italiëvaart 1590-1620', in: *Jaarboek Amstelodamum* 70 (1978) 42-60, ibidem 44. mentions 200 ships, which was according to Hart an inflated number used by a member for Zeeland in the Estates General to create animosity against the Italian trade. Van der Meulen probably had been against shipping grain, because he lacked affinity with this particular commodity: Jongbloet-Van Houtte, *Brieven Daniël van der Meulen* LI.

86 Dudok van Heel, 'Hooft' 102-104.

87 O. Schutte, *Repertorium van Nederlandse vertegenwoordigers residerende in het buitenland, 1584-1810* (The Hague 1976) 302-303, 331, 346, 347.

88 G. van Krieken, *Kapers en kooplieden, de betrekkingen tussen Algiers en Nederland1604-1830)* (Amsterdam 1999) 8-10, 13, 17.

89 Winkelman, *Bronnen Oostzeehandel* III, 536-537.

90 Israel, *Dutch primacy* 60-62; P.W. Klein, *De Trippen in de 17e eeuw* (Assen 1965) 138.

91 Winkelman, *Bronnen Oostzeehandel* III, 536.

92 Kernkamp/Klaassen-Meijer, 'Rekeningen' 14. Source of the table: Gaastra, *Geschiedenis VOC* 23; Van Goor, *Nederlandse Koloniën* 29-30.

93 Israel, *Dutch primacy* 67-68.

94 F.S. Gaastra, *De geschiedenis van de VOC* (Zutphen 1991²) 17.

95 Gaastra, *Geschiedenis VOC* 17.

96 Israel, *Dutch primacy* 70-71.

97 J. van Goor, 'A hybrid state, the Dutch economic and political network in Asia', in: C. Guillot, D. Lombard, R. Ptak, ed., *From the Mediterranean to the China Sea, miscellaneous notes* (Wiesbaden 1998) 193-214, ibidem 195.

98 L.D. Westera, 'Boekhouding en management bij de Verenigde Oostindische Compagnie', in: *Economisch- en sociaalhistorisch jaarboek* 55 (1992) 75-104, ibidem 77-78.

99 P. Musgrave, 'The economics of uncertainty, the structural revolution in the spice trade, 1480-1640', in: P.L. Cottrell, D.H. Aldcroft, ed., *Shipping, trade and commerce: essays in memory of Ralph Davis* (Leicester 1981) 9-21, ibidem 19-20; Gaastra, *Geschiedenis VOC* 23, 25; J. van Goor, *De Nederlandse koloniën, geschiedenis van de Nederlandse expansie 1600-1975* (The Hague 19972) 47,

73. The letters between Batavia and the Heren XVII published by W.Ph. Coolhaas a.o., ed., *Generale missiven van Goeverneurs-Generaal en raden aan Heren XVII der Verenigde Oostindische Compagnie* (The Hague, 1960 ff.). Nine volumes have appeared so far.

100 Van Goor, 'Hybrid state'198-204, 206-207.

101 Van Goor, *Nederlandse koloniën* 82-86.

102 H. Diferee, *Geschiedenis van den Nederlandschen handel ten tijde van den Nederlandschen handel tot den val der Republiek* (Amsterdam 1908) 244-245.

103 Van Goor, 'Hybrid state' 201-202, 208. The island of Ternate has a very tall clove tree, reputedly planted in the 17th century and now the world's oldest. It is seen as a living monument to the person who defied the VOC's prohibition to plant seeds, thus undermining the company's aspired monopoly. *The Economist* 19 December 1998, p. 82.

104 De Vries/Van der Woude, *Nederland* 454-455; Van Goor, 'Hybrid state' 201-204.

105 Israel, *Dutch primacy* 171-178.

106 Gaastra, *Geschiedenis VOC* 84-86, 94.

107 J.P. de Korte, *De jaarlijkse financiële verantwoording in de VOC* (Leiden 1984) Bijlage 6a.

108 Van Goor, 'Hybrid state' 195-196.

109 Van Goor, 'Hybrid state' 193. Van Goor puts it just the other way around, in my view incorrectly. A trading company would definitely have listed its possessions. The VOC did not write down the value of its ships, a common practice with shipping partnerships. The principle was known, however, and the directors sometimes did take the value of ships into account when calculating the cost of a particular venture: Westera, 'Boekhouding' 93.

110 J.B. Kist a.o., ed., *Van VOC tot Werkspoor, het Amsterdamse industrieterrein Oostenburg* (Utrecht 1986); R. van Gelder, L. Wagenaar, *Sporen van compagnie, de VOC in Nederland* (Amsterdam 1986).

111 On the postal communications P. Moree, 'De Verenigde Oostindische Compagnie', in: G. Hogesteeger, ed., *Naar de gordel van smaragd, de postverbindingen tussen Nederland en Nederlands-Indië 1602-1940* (The Hague 1995) 5-26

112 Quoted by Gaastra, *Geschiedenis VOC* 68. The data for the graph from Gaastra, *Geschiedenis VOC* 137.

113 Gaastra, *Geschiedenis VOC* 115, 134, 135. Source of the figure: idem, 137.

114 Gaastra, *Geschiedenis VOC* 134.

115 De Korte, *Financiële verantwoording* 60-61, Appendix 1; Israel, *Dutch primacy* 184-187.

116 The following drawn from Den Heijer, *Geschiedenis WIC*.

117 Den Heijer, *Geschiedenis WIC* 33, 102; De Korte, *Financiële verantwoording* 2, Appendix 1a: the VOC had a capital of 6.4 million guilders and, at least in 1638, outstanding bonds from the various chambers totalling 11.3 million.

118 J. Jacobs, *De scheepvaart en de handel van de Nederlandse Republiek op Nieuw-Nederland* (Amster-

dam 1989), idem, *Een zegenrijk gewest, Nieuw-Nederland in de zeventiende eeuw* (Amsterdam 1999).

119 On the slave trade J.M. Postma, *The Dutch in the Atlantic slave trade, 1600-1815* (Cambridge 1990).

120 Israel, *Dutch primacy* 162-163.

121 Den Heijer, *WIC* 151; Postma, *Slave trade* 295.

122 I.A. Wright, 'The Coymans asiento', in: *Bijdragen voor vaderlandsche geschiedenis en oudheidkunde* 6 no. 1 (1924) 23-62; Israel, *Dutch primacy* 320-324; *Nijhoffs lexicon* 137-138; J.G. van Dillen, *Het oudste aandeelhoudersregister van de Kamer Amsterdam der Oost-Indische Compagnie* (The Hague 1958) 63, 205.

123 De Vries/Van der Woude, *Nederland* 467; De Korte, *Jaarlijkse verantwoording* 60-61.

124 Den Heijer, *Geschiedenis WIC* 105, 130.

125 Den Heijer, *Geschiedenis WIC* 97-108, 113.

126 G. Jongbloet-Van Houtte, 'De belegering en de val van Antwerpen belicht vanuit een koopmansarchief', in: *Bijdragen en mededelingen van het Historisch Genootschap* 91 (1976) 23-43, ibidem 23.

127 Jongbloet-Van Houtte, *Brieven Daniël van der Meulen* XXXII; an underestimate of 50% and more mentioned for a 1635 Amsterdam tax assessment by Klein, *Trippen* 35.

128 Lindblad, 'Nederland' 8.

129 His son Jacob Poppen left an estate of about 1 million guilders eight years later, half of which in agricultural land newly created in the Beemster polder. Jan Poppen had invested 200,000 gulden in this project in 1607, rumoured to be half his capital: W. van Ravesteijn, *Onderzoekingen over de economische en sociale ontwikkeling van Amsterdam gedurende de 16e en het eerste kwart der 17e eeuw* (Utrecht 1906) 331-333; Lesger, 'Nut' 55-56; Van Dillen, *Rijkdom* 234, calls Poppen the only Amsterdam millionaire in 1607.

130 De Gast, *Beurs Rotterdam* 35; J.H. Kernkamp, *Johan van der Veken en zijn tijd* (The Hague 1952); Van der Schoor, *Stad* 173-174, 212-213.

131 Van Ravesteijn, *Onderzoekingen* 329.

132 Van Ravesteijn, *Onderzoekingen* 310-311.

133 Klein, *Trippen* 35.

134 Van Dillen, *Rijkdom* 317; The year before, Guillelmo Bartolotti had died, leaving and estate worth 1,2 million guilders: Leonhardt, *Huis* 82.

135 Van Dillen, *Rijkdom* 311.

136 Van Dillen, *Rijkdom* 143-145, 147-148, 234.

137 Enthoven, *Zeeland* 337-342; J.H. de Stoppelaar, *Balthasar de Moucheron, een bladzijde uit de Nederlandsche handelsgeschiedenis tijdens den tachtigjarigen oorlog* (The Hague 1901).

138 J.G. van Dillen, 'Isaac le Maire en de handel in actiën der Oost-Indische Compagnie', in: *Economisch-historisch jaarboek* 16 (1930) 1-165; idem, *Oudste aandeelhoudersregister* 111-113; E. Schoorl, *Le Maire* 11-15, 18; R.C. Bakhuizen van den Brink, *I. le Maire* (Amsterdam 1865) 54-55.

139 Van Dillen, *Rijkdom en regenten* 311-312; J.L. van

Zanden, *Arbeid tijdens het handelskapitalisme, opkomst en neergang van de Hollandse economie 1350-1850* (Bergen 1991) Table 3.1.

140 P.W. Klein, '"Little London", British merchants in Rotterdam during the seventeenth and eighteenth centuries', in: D.C. Coleman, P. Mathias, ed., *Enterprise and history, essays in honour of Charles Wilson* (Cambridge 1984) 116-134; see also P.Th. van der Laar, a.o., ed., *Vier eeuwen migratie bestemming Rotterdam* (Rotterdam 1998).

141 J.I. Israel, 'De Republiek der Verenigde Nederlanden tot omstreeks 1750-demografie en economische activiteit', in: J.C.H. Blom, R.G. Fuks-Mansfeld, I. Schöffer, ed., *Geschiedenis van de joden in Nederland* (Amsterdam 1995) 97-128, ibidem 114-120; O. Vlessing, 'The Portuguese-Jewish mercantile community in seventeenth-century Amsterdam', in: C. Lesger, L. Noordegraaf, ed., *Entrepreneurs and entrepreneurship in modern times, merchants and industrialists within the orbit of the Dutch staple market* (The Hague 1995) 223-244, ibidem 224-225; specifically about the sugar industry G. Novaky, 'On trade, production and relations of production, the sugar refineries of seventeenth-century Amsterdam', in: *Tijdschrift voor sociale geschiedenis* 23 (1997) 459-489.

142 About the role of copper in Swedish foreign policy Glamann, 'European trade' 446.

143 *Nijhoffs lexicon* 208.

144 Van Dillen, *Rijkdom* 317-320.

145 Glamann, 'European trade' 489; idem, *Dutch-Asiatic trade* 30-31.

146 Breedvelt-Van Veen, *De Geer* 95.

147 Klein, *Trippen* 419-432.

148 Breedvelt-Van Veen, *De Geer* 95.

149 Glamann, *Dutch-Asiatic trade* 30-31.

150 V. Barbour, *Capitalism in Amsterdam in the 17th century* (Ann Arbor 1963) 114-117; I.H. van Eeghen, 'Buitenlandse monopolies voor de Amsterdamse kooplieden in de tweede helft van de zeventiende eeuw', in: *Jaarboek Amstelodamum* 53 (1961) 176-184, ibidem 176-179. About De Ruyter's venture S. Hart, 'Michiel Adriaanszoon de Ruyter en de Noordcaepse Compagnie', in: idem, *Geschift en getal, een keuze uit de demografisch-economisch- en sociaalhistorische studiën op grond van Amsterdamse en Zaanse archivalia, 1600-1800* (Dordrecht 1976) 247-254. The Rotterdam merchant B. Geestevelt tried to get the Austrian contract in stead of Deutz, but could not raise the money: Van der Schoor, *Stad* 298-299.

151 De Vries/Van der Woude, *Nederland* 422-425.

152 Source: Bruijn, 'Vaart Europa' 213; De Korte, *Financiële verantwoording* Appendix 1a.

153 De Vries/Van der Woude, *Nederland* 467; cf. Den Heijer, *WIC* 54.

154 Den Heijer, *WIC* 130.

155 Van Tielhof, *Mother trade* (forthcoming); D.C. North, 'Sources of productivity change in ocean shipping, 1600-1850', in: *Journal of political economy* 76 (1968) 953-970.

156 Glamann, 'European trade' 427-434.

157 Lesger, 'Mythe' 12.

158 Van Ravesteyn, *Onderzoekingen* 235.

159 Van der Schoor, *Stad* 200-216.

160 Dudok van Heel, 'Hooft' 102.

161 J. de Vries, *Barges and capitalism, passenger transportation in the Dutch economy 1632-1839* (Wageningen 1978) 29, 34, 99-101; Diferee, *Geschiedenis handel* 343-344; Overvoorde, *Geschiedenis postwezen* 83-84, 114.

162 Israel, *Dutch primacy* 44-45.

163 T. Kappelhof, 'Noord-Brabant en de Hollandse stapelmarkt', in: C.A. Davids, ed., *De Republiek tussen zee en vasteland, buitenlandse invloeden op cultuur, economie en politiek in Nederland 1580-1800* (Leuven 1995) 189-206, ibidem 195-196.

164 R. Davis, 'Merchant shipping in the economy of the late seventeenth century', in: *Economic history review* 9 (1956) 59-73, ibidem 61-62.

165 Christensen, *Dutch trade* 376-379. Christensen sees a connection between the percentage of ballasted ships and the demand for grain. To my mind, this explains the annual fluctuations, but not the clear downward trend. Cf. J.W. Veluwenkamp, 'Lading voor de Oostzee' in: R. Daalder a.o., ed., *Goud uit graan, Nederland en het Oostzeegebied 1600-1850* (Zwolle 1998) 42-55, ibidem 45-46.

166 Veluwenkamp, 'Lading' 45-46, cf. 83 for details about the castle; Glamann, 'European trade' 461.

167 Winkelman, *Bronnen Oostzeehandel* III, 537.

168 J.C. van Es, 'Zestiende-eeuwse vrachtvaartbescheiden, vier scheepvaartrekeningen van 1574, 1575 en 1576', in: *Economisch-historisch jaarboek* 20 (1936) 258-293; H.A. Enno van Gelder, 'Scheepsrekeningen van enkele der vroegste Guineavaarten (eind 16^e eeuw)', in: *Economisch-historisch jaarboek* 2 (1916) 239-257; idem, 'Zestiende-eeuwse vrachtvaartbescheiden', in: *Economisch historisch jaarboek* 3 (1917) 124-290.

169 Kernkamp/Klaassen-Meijer, 'Rekeningen exploratietocht' 17-18.

170 W. Brulez, 'De scheepvaartwinst in de nieuwe tijden', in: *Tijdschrift voor geschiedeis* (1979) 1-19, see however W.G. 't Hart, P.C. van Royen, 'Het smakschip De Neufville van der Hoop, een onderzoek naar de rendabiliteit van Nederlandse vrachtvaart in de achttiende eeuw', in: *Economisch- en sociaalhistorisch jaarboek* 48 (1985) 150-169, and Bruijn, 'Productivity'.

171 G.A. Bredero, in: J.A.N. Knuttel, ed., *Werken van G.A. Bredero* (Amsterdam 1924) 97-218, ibidem 123-124.

172 Bredero, 'Moortje' 123-124.

173 W.F. Oldewelt, 'Twee eeuwen Amsterdamse faillissementen en het verloop van de conjunctuur', in: *Tijdschrift voor geschiedenis* (1962) 421-435, ibidem 421.

174 J. van den Vondel, in: A. Verwey, ed., *Vondel, volledige dichtwerken en oorspronkelijk proza*

(Amsterdam 1937) 769-772, ibidem 771.

175 E.J. Goossens, 'De rol van de beeldhouwkunst', in: J. Huisken, K. Ottenheym, G. Schwartz, *Jacob van Campen, het klassieke ideaal in de Gouden Eeuw* (Amsterdam 1995) 201-226, ibidem 216-219.

176 J. van den Vondel, 'Op den Amsterdamschen gedenkpenning', in: A. Verwey, ed., *Vondel, volledige dichtwerken en oorspronkelijk proza* (Amsterdam 1937) 790-791, ibidem 791.

177 C. Barlaeus, *Mercator sapiens*, edited by S. van der Woude (Amsterdam 1967); see H.C. Diferee, 'Een pleidooi voor handelsstudie in de zeventiende eeuw', in: *Handelsstudie* 2 No. 33 (1905) 259-262; idem, *Geschiedenis handel* 147-149; H. Brugmans, 'Het belang der economische geschiedenis', in: L. Noordegraaf, ed., *Ideeën en ideologieën, studies over economische en sociale geschiedenis in Nederland 1894-1991*, I (Amsterdam 1991) 73-98, ibidem 73-74.

178 L. Jansen, 'De koophandel van Amsterdam', een critische studie over het koopmanshandboek van Jacques le Moine de l'Espine en Isaac le Long (Amsterdam 1946) 1-3.

179 D. Grote, J. Hoock, W. Starke, 'Handbücher für den Gebrauch des Kaufmanns, Bibliographie und Analyse des Wandels einer literarische Gattung', *Tijdschrift voor geschiedenis* 103 (1990) 279-293

Chapter II, Losing the lead

1 De Vries/Van der Woude, *Nederland* 479, 567.

2 Barbour, *Capitalism* 95.

3 Barbour, *Capitalism* 96.

4 Barbour, *Capitalism* 117.

5 E. Verviers, *De Nederlandsche handelspolitiek tot aan de toepassing der vrijhandelsbeginselen* (Leiden 1914) 108.

6 Israel, *Dutch primacy* 289-291, 341-343.

7 Israel, *Dutch primacy* 303-304.

8 F. Snapper, *Oorlogsinvloeden op de overzeese handel van Holland, 1551-1719* (Amsterdam 1959) 114.

9 M. 't Hart, 'The merits of a financial revolution, public finance 1550-1700', in: M. 't Hart, J.P.B. Jonker, J.L. van Zanden, ed., *A financial history of the Netherlands* (Cambridge 1997) 11-36, ibidem 33; J.M.F., Fritschy, R. van der Voort, 'From fragmentation to unification, public finance, 1700-1914' in: M. 't Hart, J.P.B. Jonker, J.L. van Zanden, ed., *A financial history of the Netherlands* (Cambridge 1997) 64-93, ibidem 68.

10 Verviers, *Handelspolitiek* 99-103.

11 Fritschy/Van der Voort, 'From fragmentation' 70.

12 E. Laspeyres, *Geschichte der volkswirthschaftliche Anschauungen der Niederländer und ihrer Litteratur zur Zeit der Republik* (Leipzig 1863) 135-142; Van Dillen, *Rijkdom en regenten* 491-493; Israel, *Dutch primacy* 346-347, 357.

13 I.J.A. Nijenhuis, 'De ontwikkeling van het politiek-economische vrijheidsbegrip in de Republiek', in: E.O.G. Haitsma Mulier, W.R.E. Velema,

ed., *Vrijheid, een geschiedenis van de vijftiende tot de twintigste eeuw* (Amsterdam 1999) 233-252, ibidem 244-247.

14 J. Hovy, *Het voorstel van 1751 tot instelling van een beperkt vrijhavenstelsel in de Republiek (propositie tot een gelimiteerd porto-franco)* (Groningen 1966) 143. Ambassador Temple mentioned the low customs duties as a market prop: D. Roorda, *Ambassadeur in de lage landen, William Temple, Observations upon the United provinces* (Haarlem 1978) 142.

15 Israel, *Dutch primacy* 319-320, 351-354; De Vries/Van der Woude, *Nederland* 381.

16 Israel, *Dutch primacy* 289-290, 339-342.

17 Van Dillen, 'Stukken graanhandel' 70-73; Hovy, *Voorstel 1751* 121-123.

18 Hovy, *Voorstel 1751* 123-144. In 1724, an international initiative to abolish all Rhine duties launched by the Republic failed for a lack of support amongst the countries concerned: Diferee, *Geschiedenis handel* 490.

19 Joh. de Vries, *De economische achteruitgang van de Republiek in de achttiende eeuw* (Leiden 1968²) 45-49.

20 J.R. Bruijn, 'Scheepvaart in de Noordelijke Nederlanden 1650-1800', in: D.P. Blok a.o., ed., *Algemene geschiedenis der Nederlanden*, VIII, *Nieuwe Tijd* (Bussum 1979) 209-238, ibidem 215-216; De Vries, *Economische achteruitgang* 53-54.

21 J.V.T. Knoppers, 'De vaart in Europa', in: F.J.A. Broeze, J.R. Bruijn, F.S. Gaastra, ed., *Maritieme geschiedenis der Nederlanden* 3 (Bussum 1977) 226-262, ibidem 230.

22 Knoppers, 'Vaart Europa' 231; J.G. Nanninga, 'De Nederlandsche koopman in de Levant en de vrije handel (achttiende eeuw)', in: *Historische opstellen opgedragen aan prof.dr. H. Brugmans* (Amsterdam 1929) 109-140, ibidem 109; S. van Brakel, 'De Directie van den Oosterschen Handel en Reederijen te Amsterdam', in: *Bijdragen voor vaderlandsche geschiedenis en oudheidkunde* 4/IX (1910) 329-364, ibidem 336-337. There is an extensive publication of original documents on the Levant trade: K. Heeringa a.o., ed., *Bronnen tot de geschiedenis van den Levantschen handel* (The Hague, 1910 ff.). According to I. le Long, *De koophandel van Amsterdam* (Amsterdam 1704) 125, three to four fleets annually sailed for the Mediterranean, escorted by two heavily armed warships.

23 H. Brugmans, 'De notulen en munimenten van het College van Commercie te Amsterdam 1663-1665', in: *Bijdragen en mededelingen van het Historisch Genootschap* 18 (1897) 181-331, ibidem 185.

24 J.C. Westermann, *Gedenkboek van de Kamer van koophandel en fabrieken voor Amsterdam samengesteld ter gelegenheid van het 125-jarig bestaan*, I, *Het tijdvak 1811-1922* (Amsterdam 1936) 1-3.

25 Van Brakel, 'Directie' 337-338; W.A. de Clercq, 'Verleden, heden en toekomst van de Directie der Oostersche Handel en Reederijen te Amsterdam', in: *Tijdschrift voor zeegeschiedenis* 9 (1990) 5-14, ibidem 7, 9; M. van Tielhof, 'Behouden vaart!', in: R. Daalder a.o., ed., *Goud uit graan, Nederland en het Oostzeegebied 1600-1850* (Zwolle 1998) 28-41, ibidem 32-34. The term Direction came into use after the appointment of the committee to official advisory body in 1717. The Direction still exists, managing the funds collected during its active functioning.

26 Van Brakel, 'Directie' 343-349; Knoppers, 'Vaart Europa' 231.

27 Israel, *Dutch primacy* 303-304.

28 Barbour, *Capitalism* 99.

29 Israel, *Dutch primacy* 309-313, 381; Nanninga, 'Nederlandsche koopman' 119.

30 P.W. Klein, 'Handel, geld- en bankwezen in de Noordelijke Nederlanden 1650-1795', in: D.P. Blok a.o., ed., *Algemene geschiedenis der Nederlanden*, VIII, *Nieuwe tijd* (Bussum 1979) 160-184, ibidem 161; G.M. Welling, *The prize of neutrality, trade relations between Amsterdam and North America 1771-1817, a study in computational history* (Amsterdam 1998) 130.

31 Source: De Vries/Van der Woude, *Nederland* 577.

32 Welling, *Prize* 36-38; W.G. Heeres, 'Annual volumes of Amsterdam's overseas imports and exports, 1697 to 1798', in: idem a.o., ed., *From Dunkirk to Danzig, shipping and trade in the North Sea and the Baltic 1350-1850* (Hilversum 1988) 263-280, ibidem 270-271.

33 De Vries/Van der Woude, *Nederland* 567-568; Knoppers, 'Vaart Europa' 227-228.

34 Hovy, *Voorstel 1751* 361-362.

35 De Vries/Van der Woude, *Nederland* 567-568; J.V.T. Knoppers, *Dutch trade with Russia from the time of Peter I to Alexander I. A quantitative study in eighteenth century shipping* (Montreal 1976) 283 for data.

36 J.V.T. Knoppers, F. Snapper, 'De Nederlandse scheepvaart op de Oostzee vanaf het eind van de 17e eeuw tot het begin van de 19e eeuw', in: *Economisch- en sociaal-historisch jaarboek* 41 (1978) 115-153, ibidem 125-128.

37 Roorda, *Ambassadeur* 135.

38 P.D.J. van Iterson, 'Havens', in: F.J.A. Broeze, J.R. Bruijn, F.S. Gaastra, ed., *Maritieme geschiedenis der Nederlanden* III (Bussum 1977) 59-91, ibidem 68-69. In 1672, the navy had to use large wooden crates to lift its large warships over the banks: Le Long, *Koophandel* (1744, I, 15). The difficult harbour approaches provided an important argument against the building of threedecker warships for the navy, besides the high cost of these ships: J.R. Bruijn, 'In een veranderend maritiem perspectief: het ontstaan van directies voor de vaart op de Oostzee, Noorwegen en Rusland', in: *Tijdschrift voor zeegeschiedenis* 9 (1990) 15-26, ibidem 16.

39 R.M. Voortman, 'De VOC en de stad Rotterdam', in: P. Grim, *Heeren in zaken, de kemer Rotterdam van de Verenigde Oostindische Compagnie* (Zutphen 1993) 9-34, ibidem 27; F.J.A. Broeze, *De Stad Schiedam, de Schiedamse scheepsrederij en de Nederlandse vaart op Oost-Indië omstreeks 1840* (The Hague 1978) 153. The often quoted example of a passage from Rotterdam to the sea taking five weeks was very exceptional, according to Broeze.

40 Bruijn, 'Scheepvaart' 209.

41 A survey of commercial patterns in the linen trade in J.G. van Bel, *De linnenhandel van Amsterdam in de 18e eeuw* (Amsterdam 1940) 84-94; the tobacco trade between North America and Britain in J.M. Price, P.G.E. Clemens, 'A revolution of scale in British overseas trade, British firms in the Chesapeake trade 1675-1775', in: *Journal of economic history* 47 (1987) 1-43, ibidem 5-8, 22; an overall survey of developments in R.B. Westerfield, *Middlemen in English business, particularly between 1660 and 1760* (New Haven 1915) 359-361.

42 Price/Clemens, 'Revolution' 5-8.

43 De Vries, *Economische achteruitgang* 32. In 1763, the Amsterdam city liquidation office decided to release grain from Danzig merchants out of the estates of bankrupt Amsterdam merchants, because it had been sent in commission: E.E. de Jong-Keesing, *De economische crisis van 1763 te Amsterdam* (Amsterdam 1939) 204. If it required a separate decision, it was probably still unusual to send grain in commission.

44 Cf. Engels, *Merchants*; Israel, 'Merchant colonies' and idem, *Dutch primacy* 367-368; Veluwenkamp, 'Merchant colonies'.

45 An example in Veluwenkamp, 'Merchant colonies' 162.

46 Veluwenkamp, 'Merchant colonies' 150-151, 154-155, 159-161.

47 Israel, *Dutch primacy* 320-321; Van Bel, *Linnenhandel* 62-63; a similar use of cover firms in Polish inland trade in Bogucka, 'Dutch merchants' 24-25.

48 Veluwenkamp, 'Merchant colonies' 150-151, 154-155, 159-161.

49 Diferee, *Geschiedenis handel* 846-847, referring to pamphlets in Knuttel No.'s 13293, 13297, 13657, 16231.

50 For instance Israel, *Dutch primacy* 367-368, 380; but not so Veluwenkamp, 'Merchant colonies'.

51 J. Rogge, *Het handelshuis Van Eeghen, proeve eener geschiedenis van een Amsterdamsch handelshuis* (Amsterdam 1949) 29, 33, 36-37.

52 J.W. Veluwenkamp, *Ondernemersgedrag op de Hollandse stapelmarkt in de tijd van de Republiek, de Amsterdamse firma Jan Isaac de Neufville & Comp., 1730-1764* (Meppel 1981) 156; R.P.J. Tutein Nolthenius, *Het geslacht Tutein Nolthenius* (Haarlem 1914-1930) 672; GAA PA 654 Crommelin No. 6, balances.

53 D.H. Kennet, 'An English merchant in Holland in 1737 and 1738', in: *Economisch- en sociaalhistorisch jaarboek* 35 (1972) 146-186. That Pym traded from Amsterdam can be concluded from the fact that this is really the only big city in the

393

Republic not mentioned in the ledgers.

54 C.P. van Eeghen, 'Het faillissement van den frima Coenraad & Hendrick van Son in 1762', in: *Economisch-historisch jaarboek* 22 (1940-1942) 82-187, ibidem 91.

55 T.P. van der Kooy, *Hollands stapelmarkt en haar verval* (Amsterdam 1931) 19-23; criticism on this opinion in Van Eeghen, 'Faillissement' 147; a survey of the standpoints in De Vries, *Economische achteruitgang* 34-35.

56 Interview with W. van Eeghen, 13 April 1999.

57 Leonhardt, *Huis* 42-42-50, 82.

58 Van Brakel, 'Directie' 359-361; Van Tielhof, *Mother trade* (forthcoming).

59 J.E.Elias, *De vroedschap van Amsterdam 1578-1795* (Amsterdam 1963) 637, 1047-1048. Deutz first received the monopoly for Western Europe and subsequently bought the rights for Southern Europe from a Venetian firm.

60 Elias, *Vroedschap* 637, 1047, 1050.

61 De Clercq, 'Verleden' 6-7.

62 F.J.A. Broeze, 'Rederij', in: F.J.A. Broeze, J.R. Bruijn, F.S. Gaastra, ed., *Maritieme geschiedenis der Nederlanden* III (Bussum 1977) 92-141.

63 Broeze, 'Rederij' 134; J. le Moine de l'Espine, *De koophandel van Amsterdam* (Amsterdam 1715) 353. The main Dutch dictionary *Woordenboek der Nederlandsche Taal* gives 1762 for the first appearance of the term. As independent entrepreneurs, ships' agents did not organise themselves in guilds, as other commercial service providers did: H. van Driel, *Vier eeuwen veembedrijf, de voorgeschiedenis van Pakhoed 1616-1967* (Rotterdam 1992) 9-10. The city council did not provide any regulations for the ships' agents: J. Wagenaar, *Amsterdam in zijne opkomst* (Amsterdam 1760-1788) Part 4 Book 3, 547.

64 Van Tielhof, *Mother trade* (forthcoming); North, 'Sources productivity change'.

65 Broeze, 'Rederij' 134.

66 Knoppers, 'Vaart Europa' 234-235.

67 Knoppers, 'Vaart Europa' 235.

68 Davids, 'Zekerheidsregelingen' 194; F.C. Spooner, *Risks at sea, Amsterdam insurance and maritime Europe, 1766-1780* (Cambridge 1983) 29-42

69 Examples in Barbour, *Capitalism* 90-93, 100.

70 Houwink, *Acceptcrediet* 20.

71 Quoted by De Jong Keesing, *Crisis 1763* 71.

72 Wallert, *Ontwikkelingslijnen* 101-109.

73 Le Long, *Koophandel* (1715) 36-37, idem (1744) I, 106-107; Wallert, *Ontwikkelingslijnen* 109. Until now, it was generally accepted that acceptances appeared only later, i.e. around 1700: for instance De Vries, *Economische achteruitgang* 63 with references.

74 Brugmans, 'Notulen' 198, 258-259. A partnership contract from 1663 prohibited the acceptance of bills without the person concerned having sufficient money at hand: J.E. Elias, 'Contract tot oprichting van een Zweedsch factorie comptoir in Amsterdam in 1663', in: *Bijdragen en mededelingen van het Historisch Genootschap* 24 (1903) 356-

400, ibidem 393.

75 Van Dillen, *Rijkdom en regenten* 456-457. According to the literature, acceptances for foreign account came into fashion only in 1720, referring to W.M.F. Mansvelt, *Geschiedenis van de Nederlandsche Handel-Maatschappij* ([Amsterdam 1924]) I, 8.

76 Quoted by D. Grote, J. Hoock, W. Starke, 'Handbücher für den Gebrauch des Kaufmanns, Bibliographie und Analyse des Wandels einer literarische Gattung', *Tijdschrift voor geschiedenis* 103 (1990) 279-293, ibidem 289.

77 W.L. Korthals Altes, *Van £ Hollands tot Nederlandse ƒ* (Amsterdam 1996) 95-112; P.W.N.M. Dehing, M. 't Hart, 'Linking the fortunes, currency and banking 1550-1880', in: M. 't Hart, J.P.B. Jonker, J.L. van Zanden, ed., *A financial history of the Netherlands* (Cambridge 1997) 37-63, ibidem 40-42; M.S. Polak, *Historiografie en economie van de 'muntchaos', de muntproductie van de Republiek (1606-1795)* (Amsterdam 1998) 187-208.

78 Van Bel, *Linnenhandel* 103-105, 110-111.

79 J.G. van Dillen, 'Oprichting en functie der Amsterdamse Wisselbank in de zeventiende eeuw 1609-1686', in: idem, *Mensen en achtergronden* (Groningen 1964) 336-384, ibidem 383-384; idem, 'Bloeitijd der Amsterdamse Wisselbank 1687-1781', in: idem, *Mensen en achtergronden* (Groningen 1964) 385-415, ibidem 403, 411-415.

80 J.G. van Dillen, 'Amsterdam als wereldmarkt der edele metalen in de 17e en 18e eeuw', in: *Economisch-historische herdrukken* (The Hague 1964) 235-271, ibidem 245.

81 Cf. bijvoorbeeld Bruijn, 'Veranderend perspectief' 23; a disintegrating factor: Faber, 'Achttiende eeuw' 140; fit for retired merchants: Van Bel, *Linnenhandel* 5.

82 A survey of the standpoints in De Vries, *Economische achteruitgang* 33, Hovy, *Voorstel 1751* 61-62.

83 Mansvelt, *NHM* I, 3-4; Van Bel, *Linnenhandel* 5-6.

84 De Vries, *Economische achteruitgang* 32; De Vries/Van der Woude, *Nederland* 170-171, 579.

85 For instance Knoppers/Snapper, 'Nederlandse scheepvaart' 142-143.

86 Van Bel, *Linnenhandel* 78-81.

87 Knoppers/Snapper, 'Nederlandse scheepvaart' 131-133, 142-143.

88 Welling, *Prize* 130.

89 *De koopman, of bijdragen ten opbouw van Neerlands koophandel en zeevaart* (1768-1776). The title does not give away the fact that the editors nursed clear moralizing intentions, so the descriptions and criticisms voiced in it have to be treated with caution: cf. H. Brugmans, 'De koopman, Mercurius als spectator', in: *Jaarboek Amstelodamum* 10 (1917) 61-135, ibidem 61-90, 99-100; Van Dillen, *Rijkdom en regenten* 612. Examples from Dutch literature are the novel E. Wolff, A. Deken, *Historie van mejuffrouw Cornelia Wildschut* (1793-1796) and the play from P. Langendijk, *Spiegel der vaderlandsche kooplieden* (1760).

90 Van Bel, *Linnenhandel* 99.

91 Cf. P.W. Klein, J.W. Veluwenkamp, 'The role of the entrepreneur in the economic expansion of the Dutch Republic', in: C.A. Davids, L. Noordegraaf, ed., *The Dutch economy in the Golden Age* (Amsterdam 1993) 27-53, ibidem 39-43.

92 E. Harder-Gersdorff, 'Avoiding Sound traffic and Sound toll: Russian leather and tallow going west via Archangel and Narva-Lübeck (1650-1710)', in: W.G. Heeres a.o., ed., *From Dunkirk to Danzig, shipping and trade in the North Sea and the Baltic 1350-1850* (Hilversum 1988) 237-262; J.W. Veluwenkamp, 'The purchase and export of Russian commodities in 1741 by Dutch merchants established at Archangel', in: C. Lesger, L. Noordegraaf, ed., *Entrepreneurs and entrepreneurship in modern times, merchants and industrialists within the orbit of the Dutch staple market* (The Hague 1995) 85-100.

93 M.G. Buist, *At spes non fracta, Hope & Co. 1770-1815, merchant bankers and diplomats at work* (Amsterdam 1974) 431-451.

94 C. Gravesteijn, 'Amsterdam and the origins of financial journalism', in: M. North, ed., *Kommunikationsrevolutionen, die neuen Medien des 17. Und 18. Jahrhundert* (Cologne 1995) 61-72, ibidem 69, 72. In 1670 and 1683 the city fathers had tried forbid the circulation of private price currents: W.P. Sautijn Kluit, 'De Amsterdamsche prijscourantiers in de 17de en 18de eeuw' in: *Bijdragen voor vaderlandsche geschiedenis en oudheidkunde* 8 (1875) 58-66, ibidem 61-62.

95 S. Ricard, *Le negoce d'Amsterdam* (1722), quoted by L. Jansen, *'De koophandel van Amsterdam', een critische studie over het koopmanshandboek van Jacques le Moine de l'Espine en Isaac le Long* (Amsterdam 1946) 331.

96 Quoted by D. Ormrod, 'English re-exports and the Dutch staple market in the eighteenth century', in: D.C. Coleman, P. Mathias, ed., *Enterprise and history, essays in honour of Charles Wilson* (Cambridge 1984) 89-115, ibidem 109. About Senserff P. Grimm, 'Heeren in zaken, de bewindhebbers van de Kamer Rotterdam', in: idem, ed., *Heeren in zaken, de kamer Rotterdam van de Verenigde Oostindische Compagnie* (Zutphen 19972) 35-65, ibidem 51, 60-61; M. Fleurke, ''by meenigt' aan de wanden en mueren ', de portretten van de bewindhebbers van de Kamer Rotterdam', in: P. Grimm ed., *Heeren in zaken, de Kamer Rotterdam van de Verenigde Oostindische Compagnie* (Zutphen 1993) 93-100, ibidem 100.

97 A.C. Carter, 'Financial activities of the Huguenots in London and Amsterdam in the mid-eighteenth century', in: idem, *Getting, spending and investing in early modern times, essays on Dutch, English and Huguenot economic history* (Assen 1975) 91-106, ibidem 103.

98 Nanninga, 'Nederlandsche koopman' 138.

99 Carter, 'Financial activities' 101.

100 *Dictionnaire universel du commerce*, geciteerd bij Barbour, *Capitalism* 102.

101 Ricard, *Traité* (1781) I, 211, geciteerd Mansvelt,

NHM I, 4.

102 Brugmans, 'Mercurius' 99.

103 Ricard, *Traité*, geciteerd bij Jansen, *Koophandel* 322.

104 De Vries/Van der Woude, *Nederland* 491.

105 Quoted by S.D. Chapman, 'British marketing enterprise: the changing roles of merchants, manufacturers and financiers 1700-1806', in: *Business history review* 53 (1979) 205-234, ibidem 208.

106 Hildebrand, *Camera obscura* (Haarlem 1953) 53. Stastok was a manufacturer, by the way, who still had some stock after liquidating his ribbon factory.

107 B.R. Mitchell, *British historical statistics* (Cambridge 1988) 442-450.

108 C.J. French, '"Crowded with traders and a great commerce", London's domination of English overseas trade', in: *The London journal* 17 (1992) 27-35, ibidem 29.

109 De Vries/Van der Woude, *Nederland* 577-578.

110 French, 'Crowded' 29; De Vries, *Economische achteruitgang* 23.

111 Veluwenkamp, *Ondernemersgedrag* 46-47, 109-113.

112 De Vries, *Economische achteruitgang* 83-103, 137-141.

113 Van Zanden, *Handelskapitalisme* 135-150; De Vries/Van der Woude, *Nederland* 701-762.

114 By number of ships 43%, by capacity 58%. Cf. De Vries/Van der Woude, *Nederland* 567; Knoppers, 'Vaart Europa' 227.

115 P. de Buck, J.Th. Lindblad, 'Scheepvaart en handel uit de Oostzee op Amsterdam en de Republiek, 1722-1780', in: *Tijdschrift voor geschiedenis* 96 (1983) 536-562, ibidem 558.

116 N. Bang, K. Korst, *Tabeller over skibsfart og varetransport gennem Øresund 1661-1783* (Kopenhagen 1930); data for the graph from Unger, 'Publikatie' 150 and Knoppers, 'Vaart Europa' 241.

117 J.Th. Lindblad, *Sweden's trade with the Dutch Republic 1738-1795* (Assen 1982) 15-20.

118 Israel, *Dutch primacy* 384-389.

119 Unger, 'Publikatie' 159, 191; on the wine trade A. Wegener Sleeswijk, 'Les vins de Guyenne sur le marché hollandais à la fin du XVIIe et au XVIIIe siècle', in: *Chronique d'histoire maritime* 38 (1998) 31-41.

120 Calculated from Bang/Korst, *Tabeller*.

121 Unger, 'Publikatie' 188-205. In 1740, the Republic imported more grain from Britain than from the Baltic: D. Ormrod, 'Dutch commercial-industrial decline and British growth in the late seventeenth and early eighteenth centuries', in: F. Krantz, P. Hohenberg, ed., *Failed transitions to modern industrial society: renaissance Italy and seventeenth-century Holland* (Montreal 1975) 36-43, ibidem 38.

122 About the timber trade C. Lesger, 'Lange termijnprocessen en de betekenis van politieke factoren in de Nederlandse houthandel ten tijde van de Republiek', in: *Economisch- en sociaalhistorisch jaarboek* 55 (1992) 105-142.

123 For instance J.Th. Lindblad, 'Structuur en mededinging in de handel van de Republiek op de Oostzee in de achttiende eeuw', in: *Economisch- en sociaalhistorisch jaarboek* 47 (1984) 79-90, ibidem 79.

124 E. Baasch, 'Hamburg und Holland im 17. und 18. Jahrhundert', in: *Hanseatische Geschichtsblätter* 16 (1910) 45-102, ibidem 84-85.

125 Based on data in Unger, 'Publikatie' 150.

126 Knoppers, 'Vaart Europa' 227.

127 De Vries/Van der Woude, *Nederland* 567.

128 P.C. van Royen, 'Moedernegotie en kraamkamer, schippers, scheepsvolk op de Nederlandse vrachtvaart in Europese wateren vanaf de zeventiende tot in de negentiende eeuw', in: *Tijdschrift voor zeegeschiedenis* 9 (1990) 49-64, ibidem 57-58; G.J.A. Raven, '"Aanhoudend sukkelen om bootsvolk", een keerpunt in het personeelsbeleid van de marine, 1775-1795', in: *Tijdschrift voor zeegeschiedenis* 1 (1982) 132-142.

129 e Vries/Van der Woude, *Nederland* 509, 522-523.

130 About the bottlenecks in the Republic's labour supply in extenso Van Zanden, *Handelskapitalisme* 135-150; De Vries/Van der Woude, *Nederland* 701-762.

131 Knoppers, 'Vaart Europa' estimates the capacity in the European waters at 365,000 tons, De Vries/Van der Woude, *Nederland* 567, put total capacity at 400,000-450,000 tons.

132 Calculated from data in Knoppers/Snapper, 'Nederlandse scheepvaart' 132-133.

133 Unger, 'Publikatie' 157-160.

134 Den Heijer, *Geschiedenis WIC* 122; J.R. Bruijn, F.S. Gaastra, I. Schöffer, ed., *Dutch-Asiatic shipping in the 17th and 18th centuries*, I, *Introduction* (The Hague 1987) 174, 177.

135 Den Heijer, *Geschiedenis WIC* 175-181.

136 Van Goor, *Nederlandse koloniën* 93-96; Gaastra, *Geschiedenis VOC* 53, 124-127; De Korte, *Financiële verantwoording* 31, 47; De Vries/Van der Woude, *Nederland* 503-504, 522; Bruijn/Gaastra/Schöffer, *Dutch-Asiatic shipping* 187.

137 Coenraad van Beuningen did so: De Vries/Van der Woude, *Nederland* 519-520.

138 De Vries/Van der Woude, *Nederland* 502-503; Gaastra, *Geschiedenis VOC* 151.

139 Gaastra, *Geschiedenis VOC* 135.

140 Calculated from De Korte, *Financiële verantwoording* 60.

141 W. Wennekes, *Gouden handel, de eerste Nederlanders overzee, en wat zij daar haalden* (Amsterdam 1996) 189-190, 221; Glamann, *Dutch-Asiatic trade* 212.

142 Source: Gaastra, *Geschiedenis VOC,* 134

143 Baasch, 'Hamburg' 93.

144 J.J. Steur, *Herstel of ondergang, de voorstellen tot redres van de VOC 1740-1795* (Utrecht 1984) 59-60; the Rotterdam firm of J. Senserf & Sn. to Thomas Hall in London, quoted by Ormrod, 'English re-exports' 111.

145 De Vries/Van der Woude, *Nederland* 513-514.

146 J.L. van Zanden, 'Over de rationaliteit van het ondernemersgedrag van de VOC: enkele empirische bevindingen', in: C.A. Davids, J.M.F. Fritschy, L.A. van der Valk, ed., *Kapitaal, ondernemerschap en beleid, studies over economie en politiek in Nederland, Europa en Azië, afscheidsbundel voor prof.dr. P.W. Klein* (Amsterdam 1996) 409-422, ibidem 417-420.

147 De Korte, *Financiele verantwoording* 65-67.

148 Gaastra, *Geschiedenis VOC* 130.

149 Steur, *Herstel* 42-47.

150 Steur, *Herstel* 48.

151 De Korte, *Financiële verantwoording* 60-61.

Chapter III, Through a dark valley

1 For data Welling, *Prize* 193-203; about Surinam A. van Stipriaan Luïscius, *Surinaams contrast, roofbouw en overleven in een Caraïbische plantagekolonie* (Amsterdam 1993).

2 I.J. Brugmans, 'De Oost-Indische Compagnie en de welvaart in de Republiek', idem, *Welvaart en historie, tien studiën* (The Hague 19702) 28-37, ibidem 30-31. The data for the table are on 30-31.

3 De Vries/Van der Woude, *Nederland*, quoting an amount of 240 million.

4 De Vries/Van der Woude, *Nederland* 532-534; 576-579.

5 Gaastra, *Geschiedenis VOC* 86; idem, 'De VOC in Azië, 1680-1795', in: D.P. Blok a.o., ed., *Algemene geschiedenis der Nederlanden*, IX, *Nieuwe tijd* (Bussum 1980) 427-464, ibidem 433.

6 De Vries, *Economische achteruitgang* 38-45.

7 Spooner, *Risks* 80; Buist, *Hope & Co.* 12.

8 Hovy, *Voorstel 1751* 361-362; De Jong-Keesing, *Crisis 1763* 19.

9 Buist, *Hope & Co.* 46; Van Dillen, *Rijkdom en regenten* 621.

10 Source for the graph: GAA PA 735 Hope & Co. No. 592.

11 On the term merchant bankers see R. Roberts, 'What's in a name? Merchants, merchant bankers, accepting houses, issuing houses, industrial bankers and investment bankers', in: *Business History* 35 (1993) No. 3 22-39.

12 GAA PA 735 Hope & Co. No. 593, balance 1762. There are no earlier data. The VOC's initial capital was 6.4 million guilders. In addition, the company had 7.5 million guilders of bonds outstanding in 1760:: De Korte, *Financiële verantwoording* 2 and Appendix 1e.

13 GAA PA 196 Bicker No. 796, the 1755 partnership contract between Hendrick Bicker and Jan Bernd Bicker.

14 J.H. Kernkamp, 'Bengt Ferrner's dagboek van zijne reis door Nederland', in: *Bijdragen en mededelingen van het historisch genootschap* 31 (1910) 314-509.

15 J.P.B. Jonker, *Merchants, bankers, middlemen, the Amsterdam money market during the first half of the 19th century* (Amsterdam, 1996) 67.

16 Buist, *Hope & Co.* 10; Hovy, *Propositie* 111, 147,

238-640 passim.

17 Steur, *Herstel* 57-59, 65-69, 84-87, 101-104, 108-110, 277-279.

18 Buist, *Hope & Co.* 14-16; the Wisselbank's ledgers show the new name in use as early as the 1750s: De Jong-Keesing, *Crisis 1763* 69.

19 De Vries, *Economische achteruitgang* 64.

20 About these loans W.W. van der Meulen, 'Beschrijving van eenige West-Indische plantageleeningen', in: *Bijdragen en mededeelingen van het Historisch Genootschap* 25 (1904) 490-580; G. Oostindie, *Roosenburg en Monbijou, twee Surinaamse plantages 1720-1870* (Dordrecht 1989) 289-297; Van Stipriaan, *Surinaams contrast* 205-256.

21 J.C. Riley, *International government finance and the Amsterdam capital market 1740-1815* (Cambridge 1980) 16.

22 GAA PA 654 Crommelin No. 6, 7; GAA PA 447 Van Eeghen, ledgers (no inventory numbers available).

23 Jonker, *Merchants* 210-211.

24 Cf. H. Hardenberg, 'Het handelshuis Osy', in: *Rotterdams jaarboekje* (1954) 154-176.

25 Cf. S.D. Chapman, *Merchant enterprise in Britain from the Industrial Revolution to World War I* (Cambridge 1992) 90-91, 313-318.

26 Riley, *International government finance* 204.

27 A. Heertje, *David Ricardo en Amsterdam, de toekomst van de economische wetenschap als geschiedenis* (Amsterdam 1998).

28 Cf. Steur, *Herstel* 161-185; P. Moree, *Met vriend die God geleide, het Nederlands-Aziatische postverkeer ten tijde van de VOC* (Zutphen 1998).

29 Gaastra, *Geschiedenis VOC* 167-168.

30 J.G. van Dillen, 'Ondergang van de Amsterdamse Wisselbank, 1782-1820', in: idem, *Mensen en achtergronden* (Groningen 1964) 416-447, ibidem 416-425.

31 Den Heijer, *Geschiedenis WIC* 186-187.

32 Welling, *Prize* 130; L. van Nierop, 'Amsterdams scheepvaart in de Fransche Tijd', in: *Jaarboek Amstelodamum* 21 (1924) 119-139, ibidem 136.

33 A.J. Oosterwijk, *Koning van de koopvaart, Anthony van Hoboken (1756-1850)* (Rotterdam 1983) 181.

34 S. Schama, *Patriots and liberators, revolution in the Netherlands 1780-1813* ((New York 1977) 370-376; L. Noordegraaf, 'Sociale verhoudingen en structuren in de Noordelijke Nederlanden 1770-1813', in: D.P. Blok a.o., ed., *Algemene geschiedenis der Nederlanden X, Nieuwste tijd* (Bussum 1981) 361-383, ibidem 373-378.

35 Quoted by I.J. Brugmans, *Paardenkracht en mensenmacht, sociaal-economische geschiedenis van Nederland, 1795-1940* (The Hague 1983) 24.

36 Cf. E. Horlings, *The economic development of the Dutch service sector 1800-1850, trade and transport in a premodern economy* (Amsterdam 1995) 380.

37 Oldewelt, 'Amsterdamse faillissementen' 432-433.

38 Jonker, *Merchants* 189-191, 221-222.

39 Jonker, *Merchants* 190.

40 Jonker, *Merchants* 201.

41 Bruijn/Gaastra/Schöffer, *Dutch-Asiatic shipping* 194.

42 Oosterwijk, *Van Hoboken* 22, 25-29, 33, 37, 49, 56-59, 67, 78; A. Hoynck van Papendrecht, *Gedenkboek A. van Hoboken & Co., 1774-1924* (Rotterdam 1924) 38, 51, 60.

43 Crone, *Crone* 1-11.

44 Mitchell, *British historical statistics* 451; Horlings, *Economic development* 380.

45 E.S. van Eyck van Heslinga, 'De vlag dekt de lading, de Nederlandse koopvaardij in de Vierde Engelse Oorlog', in: *Tijdschrift voor zeegeschiedenis* 1 (1982) 102-113, ibidem 110.

46 Spooner, *Risks* 29-31, 33-36, 39-40, 45, 113-115.

47 Jonker, *Merchants* 154.

48 J. Sperling, 'The international payments mechanism in the seventeenth and eighteenth centuries', in: *Economic history review* 2nd ser 14 (1962) 446-468; R.C. Michie, 'The invisible stabilizer, asset arbitrage and the international monetary system since 1700', in: *Financial history review* 5 (1998) 5-26.

49 Cf. B. Kolff, 'Achter de schermen van het onder onzijdige vlag brengen van koopvaardijschepen van de Bataafsche Republiek', in: *Rotterdamsch jaarboekje* (1944) 81-108, ibidem 84-90; Knoppers, 'Vaart Europa' 229.

50 Van Eyk van Heslinga, 'Vlag'; Kolff, 'Achter de schermen' 91.

51 Kolff, 'Achter de schermen' 86-88; Rogge, *Van Eeghen* 129-131.

52 Cf. Schama, *Patriots* 403-404, 451; Oosterwijk, *Van Hoboken* 40.

53 K.J.P.F.M. Jeurgens., P.M.M. Klep, *Informatieprocessen van de Bataafs-Franse overheid 1795-1813* (The Hague 1997); P.M.M. Klep, 'Kanttekeningen bij het Bataafs-Franse beschrijvende bronnenmateriaal in Nederland, 1795-1813', in: J.P.A. Coopmans a.o., ed., *Van blauwe stoep tot citadel, varia historica Brabantica Ludovico Pirenne dedicata* (Den Bosch 1988) 257-266; idem, 'Researchwaarde en toegankelijkheid van het beschrijvende bronnenmateriaal uit de Bataafs-Franse Tijd', in: *Economisch- en sociaalhistorisch jaarboek* 55 (1992) 3-14; A. Verheusen, *Beschrijvend bronnenmateriaal van de Bataafs-Franse overheid 1795-1813* (The Hague 1995).

54 Rogge, *Van Eeghen* 135.

55 Oosterwijk, *Van Hoboken* 80-81; Westermann, *Gedenkboek* 5-13; S.W. Verstegen, 'Tussen beleid en belang, geschiedenis van de Kamers van koophandel en fabrieken in Nederland', in: J.L.J.M. van Gerwen, J.J. Seegers, S.W. Verstegen, *Mercurius' erfenis, een geschiedenis en bronnenoverzicht van de Kamers van koophandel en fabrieken in Nederland (*Amsterdam 1990) 9-56. The magazine *De Koopman* had already pleaded for such chambers: Brugmans, 'De koopman' 89-90.

56 Hoynck van Papendrecht, *Van Hoboken* 39. According to Oosterwijk, *Van Hoboken* 47, Rotterdam had only four big merchants around 1800, Van Hoboken amongst them. However, his source, Van den Berg, 'Lijst handelshuizen' does not use the particular term of *zeehandelaren* and lists an additional number of houses.

57 Hoynck van Papendrecht, *Van Hoboken* 54.

58 Hoynck van Papendrecht, *Van Hoboken* 37, 41, 57; Kolff, 'Achter de schermen' 96, 106; Rogge, *Van Eeghen* 128.

59 Oosterwijk, *Van Hoboken* 42-43; Hoynck van Papendrecht, *Van Hoboken* 54, 62.

60 Hoynck van Papendrecht, *Van Hoboken* 38, 48, 51, 60.

61 Leonhardt, *Huis* 43.

62 Oosterwijk, *Van Hoboken* 42-43, 59, 72-73.

63 Rogge, *Van Eeghen* 129-131.

64 Examples in Rogge, *Van Eeghen* 135.

65 Oosterwijk, *Van Hoboken* 73-74.

66 Oosterwijk, *Van Hoboken* 75-79; Hoynck van Papendrecht, *Van Hoboken* 65.

67 Rogge, *Van Eeghen* 126-148.

68 GAA PA 654 Crommelin Nos 6, 7.

69 Buist, *Hope & Co.* 40, 54, 57-69, 188-205, 279-329; V. Nolte, *Fifty years in both hemispheres, or reminiscences of a merchant's life* (London 1854) 75-94; G. Labouchère, 'Pierre César Labouchère (1772-1839), un financier diplomate au siècle dernier', in: *Revue d'histoire diplomatique* 27 (1913) 1-54.

70 Horlings, *Economic development* 380.

71 Jonker, *Merchants* 195-196.

72 S.D. Chapman, *The rise of merchant banking* (London 1984) 40.

73 Jonker, *Merchants* 229.

74 I.J. Brugmans, Brugmans, I.J., ed., *Statistieken van de Nederlandse nijverheid uit de eerste helft der 19e eeuw* (The Hague 1956) I, 1-245; Damsma, D., J.M.M. de Meere, L. Noordegraaf, ed., *Statistieken van de Nederlandse nijverheid uit de eerste helft der 19e eeuw, supplement* (The Hague 1979) 1-112; Z.W. Sneller, 'De toestand der nijverheid te Amsterdam en Rotterdam volgens de enquete van 1816', in: idem, *Bijdragen tot de economische geschiedenis van Nederland* (Utrecht 1968) 161-202.

75 Brugmans, *Paardenkracht* 152-154.

76 De Vries/Van der Woude, *Nederland* 568-569.

77 Knoppers, 'Vaart Europa' 233.

78 Dehing/'t Hart, 'Linking fortunes' 49; Jonker, *Merchants* 165; idem, 'The cradle of modern banking, finance in the Netherlands between the Napoleonic era and the first commercial banks, 1813-1870', in: Joh. de Vries, W. Vroom, T. de Graaf, ed., *World wide banking, ABN AMRO Bank 1824-1999* (Amsterdam 1999) 49-94, ibidem 51-52.

79 Horlings, *Economic development* 380.

80 Chapman, *Merchant enterprise* 85, 193-198; idem, 'Marketing enterprise' 217-225.

81 Horlings, *Economic development* 150.

Notes

82 Jonker, *Merchants* 195-199; N.W. Postumus, 'Nota over den toestand van de Amsterdamsche handelshuizen in het jaar 1854', in: *Economisch historisch jaarboek* 7 (1921) 196-209, ibidem 207-208.

83 Jonker, *Merchants* 35.

84 Chapman, *Merchant enterprise* 87-88; Jonker, Merchants 211, 214; J. Wake, *Kleinwort Benson, the history of two families in banking* (Oxford 1997) 44-46.

85 Jonker, *Merchants* 69; R. Walter, 'Die nordwesteuropäische Wirtschaft in mikroökonomischer Perspektive: Das Beispiel Hasenclever', in: M. North, ed., *Nordwesteuropa in der Weltwirtschaft 1750-1950* (Stuttgart 1993) 291-307, ibidem 303.

86 A.M.E. Lewe, *'Invoer te lande verboden', een verkenning van de handel over landwegen tussen Nederland en de Pruisische provincies Rheinland en Westfalen 1836-1857* (Hilversum 1995) 50-55.

87 Van Bel, *Linnenhandel* 43-44.

88 R. Miellet, 'Westfaalse ondernemers en de opkomst van het Nederlandse grootwinkelbedrijf tot circa 1920', in: *Jaarboek geschiedenis bedrijf en techniek* 3 (18986) 135-157; idem, 'Immigratie van katholieke Westfalers en de modernisering van de Nederlandse detailhandel', in: *Tijdschrif voor geschiedenis* 100 (1987) 374-393; idem, *Honderd jaar grootwinkelbedrijf in Nederland* (Zwolle s.a.).

89 P.J. Bouman, Rotterdam en het Duitse achterland 1831-1851 (Amsterdam 1931) 24-27; H.P.H. Nusteling, *De Rijnvaart in het tijdperk van stoom en steenkool 1813-1914* (Amsterdam 1974) 10-11.

90 Nusteling, Rijnvaart 3-9; J.F.E. Bläsing, *Das goldene Delta und sein eisernes Hinterland 1815-1851, von niederländisch-preussischen zu deutsch-niederländischen Wirtschaftsbeziehungen* (Leiden 1973) 56-82; Horlings, *Economic development* 194-208.

91 For instance Brugmans, *Paardenkracht* 84-85.

92 The list with merchant houses which vanished has been published in Posthumus, 'Nota 1854'. The unpublished calculations and the conclusions drawn from them by Crommelin shed another light on his considerations. They can be found in GAA PA 654 Crommelin, No. 21.

93 Oosterwijk, *Van Hoboken* 90-127; Hoynck van Papendrecht, *Van Hoboken* 15.

94 A.W. Wichers Hoeth, *De geschiedenis van het Amsterdamsche handelshuis Louis Bienfait & Soon* (Hilversum 1941) 70-74; Oostindie *Roosenburg* 294-198; Van Stipriaan, *Surinaams contrast* 243-244.

95 Posthumus, 'Nota 1854' 208.

96 Jonker, *Merchants* 214.

97 Crone, *Crone* 18-29.

98 Jonker, *Merchants* 207-209, 219-221.

99 Jonker, *Merchants* 199, 226.

100 About WIC fortresses Den Heijer, *WIC* 123-125.

101 Muller, *Zeehandelaar* 27-28. The firm's senior partner was the brother of the well-known wine merchant Jacobus Boelen.

102 Oosterwijk, *Van Hoboken* 220.

103 Mansvelt, *NHM* II, 232-233.

104 H. Muller, *Een Rotterdams zeehandelaar, Hendrik Muller Szn., (1819-1898)* (Schiedam 1977) 32-33, 35, 61-62, 198-199.

105 Jonker, *Merchants* 196, 207, 211, 219, 222.

106 Jonker, *Merchants* 47, 119; Rogge, *Van Eeghen* 184, 194, 205.

107 Posthumus, 'Nota 1854' 198, 199, 200, 204.

108 F.J.E. van Lennep, *Late regenten* (Haarlem 1962) 208-221; Mansvelt, *NHM* I, 139, 178.

109 Rogge, *Van Eeghen* 207-209, 212; H.G.Th. Crone, *Crone 1790-1940, gedenkboek ter gelegenheid van het 150-jarig bestaan van de firma* (Amsterdam 1940) 30-32, 64-66.

110 On William I's neomercantilism W.M. Zappey, 'Het Fonds voor de Nationale Nijverheid 1821-1846', in: P. Boomgaard a.o., ed., *Exercities in ons verleden, 12 opstellen over de sociale en economische geschiedenis van Nederland en koloniën 1800-1950, aangeboden aan prof.dr. W.J. Wieringa bij zijn aftreden als hoogleraar aan de Vrije Universiteit te Amsterdam* (Assen 1981) 27-42; I.J. Brugmans, 'Koning Willem I als neo-mercantilist', in: idem, *Welvaart en historie, tien studiën* (The Hague 19702) 38-50.

111 A.M. de Jong, *Geschiedenis van de Nederlandsche Bank, I, 1814-1864* (Haarlem 1967) 84-86.

112 Cf. R. Reinsma, 'De vergeten Maatschappij van koophandel en zeevaart te Amsterdam (1818-1823)', in: *Tijdschrift voor geschiedenis* 70 (1957) 189-203; idem, 'De West-Indische Maatschappij (1828-1863)', in: *Tijdschrift voor geschiedenis* 73 (1960) 58-74; Zappey, 'Fonds'; P.J. van Winter, *Een vergeten schepping van koning Willem I: de Maatschappij van landeigenaren en beklemde meiers te Groningen 1823-1878* (Amsterdam 1949); R. Filarski, *Kanalen van de Koning-koopman, goederenvervoer, binnenscheepvaart en kanalenbouw in Nederland en België in de eerste helft van de negentiende eeuw* (Amsterdam 1995).

113 J. Ratté, *De Nederlandse doorvoerpolitiek en de vrije vaart po de internationale Rijn, een schets van het ontstaan van de vrije doorvoer door Nederland* (Rotterdam 1952) 48-54.

114 Horlings, *Economic development* 118-126.

115 Posthumus, 'Nota 1854' 204-205; Th. van Tijn, *Twintig jaren Amsterdam, de maatschappelijke ontwikkeling van de hoofdstad van de jaren '50 der vorige eeuw tot 1876* (Amsterdam 1965) 35-36.

116 Ratté, *Doorvoerpolitiek* 49-54, 56-59, 90; cf. Jonker, *Merchants* 36.

117 J. van Ouwerkerk de Vries, *Verhandeling over de oorzaak van het verval en de middelen tot herstel van den Nederlandschen koophandel* (Haarlem 1827).

118 Westermann, *Kamer van Koophandel* 169-173.

119 Jonker, 'Cradle' 76.

120 Horlings, *Economic development* 136.

121 Cf. Nusteling, *Rijnvaart* 3-4, 12, on the resistance against liberating the transit trade and public bonded warehouses.

122 J. Schouwenaar, *Tussen beurs en binnenhof, J.W. van den Biesen en de politieke journalistiek van het Handelsblad (1828-1945)* (Amsterdam1999) 17-20; Jonker, *Merchants* 135-136; I.H. van Eeghen, *Uit Amsterdamse dagboeken, de jeugd van Netje en Eduard Asser 1819-1833* (Amsterdam 1964) 212.

123 Mansvelt, *NHM* I, 55; P. Boomgaard, ed., *Changing economy in Indonesia*, 9, G.J. Knaap, ed., *Transport 1819-1940* (Amsterdam 1989) 19.

124 Broeze, *Stad Schiedam* 151-153.

125 Hoynck van Papendrecht, *Van Hoboken* 137.

126 Mansvelt, *NHM* I, 57-58.

127 Posthumus, 'Nota 1854' 208.

128 Oosterwijk, *Van Hoboken* 90-127.

129 Mansvelt, *NHM* I, 54-55.

130 Bruijn/Gaastra/Schöffer, *Dutch-Asiatic shipping* I, 177; Horlings, *Economic development* 387, 389, 394-395.

131 De Korte, *Financiële verantwoording* Appendix 9E; Horlings, *Economic development* 375; Van Stipriaan, *Surinaams contrast* 429-433, 437 gives data from 1815.

132 Mansvelt, *NHM* I, 41.

133 Calculated from Bruijn/Gaastra/Schöffer, *Dutch Asiatic shipping* I, 177; De Korte, *Financiële verantwoording* 60.

134 Boomgaard, *Changing economy in Indonesia*, 12a, W.L. Korthals Altes, ed., *Regional trade statistics 1822-1940* (Amsterdam 1991) 40-43, 60-63, 80-82, 93-96.

135 Boomgaard, *Changing economy* 12a, 40-43, 60-63, 80-82, 93-96.

136 Van Ouwerkerk de Vries, *Verhandeling* 143-146.

137 Mansvelt, NHM I, 47; J.J.P. de Jong, *De waaier van het fortuin, de Nedelanders in Azië en de Indonesische archipel 1595-1950* (The Hague 1998) 193-195.

138 Boomgaard, *Changing economy* 12a, 40-43, 60-63, 80-82, 93-96.

139 Mansvelt, *NHM* I, 40-42, 54-55; idem, 'De eerste Indische handelshuizen, mededeelingen over de resultaten van een onderzoek naar de nationaliteit van het Nederlandsch-Indisch handelsapparaat in de eerste helft der 19e eeuw', typoscript Ondernemersraad voor Nederlandsch Indië in 1937, 6; Oosterwijk, *Van Hoboken* 111-113.

140 Data from Van Stipriaan, *Surinaams contrast* 437; Boomgaard, *Changing economy* 12a, 40-43, 60-63, 80-82, 93-96.

141 Cf. the introduction to the decree establishing the company in Mansvelt, *NHM* I, Appendix 1, and the King's remarks on the subject, idem 235.

142 Mansvelt, *NHM* I, 50-53.

143 Oosterwijk, *Van Hoboken* 129.

144 Cf. Oosterwijk, *Van Hoboken* 113-114, 128-129.

145 As remembered by his son Claude Crommelin in his 1854 memorandum, GAA PA 654 Crommelin, No. 21.

146 Mansvelt, *NHM* II, 332; Broeze, *Stad Schiedam* 1-12 for a survey of the relief arrangements up to

1835.

147 Oosterwijk, *Van Hoboken* 157-158.

148 Mansvelt, *NHM* II, 342-344.

149 A.J. Oosterwijk, *Reder in Rotterdam, Willem Ruys 1803-1889* (Rotterdam 1990) 27-79; Horlings, *Economic development* 147-148.

150 Oosterwijk, *Van Hoboken* 204-220.

151 Posthumus, 'Nota 1854' 207-208.

152 Mansvelt, *NHM* II, 128-129, 164, 224, 431.

153 W.M.F. Mansvelt, 'De oorsprong van den Hollandschen suikerstandaard', in: *De Indische Mercuur*, 1 May 1925, 3-11.

154 Mansvelt, *NHM* II, Appendix 1.

155 Boomgaard, *Changing economy* 12a, 40-43, 60-63, 80-82, 93-96; Mansvelt, *NHM* I, 201, II Appendix IV.

156 Mansvelt, *NHM* I, 232-233, Appendix II, III; II, Appendix V. The opium was supplied by Jacob van Lennep & Co. in Smyrna: Mansvelt, *NHM* I, 139, 178. About the semi-official opium trade in Asia E. Vanvugt, *Wettig opium, 350 jaar Nederlandse opiumhandel in de Indische archipel* (Haarlem 1985).

157 Boomgaard, *Changing economy* 12a, 40-43, 60-63, 80-82, 93-96; Mansvelt, *NHM* II, 204; data about the Cultivation System in C. Fasseur, *Kultuurstelsel en koloniale baten, de Nederlandse exploitatie van Java 1840-1860* (Leiden 1975).

158 Jonker, *Merchants* 119-121.

159 Jonker, *Merchants* 51-55, 120.

160 Jonker, *Merchants* 120.

161 Mansvelt, *NHM* I, 258-343.

162 Mansvelt, *NHM* I, Appendix III.

163 Mansvelt, *NHM* I, 403-426.

164 Horlings, *Economic development* 145-151, 375, 376, 380; about Surinam Van Stipriaan, *Surinaams contrast* Appendix 3.

165 Brugmans, 'Oostindische Compagnie' 30-31.

166 Mansvelt, *NHM* II, 204-207.

167 If one includes an extra payout from the reserves in 1849, on the occasion of the renewal of the charter, than the dividend return was as high as 9.7%: Mansvelt, *NHM* I, Appendix III; II, 210-211.

168 Jonker, *Merchants* 186; De Jong, *Nederlandsche Bank* I, Appendix 5.

169 Jonker, *Merchants* 210-211, 219, 222.

170 Mansvelt, *NHM* II, 279-281; J.L. van Zanden, *De industrialisatie van Amsterdam 1825-1914* (Bergen 1987) 42-56.

171 Mansvelt, *NHM* II, 206-280, 313-349.

172 De Jong, *Waaier* 213-226.

173 De Jong, *Nederlandsche Bank* I, 3.

174 Posthumus, 'Nota 1854' 204, De Jong, *Nederlandsche Bank* II, 112, 196; III 506 about Luden & Van Geuns. Crommelin makes no mention of Insinger.

175 Jonker, *Merchants* 229.

176 Hans Simons kindly supplied me with data on private trade with the Dutch East Indies; cf. Mansvelt, *NHM* II 228-229, quoting NHM imports in 1848 of 36 million guilders on a total for the Dutch East Indies of 64.4 million guilders; idem *NHM* II, 272-273; Rogge, *Van Eeghen* 194.

177 Oosterwijk, *Van Hoboken* 194-195.

178 Horlings, *Economic development* 375, 376, 380.

179 The rise of commercial agents charted by Chapman, 'Marketing enterprise' 217-225; on Potgieter's operations P.N. Muller, 'Potgieter ter beurze', in: *De gids* 50 (1886) 411-420.

180 Chapman, *Merchant enterprise* 193-230; idem, 'Marketing enterprise' 226-231.

181 Posthumus, 'Nota 1854' 204, 209.

182 Jonker, *Merchants* 40.

183 Posthumus, 'Nota 1854' 196-197; Van Tijn, *Twintig jaren* 30-37.

184 Cf. Posthumus, 'Nota 1854' 197.

185 D. Wanjon, *Geschiedenis van den Nederlandschen handel sedert 1795* (Haarlem 1900) 91.

186 Jonker, *Merchants* 200; GAA PA 654 Crommelin No. 7, balances 1814-1859; R.P.J. Tutein Nolthenius, *Het geslacht Tutein Nolthenius* (Haarlem 1914-1930) II, 742-745.

187 Mansvelt, *NHM* II, 272.

188 Rogge, *Van Eeghen* 206-215.

Chapter IV, A revolution in industry, traffic, and trade, 1850-1914

1 Mansvelt, *NHM* II, 245-247, 252.

2 J.J.P. de Jong, *Van batig slot naar ereschuld, de discussie over de financiële verhouding tussen Nederland en Indië en de hervorming van de Nederlandse koloniale politiek 1860-1900* (Groningen 1989) 33; M. Kuitenbrouwer, *The Netherlands and the rise of modern imperialism, colonies and foreign policy 1870-1902* (Oxford 1991) 35.

3 Mansvelt, *NHM* II, 246-254.

4 Wanjon, *Geschiedenis* 75.

5 A.G. Kenwood, A.L. Lougheed, *The growth of the international economy 1820-2000* (London 19994) 91.

6 P.J. Hugill, *Global communications since 1844, geopolitics and technology* (Baltimore 1999) 29-33, 39.

7 A specimen of this slide rule was offered for sale at a London book auction on October 28, 1999. This contraption reportedly uses the term computer for the first time to designate a device for calculations, and not a person calculating. H.R. Woudhuysen, 'Turing's legacy', *Times Literary Supplement*, 15 October 1999.

8 F.J.A. Broeze, 'The international diffusion of ocean steam navigation, the myth of the retardation of Netherlands steam navigation to the East Indies', in: *Economisch- en sociaalhistorisch jaarboek* 45 (1982) 77-95.

9 Nusteling, *Rijnvaart* 38-47.

10 *Kijk in een jarige krant: NRC 125* (Rotterdam 1969) 10, 11, 12; H.J. Scheffer, *In vorm gegoten, het Rotterdamsch Nieuwsblad in de negentiende eeuw* (The Hague 19812) 14.

11 J.A. de Jonge, *De industrialisatie in Nederland tussen 1850 en 1914* (Nijmegen 1976) 169-170. Cf. W.F. Lichtenauer, *Kamer van koophandel en*

fabrieken Rotterdam 1803-1928* (Rotterdam 1928) 634-655 about differences of opinion within the Rotterdam Chamber over commercial policy during the 1880s.

12 Brugmans, *Paardenkracht* 214-219; Ratté, *Doorvoerpolitiek* 156-199.

13 Brugmans, *Paardenkracht* 214-225; Verstegen, 'Tussen beleid en belang' 18-24.

14 Verstegen, 'Tussen beleid en belang' 18-24.

15 G. Hogesteeger, *Van lopende bode tot telematica, geschiedenis van de PTT in Nederland* (Groningen 1989) 45-54.

16 Hogesteeger, *Lopende bode* 124-132; Brugmans, *Paardenkracht* 226-228; A.J. Veenendaal jr., *De ijzeren weg in een land vol water, beknopte geschiedenis van de spoorwegen in Nederland 1834-1958* (Amsterdam 1998) 26-34, 39-50.

17 Brugmans, *Paardenkracht* 228-230.

18 De Jong, *Nederlandsche Bank* II, 73-101; for a survey of the discussion J.G.S.J. van Maarseveen, *Nicolaas Gerard Pierson, handelsman, econoom en bankier, eerste periode 1839-1877* (Rotterdam 1981) 72-77.

19 Jonker, *Merchants* 134-137; Westermann, *Gedenkboek* 300-301.

20 K. Mandemakers, *HBS en gymnasium, ontwikkeling, structuur, sociale achtergrond en schoolprestaties, Nederland, circa 1800-1968* (Amsterdam 1996) 65-70.

21 *Nederlandsch Handels-Magazijn* I, 479-483.

22 J. Bakker, *Mercurius gedurende een halve eeuw, gedenkboek ter gelegenheid van het vijftigjarig jubileum van den nationalen bond van handels- en kantoorbedienden 'Mercurius'* (Leiden 1932); Bos, D., *De opleiding voor den handel* (S.l. 1902) 13; L. van Nierop, ''Hou' en Trouw 1885-1925', in: *Gedenkboek Hou' en Trouw, Vereeniging van oud-leerlingen der openbare handelsscholen te Amsterdam 1885-1925* (Amsterdam 1925) 15-36, ibidem 24, 26-27, 32, 34; Rogge, *Van Eeghen* 307-308; J.H.H. Hülsmann, *Geschiedenis der openbare handelsschool* (Amsterdam 1899).

23 W.C. Mees, *Man van de daad, mr. Marten Mees en de opkomst van Rotterdam* (Rotterdam 1946) 526.

24 Oosterwijk, *Reder* 103-104, 141, 177-179.

25 J.L. Pierson, *Mémoires uit de jaren 1854-1926* (S.l.s.a.) 19. The periodical *De Koopman* had pleaded in vain for an academic curriculum for aspiring merchants: Brugmans, 'De koopman' 90-92.

26 Joh. de Vries, *Herinneringen en dagboek van Ernst Heldring 1871-1954* (The Hague 1970) 1009-1010.

27 J.P. Smits, E. Horlings, J.L. van Zanden, 'The measurement of grosos national product and its components, the Netherlands 1800-1913', N.W. Posthumus Instituut, Research Memorandum No. 1 (Utrecht 1997) Appendix 2.

28 De Jonge, *Industrialisatie* 19; Brugmans, *Paardenkracht* 312-313.

29 Van Zanden, *Industrialisatie Amsterdam* 42-44,

46-47; A. Heerding, *Geschiedenis van de NV Philips' Gloeilampenfabrieken*, I, *Het ontstaan van de Nederlandse gloeilampenindustrie* (The Hague 1980) 292- 299.

30 From 1865, the annual consular reports were also published. Kuitenbrouwer, *Netherlands* 250-251; Westermann, *Kamer van koophandel* 409-411.

31 Chapman, *Merchant enterprise* 195-199, 202-204

32 W.A.H. Crol, *Een tak van de familie Van Stolk honderd jaar in de graanhandel 1847-1947* (Rotterdam 1947) 31, 40.

33 J.F. Haccoû, *De termijnhandel in goederen* (Leiden 1947) 62-67; P. Geljon, 'Termijnhandel in Nederland', in: idem, ed., *Termijnhandel en termijn markten, opstellen ter gelegenheid van het 100-jarig bestaan van de georganiseerde termijnhandel in Amsterdam* (Deventer 1988) 45-70, ibidem 45-46.

34 G.H. Crone, 'De ontwikkeling der koloniale markten in Nederland', in: C. Gerretson a.o., *De sociaal-economische invloed van Nederlandsch-Indië op Nederland* (Wageningen 1938) 45-62, ibidem 58-59; Rogge, *Van Eeghen* 356-357.

35 P.N. Muller, 'Handelsstudiën', in: *De Economist* 7 (1858) 121-130, 157-167, 233-247, 398-412, ibidem 235.

36 *De Economist* 10 (1861) bijblad, 113-118, 249-255. The article is not signed, but the style renders it likely that Muller wrote it.

37 P.N. Muller, 'De handel van Nederland in de laatste vijf en twintig jaar 1847-1871', in *De economist* (1875) I, 1-37, ibidem 11.

38 See also Muller, 'Handel Nederland' 11.

39 E.C. Godée Molsbergen, *Gedenkboek Reynst & Vinju 1836-1936* (Batavia 1935) 27, 55.

40 For the techniques used see Rogge, *Van Eeghen* 216-219, 355-356.

41 Van Tijn, *Twintig jaren* 206-208.

42 H. van Driel, 'Uitschakeling van de Nederlandse koffiehandel in de negentiende- en twintigste eeuw?', in: *NEHA-jaarboek* 60 (1997) 159-203, ibidem 176-178.

43 Rogge, *Van Eeghen* 348-349.

44 Van Tijn, *Twintig jaren* 203-204.

45 Rogge, *Van Eeghen* 231.

46 Geljon, 'Termijnhandel' 53.

47 Borsumij, annual report for 1905.

48 Nusteling, *Rijnvaart* 305-317; Van Driel, *Vier eeuwen* 80-84.

49 Crol, *Van Stolk* 54-55.

50 Lichtenauer, *Gedenkboek* 467, 472.

51 Brugmans, *Paardenkracht* 360-361.

52 Nusteling, *Rijnvaart* 288-289, 304-305, 316; Van Driel, *Vier eeuwen* 96-99; Lichtenauer, *Gedenkboek* 562, 588-593.

53 Nusteling, *Rijnvaart* 280, 285-289.

54 J.H. van Stuijvenberg, *Het Centraal Bureau, een coöperatief krachtenveld in de Nederlandse landbouw, 1899-1949* (Rotterdam 1949) 137-143.

55 *Economisch archief voor Nederland en koloniën*, no page numbers.

56 W.P.M.H. van Hooff, 'Meer koopman dan ambachtsman, joodse ondernemers in de Nederlandse metaalindustrie en -handel', in: H. Berg, E.J. Fischer, T. Wijsenbeek, ed., *Venter, fabriqueur, fabrikant, joodse ondernemers en ondernemingen in Nederland 1796-1940* (Amsterdam 1994) 149-159, ibidem 149-151.

57 W.J. Hoffmann, 'Een oud-Rotterdamsche firma, J.F. Hoffmann en Zoonen 1734-1899', in: *Rotterdamsch jaarboekje* 3 (1915) 94-112; Lichtenauer, *Gedenkboek* 24, 189, 193, 231, 308, 328, 375, 424, 751, 942.

58 Miellet, *Honderd jaar* 38-41; about the distances between various social groups K. Bruin, *Een herenwereld ontleed, over Amsterdamse oude en nieuwe elites in de tweede helft van de negentiende eeuw* (Amsterdam 1980) 49-65.

59 Miellet, *Honderd jaar* 37-38.

60 Miellet, *Honderd jaar* 29-31.

61 Miellet, Honderd jaar 60-67, 80-85, 98-103; J.L. de Jager, *Arm en rijk kunnen bij mij hun inkopen doen, de geschiedenis van Albert Heijn en de Koninklijke Ahold* (Baarn 1995) 17-38.

62 Van Stuijvenberg, *Centraal bureau* 137-143.

63 See for instance Kaptein, *Hollandse textielnijverheid* 48-58; Van Bel, *Linnenhandel* 31-33; L. van Nierop, 'De zijdenijverheid te Amsterdam historisch geschetst', in: *Tijdschrift voor geschiedenis* 45 (1930) 18-40, 46 (1931) 28-55, ibidem 34-35.

64 W.F.H. Oldewelt, 'Bescherming van merk en handelsnaam', in: idem, *Amsterdamsche archiefvondsten* (Amsterdam 1942) 119-123, ibidem 120.

65 De Jager, *Arm en rijk* 22-24; J.B. Jefferys, *Retail trading in Britain, 1850-1950, a study of trends in retailing with special reference to the development of Co-operative, multiple shop and department store methods of trading* (Cambridge 1954) 1-39; P. Mathias, *Retailing revolution, a history of multiple retailing in the food trades based upon the Allied Suppliers Group of Companies* (London 1967) 35-54.

66 J.M. Welcker, 'Het dagelijks brood, de doopsgezinden, de economie en de demografie', in: S. Groenveld, S.L. Verheus, ed., *Wederdopers, menisten, doopsgezinden in Nederland 1530-1980* (Zutphen 1980) 195-218 , ibidem 206-207.

67 J.P.W.A. Smit, 'De aanleiding tot de "Wet wegens het namaken der merken en teekenen van de binnen het Koninkrijk Holland bestaande garentwijnderijen" van 26 lentemaand 1809', in: *Economisch historisch Jaarboek* 15 (1929) 218-221.

68 Oldewelt, 'Bescherming' 122-123.

69 Joh. de Vries, W. Vroom, T. de Graaf, ed., *Worldwide banking, ABN AMRO Bank 1824-1999* (Amsterdam 1999) 153.

70 M. Schrover, '"Gij zult het bokje niet koken in de melk zijner moeder", joodse ondernemers in de voedings- en genotmiddelenindustrie', in: H. Berg, E.J. Fischer, T. Wijsenbeek, ed., *Venter, fabriqueur, fabrikant, joodse ondernemers en ondernemingen in Nederland 1796-1940* (Amsterdam

1994) 160-190, ibidem 166-167.

71 *Technische Unie 75 jaar* 3, 6-7.

72 Kuitenbrouwer, *Netherlands* 189-208.

73 H.L. Wesseling, 'Nederland en de conferentie van Berlijn, 1884-1885', in: *Tijdschrift voor geschiedenis* 93 (1980) 559-577, ibidem 561, 562, 565-568; W.F. Lichtenauer, 'Lodewijk Pincoffs', in: *Biografisch woordenboek van Nederland*, I (The Hague 1979) 452-454, ibidem 453; Muller, *Zeehandelaar* 84-87; A.J. Oosterwijk, *Vlucht na victorie, Lodewijk Pincoffs 1827-1911* (Rotterdam 1979) 41-55.

74 Muller, *Zeehandelaar* 341-353.

75 Oosterwijk, *Vlucht* 57-164; Lichtenauer, 'Pincoffs'; for Mees' position, see Mees, *Man* 400-467; for Pincoffs and the club: Scheffer, *Vorm* 18-19.

76 J. Woltring, *Bescheiden betreffende de buitenlandse politiek van Nederland, 1848-1919, tweede periode, 1871-1898*, II, *1874-1880* (The Hague 1965) 372, 482, 529-530, 580; III, *1881-1885* (The Hague 1967) 331, 338, 365-366, 522, 727, 736-737, 739, 759, 761, 763.

77 Muller, *Zeehandelaar* 195-214, 341-353; Kuitenbrouwer, *Netherlands* 81-82.

78 Kuitenbrouwer, *Netherlands* 81-82, 147; circular from the AHV liquidators to creditors, 16 October 1879, Amsterdam Exchanges, records of stock quoted portfolio No. 50.

79 Wesseling, 'Nederland' 570-576; Kuitenbrouwer, *Netherlands* 81-82.

80 Muller, *Zeehandelaar* 195-214, 346-347.

81 Wesseling, 'Nederland' 572-576; A. Hochschild, *De geest van koning Leopold II en de plundering van de Congo* (Amsterdam 1998) 67-106.

82 Kuitenbrouwer, *Nederland* 93-94, 152-153; Hochschild, *Geest* 117; H.L. van der Laan, 'The NAHV 1918-1955', paper workshop Business empires in West Central Africa, London 1982.

83 G. Hogesteeger, J.W.M. Tutert, 'De overlandmail', in: G. Hogesteeger, ed., *Naar de gordel van smaragd, de postverbindingen tussen Nederland en Nederlands-Indië 1602-1940* (The Hague 1995) 27-50

84 Rogge, *Van Eeghen* 257; the cost reductions were partly undone by wage rises: idem, 299.

85 Hogesteeger/Tutert, 'Overlandmail' 56-57.

86 Godée Molsbergen, *Reynst & Vinju* 30.

87 Broeze, 'Diffusion'.

88 Hugill, *Global communications* 39; Godée Molsbergen, *Reynst & Vinju* 32, 41; Van Eeghen & Co. kocht in 1878 een codeboek: Rogge, *Van Eeghen* 235; about the situation before the telegraph and the expected changes 'De Kali Bezaar te Batavia' in: *De Economist* 1862 bijblad 153-177, ibidem 159-162.

89 Godée Molsbergen, *Reynst & Vinju* 41 (price telegram); De Jonge, *Industrialisatie* 285 (weekly wages of 5 guilders around 1850); De Vries, *Electoraat* 33 (annual income of well-to-do citizens in 1884 put at 3,500 guilders).

90 Hans Simons is preparing a thesis on this subject.

91 Cf. J.N.F.M. à Campo, *Koninklijke Paketvaart*

Maatschappij, stoomvaart en staatsvorming in de Indonesische archipel, 1888-1914 (Hilversum 1992).

92 Van Goor, *Nederlandse koloniën* 256-264; Kuiten-brouwer, *Netherlands* 253-282.

93 *De Economist* 7 (1858) 280-281.

94 C.J.M. Potting, 'De komst van Nederlandse banken naar Sumatra, 1877-1914', in: A.H.P. Clemens, J.Th. Lindblad, ed., *Het belang van de buitengewesten, economische expansie en koloniale staatsvorming in de buitengewesten van Nederlands-Indië 1870-1942* (Amsterdam 1989) 67-94; L. de Bree, *Gedenkboek van de Javasche Bank 1828-24 januari-1928* (Weltevreden 1928) 82-88.

95 J.Th. Lindblad, 'De opkomst van de buitengewesten', in: A.H.P. Clemens, J.Th. Lindblad, ed., *Het belang van de buitengewesten, economische expansie en koloniale staatsvorming in de buitengewesten van Nederlands-Indië 1870-1942* (Amsterdam 1989) 1-38.

96 The following is based on Lindblad, 'Buitengewesten' and idem, 'De handel tussen Nederland en Nederlands-Indië, 1874-1939', in: *Economisch- en sociaalhistorisch Jaarboek* 51 (1988) 240-298

97 S.W. Verstegen, 'National wealth and income from capital in the Netherlands, c. 1805-1910', in: *Economic and social history in the Netherlands* 7 (1996) 73-108, ibidem 101; D. Crena de Iongh, 'Nederlandsch-Indië als beleggingsgebied voor Nederlandsch kapitaal', in: C. Gerretson a.o., *De sociaal-economische invloed van Nederlandsch-Indië op Nederland* (Wageningen 1938) 97-113, ibidem 106-107, 110; J.Th. Lindblad, 'Foreign investment in late colonial and post colonial Indonesia', in: *Economic and social history in the Netherlands* 3 (1991) 183-208, ibidem 192-198; J.N.F.M. à Campo, 'Strength, survival and success, a statistical profile of corporate enterprise in colonial Indonesia, 1883-1913', in: *Jahrbuch für Wirtschaftsgeschichte* (1995) 45-74, ibidem 61-62.

98 *Nieuw algemeen effectenblad*, 1880, 1900, 1914.

99 D.C. Renooij, *De Nederlandse emissiemarkt van 1904-1939* (Amsterdam 1951) 115-122.

100 Jonker, *Merchants* 121-122.

101 A Campo, *KPM*, 47-48.

102 Crone, 'Koloniale markten' 51-52.

103 Mansvelt, *NHM* II, Appendix IV.

104 Mansvelt, *NHM* II, Appendix III; Lindblad, 'Handel Nederland-Nederlands-Indië' 278.

105 C.A.M. Wijtvliet, *Expansie en dynamiek, de ontwikkeling van het Nederlandse handelsbankwezen 1860-1914* (Amsterdam 1993) 107-150; Muller, *Zeehandelaar* 239-260.

106 De Jong, *Waaier* 195.

107 Rogge, *Van Eeghen* 298-299; Oosterwijk, *Van Hoboken* 274-275.

108 About the Dutch tobacco market K.E. Sluyterman, *Ondernemen in sigaren, analyse van bedrijfsbeleid in vijf Nederlandse sigarenfabrieken in de perioden 1856-1865 en 1925-1934* (Tilburg 1983) 78-90.

109 Rogge, *Van Eeghen* 194, 203-205, 211, 216-219, 355-356, 385.

110 Crone, *Crone* 36-50, 81-82.

111 A.W. Wichers Hoeth, *Van Heekeren & Co. en hunne voorgangers 1720 [1829]-1929* (Amsterdam 1929) 170-172.

112 Muller, *Zeehandelaar* 351, 401.

113 Hoynck van Papendrecht, *Van Hoboken* 14, 17, 95-96, 122-124, 125, 129, 141-142.

114 A. Goedhart, *Eerherstel voor de plantage, uit de geschiedenis van de Handelsvereeniging 'Amsterdam' (HVA) 1879-1984* (S.l. 1999) 16-23.

115 'Kali Bezaar' 153-155; more in detail about the trading houses in the Dutch East Indies Mansvelt, 'Indische handelshuizen'.

116 For instance Internatio Archive No. 41, Singapore to Batavia, 7 December 1912.

117 G. Gonggrijp, Schets ener economische geschiedenis van Nederlands-Indië/Indonesië (Haarlem 19574) 154-155, 161.

118 Crone, *Crone* 63 (1879).

119 A.C. Mees, *NV Internationale crediet- en handelsvereeniging 'Rotterdam', gedenkboek uitgegeven bij het vijf-en-zeventig jarig bestaan op 28 augustus 1938* (Rotterdam 1938) 18.

120 De Bree, *Javasche Bank* 47-49.

121 N.A. van Horn, 'Het Indische handelshuis Bauermann in de negentiende eeuw', in: *NEHA-jaarboek* 60 (1997) 137-158.

122 De Bree, *Javasche Bank* II, 243; De Jong, *Nederlandsche Bank* III, 608.

123 A. Taselaar, *De Nederlandse koloniale lobby, ondernemers en de Indische politiek 1914-1940* (Leiden 1998) 49-93; J.P.B. Jonker, 'Waterdragers van het kapitalisme, nevenfuncties van Nederlandse bankiers en de verhouding tussen bankwezen en bedrijfsleven (1910-1940)', in: *Jaarboek voor de geschiedenis van bedrijf en techniek* 6 (1989) 158-190; N.A. van Horn, 'S.P. van Eeghen, bankier', in: *Biografisch woordenboek van Nederland* III (The Hague 1989) 157-159

124 Chapman, *Merchant enterprise* 235-241.

125 Mees, *Gedenkboek Internatio* 24.

126 Mees, *Gedenkboek Internatio* 31-32.

127 Mees, *Gedenkboek Internatio* 28, 29.

128 Internatio Archive No. 46, copybook board to agents, 6 May 1910.

129 Minute book meetings non-executive board Borsumij 1894-1909, in Hagemeyer Archive, no list. The Hissink affair discussed on 15 October 1904, 29 April, 24 June, 2 October 1905. Van Heek as shareholder mentioned 9 November 1907. A Campo, *KPM* 348-350, 352, 353, 355, 356 about Schlimmer, Borsumij and the KPM. P. Zwaag, *Verloren tropische zaken, de opkomst en ondergang van de Nederlandse handel- en cultuurmaatschappijen in het voormalige Nederlands-Indië* (Meppel 1991) 226-229.

130 H. Baudet, M. Fennema, *Het Nederlands belang bij Indië* (Utrecht 1983) 52.

131 Taselaar, *Koloniale lobby* 40, 75-76, 78; *Gedenkboek aangeboden door de Handelsvereeniging 'Amsterdam'* (Amsterdam 1929) 5-10; Goedhart, *Eerherstel* 20-23; *Gedenkboek Internatio* 32; Crone, *Crone* 102. Geo. Wehry thought that the HVA had simply run a business which was too large and too expensive: Hagemeyer Archive, collection Wehry, minute book, 22 December 1903.

132 *Van Oss' Effectenboek* 1915-1916.

133 *Handboek cultuurmaatschappijen* 1892-1893; ARA 2.18.23 Jacobson & Van den Berg No.'s 437, 447, 461; Hagemeyer Archive, no list, concept press release for ANETA on the opening of the new Wehry office, 15 May 1928.

134 Archief Amsterdam Exchanges, records of stock quoted, portfolio 594; *Gedenkboek Lindeteves*, no page numbers.

135 *Handboek cultuurmaatschappijen* 1892-1893, 1912-1913; J.Th. Lindblad, 'Het bedrijfsleven in Nederlands-Indië in het Interbellum', in: *Economisch- en sociaalhistorisch jaarboek* 54 (1991) 183-211, ibidem 190.

136 J.N.F.M. à Campo, 'The rise of corporate enterprise in colonial Indonesia 1893-1913', in: J.Th. Lindblad, ed., *Historical foundations of a national economy in Indonesia, 1890s-1990s* (Amsterdam 1996) 71-94, ibidem 88.

137 Hagemeyer Archive, no inventory numbers, minutes meetings non-executive board Borsumij, 17 May 1902; annual reports Borsumij 1911, 1912, 1913, 1914, 1915.

138 ARA 2.18.23 Jacobson & Van den Berg, No. 437.

139 *Encyclopedie van Nederlandsch-Indië* s.v. Deli-Maatschappij, HVA.

140 A. Booth, *The Indonesian economy in the nineteenth and twentieth centuries, a history of missed opportunities* (Basingstoke 1998) 216-217.

141 H.J. Langeveld, *Dit leven van krachtig handelen, Hendrikus Colijn 1869-1944*, I, *1869-1933* (Amsterdam 1998) 65-66.

142 Internatio Archive No. 177, memopad A.C. Mees, 1910.

143 Internatio Archive No. 41, Batavia to Soerabaja and Semarang, 27 March 1911; Hagemeyer Archive, collection Wehry, letter from the agent in Batavia to the Amsterdam office, 8 February 1912.

144 Godée Molsbergen, *Reynst & Vinju* 41.

145 J.M. Schmiedell, *Gedenkblätter zum 50. jährigen Bestehen der Firma Erdmann & Sielcken in Java 1875-1924* (Bergen 1924) 9-11, 18; about Mincing Lane R.C. Michie, *The City of London, continuity and change 1850-1990* (London 1992) 44, 47, 50, 58.

146 Internatio Archive No. 41, Batavia to Rotterdam 24 May 1911, 1 July 1911, 21 December 1911, 28 December 1911. 10 December 1912.

147 Hagemeyer Archive, collection Wehry, letter 15 March 1899, minute book 6 October 1903; E.J. Tobi, *De uitschakeling van den groothandel in industrieele producten* (Roermond 1927) 63-64.

148 Hagemeyer Archive, no inventory numbers, account book No. 1.

149 For reasons which are not very clear, Zwaag, *Verloren zaken* 229, and De Vries, *Trek uit* 9-12, credit

Johan for taking the initiative in setting up a business. The account ledgers demonstrate this to be wrong.

150 Zwaag, *Verloren zaken*, mentions a partnership contract dated 15 June 1900 as base for the firm. This document has not been found. It remains unlikely for a firm to have been established at that date. For one, because Anton was in the Netherlands at that moment for his wedding. Moreover, his account book would certainly have listed the costs involved, and it would have listed the first transactions under the firm. Neither in effect happened.

151 Hagemeyer Archive, account book, balances, and Instructions for the Dutch East Indies.

Chapter V, On the defensive, 1914-1940

1 A.G. Kenwood and A.L. Lougheed, *The growth of the international economy 1820-2000* (4th edition, London 1999) 177-210; A. Maddison, *Monitoring the World Economy 1820-1992* (OECD 1995) 59-73.

2 Kenwood/Lougheed, *Growth of the international economy*, 211-218.

3 J.L. van Zanden, *Een klein land in de 20e eeuw. Economische geschiedenis van Nederland 1914-1995* (Utrecht 1997) 128-140; Joh. de Vries, *Een eeuw vol effecten. Historische schets van de Vereniging voor de Effectenhandel en de Amsterdamse Effectenbeurs 1876-1976* (s.a.s.l.) 130-139.

4 C. Smit, *Tien studiën betreffende Nederland in de Eerste Wereldoorlog* (Groningen 1975) 40, 89-98; C.A. van Manen, *De Nederlandsche Overzee Trustmaatschappij* (The Hague 1937) Vol. I, 75-76.

5 C. Smit, *Nederland in de Eerste Wereldoorlog (1899-1919) II 1914-1917* (Groningen 1972) 80-97; Joh. de Vries, *De Nederlandse economie tijdens de 20ste eeuw* (Utrecht 1973) 128-132.

6 A.C. Mees, *NV Internationale crediet- en handelsvereeniging 'Rotterdam'. Gedenkboek uitgegeven bij het vijf-en-zeventig jarig bestaan op 28 augustus 1938* (Rotterdam 1938) 32.

7 A.W. Wichers Hoeth, *Van Heekeren & Co en hunne voorgangers, 1720-1929* (Amsterdam 1928) 189.

8 Smit, *Nederland in Eerste Wereldoorlog* II, 55-69.

9 *Nijhoffs Geschiedenislexicon Nederland en België* (The Hague 1981).

10 E.C.van Dorp, 'Handel en nijverheid', in: H. Brugmans, *Nederland in den oorlogstijd* (Amsterdam 1920) 216.

11 R. van der Bie, *'Een doorlopende groote roes', De economische ontwikkeling vn Nederland 1913/1921* (Tinbergen Institute Research series no. 98, 1995).

12 Annual reports SHV, published in *Gedenkboek SHV*, 1996, a book without either a title or page numbers.

13 H. Baudet and M. Fennema, *Het Nederlands belang bij Indië* (Utrecht 1983) Table 2, 35.

14 P. Post, *Japanse bedrijvigheid in Indonesië, 1868-1942. Structurele elementen van Japan's vooroorlogse economische expansie in Zuidoost Azië* (Amsterdam 1991) 139-183.

15 *Lindeteves-Stokvis 1889-1939* (z.p. 1939), unnumbered pages; L. Huizinga, *'Trek jij je jas eens uit'; Kroniek van een koopmanshuis in het beeld van 75 jaar wereldgeschiedenis* (Naarden 1975) 112-126; *G. de Vries & Zonen, 1775-1950* (Amsterdam 1950) 88-89.

16 Annual reports Ceteco 1914-1920.

17 Using *Van Oss' Effectenboeken* it could be calculated that over the years 1914/1919, 12 to 14 colonial merchant houses on average paid the following dividends: 7.2%, 11.2%, 15.2%, 15.4%, 12.7%, and 14.9%.

18 Hagemeyer Archive, anual report for 1920.

19 Data on the capital expansions from: *Van Oss' Effectenboeken*, 1914-1922; about Hagemeyer see *Van Oss' Effectenboek* 1938, part I. On Stokvis see also: GA Rotterdam 255, Stokvis Archive, the introduction of the archive inventory list, iv, and No. 670 ff.

20 *Gedenkboek SHV*, 1996.

21 C. Wilson, *Geschiedenis van Unilever* (Den Haag 1954) II, 175-186; 226-232.

22 *Van Oss' Effectenboek*, 1922, 950; the quote from the report over 1920.

23 K.E. Sluyterman, *Ondernemen in sigaren. Analyse van bedrijfsbeleid in vijf Nederlandse sigarenfabrieken in de perioden 1856-1865 en 1925-1934* (Tilburg 1983) 214.

24 *Van Oss' Effectenboek*, 1922 and 1927.

25 Hagemeyer Archive, balance books 1920-1922, typed report over 1921.

26 *Van Oss' Effectenboek*, 1938, part I, prospectus, 125; Hagemeyer Archive, balance books 1920-1927. Transferring the shares to the bank in 1922 proved to have serious tax disadvantages, so in 1927 this transaction was retrospectively changed into a transaction giving the shares to the bank as collateral.

27 Borsumij Archive, minute book supervisory board, 19 June 1920-14 June 1922.

28 Internatio Archive, Annual Report 31 December 1948.

29 Hagemeyer Archive, Instructions to Dutch East Indian Branches, No. 5 and 7 (1912\13).

30 Hagemeyer Archive, Instructions to Dutch East Indian Branches, No. 2, supplement 3, 1 December 1921.

31 Hagemeyer Archive, Instructions to Dutch East Indian Branches, No. 32, 5 November 1920.

32 Hagemeyer Archive, Instructions to Dutch East Indian Branches, No. 18.

33 Hagemeyer Archive, Instructions to Dutch East Indian Branches, No. 23, supplement 10, Amsterdam, 21 March 1939.

34 Hagemeyer Archive, Instructions to Dutch East Indian Branches, No. 21, supplement 2, 1 March 1921.

35 Hagemeyer Archive, Instructions to Dutch East Indian Branches, No. 23, supplement 4, 22 December 1922.

36 Hagemeyer Archive, Instructions to Dutch East Indian Branches, No. 12, supplement 13 and 14.

37 *De Indische Mercuur, Weekblad voor Handel, Nijverheid en en Mijnwezen in Nederlandsch Oost- en West-Indië*, 15 January 1930, No. 3.

38 Hagemeyer Archive, Instructions to Dutch East Indian Branches, No. 12 plus supplments and No. 16, 31 May 1922.

39 A. van Dooren, 'Overwinning op den afstand. In den aether', in: W.H. van Helsdingen, ed., *Daar wérd wat groots verricht... Nederlandsch-Indië in de XXste eeuw* (Amsterdam 1941) 268-272.

40 Hagemeyer Archive, Instructions to Dutch East Indian Branches, No. 34; Mees, *Gedenkboek 1938*, 41: 'The rewards, in particular those paid as profit shares and bonuses in trade and plantations, increased wealth, and a sad waste came to be noticed among a large crowd'; Borsumij, minutes supervisory board, 14 June 1922.

41 J. Th. Lindblad, 'De handel tussen Nederland en Nederlands-Indië, 1874-1939', *Economisch- en sociaalhistorisch jaarboek* 51 (1988), 240-298.

42 Annual reports Ceteco, 1920-1930.

43 Annual reports Twentsche Overzee Handel Maatschappij (TOHM), 1920-1930; minutes shareholders meetings TOHM, among others 8 October 1923.

44 E.J. Tobi, *Uitschakeling van den groothandel in industrieele producten* (Roermond 1928) 45-84; 94-97.

45 Curiously enough, Delfgaauw argued in 1947 on one hand that very few data exist about wholesaling during the interwar years, and on the other that the economic significance of the independent companies had declined. Wholesaling, he argued, was partly eliminated without the public noticing. J.G.M. Delfgaauw, 'De binnenlandse groot- en kleinhandel' in: *De Nederlandse Volkshuishouding tussen Twee Wereldoorlogen* (Utrecht/Antwerpen 1947) Chapter XI.

46 According to the latest recalculations by C.A. Oomens and G.P. Bakker, 'De beroepsbevolking in Nederland 1849-1990', in: *Supplement bij de sociaal-economische maandstatistiek* 1994 No. 2 (The Hague 1994), the number of people employed in trade, i.e. retailing and wholesaling together, developed as follows in the Netherlands:

year	total	% of the working population
1899	184,000	9.5%
1909	190,000	10.0%
1920	271,000	10.0%
1930	397,000	12.5%
1960	564,000	13.5%
1990	1,084,000	17.4%

The most striking feature of this table is the continuous rise of employment in trade, both in absolute and in relative terms.

47 R. Miellet, *Honderd jaar grootwinkelbedrijf in Nederland* (Zwolle s.a.) 12 and 67.

48 *G. de Vries & Zonen*, 106-107.

49 I.J. Blanken, *Geschiedenis van Philips Electronics*

NV. *De ontwikkeling van de NV Philips' Gloeilamp-*
enfabrieken tot elektrotechnisch concern (Leiden
1992) 27-45, 304-314.

50 *Van Oss' Effectenboek*, 1939, prospectus 341-343.

51 *Gedenkboek SHV* 1996.

52 Hagemeyer, by the way, mentioned the British
office in Winston Salem in its survey.

53 A.D. Chandler jr., *The Visible Hand. The Managerial
Revolution in American Business* (Cambridge Mass.
1977), 223-224; 485-486.

54 In *Scale and Scope, the dynamics of industrial capitalism* (Cambridge Mass 1990), A.D. Chandler Jr
argues that Ford lost its lead during the 1920s by
hiring the wrong managers (207) who took the
wrong decisions: 'In the recession of 1921 Ford
demoralised his dealers by forcing cars on them
after the temporary collapse in demand'. (345)
'The new managerial team abruptly reshaped the
sales force by abolishing the wholesale distributors and insisting on exclusive retail dealerships,
and then, most serious of all, allocating these
dealers increasingly larger quotas of cars that
were increasingly difficult to sell.'

55 P. de Jong, 'Handel en wandel in de kolonie' (MA
Thesis Leiden 1995) 6: in 1940, Borsumij had 50
agency agreements, of which 29 were exclusive
ones.

56 *Van Oss' Effectenboek*, 1939, 853.

57 *Het Indische Leven, Een algemeen weekblad*, 1920.

58 *Economisch Weekblad voor Nederlandsch-Indië;
orgaan van het department van landbouw, nijverheid en handel*, 1932-1938.

59 Hagemeyer Archive, Instructions to Dutch East
Indian Branches No. 4, supplement 2, 6 October
1925.

60 Huizinga, *Trek jij je jas eens uit*, 133.

61 J.B. Jeffreys, *Retail trading in Britain, 1850-1950;
A study of trends in retailing with special reference
to the development of Co-operative, multiple shop
and department store methods of trading* (Cambridge 1954) 48.

62 Van Zanden, *Een klein land*, 128-163.

63 *Kroniek van mr. dr. A. Sternheim*, 10 (1932/33)
113.

64 J.H.Gispen, 'De practijk van de wet op het algemeen verbindend en onverbindend verklaren van
ondernemersovereenkomsten 1935', *Antirevolutionaire Staatkunde*, 14 (1938) 75-88, 128-146.

65 *Gedenkboek SHV*, 1996; *Logboek SHV 1896-1956*
(Utrecht 1956).

66 J.H. van Stuijvenberg, *Het Centraal Bureau, een
coöperatief krachtenveld in de Nederlandse landbouw, 1899-1949* (Rotterdam 1949) 233-250.

67 Sluyterman, *Winnen met papier*, 45. In addition to
price agreements, arrangements existed protecting customers, so-called 'Kundenschutz-reglung',
were not uncommon. In such contracts, manufacturers promised to respect the traders' customers,
so traders would not spoil margins with price cutting. The producer of copying paper Océ-van der
Grinten made such agreements with its trade cus-

tomers: K.E.Sluyterman, 'Uitvinden en verdienen',
in: H.F.J.M. van den Eerenbeemt, ed., *Van
boterkleursel naar fotokopieersystemen; de
ontstaansgeschiedenis van Océ-van der Grinten
1873-1956* (Leiden 1991) 240-143.

68 Internatio Archive, No. 22: papers of the board
and supervisory board, 'Enige aantekeningen naar
aanleiding van mijn reis naar het Oosten van aug.
1937 tot febr. 1938', (travel report) by A. Hombrink.

69 Mees, *Gedenkboek 1938*, 65.

70 The Dutch traders succeeded surprisingly quickly
in taking over these imports from Japanese houses. This was partly influenced by the growing animosity between China and Japan. After 1933 the
Dutch importers were supported by the colonial
government. P. Post, *Japanse bedrijvigheid in
Indonesië, 1868-1942. Structurele elementen van
Japan's vooroorlogse economische expansie in
Zuidoost Azië* (Amsterdam 1991) 162-175; 184-
210.

71 Other trading houses with offices in Japan were
Borsumij, Deli-Atjeh, Güntzel & Schumacher
together with the Molukse Handelsvereniging and
a third party, Lindeteves, Reiss & Co and Tels & Co.
Internatio was represented by the Standard Braid
and Produce Company of Japan in Kobe, originally
a German firm (travel report Hombrink, 1933/34),
but in 1939 the company had a branch in Kobe
(*Van Oss' Effectenboek*, 1939).

72 Hagemeyer Archive, Instructions to Dutch East
Indian Branches No. 22, supplement 25, 24
November 1932; No. 45, 23 November 1932.

73 Borsumij Archive, minutes supervisory board, 27
June 1934.

74 ARA, 2.18.23, Lindeteves-Jacoberg Archive, No.
437, minutes annual general meetings, 30 June
1932-16 June 1937: 'Unfortunately the general
tendency points to an overall decline of the consignment system.'

75 Internatio Archive, No. 22: papers of the board
and supervisory board, 'Enige aantekeningen naar
aanleiding van mijn reis naar het Oosten, oct.
1933 - mei 1934', (travel report) by A. Hombrink.

76 P.G. Knibbe, *Plaats en taak van den tusschenhan-
del in het tegenwoordige economische bestel* (Leiden 1938), 10-12.

77 B.G.J. de Graaff, 'Kalm temidden van woedende
golven'. *Het ministerie van KoloniNn en zijn
taakomgeving, 1912-1940* (Leiden 1997) 494-
549.

78 A.Goedhart, *Eerherstel voor de plantage. Uit de
geschiedenis van de Handelsvereeniging 'Amsterdam' (HVA) 1879-1983* (s.l. 1999) 78-82.

79 GA Amsterdam, No. 609 H.G.Th. Crone Archive,
archive inventory and No. 1, papers relating to the
firm.

80 *Economisch Archief van Nederland en Koloniën*,
Amsterdam s.a. (about 1936); W. Wennekes,
*Eeuwenoud: de lange levens van zeven Nederlandse
bedrijven* (Amsterdam 1989).

81 Internatio Archive, No. 22: papers of the board
and supervisory board, 'Enige aantekeningen naar
aanleiding van mijn reis naar het Oosten, oct.
1933 - mei 1934', (travel report) by A. Hombrink.

82 Internatio Archive, No. 22: papers of the board
and supervisory board, 'Enige aantekeningen naar
aanleiding van mijn reis naar het Oosten, oct.
1933 - mei 1934', (travel report) by A. Hombrink.

83 W.A.I.M. Segers, *Manufacturing Industry 1870-
1942* in: P. Boomgaard, ed., *Changing Economy in
Indonesia. A selection of statistical source material
from the early 19th century up to 1940*, deel 8
(Amsterdam 1987) 16-40; A. Taselaar, *De Nederlandse koloniale lobby. Ondernemers en de Indische
politiek, 1914-1940* (Leiden 1998) 472-83.

84 *Van Oss' Effectenboek* 1935.

85 G.C.P. Linssen, *Papier in Nijmegen. Voorgeschiedenis en ontwikkeling van KNP nijmegen b.v. ter gelegenheid van het tachtigjarig bestaan in 1988*
(Nijmegen 1988) 61-68.

86 W.T. Kroese, *Het begin van de industrialisatie van
Indonesië. De Stichting van de Preanger Bontweverij (PBW) te Garut* (Hengelo 1979).

87 Mees, *Gedenkboek 1938*, 57.

88 Mees, *Gedenkboek 1938*, 57; Internatio Archive,
No. 22: papers of the board and supervisory
board, 'Enige aantekeningen naar aanleiding van
mijn reis naar het Oosten, oct. 1933 - mei 1934',
(travel report) by A. Hombrink.

89 *Lindeteves-Stokvis 1889-1939* (1939) no page
numbers; *Van Oss' Effectenboek*, 1938, 815.

90 *Kroniek mr. dr. A. Sternheim*, 7 (1929/30), p. 88-9;
Van Oss' Effectenboek, 1939, 819.

91 Annual reports Borsumij, 1934-1947.

92 Internatio Archive, No. 22, papers board and
supervisory board, annex to the report of the
agents' meeting, 1 June 1927.

93 Hagemeyer Archive, employment contract with
Bödeker, 19 December 1939; Instructions to
Dutch East Indian Branches, No. 33.

94 Internatio Archive, No. 22, papers board and
supervisory board, travel report T.P. Baart De La
Faille, 15 September 1931 to 30 March 1932.

95 In 1908, Internatio founded a support fund, and a
savings fund in 1926, as a separate and independent foundation. The company had an emergency
fund for the non-European staff (Mees,
Gedenkboek 1938, 50-51). Borsumij set up a pension fund in 1928 (annual report Borsumij).
Güntzel & Schumacher had a pension fund by 1937
at the latest (*Van Oss' Effectenboek*, 1939) Ceteco
also drafted a pension arrangement for its core
European staff in 1937 (annual report 1937).

96 *Lindeteves-Stokvis*, no page numbers.

97 Internatio Archive, No. 74, board reports to
supervisory directors, June 1941; Internatio
Annual Report, 31 December 1948.

98 Historical overview R.S. Stokvis & Zonen NV,
undated document, about 1963.

99 Interview O. Bargman, staff member of Hagemeyer, 10 June 1998.

100 *Van Oss' Effectenboek*, 1915-1940. In Figure 5.2, the firms' dividend percentages have been added, and then divided by the total number of firms. There were 15 firms in 1939.

101 Other traders expanding their capital in 1937-1939 were Borsumij, Güntzel & Schumacher, Internatio, Handelsvereeniging Java, Tels & Co: *Van Oss' Effectenboek*, 1939-1941.

102 Hagemeyer Archive, papers for the annual general meeting 1940.

Chapter VI, Trade in Times of War and Decolonisation, 1940-1960

1 This survey of the Dutch economy during the Second World War is largely based on H.A.M. Klemann, 'De Nederlandse economie tijdens de Tweede Wereldoorlog', *Tijdschrift voor Geschiedenis* 110 (1997) 3-40; idem, 'De economische exploitatie van Nederland door de bezetter', in: H. Flap en W. Arts, *De organisatie van de bezetting* (Amsterdam 1997) 117-138; H.A.M. Klemann, ed., 'Mooie jaarcijfers.. Enige onderzoeksresultaten betreffende de Nederlandse economische ontwikkeling tijdens de Tweede Wereldoorlog', *Utrechtse Historische Cahiers* 18 (1997) No. 4.

2 A. Kraal, 'In- en uitschakeling van den groothandel in industrieele producten onder het huidige systeem van beheerschte prijzen', *ESB*, 24 May, 31 May, 1944.

3 Sluyterman, *Winnen met papier*, 49-59.

4 Van Stuijvenberg, *Centraal Bureau*, 374.

5 L. de Jong, *Het koninkrijk der Nederlanden in de Tweede Wereldoorlog*, Vol. 7, first half, 186-203.

6 CBS, *Economische en sociale kroniek der oorlogsjaren 1940-1945* (Utrecht 1947) 120.

7 Hagemeyer Archive, minutes supervisory board, 5 June 1945.

8 Hagemeyer Archive, papers O. Bargman, letter to the agents dated 20 November 1945.

9 Amsterdam Exchanges Archive, No. 594 file Lindeteves, report to shareholders about the years 1940-1945.

10 ARA 2.18.23, Lindeteves-Jacoberg Archive, No. 462: information about the firm during the years 1942-1944.

11 Amsterdam Exchanges Archive, No. 594 file Lindeteves, report to shareholders about the years 1940-1945.

12 D. Barnouw, ed., *Correspondentie van Mr. M.M. Rost van Tonningen*, II, *mei 1942-mei 1945* (Zulphen 1993).

13 Internatio Archive, No. 22, papers of the board 1941-1943.

14 Hagemeyer Archive, minutes of the supervisory board in the Dutch East Indies, 1941-1942; ARA 2.09.16, Nederlands Beheersinstituut Archive, No. 7559.

15 Amsterdam Exchanges Archive, No. 594 file Lindeteves, report to shareholders about the years 1940-1945.

16 Ceteco, annual report for 1945.

17 TOHM annual report for 1940-1945.

18 Hagemeyer Archive, papers Bargman, letter of 20 November 1945.

19 Huizinga, *Trek jij je jas eens uit*, 168.

20 Van der Zwaag, *Verloren tropische zaken*, 265-270.

21 Van der Zwaag, *Verloren tropische zaken*, 280-286.

22 Stokvis annual report for 1948; Lindeteves, report over the years 1940-1947.

23 GA Amsterdam, PA 609, Crone Archive, No. 21, travel report of W.F. Pahud de Mortanges.

24 Internatio Archive, No. 74, reports of the board to the supervisory directors, 24 May 1946.

25 Borsumij and Hagemeyer, annual reports for 1940-1947.

26 Van der Zwaag, *Verloren tropische zaken*, 280-282.

27 H. Baudet, M. Fennema, *Het Nederlands belang bij Indië* (Utrecht 1983) 136-144.

28 Internatio Archive, No. 74, reports of the board to the supervisory directors, 17 Janaury 1950.

29 Hagemeyer minutes supervisory board, 14 January 1950.

30 ARA 2.10.54, archive of the Colonial Ministry and its successors, files No. 1473 en 9432.

31 Internatio, Archive, No. 74, reports of the board to the supervisory directors, 17 Janaury 1950. The report added that sectarian influences appeared to have had some influence in granting the monopoly, presumably referring to Hagemeyer's Catholic background, which might have given the company better access to J.H. van Maarseveen, the Catholic minister for Union Affairs and Overseas Territories.

32 Hagemeyer Archive, index on the papers for the general meeting of shareholders, January 1950.

33 The NHM tried to change the minister's mind about the Hagemeyer monopoly by letting it be known that before the war, the company had had a reputation for not being particularly scrupulous, which made a combination of Internatio and Lindeteves a better option. ARA 2.10.54, archive of the Colonial Ministry and its successors, file No. 9432.

34 A. Booth, *The Indonesian economy in the nineteenth and twentieth centuries. A history of missed opportunities* (Basingstoke 1998) 53-63.

35 Thee Kian Wie, 'Economic policies in Indonesia during the period 1950-1965, in particular with respect to foreign investment', in: J.Th. Lindblad, ed., *Historical foundations of a national economy in Indonesia, 1890s-1990s* (Amsterdam 1996) 315-329.

36 Borsumij, minutes supervisory board, 7 July 1955.

37 Borsumij, annual reports for 1950 and 1951.

38 Hagemeyer, minutes supervisory board, 18 September 1956; Borsumij, minutes supervisory board, 7 July 1955.

39 Geo. Wehry, annual report 1956; Hagemeyer, annual reports 1955 and 1956; Hagemeyer, minutes supervisory board 20 July 1956; Borsumij, annual reports 1954 and 1959.

40 Stout, 'Van de Toko uit Rotterdam', 34-45.

41 Borsumij, minutes supervisory board 26 April 1955.

42 Geo. Wehry, annual report 1954; Lindeteves wrote in its 1952 annual report that its Indonesian operations continued the company's backbone with regards to earning capacity.

43 Internatio Archive, No. 74, reports of the board to the supervisory directors, report of 16 October 1956.

44 Hagemeyer, minutes annual general meeting of shareholders, 26 July 1954.

45 Hagemeyer, minutes supervisory board, 6 March and 20 July 1956

46 E.E. de Haan, 'Avonturen van een koopman' (Bonaire 1969) typoscript, 89-90.

47 Borsumij, minutes supervisory board 9 December 1957, 18 May 1958, 3 July 1958, 3 October 1958; Borsumij, annual reports 1957-59.

48 Borsumij, minutes supervisory board 9 December 1957; Borsumij, annual report 1957.

49 Trade conducted by the countries of the Soviet Bloc is not included in the figures just mentioned, as this was mainly internal.

50 Kenwood/Lougheed, *The growth of the international economy, 1820-2000*, 299-307.

51 M.E. Chamberlain, *Decolonization. The Fall of the European Empires* (Oxford 1985, reprint 1987) 2: 'Where Britain led the others followed. It took a generation for all the implications to be realized, but in the end most former colonial peoples found that they were pushing at an open door. The Europeans had abandoned their attempt to dominate the rest of the world politically, although perhaps not economically.'

52 J.D. Fage, *A history of Africa* (London 1997[2]), 460-490; A. Hochschild, *King Leopold's Ghost. A story of greed, terror, and heroism in colonial Africa* (1998).

53 W.G. Huff, *The economic growth of Singapore; Trade and development in the twentieth century* (Cambridge 1997).

54 Internatio Archive, No. 74, reports of the board to the supervisory directors, report of 13 December 1945.

55 Hagemeyer Archive, papers Bargman, letter from Bargman to J.M. Middeldorp dated 26 March 1946.

56 Hagemeyer Archive, papers Bargman, letter from Middeldorp (?) to Bargman, 12 August 1946.

57 Huff, *Economic growth of Singapore*, 281.

58 ARA 2.10.54, archive of the Colonial Ministry and its successors, file No. 2440.

59 ARA 2.10.54, archive of the Colonial Ministry and its successors, file No. 2440.

60 Hagemeyer, minutes supervisory board, 30 January 1959.

61 ARA 2.18.23, Archive Lindeteves-Jacoberg, No. 35, supervisory board, 4 December 1959.

62 D. Hellema, *Buitenlandse politiek van Nederland* (Utrecht 1995) 168.

63 TOHM annual reports, 1945-1965.

64 D.K. Fieldhouse, *Merchant capital and economic*

decolonization. The United Africa Company, 1929-1987 (Oxford 1994) 335-448.

65　Borsumij, minutes supervisory board 15 July 1953; Borsumij annual report 1956.

66　Stout, ' Van de Toko uit Rotterdam', 54.

67　Hagemeyer, minutes supervisory board 18 July 1955: after a fact-finding mission, the executive director Oostergo considers the opportunities to be very great, but the impossibility of working with indigenous staff renders it necessary to send more Europeans.

68　ARA 2.18.23, Archive Lindeteves-Jacoberg, No. 35, minutes supervisory board Lindeteves, 9 April 1954.

69　Laan, 'The NAHV, 1918-1955', 3-12.

70　Hagemeyer, minutes supervisory board, 16 March 1956.

71　ARA 2.18.23, Archive Lindeteves-Jacoberg No. 35, minutes supervisory board Lindeteves, 8 August 1958.

72　Hagemeyer, minutes supervisory board, 5 September 1958, 27 april 1959, 21 July 1959.

73　Internatio Archive, No. 74, reports of the board to the supervisory directors, report of 21 March 1950; Stout, 'Van de Toko uit Rotterdam', 55.

74　According to H. Stout, it was concluded that the onesidedness of the export economy and the social inequality would lead to great social unrest during the years to come: Stout, 'Van de Toko uit Rotterdam', 55.

75　Ceteco, annual report 1965.

76　Internatio Archive, No. 74, reports of the board to the supervisory directors, travel report H. Stout about a trip to America, May-June 1952.

77　Borsumij, minutes supervisory board, 1953-1962.

78　W.H. Salzmann, *Bedrijfsleven, overheid en handelsbevordering. The Netherlands Chamber of Commerce in the United States, Inc., 1903-1987* (S.l. 1994) 184-189.

79　Hellema, *Buitenlandse politiek*, 135-160.

80　J.L. van Zanden, *Een klein land in de 20e eeuw. Economische geschiedenis van Nederland 1914-1995* (Utrecht 1997) 195.

81　During the years 1946-1950, about 100 such export joint-ventures were founded with government subsidies or backing. Most of them focused their activities on the US. Nearly all these ventures failed, however, the NEC excepted. B.A. Bakker, *Export & marketing. Enige aspecten van exportmarketing en exportsamenwerking bij Nederlandse ondernemingen* (Brussel 1980) 406-448.

82　B.P. Hofstede, ed., *Veertig jaar NEC* (Soest 1992).

83　ARA 2.18.23, Archive Lindeteves-Jacoberg, minutes of the supervisory board, 13 February 1958.

84　Th. H.M. Hillen, 'Structuurwijziging in de groothandel', *ESB*, June 1955.

85　Oomens/Bakker, 'Beroepsbevolking Nederland' 39.

86　J.F. Haccoû, 'Wholesaling in the Netherlands', in; R. Bartels, *Comparative Marketing. Wholesaling in Fifteen Countries* (Homewood, Illinois, 1963) 47-56.

87　Borsumij, minutes supervisory board, 21 June 1960.

88　ARA 2.18.23, Archive Lindeteves-Jacoberg, No. 35, minutes supervisory board, 30 May 1958.

89　Details on dividends drawn from annual reports and from the *Van Oss' Effectenboeken*.

Chapter VII, Trade and industry, an awkward fit, 1960-1983

1　Kenwood/Lougheed, *Growth of the international economy* 299-307.

2　H. van der Wee, *De gebroken welvaartscirkel. De wereldeconomie, 1945-1980* (Leiden 1983) 184-193; Kenwood/Lougheed, *Growth of the international economy*, 299-307.

3　W. Overbeke, 'Naar een nieuwe internationale orde', in: W. van Spengen, *Van kolonialisme tot zelfontwikkeling* (Bussum 1978) 62-77.

4　P.F. Drucker, *The practice of management* (New York 1954).

5　H.I. Ansoff, *Corporate strategy* (1965); idem, 'The firm of the future', in: *Harvard Business Review*, 43 (1965) No. 5, 162-78.

6　H. Kahn, A.J. Wiener, 'The next thirty-three years: a framework for speculation', *Daedalus*, 96 (1967) No. 3, 705-732.

7　G.H.J. Abeln, *Het Nederlandse internationale handelshuis en de groei, prae-advies voor het verbond van de Nederlandse groothandel* (Den Haag 1969) 19-23, 40-50.

8　Table 7.1 is derived from the annual reports of the companies concerned. The Borsumij data concern the development of active investment, i.e. the sum of stocks, debtors, property, and equipment, as a percentage. Hagemeyer: the geographical spread of the capital invested in its subsidiaries. Internatio: the geographical spread of the company's own capital. Lindeteves: the spread of investment.

9　Abeln, *Nederlandse internationale handelshuis*, 30.

10　See for instance about the coffee trade: H. van Driel, 'Uitschakeling van de Nederlandse koffiehandel in de negentiende en twintigste eeuw?', in: *NEHA-jaarboek voor economische, bedrijfs- en techniekgeschiedenis* 60 (1997) 158-203.

11　H. van Driel, *Samenwerking in haven en vervoer in het containertijdperk* (Delft 1990) 103-111.

12　Tanzania, by the way, met its obligations in a decent way as had been agreed. This gave Borsumij Wehry an argument to sustain its opinion that investing in East Africa continued to be a sound proposition: Borsumij Wehry, annual report 1970.

13　Hagemeyer, minutes supervisory board, 28 August 1964.

14　Borsumij Wehry, annual report 1961.

15　Geo. Wehry, annual reports 1958 and 1959; Borsumij Wehry, annual reports 1960-1970.

16　Hagemeyer, minutes supervisory board 13 June 1967 and 5 september 1967.

17　Hagemeyer, minutes supervisory board 28 August 1964.

18　W.J.M. Blonk, 'Kartels. Bedrijfsleven vraagt richtlijnen', in: *Inkoop. Maandblad van de Nederlandse Vereniging voor Inkoop-Efficiency*, juni 1963, 128-131; M. Schrover, 'De Fiva als een bijzondere variant van collectieve verticale prijsbinding, 1928-1975', in: *NEHA-Jaarboek*, 59 (1996).

19　Borsumij, minutes supervisory board 11 May 1962 and 23 November 1966.

20　Borsumij, minutes supervisory board 9 February, 3 May, and 28 September 1972, 15 May 1973.

21　Borsumij, minutes supervisory board 16 January 1979.

22　Hagemeyer, minutes supervisory board 19 March 1962, 6 December 1966, 23 January 1968 and 17 January 1969.

23　Hagemeyer, minutes supervisory board 5 June 1975, 11 September 1975, annual report 1977. Hagemeyer's share in the joint venture was 30%.

24　H.W. de Jong, 'De concentratie in de Europese economie', in: *ESB*, 2-3-1988; idem, 'Theorie en empirie van het concentratieproces', in: J.J. van Duin a.o. (ed.), *Fusies en overnames* (Schoonhoven 1992), 119-135; idem, *Dynamische Markttheorie* (Leiden 1989).

25　*De functie van de handel. Toespraken gehouden ter gelegenheid van de uitreiking van de Internatiohandelsprijs 1964 aan J.F. Haccoû* (Rotterdam 1965) 5-8.

26　Hagemeyer, minutes supervisory board 29 July 1961, 26 November 1962 and 15 February 1963.

27　Hagemeyer, minutes supervisory board 15 February 1962, 25 March 1963.

28　Interview with G.M.A.M. Fagel, 31 March 1998.

29　Hagemeyer, minutes supervisory board 6 December 1965.

30　Hagemeyer, minutes supervisory board 21 January 1966.

31　*Sagittarius*, July 1980.

32　*Van Oss' Effectenboek*, 1964, 982 and 1036; idem 1966, 716.

33　Hagemeyer, minutes supervisory board 27 August 1968. During this meeting the board gave its consent to the acquisition, which took place during the following year.

34　Hagemeyer Archive, press release 2 April 1969.

35　Hagemeyer Archive, report Horringa & De Koning, May 1976.

36　*Sagittarius*, also published by Hagemeyer in a Dutch edition called *Boogschutter*. Data from he first volume, which appeared in 1970, and subsequent issues.

37　Hagemeyer, minutes annual general meeting, 18 March 1969.

38　*Algemeen Handelsblad*, 7 June 1969.

39　Borsumij, minutes supervisory board 9 November and 12 December 1960.

40　Hagemeyer, minutes supervisory board 2 December 1975.

41　Ceteco, annual reports 1960-1970.

42 Ceteco, annual reports 1970-1980.

43 Table 7.2 has been derived from the various annual reports for 1972.

44 Borsumij, minutes supervisory board 12 November 1965; Hagemeyer, minutes supervisory board 2 September 1965.

45 Lindeteves Jacoberg, annual report 1967.

46 M. Dendermonde, *Blik op een groei, OGEM*, 1972; R. Robijn and G.J. Laan, *De OGEM dossiers* (Amsterdam 1984) 36. The Technische Unie had been formed in 1954 by the merger of Electrocentrum with Heybroek & Co and the NV I. Zélander, a combination dating from 1946: *Uniepost*, March/April 1980.

47 ARA 2.18.23, Lindeteves Jacoberg Archive, No. 26, minutes supervisory board, 1962-1972.

48 ARA 2.18.23, Lindeteves Jacoberg Archive, No. 495, memorandum entitled 'Alleen ter inzage RvB', 28 January 1971.

49 J.J. Dankers and J. Verheul, *Hoogovens 1945-1993. Van staalbedrijf tot twee-metalenconcern. Een studie in industriële strategie* (The Hague 1993) 388.

50 ARA 2.18.23, Lindeteves Jacoberg Archive, No. 39, minutes supervisory board 20 December 1972.

51 Hagemeyer, minutes supervisory board 6 September 1973.

52 ARA 2.18.23, Lindeteves Jacoberg Archive, No. 495, memorandum entitled 'Alleen ter inzage RvB' from A.J. Klein to the supervisory board, 29 December 1970.

53 ARA 2.18.23, Lindeteves Jacoberg Archive, No. 53, minutes staff meeting 12 February 1975.

54 Hagemeyer, minutes supervisory board 39 January and 5 June 1975.

55 Hagemeyer, minutes supervisory board 1 juni 1977 (quote) and 11 September 1975.

56 Hagemeyer, minutes supervisory board 9 November 1979; annual report 1979.

57 Van Zanden, *Klein land*, 218-227.

58 B. Klaverstijn, *Samentwijnen. Via fusie naar integratie* (Arnhem 1989) 102-116, 158-159.

59 Van Zanden, *Klein land*, 217.

60 C. de Voogd, 'Uittredingsbarrières bij neergang van bedrijftakken', in: *ESB*, 4 January 1995; C. de Voogd, *De neergang van de scheepsbouw en andere industriële bedrijfstakken* (Vlissingen 1993).

61 Oomens/Bakker, 'Beroepsbevolking Nederland' 39; CBS, *Negentig jaren statistiek in tijdreeksen 1899-1989* (Voorburg 1989) 76.

62 Hagemeyer, minutes supervisory board 16 January 1970.

63 Hagemeyer, minutes supervisory board 27 April 1972.

64 Hagemeyer, minutes annual general meeting 29 May 1979.

65 Hagemeyer Archive, Report McKinsey & Company, 10 December 1976 and 28 March 1977. Mc Kinsey had been hired after the departure of Horringa & De Koning in 1976

66 Hagemeyer Archive, Report Horringa & De Koning, management consultants, May 1976 and their let-

ter to the supervisory board, 3 May 1976. Hagemeyer's supervisory board did not take this recommendation well and terminated the contract with Horringa & De Koning. Van Schaik left the company a year later, by the way.

67 Internatio-Müller, annual reports 1970-1992.

68 *Verslag van het onderzoek, ingesteld door Mr. J. van der Hoeven, dr. A. van Putten en Prof. Mr. W.J. Slagter naar het beleid en de gang van zaken bij OGEM Holding NV* (report concluded by 31 December 1986) 1987, 212. Annual reports Stokvis en Lindeteves, 1970-1978.

69 ARA 2.18.23, Lindeteves Jacoberg Archive, No. 53, minutes staff meeting 25 May 1978.

70 Miellet, *Honderd jaar grootwinkelbedrijf*, 237-245.

71 *Gedenkboek SHV* 1996 (no page numbers).

72 G. Jones, 'British trading companies and industrial development', in: F. Amatori a.o. (ed.), *Deindustrialization and reindustrialization in 20th century Europe* (Milan 1999) 345-371, quote on 371; Fieldhouse, *Merchant capital*, 716-762.

73 Internatio, annual reports 1971 and 1980.

74 Hagemeyer, minutes supervisory board 14 December 1971, 22 November 1973 (quote).

75 Goedhart, *Eerherstel voor de plantage*, 228-230.

Chapter VIII, Groping for a core business, 1983-2000

1 The 1980s saw a flood of publications about Dutch wholesaling, usually compiled by the Economisch Instituut voor het Midden- en Kleinbedrijf or EIM, an organization dedicated to the interests of small and medium-sized firms. The Verbond Nederlandse Groothandel, a sectoral organization for wholesaling founded in 1950, published its first yearbook about wholesaling trends in 1988 . This series was continued by the EIM from 1997, and entitled *Ondernemen in de Groothandel*.

2 W.J. van de Woestijne, 'De handel als motor van economisch herstel', in: *ESB*, 24-8-1983.

3 G.J. Landjouw, *Internationale handelsinstituties* (Schoonhoven 1995) 9-39.

4 Borsumij, minutes of the supervisory board, 11 February 1983, 23 September 1983, 27 January 1984.

5 Amsterdam Consulting Group, *De interne markt: een uitdaging voor de groothandel* (February 1990).

6 *Jaarboek Groothandel*, 1989; EIM, *Ondernemen in de Groothandel 1999*.

7 Het Financieele Dagblad, *De omzetcijfers van ... 1980-1984* (Amsterdam 1981-1985).

8 Borsumij, minutes of the supervisory board 12 April 1983.

9 Borsumij, minutes of the supervisory board 15 November 1983.

10 Borsumij, annual report 1986.

11 *Sagittarius*, October 1981; Hagemeyer, minutes of the supervisory board 5 September 1985, 6 February 1986; *Haagtechno bv, een betrouwbare partner*, undated; interview with H.W.N.A. Jansen,

28 April 1999.

12 Borsumij, minutes of the supervisory board 26 November 1991.

13 Borsumij, minutes of the supervisory board 4 February 1988.

14 Borsumij, minutes of the supervisory board 20 December 1985, 19 December 1986, 16 December 1988, 21 December 1989, 5 February 1990; annual reports Borsumij, 1980-1994; *Volkskrant*, 16 November 1996.

15 Borsumij, minutes of the supervisory board 22 September 1982, 11 February 1983, 23 April 1985, 19 September 1985, 4 February 1987, 17 December 1987, 26 November 1991; annual reports Borsumij, 1982-1991.

16 *Sagittarius*, July 1980; Hagemeyer, minutes of the supervisory board 2 September 1982.

17 *Sagittarius*, February 1982.

18 Hagemeyer, minutes of the supervisory board 6 June 1985, 10 November 1987, 5 November 1991, 5 May 1992; annual report Hagemeyer 1993.

19 *Sagittarius*, December 1992 (GPX) and December 1998 (Case Logic); annual reports Hagemeyer, 1991-1998; interview with A. Land, 8 June 1999.

20 Hagemeyer, minutes of the supervisory board 9 September 1986.

21 Annual report Hagemeyer, 1993.

22 Annual report Hagemeyer, 1989.

23 Hagemeyer, minutes of the supervisory board 14 December 1988 and 7 March 1989; annual report Hagemeyer, 1989. Medicopharma executed its internationalization strategy under its own steam by take-overs in the UK and the US, but filed for bankruptcy in 1992, after which parts of the company were sold to OPG: H.P.H. Nusteling, *Markant in de markt; Interpharm 1896-1996* (Den Bosch 1996) 168.

24 *Sagittarius*, October 1989.

25 *Financieele Dagblad*, 7 May 1996; interview with H.J. de Graaf, 16 June 1999; *Sagittarius*, December 1997.

26 Hagemeyer, minutes of the supervisory board 26 January 1995, 3 November 1995; 'The power to deliver across Europe', undated; interview with H.J. de Graaf, 16 June 1999.

27 Hagemeyer, minutes of the supervisory board 10 November 1987; annual reports Hagemeyer 1988-1998; interview with A. Land, 8 June 1999.

28 *Sagittarius*, December 1997.

29 René Kreileman, 'Haalt de groothandel het jaar 2001', in: *Logistiek Actueel*, No. 10, 1998, 8-9.

30 Peter van Lonkhuizen, 'De dood van de groothandel', in: *Management Team*, 9-4-1999.

31 Internatio-Müller outsourced the operations of its computerdepartment and its accountancy department in 1983, as part of an effort to reduce the size and the cost of its head office: annual report Internatio, 1983. When in 1992 one of the supervisory directors of Borsumij Wehry asked about the company's strategy concerning computerization, it turned out that the company no longer had a central computer department. The accountants

Moret Ernst & Young exercised the technical supervision, and a task force information technology was to be installed as well. However, at that moment priority was given to a task force logistical services: Borsumij, minutes of the supervisory board 26 November 1992.

32 K.R. Jonkheer, *Informatietechnologie en telematica in de groothandel. Zijn informatietechnologie en telematica een herkenbare productiefactor in de (internationale) concurrentie?* (EIM, Zoetermeer 1997); F.J. Heemstra, 'Informatietechnologie en management', *Tijdschrift voor Bedrijfsadministratie*, September 1993, 328-333.

33 Jonkheer, *IT&T in de groothandel*, 20.

34 'Groothandels bedreigd met uitschakeling', in: *Financieele Dagblad*, 30-5-1997; 'Groothandelaar spin in het web', in: *Financieele Dagblad*, 28-8-1997.

35 *Jaarboek Groothandel*, 1989.

36 *The Economist*, 26 June-2 July 1999, survey: E-business.

37 Jonkheer, *IT&T in de groothandel*, 5-8, 27-35.

38 P.Th. van de Zeijden, *Groothandel en logistieke dienstverleners: partners of concurrent?* (EIM, Zoetermeer 1991).

39 *Sagittarius*, June 1999.

40 Interview with Willem van Eeghen, 13 April 1999.

41 Hagemeyer Archive, presentation by McKinsey & Company, 1977.

42 Annual reports Internatio-Mhller, Borsumij Wehry, and Hagemeyer, 1980-1990.

43 *Tien jaar samenwerking OTRA en Sonepar* (OTRA, undated).

44 Hagemeyer, minutes of the supervisory board 18 October 1982, 9 December 1982; interview with A. Land, 8 June 1999.

45 John W. Dizard, 'Sears' humbled trading empire', in: *Fortune*, 25 June 1984.

46 Borsumij, minutes of the supervisory board 19 December 1984.

47 Hagemeyer, minutes of the supervisory board 2 May 1985-12 November 1986; interview with A. Land, 8 June 1999; annual report Hagemeyer, 1986.

48 *Jaarboeken Groothandel*, 1989-1994; EIM, *Ondernemen in de groothandel*, 1997 en 1998; J.C.G. Hensgens, *Ondernemingsconcentratie in de Nederlandse groothandel, 1989-1993* (Zoetermeer 1994); K.R. Jonkheer, *Ondernemingsconcentratie in de Nederlandse groothandel 1994* (Zoetermeer 1995).

49 Annual reports Internatio, 1990-1998.

50 Borsumij, minutes of the supervisory board 16 September 1988.

51 As late as 1982, the tanning works employed more than 700 people, including only four Europeans. However, when Kenya cut export subsidies while retaining high import duties on the chemicals needed for the tanning, producing for exports became unprofitable, while the factory was much too big for the Kenyan market alone. Borsumij, minutes of the supervisory board 17 May 1982 and 22 September 1982.

52 Annual reports Hagemeyer, 1990-1998.

53 *Sagittarius*, July 1993; annual reports Hagemeyer, 1997-1998.

54 Chandler, *Visible hand*, 209-240, 484-505.

55 Borsumij, minutes of the supervisory board 21 November 1979, 9 February 1981, 18 March 1982.

56 Borsumij, minutes of the supervisory board 26 November 1991 and memorandum 5 November 1991.

57 B. Izaks, 'Van Dorp met Despec van gedaante veranderd', in: *Beleggers Belangen*, 16 July 1999; 'Buhrmann slaat toe in de VS', in: *Beleggers Belangen*, 16 July 1999.

58 A.J.F. Boekesteijn, *Recente fusies en overnames in de Nederlandse groothandel; kenmerken en effecten* (Zoetermeer 1989) 22-26.

59 J.C.G. Hensgens, *Ondernemingsconcentratie in de Nederlandse groothandel, 1989-1993* (EIM, Zoetermeer 1994); K.R. Jonkheer, *Ondernemingsconcentratie in de Nederlandse groothandel 1994* (EIM, Zoetermeer 1995); *Ondernemen in de Groothandel 1999* (EIM, Zoetermeer 1999).

60 For instance, in its 1997 sectoral survey, the EIM puts the number of firms active in wholesaling at 57,398 for 1995, whereas the organization mentions a figure of 52,444 for the same year in the sectoral survey for 1998. The large numbers of single-person firms renders the tracing of data about wholesaling very difficult.

61 *Elan*, December 1995; *Intermediair*, 13 November 1997.

62 Draft annual report Borsumij 1993.

63 Borsumij, minutes of the supervisory board 15 November 1983.

64 Borsumij, minutes of the supervisory board 4 February 1988.

65 Hagemeyer, minutes of the supervisory board 28 January 1987.

66 Borsumij, minutes of the supervisory board 16 December 1988, 20 December 1990.

67 Borsumij, minutes of the supervisory board 9 February 1982.

68 Hagemeyer, minutes of the supervisory board 2 September 1987; Floris Hers, 'Het geheim van Hagemeyer: groot zonder massa', in: *FEM*, 18 October 1997.

69 *Elan*, February 1999.

70 Borsumij, minutes of the supervisory board 19 December 1984.

71 The data for the graphs have been derived from the annual reports published by the three companies concerned.

72 Interview with A. Land, 8 June 1999.

73 Annual report Internatio-Müller, 1991; R. Kosterman, 'Laatste kans Internatio', in: *FEM*, 17 August 1991.

74 Annual reports Internatio-Müller, 1991-1998; B. Izaks, 'Groeier Internatio-Müller drastisch veranderd', in: *Beleggers Belangen*, 28 November 1997; interview with P.J. Groenenboom, 23 September 1999.

75 Borsumij, minutes of the supervisory board 25 November 1994, 3 February 1995.

76 Borsumij, minutes of the supervisory board 19 December 1991.

77 Borsumij, minutes of the supervisory board 21 July 1993.

78 Borsumij, minutes of the supervisory board 26 November 1991; annual reports Borsumij, 1991-1994.

79 Borsumij, minutes of the supervisory board 14 April 1992, 10 February 1994.

80 Borsumij, minutes of the supervisory board 25 August 1994.

81 Hagemeyer, minutes of the supervisory board 9 September 1986, 26 April 1989; annual reports Hagemeyer, 1990-1998.

82 Hagemeyer, minutes of the supervisory board 1 July 1977.

83 *Het Financieele Dagblad*, 16 May 1995.

84 H. Schenk, 'Fuseren of innoveren', in: *ESB*, 20-3-1996; idem, 'Meerwaarde Vendex-afsplitsingen wordt teniet gedaan door fusie met KBB', in: *Elan*, July 1999.

85 Ron Kosterman, 'Handelshuis Hagemeyer lijkt niet te stuiten', in: *FEM*, 7 March 1992.

86 *Sagittarius*, June 1992, interview with Phil Betsch.

87 *Sagittarius*, December 1992.

88 B. Izaks, 'Groeier Internatio-Müller drastisch veranderd', in: *Beleggers Belangen*, 28 November 1997.

89 Annual reports Stokvis, 1970-1980; interview with A.A.M. Lauxtermann, December 1998.

90 In 1964, R. Zwolsman bought a majority stake in ARM, but ARM successfully resisted the take-over, supported by Shell. Zwolsman then sold his shares to an insurance company, the Centrale Levensverzekering in The Hague. This company retained the shares until Hagemeyer bought them in 1988. G. Meyloph and W. Bosch, *Honderd jaar handel in paardekracht, 1881-1981* (ARM, Amsterdam 1981) 82-85; Hagemeyer, minutes of the supervisory board 27 January 1988.

91 One example of this financial creativity was the fact that Hagemeyer, long before Philips and Fokker Aircraft did so, had used in 1987 a construction of sale and lease back of brands to exploit the opportunities for tax compensation on losses: Hagemeyer, minutes of the supervisory board, 10 November 1987. Though the contract was to run for ten years, Hagemeyer bought the brands back in 1995.

92 Hagemeyer, annual report for 1995.

93 *NRC-Handelsblad*, 14 March 1998.

94 MeesPierson, Hagemeyer, February 1998.

95 Jos van Hezewijk and Marcel Metze, *XXL. De macht, het netwerk, de prestaties en de wereld van de Nederlandse topmanagers* (Nijmegen 1998) 18-56.

96 *Het Financieele Dagblad*, 'Omzetcijfers van ... 1990 en 1997'.

97 G. Jones, *Merchants to multinationals. British trading companies in the nineteenth and twentieth centuries* (Oxford 2000) Chapter 11, End Game.

98 Interview with R. ter Haar, 21 October 1999.

Literature

A

Abeln, G.H.J., *Het Nederlandse internationale handelshuis en de groei, prae-advies voor het verbond van de Nederlandse groothandel* (The Hague 1969)

Algemeen Handelsblad, 7 June 1969

Amsterdam Consulting Group, *De interne markt: een uitdaging voor de groothandel* (February 1990)

Annual reports Borsumij, 1894-1994

Annual reports Ceteco, 1970-1980

Annual reports Geo. Wehry, 1947-1959

Annual reports Hagemeyer, 1936-1998

Annual reports Internatio-Müller, 1930-1998

Annual reports Lindeteves, 1916-1977

Annual reports Stokvis, 1908-1980

Annual reports Twentsche Overzee Handel Maatschappij, 1920-1963

Ansoff, H.I., *Corporate strategy* (1965)

Ansoff, H.I., 'The firm of the future', in: *Harvard Business Review*, 43 (1965) No. 5, 162-178

B

Baasch, E., 'Hamburg und Holland im 17. und 18. Jahrhundert', in: *Hanseatische Geschichtsblätter* 16 (1910) 45-102

Baasch, E., *Holländische Wirtschaftsgeschichte* (Jena 1927)

Bakhuizen van den Brink, R.C., *I. le Maire* (Amsterdam 1865)

Bakker, B.A., *Export & marketing. Enige aspecten van exportmarketing en exportsamenwerking bij Nederlandse ondernemingen* (Brussels 1980)

Bakker, J., *Mercurius gedurende een halve eeuw, gedenkboek ter gelegenheid van het vijftigjarig jubileum van den nationalen bond van handels- en kantoorbedienden 'Mercurius'* (Leiden 1932)

Bang, N., K. Korst, *Tabeller over skibsfart og varetransport gennem Øresund 1661-1783* (Copenhagen 1930)

Barbour, V., *Capitalism in Amsterdam in the 17th century* (Ann Arbor 1963)

Barlaeus, C., *Mercator sapiens*, edited by S. van der Woude (Amsterdam 1967)

Barnouw, D., ed., *Correspondentie van Mr. M.M. Rost van Tonningen*, II, *mei 1942-mei 1945* (Zutphen 1993)

Baudet, H., ed., *Handelswereld en wereldhandel, honderd jaren Internatio: tien essays* (Rotterdam 1963)

Baudet, H., M. Fennema, *Het Nederlands belang bij Indië* (Utrecht 1983)

Bel, J.G. van, *De linnenhandel van Amsterdam in de 18ᵉ eeuw* (Amsterdam 1940)

Berg, L. van den, 'Lijst der voornaamste handelshuizen te Amsterdam en Rotterdam in het jaar 1800', in: *Economisch historisch jaarboek* 6 (1920) 265-271

Beylen, J. van, 'Scheepstypen', in: L.M. Akveld, S. Hart, W.J. van Hoboken, ed., *Maritieme geschiedenis der Nederlanden*, II (Bussum 1977) 11-71

Bie, R. van der, *'Eene doorlopende groote roes'*, *De economische ontwikkeling vn Nederland 1913/1921* (Amsterdam 1995)

Blanken, I.J., *Geschiedenis van Philips Electronics NV, de ontwikkeling van de NV Philips' Gloeilampenfabrieken tot elektrotechnisch concern* (Leiden 1992)

Bläsing, J.F.E, *Das goldene Delta und sein eisernes Hinterland 1815-1851, von niederländisch-preussischen zu deutsch-niederländischen Wirtschaftsbeziehungen* (Leiden 1973)

Blonk, W.J.M., 'Kartels. Bedrijfsleven vraagt richtlijnen', in: *Inkoop. Maandblad van de Nederlandse Vereniging voor Inkoop-Efficiency*, June 1963, 128-131

Boekesteijn, A.J.F., *Recente fusies en overnames in de Nederlandse groothandel; kenmerken en effecten* (Zoetermeer 1989)

Bogucka, M., 'Dutch merchant's activities in Gdansk in the first half of the 17ᵗʰ century', in: J.P.S. Lemmink, J.S.A.M. van Koningsbrugge, ed., *Baltic affairs, relations between the Netherlands and Northeastern Europe 1500-1800* (Nijmegen 1990) 19-32

Boomgaard, P., ed., *Changing economy in Indonesia*, 6, J.T.M. van Laanen, ed., *Money and banking 1816-1940* (The Hague 1980); 8, W.A.I.M. Segers, *Manufacturing Industry, 1870-1942* (Amsterdam 1987); 9, G.J. Knaap, ed., *Transport 1819-1940* (Amsterdam 1989); 12a, W.L. Korthals Altes, ed., *Regional trade statistics 1822-1940* (Amsterdam 1991)

Booth, A., 'Growth and stagnation in an era of nation-building: Indonesian economic performance from 1950 to 1965', in: J.Th. Lindblad, ed., *Historical foundations of a national economy in Indonesia, 1890s-1990s* (Amsterdam 1996) 401-423

Booth, A., *The Indonesian economy in the nineteenth and twentieth centuries, a history of missed opportunities* (Basingstoke 1998)

Bos, D., *De opleiding voor den handel* (S.l. 1902)

Bossenbroek, M., *Holland op zijn breedst, Indië en Zuid-Afrika in de Nederlandse cultuur omstreeks 1900* (Amsterdam 1996)

Bouman, P.J., *Rotterdam en het Duitsche achterland 1831-1851* (Amsterdam 1931)

Brakel, S. van, 'De Directie van den Oosterschen Handel en Reederijen te Amsterdam', in: *Bijdragen voor vaderlandsche geschiedenis en oudheidkunde* 4/IX (1910) 329-364

Bredero, G.A., 'Moortje', in: Kruttel, J.A.N., ed., *Werken van G.A. Bredero* (Amsterdam 1924) 97-218

Bree, L. de, *Gedenkboek van de Javasche Bank 1828-24 januari-1928* (Weltevreden 1928)

Breedvelt-Van Veen, F., *Louis de Geer (1587-1652)* (Amsterdam 1935)

Broeze, F.J.A., 'The new economic history, the Navigation Acts, and the continental tobacco market, 1770-1790', in: *Economic history review* 26 (1973) 668-678

Broeze, F.J.A., 'Rederij', in: F.J.A. Broeze, J.R. Bruijn, F.S. Gaastra, ed., *Maritieme geschiedenis der Nederlanden* III (Bussum 1977) 92-141

Broeze, F.J.A., 'The international diffusion of ocean steam navigation, the myth of the retardation of Netherlands steam navigation to the East Indies', in: *Economisch- en sociaalhistorisch jaarboek* 45 (1982) 77-95

Broeze, F.J.A., *De Stad Schiedam, de Schiedamse scheepsrederij en de Nederlandse vaart op Oost-Indië omstreeks 1840* (The Hague 1978)

Brugmans, H., 'De notulen en munimenten van het College van Commercie te Amsterdam 1663-1665', in: *Bijdragen en mededelingen van het Historisch Genootschap* 18 (1897) 181-331

Brugmans, H., 'Het belang der economische geschiedenis', in: L. Noordegraaf, ed., *Ideeën en ideologieën, studies over economische en sociale geschiedenis in Nederland 1894-1991*, I (Amsterdam 1991) 73-98

Brugmans, H., 'De koopman, Mercurius als spectator', in: *Jaarboek Amstelodamum* 10 (1917) 61-135

Brugmans, I.J., 'Economische en maatschappelijke verhoudingen in het Noorden, 1840-1870', in: J.A. van Houtte a.o., ed., *Algemene geschiedenis der Nederlanden*, X, *Liberaal getij, 1840-1885* (Utrecht 1955) 253-287

Brugmans, I.J., ed., *Statistieken van de Nederlandse nijverheid uit de eerste helft der 19e eeuw* (The Hague 1956)

Brugmans, I.J., 'De Oost-Indische Compagnie en de welvaart in de Republiek', idem, *Welvaart en historie, tien studiën* (The Hague 1970²) 28-37

Brugmans, I.J., 'Koning Willem I als neo-mercantilist', in: idem, *Welvaart en historie, tien studiën* (The Hague 1970²) 38-50

Brugmans, I.J., 'Uit de geschiedenis van het kantoor', in: *Economisch- en sociaalhistorisch jaarboek* 44 (1981) 211-223

Brugmans, I.J., *De arbeidende klasse in Nederland in de 19e eeuw 1813-1870* (Utrecht 1978¹¹)

Brugmans, I.J., *Paardenkracht en mensenmacht, sociaal-economische geschiedenis van Nederland, 1795-1940* (The Hague 1983)

Bruin, C., *Een herenwereld ontleed, over Amsterdamse oude en nieuwe elites in de tweede helft van de negentiende eeuw* (Amsterdam 1980)

Bruijn, J.R., 'Postvervoer en reizigersverkeer tussen de Lage Landen en Engeland ca. 1650-ca. 1850', in: P.W. Klein, ed., *100 jaar Engelandvaart* (Bussum 1975) 19-52

Bruijn, J.R., 'De personeelsbehoefte van de VOC overzee en aan boord, bezien in Aziatisch en Nederlands perspectief', in: *Bijdragen en mededelingen betreffende de geschiedenis der Nederlanden* 91 (1976) 218-248

Bruijn, J.R., 'De vaart in Europa', in: L.M. Akveld, S. Hart, W.J. van Hoboken, ed., *Maritieme geschiedenis van Nederland* II (Bussum 1977) 200-241

Bruijn, J.R., 'Scheepvaart in de Noordelijke Nederlanden 1650-1800', in: D.P. Blok a.o., ed., *Algemene geschiedenis der Nederlanden*, VIII, *Nieuwe Tijd* (Bussum 1979) 209-238

Bruijn, J.R., F.S. Gaastra, I. Schöffer, ed., *Dutch-Asiatic shipping in the 17th and 18th centuries*, I, *Introduction* (The Hague 1987)

Bruijn, J.R., 'Productivity, profitability, and costs of private and corporate Dutch ships during the seventeenth and eighteenth centuries', in: J.D. Tracy, ed., *The rise of merchant empires, long-distance trade in the early modern world, 1350-1750* (Cambridge 1990) 174-194

Bruijn, J.R., F.S. Gaastra, ed., *Ships, sailors, spices, East India companies and their shipping in the 16ᵗʰ, 17ᵗʰ and*

407

18th centuries (Amsterdam 1993)

Bruijn, J.R., 'In een veranderend maritiem perspectief: het ontstaan van directies voor de vaart op de Oostzee, Noorwegen en Rusland', in: Tijdschrift voor zeegeschiedenis 9 (1990) 15-26

Brulez, W., De firma Della Faille en de internationale handel van Vlaamse firma's in de 16e eeuw (Brussels 1959)

Brulez, W., 'De diaspora der Antwerpse kooplui op het einde van de 16de eeuw', in: Bijdragen tot de geschiedenis der Nederlanden 15 (1960) 279-306

Brulez, W., 'The balance of trade of the Netherlands in the middle of the sixteenth century', in: Acta historiae Neerlandicae 4 (1970) 20-48

Brulez, W., 'De scheepvaartwinst in de nieuwe tijden', in: Tijdschrift voor geschiedenis (1979) 1-19

Buck, P. de, J.Th. Lindblad, 'Scheepvaart en handel uit de Oostzee op Amsterdam en de Republiek, 1722-1780', in: Tijdschrift voor geschiedenis 96 (1983) 536-562

'Buhrmann slaat toe in de VS', Beleggers Belangen, 16 juli 1999

Buist, M.G., At spes non fracta, Hope & Co. 1770-1815, merchant bankers and diplomats at work (Amsterdam 1974)

C

Campo, J.N.M.F. à, 'Wereldsysteeem in bedrijf, scheepvaartconcurrentie in Indonesië', in: Jaarboek voor de geschiedenis van bedrijf en techniek 3 (1986) 252-269

Campo, J.N.F.M. à, Koninklijke Paketvaart Maatschappij, stoomvaart en staatsvorming in de Indonesische archipel, 1888-1914 (Hilversum 1992)

Campo, J.N.F.M. à, 'Strength, survival and success, a statistical profile of corporate enterprise in colonial Indonesia 1883-1913', in: Jahrbuch für Wirtschaftsgeschichte (1995) 45-74

Campo, J.N.F.M. à, 'The rise of corporate enterprise in colonial Indonesia 1893-1913', in: J.Th. Lindblad, ed., Historical foundations of a national economy in Indonesia, 1890s-1990s (Amsterdam 1996) 71-94

Carter, A.C., 'The family and business of Belesaigne, Amsterdam 1689-1809', in: idem, Getting, spending and investing in early modern times, essays on Dutch, English and Huguenot economic history (Assen 1975) 107-122

Carter, A.C., 'Financial activities of the Huguenots in London and Amsterdam in the mid-eighteenth century', in: idem, Getting, spending and investing in early modern times, essays on Dutch, English and Huguenot economic history (Assen 1975) 91-106

Casson, M., 'The economic analysis of multinational trading companies', in: G. Jones ed., The multinational traders (London 1998) 22-47

CBS, Negentig jaren statistiek in tijdreeksen 1899-1989 (The Hague 1989)

Chamberlain, M.E., Decolonization. The fall of the European empires (Oxford 1985, reprint 1987)

Chandler Jr, A.D.,The visible hand. The managerial revolution in American business (Cambridge Mass. 1977)

Chandler Jr., A.D., Scale and Scope, the dynamics of

industrial capitalism (Cambridge Mass. 1990)

Chapman, S.D., 'British marketing enterprise: the changing roles of merchants, manufacturers and financiers 1700-1806', in: Business history review 53 (1979) 205-234

Chapman, S.D., The rise of merchant banking (London 1984)

Chapman, S.D., Merchant enterprise in Britain from the Industrial Revolution to World War I (Cambridge 1992)

Christensen, A.E., Dutch trade to the Baltic about 1600, studies in the Sound toll register and Dutch shipping records (The Hague 1941)

Clercq, W.A. de, 'Verleden, heden en toekomst van de Directie der Oostersche Handel en Reederijen te Amsterdam', in: Tijdschrift voor zeegeschiedenis 9 (1990) 5-14

Colombijn, F., 'Nostalgia for a better future, organization of economic life in a colonial trading town: Padang (West Sumatra) 1906-1942', in: Economic and social history in the Netherlands 3 (1991) 155-182

Coolhaas, W.P., a.o., ed., Generale missiven van Goeverneurs-Generaal en raden aan Heren XVII der Verenigde Oostindische Compagnie (The Hague 1960 ff)

Crena de Iongh, D., 'Nederlandsch-Indië als beleggingsgebied voor Nederlandsch kapitaal', in: C. Gerretson a.o., De sociaal-economische invloed van Nederlandsch-Indië op Nederland (Wageningen 1938) 97-113

Crol, W.A.H., Een tak van de familie Van Stolk honderd jaar in de graanhandel 1847-1947 (Rotterdam 1947)

Crone, G.H., 'De ontwikkeling der koloniale markten in Nederland', in: C. Gerretson a.o., De sociaal-economische invloed van Nederlandsch-Indië op Nederland (Wageningen 1938) 45-62

Crone, H.G.Th., Crone 1790-1940, gedenkboek ter gelegenheid van het 150-jarig bestaan van de firma (Amsterdam 1940)

D

Dankers, J.J., J. Verheul, Hoogovens 1945-1993, van staalbedrijf tot twee-metalenconcern. Een studie in industriële strategie (The Hague 1993)

Damsma, D., J.M.M. de Meere, L. Noordegraaf, ed., Statistieken van de Nederlandse nijverheid uit de eerste helft der 19e eeuw, supplement (The Hague 1979)

Davids, C.A., 'Zekerheidsregelingen in de scheepvaart en het landtransport, 1500-1800', in: J.L.J.M. van Gerwen, M.H.D. van Leeuwen, ed., Studies over zekerheidsarrangementen, risico's, risicobestrijding en verzekeringen in Nederland vanaf de Middeleeuwen (Amsterdam 1998) 183-203

Davis, R., 'Merchant shipping in the economy of the late seventeenth century', in: Economic history review 9 (1956) 59-73

Davis, R., 'English foreign trade 1700-1774', in: Economic history review 15 (1963) 285-303

Dehing, P.W.N.M., M. 't Hart, 'Linking the fortunes, currency and banking 1550-1880', in: M. 't Hart, J.P.B. Jonker, J.L. van Zanden, ed., A financial history of the Netherlands (Cambridge 1997) 37-63

Delfgaauw, J.G.M., 'De binnenlandse groot- en kleinhandel' in: De Nederlandse Volkshuishouding tussen

Twee Wereldoorlogen (Utrecht/Antwerpen 1947), Chapter XI

Dendermonde, M., Blik op een groei, OGEM (1972)

Dierickx, M., 'De eerste jaren van Filips II, 1555-1567', in: J.A. van Houtte, ed., Algemene geschiedenis der Nederlanden IV (Utrecht 1952) 305-349

Diferee, H.C., 'De fondsenhandel tijdens de Republiek', in: idem, Studiën over de geschiedenis van den Nederlandschen handel (Amsterdam 1908) 49-79

Diferee, H.C., 'Een pleidooi voor handelsstudie in de zeventiende eeuw', in: Handelsstudie 2 No. 33 (1905) 259-262

Diferee, H.C., Geschiedenis van den Nederlandschen handel tot den val der Republiek (Amsterdam 1908)

Dillen, J.G. van, 'Eenige brieven der firma Hope & Co.', in: Economisch-historisch jaarboek 1 (1916) 263-278

Dillen, J.G. van, 'Stukken betreffende den Amsterdamschen graanhandel omstreeks het jaar 1681', in: Economisch-historisch jaarboek 3 (1917) 70-74

Dillen, J.G. van, 'Stukken betreffende de termijnhandel in graan in de laatste jaren der 17e eeuw', in: Economisch-historisch jaarboek 4 (1918) 37-46

Dillen, J.G. van, 'De beurscrisis te Amsterdam in 1763', in: Tijdschrift voor geschiedenis 37 (1922) 241-253, 400-408

Dillen, J.G. van, 'Amsterdam als wereldmarkt der edele metalen in de 17e en 18e eeuw', in: Economisch-historische herdrukken (The Hague 1964) 235-271

Dillen, J.G. van, 'Stukken betreffende het verblijf van John Law in Gelderland (eerste kwart 18e eeuw)', in: Economisch-historisch jaarboek 11 (1925) 161-168

Dillen, J.G. van, 'Termijnhandel te Amsterdam in de 16e en 17e eeuw', in: De economist 76 (1927) 503-523

Dillen, J.G. van, 'Isaac le Maire en de handel in actiën der Oost-Indische Compagnie', in: Economisch-historisch jaarboek 16 (1930) 1-165

Dillen, J.G. van, 'Effectenkoersen aan de Amsterdamsche beurs 1723-1794', in: Economisch-historisch jaarboek 17 (1931) 1-46

Dillen, J.G. van, 'The Bank of Amsterdam', in: idem, ed., History of the principal public banks (The Hague 1934) 79-124

Dillen, J.G. van, 'Oprichting en functie der Amsterdamse Wisselbank in de zeventiende eeuw 1609-1686', in: idem, Mensen en achtergronden (Groningen 1964) 336-384

Dillen, J.G. van, 'Bloeitijd der Amsterdamse Wisselbank 1687-1781', in: idem, Mensen en achtergronden (Groningen 1964) 385-415

Dillen, J.G. van, 'Ondergang van de Amsterdamse Wisselbank, 1782-1820', in: idem, Mensen en achtergronden (Groningen 1964) 416-447

Dillen, J.G. van, 'Vreemdelingen te Amsterdam in de eerste helft der zeventiende eeuw, I. De Portugese joden', in: Tijdschrift voor geschiedenis 50 (1935) 4-35

Dillen, J.G. van, 'Amsterdamsche notariële acten betreffende den koperhandel en de uitoefening van mijnbouw en metaalindustrie in Zweden', in: Bijdragen en mededelingen van het Historisch Genootschap 58 (1937) 211-301

Dillen, J.G. van, Amsterdam in 1585, het kohier der capitale impositie 1585 (Amsterdam 1941)

Dillen, J.G. van, Het oudste aandeelhoudersregister van de Kamer Amsterdam der Oost-Indische Compagnie (The Hague 1958)

Dillen, J.G. van, Van rijkdom en regenten, handboek tot de economische en sociale geschiedenis van Nederland tijdens de Republiek (The Hague 1970)

Dizard, J.W., 'Sears' humbled trading empire', Fortune, 25 June 1984

Dooren, A. van, 'Overwinning op den afstand. In den aether', in: W.H. van Helsdingen, ed., Daar wèrd wat groots verricht... Nederlandsch-Indië in de XXste eeuw (Amsterdam 1941) 268-272

Dorp, E.C. van, 'Handel en nijverheid', in: H. Brugmans, Nederland in den oorlogstijd (Amsterdam 1920) 191-248

Driel, H. van, Vier eeuwen veembedrijf, de voorgeschiedenis van Pakhoed 1616-1967 (Rotterdam 1992)

Driel, H. van, 'Uitschakeling van de Nederlandse koffiehandel in de negentiende- en twintigste eeuw?', in: NEHA-jaarboek 60 (1997) 159-203

Drucker, P.F., The practice of management (New York 1954)

Dudok van Heel, S.A.C., 'Hooft, een hecht koopmansgeslacht', in: R. Breugelmans a.o., Hooft, essays over P.C. Hooft (Amsterdam 1981) 93-115

E

Economisch archief van Nederland en koloniën (Amsterdam s.a.)

Economist, The, 18 October 1997, 19 December 1998, 26 June 1999, survey: E-business

Eeghen, C.P. van, 'Het faillissement van den firma Coenraad & Hendrick van Son in 1762', in: Economisch-historisch jaarboek 22 (1940-1942) 82-187

Eeghen, I.H. van, 'Buitenlandse monopolies voor de Amsterdamse kooplieden in de tweede helft van de zeventiende eeuw', in: Jaarboek Amstelodamum 53 (1961) 176-184

Eeghen, I.H. van, Uit Amsterdamse dagboeken, de jeugd van Netje en Eduard Asser 1819-1833 (Amsterdam 1964)

Eeghen, I.H. van, 'Jacob Willem van den Biesen en Abraham Jacob Saportas', in: Maandblad Amstelodamum 54 (1967) 25-29

EIM, Ondernemen in de groothandel, 1997, 1998, 1999

Elan, December 1995, February 1999

Elias, J.E., 'Contract tot oprichting van een Zweedsch factorie comptoir in Amsterdam in 1663', in: Bijdragen en mededelingen van het Historisch Genootschap 24 (1903) 356-400

Elias, J.E., De vroedschap van Amsterdam 1578-1795 (Amsterdam 1963)

Engels, M.C., Merchants, interlopers, seamen and corsairs, the 'Flemish' community in Livorno and Genoa (1615-1635) (Hilversum 1997)

Enno van Gelder, H.A., 'Recente gegevens omtrent de 16e eeuwsche koopman', in: Tijdschrift voor geschiedenis 35 (1920) 199-223

Enno van Gelder, H.A., 'Scheepsrekeningen van enkele der vroegste Guineavaarten (eind 16e eeuw)', in:

Economisch-historisch jaarboek 2 (1916) 239-257

Enno van Gelder, H.A., 'Zestiende-eeuwse vrachtvaartbescheiden', in: Economisch historisch jaarboek 3 (1917) 124-290

Enno van Gelder, H.A., 'Zestiende-eeuwse koopmansbrieven', in: Economisch-historisch jaarboek 5 (1919) 136-191

Enthoven, V., Zeeland en de opkomst van de Republiek, handel en strijd in de Scheldedelta (Leiden 1996)

Es, J.C. van, 'Zestiende-eeuwse vrachtvaartbescheiden, vier scheepvaartrekeningen van 1574, 1575 en 1576', in: Economisch-historisch jaarboek 20 (1936) 258-293

Eyk van Heslinga, E.S. van, 'De vlag dekt de lading, de Nederlandse koopvaardij in de Vierde Engelse Oorlog', in: Tijdschrift voor zeegeschiedenis 1 (1982) 102-113

Eyk van Heslinga, E.S. van, Van compagnie naar koopvaardij, de scheepvaartverbinding van de Bataafse Republiek naar de koloniën in Azië (Amsterdam 1988)

Eyk van Heslinga, E.S. van, 'A competitive ally, the delicate balance between Great Britain and the Dutch Republic 1674-1795', in: G.J.A. Raven, N.A.M. Rodger, ed., Navies and armies, the Anglo-Dutch relationship in war and peace (Edinburgh 1990) 1-11

F

Faber, J.A., 'De achttiende eeuw', in: J.H. van Stuijvenberg, ed., De economische geschiedenis van Nederland (Groningen 1977) 119-156

Faber, J.A., 'Scheepvaart op Nederland in een woelige periode, 1784-1810', in: Economisch- en sociaalhistorisch jaarboek 47 (1984) 67-78

Faber, J.A., 'The decline of the Baltic grain trade in the second half of the seventeenth century', in: W.G. Heeres a.o., ed., From Dunkirk to Dantzig, shipping and trade in the North Sea and the Baltic 1350-1850 (Hilversum 1988) 31-52

Fage, J.D., A history of Africa (London, 1st edition 1978, reprint 1997)

Fasseur, C.F., Kultuurstelsel en koloniale baten, de Nederlandse exploitatie van Java 1840-1860 (Leiden 1975)

Fieldhouse, D.K., Merchant capital and economic decolonization. The United Africa Company, 1929-1987 (Oxford 1994)

Filarski, R., Kanalen van de Koning-koopman, goederenvervoer, binnenscheepvaart en kanalenbouw in Nederland en België in de eerste helft van de negentiende eeuw (Amsterdam 1995)

Financieele Dagblad, Het, De omzetcijfers van ... 1980-1997 (Amsterdam 1981-1998).

Financieele Dagblad, Het, 5 May 1995, 7 May 1996

Fleurke, M., ''by meenigt' aan de wanden en mueren ', de portretten van de bewindhebbers van de Kamer Rotterdam', in: P. Grimm ed., Heeren in zaken, de Kamer Rotterdam van de Verenigde Oostindische Compagnie (Zutphen 1993) 93-100

French, C.J., '"Crowded with traders and a great commerce", London's domination of English overseas trade', in: The London journal 17 (1992) 27-35

Fritschy, J.M.F., R. van der Voort, 'From fragmentation to unification, public finance, 1700-1914' in: M. 't Hart, J.P.B. Jonker, J.L. van Zanden, ed., A financial history

of the Netherlands (Cambridge 1997) 64-93

Functie van de handel. Toespraken gehouden ter gelegenheid van de uitreiking van de Internatio-handelsprijs 1964 aan J.F. Haccoû (Rotterdam 1965)

Functies van de voorraadhoudende groothandel in ijzer en staal (Leiden 1955)

G

Gaastra, F.S., 'De Verenigde Oostindische Compagnie in de zeventiende en achttiende eeuw: de groei van een bedrijf. Geld tegen goederen, een structurele verandering in het Nederlands-Aziatische handelsverkeer', in: Bijdragen en mededelingen betreffende de geschiedenis der Nederlanden 91 (1976) 249-272

Gaastra, F.S., 'The exports of precious metal from Europe to Asia by the Dutch East India Company, 1602-1795', in: J.F. Richards, ed., Precious metals in the later medieval and early modern worlds (Durham 1983) 447-475

Gaastra, F.S., 'De vaart buiten Europa: het Aziatisch gebied', in: F. Broeze, J.R. Bruijn, F.S. Gaastra, ed., Maritieme geschiedenis der Nederlanden 3 (Bussum 1977) 266-297

Gaastra, F.S., 'De VOC in Azië, 1680-1795', in: D.P. Blok a.o., ed., Algemene geschiedenis der Nederlanden, IX, Nieuwe tijd (Bussum 1980) 427-464

Gaastra, F.S., Bewind en beleid bij de VOC 1672-1702 (Zutphen 1989)

Gaastra, F.S., De geschiedenis van de VOC (Zutphen 1991²)

Gaastra, F.S., 'Private money for company trade, the role of bills of exchange in financing return cargoes of the VOC', in: Itinerario 18 (1994) 65-76

Gaastra, F.S., 'De textielhandel van de VOC', in: Textielhistorische bijdragen 34 (1994) 50-69

Gast. K. de, '...ten dienste van de commercie', vierhonderd jaar Beurs in Rotterdam (Rotterdam 1998)

Gawronski, J., De equipagie van de Hollandia en de Amsterdam, VOC bedrijvigheid in 18de eeuws Amsterdam (Amsterdam 1996)

Gedenkboek aangeboden door de Handelsvereeniging 'Amsterdam' (Amsterdam 1929)

Gedenkboek SHV 1996, untitled, no page numbers

Gelder, R. van, R. Kistemaker, Amsterdam 1275-1795, de ontwikkeling van een handelsmetropool (Amsterdam 1983)

Gelder, R. van, L. Wagenaar, Sporen van de compagnie, de VOC in Nederland (Amsterdam 1986)

Gelderblom, O., J.L. van Zanden, 'Vroegmodern ondernemerschap in Nederland', in: NEHA-Bulletin 11 (1997) No. 2, 3-15

Geljon, P., 'Termijnhandel in Nederland', in: idem, ed., Termijnhandel en termijn markten, opstellen ter gelegenheid van het 100-jarig bestaan van de georganiseerde termijnhandel in Amsterdam (Deventer 1988) 45-70

Gijsbers, W., Kapitale ossen, de internationale handel in slachtvee in Noordwest Europa (1300-1750) (Hilversum 1999)

Gispen, J.H., 'De practijk van de wet op het algemeen verbindend en onverbindend verklaren van ondernemersovereenkomsten 1935', Antirevolutionaire

Staatkunde, 14 (1938) 75-88, 128-146

Glamann, K., *Dutch-Asiatic trade 1620-1740* (The Hague 1958)

Glamann, K., 'The changing patterns of trade', in: E.E. Rich, C.H. Wilson, *The Cambridge economic history of Europe*, V, *The economic organization of early modern Europe* (Cambridge 1977) 185-289

Glamann, K., 'European trade 1500-1750' in: C.M. Cipolla, ed., *The Fontana economic history of Europe 4, The sixteenth and seventeenth centuries* (London 1974) 427-526

Godée Molsbergen, E.C., *Gedenkboek Reynst & Vinju 1836-1936* (Batavia 1935)

Goedhart, A., *Eerherstel voor de plantage, uit de geschiedenis van de Handelsvereeniging 'Amsterdam' (HVA) 1879-1984* (S.l. 1999)

Gonggrijp, G., *Schets ener economische geschiedenis van Nederlands-Indië/Indonesië* (Haarlem 1957[4])

Goor, J. van, *De Nederlandse koloniën, geschiedenis van de Nederlandse expansie 1600-1975* (The Hague 1997[2])

Goor, J. van, 'A hybrid state, the Dutch economic and political network in Asia', in: C. Guillot, D. Lombard, R. Ptak, ed., *From the Mediterranean to the China Sea, miscellaneous notes* (Wiesbaden 1998) 193-214

Goossens, E.J., 'De rol van de beeldhouwkunst', in: J. Huisken, K. Ottenheym, G. Schwartz, *Jacob van Campen, het klassieke ideaal in de Gouden Eeuw* (Amsterdam 1995) 201-226

Graaff, B.G.J. de, *'Kalm temidden van woedende golven', het ministerie van Koloniën en zijn taakomgeving, 1912-1940* (Leiden 1997)

Gravesteijn, C., J.J. Seegers, *Handel in theorie en praktijk, katalogus betreffende werken gepubliceerd vóór 1830 aanwezig in de EHB* (Amsterdam 1981)

Gravesteijn, C., 'Amsterdam and the origins of financial journalism', in: M. North, ed., *Kommunikationsrevolutionen, die neuen Medien des 17. Und 18. Jahrhundert* (Cologne 1995) 61-72

Grimm P., ed., *Heeren in zaken, de kamer Rotterdam van de Verenigde Oostindische Compagnie* (Zutphen 1997[2])

Grimm P., 'Heeren in zaken, de bewindhebbers van de Kamer Rotterdam', in: idem, ed., *Heeren in zaken, de kamer Rotterdam van de Verenigde Oostindische Compagnie* (Zutphen 1997[2]) 35-65

'Groothandels bedreigd met uitschakeling', *Het Financieele Dagblad*, 30 May 1997

'Groothandelaar spin in het web', *Het Financieele Dagblad*, 28 August 1997

Grote, D., J. Hoock, W. Starke, 'Handbücher für den Gebrauch des Kaufmanns, Bibliographie und Analyse des Wandels einer literarische Gattung', *Tijdschrift voor geschiedenis* 103 (1990) 279-293

H

Haagtechno bv, een betrouwbare partner.

Haan, E.E. de, 'Avonturen van een koopman' (Bonaire 1969) typoscript

Haccoû, J.F., *De termijnhandel in goederen* (Leiden 1947)

Haccoû, J.F., *Handel en marktwezen in goederen* (Leiden 1948)

Haccoû, J.F., 'Wholesaling in the Netherlands', in: R. Bartels, *Comparative marketing, wholesaling in fifteen countries* (Homewood 1963) 47-56

Hardenberg, H., 'Het handelshuis Osy', in: *Rotterdams jaarboekje* (1954) 154-176

Harder-Gersdorff, E., 'Avoiding Sound traffic and Sound toll: Russian leather and tallow going west via Archangel and Narva-Lübeck (1650-1710)', in: W.G. Heeres a.o., ed., *From Dunkirk to Danzig, shipping and trade in the North Sea and the Baltic 1350-1850* (Hilversum 1988) 237-262

Hart, M. 't, 'The merits of a financial revolution, public finance 1550-1700', in: M. 't Hart, J.P.B. Jonker, J.L. van Zanden, ed., *A financial history of the Netherlands* (Cambridge 1997) 11-36

Hart, S., 'De eerste Nederlandse tochten ter walvisvaart', in: *Jaarboek Amstelodamum* 49 (1957) 27-64

Hart, S., 'Amsterdamse scheepvaart en handel op Noord-Rusland in de zeventiende eeuw', in: idem, *Geschift en getal, een keuze uit de demografisch-economisch- en sociaalhistorische studiën op grond van Amsterdamse en Zaanse archivalia, 1600-1800* (Dordrecht 1976) 267-314

Hart, S., 'Michiel Adriaanszoon de Ruyter en de Noordcaepse Compagnie', in: idem, *Geschift en getal, een keuze uit de demografisch- economisch- en sociaalhistorische studiën op grond van Amsterdamse en Zaanse archivalia, 1600-1800* (Dordrecht 1976) 247-254

Hart, S., 'De Italiëvaart 1590-1620', in: *Jaarboek Amstelodamum* 70 (1978) 42-60

Hart, S., 'De handelsbetrekkingen van Amsterdam met Archangel en Lapland (Kola) in de 17e eeuw', in: *Nederlands archievenblad* 73 (1969) 66-80

Hart, S., J.J. McCusker, 'The rate of exchange on Amsterdam in London 1590-1660', in: *Journal of European economic history* 8 (1979) 689-705

Hart, W.G. 't, P.C. van Royen, 'Het smakschip De Neufville van der Hoop, een onderzoek naar de rendabiliteit van Nederlandse vrachtvaart in de achttiende eeuw', in: *Economisch- en sociaalhistorisch jaarboek* 48 (1985) 150-169

Heemstra, F.J., 'Informatietechnologie en management', in: *Tijdschrift voor Bedrijfsadministratie*, September 1993, 328-333

Heerding, A., *Geschiedenis van de NV Philips' Gloeilampenfabrieken*, I, *Het ontstaan van de Nederlandse gloeilampenindustrie* (The Hague 1980)

Heeres, W.G., 'Het paalgeld, een bijdrage tot de kennis van de Nederlandse handelsstatistiek in het verleden', in: *Economisch- en sociaalhistorisch jaarboek* 45 (1982) 1-17

Heeres, W.G., 'De heffing van het paalgeld door Kampen en Amsterdam', in: *Economisch en sociaalhistorisch jaarboek* 46 (1983) 128-141

Heeres, W.G., 'Annual volumes of Amsterdam's overseas imports and exports, 1697 to 1798', in: idem a.o., ed., *From Dunkirk to Danzig, shipping and trade in the North Sea and the Baltic 1350-1850* (Hilversum 1988) 263-280

Heeringa, K., a.o., ed., *Bronnen tot de geschiedenis van den Levantschen handel* (The Hague, 1910 e.v.)

Heertje, A., *David Ricardo en Amsterdam, de toekomst van de economische wetenschap als geschiedenis* (Amsterdam 1998)

Heijer, H. den, *De geschiedenis van de WIC* (Zutphen 1994)

Hellema, D., *Buitenlandse politiek van Nederland* (Utrecht 1995)

Hensgens, J.C.G., *Ondernemingsconcentratie in de Nederlandse groothandel, 1989-1993* (Zoetermeer 1994)

Hers, F., 'Het geheim van Hagemeyer: groot zonder massa', *FEM*, 18 October 1997

Hezewijk, J. van, en M. Metze, *XXL, de macht, het netwerk, de prestaties en de wereld van de Nederlandse topmanagers* (Nijmegen 1998)

Hochschild, A., *De geest van koning Leopold II en de plundering van de Congo* (Amsterdam 1998)

Hoes, H.J., 'Voorgeschiedenis en ontstaan van het Financieele Dagblad, 1796-1943', in: *Economisch- en sociaalhistorisch jaarboek* 49 (1986) 1-43

Hoffmann, W.J., 'Een oud-Rotterdamsche firma, J.F. Hoffmann en Zoonen 1734-1899', in: *Rotterdamsch jaarboekje* 3 (1915) 94-112

Hofstede, B.P., ed., *Veertig jaar NEC* (Soest 1992)

Hogesteeger, G., *Van lopende bode tot telematica, geschiedenis van de PTT in Nederland* (Groningen 1989)

Hogesteeger, G., J.W.M. Tutert, 'De overlandmail', in: Hogesteeger, G., ed., *Naar de gordel van smaragd, de postverbindingen tussen Nederland en Nederlands-Indië 1602-1940* (The Hague 1995) 27-50

Hoock, J., P. Jeannin, ed., *Handbücher und Traktate für den Gebrauch des Kaufmanns, 1470-1820* (Paderborn 1990)

Hoock, J., W. Reininghaus, ed., *Kaufleute in Europa, Handelshäuser und ihre Überlieferung in Vor- und Frühindustrieller Zeit* (Dortmund 1997)

Hooff, W.H.P.M. van, 'Meer koopman dan ambachtsman, joodse ondernemers in de Nederlandse metaalindustrie en –handel', in: H. Berg, E.J. Fischer, T. Wijsenbeek, ed., *Venter, fabriqueur, fabrikant, joodse ondernemers en ondernemingen in Nederland 1796-1940* (Amsterdam 1994) 149-159

Horlings, E., *The economic development of the Dutch service sector 1800-1850, trade and transport in a premodern economy* (Amsterdam 1995)

Horn, N.A. van, 'S.P. van Eeghen, bankier', in: *Biografisch woordenboek van Nederland* III (The Hague 1989) 157-159

Horn, N.A. van, 'Het Indische handelshuis Bauermann in de negentiende eeuw', in: *NEHA-jaarboek* 60 (1997) 137-158

Houtte, J.A. van, 'Handel en verkeer', in: idem a.o., ed., *Algemene geschiedenis der Nederlanden* IV (Utrecht 1952) 154-201

Houtte, J.A. van, 'Nijverheid en handel', in: D.P. Blok a.o., ed., *Algemene geschiedenis der Nederlanden* IV, *Middeleeuwen* (Bussum 1980) 87-111

Houwink, A., *Acceptcrediet, economische en bankpolitieke beschouwingen over den in het bankaccept belichaamden credietvorm* (Amsterdam 1929)

Hovy, J., *Het voorstel van 1751 tot instelling van een beperkt vrijhavenstelsel in de Republiek (propositie tot* een gelimiteerd porto-franco) (Groningen 1966)

Hoynck van Papendrecht, A., *Gedenkboek A. van Hoboken & Co., 1774-1924* (Rotterdam 1924) Huff, W.G., *The economic growth of Singapore; Trade and development in the twentieth century* (Cambridge 1994, paperback 1997)

Hugill, P.J., *Global communications since 1844, geopolitics and technology* (Baltimore 1999)

Huizinga, L., *Trek jij je jas eens uit, kroniek van een koopmanshuis in het beeld van 75 jaar wereldgeschiedenis* [Naarden 1975]

Hülsmann, J.H.H., *Geschiedenis der openbare handelsschool* (Amsterdam 1899)

I

Industrieele Club, De (Amsterdam 1918)

Intermediair, 13 November 1997

Internationale Crediet- en Handelsvereeniging Rotterdam: gedenkboek uitgegeven ter gelegenheid van het 50-jarig bestaan 1863-1913 (Rotterdam 1913)

Israel, J.I., 'The economic contribution of Dutch Sephardic Jewry to Holland's Golden Age, 1595-1713', in: *Tijdschrift voor geschiedenis* 96 (1983) 505-535

Israel, J.I., 'The phases of the Dutch Straatvaart (1590-1713), a chapter in the economic history of the Mediterranean', in: *Tijdschrift voor geschiedenis* 99 (1986) 1-30

Israel, J.I., 'The Dutch merchant colonies in the Mediterranean during the seventeenth century', in: *Renaissance and modern studies* 30 (1986) 90-99

Israel, J.I., *Dutch primacy in world trade* (Oxford 1989)

Israel, J.I., 'Englands mercantilistic response to Dutch world trade primacy, 1647-1674', in: S. Groenveld, M. Wintle, ed., *State and trade, government and the economy in Britain and the Netherlands* (Zutphen 1992) 50-61

Israel, J.I., 'De Republiek der Verenigde Nederlanden tot omstreeks 1750-demografie en economische activiteit', in: J.C.H. Blom, R.G. Fuks-Mansfeld, I. Schöffer, ed., *Geschiedenis van de joden in Nederland* (Amsterdam 1995) 97-128

Iterson, P.D.J. van, 'Havens', in: F.J.A. Broeze, J.R. Bruijn, F.S. Gaastra, ed., *Maritieme geschiedenis der Nederlanden* III (Bussum 1977) 59-91

Izaks, B., 'Van Dorp met Despec van gedaante veranderd', *Beleggers Belangen*, 16 July 1999

Izaks, B., 'Groeier Internatio-Müller drastisch veranderd', *Beleggers Belangen*, 28 November 1997

J

Jaarboek Verbond Nederlandse Groothandel, 1989

Jacobs, J., *De scheepvaart en de handel van de Nederlandse Republiek op Nieuw-Nederland* (Amsterdam 1989)

Jacobs, J., *Een zegenrijk gewest, Nieuw-Nederland in de zeventiende eeuw* (Amsterdam 1999)

Jager, J.L. de, *Arm en rijk kunnen bij mij hun inkopen doen, de geschiedenis van Albert Heijn en de Koninklijke Ahold* (Baarn 1995)

L. Jansen, *'De koophandel van Amsterdam', een critische studie over het koopmanshandboek van Jacques le Moine de l'Espine en Isaac le Long* (Amsterdam 1946)

Jansma, T.S., 'Hanze, Fugger, Amsterdam', in: *Bijdra-*

gen en mededelingen van het Historisch Genootschap (1976) 1-26

Jeannin, P., 'The seaborne and the overland trade routes of Northern Europe in the XVIth and XVIIth centuries', in: *Journal of European Economic history* 11 (1982) 5-60

Jeffreys, J.B., *Retail trading in Britain, 1850-1950, a study of trends in retailing with special reference to the development of Co-operative, multiple shop and department store methods of trading* (Cambridge 1954)

Jeurgens, K.J.P.F.M., P.M.M. Klep, *Informatieprocessen van de Bataafs-Franse overheid 1795-1813* (The Hague 1997)

Jones, G., ed., *The multinational traders* (London 1998)

Jones, G., 'British trading companies and industrial development', in: F. Amatori a.o., ed., *Deindustrialization and reindustrialization in 20th century Europe* (Milan 1999) 345-371

Jones, G., *Merchants to multinationals. British trading companies in the nineteenth and twentieth centuries* (Oxford 2000)

Jong, A.M. de, 'Zestiende- en zeventiende-eeuwse denkbeelden over de wisselkoersen', in: *Economisch-historische herdrukken* (The Hague 1964) 319-343

Jong, A.M. de, *Geschiedenis van de Nederlandsche Bank*, I, *1814-1864* (Haarlem 1967), II, III, IV, *1864-1914* (Haarlem 1967)

Jong, H.W. de, 'De concentratie in de Europese economie', in: *ESB*, 2-3-1988

Jong, H.W. de, *Dynamische markttheorie* (Leiden 1989)

Jong, H.W. de, 'Theorie en empirie van het concentratieproces', in: J.J. van Duin a.o., ed., *Fusies en overnames* (Schoonhoven 1992)

Jong, J.J.P. de, *Van batig slot naar ereschuld, de discussie over de financiële verhouding tussen Nederland en Indië en de hervorming van de Nederlandse koloniale politiek 1860-1900* (Groningen 1989)

Jong, J.J.P. de, *De waaier van het fortuin, de Nederlanders in Azië en de Indonesische archipel 1595-1950* (The Hague 1998)

Jong, L. de, *Het koninkrijk der Nederlanden in de Tweede Wereldoorlog*, VII, *Mei 1943-juni 1944* (The Hague 1976)

Jong, P. de, 'Handel en wandel in de kolonie', MA thesis Leiden 1995

Jong, Th.P.M. de, *De krimpende horizon van de Hollandse kooplieden, Hollands welvaren in het Caribisch zeegebied (1780-1830)* (Assen 1966)

Jong-Keesing, E.E. de, *De economische crisis van 1763 te Amsterdam* (Amsterdam 1939)

Jongbloet-Van Houtte, G., *Brieven en andere bescheiden betreffende Daniël van der Meulen 1584-1600*, I, *augustus 1584-september 1585* (The Hague 1986)

Jongbloet-Van Houtte, G., 'De belegering en de val van Antwerpen belicht vanuit een koopmansarchief', in: *Bijdragen en mededelingen van het Historisch Genootschap* 91 (1976) 23-43

Jonge, J.A. de, 'Vergelijking van de uitkomsten van de beroepstellingen 1849-1960', *13e Algemene Volkstelling 31 mei 1960*, Vol. 10 (Hilversum 1966)

Jonge, J.A. de, *De industrialisatie in Nederland tussen*

1850 en 1914 (Nijmegen 1976)

Jonker, J.P.B., 'Waterdragers van het kapitalisme, nevenfuncties van Nederlandse bankiers en de verhouding tussen bankwezen en bedrijfsleven (1910-1940)', in: *Jaarboek voor de geschiedenis van bedrijf en techniek* 6 (1989) 158-190

Jonker, J.P.B., *Merchants, bankers, middlemen, the Amsterdam money market during the first half of the 19th century* (Amsterdam 1996)

Jonker, J.P.B., 'The cradle of modern banking, finance in the Netherlands between theNapoleonic era and the first commercial banks, 1813-1870', in: Joh. de Vries, W. Vroom, T. de Graaf, ed., *World wide banking, ABN AMRO Bank 1824-1999* (Amsterdam 1999) 49-94

Jonker, J.P.B., K.E. Sluyterman, 'The lure of industry: Dutch trading companies entering and abandoning industrial activities', in: F. Amatori a.o., ed., *Deindustrialization and reindustrialization in 20th century Europe* (Milaan 1999) 372-382

Jonkheer, K.R., *Informatietechnologie en telematica in de groothandel. Zijn informatietechnologie en telematica een herkenbare productiefactor in de (internationale) concurrentie?* (Zoetermeer 1997)

Jonkheer, K.R., *Ondernemingsconcentratie in de Nederlandse groothandel 1994* (Zoetermeer 1995)

K

Kahn, H. en A.J. Wiener, 'The next thirty-three years: a framework for speculation', in: *Daedalus*, 96 (1967), No. 3, 705-732

'De Kali Bezaar te Batavia' in: *De Economist 1862* bijblad 153-177

Kaplan, H., *Russian overseas commerce with Great Britain during the reign of Catherine II* (Philadelphia 1995)

Kappelhof, T., 'Noord-Brabant en de Hollandse stapelmarkt', in: C.A. Davids, ed., *De Republiek tussen zee en vasteland, buitenlandse invloeden op cultuur, economie en politiek in Nederland 1580-1800* (Louvain 1995) 189-206

Kaptein, H., *De Hollandse textielnijverheid 1350-1600, conjunctuur en continuïteit* (Hilversum 1998)

Kennet, D.H., 'An English merchant in Holland in 1737 and 1738', in: *Economisch- en sociaalhistorisch jaarboek* 35 (1972) 146-186

Kenwood, A.G., A.L. Lougheed, *The growth of the international economy 1820-2000* (4th edition London 1999)

Kernkamp, G.W., 'Bengt Ferrner's dagboek van zijne reis door Nederland', in: *Bijdragen en mededelingen van het historisch genootschap* 31 (1910)

Kernkamp, J.H., *De handel op den vijand 1572-1609* (Utrecht, 2 vols. 1931, 1934)

Kernkamp, J.H., 'Scheepvaart en handelsbetrekkingen met Italië tijdens de opkomst der Republiek', in: *Economisch-historische herdrukken* (The Hague 1964) 199-234

Kernkamp J.H., A.J. Klaassen-Meijer, 'De rekeningen betreffende de exploratietocht van den Swerten Ruyter naar het Middellandse Zeegebied in 1589/1590', in: *Bijdragen en mededelingen van het Historisch*

Genootschap 73 (1958) 3-53

Kernkamp, J.H., *Johan van der Veken en zijn tijd* (The Hague 1952)

Ketner, F., *Handel en scheepvaart van Amsterdam in de vijftiende eeuw* (Leiden 1946)

Kijk in een jarige krant: NRC 125 (Rotterdam 1969)

Kist, J.B., a.o., ed., *Van VOC tot Werkspoor, het Amsterdamse industrieterrein Oostenburg* (Utrecht 1986)

Klaverstijn, B., *Samentwijnen, via fusie naar integratie* (Arnhem 1989)

Klein, P.W., *De Trippen in de 17e eeuw* (Assen 1965)

Klein, P.W., 'Kwantitatieve aspecten van de Amsterdamse roggehandel in de 17e eeuw en de Europese geschiedenis', in: Joh. de Vries a.o., ed., *Ondernemende geschiedenis, 22 opstellen geschreven bij het afscheid van mr. H. van Riel als voorzitter van de Vereniging 'Het Nederlandsch economisch-historisch archief'* (The Hague 1977) 77-88

Klein, P.W., 'De zeventiende eeuw', in: J.H. van Stuijvenberg, ed., *De economische geschiedenis van Nederland* (Groningen 1977) 79-118

Klein, P.W., 'Het mercantilisme', in: H. Baudet, H. van der Meulen, ed., *Kernproblemen der economische geschiedenis* (Groningen 1978) 117-127

Klein, P.W., 'Handel, geld- en bankwezen in de Noordelijke Nederlanden 1650-1795', in: D.P. Blok a.o., ed., *Algemene geschiedenis der Nederlanden*, VIII, *Nieuwe tijd* (Bussum 1979) 160-184

Klein, P.W., '"Little London", British merchants in Rotterdam during the seventeenth and eighteenth centuries', in: D.C. Coleman, P. Mathias, ed., *Enterprise and history, essays in honour of Charles Wilson* (Cambridge 1984) 116-134

Klein, P.W., 'De wereldhandel in edele metalen 1500-1800: centraliteit of polycentrisme?', in: *Tijdschrift voor geschiedenis* 100 (1987) 185-197

Klein, P.W., 'De Nederlandse handelspolitiek in de tijd van het mercantilisme: een nieuwe kijk op een kwestie?', in: *Tijdschrift voor geschiedenis* 102 (1989) 189-213

Klein, P.W., 'Op de klippen van een nieuwe tijd, de Nederlandsche Handel-Maatschappij en de ondergang van de traditionele Nederlandse handel in Japan tussen 1870 en 1880', in: J.F.E. Bläsing, H.H. Vleesenbeek, ed., *Van Amsterdam naar Tilburg en toch weer terug, opstellen aangeboden aan dr. Joh. de Vries ter gelegenheid van zijn afscheid als hoogleraar economische geschiedenis aan de Katholieke Universiteit Brabant op 16 oktober 1992* (Leiden 1992) 85-97

Klein, P.W., 'Ondernemen is mensenwerk, het marktgedrag van de Verenigde Oostindische Compagnie', in: E. Aerts a.o., ed., *Studia historica economica, liber amicorum Herman van der Wee* (Leuven 1993) 145-156

Klein, P.W., J.W. Veluwenkamp, 'The role of the entrepreneur in the economic expansion of the Dutch Republic', in: C.A. Davids, L. Noordegraaf, ed., *The Dutch economy in the Golden Age* (Amsterdam 1993) 27-53

Klemann, H.A.M., 'De economische exploitatie van Nederland door de bezetter', in: H. Flap, W. Arts, *De organisatie van de bezetting* (Amsterdam 1997) 705-732

Klemann, H.A.M., ed., *Mooie jaarcijfers Enige onderzoeksresultaten betreffende de Nederlandse economische ontwikkeling tijdens de Tweede Wereldoorlog*, *Utrechtse Historische Cahiers* 18 (1997) No. 4

Klemann, H.A.M., 'De Nederlandse economie tijdens de Tweede Wereldoorlog', *Tijdschrift voor Geschiedenis* 110 (1997) 3-40

Klep, P.M.M., 'Kanttekeningen bij het Bataafs-Franse beschrijvende bronnenmateriaal in Nederland, 1795-1813', in: J.P.A. Coopmans a.o., ed., *Van blauwe stoep tot citadel, varia historica Brabantica Ludovico Pirenne dedicata* (Den Bosch 1988) 257-266

Klep, P.M.M., 'Researchwaarde en toegankelijkheid van het beschrijvende bronnenmateriaal uit de Bataafs-Franse Tijd', in: *Economisch- en sociaalhistorisch jaarboek* 55 (1992) 3-14

Knoppers, J.V.T., *Dutch trade with Russia from the time of Peter I to Alexander I. A quantitative study in eighteenth century shipping* (Montreal 1976)

Knoppers, J.V.T., 'De vaart in Europa', in: F.J.A. Broeze, J.R. Bruijn, F.S. Gaastra, ed., *Maritieme geschiedenis der Nederlanden* 3 (Bussum 1977) 226-262

Knoppers, J.V.T., F. Snapper, 'De Nederlandse scheepvaart op de Oostzee vanaf het eind van de 17e eeuw tot het begin van de 19e eeuw', in: *Economisch- en sociaalhistorisch jaarboek* 41 (1978) 115-153

Knuttel, J.A.N., ed., *Werken van G.A. Bredero* (Amsterdam 1924)

Kolff, B., 'Achter de schermen van het onder onzijdige vlag brengen van koopvaardijschepen van de Bataafsche Republiek', in: *Rotterdamsch jaarboekje* (1944) 81-108

De koopman, of bijdragen ten opbouw van Neerlands koophandel en zeevaart (1768-1776)

Kool, M., *Die conste vanden getale, een studie over Nederlandstalige rekenboeken uit de vijftiende en zestiende eeuw, met een glossarium van rekenkundige termen* (Hilversum 1999)

Kooy, T.P. van der, *Hollands stapelmarkt en haar verval* (Amsterdam 1931)

Korte, J.P. de, *De jaarlijkse financiële verantwoording in de VOC* (Leiden 1984)

Korthals Altes, W.L., *Van £ Hollands tot Nederlandse ƒ* (Amsterdam 1996)

Kosterman, R., 'Handelshuis Hagemeyer lijkt niet te stuiten', in: *FEM*, 7 March 1992

Kosterman, R., 'Laatste kans Internatio', in: *FEM*, 17 August 1991

Kraal, A., 'In- en uitschakeling van den groothandel in industrieele producten onder het huidige systeem van beheerschte prijzen', in: *ESB*, 24 May, 31 May 1944

Kreileman, R., 'Haalt de groothandel het jaar 2001', in: *Logistiek Actueel*, No. 10 (1998)

Krieken, G. van, *Kapers en kooplieden, de betrekkingen tussen Algiers en Nederland (1604-1830)* (Amsterdam 1999)

Kroese, W.T., *Het begin van de industrialisatie van Indonesië. De Stichting van de Preanger Bontweverij (PBW) te Garut* (Hengelo 1979)

Kroniek van mr. dr. A. Sternheim, 1920-1939

Kuitenbrouwer, M., *The Netherlands and the rise of modern imperialism, colonies and foreign policy 1870-1902* (Oxford 1991)

L

Laan, H. Laurens van der, 'The NAHV 1918-1955', paper workshop Business empires in West Central Africa, London 1982

Laar, P.Th. van der, a.o., ed., *Vier eeuwen migratie bestemming Rotterdam* (Rotterdam 1998)

Labouchère, G., 'Pierre César Labouchère (1772-1839), un financier diplomate au siècle dernier', in: *Revue d'histoire diplomatique* 27 (1913) 1-54

Landjouw, G.J., *Internationale handelsinstituties* (Schoonhoven 1995)

Langeveld, H., *Dit leven van krachtig handelen, Hendrikus Colijn 1869-1944*, I, *1869-1933* (Amsterdam 1998)

Laspeyres, E., *Geschichte der volkswirthschaftliche Anschauungen der Niederländer und ihrer Litteratur zur Zeit der Republik* (Leipzig 1863)

Lennep, F.J.E. van, *Late regenten* (Haarlem 1962)

Leonhardt, G., *Het huis Bartolotti en zijn bewoners* (Amsterdam 1979)

Lesger, C., 'Tussen stagnatie en expansie, economische ontwikkeling en levensstandaard tussen 1500 en 1600', in: *Woelige tijden, Amsterdam in de eeuw van de beeldenstorm* (Amsterdam 1987) 9-29

Lesger, C., 'Lange termijnprocessen en de betekenis van politieke factoren in de Nederlandse houthandel ten tijde van de Republiek', in: *Economisch- en sociaalhistorisch jaarboek* 55 (1992) 105-142

Lesger, C., 'Intraregional trade and the port system of Holland, 1400-1700', in: C.A. Davids, L. Noordegraaf, ed., *The Dutch economy in the Golden Age* (Amsterdam 1993) 186-217

Lesger, C., 'Over het nut van huwelijk, opportunisme en bedrog, ondernemen en ondernemerschap tijdens de vroeg-moderne tijd in theoretisch perspectief', in: C.A. Davids, J.M.F. Fritschy, L.A. van der Valk, ed., *Kapitaal, ondernemerschap en beleid, studies over economie en politiek in Nederland, Europa en Azië, afscheidsbundel voor prof.dr. P.W. Klein* (Amsterdam 1996) 55-76

Lesger, C., 'De mythe van de Hollandse wereldstapelmarkt in de zeventiende eeuw', in: *NEHA Jaarboek* 62 (1999) 6-25

Lesger, C., L. Noordegraaf, ed., *Entrepreneurs and entrepreneurship in modern times, merchants and industrialists within the orbit of the Dutch staple market* (The Hague 1995)

Lewe, A.M.E., *'Invoer te lande verboden', een verkenning van de handel over landwegen tussen Nederland en de Pruisische provincies Rheinland en Westfalen 1836-1857* (Hilversum 1995)

Lichtenauer, W.F., *Kamer van koophandel en fabrieken Rotterdam 1803-1928* (Rotterdam 1928)

Lichtenauer, W.F., *Geschiedenis van de wetenschap van het handelsrecht in Nederland tot 1809* (1956)

Lichtenauer, W.F., 'Lodewijk Pincoffs', in: *Biografisch woordenboek van Nederland*, I (The Hague 1979) 452-454

Lindblad, J.Th., *Sweden's trade with the Dutch Republic 1738-1795* (Assen 1982)

Lindblad, J.Th., 'Structuur en mededinging in de handel van de Republiek op de Oostzee in de achttiende

412

eeuw', in: *Economisch- en sociaalhistorisch jaarboek* 47 (1984) 79-90

Lindblad, J.Th., 'Economische aspecten van de Nederlandse expansie in de Indonesische archipel', in: J. van Goor, ed., *Imperialisme in de marge, de afronding van Nederlands-Indië* (Utrecht 1985) 227-265

Lindblad, J.Th., 'De handel tussen Nederland en Nederlands-Indië, 1874-1939', in: *Economisch- en sociaalhistorisch Jaarboek* 51 (1988) 240-298

Lindblad, J.Th., 'De opkomst van de buitengewesten', in: A.H.P. Clemens, J.Th. Lindblad, ed., *Het belang van de buitengewesten, economische expansie en koloniale staatsvorming in de buitengewesten van Nederlands-Indië 1870-1942* (Amsterdam 1989) 1-38

Lindblad, J.Th., 'The economic history of colonial Indonesia, an historiographical survey', in: *Economic and social history in the Netherlands* 1 (1989) 31-47

Lindblad, J.Th., 'Bedrijfsgeschiedenis betreffende Nederlands-Indië (1602-1958)', in: *Jaarboek voor de geschiedenis van bedrijf en techniek* 7 (1990) 127-142

Lindblad, J.Th., 'Het bedrijfsleven in Nederlands-Indië in het Interbellum', in: *Economisch- en sociaalhistorisch jaarboek* 54 (1991) 183-211

Lindblad, J.Th., 'Foreign investment in late colonial and post colonial Indonesia', in: *Economic and social history in the Netherlands* 3 (1991) 183-208

Lindblad, J.Th., 'Ondernemen in Nederlands-Indië c. 1900-1940', in: *Bijdragen en mededelingen betreffende de geschiedenis der Nederlanden* 108 (1993) 699-710

Lindblad, J.Th., 'De handel in katoentjes op Nederlands-Indië, 1824-1939', in: *Textielhistorische bijdragen* (1994) 89-103

Lindblad, J.Th., 'Between Singapore and Batavia, the Outer Islands in the Southeast Asian economy during the nineteenth century', in: C.A. Davids, J.M.F. Fritschy, L.A. van der Valk, ed., *Kapitaal, ondernemerschap en beleid, studies over economie en politiek in Nederland, Europa en Azië, afscheidsbundel voor prof.dr. P.W. Klein* (Amsterdam 1996) 529-548

Lindblad, J.Th., 'Nederland en de Oostzee, 1650-1800', in: R. Daalder, ed., *Goud uit graan, Nederland en het Oostzeegebied 1600-1850* (Zwolle 1998) 8-27

Lindblad, J.Th., J.L. van Zanden, 'De buitenlandse handel van Nederland, 1872-1913', in: *Economisch- en sociaalhistorisch jaarboek* 52 (1989) 231-269

Linden, W.H. van der, *Jacobus Boelen 1733-1958* (Amsterdam s.a.)

Lindeteves-Stokvis 1889-1939 (1939)

G.C.P. Linssen, *Papier in Nijmegen. Voorgeschiedenis en ontwikkeling van KNP nijmegen b.v. ter gelegenheid van het tachtigjarig bestaan in 1988* (Nijmegen 1988)

Logboek SHV 1896-1956 (Utrecht 1956)

Long, I. le, *De koophandel van Amsterdam* (Amsterdam 1704, 1744)

M

Maarseveen, J.G.J.S. van, *Nicolaas Gerard Pierson, handelsman, econoom en bankier, eerste periode 1839-1877* (Rotterdam 1981)

Maassen, H.A.J., *Tussen commercieel en sociaal krediet, de ontwikkeling van de bank van lening in Nederland van*

lombard tot gemeentelijke kredietbank 1260-1940 (Hilversum 1994)

Maddison, A., *Monitoring the World Economy 1820-1992* (OECD 1995)

Mandemakers, K., *HBS en gymnasium, ontwikkeling, structuur, sociale achtergrond en schoolprestaties, Nederland, circa 1800-1968* (Amsterdam 1996)

Manders, M., 'Raadsels rond een gezonken Oostzeevaarder' in: R. Daalder, ed., *Goud uit graan, Nederland en het Oostzeegebied 1600-1850* (Zwolle 1998) 70-81

Manen, C.A.. van, *De Nederlandsche Overzee Trustmaatschappij* (The Hague 1937)

Mansvelt, W.M.F., *Geschiedenis van de Nederlandsche Handel-Maatschappij* ([Amsterdam 1924])

Mansvelt, W.M.F., 'De oorsprong van den Hollandschen suikerstandaard', in: *De Indische Mercuur*, 1 May 1925, 3-11

Mansvelt, W.M.F., 'De eerste Indische handelshuizen, mededeelingen over de resultaten van een onderzoek naar de nationaliteit van het Nederlandsch-Indisch handelsapparaat in de eerste helft der 19e eeuw', typoscript Ondernemersraad voor Nederlandsch Indië in 1937

Mathias, P., *Retailing revolution, a history of multiple retailing in the food trades based upon the Allied Suppliers Group of Companies* (London 1967)

McCusker, J.J., C. Gravesteijn, *The beginnings of commercial and financial journalism, the commodity price currents, exchange rate currents, and money currents of early modern Europe* (Amsterdam 1991)

Mechelen, P.A.A. van, *Zeevaart en zeehandel van Rotterdam (1813-1830)* ((Rotterdam 1929)

Mees, A.C., *NV Internationale crediet- en handelsvereeniging 'Rotterdam', gedenkboek uitgegeven bij het vijf-en-zeventig jarig bestaan op 28 augustus 1938* (Rotterdam 1938)

Mees, W.C., *Man van de daad, mr. Marten Mees en de opkomst van Rotterdam* (Rotterdam 1946)

Meilink, P.A., 'Gegevens aangaande bedrijfskapitalen in den Hollandschen en Zeeuwschen handel in 1543', in: *Economisch-Historisch Jaarboek* 8 (1922) 262-277

Meilink-Roelofsz, M.A.P., 'Een vergelijkend onderzoek van bestuur en handel van Nederlandse en Engelse handelscompagnieën op Azië in de eerste helft van de zeventiende eeuw', in: *Bijdragen en mededelingen betreffende de geschiedenis der Nederlanden* 91 (1976) 196-217

Meilink-Roelofsz, M.A.P., 'Hoe rationeel was de organisatie van de Nederlandse Oostindische Compagnie?', in: *Economisch- en sociaalhistorisch jaarboek* 44 (1981) 170-190

Meyloph, G., W. Bosch, *Honderd jaar handel in paardekracht, 1881-1981* (Amsterdam 1981)

Michie, R.C., *The City of London, continuity and change 1850-1990* (London 1992)

Michie, R.C., 'The invisible stabilizer, asset arbitrage and the international monetary system since 1700', in: *Financial history review* 5 (1998) 5-26

Miellet, R., 'Westfaalse ondernemers en de opkomst van het Nederlandse grootwinkelbedrijf tot circa 1920', in: *Jaarboek geschiedenis bedrijf en techniek* 3 (1986) 135-157

Miellet, R., 'Immigratie van katholieke Westfalers en de modernisering van de Nederlandse detailhandel', in: *Tijdschrif voor geschiedenis* 100 (1987) 374-393

Miellet, R., *Honderd jaar grootwinkelbedrijf in Nederland* (Zwolle s.a.)

Mitchell, B.R., *British historical statistics* (Cambridge 1988)

Moine de l'Espine, J., *De koophandel van Amsterdam* (Amsterdam 1715)

Moree, P., 'De Verenigde Oostindische Compagnie', in: G. Hogesteeger, ed., *Naar de gordel van smaragd, de postverbindingen tussen Nederland en Nederlands-Indië 1602-1940* (The Hague 1995) 5-26

Moree, P., *Met vriend die God geleide, het Nederlands-Aziatische postverkeer ten tijde van de VOC* (Zutphen 1998)

Muller, H., *Een Rotterdams zeehandelaar, Hendrik Muller Szn., (1819-1898)* (Schiedam 1977)

Muller, P.N.,'Handelsstudiën' in: *De Economist* 7 (1858) 121-130, 157-167, 233-247, 398-412

Muller, P.N., 'De handel van Nederland in de laatste vijf en twintig jaar 1847-1871', in *De economist* (1875) I, 1-37

Muller, P.N., 'Potgieter ter beurze', in: *De gids* 50 (1886) 411-420

Musgrave, P., 'The economics of uncertainty, the structural revolution in the spice trade, 1480-1640', in: P.L. Cottrell, D.H. Aldcroft, ed., *Shipping, trade and commerce: essays in memory of Ralph Davis* (Leicester 1981) 9-21

N

Nanninga, J.G., 'De Nederlandsche koopman in de Levant en de vrije handel (achttiende eeuw)', in: *Historische opstellen opgedragen aan prof.dr. H. Brugmans* (Amsterdam 1929) 109-140

Nanninga Uitterdijk, J., *Een Kamper handelshuis te Lissabon 1572-1594, handelscorrespondentie, rekeningen en bescheiden* (Zwolle 1904)

Nederlandsch handelsmagazijn, of algemeen zamenvattend woordenboek voor handel en nijverheid (Amsterdam 1843)

Nierop, L. van, 'De honderd hoogst aangeslagenen te Anmsterdam van 1813', in: *Economisch historisch jaarboek* 11 (1923) 1-76

Nierop, L. van, ''Hou' en Trouw 1885-1925', in: *Gedenkboek Hou' en Trouw, Vereeniging van oud-leerlingen der openbare handelsscholen te Amsterdam 1885-1925* (Amsterdam 1925) 15-36

Nierop, L. van, 'Toevoegingen tot de aanvullingen bij de honderd hoogst aangeslagenen van Amsterdam in 1813', in: *Economisch historisch jaarboek* 13 (1927) 247-249

Nierop, L. van, 'De zijdenijverheid te Amsterdam historisch geschetst', in: *Tijdschrift voor geschiedenis* 45 (1930) 18-40, 151-172; 46 (1931) 28-55, 113-143

Nierop, L. van, 'Eenige handelsbetrekkingen van het huis Braunsberg & Co. te Amsterdam in 1815', in: *Economisch historisch jaarboek* 19 (1935) 89-96

Nierop, L. van, 'Amsterdams scheepvaart in de Fransche Tijd', in: *Jaarboek Amstelodamum* 21 (1924) 119-139

Nierop, L. van, 'Over het huis Thomas en Adrian Hope te Amsterdam', in: *Maandblad Amstelodamum* 27 (1940) 47

Nijenhuis, I.J.A., 'De ontwikkeling van het politiek-economische vrijheidsbegrip in de Republiek', in: E.O.G. Haitsma Mulier, W.R.E. Velema, ed., *Vrijheid, een geschiedenis van de vijftiende tot de twintigste eeuw* (Amsterdam 1999) 233-252

Nijhoffs Geschiedenislexicon Nederland en België (The Hague 1981)

Nolte, V., *Fifty years in both hemispheres, or reminiscences of a merchant's life* (London 1854)

Noordegraaf, L., 'Sociale verhoudingen en structuren in de Noordelijke Nederlanden 1770-1813', in: D.P. Blok a.o., ed., *Algemene geschiedenis der Nederlanden* X, *Nieuwste tijd* (Bussum 1981) 361-383

Noordkerk, H., ed., *Handvesten ofte privilegien der stad Amsterdam* (Amsterdam 1748-1778)

North, D.C., 'Ocean freight rates and economic development 1750-1913', in: *Journal of economic history* 18 (1958) 537-555

North, D.C., 'Sources of productivity change in ocean shipping, 1600-1850', in: *Journal of political economy* 76 (1968) 953-970.

Novaky, G., 'On trade, production and relations of production, the sugar refineries of seventeenth-century Amsterdam', in: *Tijdschrift voor sociale geschiedenis* 23 (1997) 459-489 NRC-Handelsblad, 14 March 1998

Nübel, O., *Pompeius Occo 1483-1537, Fuggerfaktor in Amsterdam* (Tübingen 1972)

Nusteling, H.P.H., *De Rijnvaart in het tijdperk van stoom en steenkool 1813-1914* (Amsterdam 1974)

Nusteling, H.P.H., *Welvaart en werkgelegenheid in Amsterdam 1540-1860, een relaas over demografie, economie en sociale politiek van een wereldstad* (Amsterdam 1985)

Nusteling, H.P.H., 'Kritische beschouwingen aangaande de Amsterdamse volkstellingen in de periode 1795-1859', in: *Economisch- en sociaal-historisch jaarboek* 55 (1992) 189-236

Nusteling, H.P.H., *Markant in de markt Interpharm 1896-1996* (Den Bosch 1996)

NV Handelmaatschappij v/h Joh. Wolff & Co., Gouda 1908-1958 (Gouda 1958)

O

Oldewelt, W.F.H., 'Bescherming van merk en handelsnaam', in: idem, *Amsterdamsche archiefvondsten* (Amsterdam 1942) 119-123

Oldewelt, W.F.H., 'De desolate boedelkamer', in: idem, *Amsterdamsche archiefvondsten* (Amsterdam 1942) 135-139

Oldewelt, W.F.H., 'Een beroepstelling uit den jare 1688', in: idem, *Amsterdamsche archiefvondsten* (Amsterdam 1942) 172-176

Oldewelt, W.F.H., ed., *Kohier van de personeele quotisatie te Amsterdam over het jaar 1742* (Amsterdam 1945)

Oldewelt, W.F.H., 'De scheepvaartstatistiek van Amsterdam in de 17de en 18de eeuw', in: *Jaarboek Amstelodamum* 45 (1953) 114-151

Oldewelt, W.F.H., 'Twee eeuwen Amsterdamse faillissementen en het verloop van de conjunctuur', in: *Tijd-schrift voor geschiedenis* (1962) 421-435

Oomens, C.A., G.P. Bakker, 'De beroepsbevolking in Nederland 1849-1990', *Supplement bij de sociaal-economische maandstatistiek 1994, dl. 2* (The Hague 1994)

Oosterwijk, A.J., *Vlucht na victorie, Lodewijk Pincoffs 1827-1911* (Rotterdam 1979)

Oosterwijk, A.J., *Koning van de koopvaart, Anthony van Hoboken (1756-1850)* (Rotterdam 1983)

Oosterwijk, A.J., *Reder in Rotterdam, Willem Ruys 1803-1889* (Rotterdam 1990)

Oostindie, G., *Roosenburg en Mon Bijou, twee Surinaamse plantages 1720-1870* (Dordrecht 1989)

Ormrod, D.J., 'Dutch commercial-industrial decline and British growth in the late seventeenth and early eighteenth centuries', in: F. Krantz, P. Hohenberg, ed., *Failed transitions to modern industrial society: renaissance Italy and seventeenth-century Holland* (Montreal 1975) 36-43

Ormrod, D.J., 'English re-exports and the Dutch staple market in the eighteenth century', in: D.C. Coleman, P. Mathias, ed., *Enterprise and history, essays in honour of Charles Wilson* (Cambridge 1984) 89-115

Van Oss' Effectenboeken, 1904-1939

Ouwerkerk de Vries, J. van, *Verhandeling over de oorzaak van het verval en de middelen tot herstel van den Nederlandschen koophandel* (Haarlem 1827)

Overbeke, W., 'Naar een nieuwe internationale orde', in: W. van Spengen, *Van kolonialisme tot zelfontwikkeling* (Bussum 1978) 62-77

Overvoorde, J.C., *Geschiedenis van het postwezen in Nederland vóór 1795 met de voornaamste verbindingen met het buitenland* (Leiden 1902)

P

Pierson, J.L., *Mémoires uit de jaren 1854-1926* (S.l. s.a.)

Polak, M.S., *Historiografie en economie van de 'muntchaos', de muntproductie van de Republiek (1606-1795)* (Amsterdam 1998)

Post, P., *Japanse Bedrijvigheid in Indonesië, 1868-1942. Structurele elementen van Japan's vooroorlogse economische expansie in Zuidoost Azië* (Amsterdam 1991)

Posthumus, N.W., 'Statistiek van den in- en uitvoer van Amsterdam in het jaar 1774', in: *Bijdragen en mededeelingen van het Historisch Genootschap* 34 (1913) 516-528

Posthumus, N.W., 'Statistiek van den in- en uitvoer van Rotterdam en Dordrecht in het jaar 1680', in: *Bijdragen en mededeelingen van het Historisch Genootschap* 34 (1913) 529-537

Posthumus, N.W., 'Eene kartelovereenkomst in de zeventiende eeuw in de Amsterdamsche zijdehandel', in: *Economisch historisch Jaarboek* 6 (1920) 215-222

Posthumus, N.W., 'Nota over den toestand van de Amsterdamsche handelshuizen in het jaar 1854', in: *Economisch historisch jaarboek* 7 (1921) 196-209

Posthumus, N.W., 'Een schrijven uit het jaar 1860 van Hendrik Muller Szoon aan Prof. S. Vissering over personen en toestanden in Twente', in: *Economisch historisch jaarboek* 14 (1928) 282-295

Posthumus, N.W., *De oosterse handel te Amsterdam, het oudst bewaard gebleven koopmansboek van een Amsterdamse vennootschap betreffende de handel op de Oostzee 1485-1490* (Leiden 1953)

Posthumus, N.W., 'Rumor in casa, het Huis der Waarden te Amsterdam', in: *Jaarboek Amstelodamum* 49 (1957) 1-9

Posthumus, N.W., *Inquiry into the history of prices in Holland*, I (Leiden 1946)

Posthumus, N.W., *De uitvoer van Amsterdam 1543-1545* (Leiden 1971)

Postma, J.M., *The Dutch in the Atlantic slave trade, 1600-1815* (Cambridge 1990)

Pot, J.E. van der, *Abram, Huibert en Elie van Rijckevorsel* (Rotterdam 1957)

Potting, C.J.M., 'De komst van Nederlandse banken naar Sumatra, 1877-1914', in: A.H.P. Clemens, J.Th. Lindblad, ed., *Het belang van de buitengewesten, economische expansie en koloniale staatsvorming in de buitengewesten van Nederlands-Indië 1870-1942* (Amsterdam 1989) 67-94

Price, J.M., 'Directions for the conduct of a merchant's counting house, 1766', in: *Business history* 28 (1986) 134-150

Price, J.M., 'What did merchants do? Reflections on British overseas trade, 1660-1790', in: *Journal of economic history* 49 (1989) 267-284

Price, J.M., P.G.E. Clemens, 'A revolution of scale in British overseas trade, British firms in the Chesapeake trade 1675-1775', in: *Journal of economic history* 47 (1987) 1-43

R

Ratté, J., *De Nederlandse doorvoerpolitiek en de vrije vaart op de internationale Rijn, een schets van het ontstaan van de vrije doorvoer door Nederland* (Rotterdam 1952)

Raven, G.J.A., '"Aanhoudend sukkelen om bootsvolk", een keerpunt in het personeelsbeleid van de marine, 1775-1795', in: *Tijdschrift voor zeegeschiedenis* 1 (1982) 132-142.

Ravesteijn, W., *Onderzoekingen over de economische en sociale ontwikkeling van Amsterdam gedurende de 16e en het eerste kwart der 17e eeuw* (Utrecht 1906)

Reinsma, R., 'De vergeten Maatschappij van koophandel en zeevaart te Amsterdam (1818-1823)', in: *Tijdschrift voor geschiedenis* 70 (1957) 189-203

Reinsma, R., 'De West-Indische Maatschappij (1828-1863)', in: *Tijdschrift voor geschiedenis* 73 (1960) 58-74

Renooij, D.C., *De Nederlandse emissiemarkt van 1904-1939* (Amsterdam 1951)

Ricard, J.P., *Le negoce d'Amsterdam* (Amsterdam 1722)

Ricard, S., *Traité général du commerce de la Hollande ou d'Amsterdam* (Amsterdam 1705²; 1721⁴; 1781 2 vols edited by M. de M.)

Riley, J.C., *International government finance and the Amsterdam capital market 1740-1815* (Cambridge 1980)

Roberts, R., 'What's in a name? Merchants, merchant bankers, accepting houses, issuing houses, industrial bankers and investment bankers', in: *Business History*

35 (1993) No. 3 22-39

Robijn, R., G.J. Laan, *De OGEM dossiers* (Amsterdam 1984)

Rogge, J., 'Inlichtingen omtrent een aantal Amsterdamsche en buitenlandsche handelshuizen, in 1804 verstrekt door P. & C. van Eeghen', in: *Economisch historisch jaarboek* 22 (1940-1942) 188-192

Rogge, J., 'Inlichtingen omtrent een aantal handelshuizen in Amsterdam, in het najaar van 1816 verstrekt door de firma Van Eeghen & Co.', in: *Economisch historisch jaarboek* 22 (1940-1942) 193-195

Rogge, J., *Het handelshuis Van Eeghen, proeve eener geschiedenis van een Amsterdamsch handelshuis* (Amsterdam 1949)

Rogier, L.J., *Rotterdam tegen het midden van de negentiende eeuw* (Rotterdam 1948)

Rogier, L.J., *Rotterdam in het derde kwart van de negentiende eeuw* (Rotterdam 1953)

Romein, J., A. Romein-Verschoor, *Erflaters van onze beschaving, Nederlandse gestalten uit zes eeuwen* (Amsterdam 1977¹²)

Roorda, D., *Ambassadeur in de lage landen, William Temple, Observations upon the United provinces* (Haarlem 1978)

Roover, R. de, 'The organization of trade', in: M.M. Postan, E.E. Rich, E. Miller, ed., *The Cambridge economic history of Europe*, III, *Economic organization and policies in the Middle Ages* (Cambridge 1963) 42-118

Rooy, M. van, *Amsterdam en het beurzenspektakel* (Aarlanderveen 1982)

Royen, P.C. van, 'Foreigners aboard the Dutch merchant marine about 1700', in: W.G. Heeres a.o., ed., *From Dunkirk to Danzig, shipping and trade in the North Sea and the Baltic 1350-1850* (Hilversum 1988) 391-404

Royen, P.C. van, 'Modernegotie en kraamkamer, schippers, scheepsvolk op de Nederlandse vrachtvaart in Europese wateren vanaf de zeventiende tot in de negentiende eeuw', in: *Tijdschrift voor zeegeschiedenis* 9 (1990) 49-64

S

Sautijn Kluit, W.P., 'De Amsterdamsche prijscourantiers in de 17*de* en 18*de* eeuw' in: *Bijdragen voor vaderlandsche geschiedenis en oudheidkunde* 8 (1875) 58-66

Sagittarius, staff newsletter published by Hagemeyer, 1970-1999

Salzmann, W.H., *Bedrijfsleven, overheid en handelsbevordering. The Netherlands Chamber of Commerce in the United States, Inc., 1903-1987* (S.l. 1994)

Sayous, A.E., 'Die grössen Händler und Kapitalisten in Amsterdam gegen das Ende des sechzehnten und während das siebzehnten Jahrhunderts', in: *Weltwirthschaftliches Archiv* 47 (1938) 115-144

Schama, S., *Patriots and liberators, revolution in the Netherlands 1780-1813* (New York 1977)

Scheffer, H.J., *In vorm gegoten, het Rotterdamsch Nieuwsblad in de negentiende eeuw* (The Hague 1981²)

Schenk, H., 'Fuseren of innoveren, in: *ESB*, 20 March 1996

Schenk, H., 'Meerwaarde Vendex-afsplitsingen wordt teniet gedaan door fusie met KBB', in: *Elan*, July 1999

Schillemans, C.A., *De houtveilingen van Zaandam in de*

jaren 1855-1911 (The Hague 1947)

Schmiedell, J.H., *Gedenkblätter zum 50. jährigen Bestehen der Firma Erdmann & Sielcken in Java 1875-1924* (Bergen 1924)

Schmitz, H., *Schiedam in de tweede helft van de negentiende eeuw, een onderzoek naar enige aspecten van de sociale en economische geschiedenis van de stad in de jaren 1850-1890* (Schiedam 1962)

Schoor, A. van der, *Stad in aanwas, geschiedenis van Rotterdam tot 1813* (Zwolle 1999)

Schoorl, H., *Isaac le Maire, koopman en bedijker* (Haarlem 1969)

Schouwenaar, J., *Tussen beurs en binnenhof, J.W. van den Biesen en de politieke journalistiek van het Handelsblad (1828-1845)* (Amsterdam 1999)

Schrover, M., '"Gij zult het bokje niet koken in de melk zijner moeder", joodse ondernemers in de voedings- en genotmiddelenindustrie', in: H. Berg, E.J. Fischer, T. Wijsenbeek, ed., *Venter, fabriqueur, fabrikant, joodse ondernemers en ondernemingen in Nederland 1796-1940* (Amsterdam 1994) 160-190

Schrover, M., 'De Fiva als een bijzondere variant van collectieve verticale prijsbinding, 1928-1975', in: *NEHA-Jaarboek* 59 (1996) 292-329

Schutte, O., *Repertorium van Nederlandse vertegenwoordigers residerende in het buitenland, 1584-1810* (The Hague 1976)

Sigmond, J.P., 'Havens', in: L.M. Akveld, S. Hart, W.J. van Hoboken, ed., *Maritieme geschiedenis der Nederlanden*, II (Bussum 1977) 78-105

Sillem, J.A., ed., 'Herinneringen van mr. J.A. Sillem, 1840-1912', in: *Jaarboek van het genootschap Amstelodamum* 62 (1970) 131-192

Sluyterman, K.E., *Ondernemen in sigaren, analyse van bedrijfsbeleid in vijf Nederlandse sigarenfabrieken in de perioden 1856-1865 en 1925-1934* (Tilburg 1983)

Sluyterman, K.E., 'Uitvinden en verdienen', in: H.F.J.M. van den Eerenbeemt, ed., *Van boterkleursel naar fotokopieersystemen; de ontstaansgeschiedenis van Océ-van der Grinten 1873-1956* (Leiden 1991) 171-264

Sluyterman, K.E., *Winnen met papier. Vijftig jaar uit de 250-jarige geschiedenis van Proost en Brandt, 1942-1992* (Diemen 1992)

Sluyterman, K.E., 'Dutch multinational trading companies in the twentieth century', in: G. Jones ed., *The multinational traders* (London 1998) 86-101

Smit, C., *Nederland in de Eerste Wereldoorlog (1899-1919), dl II 1914-1917* (Groningen 1972)

Smit, C., *Tien studiën betreffende Nederland in de Eerste Wereldoorlog* (Groningen 1975)

Smit, J.P.W.A., 'De aanleiding tot de "Wet wegens het namaken der merken en teekenen van de binnen het Koninkrijk Holland bestaande garentwijnderijen" van 26 lentemaand 1809', in: *Economisch historisch Jaarboek* 15 (1929) 218-221

Smith, M.F.J., *Tijdaffaires aan de Amsterdamsche beurs* (The Hague 1919)

Smits, J.P.H., E. Horlings, J.L. van Zanden, 'The measurement of gross national product and its components, the Netherlands 1800-1913', N.W. Posthumus Instituut, Research Memorandum No. 1, Utrecht 1997

Snapper, F., *Oorlogsinvloeden op de overzeese handel*

van Holland, 1551-1719 (Amsterdam 1959)

Snapper, F., 'Veranderingen in de Nederlandse scheepvaart op de Oostzee in de achttiende eeuw', in: Joh. de Vries a.o., ed., *Ondernemende geschiedenis, 22 opstellen geschreven bij het afscheid van mr. H. van Riel als voorzitter van de Vereniging 'Het Nederlandsch economisch-historisch archief* (The Hague 1977) 124-139

Snapper, F., 'De generale lijsten van de schepen die in de perioden 1758-1761 en 1783-1786 in Holland zijn binnengelopen', in: *Economisch- en sociaalhistorisch jaarboek* 42 (1979) 26-44

Sneller, Z.W., 'De stapel der Westfaalsche linnens te Rotterdam, 1669-1772', in: idem, *Rotterdams bedrijfsleven in het verleden* (Amsterdam 1940) 64-106

Sneller, Z.W., 'Het bedrijf der Thorbeckes te Zwolle in de achttiende eeuw', in: idem, *Bijdragen tot de economische geschiedenis van Nederland* (Utrecht 1968) 147-160

Sneller, Z.W., 'De Rotterdamsche Wisselbank', in: idem, *Rotterdamsch bedrijfsleven in het verleden* (Amsterdam 1940) 107-184

Sneller, Z.W., 'De toestand der nijverheid te Amsterdam en Rotterdam volgens de enquete van 1816', in: idem, *Bijdragen tot de economische geschiedenis van Nederland* (Utrecht 1968) 161-202

Sneller, Z.W., 'Beurshandel in Nederland', in: idem, *Bijdragen tot de economische geschiedenis van Nederland* (Utrecht 1968) 134-146

Sperling, J., 'The international payments mechanism in the seventeenth and eighteenth centuries', in: *Economic history review* 2nd ser 14 (1962) 446-468

Spooner, F.C., *Risks at sea, Amsterdam insurance and maritime Europe, 1766-1780* (Cambridge 1983)

Steensgaard, N., 'The Dutch East India Company as an institutional innovation', in: M. Aymard., ed., *Dutch capitalism and world capitalism* (Cambridge 1982) 235-257

Steur, J.J., *Herstel of ondergang, de voorstellen tot redres van de VOC 1740-1795* (Utrecht 1984)

Stipriaan Luïscius, A. van, *Surinaams contrast, roofbouw en overleven in een Caraïbische plantagekolonie* (Amsterdam 1993)

Stoppelaar, J.H. de, *Balthasar de Moucheron, een bladzijde uit de Nederlandsche handelsgeschiedenis tijdens den tachtigjarigen oorlog* (The Hague 1901)

Stout, H., 'Van de Toko uit Rotterdam en van wat daarna kwam' in: H. Baudet, ed., *Handelswereld en wereldhandel, honderd jaren Internatio: tien essays* (Rotterdam 1963) 17-74

Stuijvenberg, J.H. van, *Het Centraal Bureau, een coöperatief krachtenveld in de Nederlandse landbouw, 1899-1949* (Rotterdam 1949)

Stuijvenberg, J.H. van, *De Nederlandse Economische Hoogeschool 1913-1963, van handelshoogeschool naar hogeschool voor maatschappijwetenschappen* (Rotterdam 1963)

Supple, B.S., 'The nature of enterprise', in: E.E. Rich, C.H. Wilson, *The Cambridge economic history of Europe*, V, *The economic organization of early modern Europe* (Cambridge 1977) 394-461

T

Taselaar, A., *De Nederlandse koloniale lobby, onderne-mers en de Indische politiek 1914-1940* (Leiden 1998)

Technische Unie 1880-1955 (Amsterdam 1955)

Thee Kian Wie, 'Economic policies in Indonesia during the period 1950-1965, in particular with respect to for-eign investment', in: J.Th. Lindblad, ed., *Historical foundations of a national economy in Indonesia, 1890s-1990s* (Amsterdam 1996) 315-329

Tielhof, M. van, *De Hollandse graanhandel 1470-1570, koren op de Amsterdamse molen* (The Hague 1996)

Tielhof, M. van, 'Handel en politiek in de 16e eeuw, een Amsterdamse Oostzeehandelaar tijdens de eerste jaren van de Opstand', in: *Holland* 29/1 (1997) 37-52

Tielhof, M. van, 'Behouden vaart!', in: R. Daalder a.o., ed., *Goud uit graan, Nederland en het Oostzeegebied 1600-1850* (Zwolle 1998) 28-41

Tielhof, M. van, *The mother of all trades, the Baltic grain trade in Amsterdam from the late 16th to the early 19th century* (forthcoming)

Tien jaar samenwerking OTRA en Sonepar (OTRA s.a.)

Tijn, Th. van, 'Op de drempel van de nieuwe tijd: Neder-land omstreeks 1870', in: J.A. van Houtte a.o., ed., *Algemene geschiedenis der Nederlanden, X, Liberaal getij, 1840-1885* (Utrecht 1955) 288-313

Tijn, Th. van, *Twintig jaren Amsterdam, de maatschap-pelijke ontwikkeling van de hoofdstad van de jaren '50 der vorige eeuw tot 1876* (Amsterdam 1965)

Tijn, Th. van, W.M. Zappey, 'De negentiende eeuw', in: J.H. van Stuijvenberg, ed., *De economische geschiede-nis van Nederland* (Gronignen 1977) 201-260

Tobi, E.J., *De uitschakeling van den groothandel in industrieele producten* (Roermond 1927)

Touwen, J., *Extremes in the archipelago, trade and development in the outer islands of Indonesia, 1900-1942* (Leiden 1997)

Tracy, J.D., ed., *The rise of merchant empires, long-dis-tance trade in the early modern world, 1350-1750* (Cam-bridge 1990)

Tracy, J.D., ed., *The political economy of merchant empires, state power and world trade, 1350-1750* (Cam-bridge 1991)

Tutein Nolthenius, R.P.J., *Het geslacht Tutein Nolthe-nius* (Haarlem 1914-1930)

U

Unger, R.W., 'The Dutch trade in rye, comparative capi-tal requirements in the seventeenth and eighteenth centuries', in: C.A. Davids, J.M.F. Fritschy, L.A. van der Valk, ed., *Kapitaal, ondernemerschap en beleid, studies over economie en politiek in Nederland, Europa en Azië, afscheidsbundel voor prof.dr. P.W. Klein* (Amsterdam 1996) 121-140

Unger, W.S., 'Middelburg als handelsstad, 13e-16e eeuw', in: *Archief Zeeuwsch Genootschap voor Weten-schappen* (1935) 1-173

Unger, W.S., 'De publikatie der Sonttabellen voltooid', in: *Tijdschrift voor geschiedenis* 71 (1958) 147-205

V

Vanvugt, E., *Wettig opium, 350 jaar Nederlandse popi-umhandel in de Indische archipel* (Haarlem 1985)

Veenendaal jr., A.J., *De ijzeren weg in een land vol water, beknopte geschiedenis van de spoorwegen in Ned-erland 1834-1958* (Amsterdam 1998)

Veluwenkamp, J.W., 'Lading voor de Oostzee' in: R. Daalder a.o., ed., *Goud uit graan, Nederland en het Oostzeegebied 1600-1850* (Zwolle 1998) 42-55

Veluwenkamp, J.W., 'n Huis op Archangel, de Amster-damse koopmansfamilie Thesingh, 1650-1725', in: *Jaarboek Amstelodamum* 69 (1977) 123-139

Veluwenkamp, J.W., *Ondernemersgedrag op de Hol-landse stapelmarkt in de tijd van de Republiek, de Ams-terdamse firma Jan Isaac de Neufville & Comp., 1730-1764* (Meppel 1981)

Veluwenkamp, J.W., 'Familienetwerken binnen de Ned-erlandse koopliedengemeenschap van Archangel in de eerste helft van de achttiende eeuw', in: *Bijdragen en mededelingen betreffende de geschiedenis der Nederlan-den* 108 (1993) 655-672

Veluwenkamp, J.W., 'De buitenlandse textielhandel van de Republiek in de achttiende eeuw', in: *Textielhis-torische bijdragen* 34 (1994) 70-88

Veluwenkamp, J.W. 'The purchase and export of Russ-ian commodities in 1741 by Dutch merchants estab-lished at Archangel', in: C. Lesger, L. Noordegraaf, ed., *Entrepreneurs and entrepreneurship in modern times, merchants and industrialists within the orbit of the Dutch staple market* (The Hague 1995) 85-100

Veluwenkamp, J.W., 'Merchant colonies in the Dutch trade system (1550-1750)', in: C.A. Davids, J.M.F. Fritschy, L.A. van der Valk, ed., *Kapitaal, ondernemer-schap en beleid, studies over economie en politiek in Nederland, Europa en Azië, afscheidsbundel voor prof.dr. P.W. Klein* (Amsterdam 1996) 141-164

Verheusen, A., *Beschrijvend bronnenmateriaal van de Bataafs-Franse overheid 1795-1813* (The Hague 1995)

Verslag van het onderzoek, ingesteld door mr. J. van der Hoeven, dr. A. van Putten en prof. mr. W.J. Slagter naar het beleid en de gang van zaken bij OGEM Holding NV (1987)

Verstegen, S.W., 'Tussen beleid en belang, geschiede-nis van de Kamers van koophandel en fabrieken in Ned-erland', in: J.L.J.M. van Gerwen, J.J. Seegers, S.W. Ver-stegen, *Mercurius' erfenis, een geschiedenis en bronnenoverzicht van de Kamers van koophandel en fab-rieken in Nederland (*Amsterdam 1990) 9-56

Verstegen, S.W., 'National wealth and income from cap-ital in the Netherlands, c. 1805-1910', in: *Economic and social history in the Netherlands* 7 (1996) 73-108

Verviers, E., *De Nederlandsche handelspolitiek tot aan de toepassing der vrijhandelsbeginselen* (Leiden 1914)

Verwey, A., ed., *Vondel, volledige dichtwerken en oor-spronkelijk proza* (Amsterdam 1937)

Vlessing, O., 'The Portuguese-Jewish mercantile com-munity in seventeenth-century Amsterdam', in: Lesger, C., L. Noordegraaf, ed., *Entrepreneurs and entrepreneur-ship in modern times, merchants and industrialists with-in the orbit of the Dutch staple market* (The Hague 1995) 223-244

Volkskrant, 16 November 1996

Vondel, J. van den, 'Zeemagazijn', in: A. Verwey, ed., *Vondel, volledige dichtwerken en oorspronkelijk proza* (Amsterdam 1937) 769-772

Vondel, J. van den, 'Op den Amsterdamschen gedenkpenning', in: A. Verwey, ed., *Vondel, volledige dichtwerken en oorspronkelijk proza* (Amsterdam 1937) 790-791

Voogd, C. de, *De neergang van de scheepsbouw en andere industriële bedrijfstakken* (Flushing 1993)

Voogd, C. de, 'Uittredingsbarrières bij neergang van bedrijftakken', in: *ESB,* 4 January 1995

Voortman, R.M., 'De VOC en de stad Rotterdam', in: P. Grimm, ed., *Heeren in zaken, de kemer Rotterdam van de Verenigde Oostindische Compagnie* (Zutphen 1993) 9-34

Vries, B. de, *Electoraat en elite, sociale structuur en sociale mobiliteit in Amsterdam, 1850-1895* (Amster-dam 1986)

G. de Vries & Zonen, 1775-1950 (Amsterdam 1950)

Vries, J. de, *Barges and capitalism, passenger trans-portation in the Dutch economy 1632-1839* (Wagenin-gen 1978)

Vries., J. de, A. van der Woude, *Nederland 1500-1815, de eerste ronde van moderne economische groei* (Ams-terdam 1995)

Vries, Joh. de, 'De ontduiking der convooien en licen-ten in de Republiek tijdens de achttiende eeuw', in: *Tijdschrift voor geschiedenis* 71 (1958) 349-361

Vries, Joh. de, *De economische achteruitgang van de Republiek in de achttiende eeuw* (Leiden 2nd edition 1968)

Vries, Joh. de, ed., *Herinneringen en dagboek van Ernst Heldring 1871-1954* (The Hague 1970)

Vries, Joh. de, *De Nederlandse economie tijdens de 20ste eeuw, een verkenning van het meest kenmerkende* (Utrecht 1973)

Vries, Joh. de, *Een eeuw vol effecten, historische schets van de Vereniging voor de Effectenhandel en de Amster-damse Effectenbeurs 1876-1976* (Amsterdam 1976)

Vries, Joh de, W. Vroom, T. de Graaf, ed., *Worldwide banking, ABN AMRO Bank 1824-1999* (Amsterdam 1999)

W

Waal, P.G.A. de, *Van Paciolo tot Stevin, bijdrage tot de leer van het boekhouden in Nederland* (Roermond 1927)

Wagenaar, J., *Amsterdam in zijne opkomst* (Amsterdam 1760-1788)

Wake, J., *Kleinwort Benson, the history of two families in banking* (Oxford 1997)

Wallert, J.A.F., *Ontwikkelingslijnen in praktijk en theorie van de wisselbrief 1300-2000* (Amsterdam 1996)

Wallis de Vries, R.D.H., *D.H. de Vries, een Amsterdamse koopman in de Molukken 1883-1901* (Amsterdam 1996)

Walsum, G.E. van, 'Abram van Rijckevorsel Hzn., man van de vooruitgang', in: *Rotterdams jaarboekje* VII/3 (1965) 148-174

Walter, R., 'Die nordwesteuropäische Wirtschaft in mikroökonomischer Perspektive: Das Beispiel Hasen-clever', in: M. North, ed., *Nordwesteuropa in der Weltwirtschaft 1750-1950* (Stuttgart 1993) 291-307

Wanjon, D., *Geschiedenis van den Nederlandschen han-*

del sedert 1795 (Haarlem 1900)

Wee, H. van der, 'Handel in de zuidelijke Nederlanden', in: D.P. Blok a.o., ed., *Algemene geschiedenis der Nederlanden*, VI, *Nieuwe tijd* (Bussum 1979) 75-97

Wee, H. van der, *De gebroken welvaartscirkel, de wereldeconomie 1945-1980* (Leiden 1983)

Wegener Sleeswijk, A., 'Les vins de Guyenne sur le marché hollandais à la fin du XVIIe et au XVIIIe siècle', in: *Chronique d'histoire maritime* 38 (1998) 31-41

Welcker, J.M., 'Het dagelijks brood, de doopsgezinden, de economie en de demografie', in: S. Groenveld, S.L. Verheus, ed., *Wederdopers, menisten, doopsgezinden in Nederland 1530-1980* (Zutphen 1980) 195-218

Welling, G.M., *The prize of neutrality, trade relations between Amsterdam and North America 1771-1817, a study in computational history* (Amsterdam 1998)

Wennekes, W., *Eeuwenoud: de lange levens van zeven Nederlandse bedrijven* (Amsterdam 1989)

Wennekes, W., *Gouden handel, de eerste Nederlanders overzee, en wat zij daar haalden* (Amsterdam 1996)

Wesseling, H.L., 'Nederland en de conferentie van Berlijn, 1884-1885', in: *Tijdschrift voor geschiedenis* 93 (1980) 559-577

Westera, L.D., 'Boekhouding en management bij de Vereenigde Oostindische Compagnie', in: *Economisch- en sociaalhistorisch jaarboek* 55 (1992) 75-104

Westera, L.D., 'Het maatschappelijke vermogen van de familie Brants, een doopsgezinde ondernemersfamilie in de achttiende eeuw', in: *NEHA-jaarboek* 58 (1995) 114-148

Westerfield, R.B., *Middlemen in English business, particularly between 1660 and 1760* (New Haven 1915)

Westermann, J.C., 'Bescheiden betreffende den Amsterdamschen handel in de eerste helft der 19e eeuw, naar aanleiding van de invoering van de nieuwe maten en gewichten', in: *Economisch historisch jaarboek* 20 (1936) 294-328

Westermann, J.C., *Gedenkboek van de Kamer van koophandel en fabrieken voor Amsterdam samengesteld ter gelegenheid van het 125-jarig bestaan*, I, *Het tijdvak 1811-1922* (Amsterdam 1936)

Wichers Hoeth, A.W., *Van Heekeren & Co. en hunne voorgangers 1720 [1829]-1929* (Amsterdam 1929)

Wichers Hoeth, A.W., *De geschiedenis van het Amsterdamsche handelshuis Louis Bienfait & Soon* (Hilversum 1941)

Wijtvliet, C.A.M., *Expansie en dynamiek, de ontwikkeling van het Nederlandse handelsbankwezen 1860-1914* (Amsterdam 1993)

Wilczek, B., J. van Waterschoot, ed., *Amsterdam 1585-1672, Morgenröte des bürgerlichen Kapitalismus* (Bühl-Moos 1993)

Wilson, C., *Geschiedenis van Unilever* (The Hague 1954)

Winkelman, P.H., ed., *Bronnen voor de geschiedenis van de Nederlandse Oostzeehandel in de zeventiende eeuw* (The Hague 1971-1983, 6 vols.)

Winter, P.J. van, 'Een vergeten schepping van koning Willem I: de Maatschappij van landeigenaren en beklemde meiers te Groningen 1823-1878', in: *Verslagen van de KNAW afd. Letterkunde* New Series 53 No. 1 (1949)

Winter, P.J. van, *Het aandeel van den Amsterdamschen handel aan de opbouw van het Amerikaansche Gemeenebest* (The Hague 1933)

Woestijne, W.J. van de, 'De handel als motor van economisch herstel', in: *ESB*, 24 August 1983

Woltring, J., *Bescheiden betreffende de buitenlandse politiek van Nederland, 1848-1919, tweede periode, 1871-1898*, II, *1874-1880* (The Hague 1965); III, *1881-1885* (The Hague 1967)

Woudhuysen, H.R., 'Turing's legacy', *Times Literary Supplement*, 15 October 1999

Wright, H.R.C., *Free trade and protection in the Netherlands 1816-1830, a study of the first Benelux* (Cambridge 1955)

Wright, I.A., 'The Coymans asiento', in: *Bijdragen voor vaderlandsche geschiedenis en oudheidkunde* 6 No. 1 (1924) 23-62

Y

Yonokama, S., ed., *General trading companies: a comparative and historical study* (Tokio 1990)

Z

Zanden, J.L. van, *De industrialisatie van Amsterdam 1825-1914* (Bergen 1987)

Zanden, J.L. van, 'De economie van Holland in de periode 1650-1805: groei of achteruitgang?', in: *Bijdragen en mededelingen betreffende de geschiedenis der Nederlanden* 102 (1987) 562-609

Zanden, J.L. van, 'Dutch economic history of the period 1500-1940: a review of the present state of affairs', in: *Economic and social history in the Netherlands* 1 (1989) 9-29

Zanden, J.L. van, 'De introductie van stoom in de Amsterdamse meelfabricage 1828-1855, over de rol van marktstructuren, ondernemersgedrag en de overheid', in: *Jaarboek voor de geschiedenis van bedrijf en techniek* 8 (1991) 63-80

Zanden, J.L. van, *The rise and decline of Holland's economy, merchant capitalism and the labour market* (Manchester 1993)

Zanden, J.L. van, 'Over de rationaliteit van het ondernemersgedrag van de VOC: enkele empirische bevindingen', in: C.A. Davids, J.M.F. Fritschy, L.A. van der Valk, ed., *Kapitaal, ondernemerschap en beleid, studies over economie en politiek in Nederland, Europa en Azië, afscheidsbundel voor prof.dr. P.W. Klein* (Amsterdam 1996) 409-422

Zanden, J.L. van, *Een klein land in de 20e eeuw. Economische geschiedenis van Nederland 1914-1995* (Utrecht 1997)

Zappey, W.M., 'Het Fonds voor de Nationale Nijverheid 1821-1846', in: P. Boomgaard a.o., ed., *Exercities in ons verleden, 12 opstellen over de sociale en economische geschiedenis van Nederland en koloniën 1800-1950, aangeboden aan prof.dr. W.J. Wieringa bij zijn aftreden als hoogleraar aan de Vrije Universiteit te Amsterdam* (Assen 1981) 27-42

Zeijden, P.Th. van de, *Groothandel en logistieke dienstverleners: partners of concurrent?* (Zoetermeer 1991)

Zonneveld, P. van, ed., *Naar de Oost! Verhalen over vier eeuwen reizen naar Indië* (Amsterdam 1997)

Zwaag, P., *Verloren tropische zaken, de opkomst en ondergang van de Nederlandse handel- en cultuurmaatschappijen in het voormalige Nederlands-Indië* (Meppel 1991)

417

Index

425

427

Picture credits

We have tried to trace all the rightful claimants of the illustrations. However, if you claim to hold the rights to any illustration, please contact the publisher.

ABN AMRO Historisch Archief Amsterdam 96, 160, 161,162,163, 167, 169, 173, 199, 200, 221, 228, 241, 376

ANP Fotoarchief, 314o, 328, 332-333, 356, 369, 382

Amsterdams Historisch Museum 32, 48, 70, 85, 110, 154, 164, 372o, 375

Atlas van Stolk Rotterdam 33, 34, 69, 74, 78, 80, 103, 126, 127, 128, 130, 132, 135, 139, 141, 143, 148, 150, 166, 191

Archief Hagemeijer Naarden 89. 90, 184, 206, 208, 210, 211, 215o, 216, 217 225o, 226, 229, 231, 235, 238, 243, 250, 258, 260, 261, 263, 265, 266, 268, 270, 271, 272, 276, 277, 281, 282, 286, 287, 289, 290, 292, 294, 298, 301, 302l, 306, 307, 308, 309, 311, 316-317, 318, 330, 335o, 335b, 336, 339, 340, 341, 342r, 343, 344, 346, 348, 350, 353, 354-355, 356, 359, 362, 370, 376, 378, 380, 381, 382, 384-385

Archief Internatio-Müller Rotterdam 202, 207, 213, 218, 230l, 234, 247, 249, 257r, 274, 275, 278, 296r, 297, 304, 319, 341, 348, 366b, 372

Bayerische Staatsbibliothek München 14m

Belastingmuseum van der Poel Rotterdam 77

Bymuseum Helsingør 66o

Gemeentemuseum Breda 189

Collection Algemeen Rijksarchief 's Gravenhage 277l, 280, 283

Collection audio-visual materials De Nederlandsche Bank NV 128o

Collection Gemeente Archief 's Gravenhage 133

Collection Gemeente Archief Amsterdam 37, 58, 63, 92, 115, 120, 122, 131, 147, 148o,150o,151, 167o, 172, 176, 187, 200o, 236, 244, 245, 300, 315, 378, 380

Collection Gemeente Archief Kampen 16o

Collection Gemeente Archief Rotterdam 10, 93, 94, 116, 135o, 136, 137, 138, 186, 188, 237, 239, 241o, 285, 296l

Collection Gemeente Archief Utrecht 125

Collection Mees Pierson 140

Fries Scheepvaart Museum Sneek 82

Germanisches Nationalmuseum Nürnberg 16, 22

Hidde Nijland Museum Hindelopen 106

Historisch Museum Rotterdam 72o, 86, 107

Hollandse Hoogte Fotoarchief 328, 329, 331, 342, 349, 351, 366

Internationaal Instituut voor Sociale Geschiedenis Amsterdam 17, 71, 95, 99, 179, 180, 218b, 220, 221o, 222, 223, 225, 240

Instituut Collectie Nederland Amsterdam 87

Koninklijk Instituut voor de Tropen Fotoarchief Amsterdam 168, 183, 192, 193, 197, 198, 202o, 203, 204, 205, 209, 212, 215, 242, 381

Koninklijke Bibliotheek 's Gravenhage 51, 165

Maritiem Museum Prins Hendrik Rotterdam 25, 113, 119, 156

Museum Boymans van Beuningen Rotterdam 38, 54, 68, 100

Museum Kröller- Müller Otterlo 196

Museum Mauritshuis 's Gravenhage 76

Museum voor Communicatie 's Gravenhage 28, 29, 174, 178, 195

Museum voor Geschiedenis en Scheepvaart Riga 26

Nederlands Instituut voor Oorlogsdocumentatie 257

Noord Brabants Museum 's Hertogenbosch 14

Ottawa National Gallery 101

Prive-collection 11,12, 232

Rijksmuseum Amsterdam 8, 23, 24, 34, 36, 40, 45, 46, 47, 50, 55, 57, 59, 61, 72, 108, 110, 114, 121, 145, 158, 159

Scheepvaartmuseum Amsterdam 20, 31,42, 43, 83, 171

Scheepvaartmuseum Antwerpen 19

SHV Nederland Utrecht 321

Spaarnestad Fotoarchief 252, 254, 255, 258, 259, 262, 296r, 302r, 314, 323, 325, 334, 337, 345, 383

Spoorwegmuseum Utrecht 146, 174o

Stedelijk Museum Vlissingen 64

Stichting Collectie Cultuurgeschiedenis Nederlanders Overzee Amsterdam 112

Walter de Maar BV Rijswijk 123

Wereldmuseum Rotterdam 190

Zaans Museum, Zaandijk 66